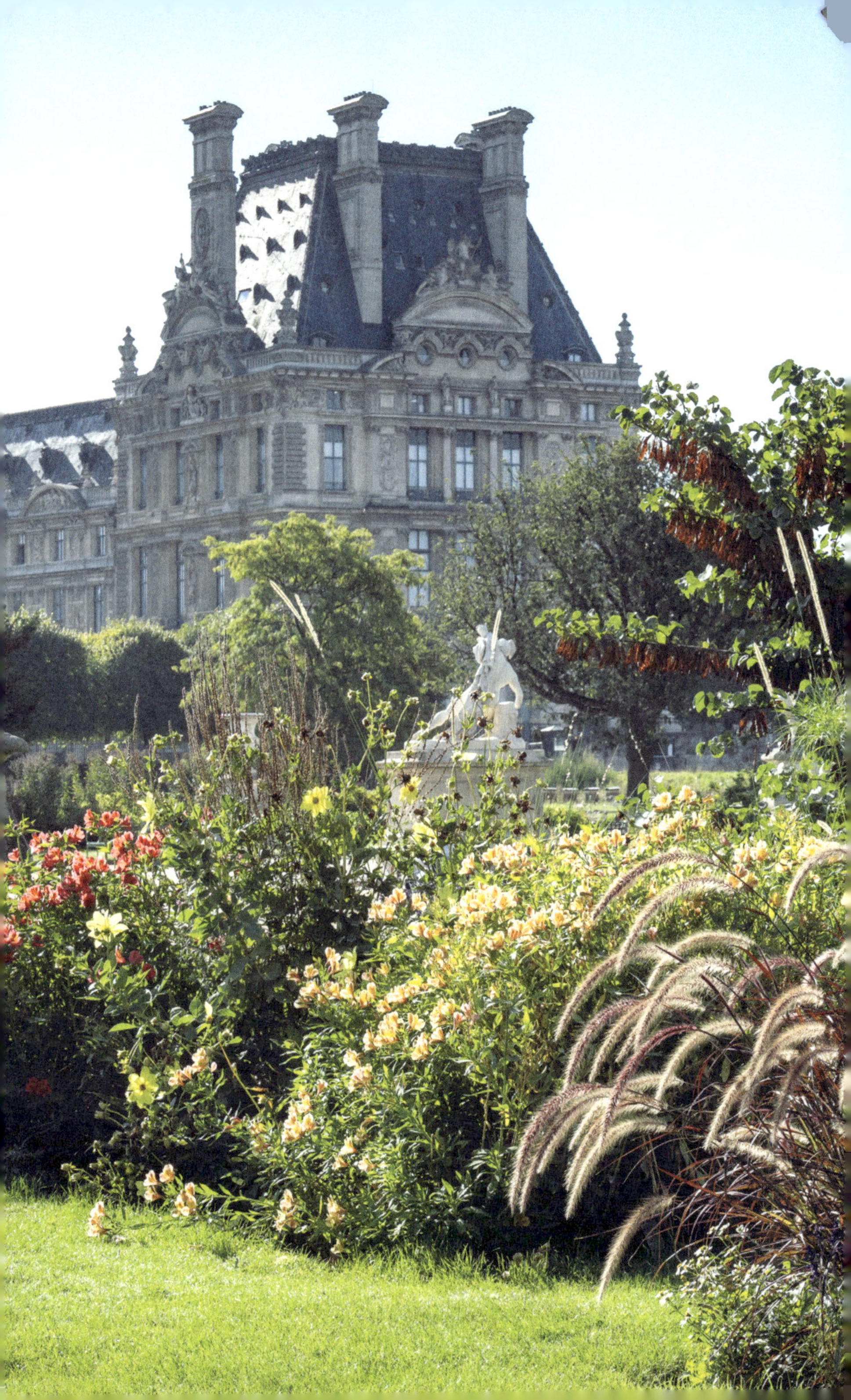

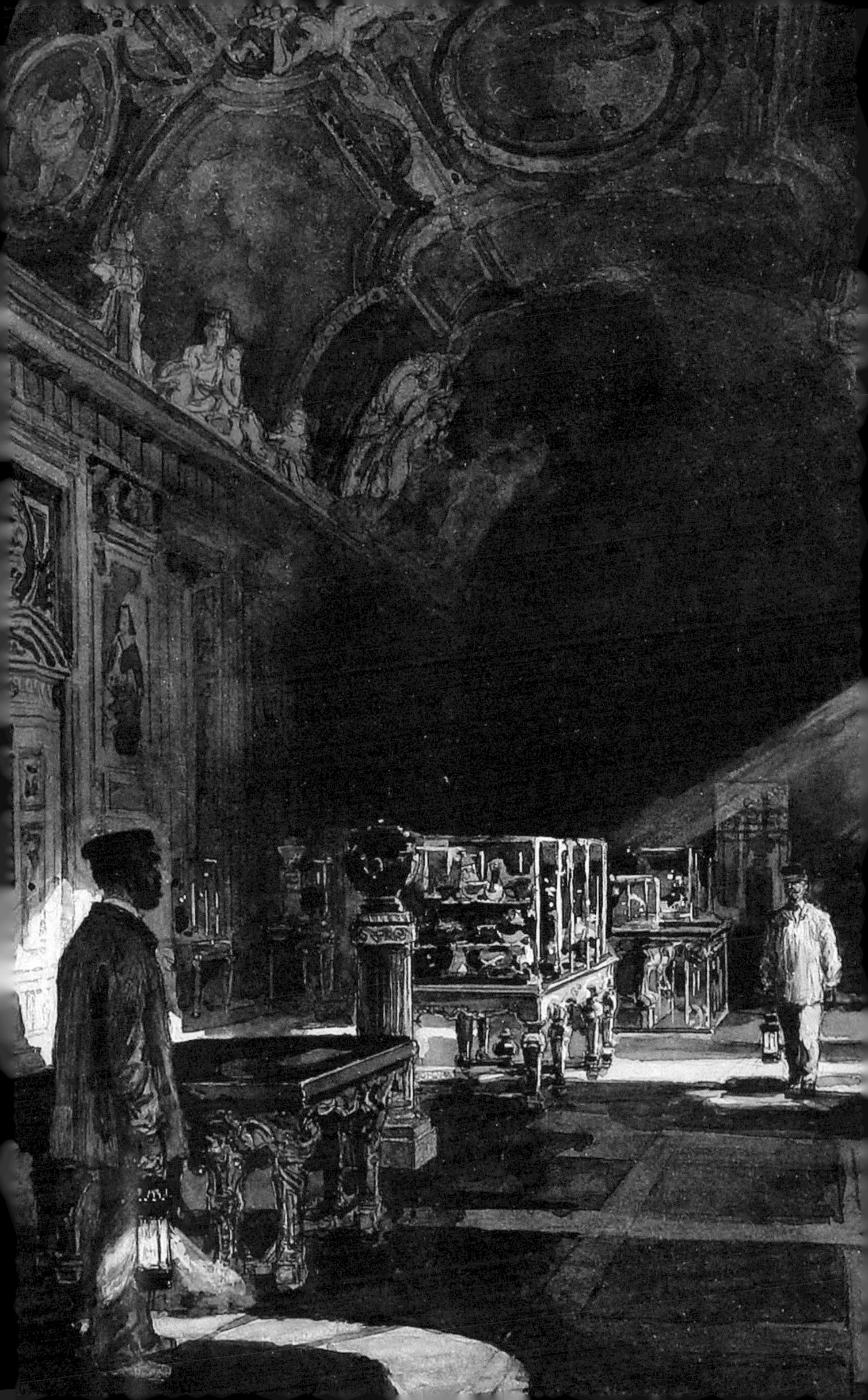

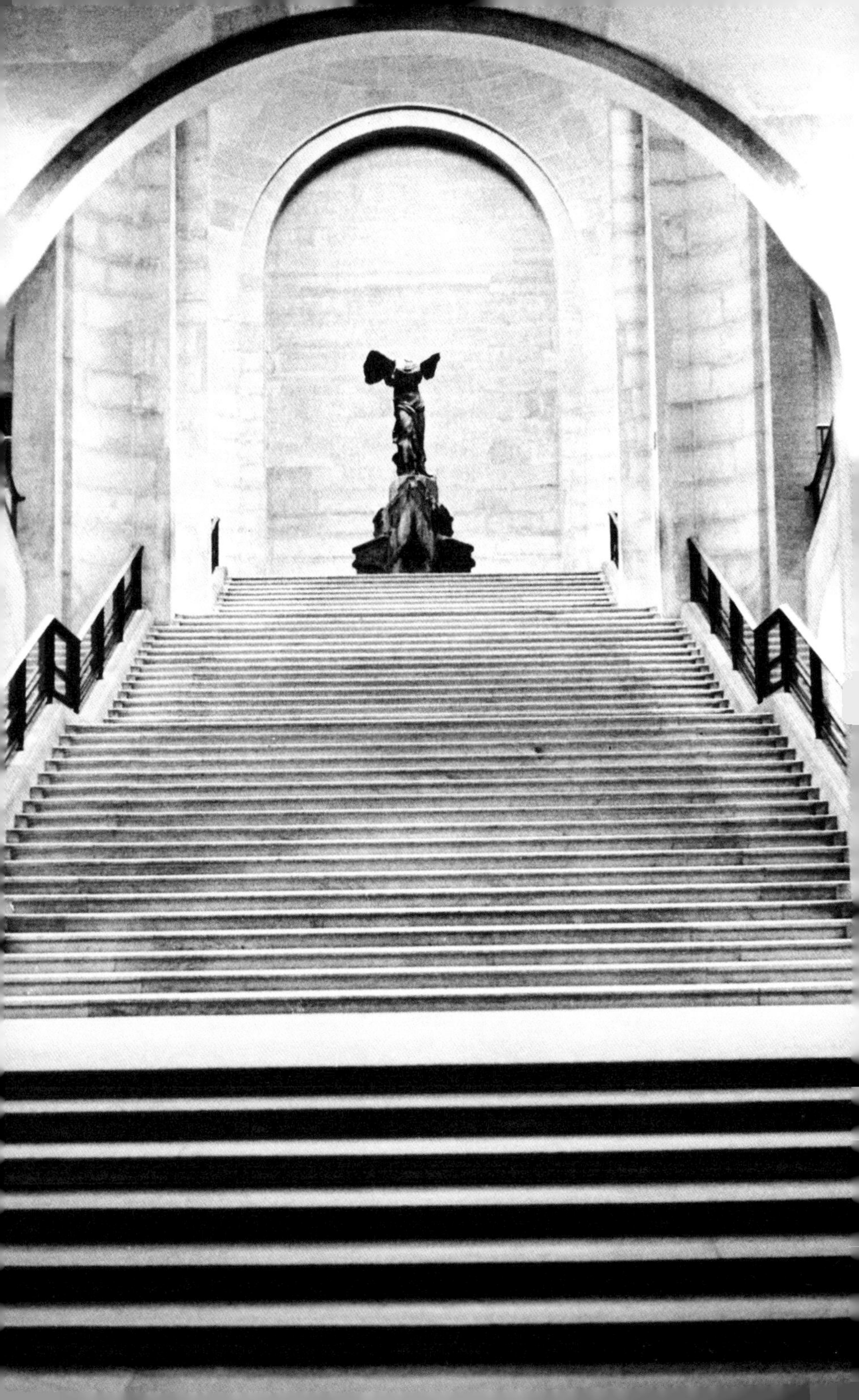

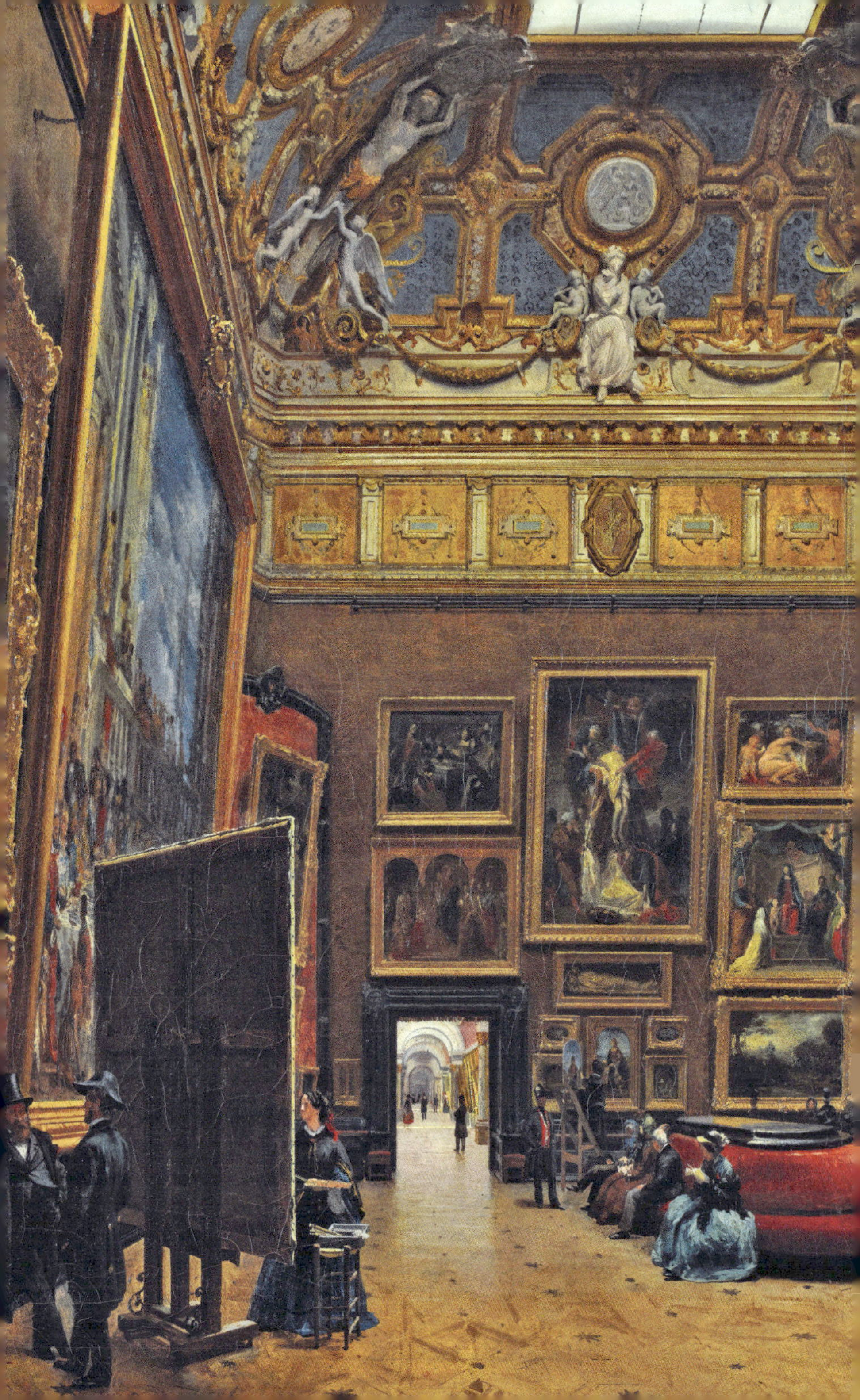

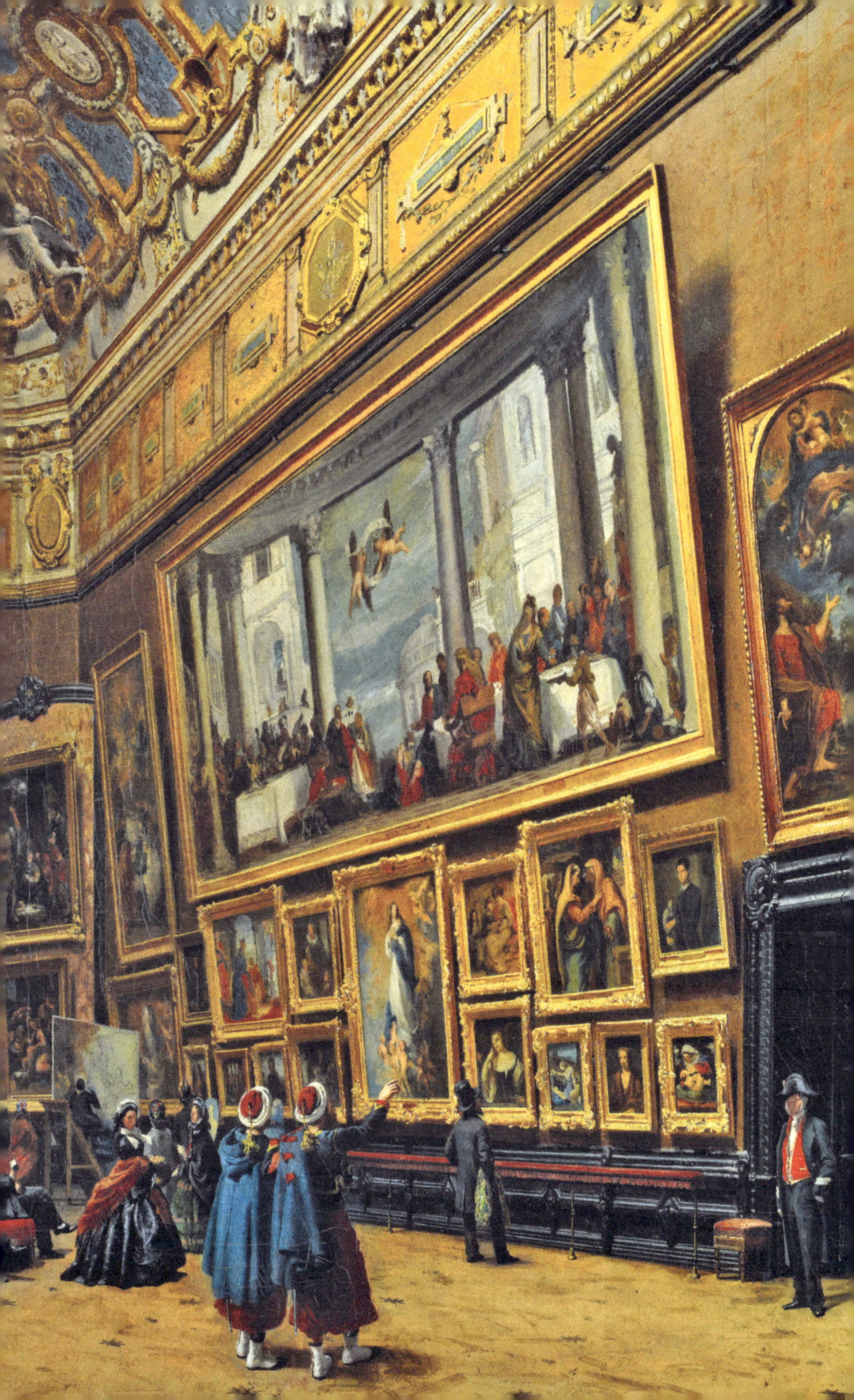

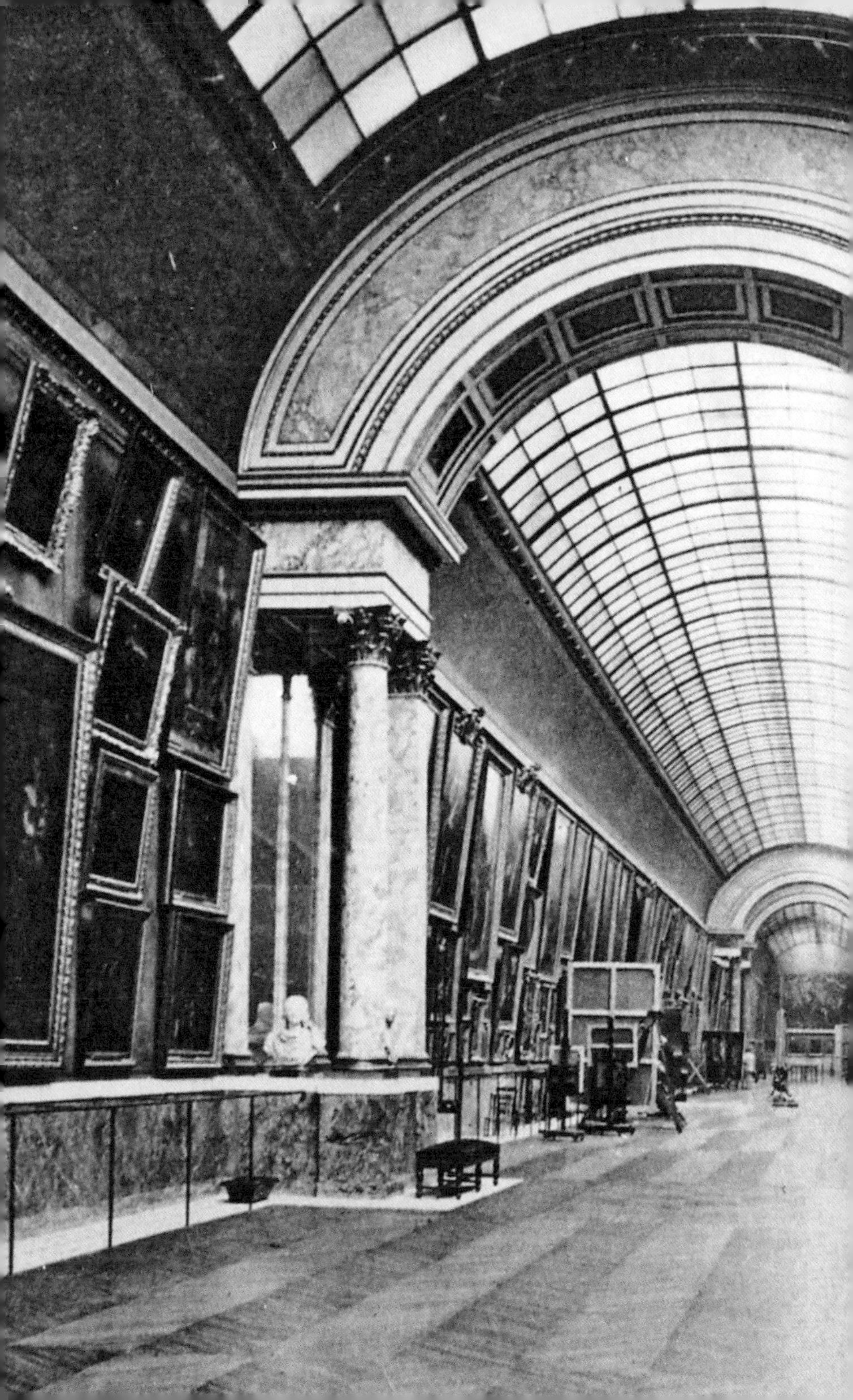

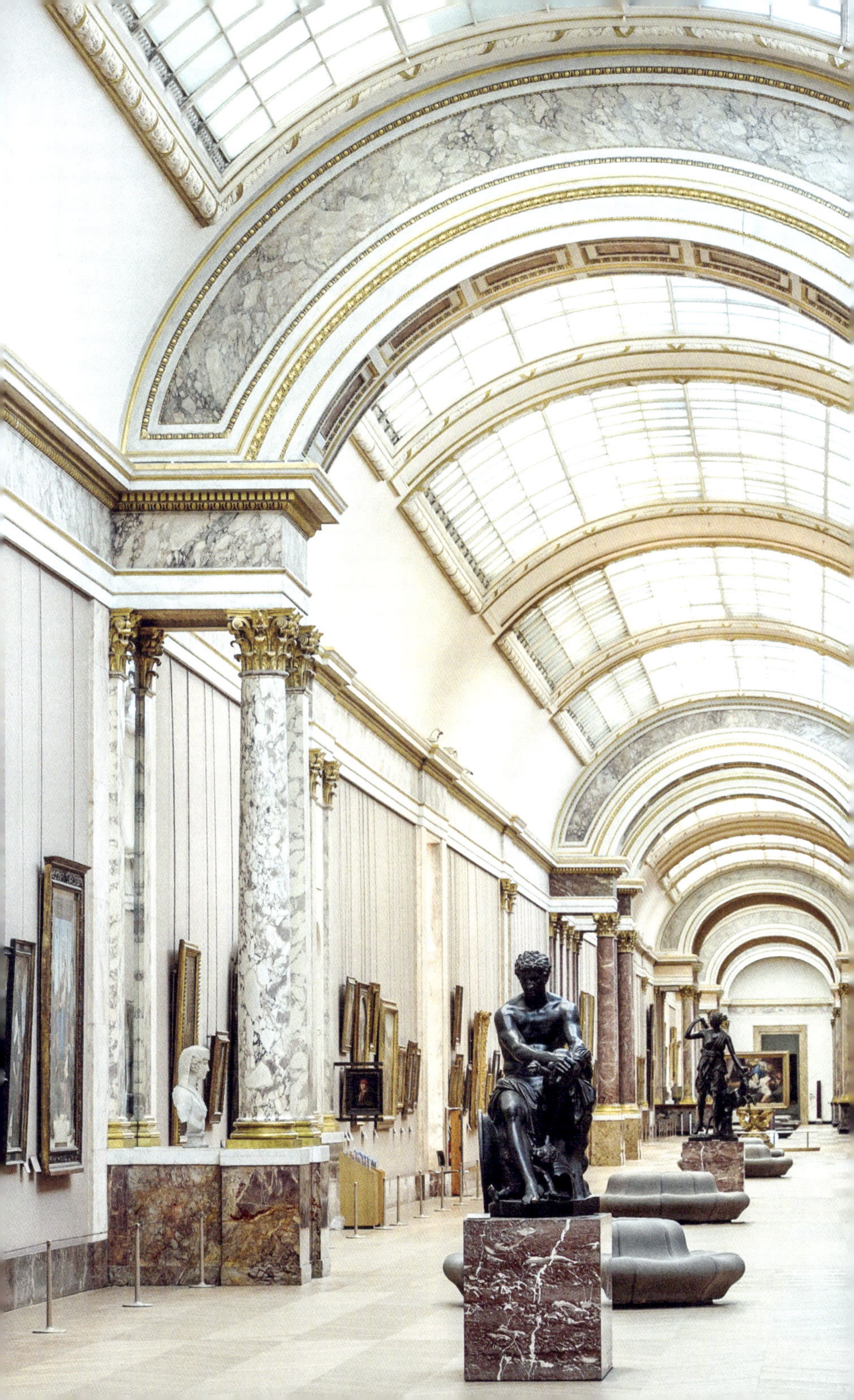

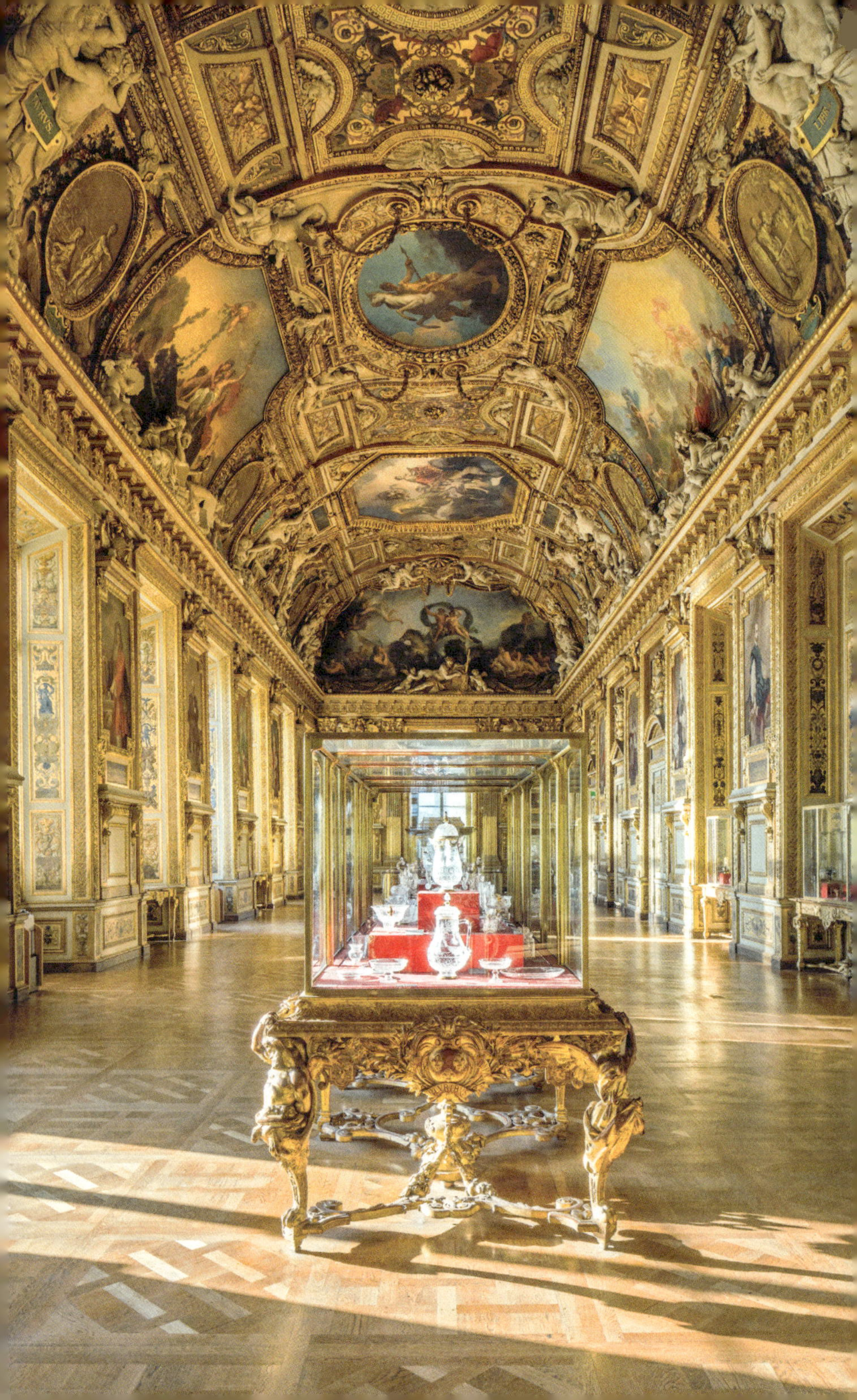

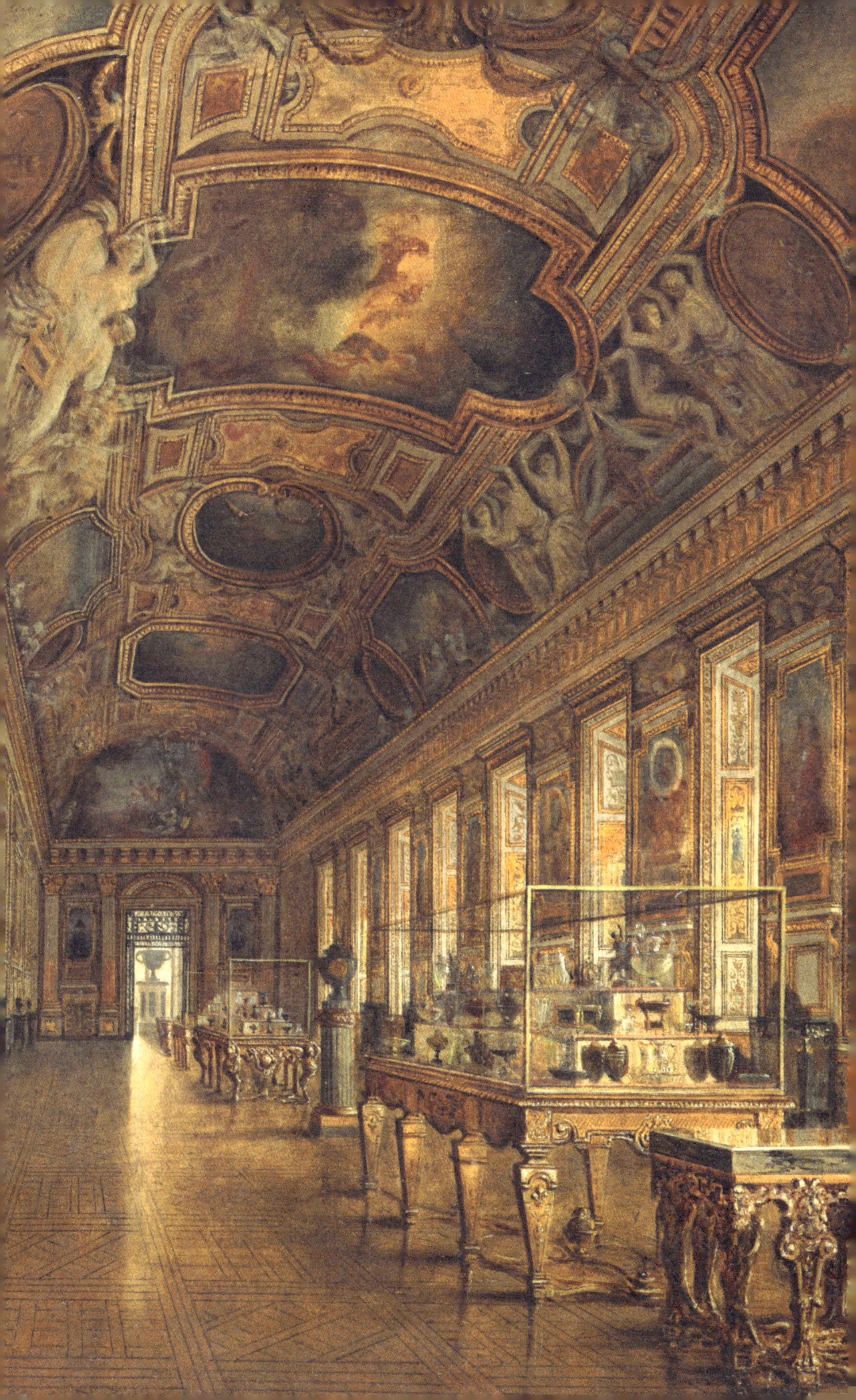

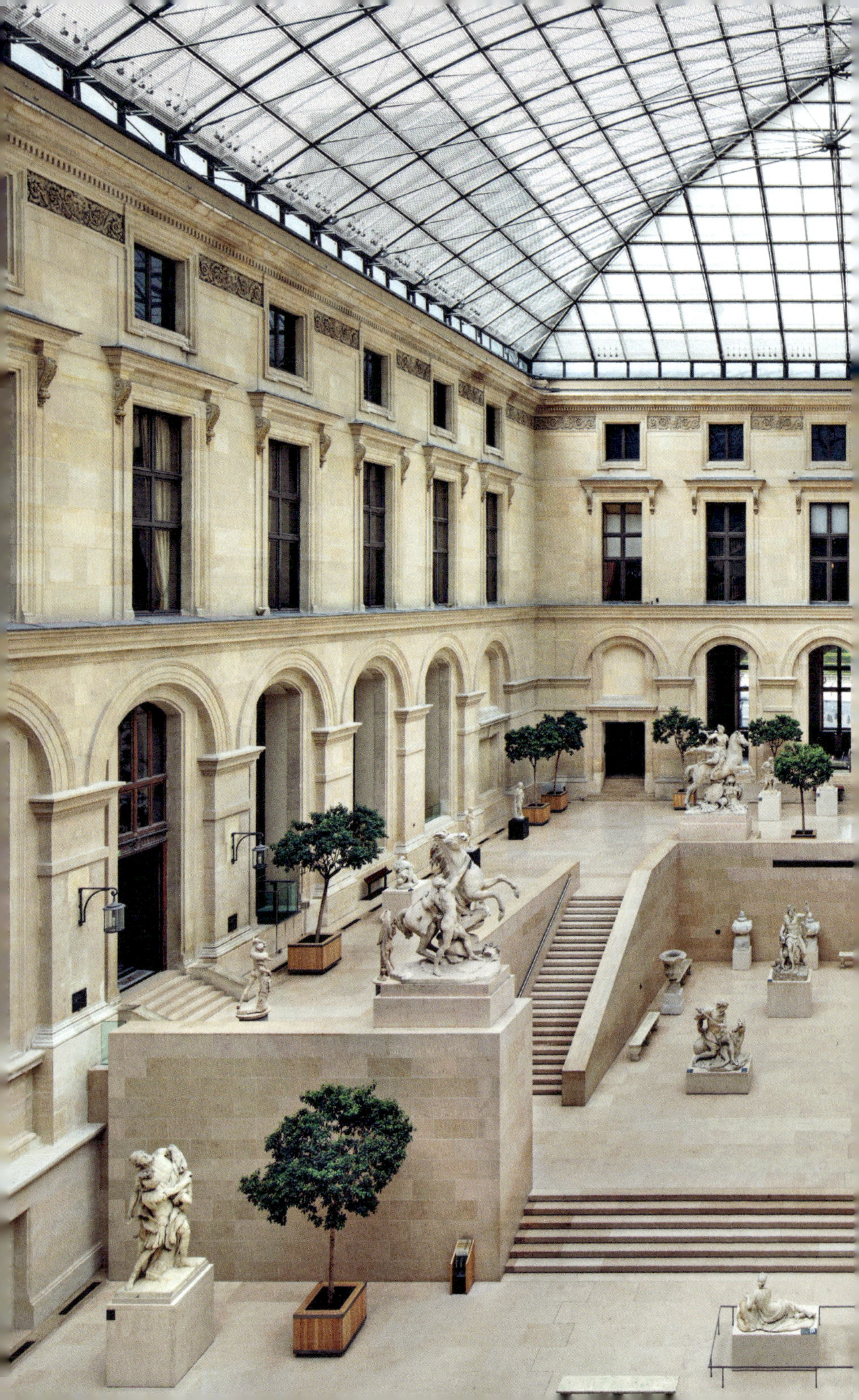

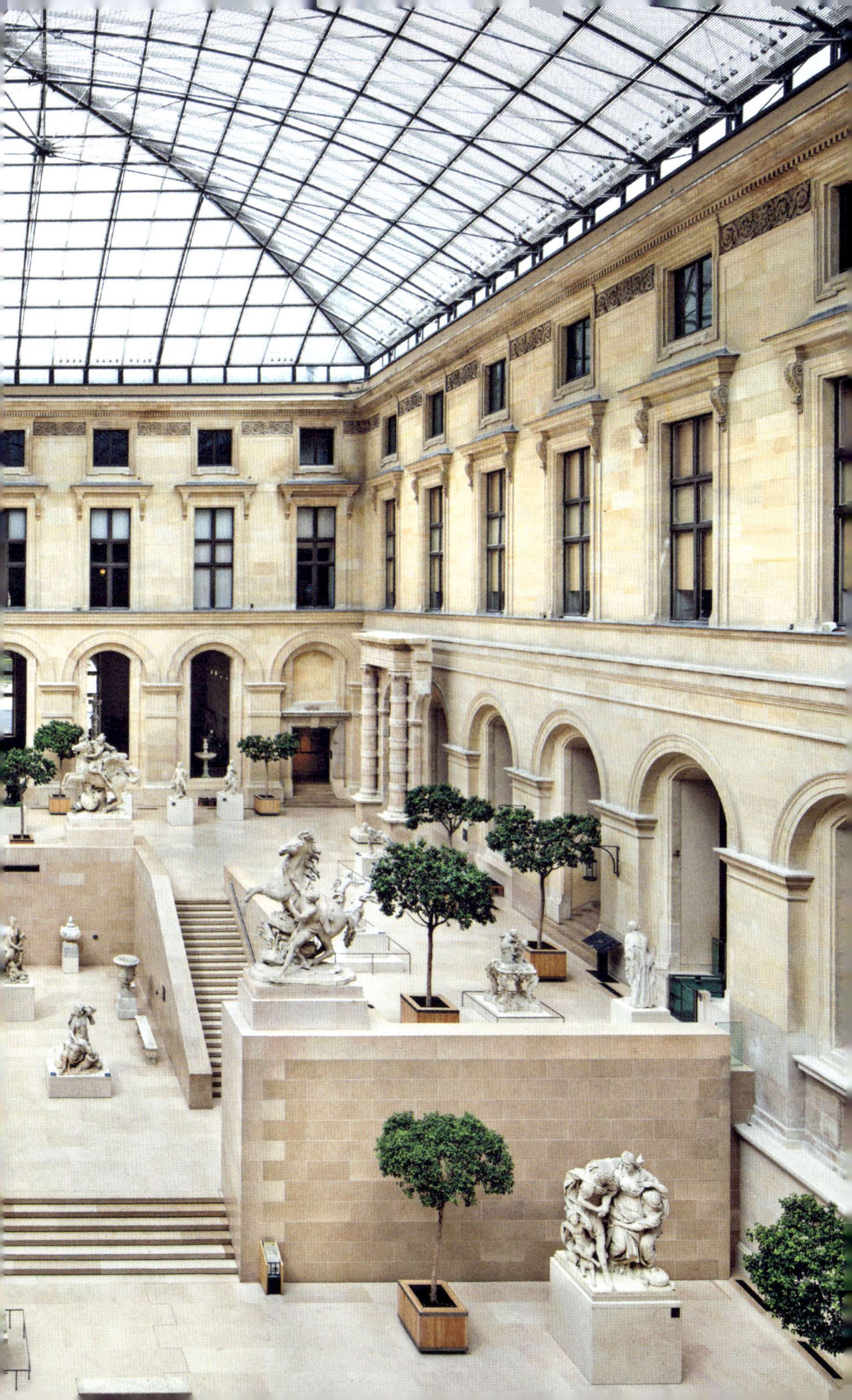

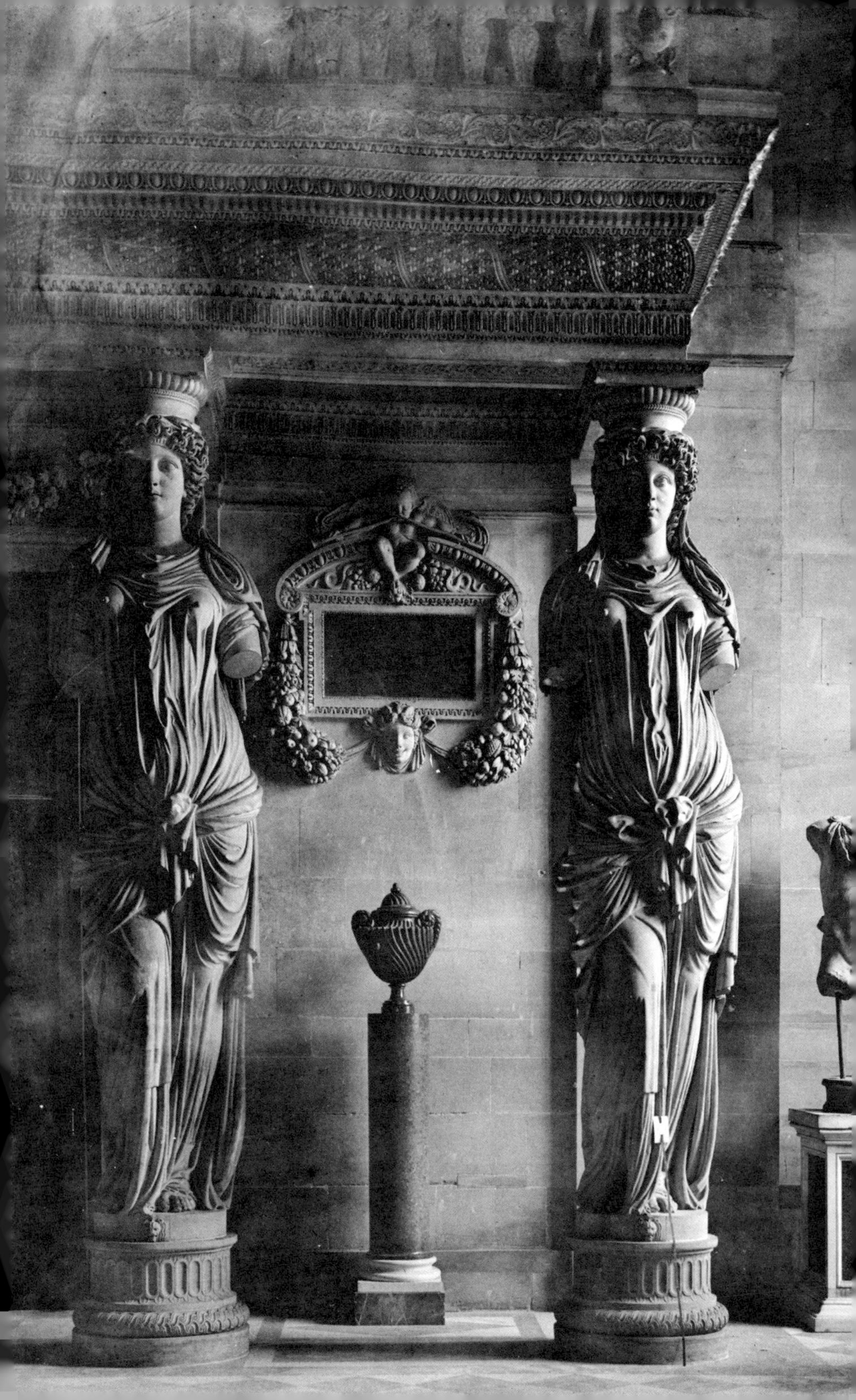

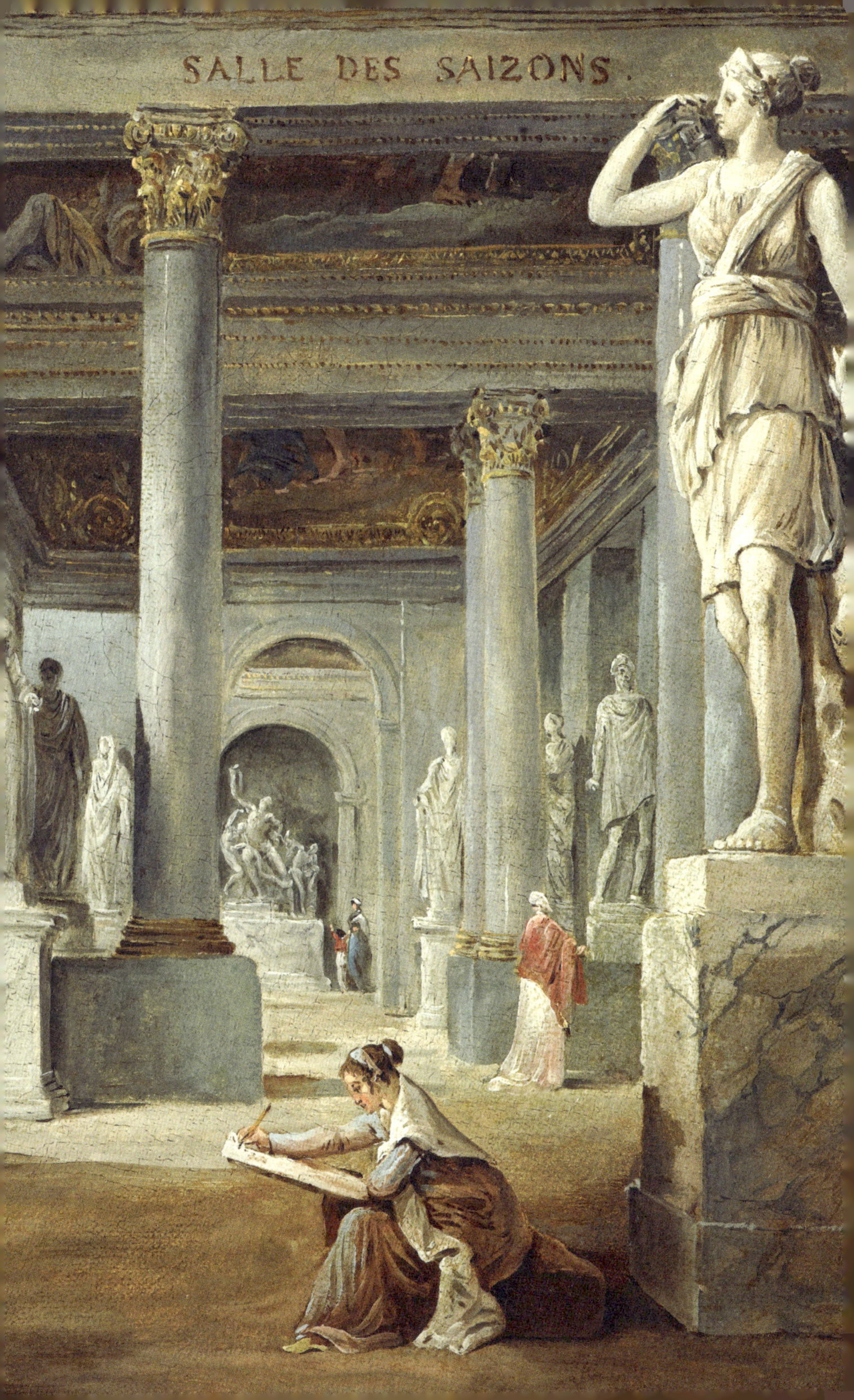
SALLE DES SAIZONS.

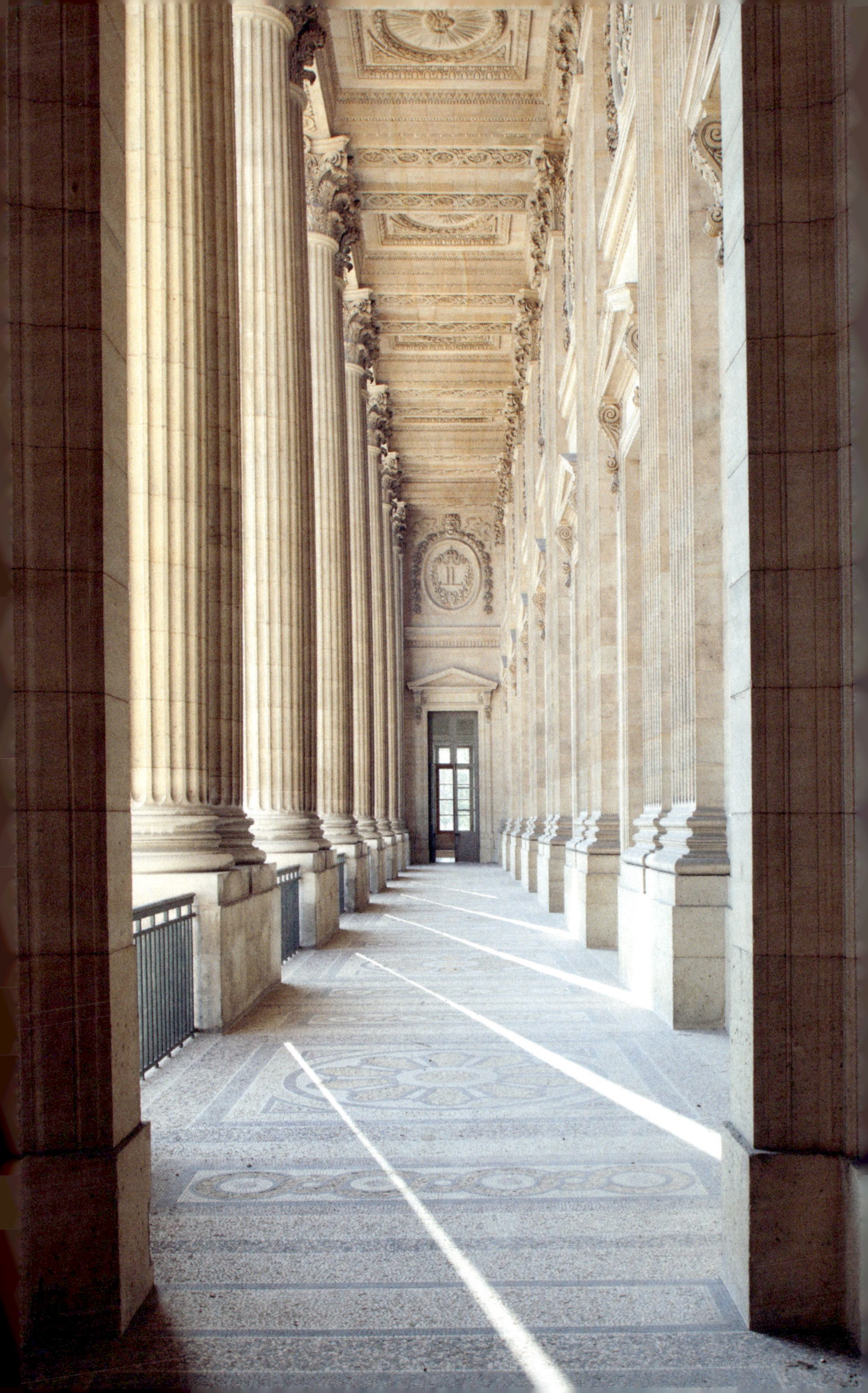

THE LOUVRE

the guide

text by
Dominique de Font-Réaulx

LOUVRE éditions
GrandPalais RmnÉditions

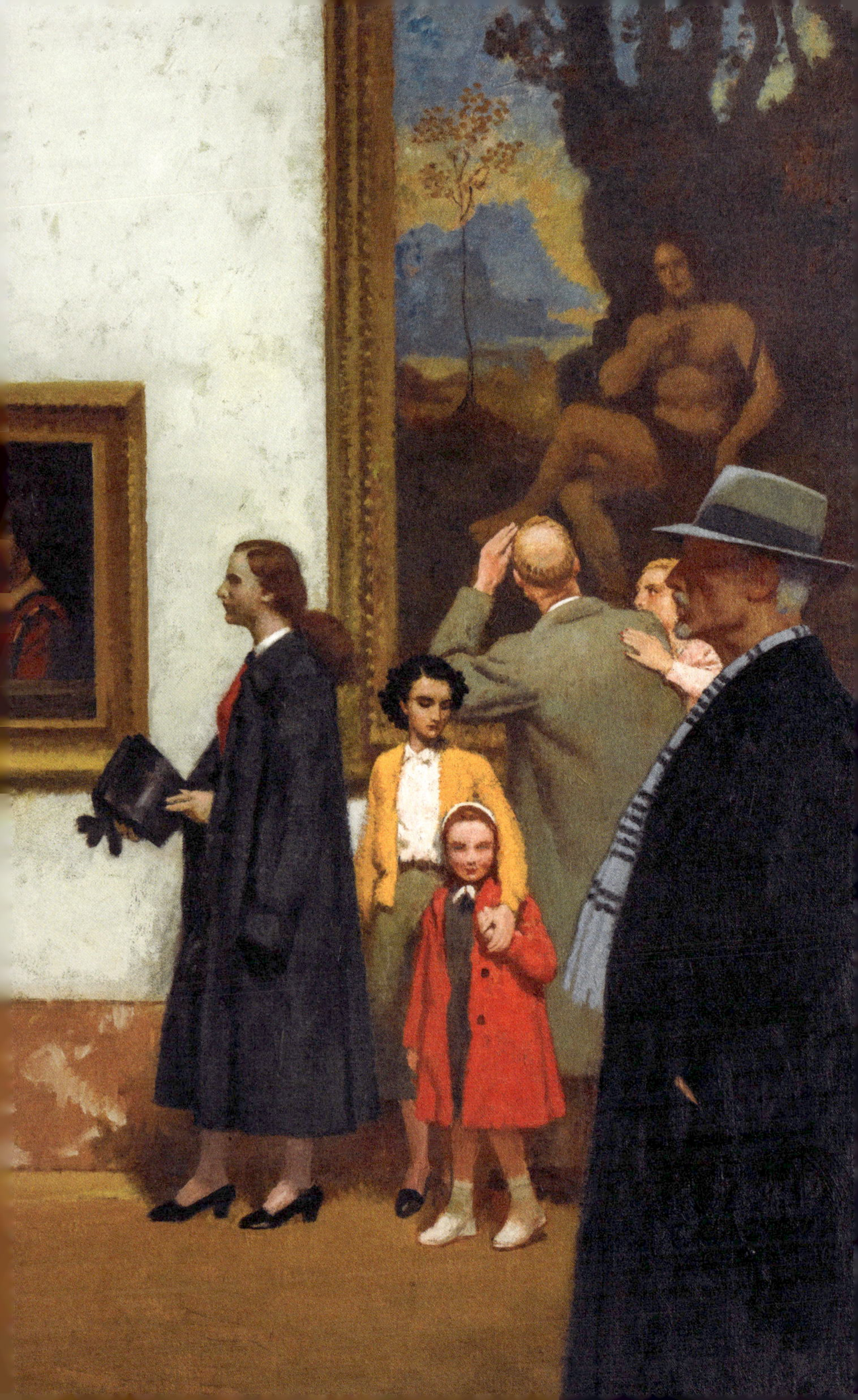

FOREWORD

Founded in 1793, in what had been a royal palace, the Louvre celebrated its 230th anniversary in 2023. Its collections, in all their historical scope and diversity, make it a unique place where the past, cast in a new light, brings substance and meaning to the present.

As we move from one civilisation and one technique to another, a pleasure made greater still by the freedom to wander and explore, stories take shape that are rooted in the connections and counterpoints that emerge between the works; in the mutual admiration and, sometimes, envy or desire for conquest they represent. Transforming these narratives into something we see and experience enhances the Louvre's relation with today's world.

The Musée du Louvre is an encyclopaedia whose entries are constantly being composed, inviting comparisons that bring fresh perspectives to its collections. This guide is intended to bring these relations to the fore, and I would like to thank its author, Dominique de Font-Réaulx, for her wonderful work.

In times of peace as in times of war, history has been written by the connections between peoples and civilisations. In its ambition to be a universal museum, in its determination to remain a window onto the world, the Louvre is a book whose pages are continually rewritten, a place to discover and rediscover, finding new enjoyment each time.

Laurence des Cars
President-Director, Musée du Louvre

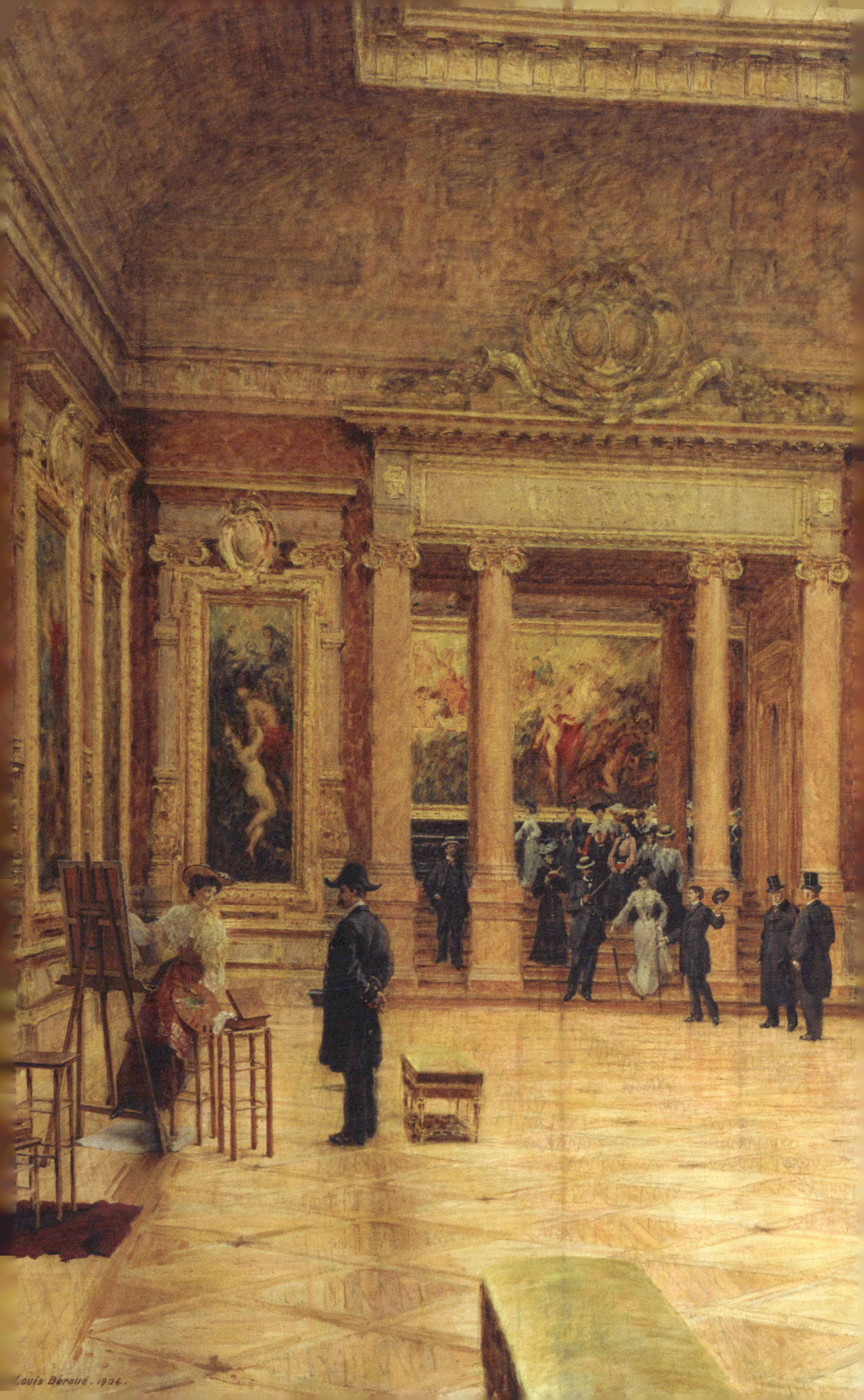
Louis Béroud . 1904 .

Introduction 21

Before writing 26

The invention of writing, 3500–3100 BCE 32

Discovering ancient civilisations 36

The fall of Babylon, 6th century BCE 68

New perspectives on ancient art 72

The Augustan Age, 25 BCE–25 CE 88

The Roman and Byzantine empires 92

Hijrah, the birth of a new religion, 622 116

Cross-cultural inspirations 120

The powerful Ghana Empire, 11th century 128

The Louvre, heir to the Musée des Monuments Français 132

The travels of Marco Polo, late 13th century–14th century 146

Powerful patrons: The origins of the Louvre collections 150

The invention of printing, c. 1452 162

Renaissances 166

The Edict of Nantes, 1598 208

Accomplished masters 212

The Seven Years' War, 1756–1763 244

Virtuosities 248

Creation of the Muséum Central at the Louvre, 1793 264

Inventing the museum 268

The abolition of slavery in France, 1848 298

From one museum to another 302

Index 314

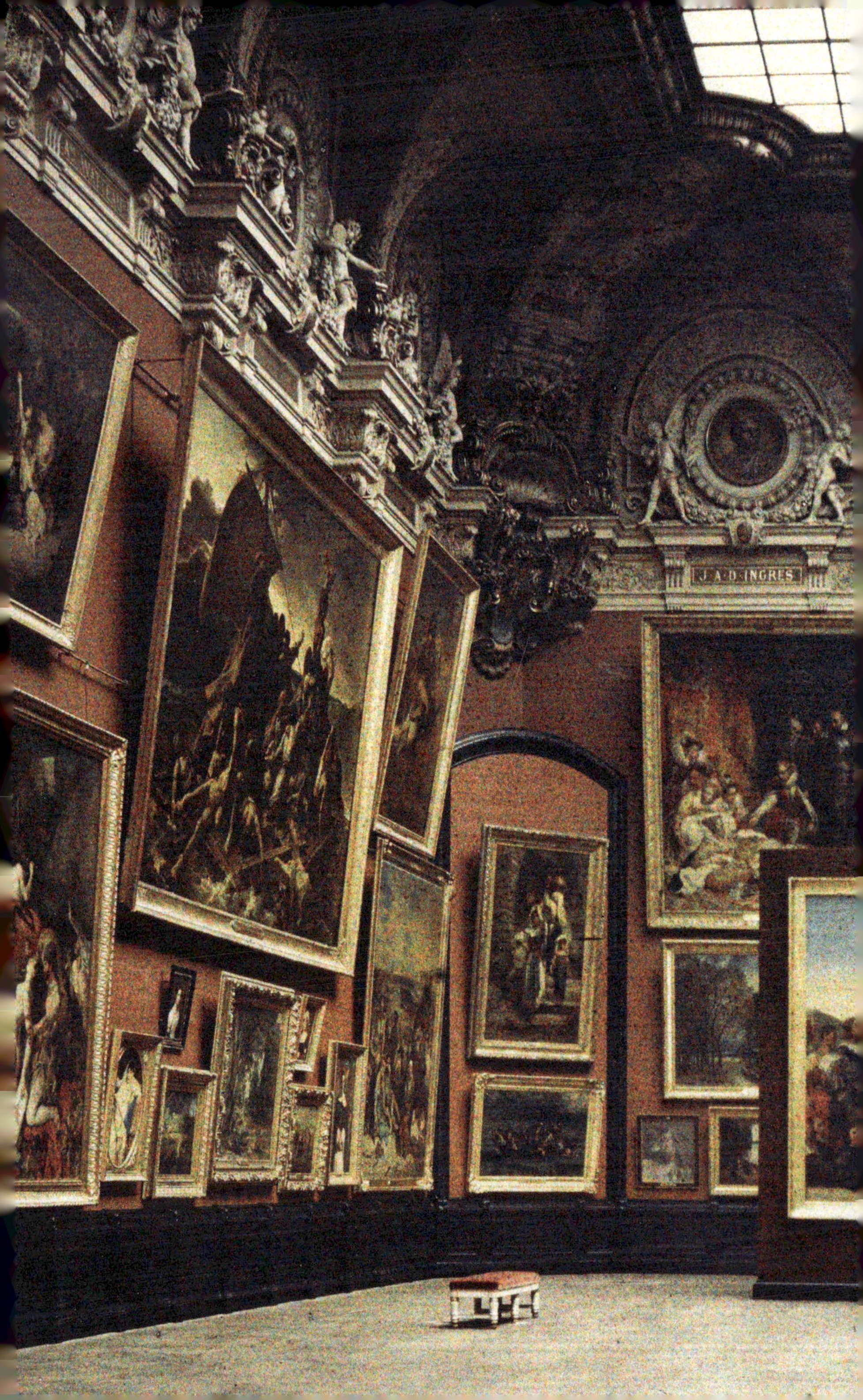
J.A.D. INGRES

When the Louvre was founded in the summer of 1793 its purpose was to be an encyclopaedic museum, presenting the most remarkable examples of artistic creation since the dawn of humanity for all to enjoy. Heir to the ideas of the Enlightenment, today's Louvre forms one small part of this ambition, accomplished in a dimension that is both realistic and utopian. Extending across more than 75,000 square metres (807,300 sq. ft) and assembling thousands of works produced since the invention of writing up to the mid-nineteenth century, the Louvre's galleries are a succession of surprises and revelations. A monument that has taken shape over multiple centuries, once the home of France's kings and expanded during the Second Empire by Napoleon III, its meanders are an invitation to delve left and right, to double back and change trajectories. Its decor is still that of the palace it once was, with ancient Greek sculpture in Henry II's ballroom, Roman antiquities in Anne of Austria's apartments, and the Egyptian collections displayed beneath ceilings commissioned by Charles X from the up-and-coming artists of the day. The Louvre is an extraordinary playground. It is a place to learn to see, exploring its spaces in whichever order you wish, inventing a different path every time.

The Louvre remains true to the idea of universality, to be open to all. This is a reality observed each day in the galleries and an axiom that underlies all its projects, the presentation of the works and the contextualisation of the collections. Created to spark aesthetic delectation, as it was then called, the museum is a space where pleasure blooms: the pleasure of discovery, of wonderment, of new encounters. In its very essence, the Louvre is a place where connections are made, between the works themselves, the visitors, and between visitors and the museum's staff. To see objects from so many civilisations and places in such close proximity invites dialogue and provides perspective.

Shaped by the aesthetic concepts and artistic tastes that preceded and informed its development, the narrative the Louvre presents is not linear; collections are not set out in the established order of a dictionary or a textbook. To visit the Louvre is to travel through time, jumping from one civilisation to another and moving between timescales in a constantly renewed experience. We contemplate objects whose presence reflects choices that were not governed by the same criteria that would be used today. A museum of fine arts, heir to the royal collections that began in the fourteenth century, the Louvre is also an archaeological museum that continues to conduct excavations, working with the countries concerned, as well as a social museum reflecting humanity's aspirations, the thirst for knowledge, the desire to collaborate, and the need to share and exchange. It does not gloss over the difficulties humans face. In this, the first third of the twenty-first century, the dangers of a sometimes benevolent, sometimes menacing nature are evident. This nature is resistant to humanity's vain attempts to control its force, of which our predecessors were so careful. The desire for peace but also the upheavals of war, the decision to not see or create a certain distance exist now as then. Thus, works from the past are still relevant today, enriched by our own point of view and the questions we ask ourselves.

As home to some of the greatest accomplishments of the human mind and hand, the Louvre is also a place of storytelling. The founding myths of civilisations and many of the most important written manifestations of human thought are contained in its collections: the *Epic of Gilgamesh*, the Sumerian hero whose exploits inspired the legend of the Greek hero Heracles; the books of the Old Testament, shared by Judaism, Christianity and Islam;

the *Odyssey*, which describes the Greek warrior Ulysses's journey home, from victory in the Trojan War to the island of Ithaca, and the violent winds, treacherous currents and dangerous shoals he encountered as he crossed the Mediterranean; as well as Virgil's *Aeneid*, Ovid's *Metamorphoses* and the *Song of Roland*.

Founded as a place of education, the Louvre's doors have always been open to artists. The latter have spent time in the museum, admiring the work of the ancient masters, sharpening their gaze and technique, until their creations found a final home within its walls: the ultimate distinction and their greatest aspiration. The museum displays paintings by Jean-Auguste-Dominique Ingres, Théodore Géricault and Eugène Delacroix alongside sculptures by Antoine-Louis Barye, all of whom made copies in the Louvre before their own work was exhibited in turn, for others to interpret. Reviving a practice inaugurated in the 1820s, the Louvre has commissioned Georges Braque, Anselm Kiefer, François Morellet and Cy Twombly to create permanent works for its galleries. Each year, the museum extends invitations to visual artists, photographers, writers and poets. Their creative vision establishes fresh connections and new bridges between past and present achievements.

The history of art that unfolds in the Louvre did not exist before the museum opened its doors. The Louvre is writing a history of art as its collections grow. Space had to be found – and must still be made – for new objects, new knowledge and new places which have sometimes challenged existing theories, redefined representations of the human body, or introduced fresh frames of reference. The museum's temporal limits, geographic boundaries and aesthetic canons have thus been transformed. In 1827 the Louvre opened a department of Egyptian antiquities, directed by Jean-François Champollion, who deciphered hieroglyphs. The arrival of architectural and sculpted remains from the palace of Sargon II in Khorsabad in 1847 were the starting point for the collections of Near Eastern antiquities. Towards the middle of the nineteenth century, the Louvre acquired a collection of American antiquities. The opening, in spring 2000, of the Pavillon des Sessions, which displays works from African, Oceanian and American civilisations from the collections of the Musée du Quai Branly – Jacques Chirac, celebrates a global artistic heritage. The creation of the Department of Islamic Art in 2004, and its presentation in the Cour Visconti, and of the Department of Byzantine and Eastern Christian Art, initiated in 2022 for launch in 2026, confirm that the Louvre is open to the world. This ongoing enveloping of successive discoveries shows that the Louvre is a living museum designed to be part of its time and committed to reinventing itself. It also explains the complex nature of a place where the history of men, women and their artistic creations is constantly written and recomposed.

In this twenty-first century, the Louvre's universal premise may appear to be dominated by a Western view: other French institutions conserve works that reflect how other cultures see the world. Yet the Louvre has remained open to the artistic creation gradually brought to light through voyages, exchanges and study. Its inventories list objects from Europe, Africa, Asia, and North and South America. The artefacts exhibited in its galleries comprise materials from all around the globe. The story of their origins tells of a sometimes peaceful history of trade and exchange, and at other times, of a painful past in which peoples were denied their right to freedom.

A visit to the Louvre elicits many different emotions; to try and contain them in a few hundred pages would be a dizzying task. No single publication can hope to reproduce every one of the works on display, nor have the presumption to guide the reader through the museum. Rather, the purpose of this book is to make people want to visit the Louvre or, for those who have already explored its galleries, to be a reminder of a rich experience, and it serves as a guide to the history of art through the Louvre collection. It juxtaposes selected works from the collections managed by the Louvre's nine departments and from the collections of the Musée du Quai Branly – Jacques Chirac shown in the Pavillon des Sessions. Read it from cover to cover or, better still, browse through its pages and imagine your own path around the museum. Referencing major world events from the seventh millennium BCE until 1848, this guide establishes common markers that highlight the Louvre's place within the world and its ties with every civilisation. Some of the stories that take shape inside the museum – stories about the artists and their creations, stories the works tell, stories about how they came to the Louvre and the reaction they inspired – are interwoven here. Some, not all: these pages can only contain a small part of the narratives whose origins and home are within the Louvre's walls.

Works of art cannot be explained in a few brief lines. They reveal themselves through contemplation, divulging a different secret each time. The choice of images as well as the design of this guide are therefore intended to appeal to the eye in a way that will mirror the enchantment of a walk through the Louvre's galleries, with its multiple perspectives. Along the way, six poetic associations of celebrated works are an invitation to imagine your own connections and stories. We hope this guide will achieve its aim: that you should return to the Louvre, as often as possible.

Before writing

As a museum whose collections form a multitude of intersecting, interwoven narratives, writing is at the heart of the Louvre. Part of history, these collections underpin a process of transmission that draws on the ability to decipher languages, especially ancient languages, and an understanding of texts. Yet several of the museum's acquisititions predate the invention of writing systems, believed to have begun between 3500 and 3100 BCE. These works are a reminder that the Louvre, a museum of fine art, is also an important archaeological museum. Beginning in the 1820s, excavations conducted in Egypt, the Near East, the Middle East, Greece and Italy were driven by curiosity about the ancient civilisations whose names appear in the Bible, and which were brought to light by the first discoveries, particularly in Egypt. Over the course of the nineteenth century, what began as an appreciation of beauty became a desire for knowledge and exploration. By delving into the past, digging through earth and exploring ruins, modern archaeology has also sought answers to questions about the present, in order to forge links across history leading to our lives today, and to give substance to our founding mythological and religious texts.

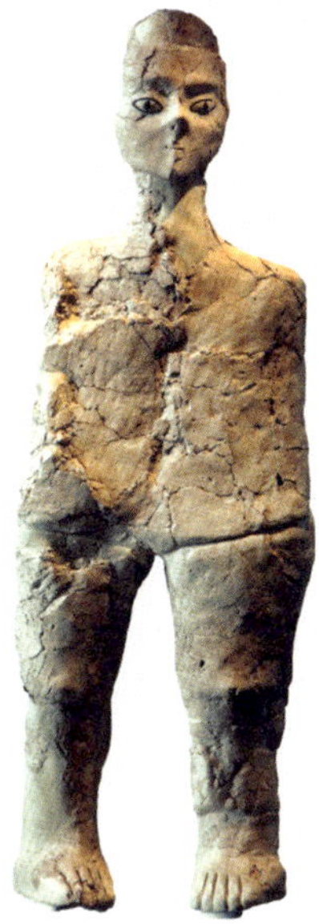

[1]
Ain Ghazal Statue
'Ain Ghazal, Jordan
c. 7000–6000 BCE
Plaster and bitumen
H. 105; W. 33; D. 13 cm
(H. 3 ft 5¼ in.; W. 1 ft 1 in.;
D. 5⅛ in.)
⊻ 1997 (on deposit from the Jordan Archaeological Museum, Amman)
DNEA

EXPLORING AND DECIPHERING In 1827 Jean-François Champollion was put in charge of the Louvre's collections of Egyptian antiquities. Intellectually curious, this gifted young scholar had, thanks to the Rosetta Stone (now held in the British Museum in London), deciphered the secret of hieroglyphics. In 1847 Paul-Émile Botta, the French consul in Mosul, in present-day Iraq, discovered the remains of Assyrian palaces in Khorsabad while searching for the city of Nineveh, mentioned in the Bible. French archaeologists continued and extended early explorations at various locations, including Memphis and Saqqara in Egypt, Susa in what is now Iran, Babylon (Hillah) in present-day Iraq, Mari in today's Syria, Bahrain, and in Delphi and Delos in Greece. At several sites these excavations are ongoing, in close cooperation with archaeologists from the countries in question.

The discovery of a number of large statues, standing almost a metre (3 ft) high, at the 'Ain Ghazal site in Jordan in 1983 was a revelation. Dating from around 7000 BCE, they are remarkable, both for the materials from which they are made – plaster applied to a reed core, implying preparatory

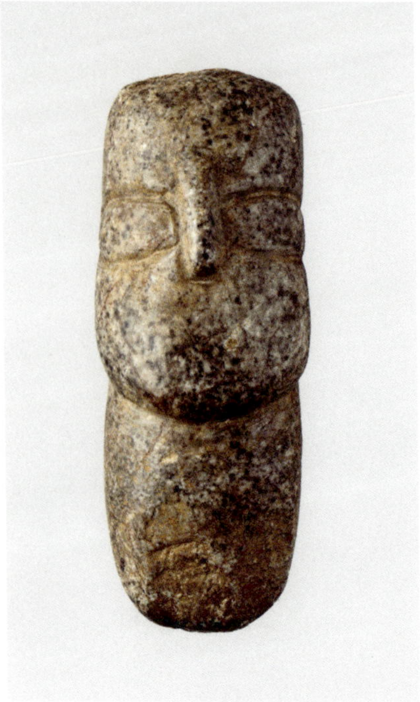

[2]
Head of a Statuette
Anatolia, Turkey
c. 6900–5300 BCE
Marble
H. 11.4; W. 4.5; D. 3.6 cm
(H. 4½; W. 1¾; D. 1⅜ in.)
⩡ 1899 (gift of Paul Gaudin)
DNEA

work – and for their size, being significantly larger than any other prehistoric human representation. Their purpose is unknown; they had been carefully buried in a pit that protected them for almost nine thousand years. Their careful construction and naturalist human form strongly suggest that this was already an established and organised society. The *Ain Ghazal Statue* **[1]** was placed on deposit at the Louvre by the state of Jordan and the Jordan Archaeological Museum in Amman.

Head of a Statuette **[2]**, from Anatolia in what is now Turkey, is one of the oldest works in the Louvre's inventories. Sculpted from grey marble, the elongated face is rendered schematically, with incisions to represent the eyes; the nose is prominent in relation to the rest of the figure, whose neck has been preserved. This particularly large head would have been inserted on a figurine standing some seventy centimetres (27½ in.) high, almost certainly in wood, a perishable material.

The site of Susa, founded around 4200 BCE in western Iran, in what is now Khuzestan province, is proof that

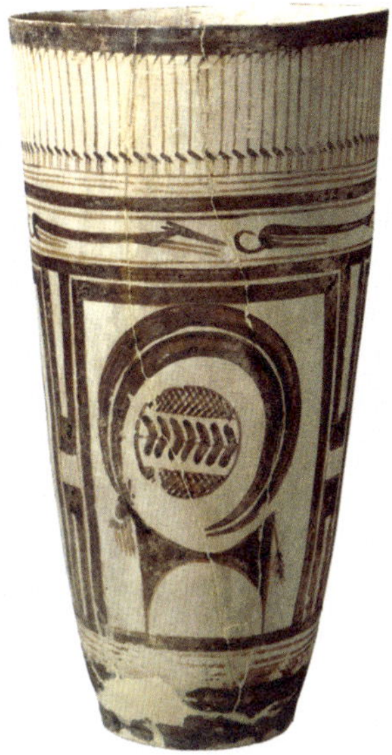

[3]
Vase
Susa, present-day Iran
c. 4000–3500 BCE
Painted terracotta
H. 28.8; Diam. 16.4 cm
(H. 11¼; Diam. 6½ in.)
⩡ 1910–1911
DNEA

an urban settlement with a stratified society existed from this period. During digs by French archaeologists Marcel Dieulafoy and Jane Dieulafoy, which began in 1884, two thousand tombs were discovered in the centre of a vast necropolis. These burial sites were richly furnished with grave goods, mainly terracotta vases of exceptional quality. These vessels exhibit a wide range of decorative motifs, painted in black or brown on the light ochre ground formed by the clay paste and slip. Tall vases with conical bases make up one of the main types **[3]**. Designs are geometric – vertical and horizontal lines, solid triangles, lozenges, squares and chevrons that overlap to varying degrees – or depict animals – stylised birds with long necks, ibexes with exaggeratedly large horns, or Sloughis, long-bodied dogs running as a frieze around certain vases.

The *Gebel el-Arak Knife* **[4]** is one of the finest artefacts from Predynastic Egypt, a period referred to as Naqada (3900–3150 BCE). Purchased by the Louvre in the early twentieth century, it is believed to originate from the region around Thebes. The blade is flint, while the handle is ivory,

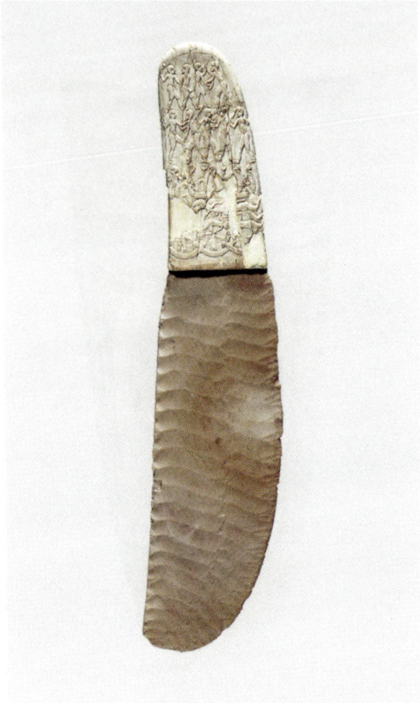

[4]
Gebel el-Arak Knife
Gebel el-Arak, Egypt
c. 3600–3300 BCE
Hippopotamus ivory and flint
H. 25.5; W. 4.5 cm
(H. 10; W. 1¾ in.)
⊻ 1914
DEA

probably from a hippopotamus tooth. It has been elaborately carved with scenes that suggest a Sumerian influence, from Mesopotamia. They depict a bearded male figure between two lions he is controlling, with other animals carved at the top, including dogs, lionesses and ibexes. This Master of Animals motif indicates that close ties existed between the two geographic regions from the fourth millennium BCE, which would have facilitated trade and artistic exchanges.

Dating from the last years of the Naqada period, the *Stele of the Serpent King* **[5]** was found in a tomb at the site of Abydos in the late nineteenth century. It provides evidence of a first proto-hieroglyphic writing system that combines iconographic forms with signs. The falcon, symbol of the god Horus, surmounts the outline of a palace and a serpent, the hieroglyph for Djet, a First Dynasty king.

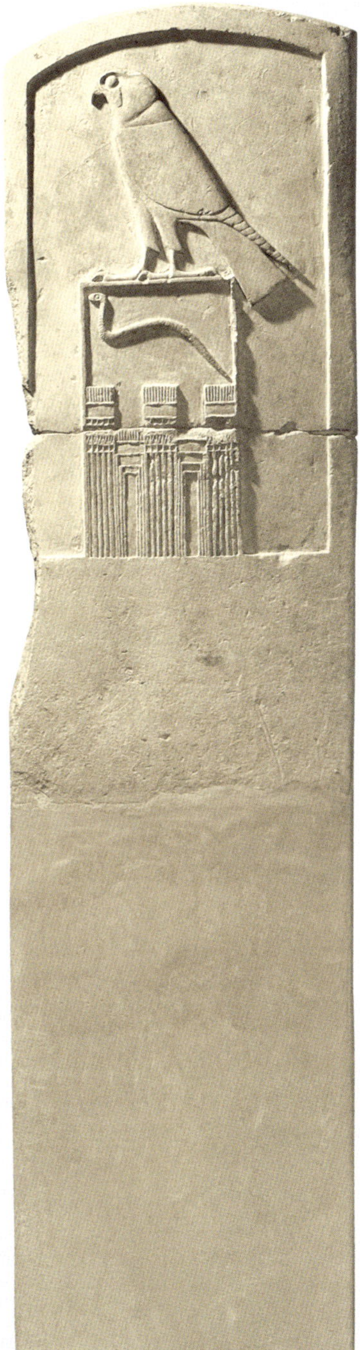

[5]
Stele of the Serpent King
Tomb of Djet, Abydos,
Egypt
c. 3100–2900 BCE
Limestone
H. 143; W. 65.5; D. 25 cm
(H. 4 ft 8¼ in.; W. 2 ft 1¾ in.;
D. 9¾ in.)
⊻ 1904
DEA

Writing came into use around 3400 BCE in Sumer in southern Mesopotamia, a fertile region of the Near East between the Tigris and Euphrates rivers. The emergence of writing systems was tied to the development of urban settlements, often adjacent to religious sanctuaries, which encouraged trade as well as social interaction and artistic production. The Sumerians appear to have considered Uruk, in the south of present-day Iraq, a model city, because of its organisation and dynamism **[6]**. Scribes used a sharpened reed as a stylus to impress signs on clay tablets. These signs were wedge-shaped, *cuneus* in Latin, hence cuneiform, the name given to this early writing system. Clay had the advantage of being readily available and easy to model, but is also a noble material with symbolic importance, as it was the material the god Enki used to create humankind. Thus, writing is as much a spiritual creation as a physical one.

The first written texts appear to have recorded transactions and exchanges of goods, vital in ensuring the fortunes of a region at the intersection of numerous trade routes. Initially, writing was formed by pictographs that produced meaning when combined. For example, the head and bread on the Uruk tablet **[8]**, one of the first known written documents, signify a ration of food; on the reverse side, the palace is indicated by a sceptre next to a dwelling. The symbol at the top left is that of the city of Uruk, while the symbol at the bottom right corresponds to the region of Dilmun – present-day Bahrain – a busy trading centre.

Mesopotamia, with its long history and despite a succession of wars and conflicts between the different peoples who lived there, was an extremely stable region in terms of the transmission of languages, texts and myths. Because of its presence in the Bible and its influence on early mythological texts, it is considered the cradle of Western thought. The individuals who discovered these vanished civilisations in the nineteenth century set out in search of the traces of biblical settings, especially Nineveh, the mythical Babylon. The first cuneiform texts to be discovered were written in Akkadian, a language that dates from the twelfth century BCE. The initial tablet to enter the Louvre's

[6]
Statue
Sumer, present-day Iraq
c. 3500–3100 BCE
Limestone
H. 30.5; W. 10.4; D. 7 cm
(H. 12; W. 4; D. 2¾ in.)
DNEA

[7]
Pin
Telloh, present-day Iraq
c. 3500–3100 BCE
Copper
L. 18.1 cm
(L. 7¼ in.)
⊻ 1931
DNEA

[8]
Tablet
Uruk, present-day Iraq
c. 3500–3100 BCE
Clay
H. 4.5; W. 7.2; D. 1.5 cm
(H. 1¾; W. 2⅞; D. ½ in.)
⊻ 1988
DNEA

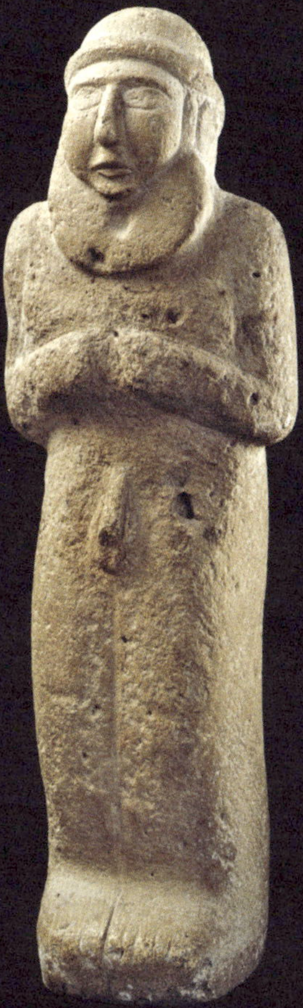

6

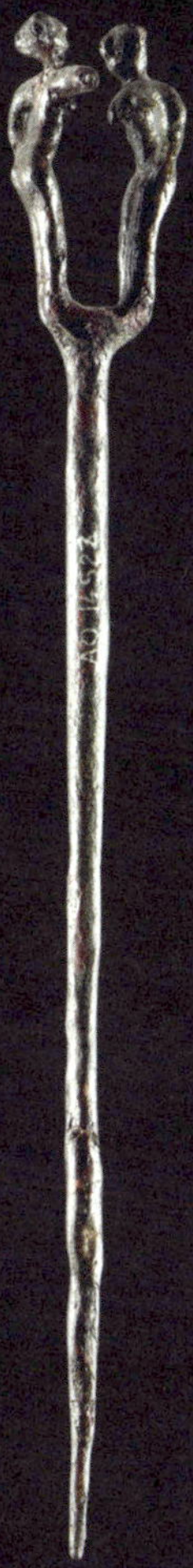

7

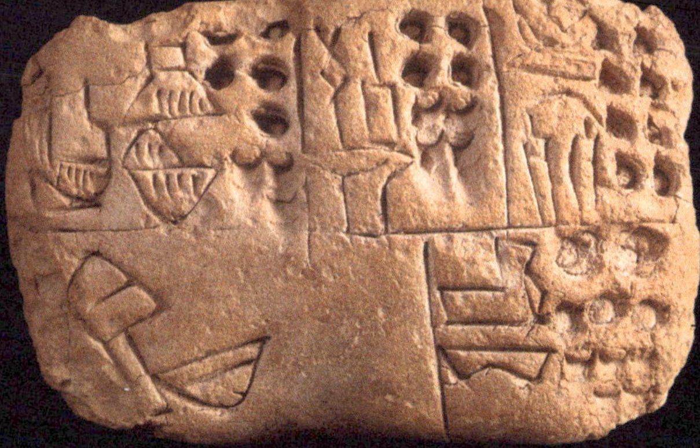

8

collections came from digs carried out in Khorsabad in northern Iraq in the mid-nineteenth century.

Large numbers of clay tablets arrived at the Louvre from excavations conducted in Telloh by Ernest de Sarzec and later by others. In 1905 the linguist François Thureau-Dangin deciphered the Sumerian language. Continued research and fresh revelations bolstered knowledge. Under terms agreed with the Ottoman government, which was then in charge of the region, artefacts **[7]** were brought to the Louvre, where history takes shape around them.

[9]
Figurine
Lower Egypt (?)
c. 3600–3300 BCE
Chlorite
H. 2.75; L. 3.85; W. 1.75 cm
(H. 1; L. 1½; W. ⅝ in.)
⊻ 1979 (gift of the Société des Amis du Louvre)
DEA

[10]
Violin-Shaped Figurine
Cyclades, Greece
c. 3200–3000 BCE
Marble
H. 10.2; W. 4.5; D. 1 cm
(H. 4; W. 1¾; D. ⅜ in.)
⊻ 1949 (gift of Nicolas Koutoulakis)
DGERA

[11]
Jar
Naqada (?), Egypt
c. 3900–3600 BCE
Basalt
H. 37.1; Diam. 12.8 cm
(H. 14½; Diam. 5 in.)
⊻ 1938 (bequest of Mr and Mrs Curtis)
DEA

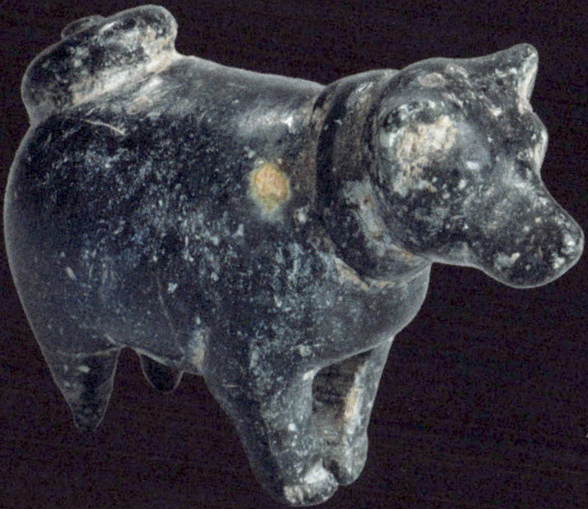

9

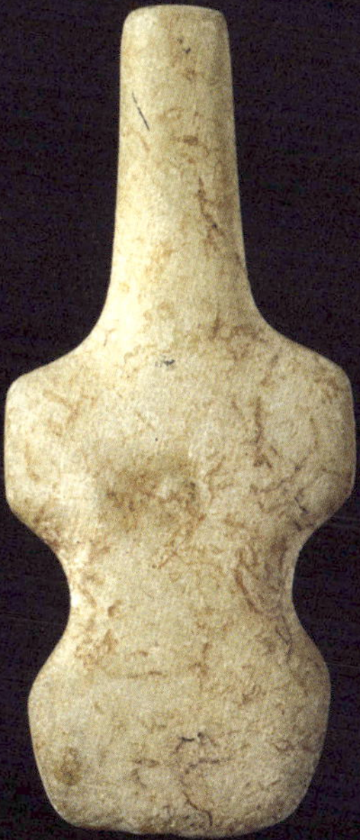

10

11

Discovering ancient civilisations

The Louvre's collections of antiquities are among the world's richest holdings of ancient artefacts. They trace the way artists thousands of years ago created multiple representations of the world around them. They illustrate the vitality of structured societies that built busy cities, watched over by divinities who were honoured in magnificent temples. These societies arose in the eastern Mediterranean, in an area stretching from Mesopotamia, between the Tigris and Euphrates rivers, to ancient Egypt, and extending the length of the Nile, one of the longest and most powerful rivers, as far as Asia Minor and Greece. These are lands of storytelling. Many of the texts that have formed the basis of human thought originated here, rooted in meteorological phenomena or historical events.

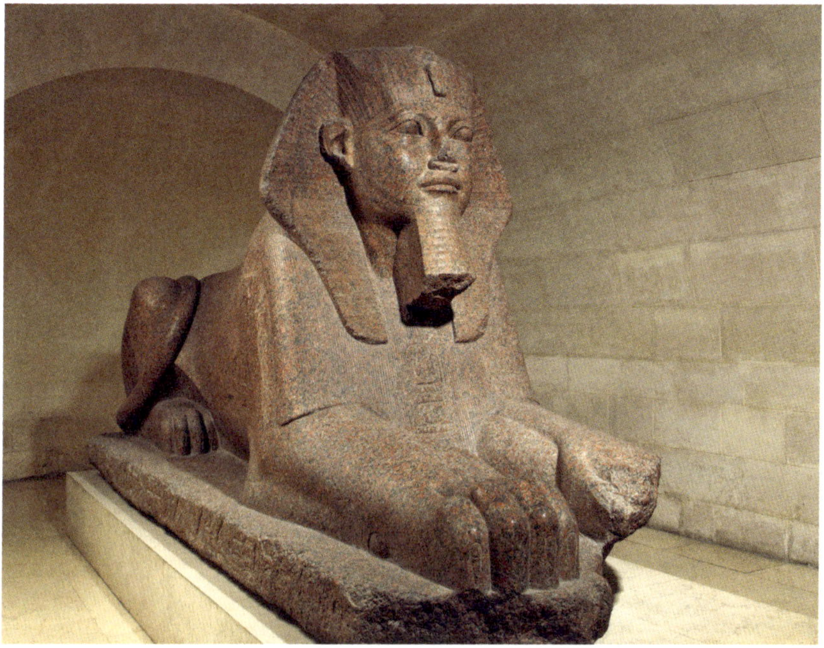

[12] ***Great Sphinx of Tanis***. Tanis, Egypt. c. 2620–1866 BCE. Pink granite
H. 183; L. 480; W. 154 cm (H. 6 ft; L. 15 ft 9 in.; W. 5 ft). A 1826. DEA

Their authors, reprising an oral tradition, gave these narratives a far greater dimension: that of human destiny – the constant inner battle to lend meaning to a brief existence that ends, inevitably, in death. Running through many of these representations is the desire for eternal life.

RECONSTRUCTING HISTORY Relations to power are central to the history recounted in the works that have survived. Often discovered in the ruins of palaces, in the elaborate tombs of necropolises, in the remains of temples dug free from earth and sand, they tell the stories of powerful individuals and the gods they honoured. Stone, granite and marble have triumphed over the passage of time while other, more fragile materials have perished. We know more about the monumental features and sculpted decorations of palaces and temples than we do about more modest dwellings. Thanks to these vestiges, we are able to establish the succession of pharaonic dynasties in Egypt, untangle the strands of Mesopotamia's empires, or study the development of ancient Greece's different cities. Details of everyday life have emerged, such as the relationship

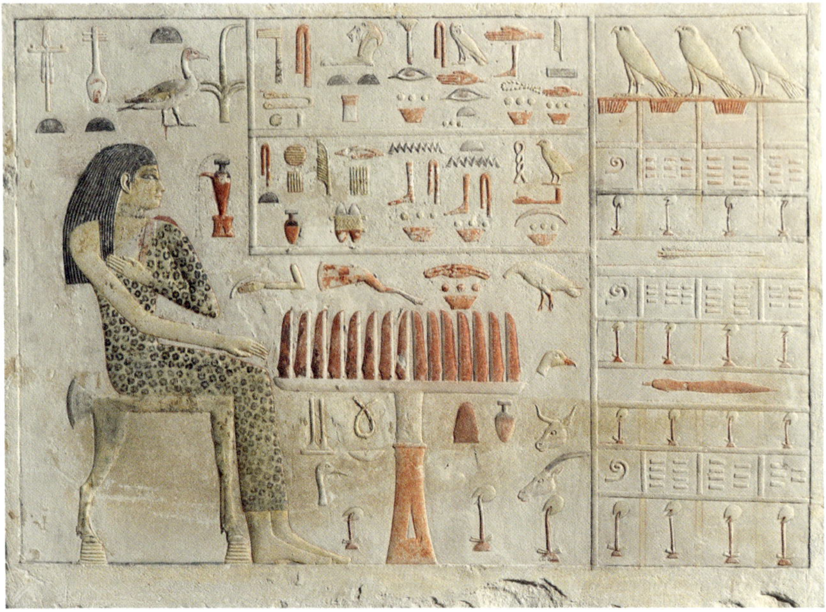

[13] ***Stele of Nefertiabet***. Mastaba G 1225, Giza, Egypt. c. 2590–2533 BCE. Painted limestone
H. 37.7; W. 52.5; D. 8.3 cm (H. 14¾; W. 20¾; D. 3¼ in.). A 1938 (gift of Mr and Mrs Curtis). DEA

with nature, a preference for certain foods, or the experience of art, poetry and music.

This history did not fall into place easily. Rather, it was woven together thread by thread over the past two centuries, by men and women who studied texts – which first had to be deciphered – and observed the objects themselves, as well as the sites where they were found. This was a gradual process that required methodical analysis in addition to a fertile and erudite imagination, necessary for the formulation of lucid hypotheses to serve as the base for solid interpretations. The memory of this incremental process, grounded in science and the imagination, resonates within the Louvre's walls, where it continues to this day.

IN THE STEPS OF THE POWERFUL AND THE DIVINE The *Great Sphinx of Tanis* **[12]**, acquired by the Louvre in 1826, is one of the largest sphinxes outside Egypt. Discovered in Tanis, in the eastern Nile Delta, this colossal granite statue measures almost five metres (16 ft 4¾ in.) long and weighs several tonnes. A lion with the head of a man, this protective figure combines

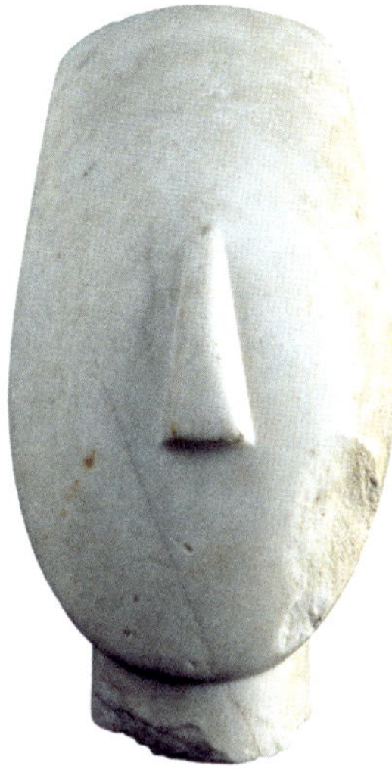

[14]
Head of a Female Statue, Spedos type
Keros, Cyclades, Greece
c. 2600–2400 BCE
Marble
H. 27; W. 14; D. 10 cm
(H. 10½; W. 5½; D. 4 in.)
⩡ 1873 (gift of Olivier Rayet)
DGERA

the animal's power with the wisdom of the Egyptian ruler, who is adorned with the pharaoh's headdress – the nemes – a false beard and an upright cobra – the uraeus – all symbols of power. Built for a pharaoh during the Fourth Dynasty, the monument was adopted by later pharaohs, up to the early first millennium BCE, and shows the permanence of symbolic representations in ancient Egypt. The *Stele of Nefertiabet* **[13]**, in painted limestone, was found in the early twentieth century close to the Great Pyramid of Giza. It depicts the meal that will accompany Nefertiabet, the pharaoh's daughter, after her earthly demise and throughout eternal life. The slab's naturalist carvings bear witness to the talent of the Egyptian sculptors and to the pictorial nature of the hieroglyphic writing system.

Dating from the same period, the marble head found on the island of Keros **[14]** is part of what we can imagine must have been an impressively large statue of a woman, the body of which is missing. Sometimes referred to as "the *Mona Lisa* of Cycladic art", it belongs to a body of works uncovered during the latter half of the nineteenth century in the Cyclades, a group of islands in the Aegean. Because of the pure, simple beauty

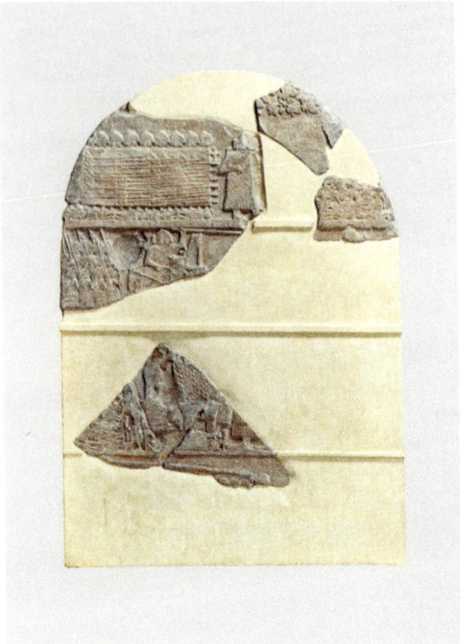

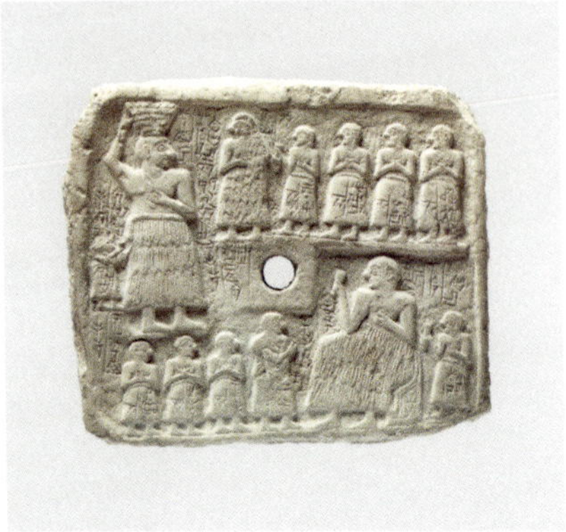

[15]
Stele of the Vultures
Telloh, present-day Iraq
c. 2450–2425 BCE
Limestone
H. 180; W. 130; D. 11 cm
(H. 5 ft 10¾ in.;
W. 4 ft 3¼ in.; D. 4⅜ in.)
⩡ 1881 (gift of the Ottoman government)
DNEA

[16]
Relief of Ur-Nanshe
Telloh, present-day Iraq
c. 2495–2465 BCE
Limestone
H. 39; W. 46.5; D. 6.5 cm
(H. 15¼; W. 18¼ in.; D. 2½ in.)
⩡ 1890 (gift of the Ottoman government)
DNEA

of their shape and features, they are often considered as "idols", although there is nothing to suggest any sacred use. The painter Pablo Picasso was among the admirers who visited this exceptional work – which has become a modern icon – at the Louvre.

The *Relief of Ur-Nanshe* **[16]** is named after the king of Lagash – a city in Mesopotamia, in what is now Iraq – and dedicated to him. It was found at the site of Telloh by the archaeologist and diplomat Ernest de Sarzec in 1888. Dating from around 2500 BCE and particularly well preserved, it illustrates episodes from the king's life in two registers. On the top, the king carries a basket of bricks that will be used for construction; facing him are his wife and children. In the bottom register, Ur-Nanshe is taking part in a banquet, alongside his sons and servants. Cuneiform script carved in the stone tells the story of his life. The king and his family wear a *kaunakes*, a fleece skirt. The *Stele of the Vultures* **[15]**, also discovered in Telloh by de Sarzec, in 1881, shows the victory of Eannatum, king of Lagash and successor to Ur-Nanshe, over the neighbouring city of Umma. The limestone stele has been partly reconstructed. It depicts human figures as well

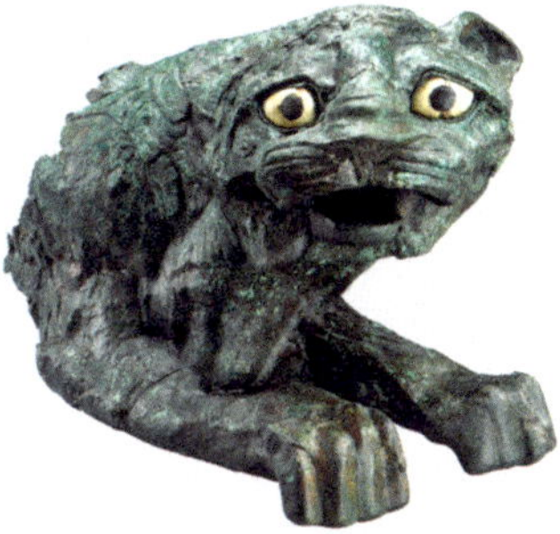

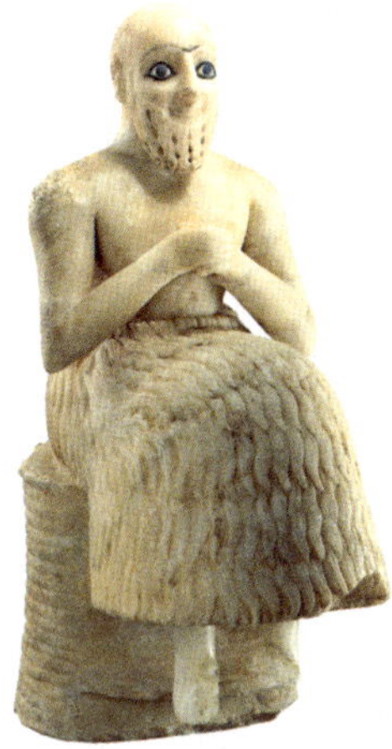

[17]
Mari Lion
Temple of Dagan, Mari, Syria
c. 2500–1759 BCE (?)
Copper, limestone and steatite
H. 53; W. 77.5; D. 43 cm
(H. 20¾; W. 30½; D. 17 in.)
⊻ 1937
DNEA

[18]
Nu-banda Ebih-Il
Temple of Ishtar, Mari, Syria
c. 2500–2340 BCE
Alabaster, shell, lapis lazuli and bitumen
H. 52.5; W. 20.6; D. 30 cm
(H. 20¾; W. 8; D. 11¾ in.)
⊻ 1934
DNEA

as representations of animals, many symbolic: vultures, an eagle, a bull and a lion. The Sumerian text recounts the battle and the cruel nature of the fighting.

Almost contemporary to these works, the statue of the *Nu-banda Ebih-Il* **[18]**, in alabaster and lapis lazuli, portrays Ebih-Il, the superintendent of Mari, a city founded in the early third millennium BCE on the western bank of the Euphrates, in modern-day Syria. Seated on a wicker stool, his hands clasped in prayer, he also wears a *kaunakes*. The cuneiform inscription, in Akkadian, dedicates the statue to the goddess Ishtar, in whose temple André Parrot uncovered it in 1934. Similarities in clothing and attitude indicate that despite being divided into often rival city-states, ancient Mesopotamia maintained cultural coherence. The *Mari Lion* **[17]**, a metal statue with inlaid eyes, was also discovered by Parrot in Mari. The lion's attributes of power and protection explain why this representation would have been chosen to guard the Temple of Dagan, where it was found.

The *Mastaba of Akhethetep*, the funeral chapel of the priest of that name, comes from the Saqqara necropolis.

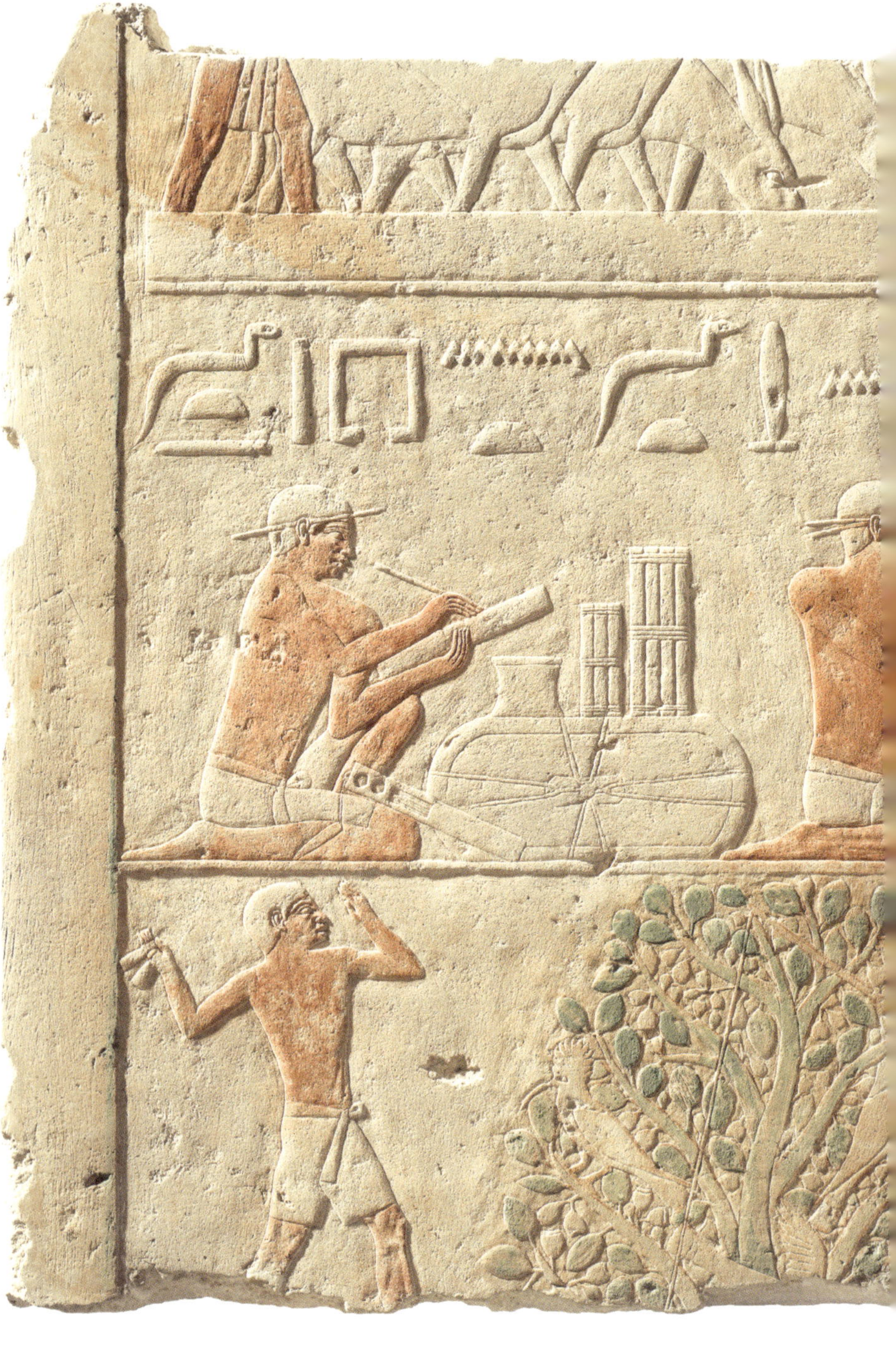

[19] ***Mastaba of Akhethetep*** (detail). Saqqara, Egypt. c. 2445–2385 BCE. Painted limestone
H. 432; W. 483; D. 380 cm (H. 14 ft 2 in.; W. 15 ft 10 in.; D. 12 ft 5½ in.). A 1903. DEA

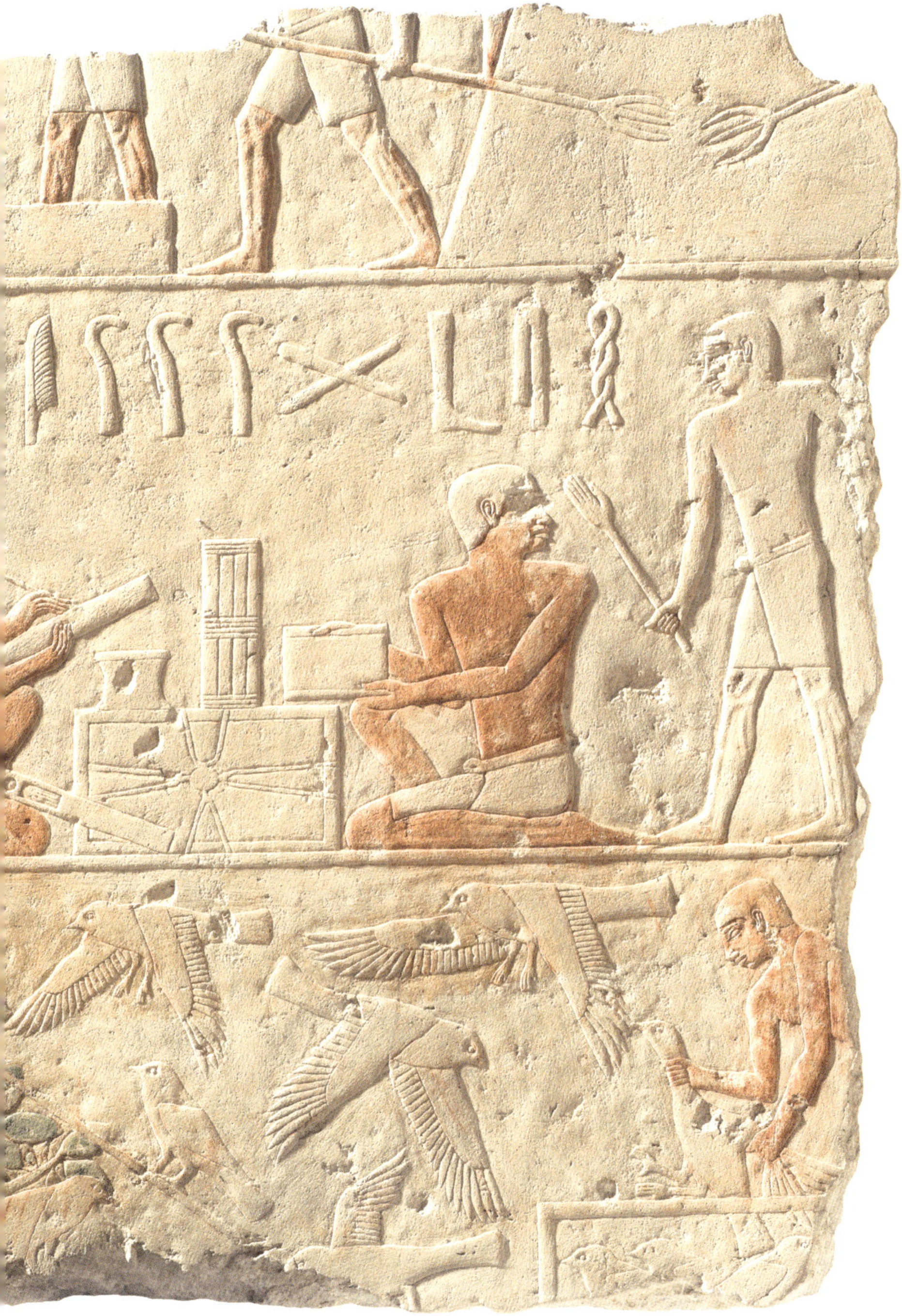

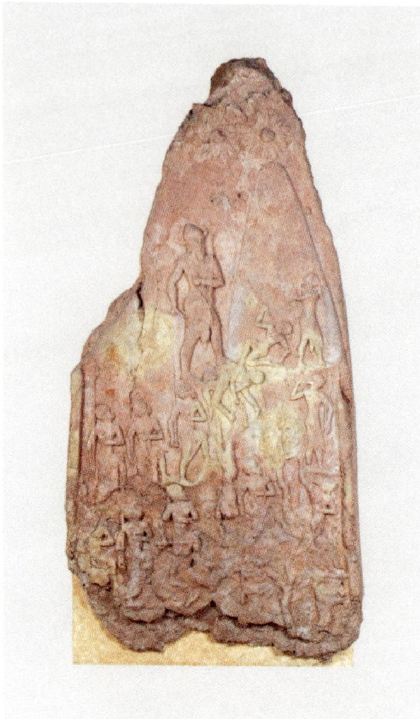

[20]
Victory Stele of Naram-Sin
Susa, present-day Iran
c. 2254–2218 BCE
Limestone
H. 200; W. 105 cm
(H. 6 ft 6¾ in.; W. 3 ft 5¼ in.)
⊻ 1898
DNEA

Acquired in the early twentieth century from Egypt's Antiquities Authority, it dates from the middle of the third millennium BCE, the period known as the Old Kingdom. The quality of this limestone construction, with its geometric trapezoid shapes, and the beauty of the decorations **[19]**, executed in different colour and pleasingly arranged in registers, is proof of the ancient Egyptians' belief in life after death. Each of the painted and carved elements is intended to bring the deceased prosperity, sustenance and comfort in the hereafter. This monument, which has been reconstructed inside the Louvre, provides valuable insight into ancient Egyptian architecture.

The *Victory Stele of Naram-Sin* **[20]**, king of Akkad in Mesopotamia, shows the victory of this ruler – bearded and wearing a horned helmet – over his enemies, the Lullubi. Carved from limestone and dating from the second half of the third millennium BCE, it was found almost intact in 1898 by archaeologist Jacques de Morgan at the site of Susa in modern-day Iran, far from where it was made, in the ancient city of Sippar in present-day Iraq. The stele was taken as a spoil of war by king Shutruk-Nakhunte in the twelfth century BCE,

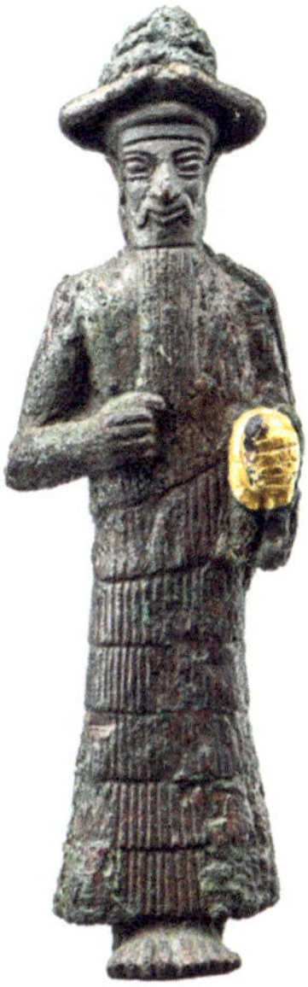

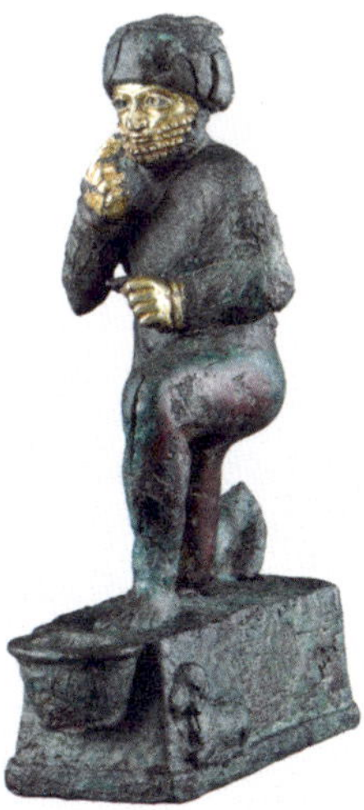

[21]
***Figurine*, known as**
The God with the Golden Hand
Susa, present-day Iran
c. 2000–1800 BCE
Copper and gold
H. 17.5; W. 5.5; D. 3.8 cm
(H. 6¾, W. 2⅛; D. 1½ in.)
⊻ 1906–1908
DNEA

[22]
***Figurine*, known as**
The Worshipper of Larsa
Senkereh, present-day Iraq
c. 1792–1750 BCE
Copper and gold
H. 19.6; W. 7; D. 14.8 cm
(H. 7¾; W. 2¾; D. 5⅞ in.)
⊻ 1931
DNEA

[23]
Babylon, present-day Iraq
Code of Hammurabi
Susa, present-day Iran
c. 1792–1750 BCE
Basalt
H. 225; W. 79; D. 47 cm
(H. 7 ft 4½ in.; W. 31 in.; D. 18½ in.)
⊻ 1901–1902
DNFA

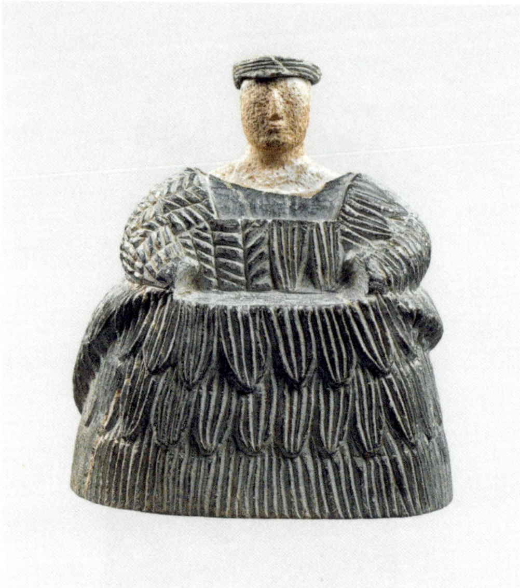

[24]
Bactrian Princess
Bactria, present-day Afghanistan
c. 2500–1800 BCE
Serpentine and limestone
H. 18.1; W. 16; D. 14.4 cm
(H. 7½; W. 6½; D. 5⅝ in.)
⚒ 1969
DNEA

almost a thousand years after its creation. That the Shutrukid king was compelled to take this representation of power speaks volumes about the force that emanates from it, its beauty and how vividly nature is depicted, in particular the mountain Naram-Sin has scaled and the forest he has crossed.

Reliefs that had decorated the palace of the Shutrukid kings were also uncovered in Susa. They depict human creatures with bull's hooves, their headdress similar to that of the Akkadian king. As well, *The God with the Golden Hand* **[21]** was discovered during excavations in Susa. Made from copper, it would originally have been entirely overlaid with gold. Only one hand retains this gilding. The statue's origin is unknown; the horned helmet and the *kaunakes* suggest it was made in Sumer. The *Code of Hammurabi* **[23]**, a black basalt monolith, was also found in Susa. Hammurabi, one of the first kings of Babylon, in what is now Iraq, was an influential lawmaking sovereign. This was one of the first legal codes. A sculpted relief at the stele's summit, which is inscribed with cuneiform script, shows Hammurabi standing opposite the god Shamash, enthroned and holding a rod. The description of their

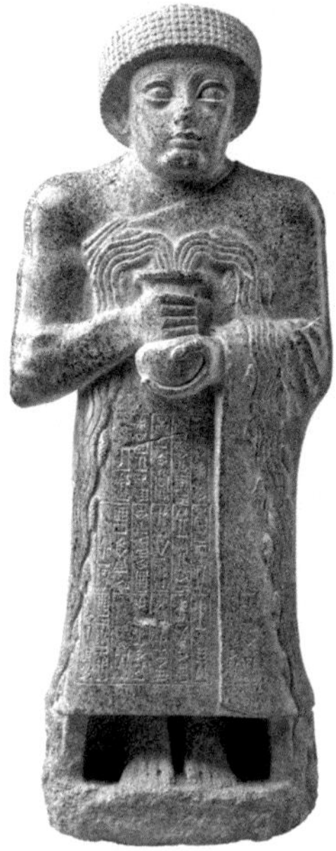

[25]
Gudea with Gushing Vase
Bactria, Central Asia
c. 2120–2110 BCE.
Dolerite
H. 62; W. 25.6; D. 16 cm
(H. 24½; W. 10; D. 6¼ in.)
⊻ 1967
DNEA

meeting legitimises the king as chosen and acknowledged by the deity. The *Worshipper of Larsa* **[22]**, a copper statuette that would originally have been covered with gold leaf, pays homage to Hammurabi. A long cuneiform text reads: "To Martu [Amurru, patron god of the Amorites], his god, for the life of Hammurabi, king of Babylon." The region known as Bactrian, in what is now Afghanistan, belonged to the world of ancient Iran. A *Bactrian Princess* **[24]** is a statuette of a female figure, standing or seated in a hieratic position, wrapped in a robe and wearing a *kaunakes*. To date around a dozen of these works have been uncovered. They are thought to depict tutelary deities. Three are conserved in the Louvre, having entered the museum's collections between the 1960s and the early 2000s. In the Greco-Roman era, Bactria was the limit of the known world.

Sculptures representing Gudea, prince of Lagash, were found at the site of Telloh. These diorite figures, dating from around 2100 BCE, show the prince with a round head, covered by a band, large eyes and prominent eyebrows that meet at the bridge of the nose. *Gudea with Gushing Vase* **[25]** portrays

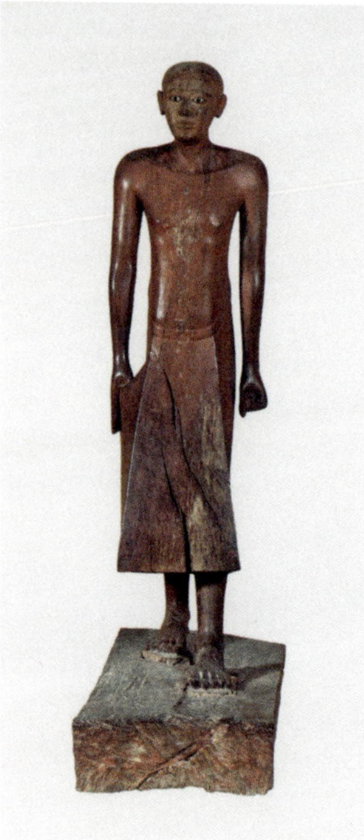

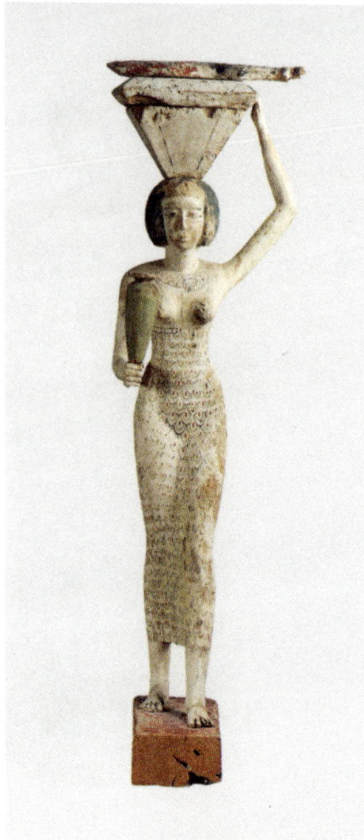

[26]
Statue
Tomb 7, Nakht, Asyut, Egypt
c. 1963–1862 BCE
Acacia, Egyptian alabaster, copper alloy, obsidian and paint
H. 178.5; W. 49.5; D. 110 cm
(H. 5 ft 10½ in.; W. 19½ in.; D. 3 ft 7¼ in.)
⩡ 1903
DEA

[27]
Offering Bearer
Egypt
c. 1963–1862 BCE
Painted fig wood
H. 108.5; W. 14; D. 32.7 cm
(H. 3 ft 6¾ in.; W. 5½ in.; D. 12¾ in.)
⩡ 1899
DEA

a sovereign who brings fertility and prosperity to his country. These virtues are symbolised by the streams of fish-filled water pouring from the vessel that the prince holds between his hands.

BEYOND THE LIVING AND THE DEAD The tomb of Nakhti was excavated in the early twentieth century by Émile Gaston Chassinat and Charles Palanque. This acacia wood statue **[26]** shows a figure standing erect, his left foot forward, as per the aesthetic norms of ancient Egyptian art, which combines naturalism with the artistic canon. The work dates from the beginning of the second millennium BCE, which corresponds to ancient Egypt's Middle Kingdom. The *Model of a Boat* **[29]**, in painted wood, was also found in Nakhti's tomb. The boat refers to actual navigation along the Nile, which flows the entire length of the country, as well as the idea of crossing from the world of the living to that of the dead and the promise of eternal life. *Offering Bearer* **[27]**, in painted fig wood, dates from the same period. This graceful figure also evokes life and death, as she brings sustenance for the deceased.

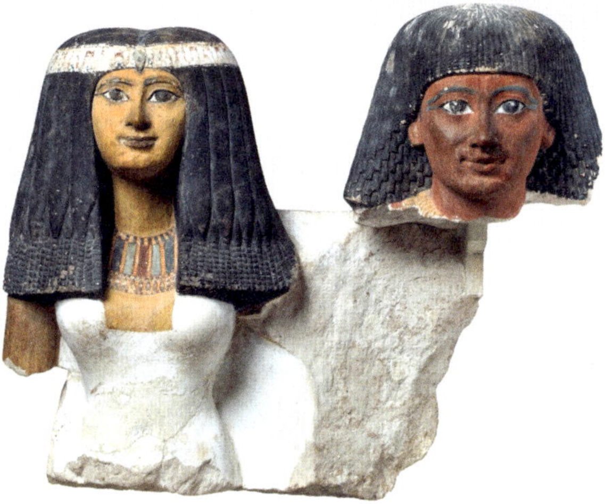

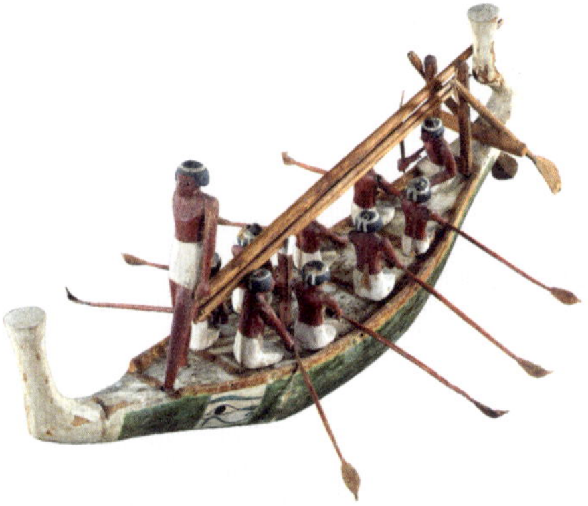

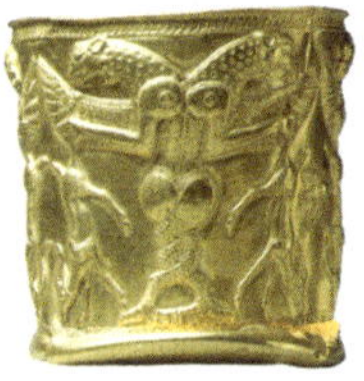

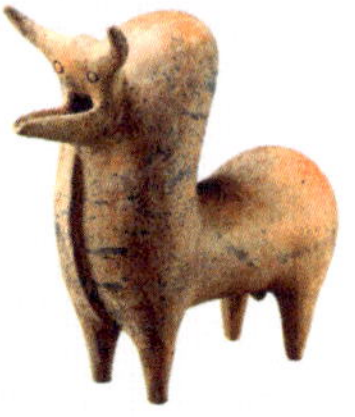

[28]
Statue of a Couple*, known as *Sennefer and His Wife
Thebes, Egypt
c. 1425–1400 BCE
Painted sandstone
H. 66; W. 85; D. 29.4 cm
(H. 26; W. 33½; D. 11½ in.)
⩡ 1978
DEA

[29]
Model of a Boat
Tomb 7, Nakht,
Asyut, Egypt
c. 1963–1862 BCE
Painted wood
H. 38.5; L. 81 cm
(H. 15¼; L. 32 in.)
⩡ 1903
DEA

[30]
Vase
Marlik, present-day Iran
c. 1400–1100 BCE
Electrum
H. 11; Diam. 11.2 cm
(H. 4⅜; Diam. 4⅜ in.)
⩡ 1956
DNEA

[31]
Vase
Marlik, present-day Iran
c. 1400–1100 BCE
Painted terracotta
H. 21.2; L. 21.3; D. 10 cm
(H. 8¼; L. 8½; D. 3⅞ in.)
⩡ 1960 (gift of Mohsen Foroughi)
DNEA

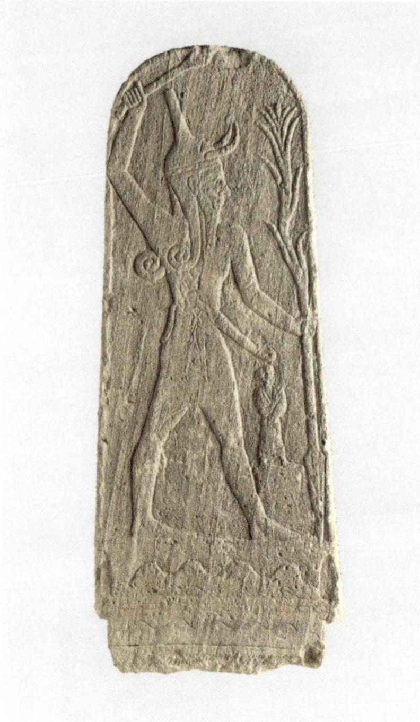

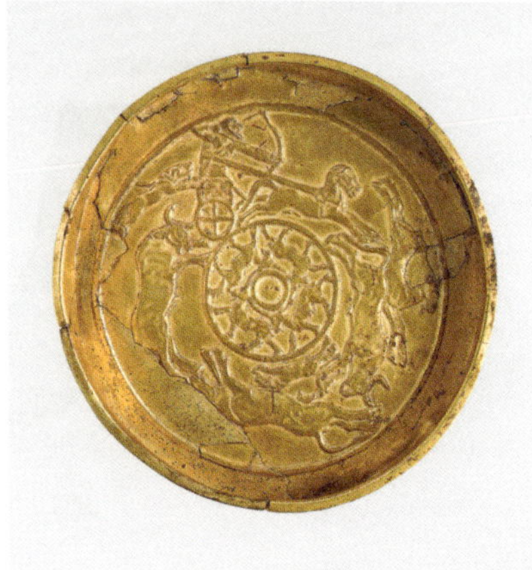

[32]
Baal with Thunderbolt Stele
Ras Shamra/Ugarit, present-day Syria
15th–13th century BCE
Sandstone
H. 144; W. 57.5; D. 29 cm
(H. 4 ft 8¾ in.; W. 1 ft 10¾ in.; D. 11½ in.)
⊻ 1932
DNEA

[33]
Patera with Hunting Scene
Acropolis of Ras Shamra/Ugarit, present-day Syria
c. 1400–1200 BCE
Gold
H. 3.1; Diam. 18.8 cm
(H. 1¼; Diam. 7½ in.)
⊻ 1933
DNEA

A hieroglyphic inscription indicates that the fragment of a group statue in painted sandstone **[28]** depicts Sennefer, priest of the great Egyptian deity Amun, and his wife. The work, which would have been life-size, dates from Egypt's early New Kingdom, as shown by the less formal treatment of its subject. It was acquired by the Louvre in the 1970s.

The prehistoric site of Marlik is located in the Gilan mountains, in the north of what is now Iran. Excavations of several dozen tombs during the 1950s and 1960s revealed a group of artefacts of remarkable quality. Representations of real and imaginary animals abound, for example the bull-shaped vase in terracotta **[31]** or the two-headed winged monsters grasping gazelles, finely embossed onto a precious metal cup **[30]**. These hybrid creatures have a lion's head and body, and the talons of a bird of prey. Its base is decorated with a rosace and four fish. Artists in Marlik would not have been familiar with written text. The Louvre acquired these works in the mid-twentieth century, shortly after they were unearthed.

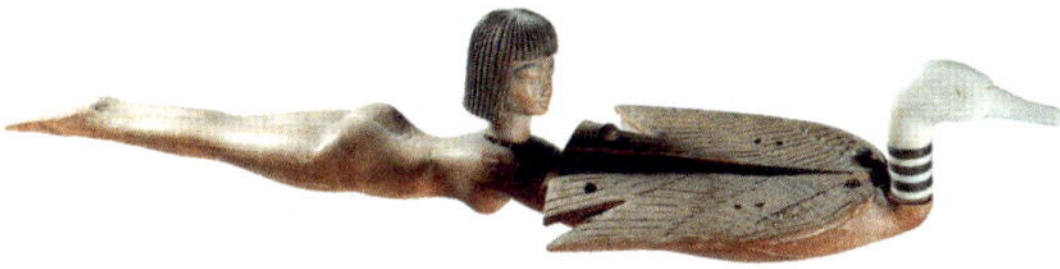

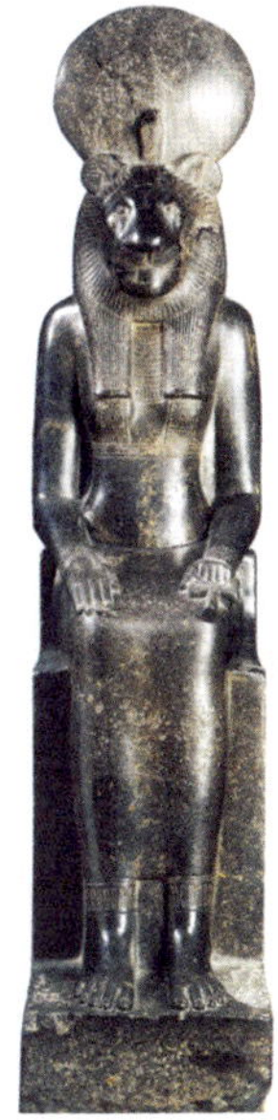

[34]
Cosmetic Spoon with Young Woman Swimming
Egypt
c. 1390–1352 BCE
Wood and ivory (?)
H. 5.8; L. 29.3; D. 5.3 cm
(H. 2½; L. 11½; D. 2 in.)
⩡ 1852
DEA

[35]
Statue of the Goddess Sekhmet
Temple of Mut, Thebes, Egypt
c. 1390–1352 BCE
Diorite
H. 218; W. 49; D. 93.5 cm
(H. 7 ft 1¾ in.;
W. 1 ft 7¼ in.; D. 3 ft)
⩡ 1817
DEA

ARTISTIC CREATION IN THE MEDITERRANEAN The ancient site of Ugarit in Ras Shamra, in present-day Syria, was discovered in the 1920s. Decades of excavations revealed a prosperous city with a wealth of written and artistic production centred on the Mediterranean. The *Patera with Hunting Scene* **[33]**, in embossed gold, was found on the acropolis, near the Temple of Baal. Its circular decoration, which mirrors the bowl's shape, depicts a hunting scene in which a king, standing in a chariot, pursues a deer. The *Baal with Thunderbolt Stele* **[32]**, in sandstone, shows the god Baal wearing a horned helmet and brandishing a thunderbolt above his head, a prelude to rain, which he controls. The large reed he holds in front of him indicates that he is a god of fertility and protection. Baal is mentioned in the books of the Old Testament as one of the deities who might turn those who worship them away from the one god, Yahweh.

During this same period, the thirty-eight-year reign of Amenhotep III was marked by prosperity and artistic achievement. The elegant *Cosmetic Spoon with Young Woman Swimming* **[34]** is proof of the refinement of ancient Egyptian

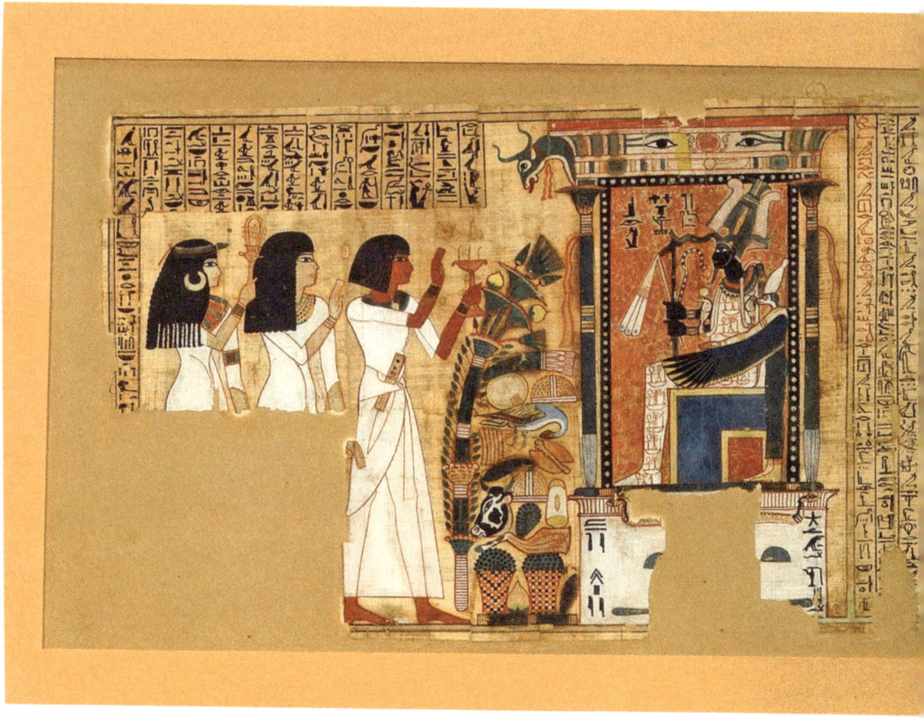

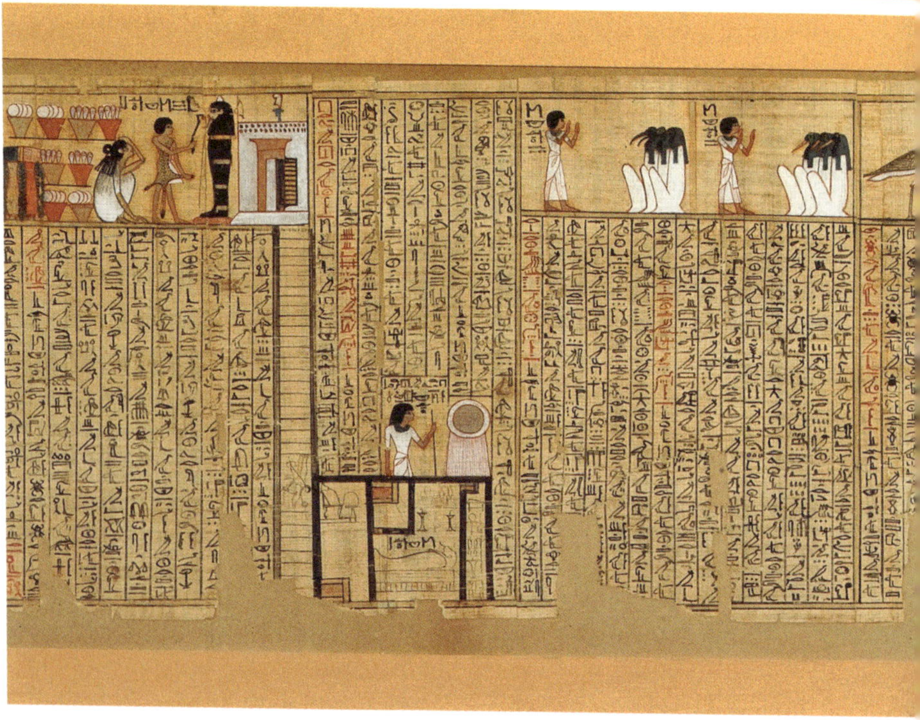

[36] ***Funerary Papyrus***. Egypt. c. 1400–1352 BCE. Painted papyrus. H. 31; W. 630 cm (H. 1 ft; W. 20 ft 8 in.). ⊻ 1827. DEA

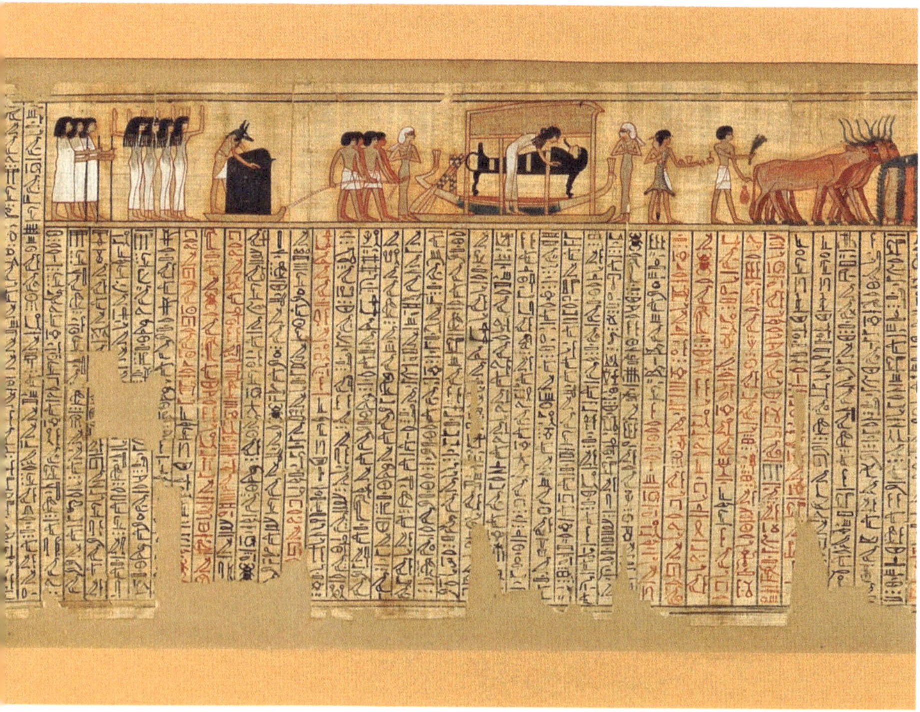

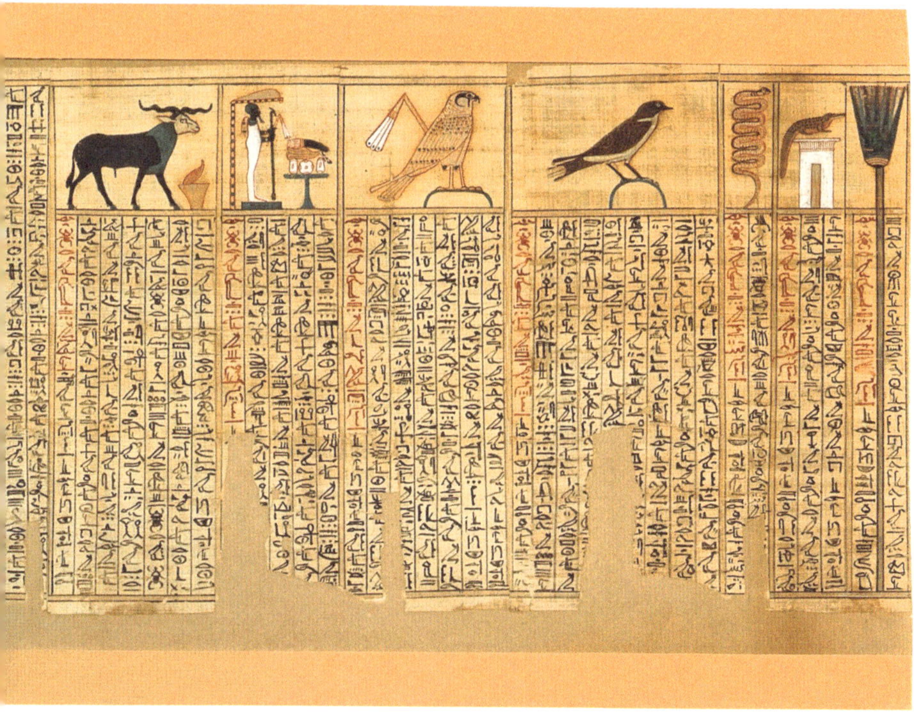

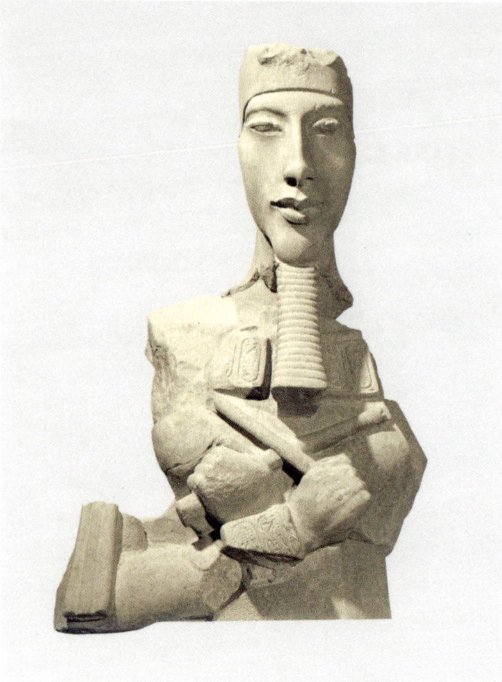

[37]
Bust of Akhenaten
Temple of Amenhotep IV/Akhenaten, Thebes, Egypt
c. 1352–1335 BCE
Sandstone
H. 135; W. 87; D. 49 cm
(H. 4 ft 5¼ in.; W. 2 ft 10¼ in.; D. 1 ft 7¼ in.)
⊻ 1972 (gift)
DEA

societies. Made from wood and ivory, the wings of the duck that guides and pulls the swimmer along open to allow access to a compartment that would have held some kind of cosmetic. It was acquired by the Louvre in 1852. Books of the Dead, such as the *Funerary Papyrus* **[36]**, were rolled and placed next to the deceased so that they might come forth by day into eternal life. The custom spread during the New Kingdom. The coloured vignettes that adorn the *Funerary Papyrus*, made of woven reed, demonstrate the scribes' creativity and dexterity. The statue of the goddess Sekhmet **[35]**, originating from the Temple of Mut in Karnak, was acquired by the Louvre in 1817. Its acquisition illustrates the strength of the interest in ancient Egypt following Napoleon Bonaparte's Egyptian campaign of 1798. The lion-headed goddess Sekhmet was a powerful deity. Daughter of the sun god Ra, she accompanied and assisted the pharaohs in battle. Her chimerical appearance shows how ancient Egyptian imagery combined human and animal figures, through a sophisticated understanding of nature that glorified their strengths. Representations of Akhenaten, son of Amenhotep III, are easily recognised by their

[38]
***Brick Panel* (architectural decoration)**
Apadana, Susa, present-day Iran
c. 1150–1120 BCE
(Shutrukid Dynasty)
Clay
H. 136; W. 73.5; D. 17 cm
(H. 4 ft 5½ in.;
W. 2 ft 5 in.; D. 6¾ in.)
⩡ 1913–1921
DNEA

[39]
Relief of Seti I and Hathor
Tomb of Seti I, Valley of the Kings, Thebes, Egypt
c. 1294–1279 BCE
Painted limestone
H. 226.5; W. 105 cm
(H. 7 ft 5¼ in.;
W. 3 ft 5¼ in.)
⩡ 1830
DEA

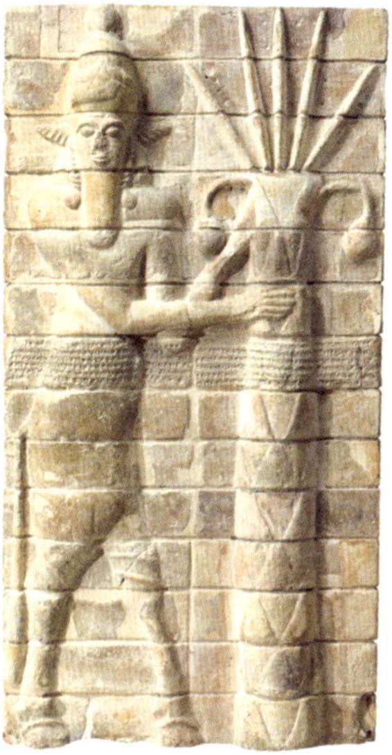

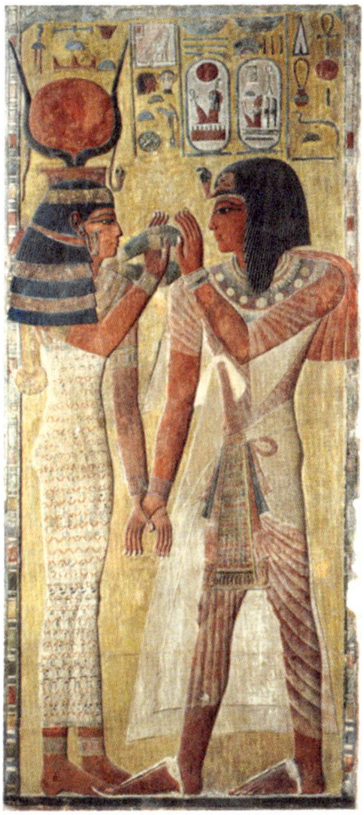

characteristic long face and prominent nose and mouth **[37]**. Akhenaten took this name because he considered Aten – the sun depicted as a disc – as the one and only god. He moved his capital from Thebes to Tell el-Amarna, which he founded.

In 1828–1829 Jean-François Champollion, who would decipher hieroglyphs, joined a mission to Egypt. His encounter with Egyptian artefacts filled him with wonder. While there, he acquired the *Relief of Seti I and Hathor* **[39]**, the latter being the goddess of love, joy and music; the deity and the pharaoh stand face to face. The panel, from the tomb of Seti I in Thebes, is the work of an artist sufficiently skilled to render the transparency of the pharaoh's robe. Champollion also returned to France with the richly decorated *Mummiform Coffin of Tamutnofret* **[40]**, who served in the Temple of Amun. An inscription appeals for the divine protection of Osiris, Isis and Thoth, the ibis-headed god, so that the deceased might go on to life in the hereafter. One work in particular, the statue of Karomama **[41]**, captivated Champollion with its allure. In 1829 he wrote: "I am bringing to the Louvre the most beautiful bronze yet discovered in Egypt; Karomama,

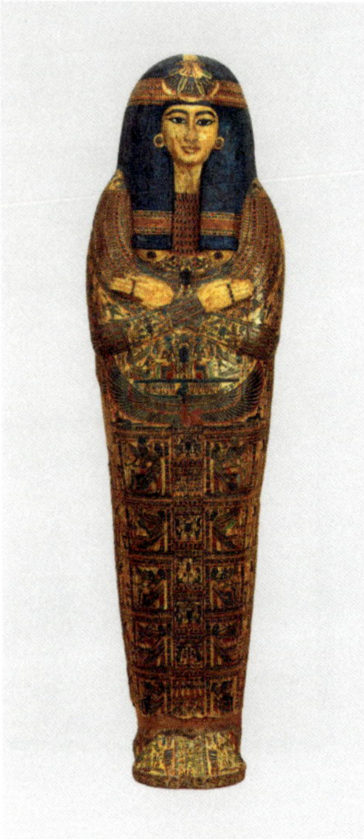

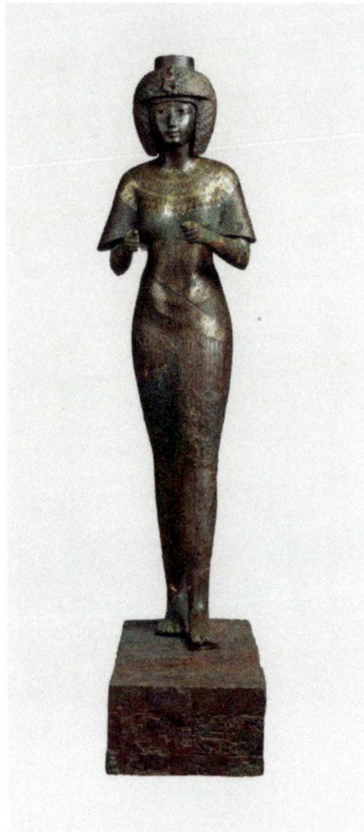

[40]
Mummiform Coffin of Tamutnofret
Thebes, Egypt
c. 1069–943 BCE
Painted wood
L. 189; W. 55; D. 31 cm
(L. 6 ft 2½ in.;
W. 1 ft 9¾ in.; D. 1 ft)
⩡ 1828–1829
DEA

[41]
Statue of Karomama
Thebes, Egypt
865–809 BCE
Bronze and gold
H. 53; W. 15.5; D. 35.2 cm
(H. 20¾ in.; 6 in.; D. 13¾ in.)
⩡ 1828–1829
DEA

the Divine Adoratrice of Amon." The pharaoh's authority was weakened under the reign of Osorkon I, and so the title of Divine Adoratrice of Amon was created to win the favours of the powerful priests of Upper Egypt.

The *Triad of Osorkon* **[42]** is a precious object in gold and lapis lazuli that was found in Karnak. The goddess Isis, wearing a headdress composed of a solar disc framed by horns, and Horus, the falcon-headed god, flank Osiris, their brother, husband and father. The god is wrapped in a shroud and wears the *atef* crown, adorned with plumes on each side. The reverse of the triad is engraved with a hieroglyphic text dedicated to Osorkon II.

The monumental granite statue of Ramses II **[43]** comes from the Temple of Tanis. It was acquired by the Louvre in 1827. Of all the ancient Egyptian pharaohs, Ramses II is without doubt one of the best known. Son of Seti I, he triumphed over his country's enemies: the Hittites, from Asia Minor, and the Assyrians who dominated Mesopotamia. A prolific builder, he consolidated his kingdom as far as the Nile's second cataract and ordered construction of the impressive

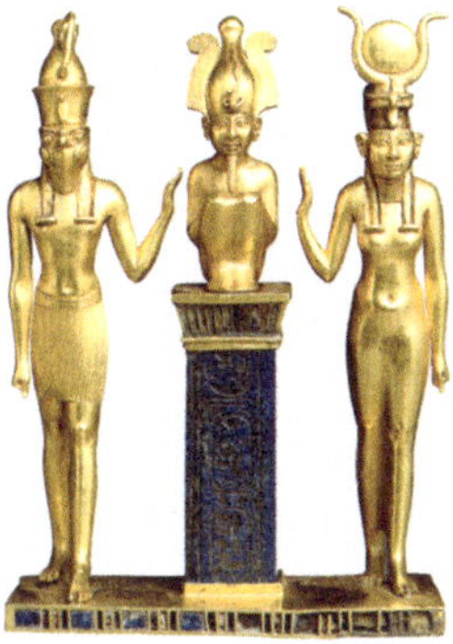

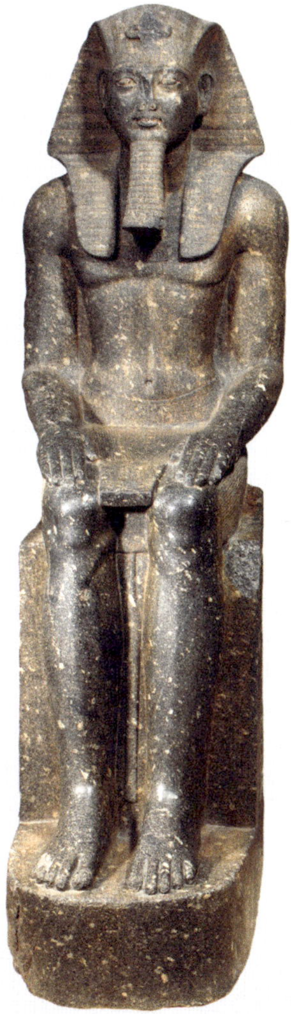

[42]
Triad of Osorkon
Karnak, Egypt
c. 865–830 BCE
Gold and lapis lazuli
H. 9; W. 6.6 cm
(H. 3½; W. 2⅝ in.)
⊻ 1872
DEA

[43]
Statue of Ramses II
Tanis, Egypt
c. 1279–1213 BCE
Diorite
H. 259; W. 80; D. 117 cm
(H. 8 ft 6 in.; W. 2 ft 7½ in.;
D. 3 ft 10 in.)
⊻ 1827
DEA

[44]
Pectoral
Tomb of Ramses II,
Saqqara, Egypt
c. 1279–1213 BCE
Gold, carnelian, lapis lazuli
and turquoise
H. 7.1; W. 13.7 cm
(H. 2¾; W. 5⅜ in.)
⊻ 1852
DEA

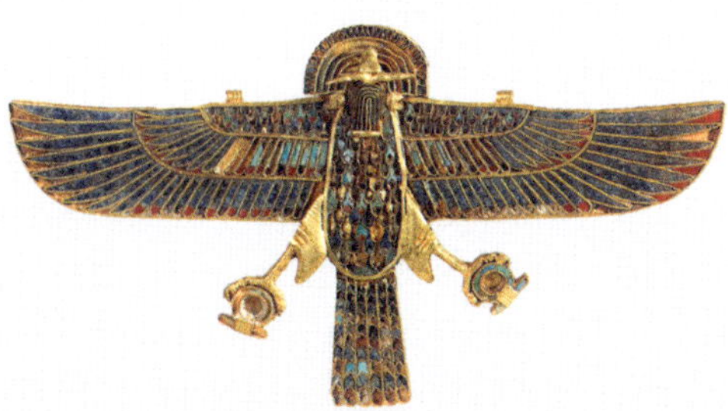

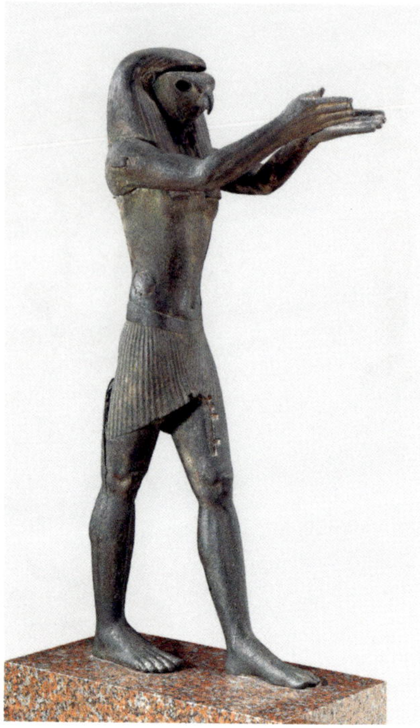

[45]
Statue,
known as the *Posno Horus*
Memphis (?), Egypt
c. 1069–664 BCE
Copper alloy
H. 95.5; W. 26; D. 39 cm
(H. 3 ft 1½ in.; W. 10¼ in.;
D. 1 ft 3¼ in.)
⊻ 1884
DEA

Great Temple at Abu-Simbel. The *Pectoral* **[44]** was discovered in 1852, in the tomb of Ramses II in the Serapeum at Memphis, by Auguste Mariette, a leading ancient Egyptian scholar who went on to found the Cairo Museum. In gold with cloisonné lapis lazuli, turquoise and carnelian, it depicts a vulture with the head of a ram and wings spread as a symbol of protection.

The *Posno Horus* **[45]**, named after one of its owners, depicts the falcon-headed god. Sculpted from metal, it illustrates the taste of that period, at the cusp of the second and first millennium BCE, for a more archaic aesthetic and a return to more formal conventions. Horus, son of Isis and Osiris, was the god of the sky and protector of the pharaohs. The Louvre acquired the statue in 1884.

Scholars and artists of the early nineteenth century were fascinated by the Near East, whose memory is captured in biblical texts. The first French exploratory missions set out in 1834. In 1843 the French consul in Mosul, Paul-Émile Botta, while searching for the biblical Nineveh, discovered the site of Khorsabad in the fertile crescent formed by the waters of the Tigris and its tributaries in present-day Iraq. The findings

[46]
Wall Relief, Human-Headed Winged Bulls, Lamassu
Palace of Sargon II, Khorsabad, Iraq
c. 721–705 BCE
Gypsum alabaster
H. 420; W. 436; D. 97 cm
(H. 13 ft 9¼ in.; W. 14 ft 3½ in.; D. 3 ft 2¼ in.)
⩡ 1847
DNEA

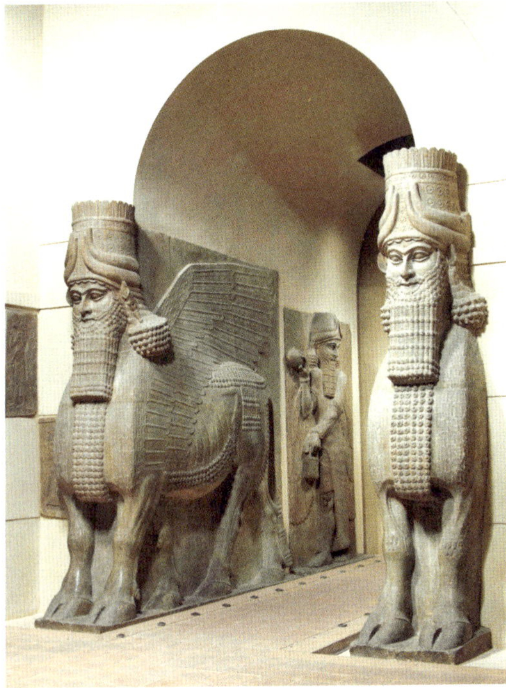

of these excavations were published as *The Monuments of Nineveh*. The dig was nothing less than a revelation: shown for the first time at the Louvre in 1847, monumental reliefs from the palace of Sargon II, an Assyrian king in the eighth century BCE, were enthusiastically admired and Assyria became all the rage. Built in a newly founded city, this vast palace seems to have been abandoned following the king's death. The *Lamassu* **[46]**, human-headed winged bulls, give an idea of its colossal size and footprint. Protective figures, they guarded the gates to the palace. In order to convey the building's imposing nature within the Louvre, in the 1990s two plaster casts were added to the original statues. The palace walls were adorned with finely sculpted reliefs, some of which relate the challenges such a construction entailed. *Naval Expedition* **[49]** describes in detail a voyage to bring precious cedarwood from the Tyre region in today's Lebanon. Propelled by oarsmen, boats with horse's heads at their bows carry men and wood through waters filled with real and imagined creatures: fish, turtles and winged bulls. Two buildings in the top section represent the fortified cities of Tyre and Arwad. This sculpted relief illustrates the power of the Assyrian Empire

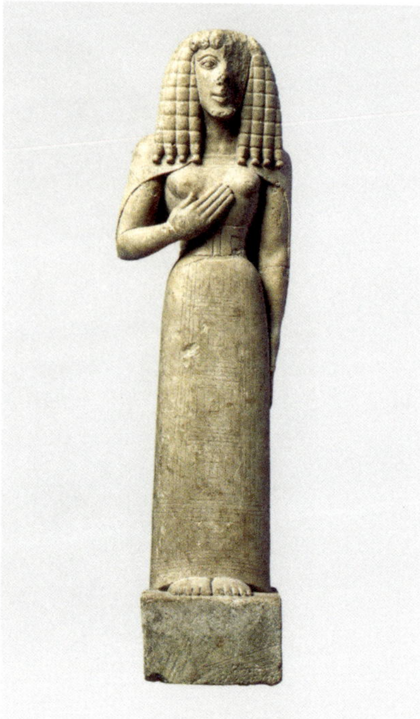

[47]
Lady of Auxerre
Eleutherna (?), Crete, Greece
c. 640–620 BCE
Painted limestone
H. 75; W. 20.5; D. 16 cm
(H. 29½; W. 8; D. 6¼ in.)
⩡ 1909 (exchanged from Auxerre)
DGERA

and its ties with neighbouring regions, whether for trade as depicted here, or in the conquest of new territories. The reign of Ashurbanipal in the seventh century BCE is a striking illustration of Assyrian dominance. For Assyria this was a period of unprecedented expansion: Ashurbanipal extended his power to Lower Egypt and all of Mesopotamia, as far as what is now Iran. The *Relief of Ashurbanipal* **[48]**, from the king's palace in Nineveh, shows the ruler in his chariot, crushing men, women and children who have been taken prisoner. They are Elamites, who inhabited the area in present-day Iran before the Persians. A learned king who assembled a library of every literary and scientific text of his day, Ashurbanipal was nonetheless feared by surrounding populations for his cruelty, as were his troops.

The *Lady of Auxerre* **[47]** dates from the late seventh century BCE and is believed to come from the site of Eleutherna in Crete, a large Greek island in the eastern Mediterranean where similar works have been uncovered. In 1909 this stone statuette left Auxerre, Burgundy, where it had been kept, for the Louvre. Its arrival at the museum coincided with the identification of a new artistic style,

[48]
Orthostate, Relief of Ashurbanipal (detail)
Palace of Ashurbanipal, Nineveh, present-day Iraq
c. 668–627 BCE
Gypsum alabaster
H. 163; W. 77 cm
(H. 5 ft 4¼ in.; W. 2 ft 6¼ in.)
DNEA

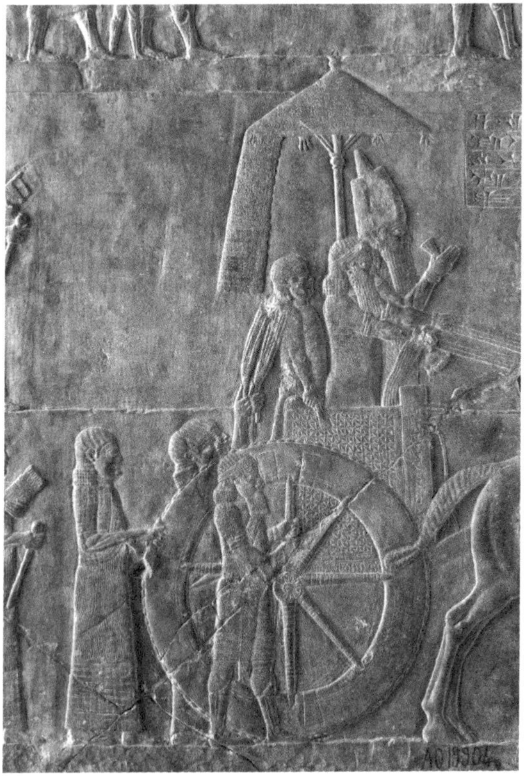

[49]
Naval Expedition
Palace of Sargon II, Khorsabad, Iraq
c. 721–705 BCE
Gypsum alabaster
H. 38; W. 49; D. 32 cm
(H. 15; W. 19¼; D. 12½ in.)
⊻ 1844
DNEA

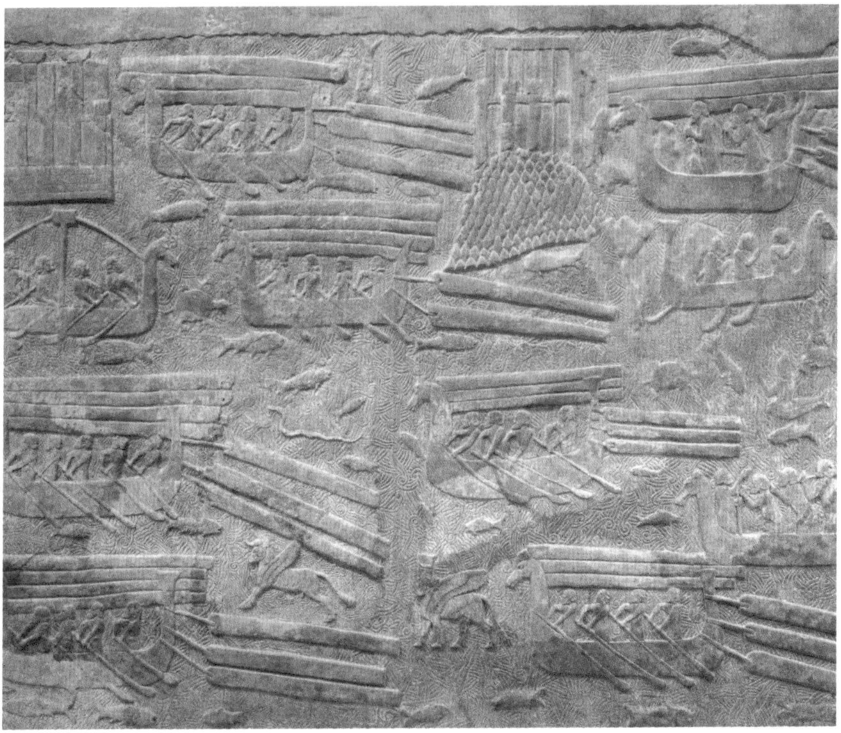

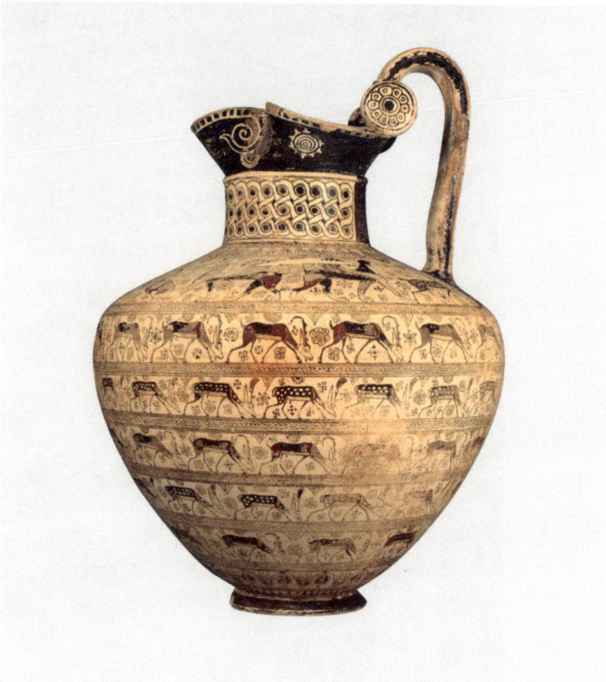

[50]
Levy Oenochoe
Miletus, present-day Turkey
c. 630 BCE
Clay
H. 39.5; Diam. 30.1 cm
(H. 15½; Diam. 11¾ in.)
⩝ 1891
DGERA

which historians and archaeologists dubbed "daedalic", after Daedalus, the father of Icarus and architect of the Minotaur's palace. The woman's upright posture, her large, incised eyes, one of which is missing, and the voluminous wig that covers her head, point to an Eastern influence, from Mesopotamia and Egypt. The emergence of such works renewed thinking as to the origins of the art of Greek sculpture and added a new branch to knowledge about the reproduction of the human form. Discovered at the site of Miletus, an ancient Greek city on the Ionian coast, in present-day Turkey, the *Levy Oenochoe* **[50]** – an oenochoe is a jug used to scoop wine from a vessel called a krater – is another example of Eastern influence on Greek art. Objects such as this, decorated with several registers of animals grazing in a landscape, belong to the so-called "wild goat style". This elegant zoomorphic motif, made all the more graceful by lines of black paint, recalls ancient Mesopotamian representations. Such a large and beautifully embellished object could only have existed in a society with particularly refined customs.

WRITING

"Writing is the painting of the voice; the closer the resemblance, the better it is."

Voltaire,
Dictionnaire philosophique,
1764

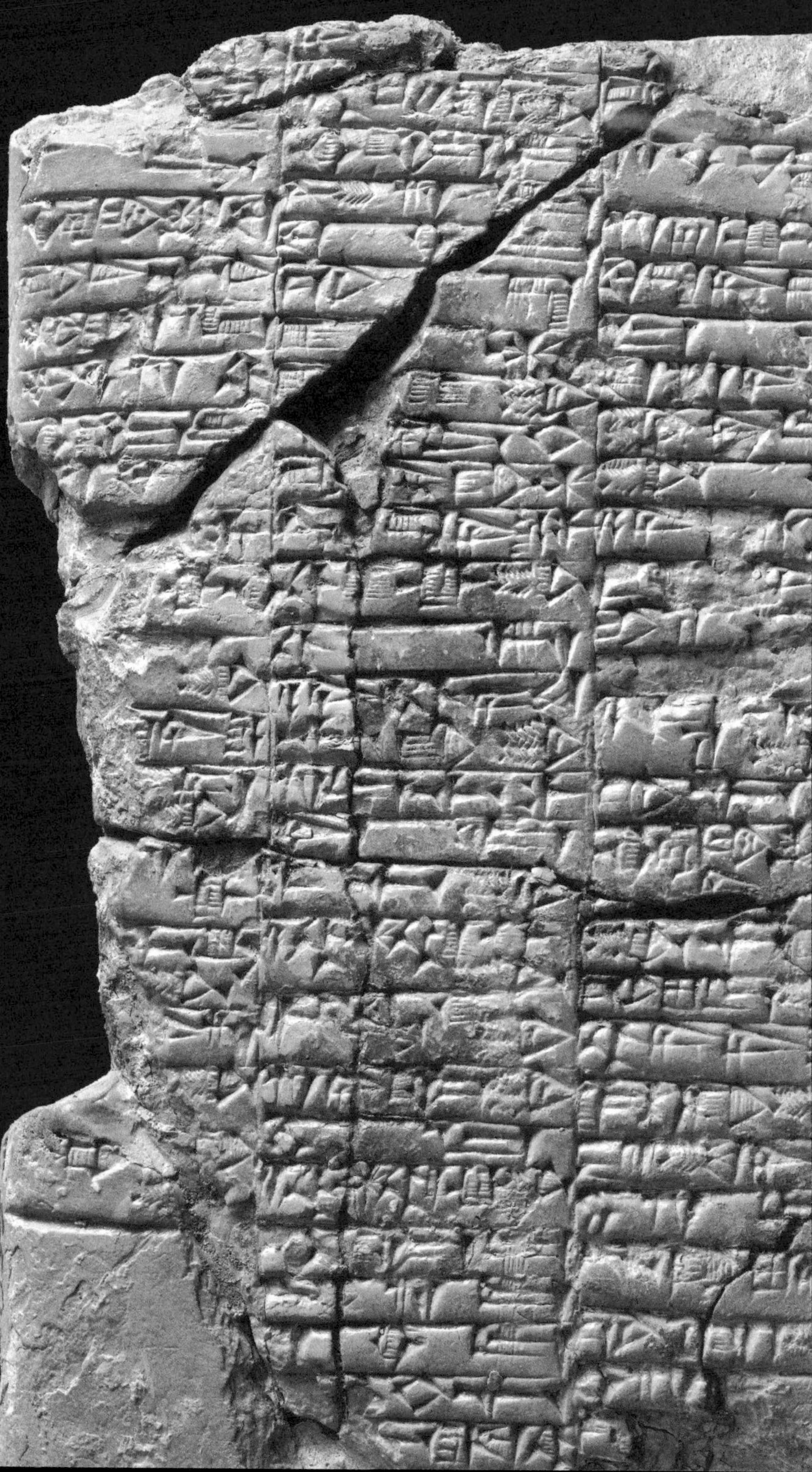

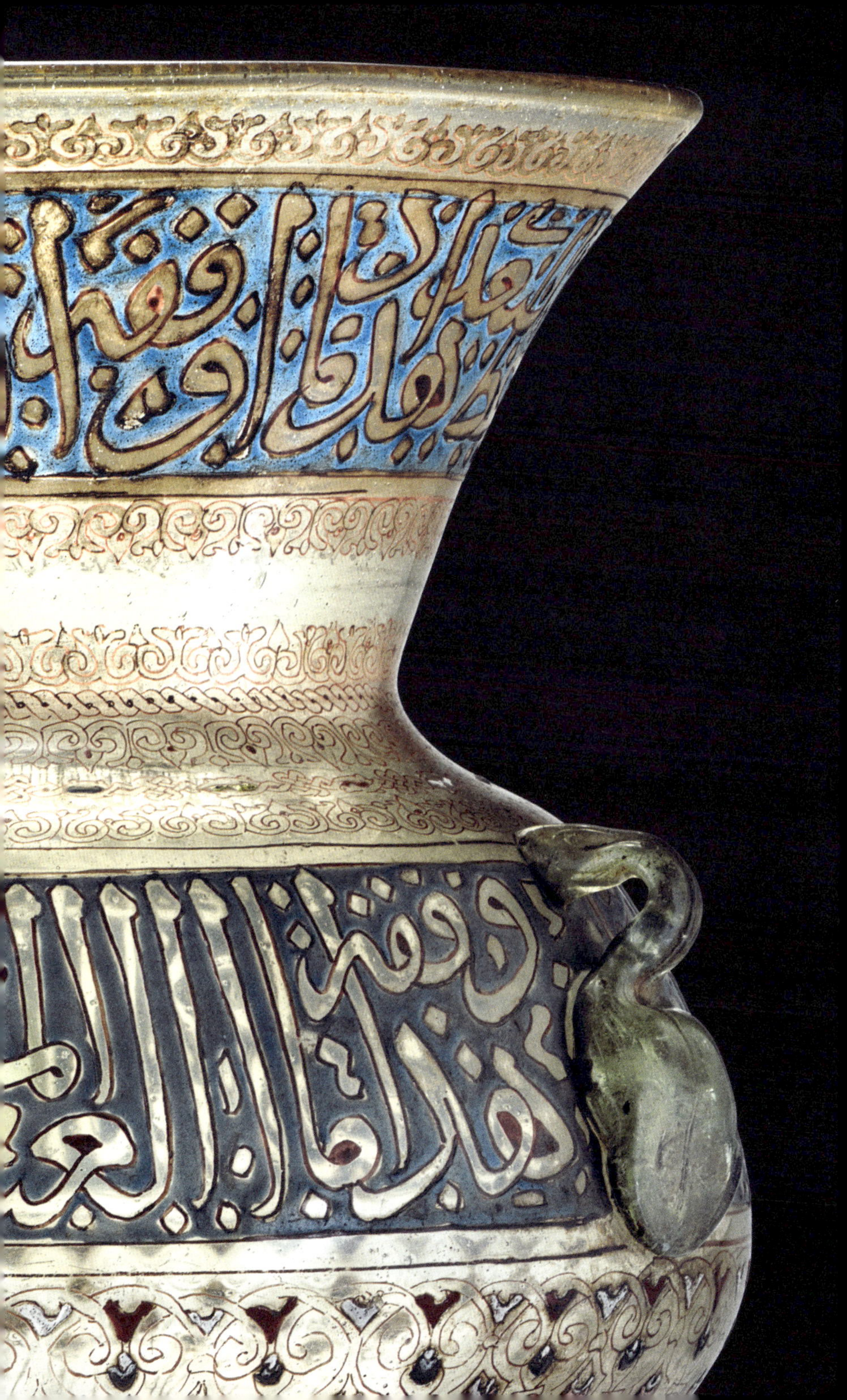

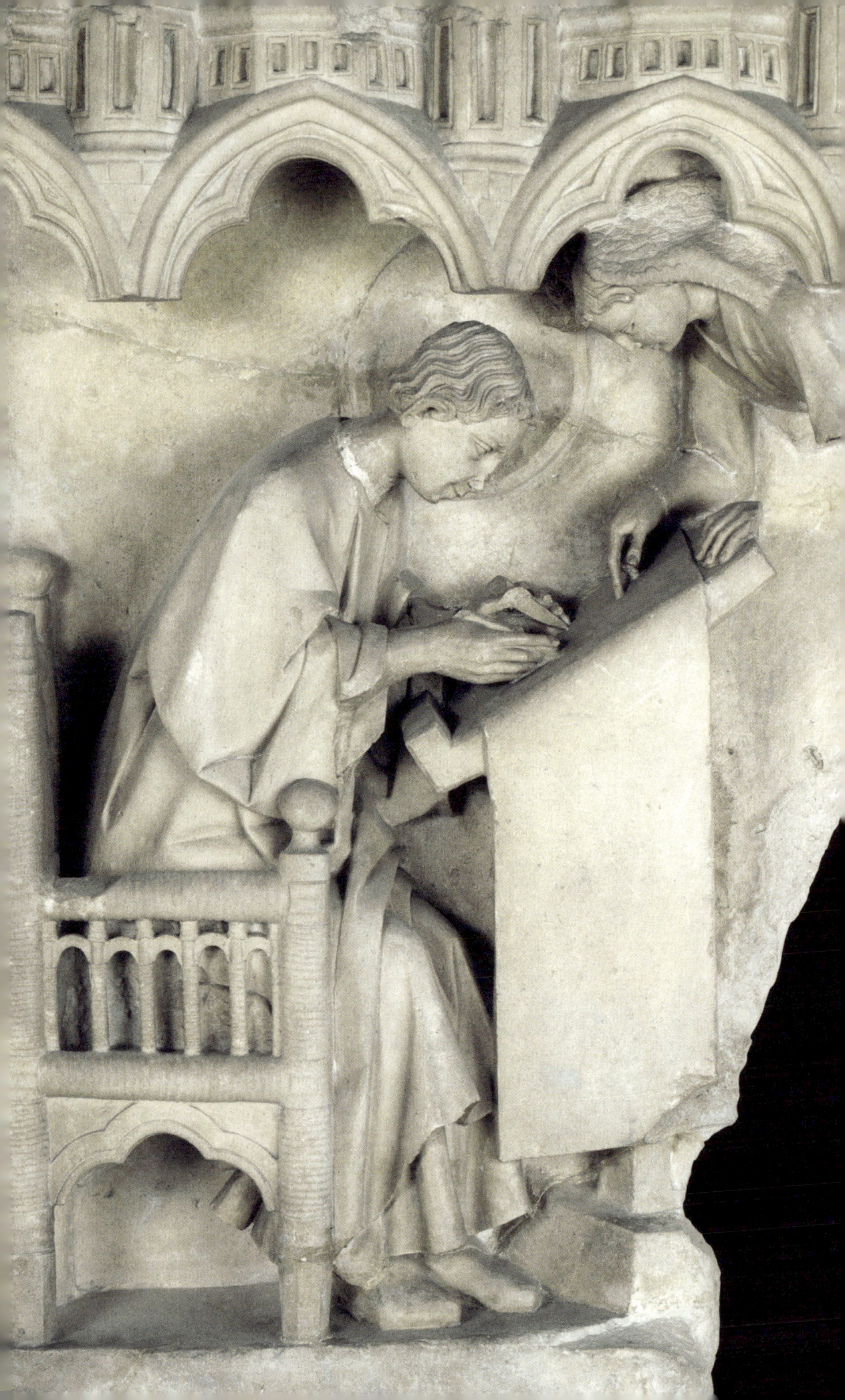

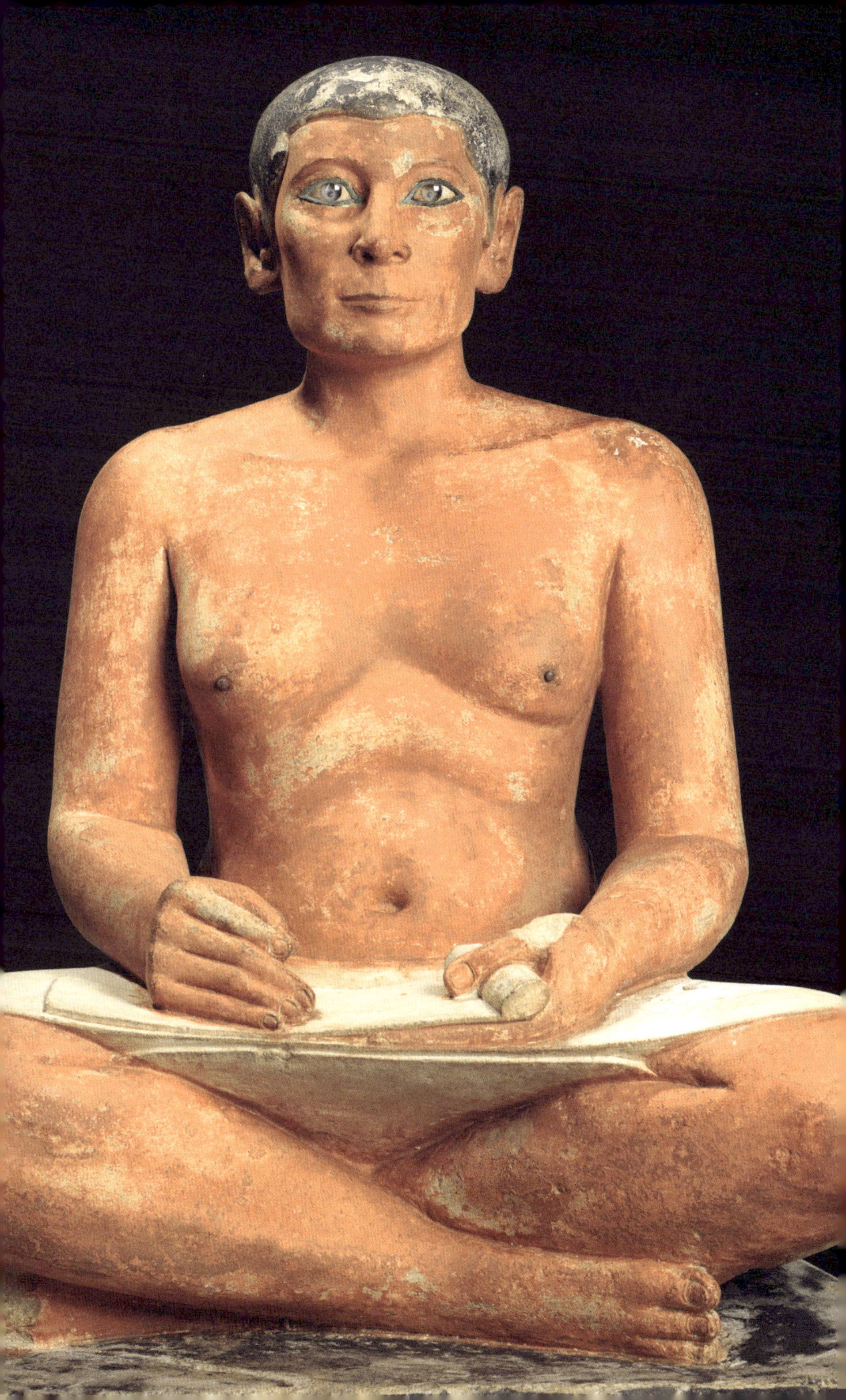

The fall of Babylon

The city of Babylon, in modern-day Iraq, was Mesopotamia's largest urban centre in the first millennium BCE. From the early second millennium BCE, under king Hammurabi, it became a place of great cultural importance, governed by efficient administrative and legal systems. Babylon reached its apogee under Nebuchadnezzar II, whose vast palace was entered via the 180-metre-long (591-foot-long) Processional Way, lined with polychrome ceramic bricks depicting 120 roaring lions **[51]**. A city of refinement and splendour, adorned with hanging gardens, Babylon was both envied and mistrusted by its neighbours. Images of dragons, the symbol of Babylon's patron god, Marduk, were present throughout the city and would have filled visitors with awe. Following the capture of the inhabitants of Judea, Babylon became a place of exile for the Hebrews, as recounted in the Old Testament. According to the Bible, the Tower of Babel was built in defiance of God in an attempt to reach heaven, its architecture inspired by Babylonian ziggurats, tall constructions with a succession of receding levels.

After Nebuchadnezzar's death and disputed succession, the power of the reigning dynasty was greatly undermined. The image of a splendid, sumptuous and cruel city endures nonetheless and continues to fuel modern-day narratives, from cinema to video games. Babylon's presence in the Louvre is tied to an archaeology of objects and places, but more so to an archaeology of writing and narratives. The Code of Hammurabi **[23]**, the *Epic of Gilgamesh* – the first hero, who went on to inspire Greek mythology – and the exile of the inhabitants of Judea have all informed the museum's vision.

The statue of Neshor **[52]**, a group sculpture of a kneeling man holding three statues of Egyptian gods – Khnum, with a ram's head, Satis and Anuket – is contemporary with the last years of Nebuchadnezzar II's reign. It was discovered in Rome in the seventeenth century, where it joined the prestigious collection amassed by Cardinal Albani. The presence of such a work in ancient Rome shows how ancient Egypt captured people's imagination, even in antiquity.

Kouros – "young man" – is the name given to ancient Greek statues depicting nude males. This one **[53]** was uncovered in 1867 in Actium, on the east coast of Greece,

[51]
Brick panel
Babylon, present-day Iraq
c. 604–562 BCE
(Nebuchadnezzar II)
Glazed siliceous clay
ceramic
H. 105; W. 227; D. 12 cm
(H. 3 ft 5¼ in.;
W. 7 ft 5¼ in.; D. 4¾ in.)
⩡ 1938 (on deposit from
the Pergamonmuseum,
Berlin)
DNEA

[52]
Statue of Neshor
Rignano, Italy
c. 589–570 BCE
Diorite
H. 105; W. 37.5; D. 51.1 cm
(H. 3 ft 5¼ in.;
W. 1 ft 2¾ in.; D. 1 ft 8 in.)
⩡ 1815
DAE

[53]
Kouros, Statue of a Man
Temple of Apollo,
Actium, Greece
c. 570 BCE
Marble
H. 94.5; W. 47; D. 31 cm
(H. 3 ft 1¼ in.;
W. 1 ft 6½ in.; D. 1 ft)
⩡ 1874
DGERA

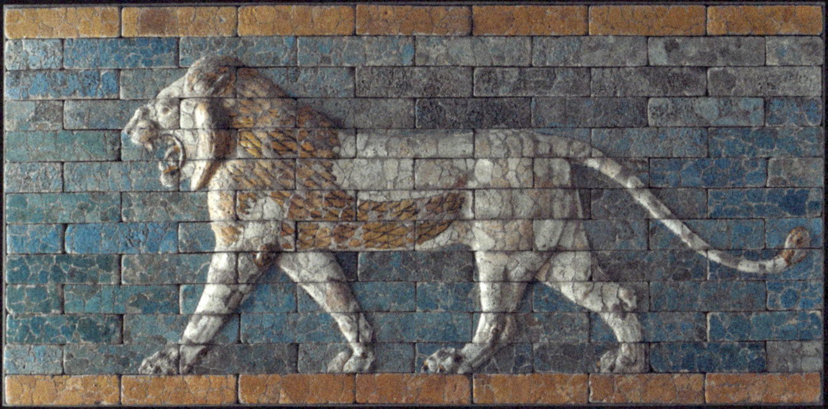

51

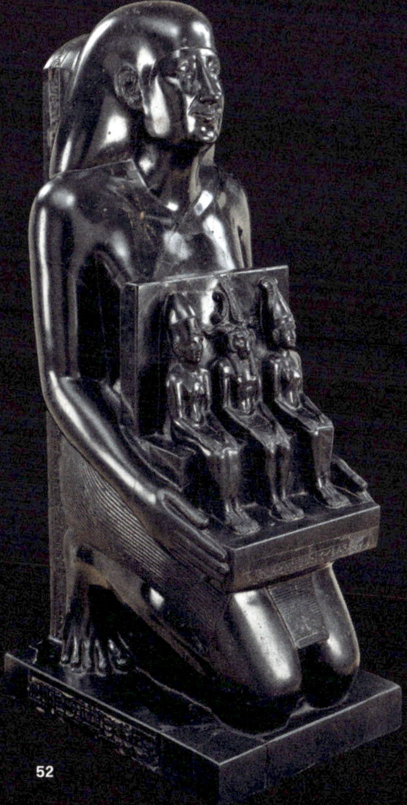

52

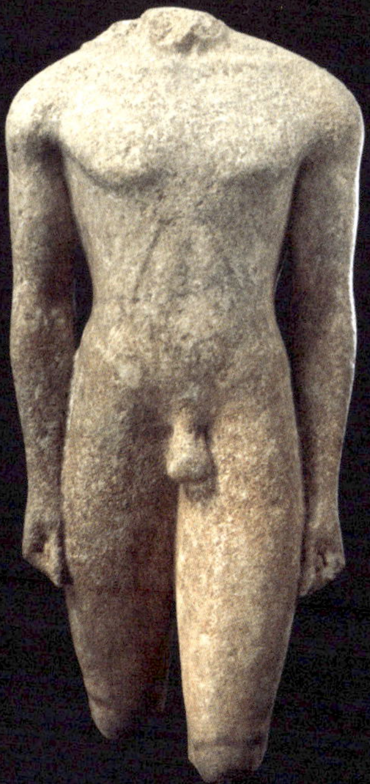

53

by Charles Champoiseau, who also discovered the *Winged Victory of Samothrace* **[59]**. It adopts a hieratic, slightly stiff pose. Another example of a kouros **[56]** was found in 1902 on Paros, one of the Cyclades islands. The emergence of this type of statue redefined understanding of the art of Greek sculpture. These works, labelled as archaic, show a stage prior to the classical Greek art that until then had fuelled Western taste. Their arrival at the Louvre was an opportunity to consider ancient creation in a new light: finding them a place within the museum would necessarily imply a vision that embraced the notion of evolution.

Through this union of Mesopotamian, Egyptian **[55]** and Greek **[53]** works, the discontinuous but underlying thread between forgotten civilisations was restored, shaping new historical and aesthetic thinking. These ideas were profoundly challenged by the emergence of works from other continents and the (welcome) decentred perspective that came with them. From Mexico, the *Anthropomorphic Statuette* **[54]**, in coloured ceramic, is a very different representation of the human body to those produced in the same period by the civilisations so far mentioned, yet is instantly identifiable. The coloured triangles on the figure's torso emphasise the connection between humans, nature and the cosmos in a singular vision, where humanity is just one part of creation.

[54]
Anthropomorphic Statuette
Mexico
c. 600 BCE–200 CE
Modelled slip-cast terracotta
H. 31; W. 22.5; D. 14 cm
(H. 12¼ in.; W. 8¾ in.; D. 5½ in.)
MQB–JC

[55]
Donor Figure
Egypt
c. 589–570 BCE
Alloy of copper, silver, electrum and gold
H. 51; W. 10.5; D. 30 cm
(H. 20; W. 4⅛; D. 11¾ in.)
⊻ 1826
DEA

[56]
Kouros, Statue of a Man
Asklepion, Paros, Greece
c. 540–530 BCE
Marble
H. 103; W. 40; D. 25 cm
(H. 3 ft 4½ in.; W. 1 ft 3¾ in.; D. 9¾ in.)
⊻ 1910
DGERA

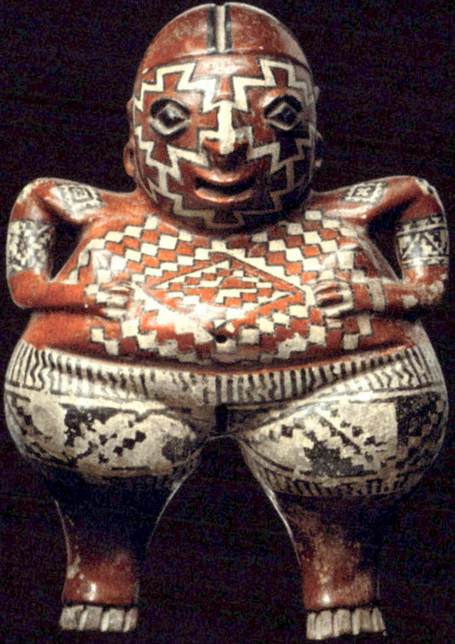
54

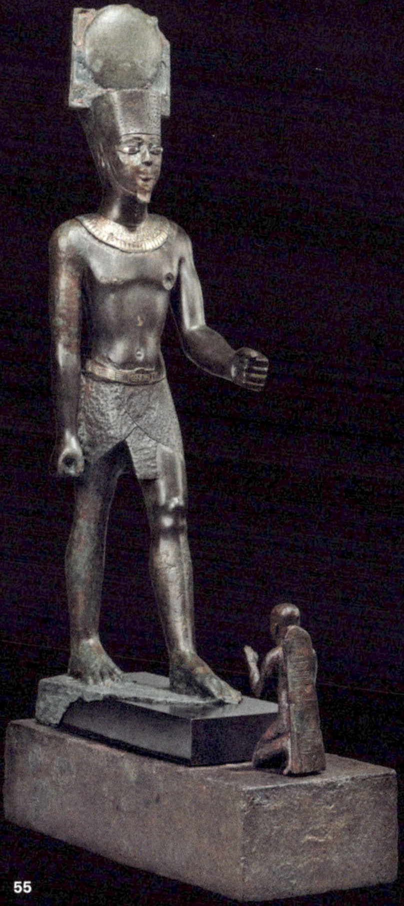
55

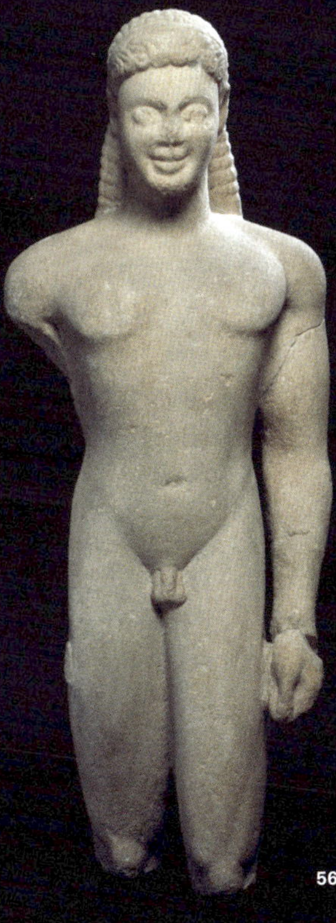
56

New perspectives on ancient art

The growth of the Louvre's collections of antiquities throughout the nineteenth century expanded the scope and depth of understanding of the art of ancient civilisations. These works were like new roots, giving fresh impetus to the study of Greek art, which since antiquity had formed the Western ideal for representations of the human body. The art of certain neighbouring, sometimes rival, civilisations was also brought to light, most notably the Achaemenid Persians. More was revealed of the Etruscans, a previously little-known civilisation established on the Italian Peninsula. In addition to their own artistic production, marked by a distinct and pronounced aesthetic sensibility, the Etruscans owned many Greek artefacts, including numerous beautiful painted vases.

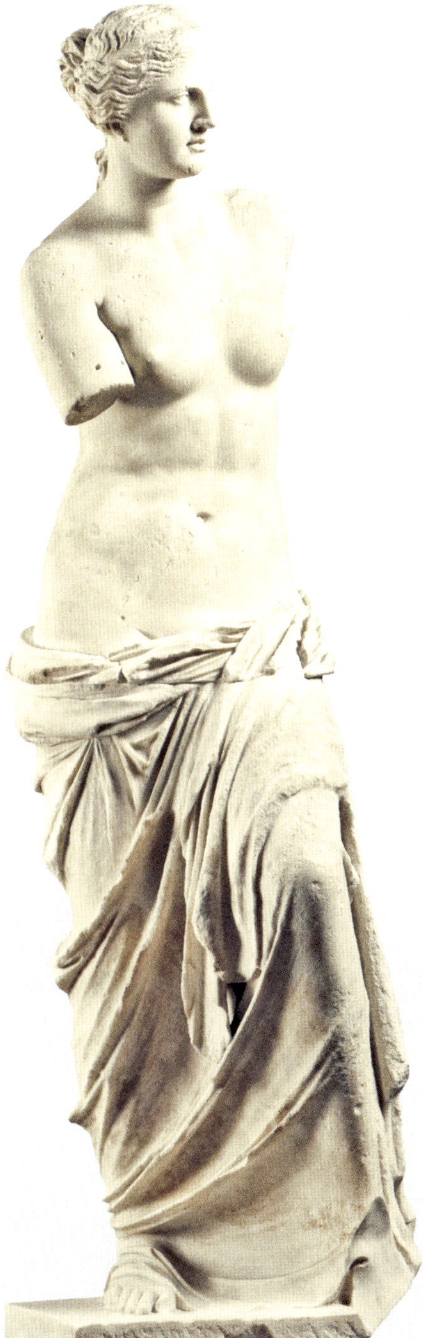

[57]
Venus de Milo
Milos, Greece
c. 150–125 BCE
Parian marble
H. 204 cm
(H. 6 ft 8¼ in.)
⊻ 1821 (gift of
Louis XVIII)
DGERA

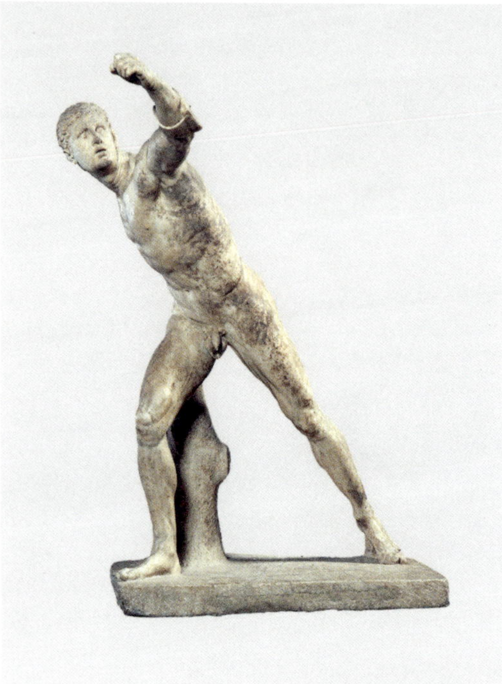

[58]
Agasias
Active in the 1st century BCE
Borghese Gladiator
Anzio, Italy
c. 100 BCE
Marble
H. 173; W. 172; D. 169 cm
(H. 5 ft 8 in.; W. 5 ft 7¾ in.;
D. 5 ft 6½ in.)
⩡ 1807 (former collection of
Camillo Borghese)
DGERA

The arrival of the *Venus de Milo* **[57]** at the Louvre in 1821 was an event for the entire art world. Discovered the previous year, this Hellenistic statue marked the introduction of an original Greek work into the museum's collection. Its elegant lines and subtly balanced proportions made it a model of beauty and soon an inspiration for artists. Another Hellenistic Greek sculpture, found during excavations conducted in the early seventeenth century at the ancient site of Antium, south of Rome, the *Borghese Gladiator* **[58]** was admired for the vividness and grace of the warrior's pose. It was acquired by the Louvre in 1807, together with the entire Camillo Borghese collection. Since 1883, from its place at the top of the largest staircase, the monumental *Winged Victory of Samothrace* **[59]** appears to embrace the entire museum in its outstretched wings. This triumphant figure was uncovered on the island of Samothrace during excavations that began in the early 1860s. Later digs were organised in an attempt to locate the statue's head, unsuccessfully. Alongside the *Mona Lisa* **[207]**, it is one of the Louvre's most visited works.

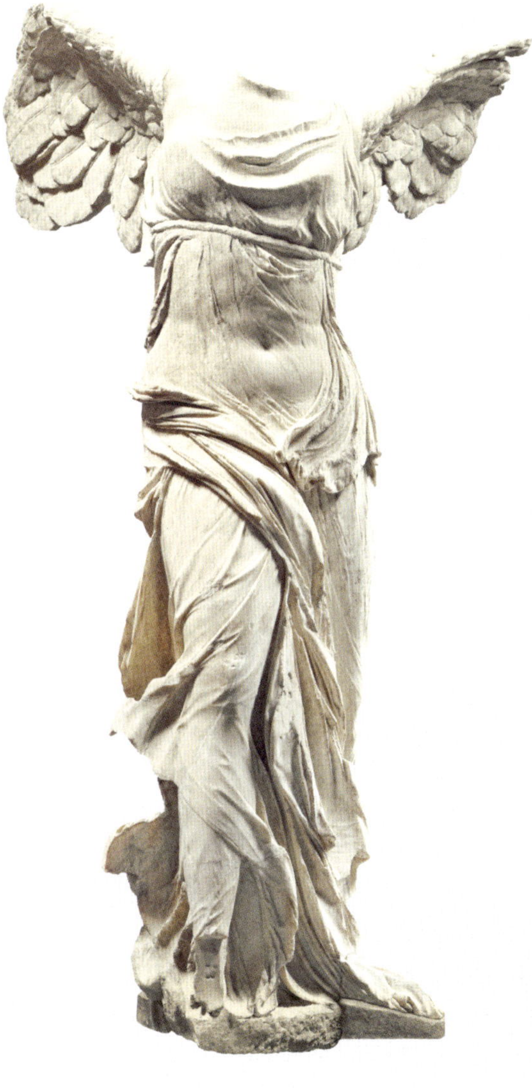

[59]
Winged Victory of Samothrace
Palaeopolis, Samothrace, Greece
c. 200–175 BCE
Parian and grey Lartos marble
H. 511 (total), 275 (statue), 200 cm (ship)
(H. 16 ft 9¼ in. [total], 9 ft [statue],
6 ft 6¾ in. [ship])
⊻ 1864
DGERA

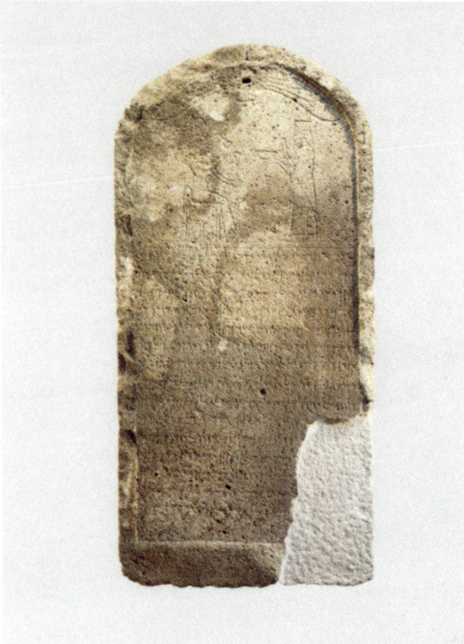

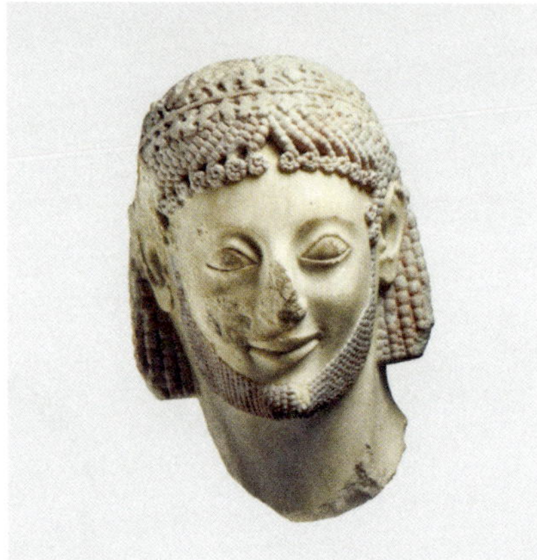

[60]
Yehawmilk Stele
Byblos, present-day Lebanon
c. 450 BCE
Limestone
H. 112; W. 56; D. 24 cm (H. 3 ft 8 in.; W. 1 ft 10 in.; D. 9½ in.)
⩡ 1967 (gift of Henri Louis Marie Martin de Boisgelin)
DNEA

[61]
Rampin Horseman
Acropolis of Athens, Greece
c. 560–540 BCE
Painted Pentelic marble
H. 27 cm (H. 10¾ in.)
⩡ 1896 (bequest of Georges Rampin)
DGERA

THE MEDITERRANEAN, A CROSSROADS OF CIVILISATIONS The head of the *Rampin Horseman* **[61]**, his jovial features skilfully rendered, was uncovered in the 1860s on the Acropolis in Athens. Several fragments of the same statue, including the young man's torso and mount, are now conserved in Athens. The sculpture was greatly admired when it was shown at the 1878 Universal Exposition in Paris. It was bequeathed to the Louvre by its owner, Georges Rampin, in 1896.

Frequent contact between the different civilisations of the Mediterranean Basin resulted in many reciprocal influences. The capital discovered on the island of Cyprus in the 1880s, which depicts the Phoenician goddess Astarte **[63]**, borrows motifs from ancient Egyptian art such as references to the goddess Hathor. The Phoenicians were established primarily in the Levant, where Lebanon is today. These experienced navigators and merchants set up numerous trading posts along the shores of the Mediterranean.

The Achaemenid Empire stood as a powerful rival to the Greek city-states; the two opposed each other during

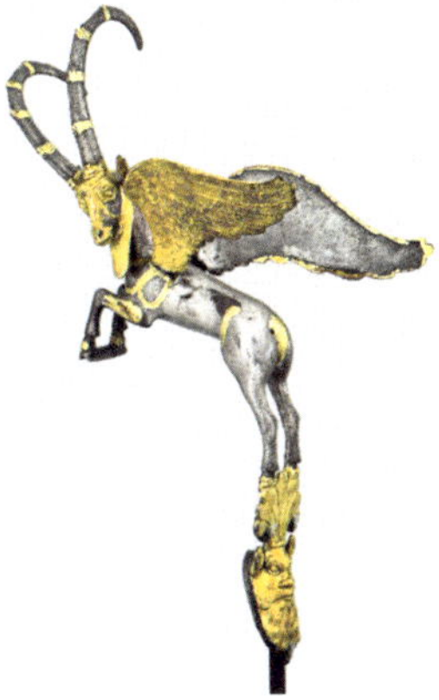

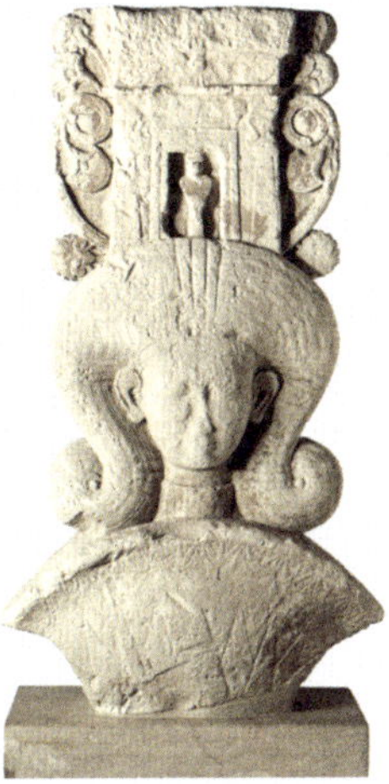

[62]
Vase Handle
Urartu (?), Armenia
c. 539–330 BCE
Gilded silver
H. 26.5; W. 15; D. 10 cm
(H. 10½; W. 5⅞; D. 3⅞ in.)
⩡ 1898
DNEA

[63]
Stele, Capital, Votive Object
Sanctuary of Astarte, Larnaca, Cyprus
c. 600–475 BCE
Limestone
H. 133; W. 74; D. 37 cm
(H. 4 ft 4¼ in.;
W. 2 ft 5¼ in.; D. 1 ft 2½ in.)
⩡ 1887
DNEA

the Greco-Persian Wars of the early fifth century BCE. Art at the courts of Darius I and Xerxes reflected the wealth and strength of the Persian Empire, as well as the quality of the artists who served it **[62]**. The Louvre holds architectural elements and part of the polychrome glazed brick decor from the palace of Darius I. They were uncovered in Susa, as were numerous ensembles of Mesopotamian art whose influence on Persian art can be seen, for example, in the hieratic procession of soldiers in the *Frieze of Archers* **[64]** and in the prominence of animal figuration. The introduction of these works to the Louvre gave life and substance to these enemies of the Greeks, already well documented in historic texts.

The two were opposed not just in battle. The opportunity to view Greek and Persian masterpieces from the same period at the Louvre reveals differences in the two civilisations' conception of beauty. The *Miletus Torso* **[67]** was discovered in Miletus, in modern-day Turkey, in the remains of the city's Roman theatre, during excavations initiated by Gustave and Edmond de Rothschild.

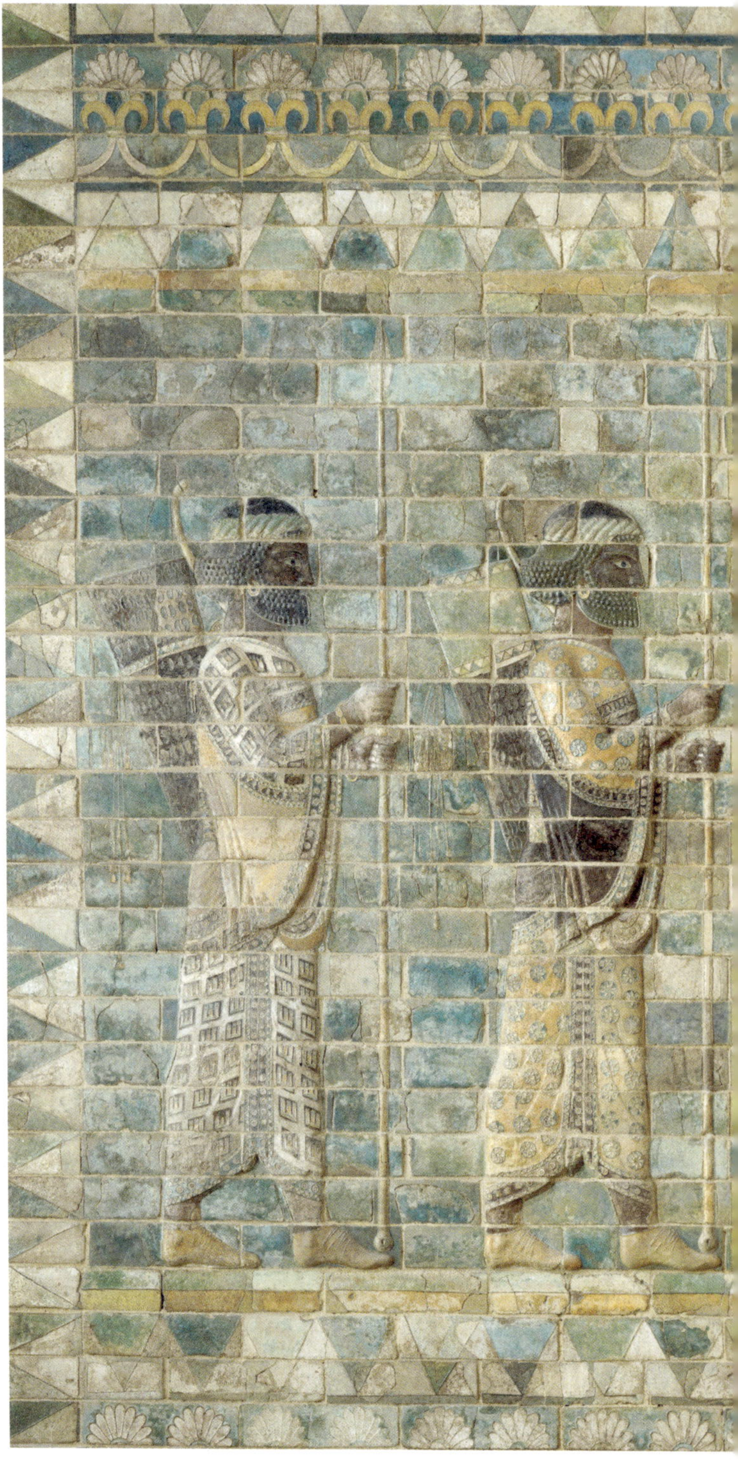

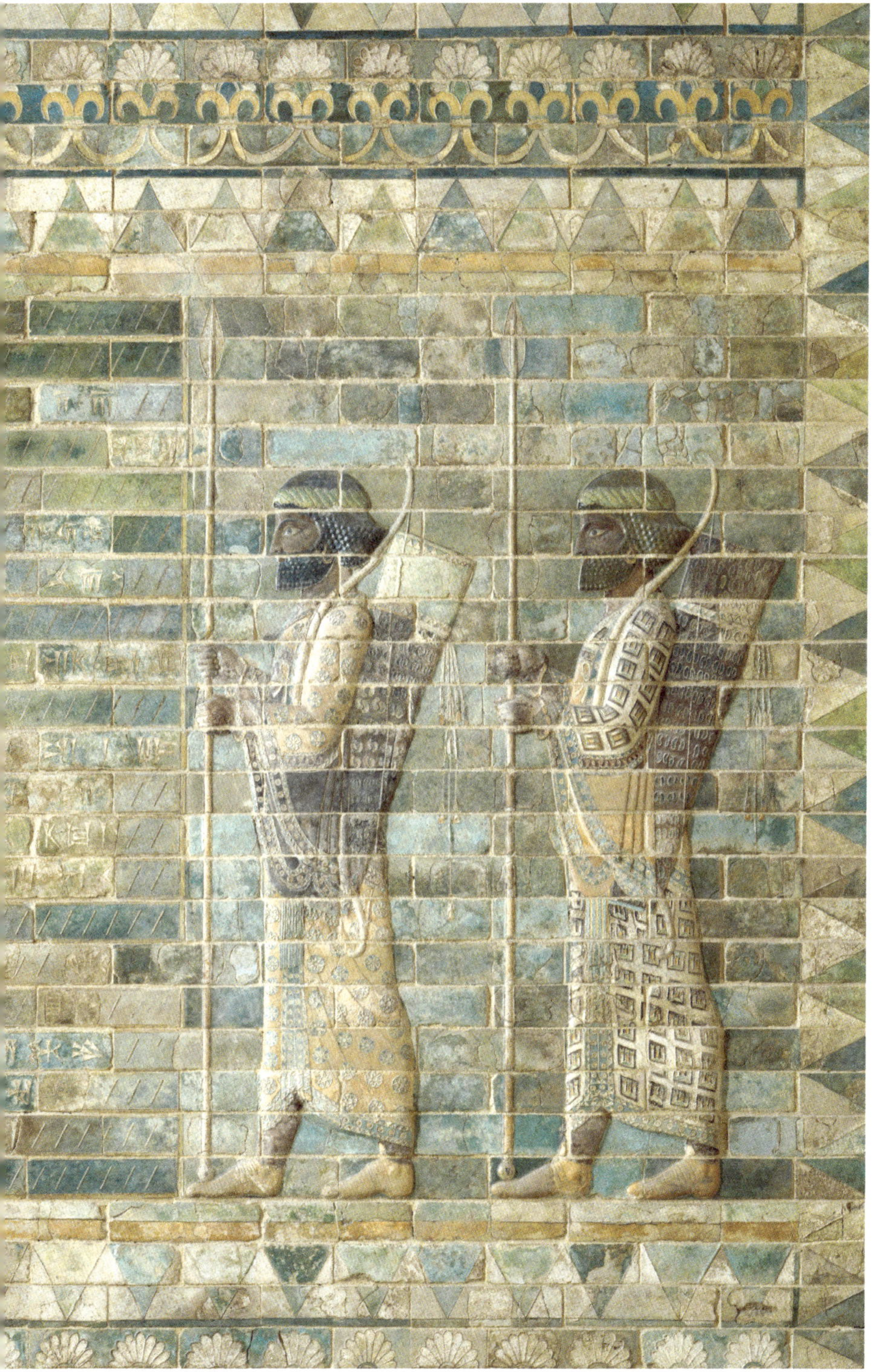

[64] ***Frieze of Archers***. Palace of Darius I, Susa, present-day Iran. c. 522–486 BCE. Glazed siliceous clay ceramic. H. 475; W. 375; D. 17 cm (H. 15 ft 7 in.; W. 12 ft 3½ in.; D. 6¾ in.). ⩡ 1884–1886. DNEA

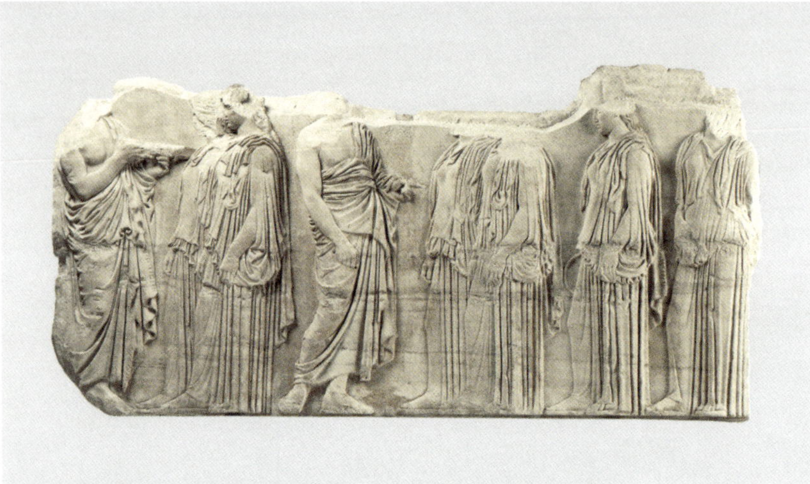

[65] Phidias. c. 490–431 BCE. ***Parthenon Frieze***. Parthenon, Acropolis of Athens, Greece. c. 445–438 BCE
Marble. H. 101; W. 207; D. 13 cm (H. 3 ft 3¾ in.; W. 6 ft 9½ in.; D. 5⅛ in.). ⊻ 1798. DGERA

This superb marble fragment was an aesthetic revelation, as it illustrates the evolution of Greek art over the course of the fifth century BCE. The quivering muscles are conveyed with an aesthetic sensibility grounded in a new naturalist approach that would blossom in so-called classical Greek art. *Heracles and the Cretan Bull* **[66]**, a relief from the Temple of Zeus at Olympia, which resurfaced in 1830, shows Heracles fighting the mythical creature. The sculptor plays on the diagonal formed by man and beast to convey the strength and suppleness of Heracles (Hercules for the Romans) with rare intensity. The *Parthenon Frieze* **[65]** ran around the Parthenon, which stood at the top of the Acropolis in Athens. Built between 447 and 432 BCE, this temple and treasury housed a monumental sculpture, now vanished, of Athena, the patron and protector of the city. Each year the goddess was celebrated at the Panathenaic festival which culminated in a grand procession, the subject of the frieze. The human figures have been sculpted with grace but also with the intention to distinguish not just the various groups but the

[66]
Heracles and the Cretan Bull
Temple of Zeus, Olympia, Greece
c. 460 BCE
Marble
H. 114; W. 152; D. 31 cm
(H. 3 ft 8¾ in.; W. 4 ft 11¾ in.; D. 1 ft)
⊻ 1830 (gift)
DGERA

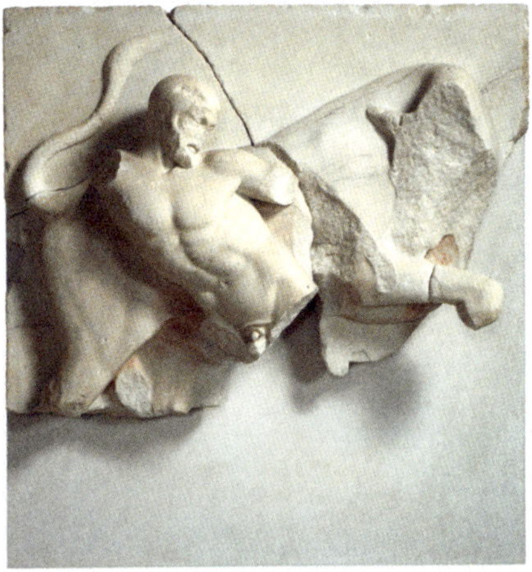

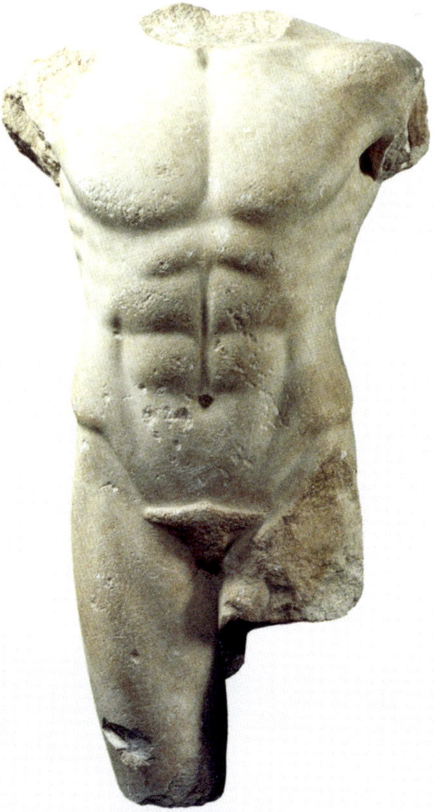

[67]
Miletus Torso
Miletus theatre, present-day Turkey
c. 490–385 BCE
Marble
H. 132; W. 76.5; D. 43 cm
(H. 4 ft 4 in.; W. 2 ft 6 in.; D. 1 ft 5 in.)
⊻ 1873 (gift of Gustave and Edmond de Rothschild)
DGERA

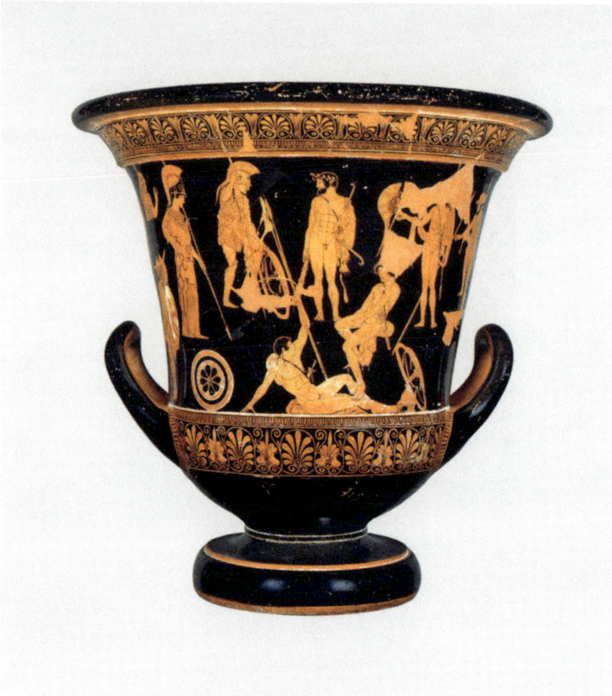

[68]
Athens, Greece
Niobid Krater
Orvieto, Italy
c. 460–450 BCE
Painted clay
H. 54; Diam. 51.5 cm
(H. 21½; Diam. 20½ in.)
⊻ 1883
DGERA

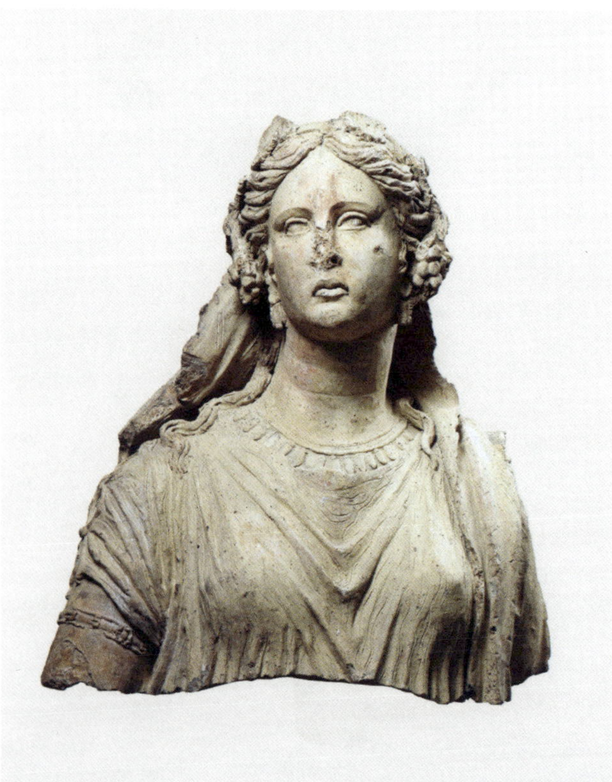

[69]
Bust of Ariadne
Falerii, present-day Italy
c. 300–200 BCE
Painted clay
H. 61; W. 58; D. 31 cm
(H. 24; W. 22¾; D. 12¼ in.)
⊻ 1862 (former collection of Giampietro Campana)
DGERA

[70]
Euphronios
Late 6th–first half of the 5th century BCE
Antaeus Krater
Etruria, Italy
c. 515–510 BCE
Painted clay
H. 45.5; Diam. 56 cm
(H. 18; Diam. 22 in.)
⩝ 1862 (former collection of Giampietro Campana)
DGERA

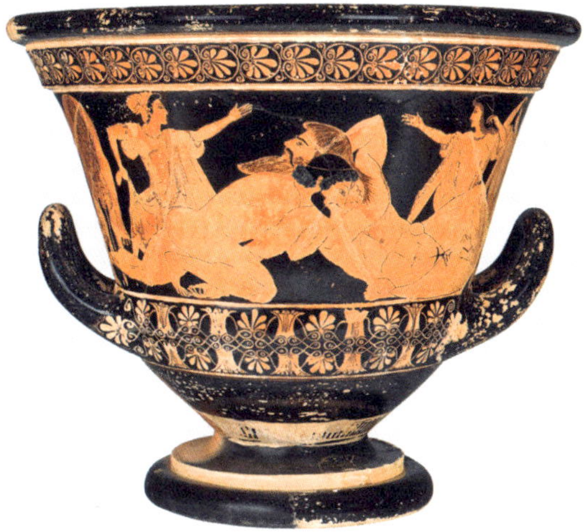

individuals within them, shown by the care taken to give each one a different pose.

Already in their day, Greek potters were praised for their talent and expertise. Painted ceramic vases were used at different stages of a banquet, their shape and size adapted to their purpose. These works, decorated with scenes narrating the exploits of the gods and heroes of ancient mythology **[68]**, have taught us much about the Greek art of painting. The *Antaeus Krater* **[70]** by Euphronios shows Heracles fighting the mythical giant Antaeus, son of the Earth goddess Gaea and Poseidon, god of the sea. The Louvre holds a fine collection of Greek vases, much of which was acquired in the early 1860s from the collection assembled by Giampietro Campana. Many of these vases were found in Italy, in the remains of Etruscan tombs. Before the advent of the Roman Republic, the Etruscans were among the leading civilisations on the Italian Peninsula. Skilled mariners and craftsmen, they had a particular appreciation for Greek ceramics, which they obtained in exchange for minerals found in the region. The Etruscans, who believed in life after death,

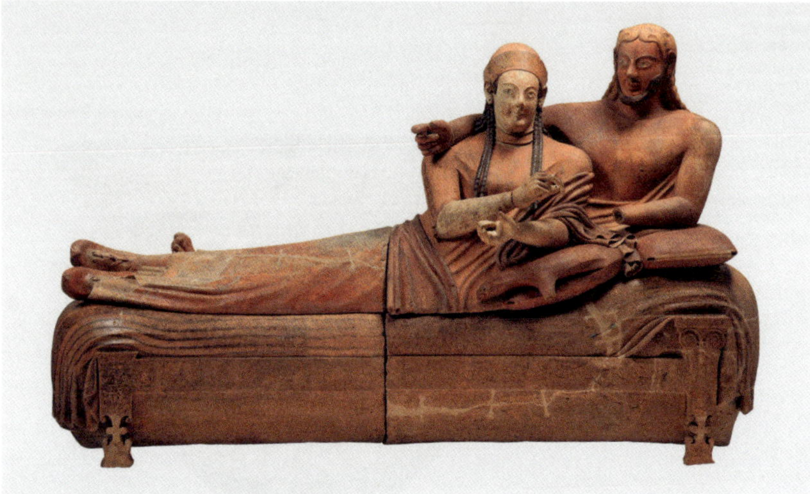

[71]
Sarcophagus of the Spouses
Necropolis of the Banditaccia, Cerveteri, Italy
c. 520–510 BCE
Painted clay
H. 114; W. 194; D. 74 cm
(H. 3 ft 8¾ in.; W. 6 ft 4¼ in.; D. 2 ft 5¼ in.)
⩡ 1862 (former collection of Giampietro Campana)
DGERA

placed Greek vases in their tombs so that the deceased might enjoy an eternal banquet. Etruscan art reflects the artistic concepts of the period but is also inventive in its forms and themes. The *Sarcophagus of the Spouses* **[71]** is a monumental terracotta funeral urn; the couple recline side by side, their pose reminiscent of participants in a banquet. The Etruscans were also talented goldsmiths, as demonstrated by the *Pendant with the Head of Achelous* **[73]**, a representation of the river god's bearded head.

A SHIFTING PARADIGM Of Etruscan ancestry, Lucius Tarquinius Superbus (Tarquin the Proud) was the last king of Rome. His fall marked the (partly mythical) establishment of the Roman Republic, at the very end of the sixth century BCE. The strengthening of the regime, which was dominated by a patrician class, enabled Rome to develop, its influence to spread, and a major civilisation to emerge in the West. The architectural relief of the *Altar of Domitius Ahenobarbus* **[74]** reveals the influence of Greek art. Constructed as a frieze, it is distinguished by the austere

[72]
Statue, Head **(fragment)**
Fiesole, Italy
c. 300 BCE
Bronze
H. 29.6; W. 16; D. 23 cm
(H. 11¾; W. 6¼; D. 9 in.)
⊻ 1864
DGERA

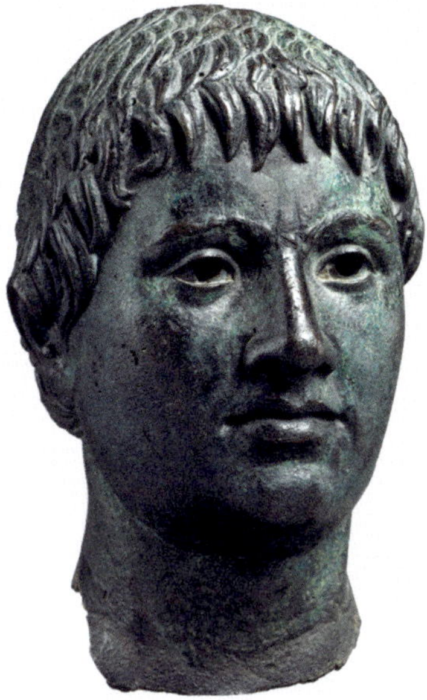

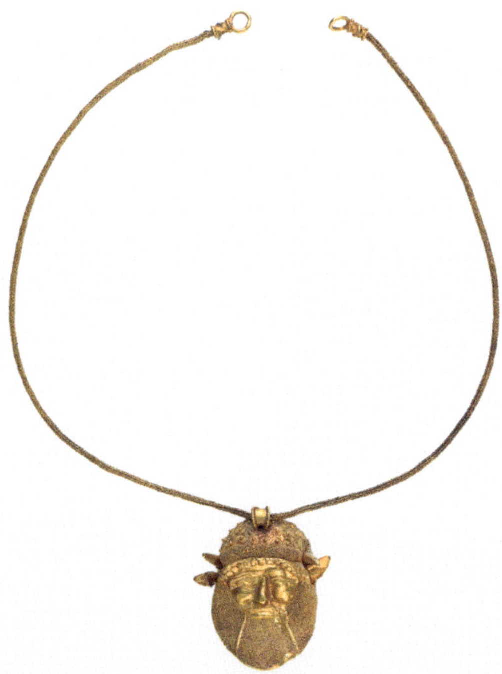

[73]
Etruria, Italy
Pendant with the Head of Achelous
Chiusi, Italy
c. 480–460 BCE
Gold
H. 22; W. 3.6; D. 1.4 cm
(H. 8¾; W. 1⅜; D. ½ in.)
⊻ 1862 (former collection of Giampietro Campana)
DGERA

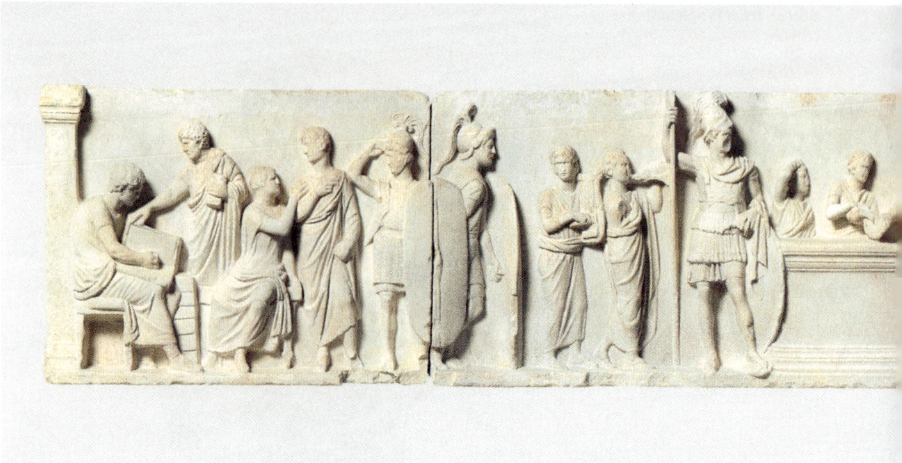

[74]
Altar of Domitius Ahenobarbus
Campus Martius, Rome, Italy
c. 150–100 BCE
Marble
H. 84; W. 566; D. 22 cm
(H. 2 ft 9 in.; W. 18 ft 6¾ in.; D. 8¾ in.)
⊻ 1824
DGERA

beauty of the figures depicted. Just as Greece had the Persian Empire as an adversary, Rome had Carthage, in what is now Tunisia. In the third and second centuries BCE, these rival cities clashed in the Punic Wars ("Punic" being another name for "Carthaginian"). The victorious Romans destroyed Carthage. The Louvre's collection of Punic funerary steles illustrates this civilisation's artistic creation **[76]**.

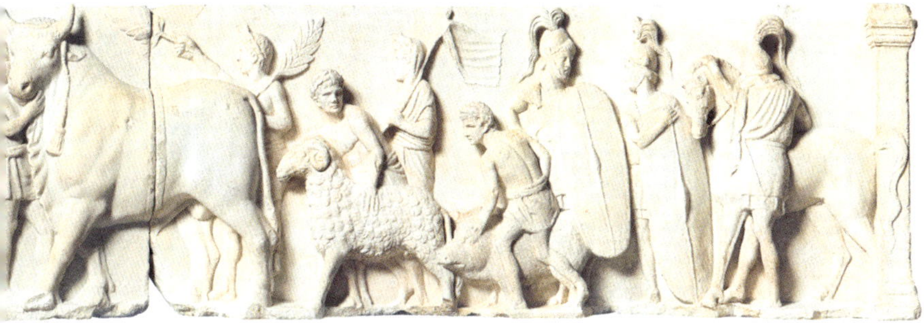

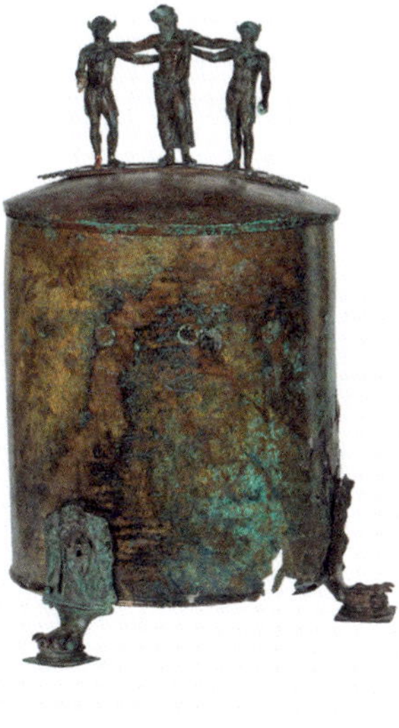

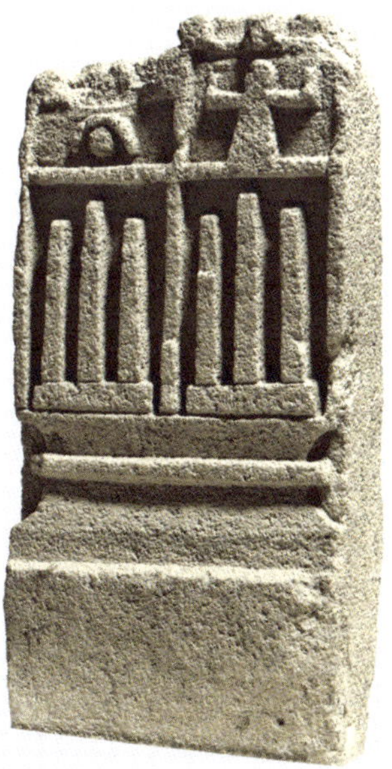

[75]
Napoleon Cista
Palestrina, Italy
c. 375–350 BCE
Bronze
H. 71; Diam. 42 cm
(H. 28; Diam. 16½ in.)
⊻ 1862
DGERA

[76]
Stele
Hadrumetum, present-day Tunisia
c. 400–200 BCE
Limestone and sandstone (?)
H. 110; W. 45; D. 10 cm
(H. 3 ft 7¼ in.; W. 17¾ in.; D. 4 in.)
⊻ 1896 (gift of Théodore Trihidez)
DNEA

From the third century BCE, the Roman Republic gradually extended its power to encompass the entire Mediterranean Rim. By the Augustan Age, thanks to the proficiency and coherence of its military legions, and by astutely granting Roman citizenship to the vanquished, Rome conquered much of the world as it was then known by the West. The Mediterranean became the Romans' mare nostrum, "our sea" – its shores bathed in Roman civilisation. The figurine of Isis **[80]**, which displays the attributes of both the Egyptian goddess and Venus, the Roman goddess of beauty, is typical of the creativity sparked by Roman acculturation. The *Venus of Arles* **[77]** takes its name from the city where it was found in 1651, situated in one of the first Roman provinces in the territory that is now France. It entered the collection of the reigning monarch, Louis XIV. Discovered in several pieces and restored by the sculptor François Girardon, it is considered an ideal of feminine beauty. In 27 BCE Gaius Octavius, the adopted son of Julius Caesar, became Augustus **[78]**, the first Roman emperor. This marked the beginning of a long period of political stability, lasting several centuries.

Still today, this political, economic and cultural continuity serves as a historical model. The hierarchy of the Catholic Church and the structure of the Holy Roman Empire were fashioned after Rome. The great conquerors also looked to Rome: Charlemagne in the ninth century CE and Napoleon Bonaparte in the early nineteenth century. Rome itself played a part in the edification of its glory. At the beginning of Augustus's reign, Virgil wrote the *Aeneid*, the story of Aeneas that links the foundation of Rome to the legend of Troy. In the second century CE, Suetonius recorded the deeds of the first emperors in *The Twelve Caesars*.

The Roman elite enjoyed a life of refinement. The *Augustus Cameo* **[81]** was uncovered in Rome, at the site known as the Catacomb of Priscilla. It entered the Vatican's collections under Pope Benedict XIV, then came to the Louvre with works seized by Bonaparte's army. The silverware unearthed in 1895 in Boscoreale, near Naples, constitutes one of the finest decorative Roman ensembles known. One of the major pieces in this Boscoreale treasure, the *Africa Dish* **[83]** depicts

[77]
Venus of Arles
Roman Theatre of Arles, France
c. last 3rd of the 1st century BCE
Hymettus marble
H. 220; W. 102; D. 65 cm
(H. 7 ft 2½ in.; W. 3 ft 4¼ in.; D. 2 ft 1½ in.)
⊻ 1798 (former royal collection, collection of Louis XIV)
DGERA

[78]
Bust of Augustus
Rome (?), Italy
c. 25 BCE–25 CE
Marble
H. 36.5; W. 19.5; D. 21 cm
(H. 14¼; W. 7¾; D. 8½ in.)
⊻ 1807 (former collection of Camillo Borghese)
DGERA

[79]
Statue of Artemis
Pyla (?), Greece
1st century
Limestone
H. 20; W. 12; D. 14.5 cm
(H. 7¾; W. 4¾; D. 5¾ in.)
⊻ 1874 (gift of Robert Hamilton Lang)
DNEA

[80]
Figurine of Isis
c. last 3rd of the 1st century BCE
Terracotta and paint
H. 23.8 cm
(H. 9¼ in.)
⊻ 1948 (former collection of the Musée Guimet, Paris)
DEA

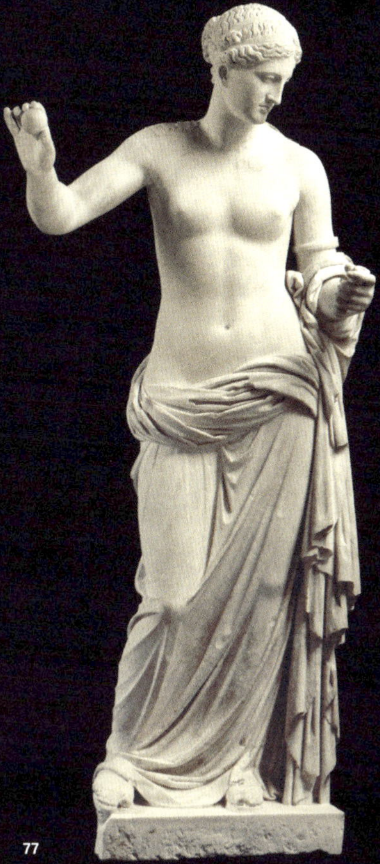

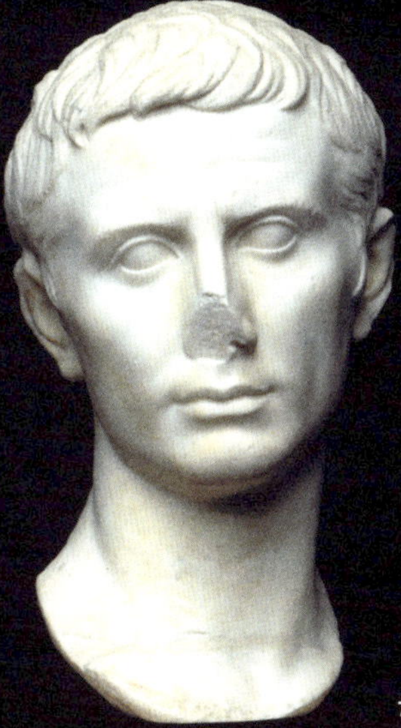

78

77

80

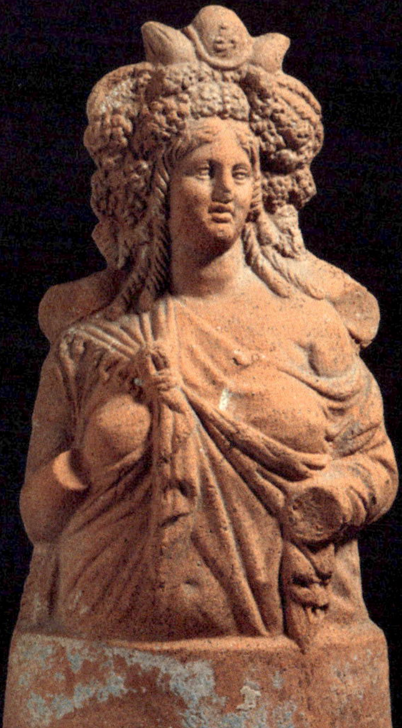

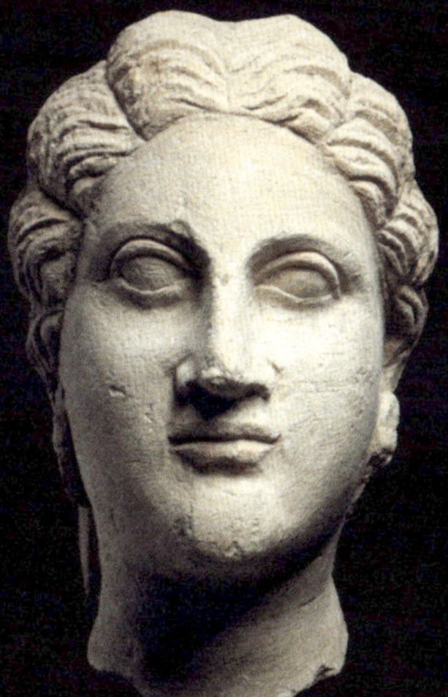

79

a woman – possibly Cleopatra, possibly Selene, goddess of the moon – surrounded by miniature renderings of an elephant, lion and panther. The delicate chasing and the silversmith's expertise in forming the different reliefs are quite striking.

The Nok, whose culture extended across an area corresponding to present-day Nigeria, became known to the West only in the 1920s. Nok sculptors – who most likely were unaware of their Greek and Roman contemporaries – display their remarkable skill in terracotta sculptures **[82]** whose beauty, purity and simplicity, elegantly blending naturalism and idealism, still fascinate.

[81]
Cameo of Augustus
(partial view of a 1785 monument comprising a cameo and nine ancient phalerae)
Catacomb of Priscilla, Rome, Italy
1st century
Chalcedony
H. 14 cm
(H. 5½ in.)
⩡ 1801
DGERA

[82]
Sculpture
Nigeria, Nok culture
500 BCE–500 CE
Terracotta
H. 54; W. 50; D. 50 cm
(H. 21¼; W. 19¾; D. 19¾ in.)
MQB–JC

[83]
Africa Dish, Boscoreale Treasure
Villa della Pisanella, Boscoreale, Italy
c. 25 BCE–50 CE
Partially gilded silver
H. 8; Diam. 22.6 cm
(H. 3⅛; Diam. 9 in.)
⩡ 1895 (gift of Edmond de Rothschild)
DGERA

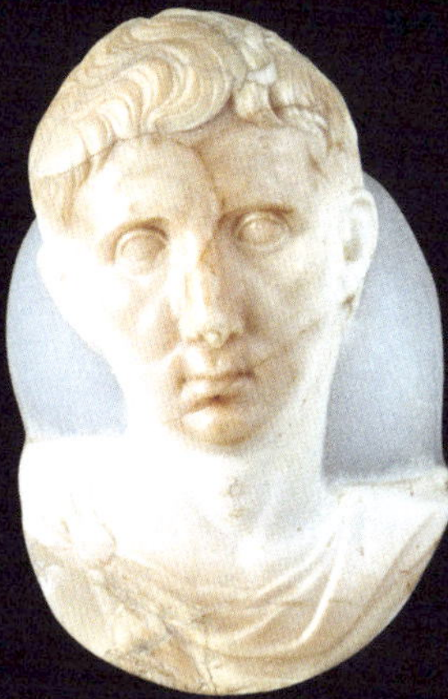
81

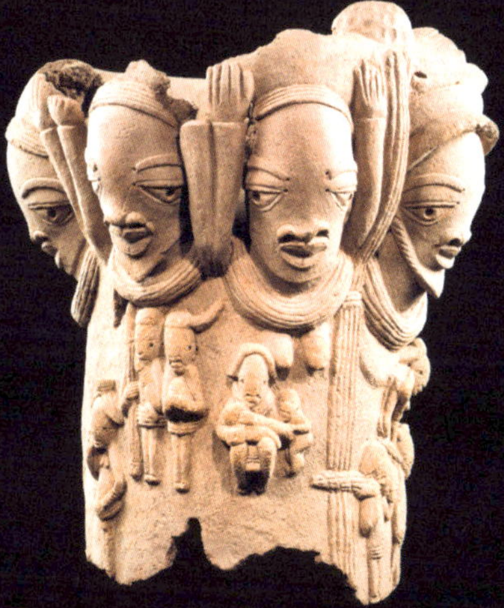
82

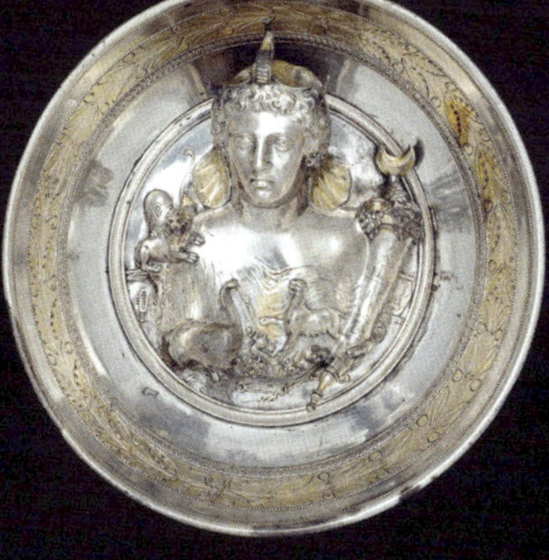
83

The Roman and Byzantine empires

The Roman Empire was a military and political power that progressively extended its influence to every known territory, from North Africa to Britain, from Spain to Asia Minor. The Romans were clearly enamoured of Greek art, seduced by the ability of Hellenic artists to reproduce the human body through naturalistic representations, founded on a sense of equilibrium and the desire to portray an idealised beauty. That Rome adopted a mythology similar to that of the Greeks further encouraged this artistic appropriation. These words, taken from the *Aeneid* – the epic story of the Trojan hero Aeneas, the mythical ancestor of the Romans, written by the poet Virgil in honour of Emperor Augustus – illustrate Rome's relationship to artistic creation: "Let others better mould the running mass / Of metals, and inform the breathing brass, / And soften into flesh a marble face / ... / But, Rome, 'tis thine alone, with awful sway, / To rule mankind, and make the world obey. / Disposing peace and war by thy own majestic way; / To tame the proud, the fetter'd slave to free."

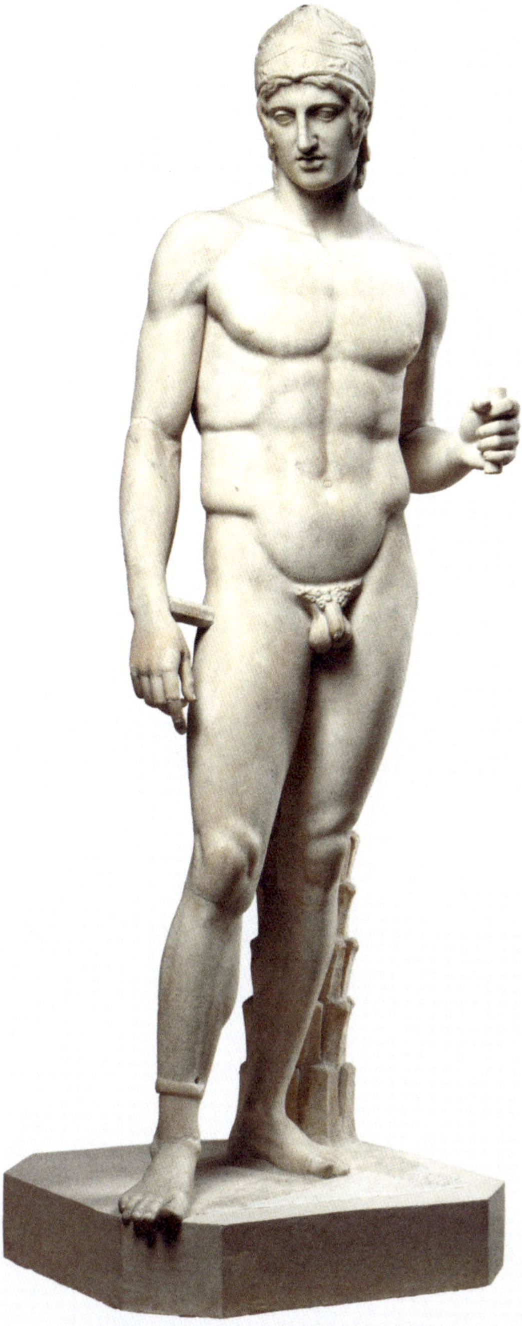

[84]
Ares Borghese
Rome (?), Italy
c. 100 BCE–50 CE
Marble
H. 220; W. 85; D. 76 cm
(H. 7 ft 2½ in.; W. 2 ft 9½ in.;
D. 2 ft 6 in.)
⊻ 1807 (former collection
of Camillo Borghese)
DGERA

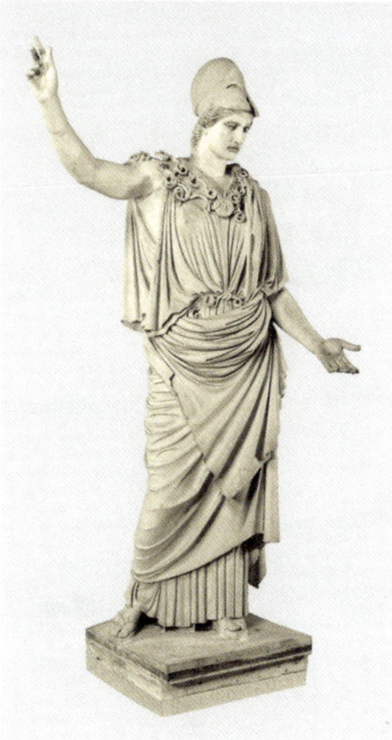

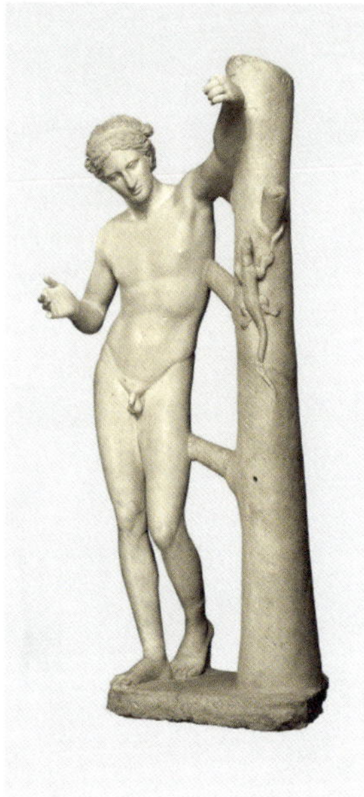

[85]
Velletri Pallas
Velletri, Italy
c. 1st century
Parian marble
H. 305; W. 177; D. 112.5 cm
(H. 10 ft; W. 5 ft 9¾ in.;
D. 3 ft 8¼ in.)
⊻ 1803
DGERA

[86]
Apollo Sauroctonos
Italy
c. 25–50
Marble
H. 167; W. 78; D. 85 cm
(H. 5 ft 5¾ in.;
W. 2 ft 6¾ in.; 2 ft 9½ in.)
⊻ 1807 (former collection of
Camillo Borghese)
DGERA

"SOFTEN INTO FLESH A MARBLE FACE" Roman art lovers had marble replicas made of Greek sculptures **[84–89]** (most of the originals would have been bronze). The *Ares Borghese* **[84]**, for example, a sculpture of the Greek god of war, is taken from a work by Alcamenes, from the fifth century BCE. The graceful *Apollo Sauroctonus* **[86]**, which shows the god of the sun and the arts about to catch a lizard, reprises a work by the Athenian sculptor Praxiteles, one of the most renowned Greek artists of the fourth century BCE. At first sight, *Sleeping Hermaphroditus* **[88]** depicts a beautiful young woman in slumber. Only by walking around the statue – believed to be an interpretation of a bronze from the third century BCE – is its dual nature, feminine and masculine, revealed. Having reappeared in Rome in the early seventeenth century, it now reclines on a soft pillow and thick mattress that were sculpted in 1620 by Gian Lorenzo Bernini, one of the great Italian artists of his day. Acquired by the Louvre in 1807 as part of the Borghese collection, it is admired as much today as it was centuries ago, dazzling proof of the enduring attraction of Greek art.

[87]
Child and Goose
Villa of the Quintilii,
Rome, Italy
c. 2nd century
Pentelic marble
H. 93; W. 69.5; D. 65 cm
(H. 36½; W. 27¼; D. 25½ in.)
⊻ 1801
DGERA

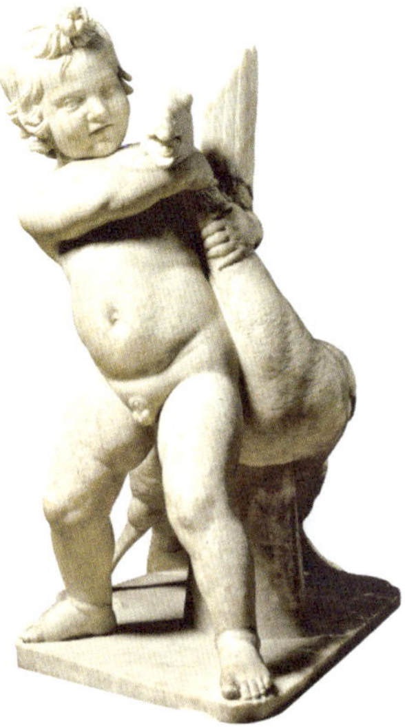

[88]
Sleeping Hermaphroditus
Baths of Diocletian,
Rome, Italy
c. 100–150
Marble
H. 46.5; W. 173.5; D. 90.5 cm
(H. 1 ft 6¼ in.; W. 5 ft 8¼ in.;
D. 2 ft 11¾ in.)
⊻ 1807 (former collection of
Camillo Borghese)
DGERA

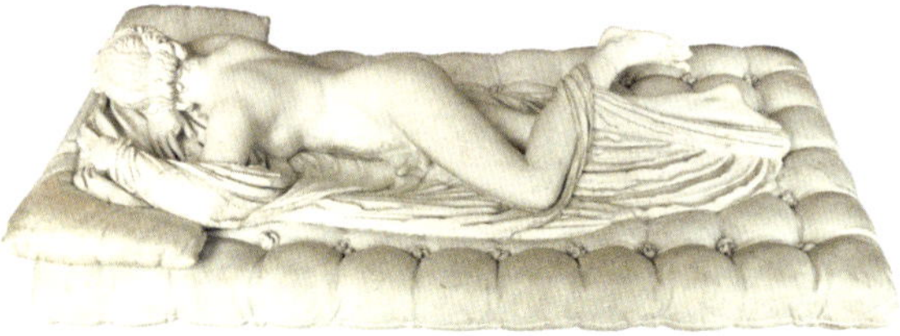

[89]
Statue of the Tiber River with Romulus and Remus
Campus Martius, Rome, Italy
c. 75–150
Pentelic marble
H. 222; W. 317; D. 131 cm
(H. 7 ft 3½ in.;
W. 10 ft 4¾ in.; D. 4 ft 3½ in.)
⊻ 1804
DGERA

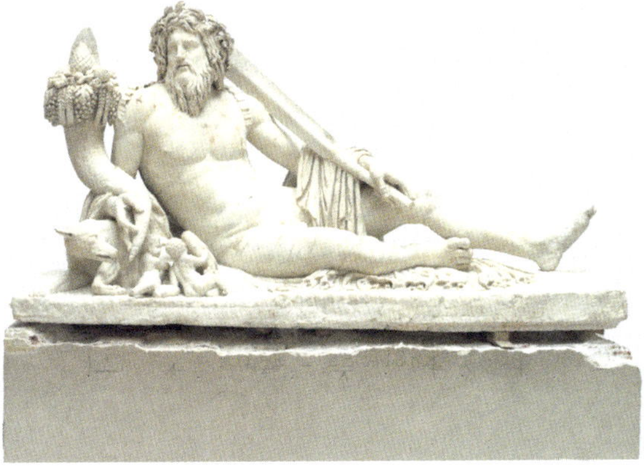

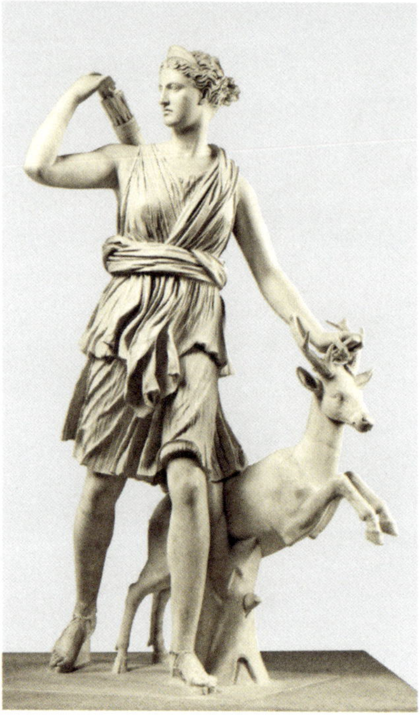

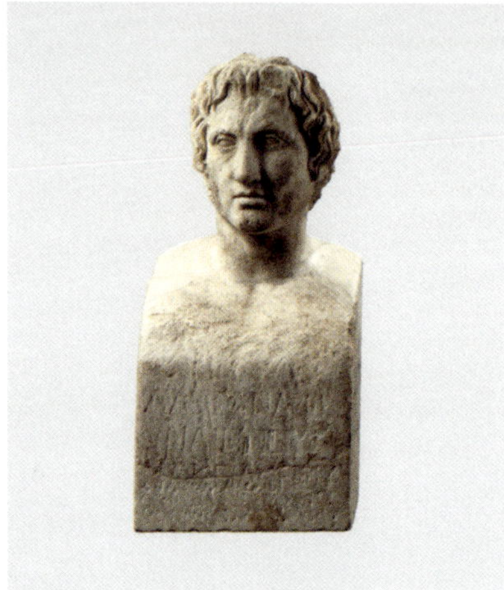

[90]
Diana of Versailles
Italy
c. 125–150
Marble
H. 200; W. 139; D. 103 cm
(H. 6 ft 6¾ in.; W. 4 ft 6¾ in.; D. 3 ft 4½ in.)
⊻ 1798
DGERA

[91]
Italy
Azara Herm
Tivoli, Italy
1–50
Marble
H. 68; W. 32; Th. 27 cm
(H. 26¾; W. 12½; Th. 10¾ in.)
⊻ 1803 (gift)
DGERA

France's monarchs shared this taste for ancient art. Indeed, in the mid-sixteenth century Pope Paul IV gifted *Diana of Versailles* **[90]** to Henry II. Originally displayed at the Château de Fontainebleau, it was later moved to Versailles at the request of Louis XIV. This goddess of hunting was almost certainly sculpted during the reign of Emperor Hadrian, in the second century, and was partially restored in the early seventeenth century, when she was joined by a small deer. The *Azara Herm* **[91]** is a portrait of Alexander the Great that was copied from an original made by Lysippus in the fourth century BCE. It was given to Napoleon Bonaparte, who would have recognised in the young Macedonian king one of his most illustrious predecessors, one who succeeded in extending his empire as far as the Indus River.

INVENTORS OF MODELS The Romans, though not the creators of this ancient art, reinvented and thus helped establish it as a model for beauty in Western Europe. For a long time, based on their observation of Roman replicas, artists

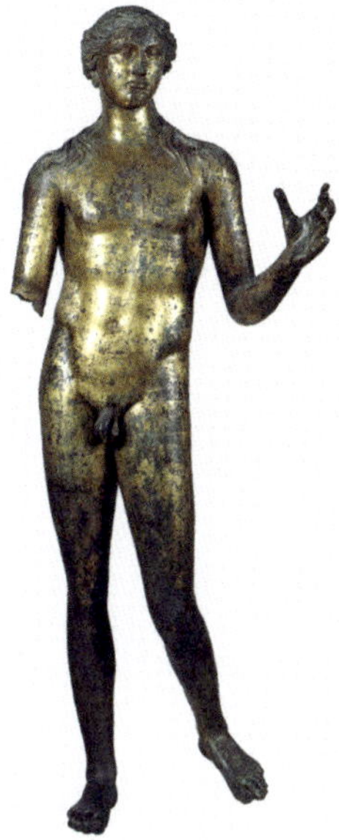

[92]
Apollo of Lillebonne
Lillebonne, France
c. 100–299
Bronze and gold
H. 194; W. 74; D. 65 cm
(H. 6 ft 4½ in.; W. 2 ft 5¼ in.; D. 2 ft 1½ in.)
⩡ 1853
DGERA

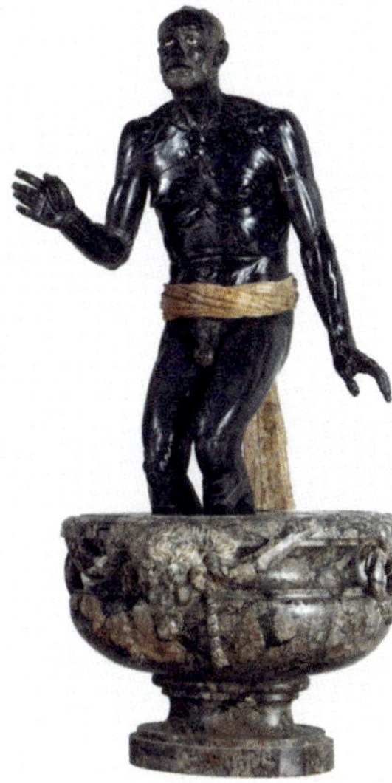

[93]
Death of Seneca
Esquiline Hill, Rome, Italy
c. 125–175 and 1585–1625
Black marble, enamel and alabaster
H. 183; W. 90; D. 99 cm
(H. 6 ft; W. 2 ft 11½ in.; D. 3 ft 3 in.)
⩡ 1807 (former collection of Camillo Borghese)
DGERA

and connoisseurs imagined Greece as a blanket of white, until archaeological investigations carried out from the nineteenth century revealed polychromatic works, many in bronze. Even then, this model persisted: white marble remained, to Western eyes, the most noble medium in which to represent the human form. The so-called *Apollo of Lillebonne* **[92]** was discovered on 24 July 1823, in the ruins of a Roman amphitheatre, in the town in Normandy from which it takes its name. Almost two metres (6½ ft) high, in gilded bronze, it is believed to have been cast in Lyon, in Roman Gaul, during the second century. Purchased by an English collector, it was acquired by the Louvre in 1853. There are few surviving examples of ancient painting, described by Pliny the Elder in his *Natural History* in the first century CE. The mid-eighteenth-century discovery of Pompeii – destroyed when Vesuvius erupted in 79 – revealed villas in an almost perfect state of conservation, down to their decoration. A wall painting from the house of Julia Felix shows Calliope **[94]**, the muse of eloquence. She is one of the nine muses, daughters

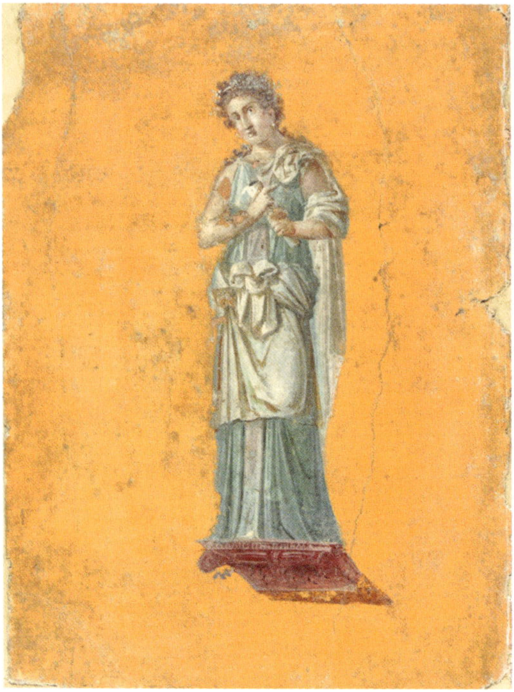

[94]
Wall painting, Calliope
Villa of Julia Felix, Pompeii, Italy
c. 62–79
Fresco on plaster
H. 51.7; W. 40.9; D. 6 cm
(H. 20¼; W. 16; D. 2⅜ in.)
⊻ 1825
DGERA

of Zeus, each of whom presides over one of the liberal arts. The refinement of Roman art culminates in the rhythm of the colours and the carefully drawn lines. A mosaic **[95]** discovered in 1932 in Antioch in present-day Turkey leaves no doubt as to Roman artists' mastery of this polychromatic art. The scene, the Judgement of Paris, is a homage to beauty. Asked who of Hera, Athena and Aphrodite was the fairest, the foolhardy son of the king of Troy chose the goddess of love.

THE ORIGINS OF PORTRAITURE The art of portraiture as a faithful reproduction of an individual's features was invented under the Roman Republic and developed during the Roman Empire, through the multiple likenesses of successive emperors and their circle. Displayed across the empire, the emperor's face was also stamped on coins. The empire was made up of different peoples; that citizens should recognise their emperor was an essential element in promoting the regime's unity. Augustus, the first Roman emperor, established rules that governed the form

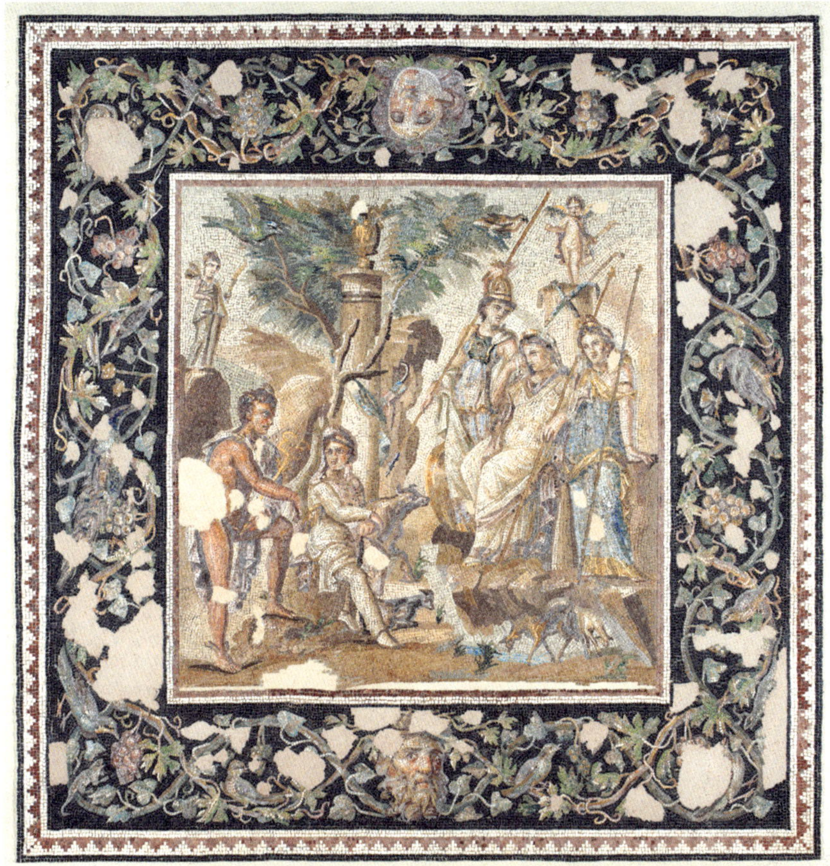

[95]
Mosaic
Atrium House, Antioch,
present-day Turkey
c. 115–150
Marble, limestone and
glass paste
H. 196; W. 196; D. 15 cm
(H. 6 ft 5¼ in.;
W. 6 ft 5¼ in.; D. 5⅜ in.)
⊻ 1936
DGERA

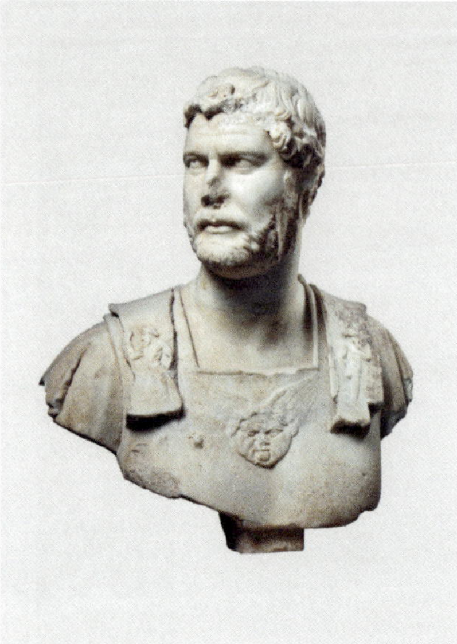

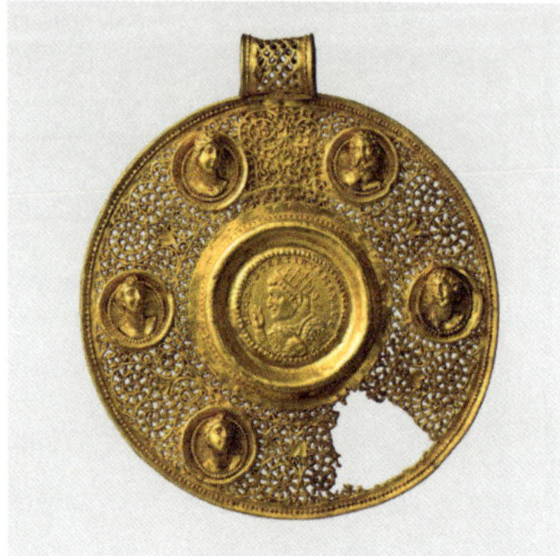

[96]
Bust of Hadrian
Heraklion, Crete, Greece
c. 130
Marble
H. 64; W. 60; D. 33 cm
(H. 25¼; W. 23½; D. 13 in.)
⊻ 1898
DGERA

[97]
Constantinople, now
Istanbul, Turkey
Medallion
Cyrenaica region, Libya
c. 350–400
Gold
H. 10.2; D. 1.5; Diam. 9.3 cm
(H. 4; D. ⅝; Diam. 3⅝ in.)
⊻ 1973
DGERA

the emperor's portrait must take, linking his specific features to his military prowess and the monarch's sacred nature. The *Bust of Hadrian* **[96]** was discovered in Heraklion in Crete. This great second-century emperor, as renowned for his military victories as for his love of the arts, wears the commander's cuirass. It is adorned with a gorgoneion, or head of a gorgon, in this instance Medusa, a terrifying mythical figure who turned anyone who gazed upon her to stone. This motif, which was said to protect its wearer in combat, can be seen, for example, in representations of Athena, the Greek goddess of war and wisdom. The *Head of Livia* **[98]** is a portrait of the wife of Augustus and mother to the emperor Tiberius, who was deified after his death. It borrows the strict simplicity of the art of the Roman Republic, while the use of basanite, a black stone, is a tribute to the monumental art of ancient Egypt.

The Roman Empire owed its success and longevity to its leaders' ability to maintain unity between multiple peoples while respecting their differences. Roman influence fused with existing customs. Painted on gilded wood, mummy

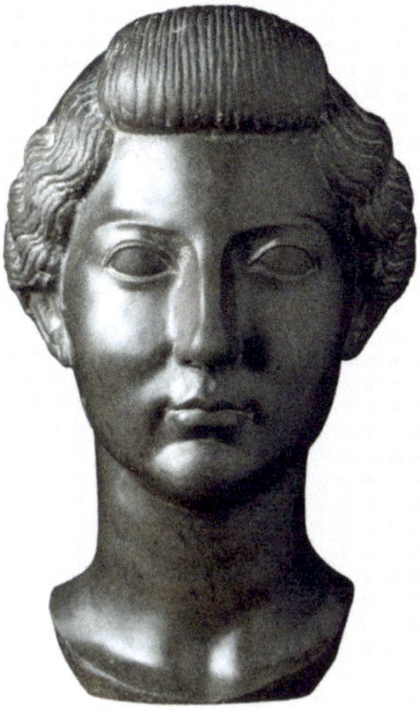

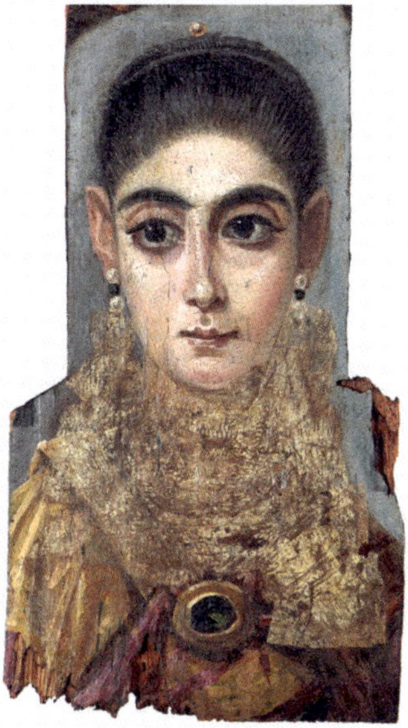

[98]
Head of Livia
Rome (?), Italy
c. 25–50
Basanite
H. 31.5; W. 19; D. 23 cm
(H. 12½; W. 7½; D. 9 in.)
⊻ 1860
DGERA

[99]
Portrait of a Mummy*, known as *The European
Antinoe, present-day Egypt
c. 100–150
Painted cedar, gold and linen
H. 42.5; W. 24; D. 1.6 cm
(H. 16¾; W. 9½; D. ⅝ in.)
⊻ 1951
DEA

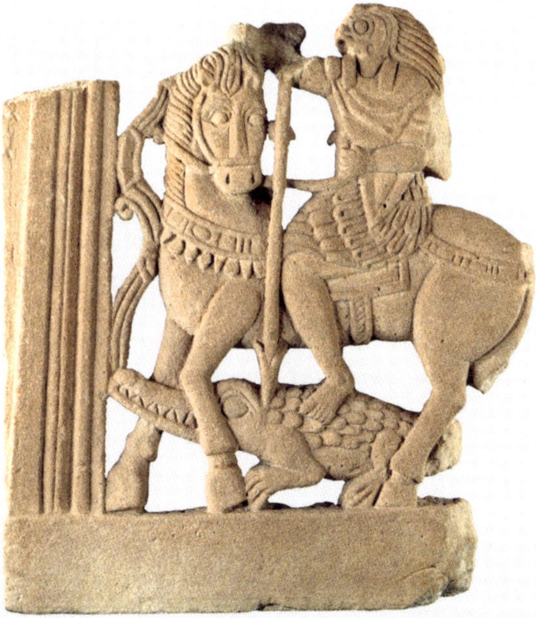

[100]
Horus Horseman
Faras, present-day Egypt
Sandstone
H. 47; W. 43; D. 7.5 cm
(H. 18½; W. 17; D. 3 in.)
⊻ 1864
DAE

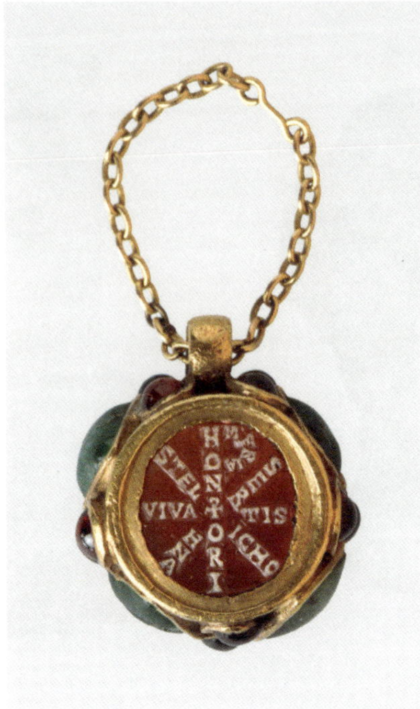

[101]
Milan (?), Italy
Pendant of the Empress Maria
c. 398–407
Cameo of agate, gold, ruby (or garnet) and mother-of-emerald
H. 2.6; W. 1.8; D. 1 cm
(H. 1; W. ¾; D. ⅜ in.)
⊻ 1951 (gift of Blaise de Montesquiou-Fezensac)
DDA

portraits **[99]** from Roman Egypt combine Roman figuration with Egyptian burial practices. These faces are captivating for their beauty and the sensation of their very real presence. *Horus Horseman* **[100]** bears witness to the art of the Meroë civilisation, in what is now Sudan, only the Egyptian god is depicted on horseback, like a Roman general.

VANITAS Marble sarcophagi were an important characteristic of Roman funerary art, especially from the second century. These stone coffins were embellished with relief carvings whose subject was often chosen to reflect the image the deceased wished to leave behind: the nine muses for an art lover, for example. Several thousand sarcophagi have been found, suggesting that production centres existed in different regions of the empire. The wealthier the deceased, the more richly ornamented these monuments were. Why lavish such decoration, intended for the living to admire, on a sarcophagus that would then be placed out of sight, in a mausoleum? No doubt the customer took pleasure simply from seeing these works of art take shape:

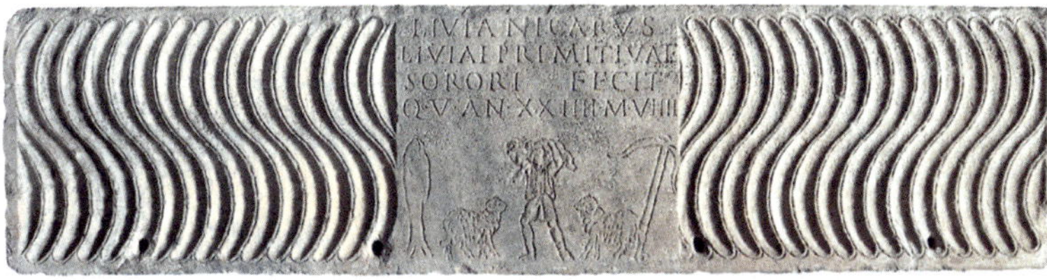

[102]
Sarcophagus of Livia Primitiva
St Peter's Basilica, Rome, Italy
c. 250
Marble
H. 50.5; W. 207; D. 37.5 cm
(H. 1 ft 8 in.; W. 6 ft 9½ in.; D. 1 ft 2¾ in.)
⊻ 1862 (former collection of Giampietro Campana)
DBECA

partly or completely, depending on the circumstances. These decorations became even more valued with the spread of Christianity across the Roman Empire. Having appeared during Tiberius's reign, Christianity was at first outlawed and its followers persecuted. The Roman elite's gradual conversion, particularly during the third century, resulted in greater tolerance. Religious peace came in 313, when Constantine's Edict of Milan authorised Christian worship **[101]**.

Dating from the middle of the third century, the *Sarcophagus of Livia Primitiva* **[102]** is inscribed with several symbols: the Good Shepherd, represented by a man carrying a lamb, with a lamb on either side, and these flanked by an anchor, a sign of perseverance in the Christian faith, and by a fish, a sign of abundance and an evocation of Christ himself. A fragment from a late-third-century sarcophagus **[103]**, discovered in the Catacomb of Priscilla in Rome, displays what can be read as a metaphor for the resurrection of Christ, as it refers to the Bible story of Jonah, who was swallowed by a whale yet came out of its belly alive.

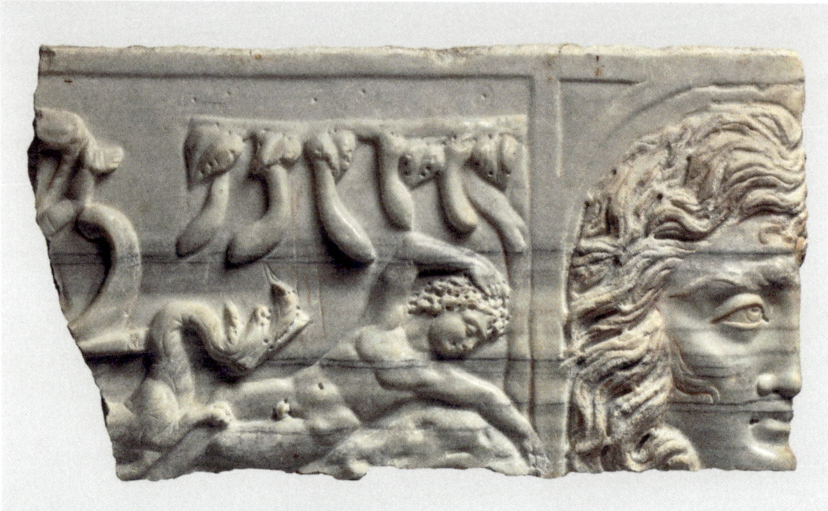

[103]
Sarcophagus Lid
Catacomb of Priscilla, Rome, Italy
c. 275–300
Marble
H. 41; W. 77; D. 6 cm
(H. 16¼; W. 30¼;. D. 2⅜ in.)
⊻ 1923
DGERA

[104]
Carthage, present-day Tunisia
Sarcophagus Lid
Caesarea in Mauretania,
present-day Algeria
c. 300–350
Marble
H. 33; W. 181; D. 7.5 cm
(H. 1 ft 1 in.; W. 5 ft 11¼ in.; D. 3 in.)
⊻ 1903 (gift of Joanny Benoît Peytel)
DBECA

[105]
Rome, Italy
Sarcophagus
Saint-Médard-d'Eyrans, France
c. 235
Marble
H. 95; W. 211; D. 62 cm
(H. 3 ft 1½ in.; W. 6 ft 11 in.;
D. 2 ft½ in.)
⊻ 1817
DGERA

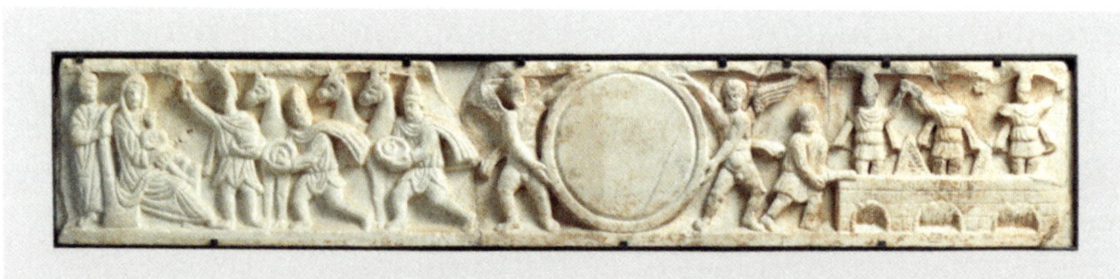

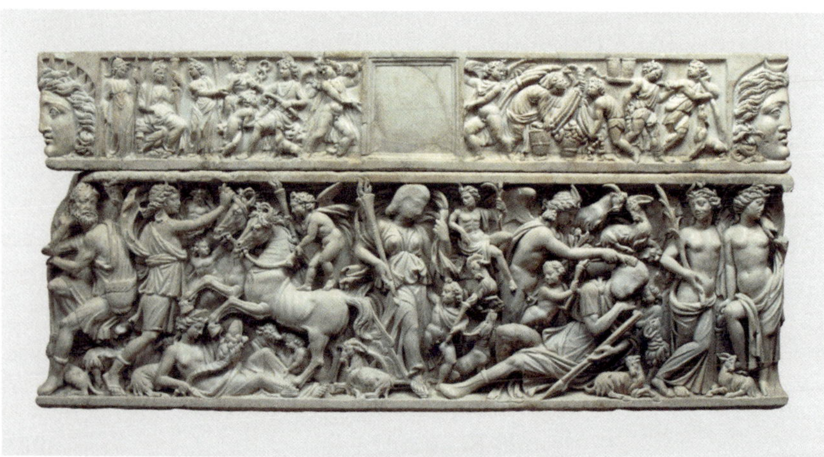

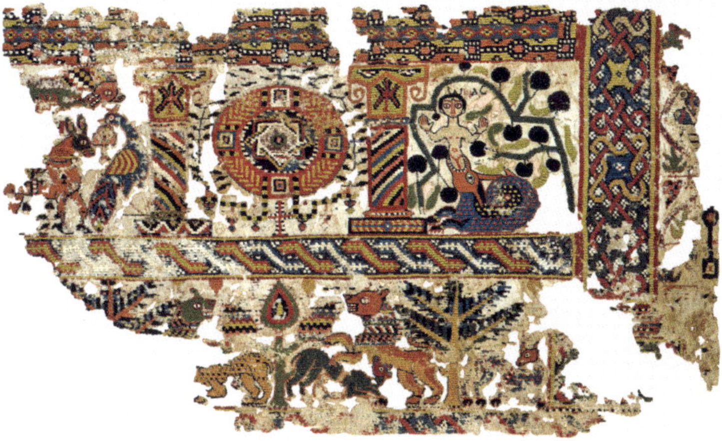

[106]
Jonah Tapestry
Egypt
c. 320–420
Linen and wool
H. 120; W. 208.5 cm
(H. 3 ft 11¼ in.; W. 6 ft 10 in.)
⊻ 1968
DBECA

Jonah's languid position can be likened to an image from mythology: that of Endymion **[105]**, a youth loved by Selene, goddess of the moon. Burgeoning Christian art looked to the forms and representations of Roman art. The *Jonah Tapestry* **[106]**, acquired by the Louvre in 1968, evokes the same biblical episode. A young Jonah is shown emerging from the jaws of a sea creature, in what almost resembles an epiphany, the manifestation of divine presence. Made in Carthage, in modern-day Tunisia, this *Lid of a Sarcophagus* **[104]** depicts the Magi, the three wise men who travelled to Bethlehem to honour the new-born Jesus Christ. The composition is devised as a frieze, with two scenes separated by a central medallion. On one side, the Magi, each with a camel, bring gifts to Joseph, Mary and their son. On the other, we have the terrible sight of three young Hebrews thrown into a furnace, martyrs of the Babylonian king Nebuchadnezzar II. This dramatic biblical scene hints at the suffering endured by the first Christians, who were persecuted for their faith. The same iconography appears on a fifth-century mosaic **[107]**, created

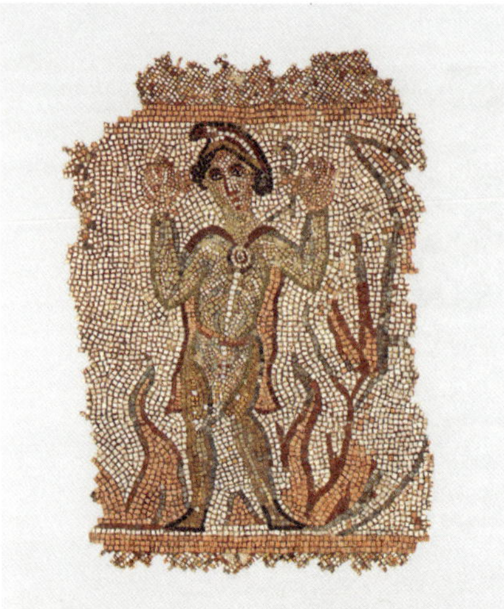

[107]
Mosaic, Hebrews in the Furnace
Syria
c. 400–600
Marble and limestone
H. 112; W. 75 cm
(H. 3 ft 8 in.; W. 2 ft 5½ in.)
⊻ 1971
DBECA

[108]
Phoenix Mosaic
Antioch, present-day Turkey
c. 475–500
Marble and limestone
H. 573; W. 432.3; D. 6.3 cm
(H. 18 ft 9½ in.; W. 14 ft 2¼ in.; D. 2½ in.)
⊻ 1936
DBECA

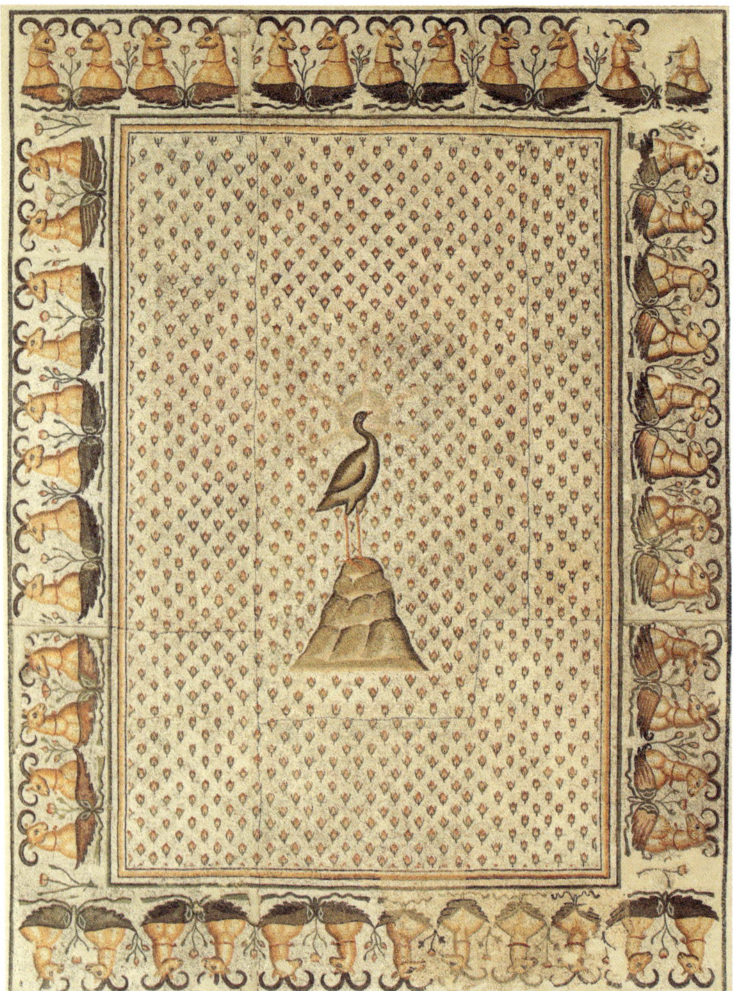

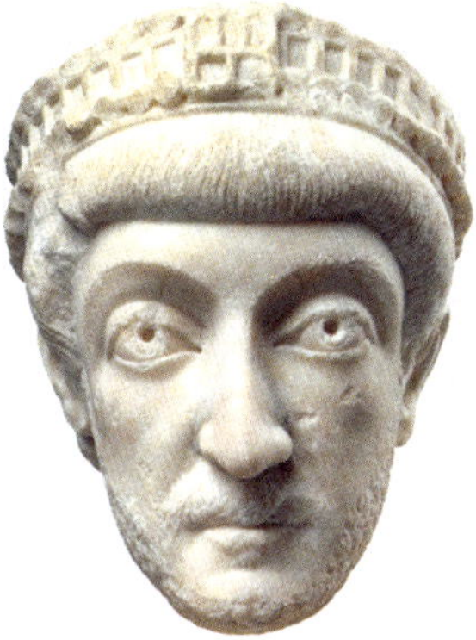

[109]
Constantinople,
now Istanbul, Turkey
Emperor's Head
c. 425–450
H. 28.5; W. 23.5; D. 24 cm
(H. 11¼; W. 9½; D. 9½ in.)
⩡ 1793 (former royal collection)
DBECA

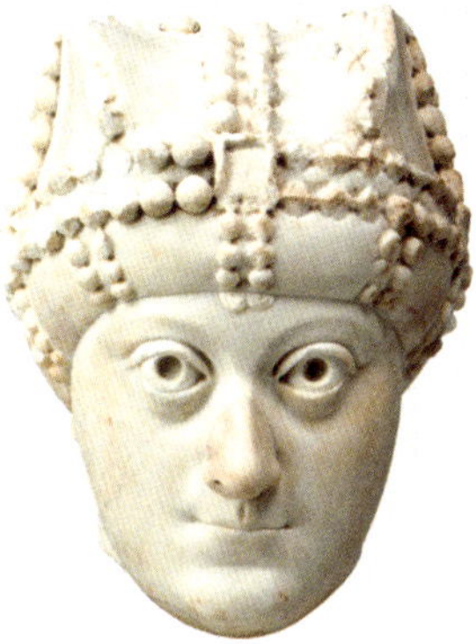

[110]
Constantinople,
now Istanbul, Turkey
Head of the Byzantine Empress Ariane (?)
c. 500–515
Marble
H. 25.7; W. 22.8; D. 23 cm
(H. 10; W. 9; D. 9 in.)
⩡ 1911 (bequest of Isaac de Camondo)
DBECA

in what is now Syria. Dating from the late fifth century, the *Phoenix Mosaic* **[108]**, uncovered in Antioch in 1934, superbly illustrates the vitality of a still practised Roman art. The central figure of the mythical bird rising from its ashes can also be seen as a symbol of Christ.

BYZANTIUM AND THE EASTERN CHRISTIANS Christianity became the Roman state religion under Emperor Theodosius **[109]**. On his death in 395 the empire was divided into the Western Roman Empire and the Eastern Roman Empire. The former kept Rome as its capital, while the latter chose Constantinople, founded by Constantine in the early fourth century. Whereas the Western Roman Empire declined and ultimately fell, in 476, the Eastern Roman Empire, also known as the Byzantine Empire in reference to Byzantium, the ancient name of its capital, existed until 1453. Byzantine influence spread across a large part of the Mediterranean Basin, reaching as far as Central Europe and Africa. Thus, in the sixth century, Emperor Justinian **[p. 204]** conquered the city of Ravenna, on the east coast of Italy. The opening of the Department

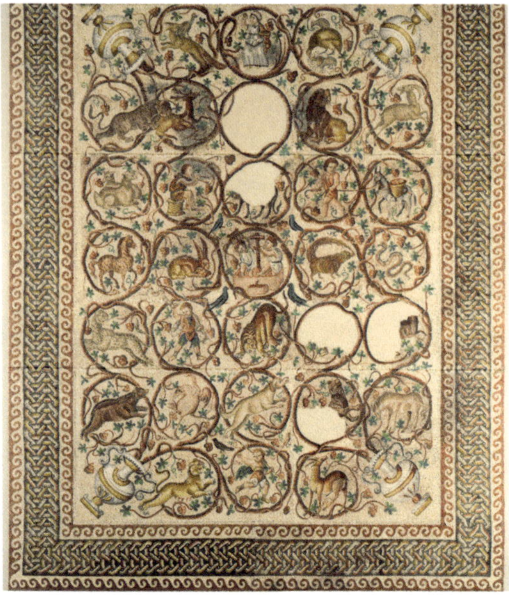

[111]
Qabr Hiram Mosaic
Church of Saint Christopher,
Qabr Hiram, Lebanon
c. 550–600
Marble, limestone and glass paste
H. 548; W. 426 cm
(H. 17 ft 11¾ in.; W. 13 ft 11¾ in.)
⊻ 1862
DBECA

of Byzantine and Eastern Christian Art at the Louvre in 2026 will provide the opportunity to exhibit the scope, diversity and importance of Byzantine civilisation **[110–114]**.

The Byzantine site of Bawit is located in Middle Egypt, on the west bank of the Nile. *Bawet* means "monastery" in Coptic. Excavations of the site in the early twentieth century revealed the presence of two churches. The remains of the southern church were transferred to the Louvre where they have been reconstructed. This building and elements from it – sculpted decors **[112]** and textiles – bear witness to Christian art as it developed in Egypt from the religion's beginnings. In the sixth century, the large – 20 square metres (215 sq. ft) – *Qabr Hiram Mosaic* **[111]** would have decorated the pavement of the nave of the Church of Saint Christopher, in what is now Lebanon. Agricultural and hunting scenes are set in medallions, connected by scrolls of foliage, in a celebration of the bounty of divine creation. It has been executed with exemplary skill, indicating the existence of talented mosaic workshops and the ongoing presence of this Roman tradition. This mosaic joined the Louvre's collections

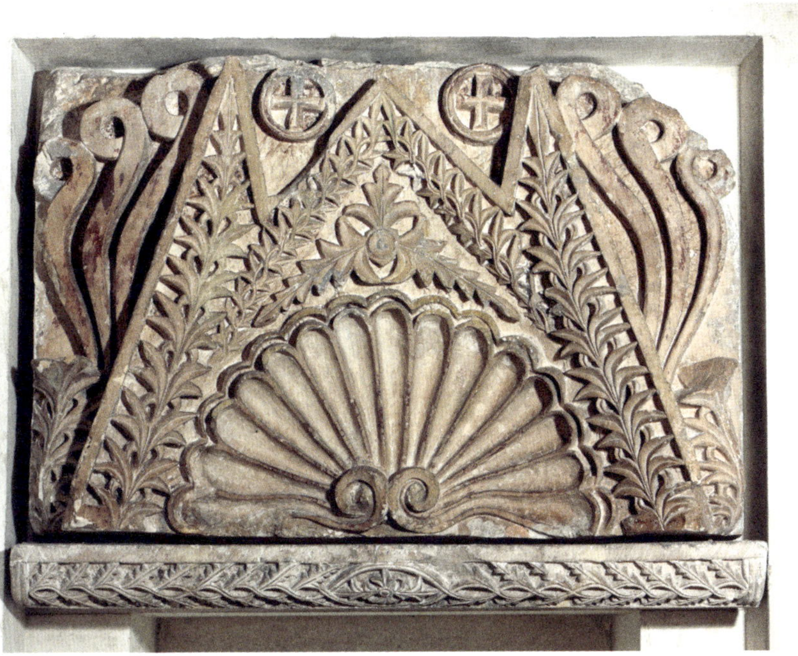

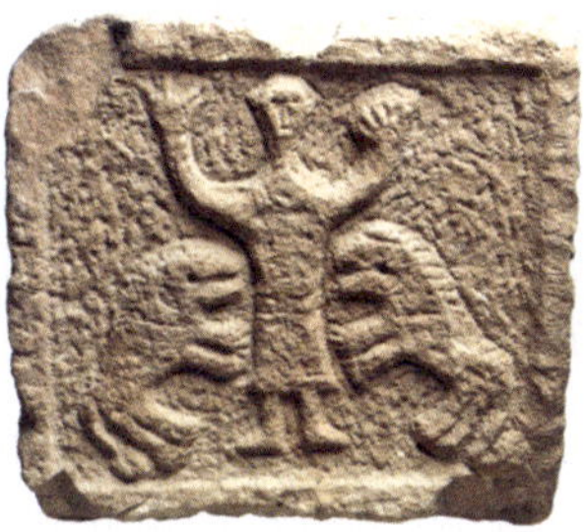

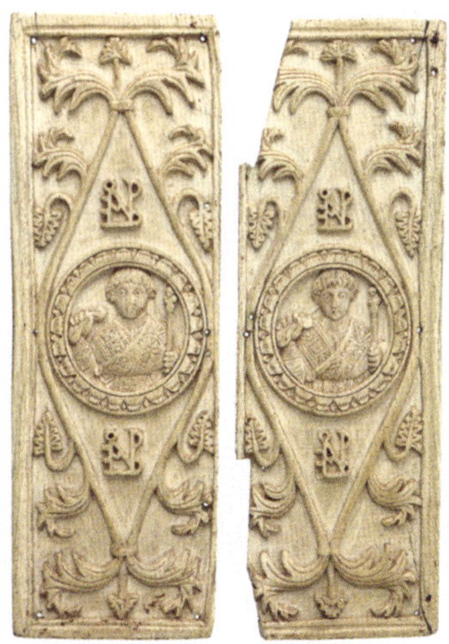

[112]
Niche
South Church,
Bawit, Egypt
c. 480–640
Painted limestone
H. 60; W. 97; D. 22 cm
(H. 1 ft 11½ in.;
W. 3 ft 2¼ in.; D. 8¾ in.)
⊻ 1903
DBECA

[113]
Dosseret,
Daniel in the Lions' Den
Tigzirt Church, Algeria
c. 475–525
Sandstone
H. 43; W. 55; D. 39 cm
(H. 17; W. 21¾; D. 15¼ in.)
⊻ 1894
DBECA

[114]
Constantinople,
now Istanbul, Turkey
Consular Diptych of
Areobindus
Byzantium
506
Elephant ivory
H. 34; W. 11.8; D. 0.9 cm
(H. 13½; W. 4⅝; D. ⅜ in.)
(each panel)
⊻ 1951 (gift)
DBECA

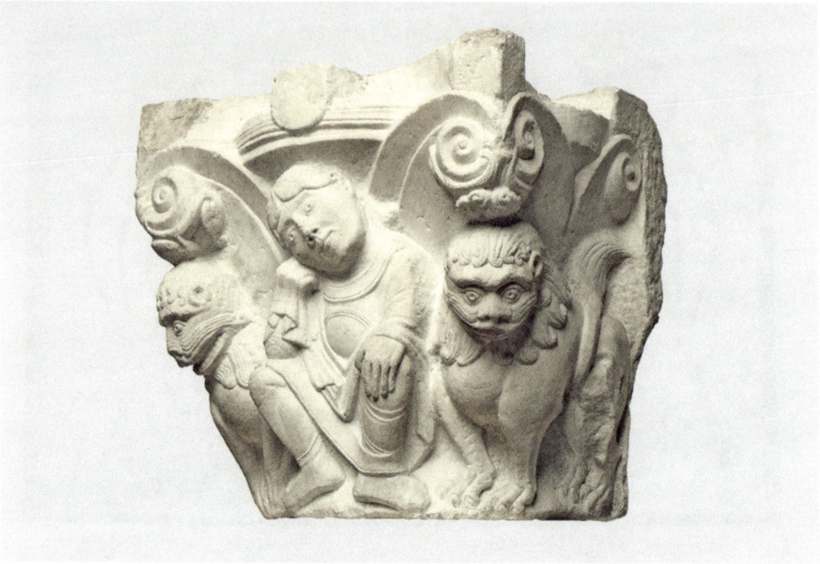

[115] ***Capital, Daniel in the Lions' Den.*** Abbey of Saint Geneviève, France. c. 500–600
Carrara marble. H. 49.5; W. 53; D. 51 cm (H. 19½; W. 20¾; D. 20 in.). ⩡ 1881 (Saint-Denis excavations). DS

in 1862, thanks to the mission led by the writer and philosopher Ernest Renan. Originating much closer to the museum, from the Abbey of Saint Geneviève in Paris, this capital **[115]** is one of the oldest conserved at the Louvre that has been historiated, meaning inscribed with scenes inspired by history, Holy Scriptures, as here, or mythology. As its title, *Daniel in the Lions' Den*, suggests, it shows the biblical figure of Daniel.

"Contribute to the definition
of a true humanism,
universal humanism,
for there can be no humanism
that is not universal
and no humanism
without dialogue."

Aimé Césaire,
Dakar,
1966

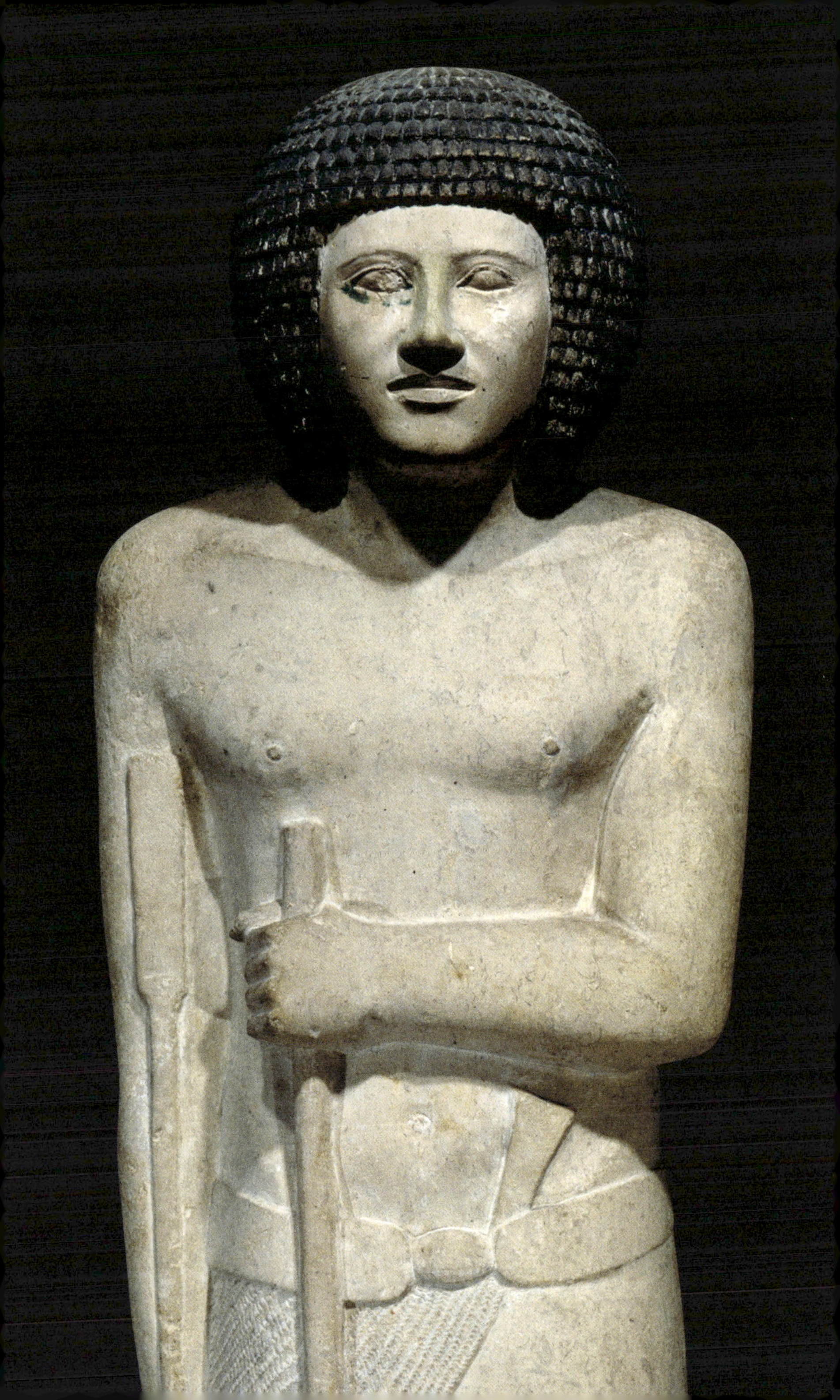

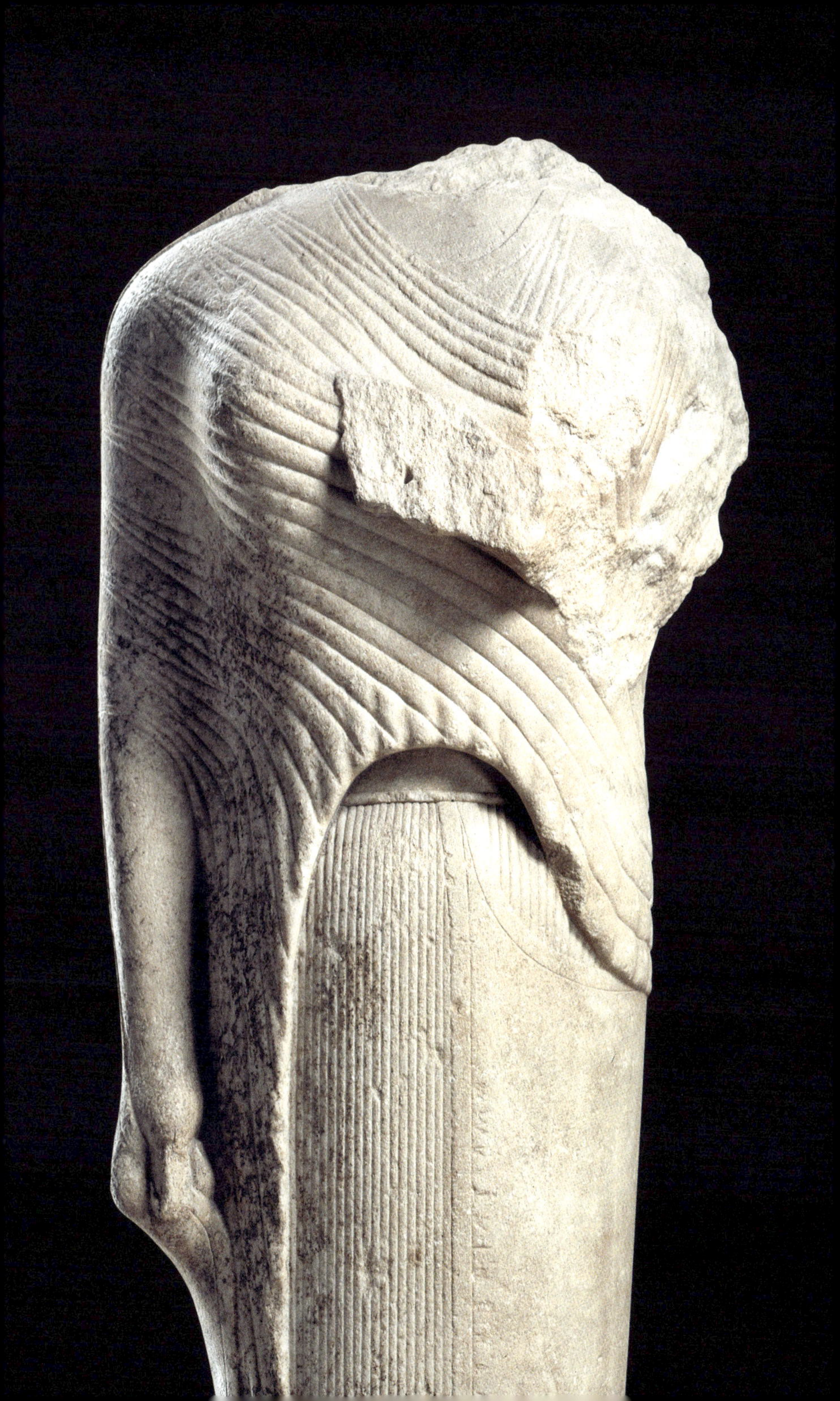

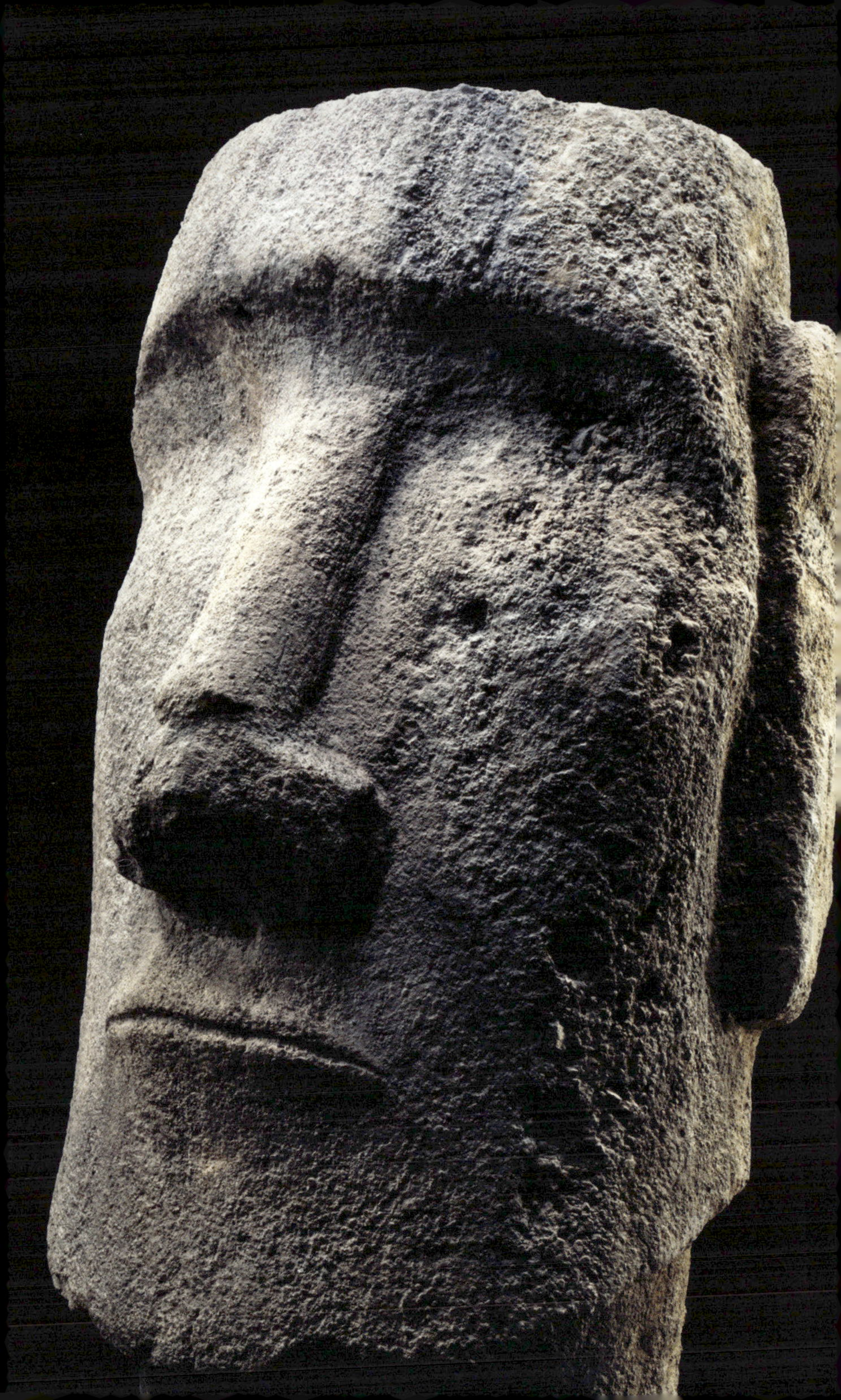

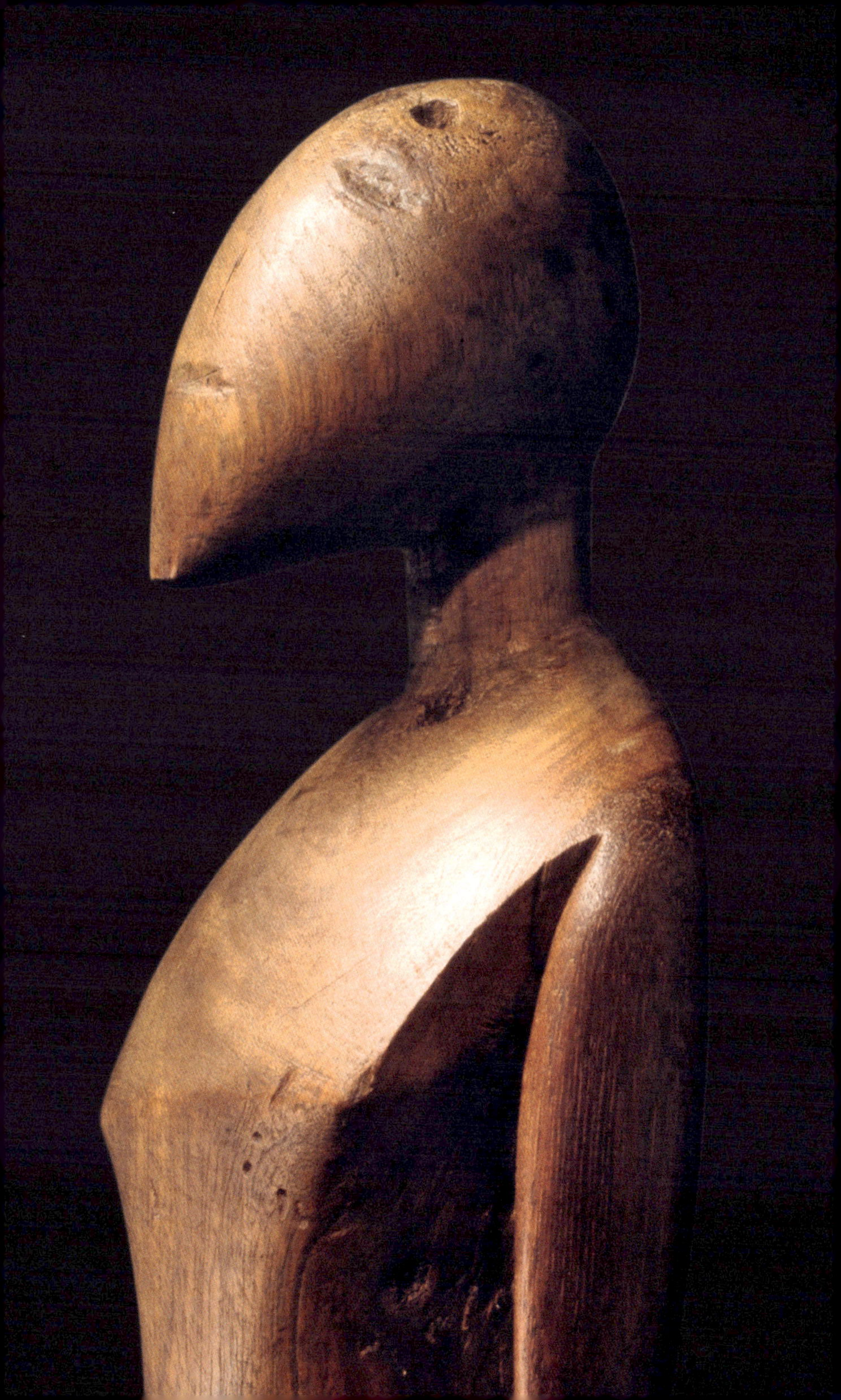

The artistic influence of Rome did not disappear with the fall of the Western Roman Empire in the late fifth century. The peoples of northern and eastern Europe who brought Rome's political power to an end introduced elements of ancient art into their own traditions **[118]**. The *Pillar Capital with Stylised Leaves* **[117]**, produced in a region that is now part of Spain, is a Visigothic work that borrows the structure and leaf decoration of Roman capitals.

The Eastern Christian Empire was strongest during the long reign of Emperor Justinian, in the sixth century **[p. 204]**. Byzantium's power and influence extended from the Adriatic coast to southern Spain, along the entire Mediterranean. A military leader, Justinian also embodied Christian religious authority, as well as being a great patron of the arts. The beautiful *Ganay Chalice* **[119]** illustrates the extent of Byzantine influence; a later inscription in Coptic, probably added in the ninth century, shows that it was used in Egypt as a liturgical object. Donated to the Louvre by the de Ganay family, it is typical of the precious decorative art objects that were so sought-after in the nineteenth and twentieth century by Western collectors, whose curiosity is behind many of the Louvre's treasures.

The life and deeds of Muhammad, who was born in Mecca, Arabia, at the end of the sixth century, deeply transformed world history. The founding prophet of a new religion, Islam, his teachings are contained within its central text, the Quran. Muhammad immersed himself in the sacred texts of the Bible. His revelations were, he reported, brought to him by archangel Gabriel while in seclusion in a mountain cave. For Muhammad and his followers – Muslims – Abraham is the father of the faithful, as he is for Jews and for Christians. Despite opposition from certain of his contemporaries in Arabia, Muhammad's influence grew rapidly, and from the seventh century, this new religion drew many more disciples. Caliphs, regarded as the successors to Muhammad, held both religious and political authority. The magnificent *Sasanian Oval Dish* **[116]**, in gold and rock crystal, is one of the last works created before Persia's conversion to Islam.

The first collections of Islamic art were assembled in the nineteenth century by artists and enthusiasts during

[116]
Sasanian Oval Dish
Susa, present-day Iran
c. 600–700
Gold and rock crystal
L. 9.1; W. 6.6; D. 1.3 cm
(H. 3⅝; W. 2⅝; D. ½ in.)
⊻ 1912
DNEA

[117]
Visigoth Spain (?)
Pillar Capital with Stylised Leaves
c. 600–700
Marble
H. 36; W. 33.5; D. 33.5 cm
(H. 14¼; W. 13¼; D. 13¼ in.)
DS

[118]
Merovingian Fibula
c. 600–650
Gold, cloisonné garnets and blue glass
H. 5.2; W. 6; D. 0.7 cm
(H. 2; W. 2⅜; D. ¼ in.)
⊻ 1997 (gift of Guy Ladrière)
DDA

116

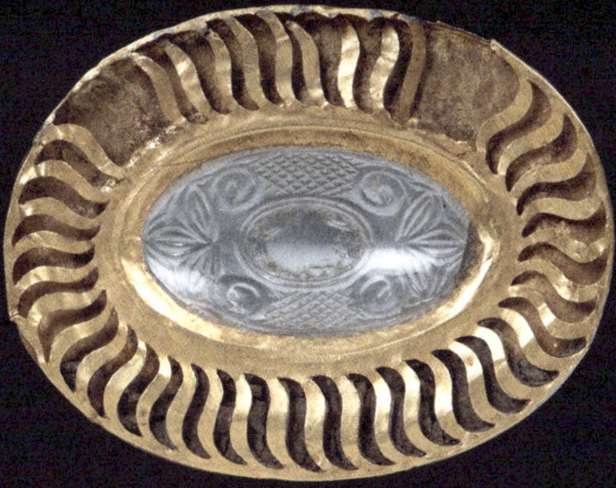

117

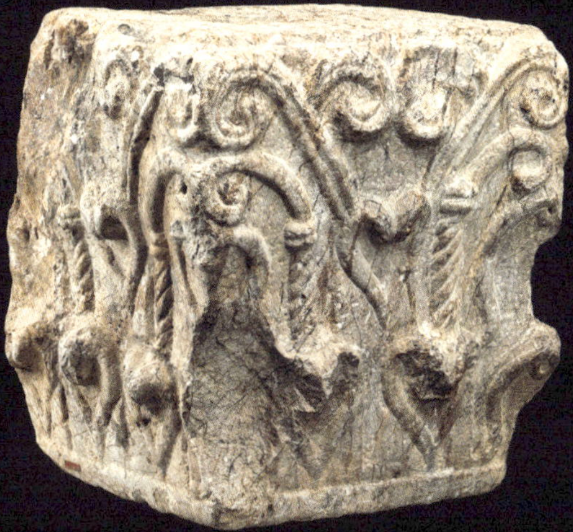

118

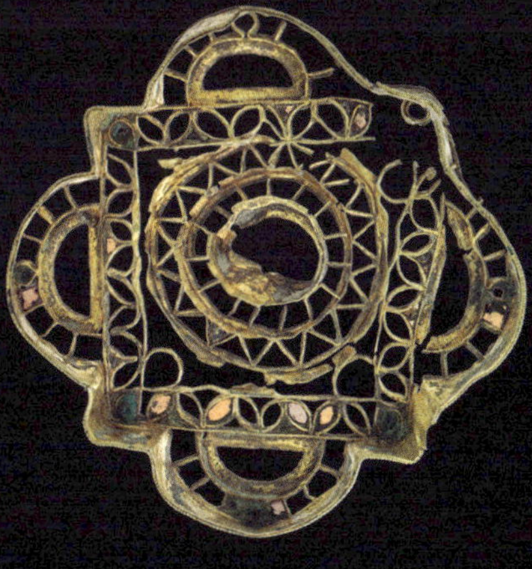

their travels to the East. Initially, they joined the Louvre's decorative arts collections. Islamic artefacts **[120]** revealed by archaeological investigations conducted in Susa, Iran, were added to the museum's collections of Eastern antiquities. The Department of Islamic Art was created in 2004, and in 2012 the collections were moved to a purpose-built space in the Louvre's Cour Visconti.

[119]
Ganay Chalice
Byzantium
c. 585–615
Silver and gilded silver
H. 20; Diam. 15.5 cm
(H. 7¾; Diam. 6 in.)
⩡ 1990 (gift of
Hubert de Ganay)
DDA

[120]
Jug with "Rope" Decoration
Susa, present-day Iran
c. 600–700
Unglazed ceramic
H. 24.2; Diam. 12.8 cm
(H. 9½; Diam. 5 in.)
DIA

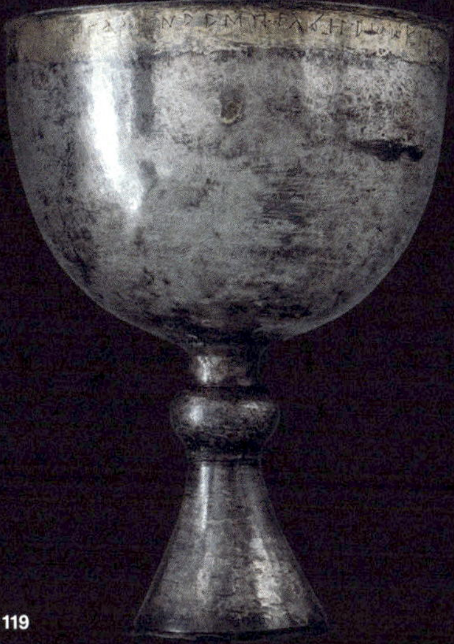

119

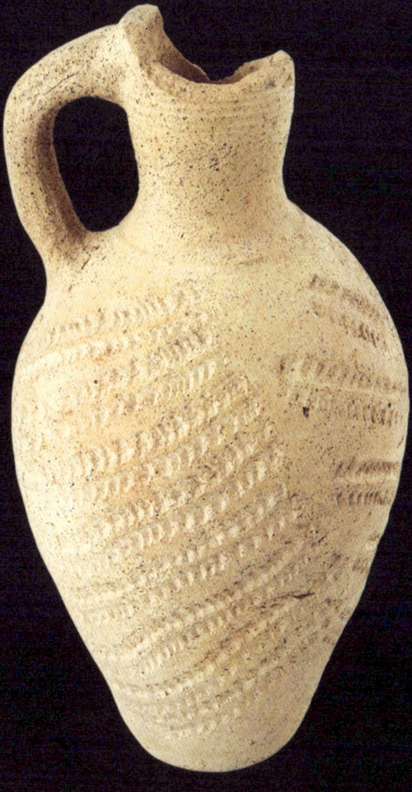

120

Cross-cultural inspirations

The Louvre's collections, which are organised into different groups of objects, point to the virtuosity of their makers' skill and technique, and the desire to use only the finest materials. They also shed light on how certain of these works were made, incorporating elements from antiquity or artefacts produced in other parts of the world. These practices resulted in hybrid objects, evidence of encounters and exchanges between multiple cultures, in spite of differing beliefs and hostilities.

[121]
Plaque, the Prophet Joel
Palestine (?), Italy (?), Syria (?)
c. 685–900
Elephant ivory
H. 10.2; W. 8.7; D. 0.7 cm
(H. 4; W. 3⅜; D. ¼ in.)
⊻ 1962 (bequest of Marie-Françoise Côte, in memory of her husband)
DBECA

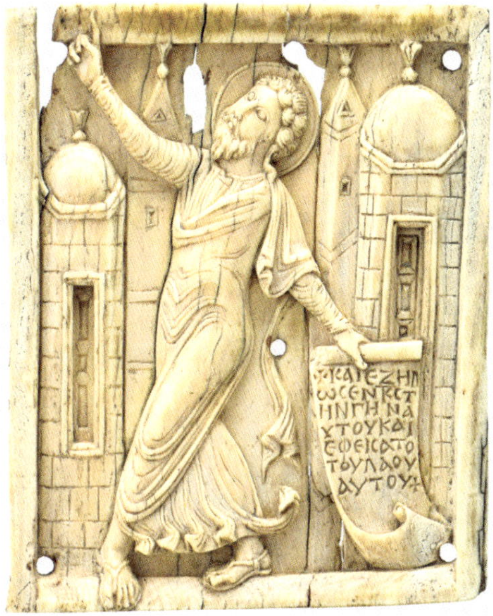

THE POWER OF THE IMAGE In the wake of the Iconoclastic Period, when representations of the human form were prohibited, the Byzantine emperors of the Macedonian Dynasty (867–1057), approving of new figurations, paved the way for an artistic renaissance. This was founded on a return to the art of antiquity, along with renewed interest in the artistic conventions of the East. The Louvre's collections hold many remarkable works to have come out of this revival, such as the carved ivory plaque, probably of Palestinian provenance, depicting Joel **[121]**, a prophet of the Old Testament. The *Harbaville Triptych* **[122]**, named after its collector, illustrates the talent of such sculptural artists. When closed, the back panel depicts a scene that melds Christian and other traditions: an abundant, idealised nature in a garden of paradise. The polychrome ceramic plaque **[123]** would, along with other plaques, have formed an iconostasis, a screen decorated with icons that separates the nave from the sanctuary in a Byzantine church. The peacock motif, symbolising the splendour of the gardens of paradise as well as the concept of renewal, can be traced to classical antiquity.

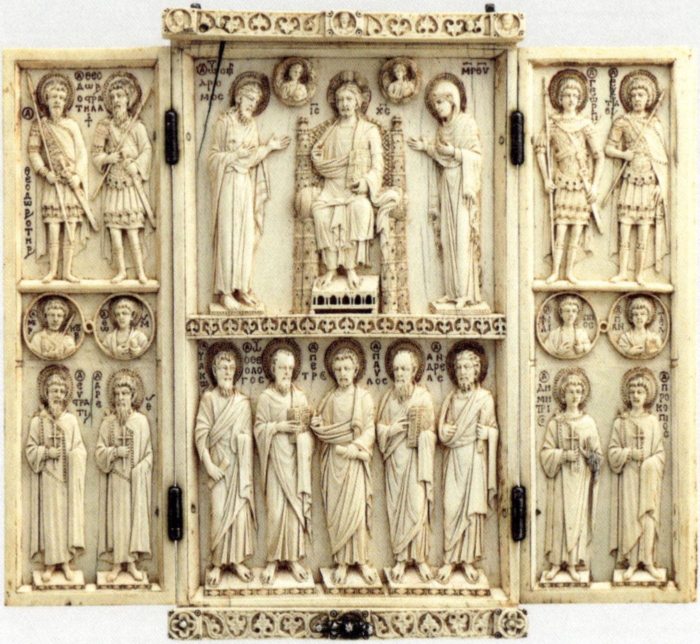

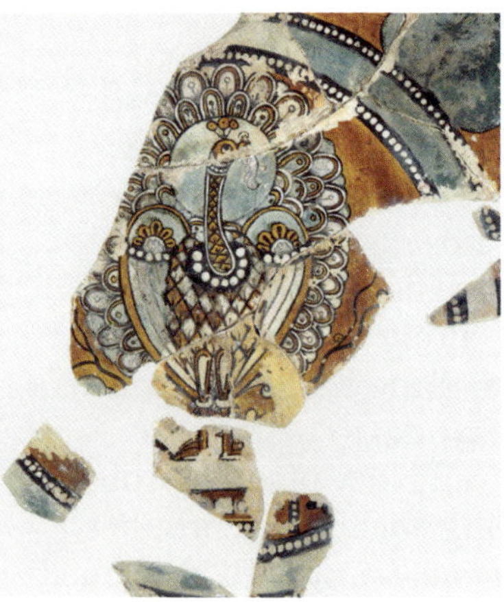

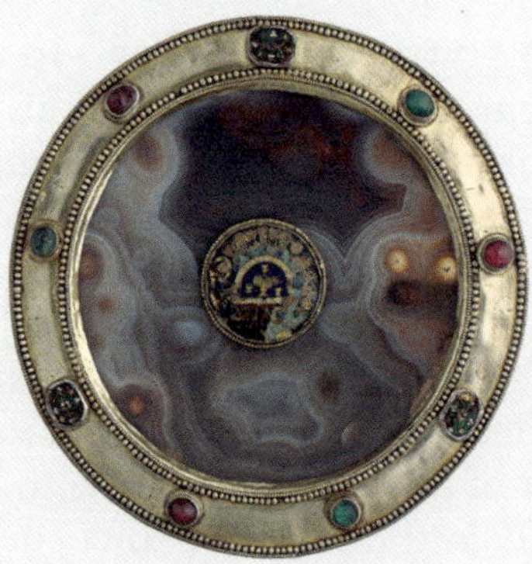

[122]
Romanos group,
Constantinople,
now Istanbul, Turkey
Harbaville Triptych
Byzantium
c. 940–960
Gilded and painted
elephant ivory
H. 24.2; W. 28.2; D. 2.5 cm
(H. 9½; W. 11; D. 1 in.)
⩡ 1891
DBECA

[123]
Workshop, Constantinople,
now Istanbul, Turkey
Plaque from an Iconostasis, Peacock
Byzantium
Prusias ad Hypium,
present-day Turkey
c. 800–1000
Ceramic
H. 33; W. 33; D. 1 cm
(H. 13; W. 13; D. ⅜ in.)
⩡ 1955
DBECA

[124]
Workshop, Constantinople,
now Istanbul, Turkey, and
Paris, France
"Stoclet" Paten
Byzantium
c. 885–915 (mount);
c. 1300 (paten)
Sardonyx, silver gilt,
gemstones and enamel
Diam. 12.6 cm
(Diam. 5 in.)
⩡ 1998
DBECA

[125]
Serpentine Paten from the Treasury of Saint-Denis
Treasury of Saint-Denis, France
c. 100 BCE–100 CE (paten); c. 850–900 (mount)
Serpentine, gold, gemstones and green glass
Diam. 17 cm (Diam. 6¾ in.)
⊻ 1793
DDA

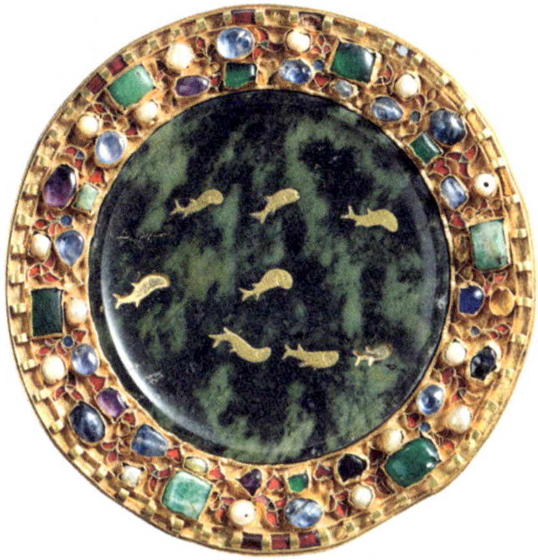

The *"Stoclet" Paten* **[124]** – a paten is a small plate used to carry the Host before consecration, when it is transformed into the Body of Christ – is a superb illustration of how different times and places can come together. A sardonyx dish dating from late antiquity is set in a gilded silver mount. A central medallion depicts the Last Supper, Christ's final meal before his arrest and ultimate crucifixion. While the cloisonné enamelwork is typical of Byzantine workshops, the three enamel plaques that alternate with the cabochons around the rim were almost certainly produced in the West, sometime in the early fourteenth century. The paten would have been brought to the West following the Sack of Constantinople in 1204.

HYBRIDISATION AND REUSE The Treasury of Saint-Denis, assembled since the reign of Charles the Bald, was confiscated during the French Revolution because of its royal and religious associations and transferred to the Louvre in 1793. It contains several eloquent examples of hybridisation and reuse. These include the *Serpentine Paten from the Treasury of Saint-*

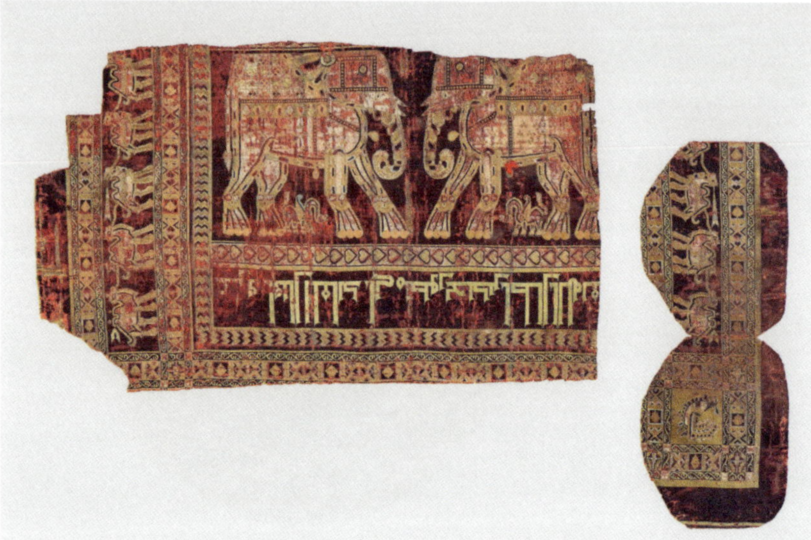

[126] Khorasan region, Iran. ***Shroud of Saint Josse***. Abbey of Saint Josse, France
Before 961. Silk. H. 94; W. 143; D. 2 cm (H. 3 ft 1 in.; W. 4 ft 8¼ in.; D. ¾ in.). ⩡ 1922. DIA

Denis **[125]**, which is made from an ancient serpentine dish inlaid with gold fish, probably from the same period. An early Christian symbol, these fish would have destined this charming object for its new use as a paten. Similarly, the *Rock Crystal Ewer from the Treasury of Saint-Denis* **[127]** combines multiple origins. Its decoration of face-to-face birds engraved in the rock crystal – one of the purest stones, as transparent as liquid – ties it to the Egypt of the Fatimid caliphs (909–1171). An inscription in Kufic requests a blessing on its owner. As for its gold lid, this was probably fashioned in Italy at the request of whoever brought the ewer to the West, before offering it to the treasury. Abbot Suger, the abbot of Saint-Denis in the early twelfth century, was so taken with a vase in porphyry – a red stone favoured by ancient sovereigns – that he had it mounted in the form of an eagle to create the singular and striking *Porphyry Vase*, known also as *Suger's Eagle* **[128]**.

The *Shroud of Saint Josse* **[126]** is another illustration of exchanges between different cultures. No doubt brought from the East in the eleventh century – its ornamentation suggests it would have originated in Iran – it was transformed

[127]
Egypt (vase), Italy (lid)
Rock Crystal Ewer from the Treasury of Saint-Denis
Treasury of Saint-Denis, France
c. 985–1015 (ewer);
1000–1100 (lid)
Rock crystal and gold
H. 24; W. 13.5 cm
(H. 9½; W. 5¼ in.)
⩡ 1793
DIA

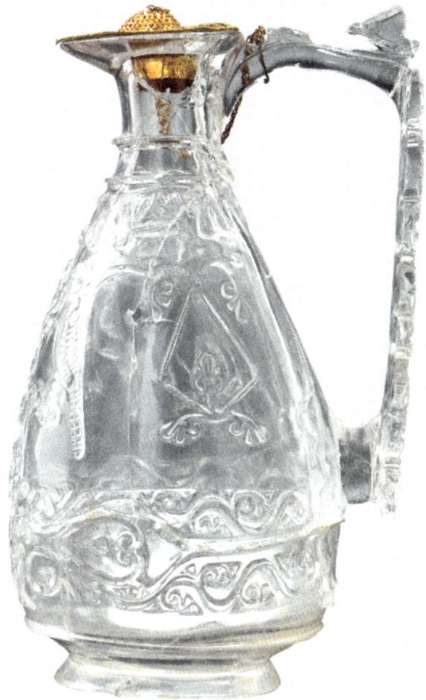

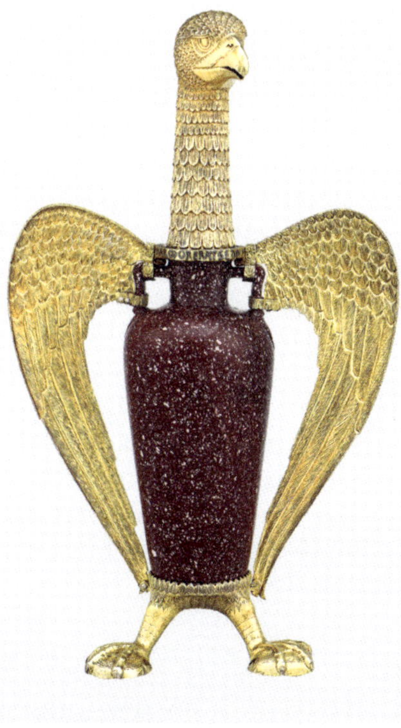

[128]
Egypt (?),
Rome (?), Italy (vase),
Saint-Denis, France (mount)
Porphyry Vase*, known as *Suger's Eagle
Treasury of Saint-Denis, France
Before 1147 (mount)
Red porphyry, silver and gold
H. 43.1; W. 27; D. 15.5 cm
(H. 17; W. 10¾; D. 6 in.)
⩡ 1795
DDA

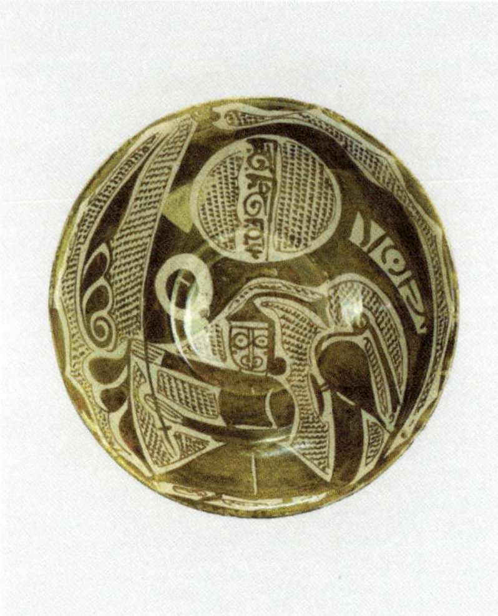

[129]
Bowl with Standard Bearer
Iraq
c. 900–1000
Ceramic
H. 9.8; Diam. 31.7 cm (H. 3⅞; Diam. 12½ in.)
⊻ 1949 (gift of Mr and Mrs Michel Maurice-Bokanowski in memory of their uncle Alphonse Kann)
DIA

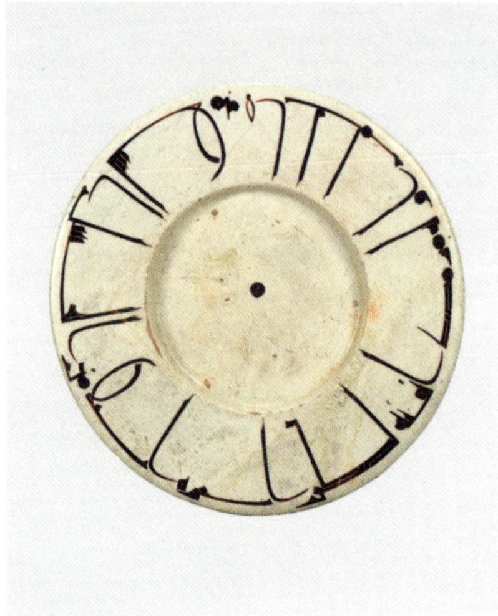

[130]
Dish with Radial Inscription
Samarkand, Uzbekistan
c. 975–1000
Ceramic
H. 5.3; Diam. 37.6; D. 0.7 cm
(H. 2; Diam. 14¾; D. ¼ in.)
⊻ 1935 (gift of Alphonse Kann)
DIA

into a kind of reliquary. Founded in the seventh century, Islam quickly spread. Precious objects created by artists in Islamic regions – such as Cairo in Egypt, Samarkand in present-day Uzbekistan, or the territories of modern-day Iraq, Afghanistan and Spain – attest to their makers' skill and stand out for their extraordinary variety of shapes and motifs **[129–133]**. Writing blends deftly into the decoration of the *Bowl with Standard Bearer* **[129]** or, in the case of the *Dish with Radial Inscription* **[130]**, forms the very essence of a design composed of an epigraph in Kufic script, written in elegant, elongated strokes. Originating in Islamic Spain, the *Pyxis of al-Mughira* **[132]** is a uniquely fascinating object. Carved from a single piece of ivory, this cylindrical box was slow to reveal its secrets. Such an exquisite and abundant decoration initially suggested that this was an object designed for peaceful contemplation; recent research has shown that it in fact illustrates the bloody struggle for the Umayyad Caliphate in Córdoba, Andalusia.

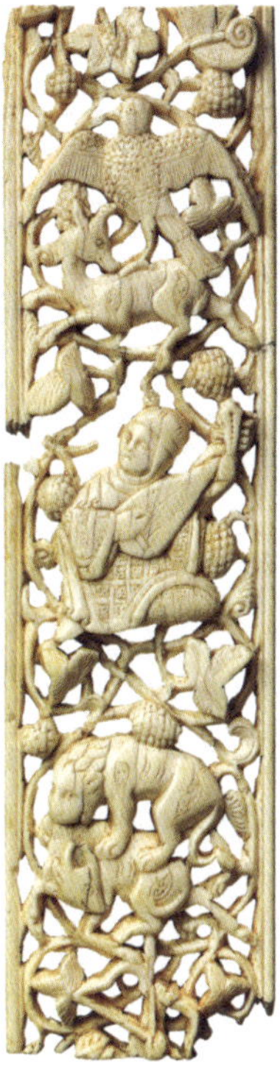

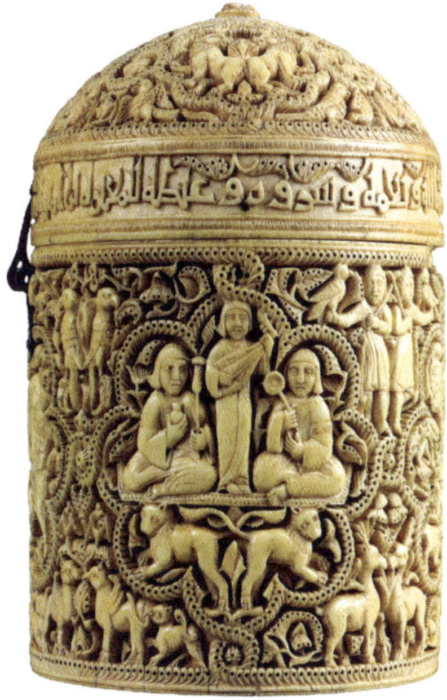

[131]
Panel with Lute Player
Egypt
c. 1000–1200
Carved and painted ivory
H. 21.3; W. 5.7; D. 1.1 cm
(H. 8½; W. 2¼; D. ⅜ in.)
⩡ 1909
DIA

[132]
Pyxis of al-Mughira
Madinat al-Zahra, Spain
968
Elephant ivory
H. 18; Diam. 11.8; D. 0.4 cm
(H. 7; Diam. 4⅝; D. 1¾ in.)
⩡ 1898
DIA

[133]
Pourer with Votive Inscription
Afghanistan (?), Iran (?)
c. 900–1100
Metal
H. 15.2; Diam. 8.2 cm
(H. 6; Diam. 3¼ in.)
⩡ 1934 (gift of
Joseph Hackin)
DIA

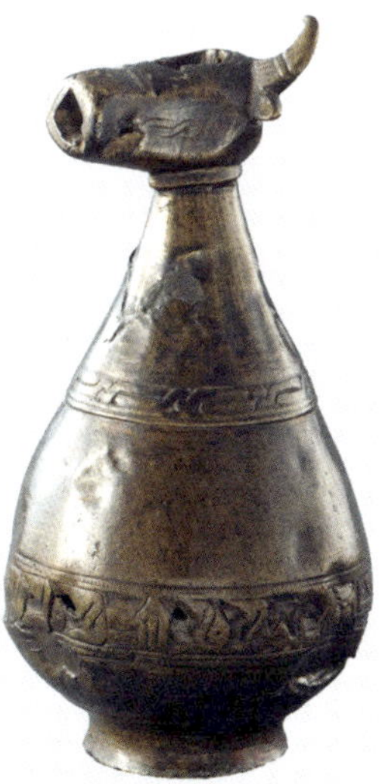

The Ghana Empire was at the height of its power in the tenth and eleventh centuries, continuing into the twelfth century across an area that now comprises much of Mauritania and Mali. Its wealth, art and political importance were renowned beyond its borders; the empire is mentioned in Arabic writings as early as the seventh century. An example of this creativity, the hermaphrodite sculpture **[134]**, with female and male attributes, depicts a high-ranking individual who brings peace, protection, food and fertility to a community.

From the Near East to the Atlantic, the Early Middle Ages were not the "dark ages" they were long made out to be. Philosophical and religious thinking forged different political and spiritual visions of the world, which in turn gave rise to events that would crystallise relations. Sometimes this was through conflict, but also peaceful encounters that fostered new links. These included conquests, such as the establishment of the Umayyad caliphate in Spain, Vladimir the Great's conversion to Christianity under the influence of the Macedonian Dynasty of Byzantine emperors, as well as the First Crusade, called by Pope Urban II during the Council of Clermont, against the Seljuk Turks who controlled entrance to Jerusalem. The Louvre, through its collections, reflects the range of situations and transformations that took place at this point in history.

Carved with leaves and motifs inspired by ancient art, the *Corinthian Capital of Caliph al-Hakam II al-Mustansir bi-Ilâh* **[135]** originates in Islamic Córdoba; by 711 the Muslims had conquered a large part of the Iberian Peninsula. The work is dedicated to Caliph al-Hakam II, a learned ruler and defender of the arts. As his capital, Córdoba prospered under his reign, not least with the construction of a great mosque, now a cathedral. The *Icon of Saint Demetrios* **[137]** portrays the saint as a warrior. Born in Thessaloniki, Demetrios served in the Roman army in the early sixth century. Martyred for his faith, he was among the saints venerated by the Byzantines. For a long time the *Maastricht Binding-Case* **[138]** contained the manuscript on which the Dukes of Brabant took their oath. This elaborate object is the work of the talented craftsmen and artists who served the Ottonian emperors, founders of the Holy Roman Empire, and calls upon various

[134]
Soninke Hermaphrodite Statue
Bandiagara, Mali
c. 1050–1095
Wood
H. 210; W. 37; D. 22 cm
(H. 6 ft 10¾ in.;
W. 1 ft 2½ in.; D. 8¾ in.)
MQB–JC

[135]
Corinthian Capital of Caliph al-Hakam II al-Mustansir bi-Ilâh
Córdoba, Spain
c. 961–970
Marble
H. 30.5; W. 35 cm
(H. 12; W. 13¾ in.)
⊻ 1900
DIA

[136]
Constantinople,
now Istanbul, Turkey
Chest with Mythological Scenes
Byzantium
c. 950–1000
Bone and wood
H. 16.5; W. 26.5; D. 17.2 cm
(H. 6½; W. 10½; D. 6¾ in.)
⊻ 1922
DBECA

[137]
Constantinople,
now Istanbul, Turkey
Icon of Saint Demetrios
Byzantium
c. 1040–1060
Steatite
H. 9.4; W. 6.3; D. 0.6 cm
(H. 3¾; W. 2½; D. ¼ in.)
⊻ 1897
DBECA

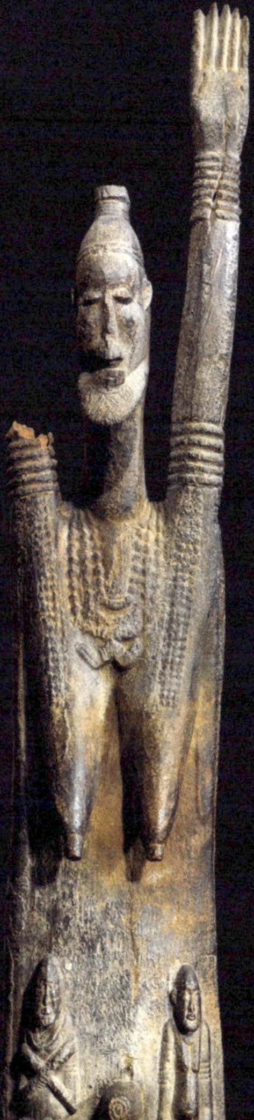

134

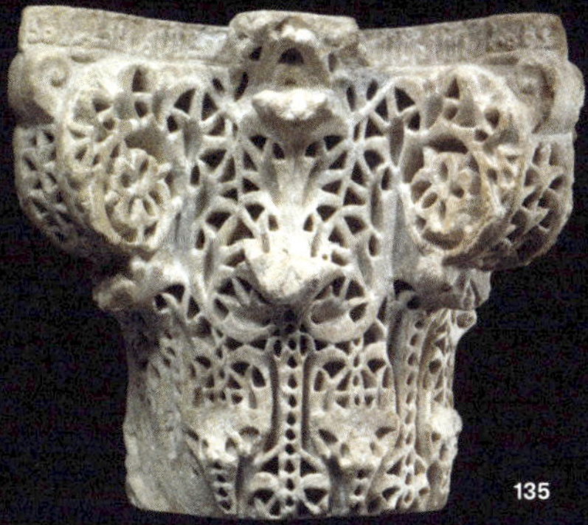

135

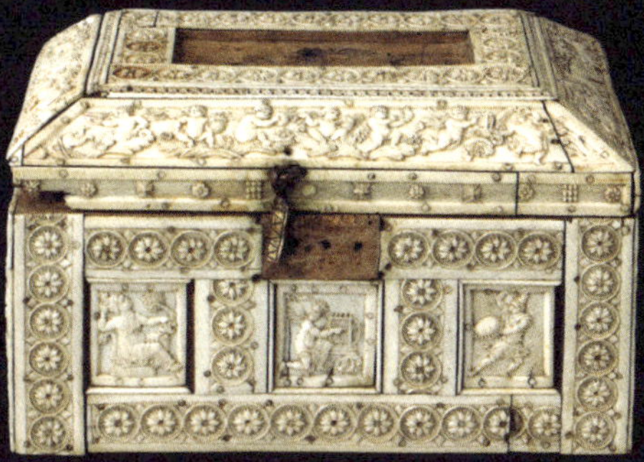

136

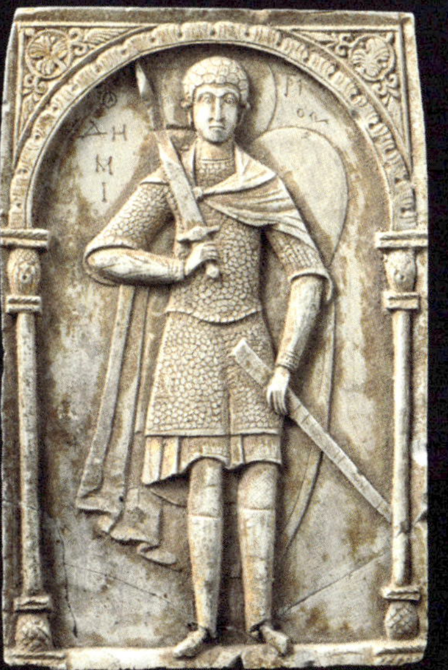

137

techniques. Skilfully crafted in gold, it is decorated with cloisonné enamel and encrusted with precious stones. It arrived at the Louvre after being confiscated during the French Revolution.

The capital **[139]** from the Benedictine abbey of Saint Pierre in Flavigny draws attention to the visual and imaginative quality of the Romanesque style, which was gaining prominence during the eleventh century. Emphasising the depiction of nature, this art, in its simplicity, exalted its architectural setting. Nineteenth-century historians looked with interest at the Romanesque style, and this is reflected in the Louvre's acquisition of the capital. A gradual rediscovery of Romanesque art would significantly influence artists of the late nineteenth and twentieth centuries.

This olifant **[140]** – a horn blown to attract attention – belonged to the painter Pierre Révoil, who was also a prominent art collector. An ornate mixture of ancient art – such as the foliage around the procession of animals – and Eastern influence, it was made from an elephant's tusk by Muslim craftsmen in southern Italy. Knights returning from the crusades would bring back olifants as a reminder of lands that many had discovered with wonder. No doubt they were also familiar with such objects from an episode in the *Song of Roland*, an immensely popular eleventh-century epic poem in which Roland, one of Charlemagne's loyal knights, blows into an olifant to summon help during the Battle of Roncevaux Pass, to no avail.

The eleventh century was a prosperous time for the cities of north-west South America. Gold artefacts, such as the *Anthropomorphic Pendant* **[141]** from present-day Colombia, would have fascinated sixteenth-century Spanish conquistadors. Populations continued to resist the Spanish occupants until the late nineteenth century.

[138]
Germany (?)
Maastricht Binding-Case
Treasury of the Basilica of Saint Servatius, Maastricht
c. 1000–1050
Gold, cloisonné enamel, silver, pearls, gemstones and wood
H. 38.6; W. 33.5; D. 7.5 cm
(H. 15¼; W. 13¼; D. 3 in.)
⩡ 1795
DDA

[139]
Capital decorated on three sides with two eagles, wings outstretched, two quadrupeds devouring each other by the tail, and a wicker motif
Abbey of Saint Pierre, Flavigny-sur-Ozerain, France
11th century
Limestone
H. 40.5; W. 30; D. 31 cm
(H. 16; W. 11¾; D. 12¼)
⩡ 1891
DS

[140]
Southern Italy
Olifant: Circles with Animals
c. 1085–1100
Elephant ivory
H. 48; W. 51.5; Diam. 11.3 cm
(H. 19; W. 20¼; Diam. 4½ in.)
⩡ 1828 (former collection of Pierre Révoil)
DDA

[141]
Anthropomorphic Pendant
Present-day Colombia
c. 1000–1500
Gold
H. 13; W. 13; D. 4.5 cm
(H. 5⅛; W. 5⅛; D. 1¾ in.)
MQB–JC

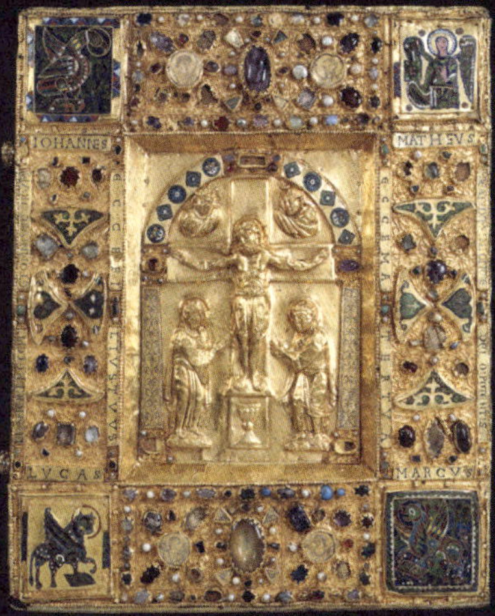

138

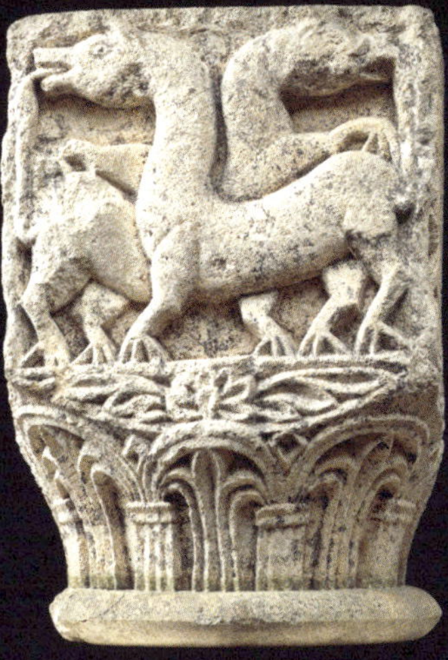

139

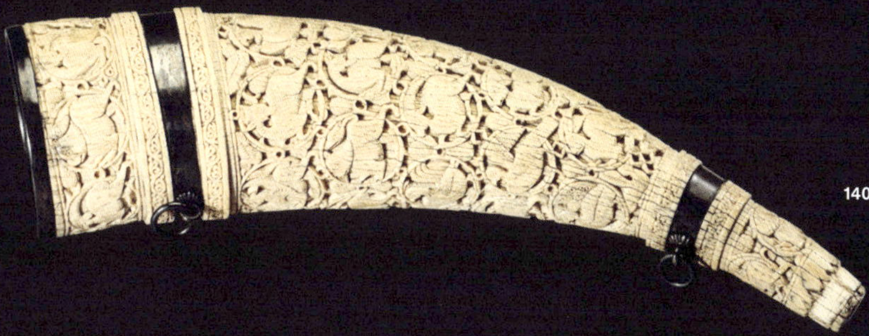

140

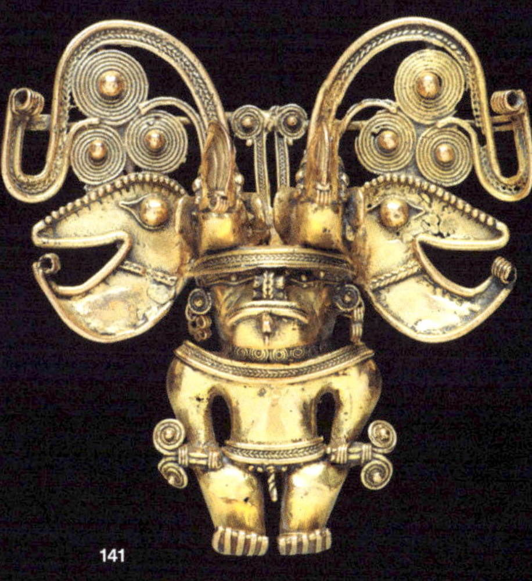

141

The Louvre, heir to the Musée des Monuments Français

During the French Revolution at the end of the eighteenth century, many religious buildings in France were desacralised and property was confiscated from the clergy: conditions were ripe for a reconsideration of how ancient religious art was perceived. The nature of these artefacts was of course transformed: the moment they entered the museum's collections, their spiritual and liturgical dimension was lost. Most of all, they underwent a major aesthetic transformation as they became incorporated into the history and evolution of styles. In 1795 the painter and collector Alexandre Lenoir opened the Musée des Monuments Français in the former convent of the Petits Augustins in Paris, to house works that had been removed from churches or monasteries and which might otherwise be destroyed. It was, to a degree, thanks to Lenoir's categorisation of these objects per era, and his insistence that they be properly displayed, that they were recognised as art. Interest in the study of religious art in France and the identification of different styles – first Gothic then the earlier Romanesque – took root there, in an institution celebrated by artists and connoisseurs.

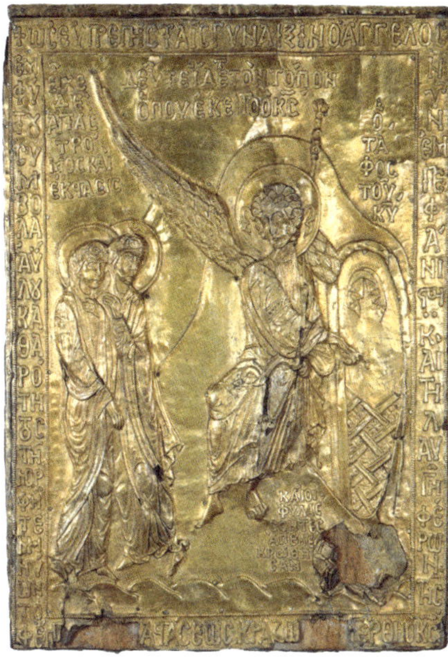

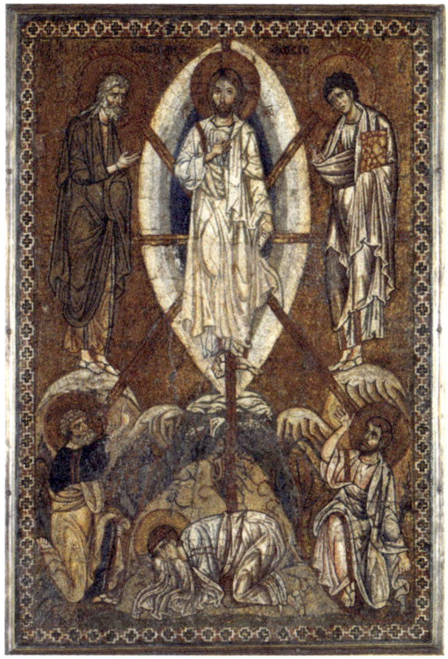

[142]
Constantinople,
now Istanbul, Turkey
Plaque of the Reliquary of the Stone from Christ's Sepulchre, the Holy Women at the Tomb
Byzantium
c. 1150–1200
Wood and gilded silver
H. 42.6; W. 31; D. 3 cm
(H. 16¾; W. 12¼; D. 1⅛ in.)
⊻ 1793
DBECA

[143]
Constantinople,
now Istanbul, Turkey
Portable Icon, the Transfiguration of Christ
Byzantium
c. 1200
Gilded copper, marble, lapis lazuli, glass, wax, mastic (restoration) on slate and copper frame
H. 52; W. 35 cm
(H. 20½; W. 13¾ in.)
⊻ 1852
DBECA

[144]
Constantinople,
now Istanbul, Turkey
Diptych, Nativity, Crucifixion and Prophets
Byzantium
c. 1200–1300
Ivory
H. 29; W. 10.8; D. 1.2 cm
(H. 11½; W. 4¼; D. ½ in.)
⊻ 2012
DBECA

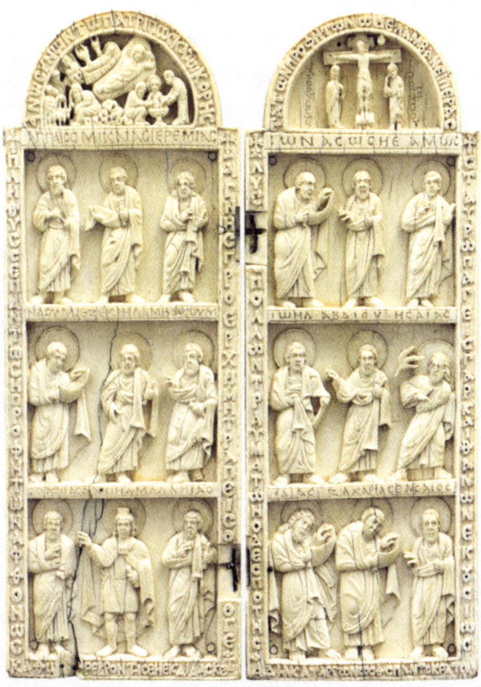

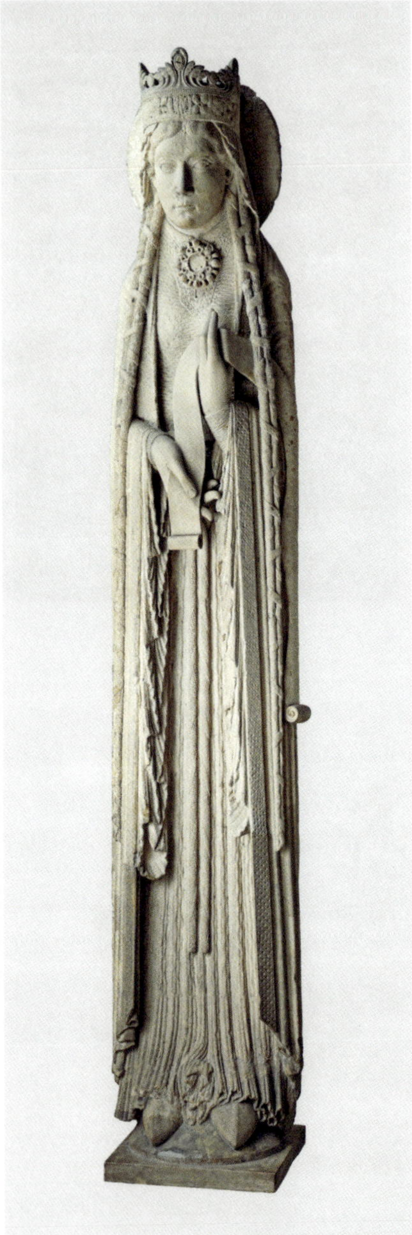

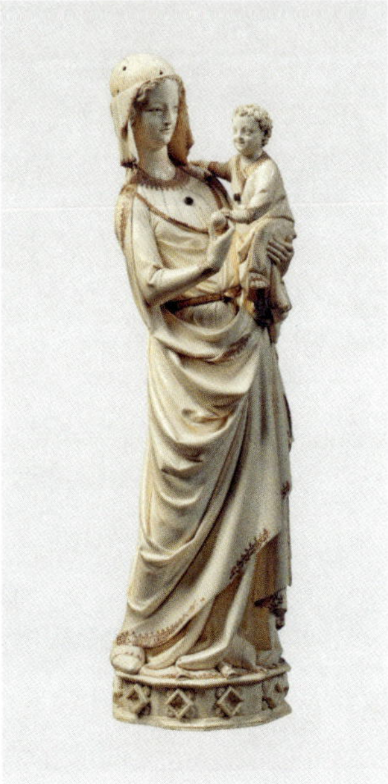

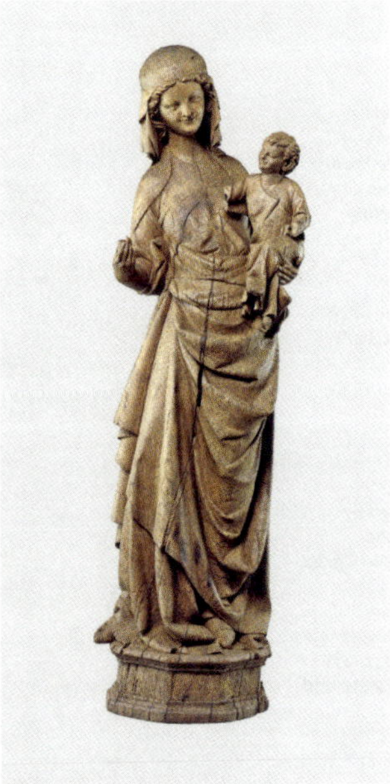

[145]
A Queen (the Queen of Sheba?)
Former collegial church of
Notre-Dame, Corbeil-Essonnes,
France
c. 1175–1200
Limestone
H. 235; W. 44; D. 38.5 cm
(H. 7 ft 8½ in.;
W. 1 ft 5¼ in.; D. 1 ft 3¼ in.)
⩡ 1916 (former collection of the
Musée Monuments Français)
DS

[146]
Paris, France
Sainte-Chapelle Virgin and Child
Treasury of the Sainte-Chapelle,
Paris, France
c. 1260–1270
Polychrome elephant ivory
H. 41; W. 12.4 cm
(H. 16¼; W. 4⅞ in.)
⩡ 1861
DS

[147]
Picardy region, France
Virgin of Wargnies
c. 1270
Polychrome oak
H. 116; W. 32; D. 30 cm
(H. 3 ft 9¾ in.;
W. 1 ft ½ in.; D. 11¾ in.)
⩡ 1907
DS

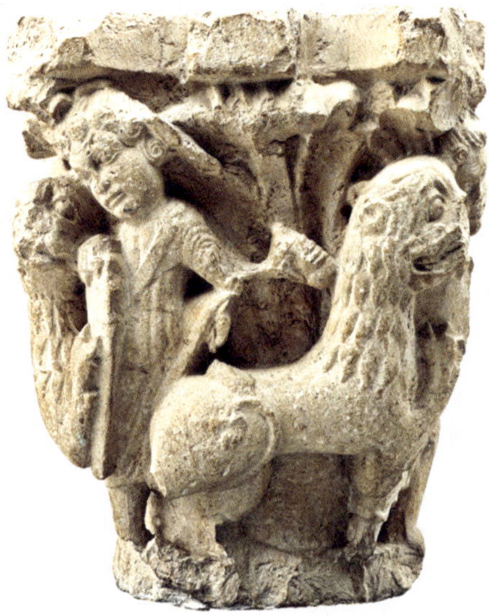

[148]
Capital with Armed Men Fighting Lions
Cloister of Girona Cathedral, Spain
c. 1185–1200
Limestone
H. 30; W. 25; D. 25 cm
(H. 11¾; W. 9¾; D. 9¾ in.)
⊻ 1925
DS

After the museum was dismantled in 1816, many of the works Lenoir had preserved there entered the Louvre's collections, including its sculptures. One example is the column-statue **[145]** – almost certainly a representation of the Queen of Sheba – from the church in Corbeil, south of Paris. One of a pair, its counterpart depicts another biblical figure, King Solomon, which is also in the Louvre. Both sculptures were incorporated as decorative elements into the church's architecture, hence their exaggeratedly elongated proportions.

The delightful *Sainte-Chapelle Virgin and Child* **[146]**, which belonged to Lenoir, shows how artists in the thirteenth century strived and succeeded in producing figures in more supple postures – the Virgin stands with one hip slightly forward – and with softer features. It offers a stunning example of the virtuosity of Parisian ivory sculptors. The same desire for a new naturalism is apparent in other sculptures of the same period, such as the *Virgin of Wargnies* **[147]**. Having identified previously overlooked styles, nineteenth-century historians felt encouraged to turn their attention to little-known centres of artistic production, many in small towns

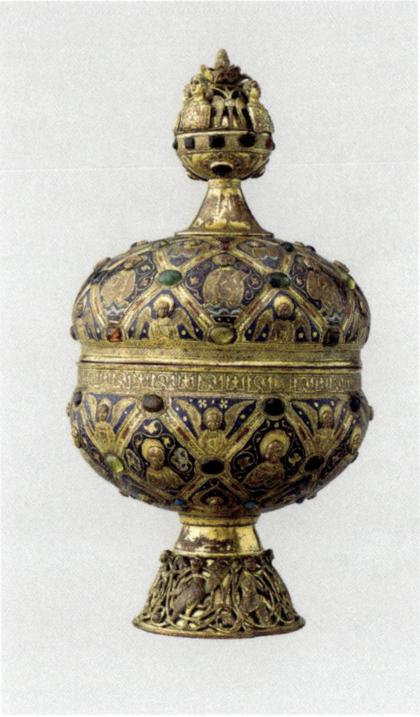

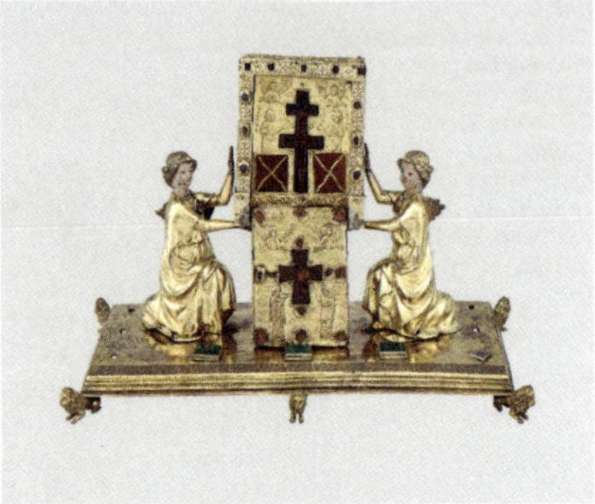

[149]
Attributed to Master Alpais, Limoges, France
Master Alpais Ciborium
Montmajour (?), France
c. 1200
Enamelled and gilded copper
H. 30.1; Diam. 16.8 cm
(H. 11¾; Diam. 6½ in.)
⊻ 1828 (former collection of Pierre Révoil)
DDA

[150]
Workshops in Constantinople, now Istanbul, Turkey, and in the Champenois region, France
Jaucourt Reliquary
c. 1100–1360
Copper, gold, silver and enamel
H. 26.4; W. 37.8; D. 17.2 cm
(H. 10½; W. 15; D. 6¾ in.)
⊻ 1915
DDA

and villages throughout France, Italy and Spain. The study of Romanesque and Gothic art contributed to the historical construction of a national artistic expression in most countries on the European continent.

NATIONAL ARTISTIC EXPRESSIONS Originally from Girona, Spain, *Capital with Armed Men Fighting Lions* **[148]** is characteristic of a Romanesque style in which decoration and architecture interconnect. With its simplicity of forms, the *Courajod Christ* **[151]**, from Burgundy, is a particularly beautiful example of Romanesque art. Shown at the 1878 Universal Exposition, it was purchased by Louis Courajod, a curator at the Louvre. It no doubt comes from a group of sculptures depicting the descent from the cross, when Christ's body was taken down before being placed in the tomb. This precise moment, when the grief of those closest to him is at its most intense, brings Christ's humanity into sharp focus. The scene, a new subject for artists at the time this work was made, is also depicted in the large *Descent from the Cross* **[152]**, from Umbria in Italy. In this later work the bodies

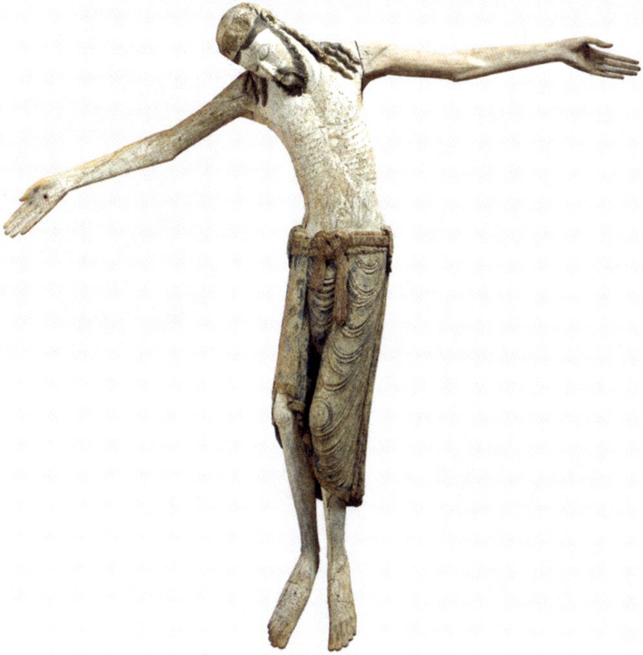

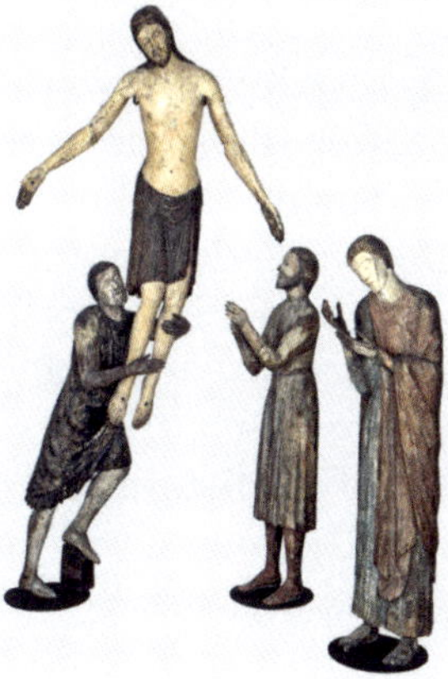

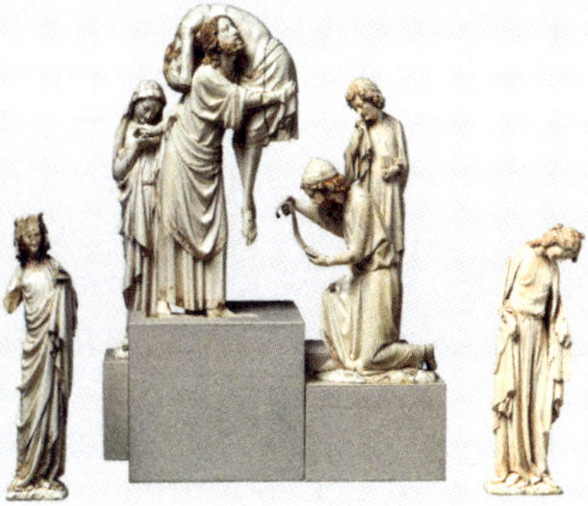

[151]
Bourgogne region, France
Courajod Christ
c. 1125–1150
Polychrome linden and alder
H. 155; W. 168; D. 30 cm
(H. 5 ft 1 in.; W. 5 ft 6¼ in.; D. 11¾ in.)
⊻ 1895 (gift of Louis Courajod)
DS

[152]
Umbria region (?), Italy
Descent from the Cross, Christ
c. 1225–1250
Polychrome poplar and walnut
H. 184; W. 123; D. 43 cm
(H. 6 ft ½ in.; W. 4 ft ½ in.; D. 1 ft 5 in.)
⊻ 1968
DS

[153]
Paris, France
Descent from the Cross, Group
c. 1270–1280
Polychrome elephant ivory
H. 40; W. 52 cm (H. 15¾; W. 20½ in.)
⊻ With the participation of the Société des Amis du Louvre and crowdfunding
DDA

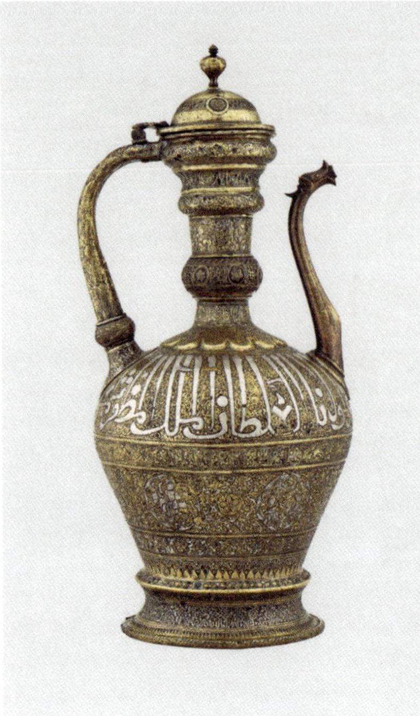

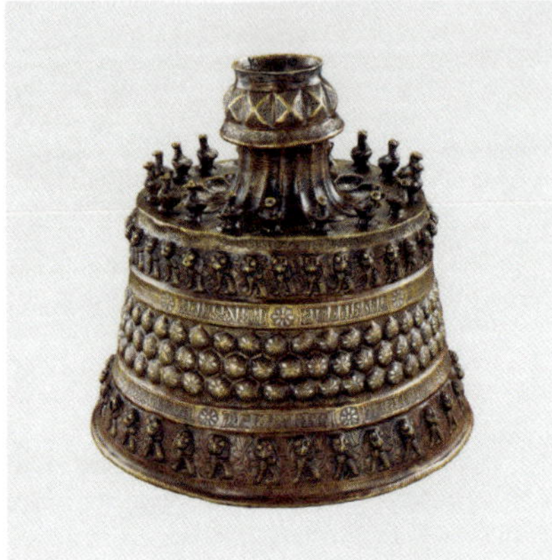

[154]
Ali ibn Husayn ibn Muhammad al-Mawsili, Cairo, Egypt
Ewer inscribed with the name of the Sultan al-Malik al-Muzaffar Shams al-Din Yusuf
c. 1275–1276
Copper and silver
H. 49.5; W. 22.7; Diam. 10.2 cm
(H. 19½; W. 9; Diam. 4 in.)
⩡ 1888
DIA

[155]
Candlestick with Ducks
Herat, Afghanistan
c. 1150–1200
Brass, silver, copper and black paste
H. 34; Diam. 35.5; D. 0.5 cm (H. 13½; Diam. 14; D. ¼ in.)
⩡ 1909 (bequest of Charles Piet-Lataudrie)
DIA

are treated in a more realistic manner, with the still visible colour suggesting the artist's intention to elicit the viewer's emotions. It took more than a century to reunite the ivory figures in the poignant *Descent from the Cross* **[153]**, sculpted in Paris in the mid-thirteenth century. Craftsmen applied their highly refined skills to the making of these devotional objects, of which the *Master Alpais Ciborium* **[149]** is an example. One of the finest pieces of champlevé enamel, a technique in which the master enamellists of Limoges excelled, it is outstanding as much for the richness of its decoration as for the beauty of its cupola-like shape. It belonged to Pierre Révoil, who began his collection of medieval artworks in the early nineteenth century.

Crafted from a single sheet of metal, *Candlestick with Ducks* **[155]** is a reminder of the prodigious talent of the metalsmiths working in Iran from the twelfth century. The combination of repoussé, chasing and inlays across its entire surface is a technical feat. Acquired in 1999, the graceful *Prince's Head* **[156]**, also from Iran, has become one of the most acclaimed works in the Department of Islamic Art. It shows the great skill

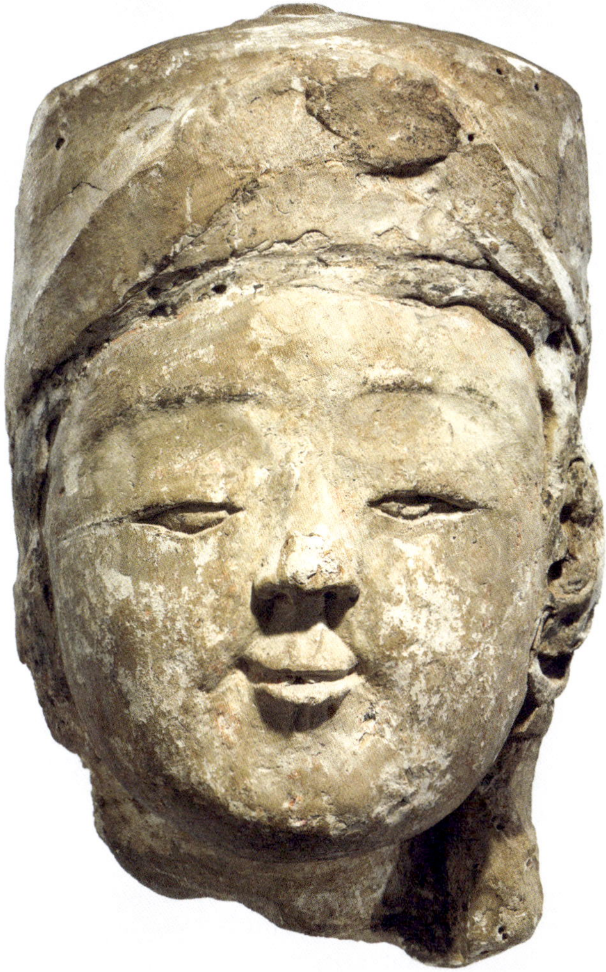

[156]
Prince's Head
Rayy, present-day Iran
c. 1185–1215
Painted stucco
H. 32.5; W. 16.7; D. 18.5 cm
(H. 12¾; W. 6½; D. 7¼ in.)
⊻ 1999
DIA

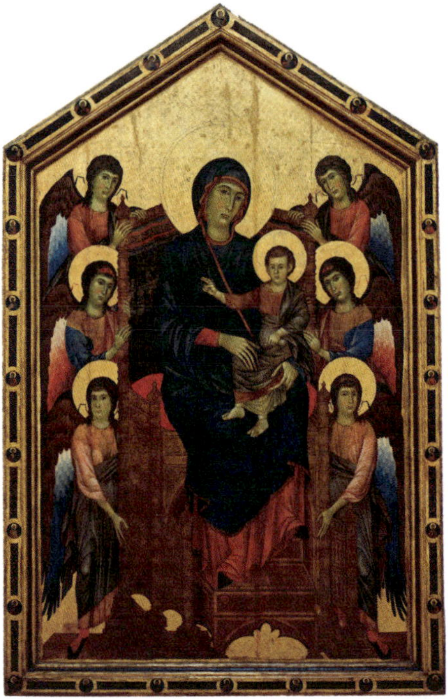

[157]
Cenni di Pepo,
known as Cimabue
c. 1240–1301/1302
The Virgin and Child in Majesty Surrounded by Six Angels, Maestà
c. 1275–1300
Tempera and gold ground
on poplar wood
H. 427; W. 280 cm
(H. 14 ft; W. 9 ft 2¼ in.)
⩡ 1812
DP

with which Muslim artists portrayed the human form, even though such representations were banned.

Cimabue's *Maestà* **[157]** is considered one of the founding works of a specifically Italian school of painting that broke away from the influence of Byzantine art. While the artist remains indebted to the sense of symmetry and hieratics of the Byzantine tradition, and retains gold for the scene's backdrop, he also introduces new forms of visual expression. Inspired by his observation of contemporary sculpture, he transfers the three-dimensionality of the bodies and objects to the wood panel's flat surface. His treatment of the fabric and drapery further indicates this quest for greater realism. The painter also attaches importance to the facial expressions of the various figures. The work of Cimabue inspired the artists who came after him. Napoleon's armies took this panel from Pisa and it entered the Louvre in 1812.

INTERWEAVING

"What do these objects
tell us of the world?
Our children belong
to the world
of tomorrow, a world
we will never experience,
not even in our dreams.
Our ancestors belong
to the world of yesterday,
a world we will never see again,
no matter how much we long
for it. ... Objects are reefs
in a mysterious ocean.
They are remote
and enigmatic, observing
us more thoroughly
than we observe them."

Jean-Marie Gustave Le Clézio,
Les musées sont des mondes, 2011

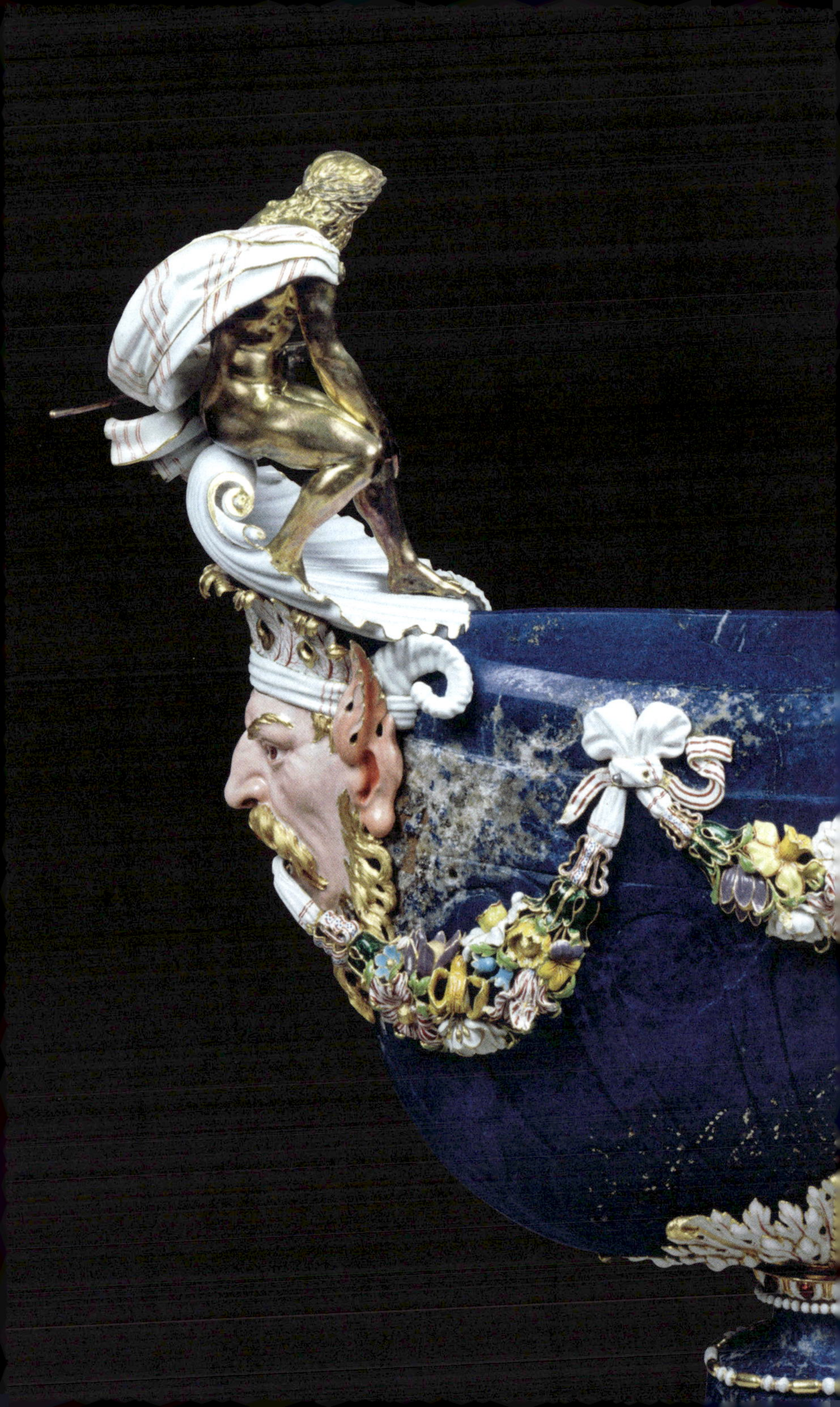

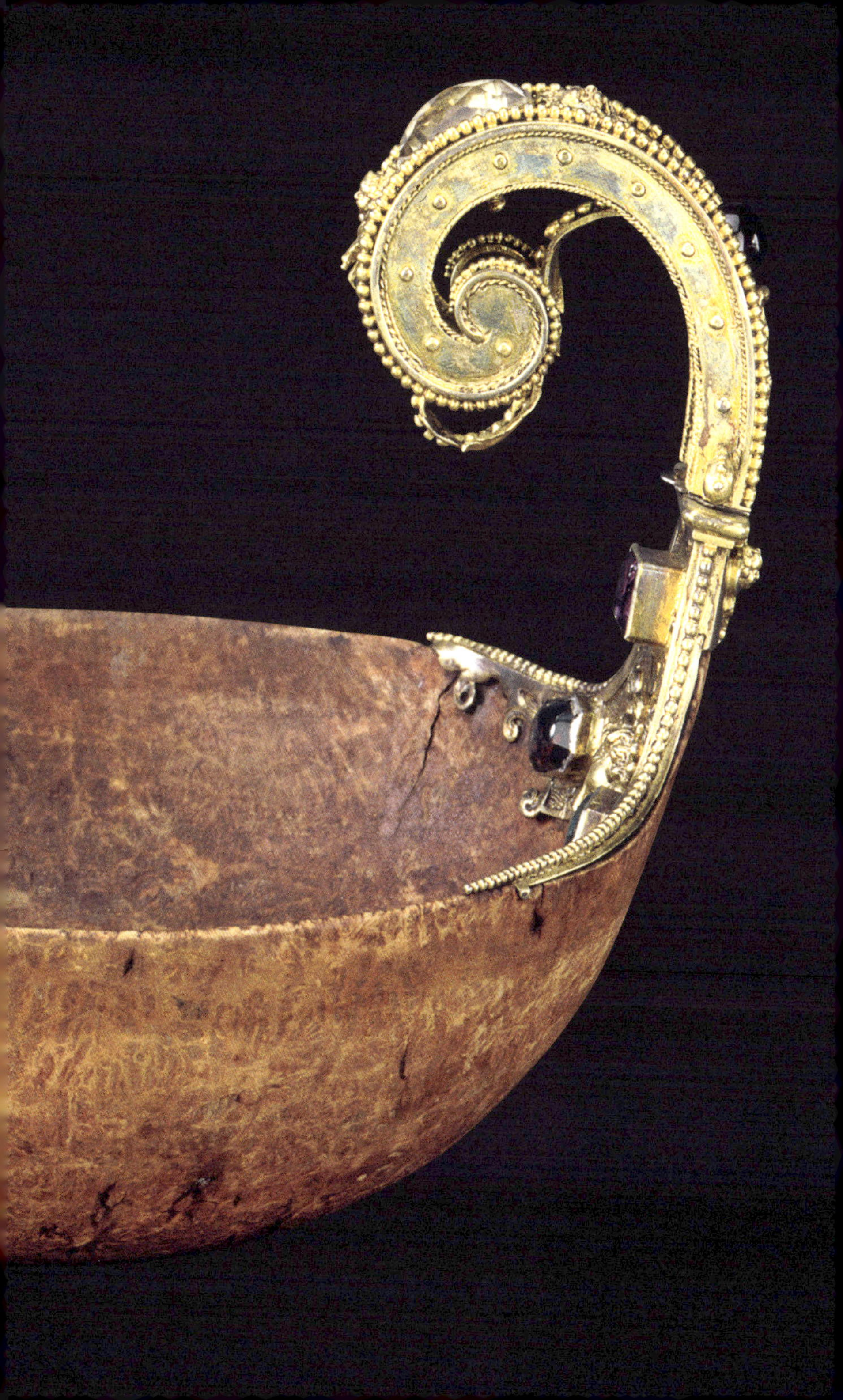

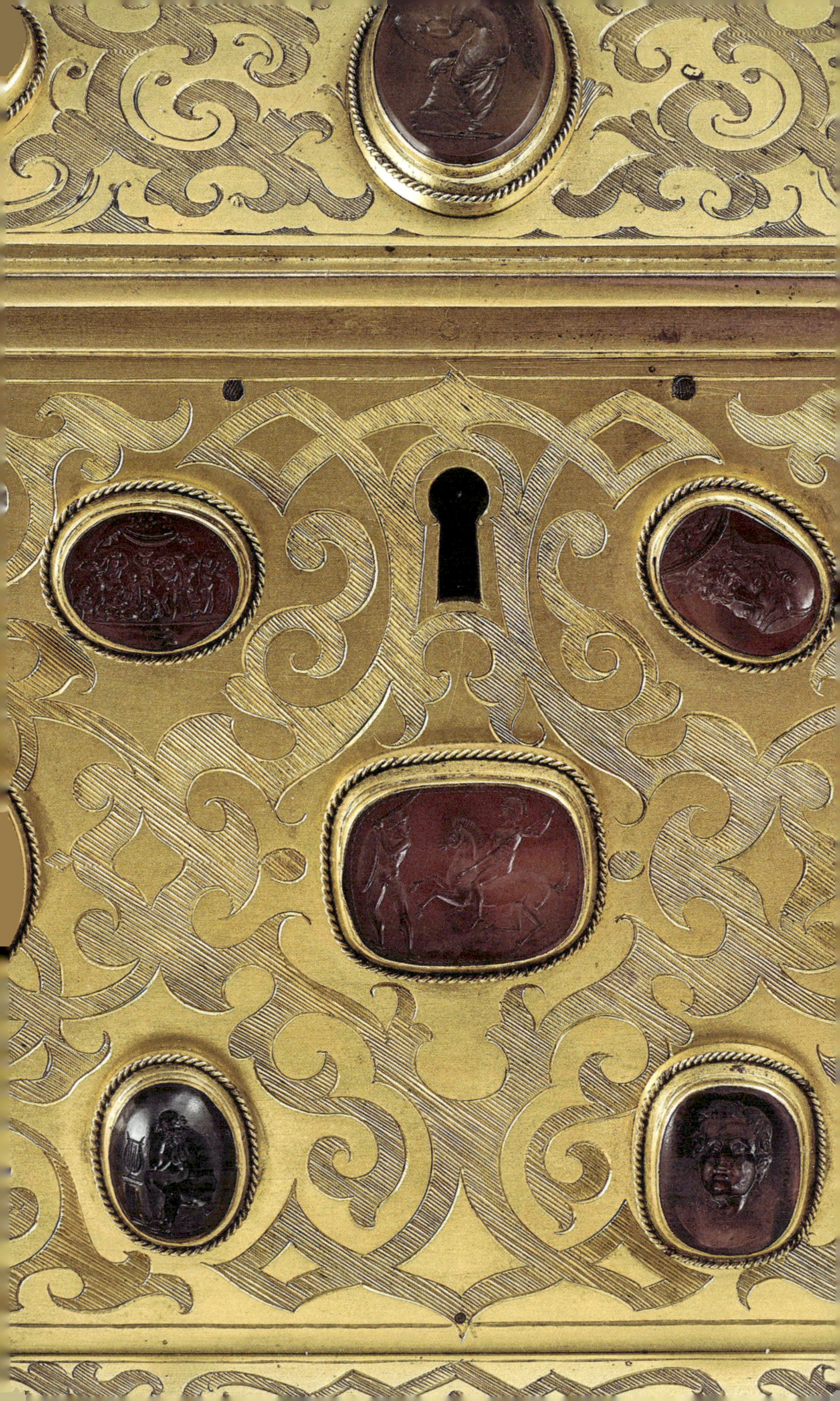

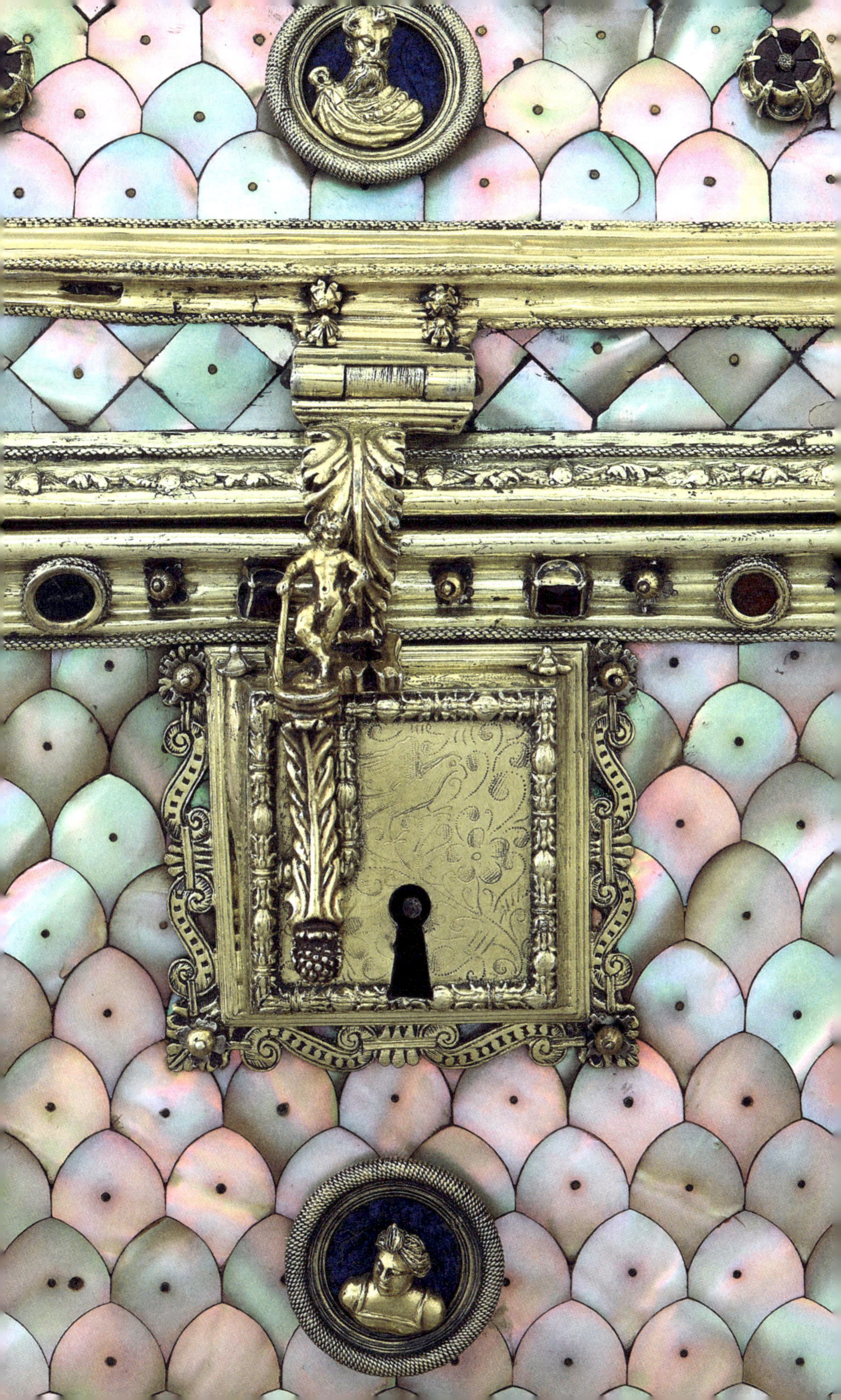

The travels of Marco Polo

Late 13th century–
14th century

Marco Polo, a Venetian merchant, travelled with his father and uncle on two long voyages that took him from Italy all the way to present-day China. On his return, he dictated stories of his adventures, which were published in 1298 as *Description of the World*, also known as *The Travels of Marco Polo*. Western readers were enthralled by these tales; when Christopher Columbus set sail in the late fifteenth century, he carried a copy with him. Polo describes the outbound journey over land, through the Near East, Asia Minor and Central Asia, his time in Cathay – China – and his return by sea, along the coasts of Southeast Asia and India. The routes Polo took followed paths that had been traced thousands of years earlier, such as between Mesopotamia and Central Asia where lapis lazuli, a rich blue stone set into jewellery and sculpted objects, was mined. Countless objects bear witness to the interactions and exchanges between distant societies that these ancient routes made possible. While we can consider the *Dish with Phoenixes in Flight* **[158]** to be Iranian, because of its provenance and because the phoenix is a recurrent motif in Persian art, Chinese influences are nonetheless discernible. As early as the fourteenth century, Iranian ceramists, already highly skilled, were incorporating techniques borrowed from their counterparts in China's artistic centres. Saint Andrew **[163]**, one of Christ's apostles, travelled through the countries bordering the Black Sea. He is celebrated by the Catholic Church and Orthodox churches.

The fourteenth century was a period of economic and social transformation for the Italian Peninsula, as cities prospered and the governing families extended their influence. Trade and the stories brought back by travelling merchants were a window on the world. The inhabitants of these cities are captured in *Group of Figures in Civilian Dress* **[164]**, a sculpture from Emilia-Romagna in northern Italy. The expressions of each figure and their sense of movement brings them vividly to life. The painter Simone Martini originated from a different region of Italy. From his birthplace in Sienna, a Tuscan city and rival to neighbouring Florence, he travelled to southern France and joined the papal court in Avignon. Here he painted a polyptych – a work composed of several panels – depicting episodes from the Passion and

[158]
Iran
Dish with Phoenixes in Flight
c. 1300–1350
Ceramic
H. 12; Diam. 25.3 cm
(H. 4¾; Diam. 10 in.)
⩡ 1931
DIA

[159]
Simone Martini
1284–1344
Christ Carrying the Cross
Second quarter of the 14th century
Tempera and gold ground on wood
H. 30; W. 20.5 cm
(H. 11¾; W. 8 in.)
⩡ 1834
DP

[160]
Constantinople,
now Istanbul, Turkey
Mosaic*, known as *Saint George (?) Slaying the Dragon
Byzantium
c. 1300–1350
Mosaic and wood
Diam. 22; D. 1.1 cm
(Diam. 8¾; D. ⅜ in.)
⩡ 1883 (bequest of Jean-Charles Davillier)
DDA

[161]
Ceremonial Duho
Taíno people, Caribbean
14th century
Guayacan wood
H. 42.4; W. 30.36;
D. 71.5 cm (H. 16¾;
W. 12; D. 28¼ in.)
⩡ Gift of Flora Raphaël and David David-Weill, former collection of the Muséum National d'Histoire Naturelle
MQB-JC

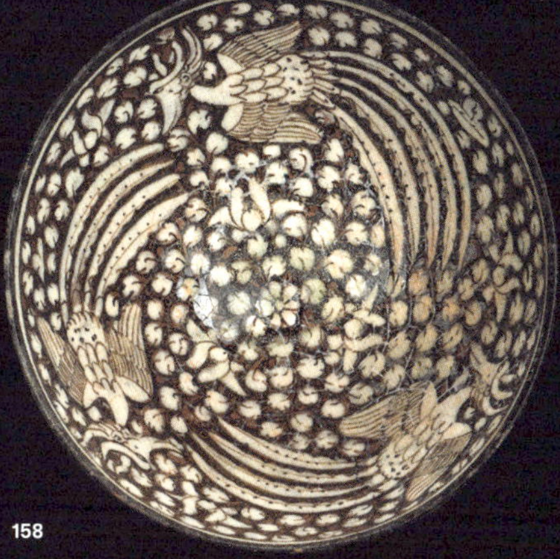

158

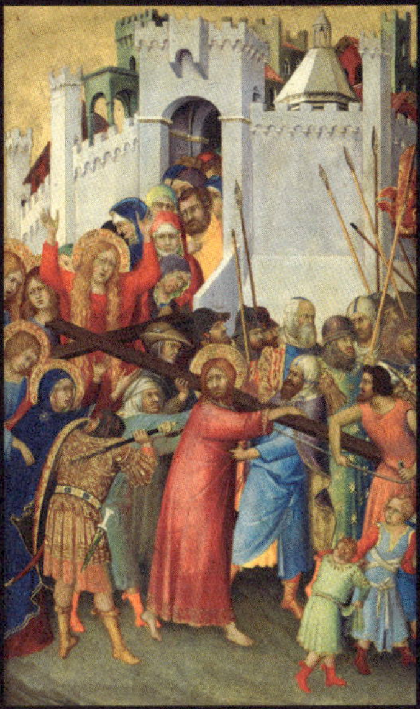

159

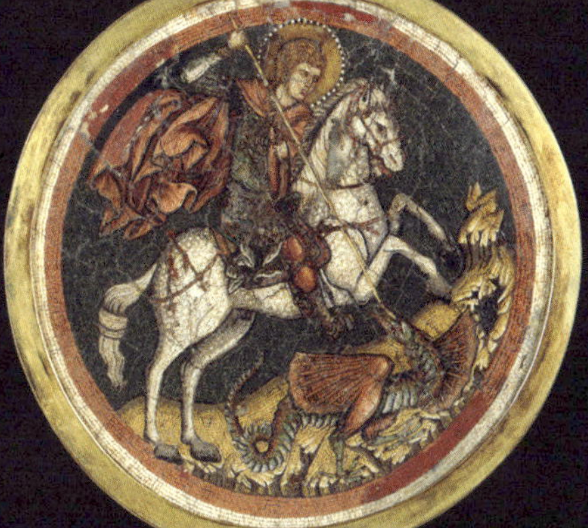

160

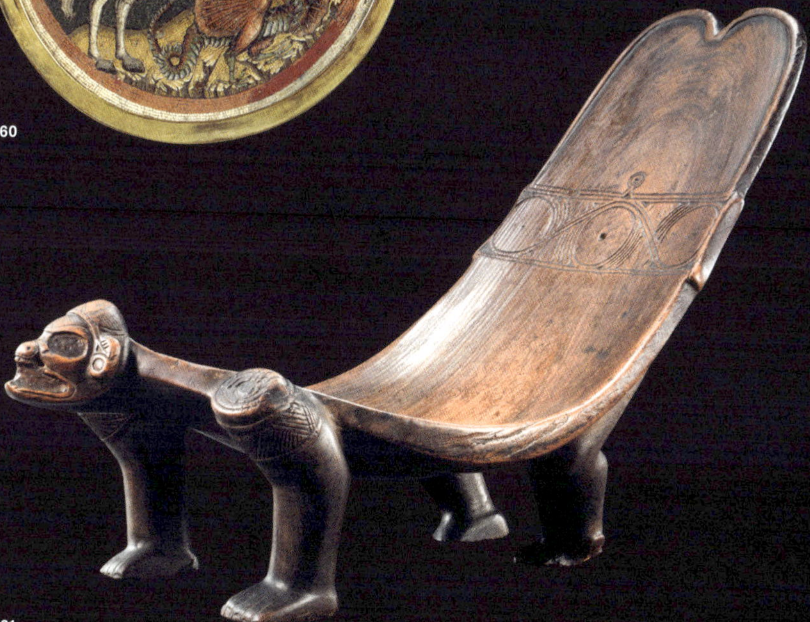

161

death of Christ for Cardinal Napoleone Orsini. Martini's time in Avignon helped spread Italian models in France. For many years the panels of his polyptych resided at the Chartreuse de Champmol, a monastery in Burgundy. Its dispersal and Louis-Philippe of France's 1834 acquisition of *Christ Carrying the Cross* **[159]** indicates a burgeoning interest in the Italian Primitives.

Created much further east in the Mediterranean Basin, *Saint George Slaying the Dragon* **[160]** features one of the great saints venerated by the Orthodox Church of Constantinople. The only known mosaic tondo – the name given to a circular work of art – its remarkable aesthetic qualities are characteristic of the artistic renaissance taking place under the Palaiologos Dynasty of Byzantine emperors.

Comparable artistic accomplishments existed in more distant lands. In Africa, for example, and more specifically Nigeria, Ife, an important centre of Yoruba culture, came to the attention of the Western world in the early twentieth century. Of the exceptional works produced in West Africa, Europeans were already familiar with those of the Kingdom of Benin (thirteenth–nineteenth centuries) – which was also situated, at least in part, in present-day Nigeria – whose treasures were looted at the end of the nineteenth century. Ife heads **[162]**, in metal or terracotta, combine realism with an idealised representation. They reflect the belief that the head is the seat of the human soul, where a person's destiny is determined.

Dating from this same period, specifically the fourteenth century, in the Americas, the *Ceremonial Duho* **[161]** – gifted by the leading French-American collector and patron David David-Weill – is characteristic of the art of the Taíno people in its simple, flowing lines. Indigenous to what is now the Caribbean, these farmers and fishermen were the first people encountered by European explorers. The navigators arriving on these shores dubbed this the "New World", yet these were already established civilisations, with their own customs and concepts, who hadn't waited for the Western world to "discover" them in order to produce remarkable works. A seat such as this would have been for a cacique, to emphasise their power and importance.

[162]
Head
Kingdom of Ife, Nigeria
c. 12th–14th century
Terracotta
H. 17; W. 12; D. 14 cm
(H. 6¾; W. 4¾; D. 5½ in.)
MQB–JC

[163]
Pacino di Bonaguida
14th century
Saint Andrew's Vocation
c. 1330
Illuminated manuscript on parchment
H. 47; W. 34 cm
(H. 18½; W. 13½ in.)
⩡ 1857 (gift of Louis Charles Auguste Steinheil)
DPD

[164]
Bologna, Italy
Group of Figures in Civilian Dress (Reconciliation Scene?)
c. 1300–1350
Marble
H. 57.8; W. 53.3; D. 5.8 cm
(H. 22¾; W. 21; D. 2¼ in.)
⩡ 1919 (gift of Jules-Marie Jeuniette)
DS

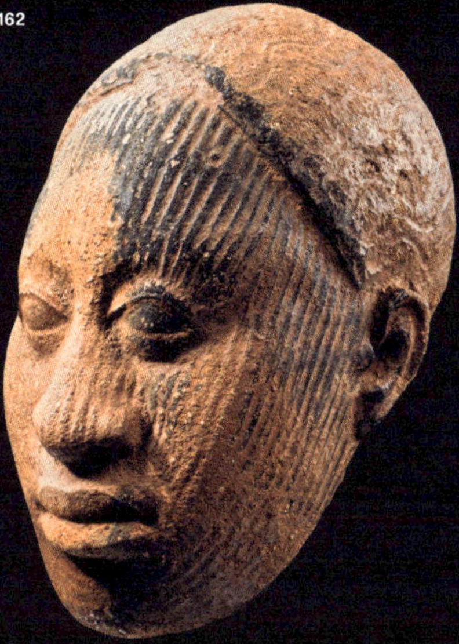

162

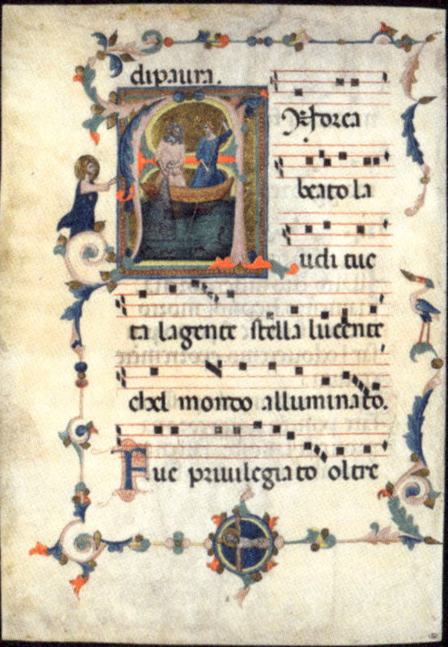
dipaura.
beato la
udi tue
ta la gente stella lucente
chel mondo alluminato.
Fue privilegiato oltre

163

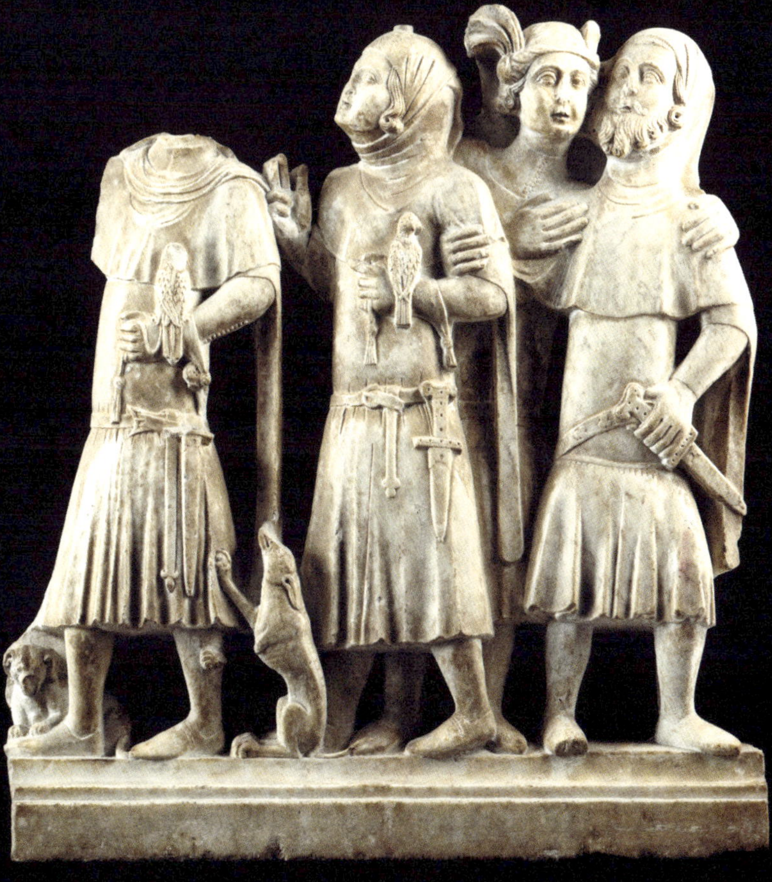

164

Powerful patrons: The origins of the Louvre collections

First a fortress, then a royal residence in the heart of Paris, the Louvre had many incarnations before becoming a museum filled with exceptional collections. Its very history embodies the evolutions that fostered the development of artistic creation, thanks to the enlightened support of powerful patrons. An important turning point came during the reign of Charles V, when the fortress built by Philip II at the turn of the thirteenth century was converted into a palace. The new buildings housed the king's apartments and his library. Despite the pressing issue of the Hundred Years' War between France and England, resulting from claims to the French throne following Charles IV's death without a male heir, Charles V, a man known for his love of art, encouraged creation. Eager to show the treasures thus accumulated, he opened his library to the professors and students of the Sorbonne, France's first university.

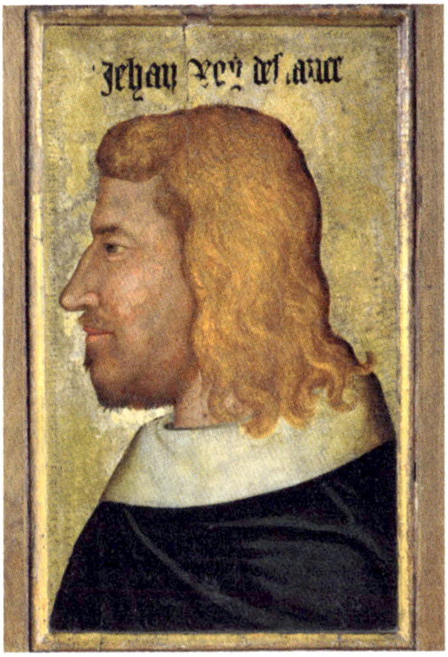

[165]
Île-de-France, France
John the Good
c. 1350–1375
Distemper on gold ground on canvas mounted on oak wood
H. 60; W. 45 cm
(H. 23½; W. 17¾ in.)
⩡ 1925
DP

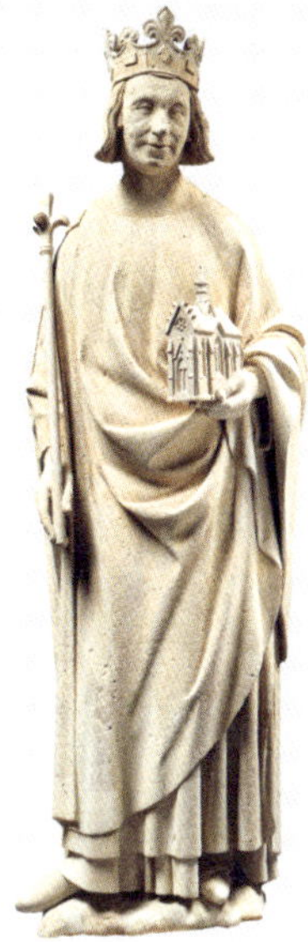

[166] Île-de-France, France. ***Charles V, King of France***
Decoration for the Louvre Palace, Paris, France. c. 1365–1370
Limestone. H. 195; W. 71; D. 40 cm (H. 6 ft 4¾ in.; W. 2 ft 4 in.; D. 1 ft 3¾ in.). ⩡ 1904. DS

The statue of Charles V **[166]** and that of his consort, Jeanne de Bourbon, were once part of the Louvre's decorations, probably adorning the facade of the east entrance, which was destroyed in the seventeenth century. The monarchs' faces are intended to be as lifelike as possible and their bodies are in no way idealised. Traces of colour indicate that both statues were painted.

The same desire for a genuine resemblance prevails in the portrait of John the Good **[165]**. The father of Charles V, he was captured at the Battle of Poitiers in 1356 and died in exile in London. The application of gold ground on the wood panel draws from ancient tradition, whereas the treatment of the king's facial expression and the unruly curls point to new styles of figurative description. During excavation work for the Grand Louvre in the 1980s, 150 fragments of a royal ceremonial helmet **[169]** were uncovered, most probably that of Charles VI, son of Charles V. The fleurons on the crown and the rows of fleurs-de-lys in rectangular enamelled medallions confirm its royal provenance.

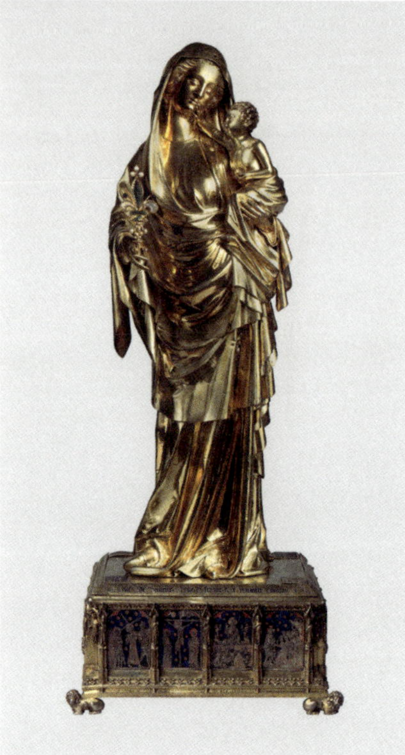

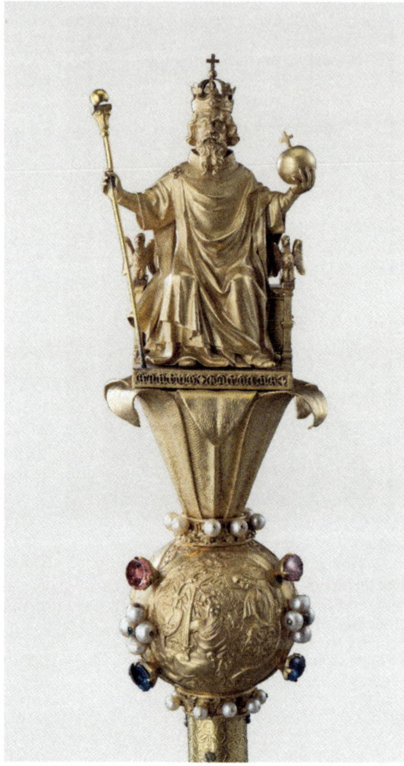

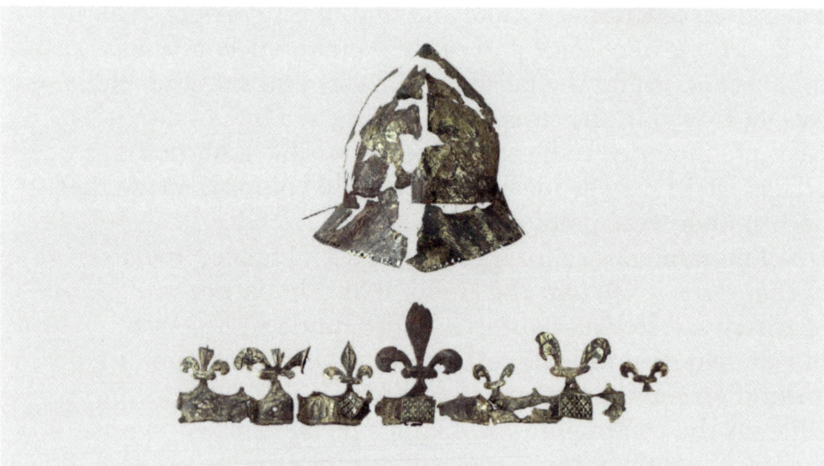

[167]
Paris, France
***Virgin and Child*, known as**
Virgin of Jeanne d'Évreux
Treasury of Saint-Denis, France
c. 1324–1339
Silver, gold, crystal, gemstones, pearls and enamel
H. 68; W. 29; D. 22.8 cm
(H. 26¾; W. 11½; D. 9 in.)
⊻ 1793
DDA

[168]
Hennequin du Vivier (?), active before 1380; Martin Guillaume Biennais, 1764–1843
Sceptre of Charles V
Treasury of Saint-Denis, France
Before 1380; 1804
Gold (previously enamelled), silver, pearls, balas ruby, blue and green glass
H. 60; W. 7 cm (H. 23½; W. 2¾ in.)
⊻ 1793
DDA

[169]
Île-de-France, France
***Gilded Kettle Hat*, known as**
Charles VI's Helmet
Excavations for the Grand Louvre
c. 1380–1385
Enamelled and gilded copper
H. 22.5; W. 24.2; D. 29.1 cm
(H. 8¾; W. 9½; D. 11½ in.)
⊻ 2003
DDA

[170]
Jacob de Littemont (?)
Dais of Charles VII: Two Angels Holding a Crown
c. 1425–1450
Wool and silk
H. 292; W. 285 cm
(H. 9 ft 7 in.; W. 9 ft 4¼ in.)
⩡ 2010
DDA

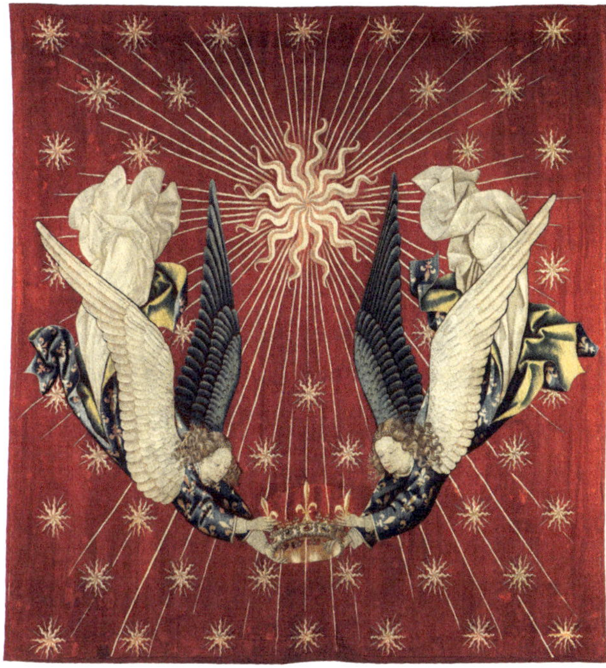

A lifelong patron of the arts, Jeanne d'Évreux, widow of Charles IV, was famed in her day for her foundations, endowments and commissions. The exceptional *Virgin and Child,* known as the *Virgin of Jeanne d'Évreux* **[167]**, in gilded silver embellished with precious stones, pearls, gold and coloured enamel, is testament to the goldsmiths' expertise. Along with the *Sceptre of Charles V* **[168]**, it was part of the Treasury of Saint-Denis. The bond between mother and child is conveyed with immense delicacy and tenderness. A symbol of purity, the fleur-de-lys in the young woman's right hand formed a reliquary that would have enclosed relics of the Virgin. On her tomb effigy, made between 1371 and 1372 and conserved in the Louvre, Jeanne holds a bag containing her entrails. The queen appears softly featured, her expression peaceful: a tribute to the talent of the sculptor, Jean de Liège, who was active at the French and English courts.

EASTERN SPLENDOURS The craftsmen of Mamluk Egypt were held in great esteem by their contemporaries, thanks to their mastery of ceramics, metalwork and glass: techniques which

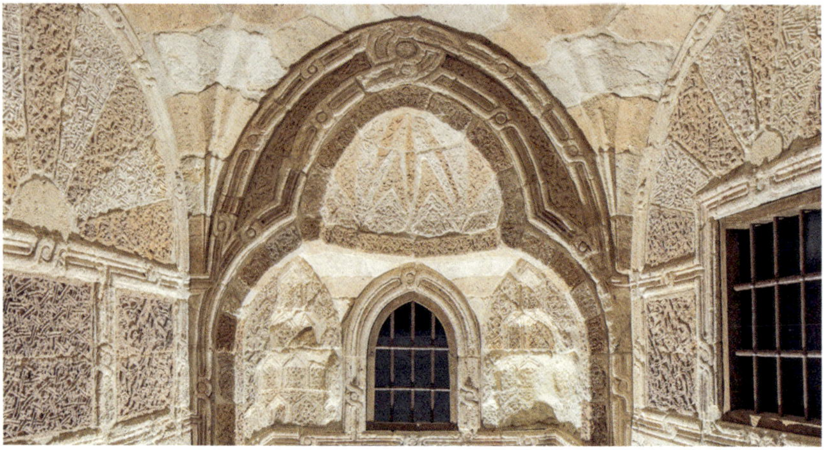

[171]
Porch from a Mamluk House in Cairo
Cairo, Egypt
c. 1400–1500
Limestone, iron and wood
H. 250; W. 300; D. 250 cm
(H. 8 ft 2½ in.; W. 9 ft 10 in.; D. 8 ft 2½ in.)
⊻ 2012 (deposit from the Union Centrale des Arts Décoratifs, Paris)
DIA

use fire to transform matter. Under the Mamluk Dynasty, founded by the heirs of freed slave soldiers, the country thrived economically and artistically. Sumptuous objects were presented as diplomatic gifts that were highly prized by their recipients, for example the basin given to Hugh IV, King of Cypress **[173]**. Signed by its maker, the coppersmith Muhammad ibn al-Zayn, the *Baptistery of Saint Louis* **[172]**, in hammered brass inlaid with gold and silver, is a dazzling example of Western courts' taste for Eastern artefacts. Its wealth of decoration, both inside and outside, includes multiple scenes ranging from men on horseback to animals and foliage. Despite its name, the basin was not brought back from the crusades by Louis IX, who was canonised as Saint Louis; it was made long after the French king's death. It did, however, serve as a baptismal font for several royal children, including the future Louis XIII. Also from the Mamluk period, the porch from a house in Cairo **[171]** has been rebuilt inside the Department of Islamic Art, one of several architectural reconstructions inside the museum. The variety of patterns chiselled into the stone

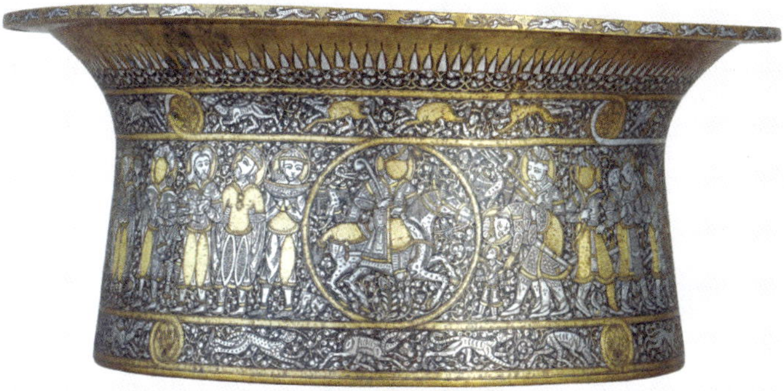

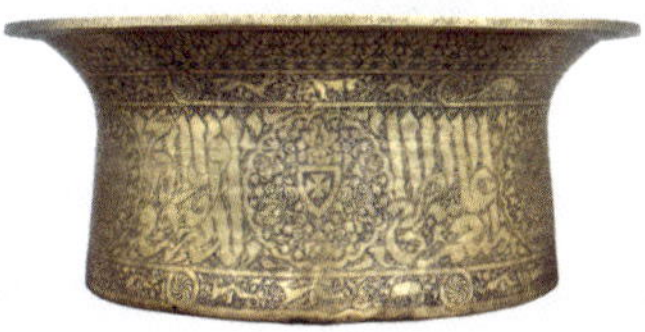

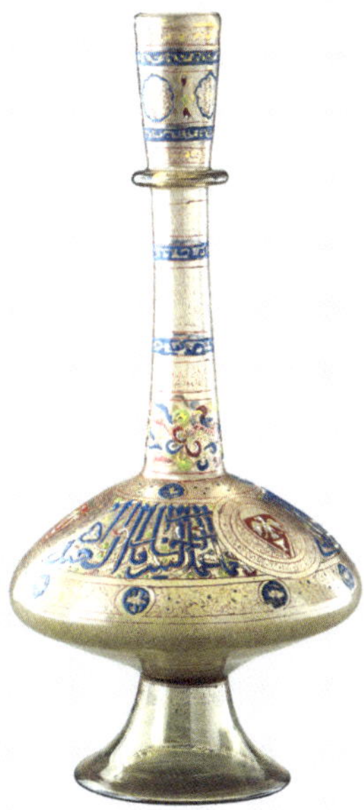

[172]
Muhammad ibn al-Zayn
***Basin*, known as**
Baptistery of Saint Louis
Egypt (?), Syria (?)
c. 1325–1340
Brass, silver and gold
H. 23.2; Diam. 50.5 cm
(H. 9¼; Diam. 20 in.)
⊻ 1793
DIA

[173]
Basin inscribed with the name of Hugh IV of Cyprus and with the coat of arms of the Ibelin and of Jerusalem
Egypt (?), Syria (?)
c. 1324–1359
Copper, silver and black organic matter
H. 25.5; Diam. 57.5 cm
(H. 10; Diam. 22¾ in.)
⊻ 1951 (gift of the heirs of Henri René d'Allemagne)
DIA

[174]
Bottle with the coat of arms of Tankiz, viceroy of Syria
Egypt (?), Syria (?)
c. 1350
Enamelled and gilded glass
H. 51; Diam. 24.4 cm
(H. 20; Diam. 9½ in.)
⊻ 1893
DIA

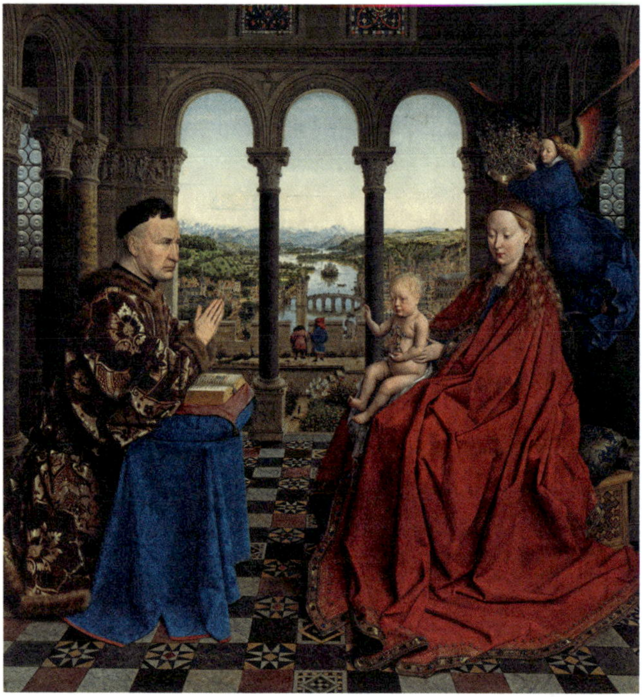

[175]
Jan van Eyck
c. 1390/1395–1441
Madonna of Chancellor Rolin
c. 1400–1450
Oil on wood
H. 66; W. 62 cm
(H. 26; W. 24½ in.)
⊻ 1800
DP

are typical of the vast lexicon of Cairo's artists, informed by geometric and organic shapes.

A NEW HUMANISM The visual innovations introduced by Cimabue in the late thirteenth century – the quest for a greater resemblance to reality and the rendering of bodies in three dimensions – significantly influenced later artists. In his most famous work, *Lives of the Most Excellent Painters, Sculptors and Architects*, published in the mid-sixteenth century, Giorgio Vasari tells how Cimabue, while walking through the countryside, spotted Giotto, a shepherd boy, and was struck by his talent for sketching. Giotto's painting for the Church of San Francesco in Pisa, *Saint Francis Receiving the Stigmata* **[176]**, is unique for the artist's decision to portray an event as it takes place: the exact moment the stigmata appear on the saint's palms, feet and side, in memory of Christ's suffering and death, known as the Passion. The rays reaching down towards the saint's body form lines of force in a composition that reveals the effort Giotto made to place his subjects in a realistic landscape.

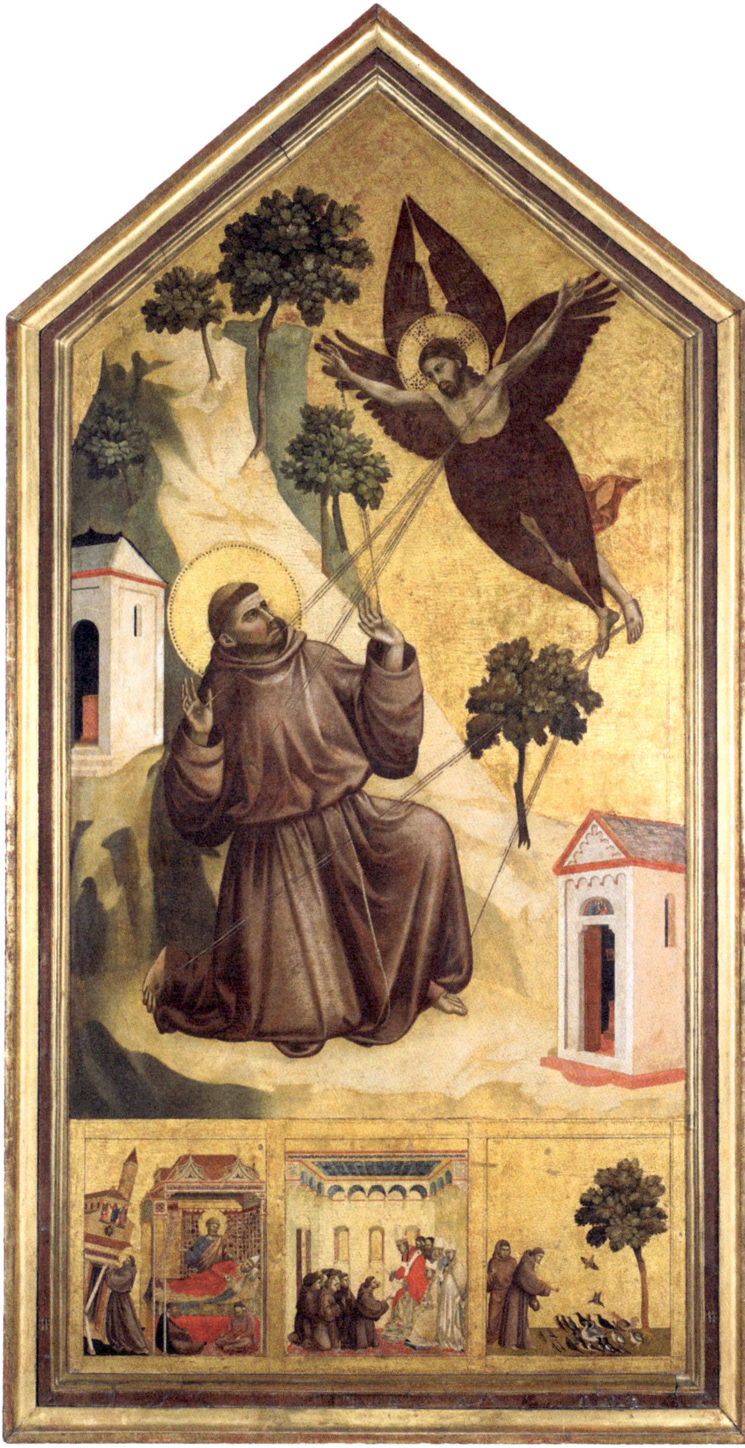

[176] Giotto di Bondone. 1267–1337. ***Saint Francis Receiving the Stigmata***. c. 1300–1325
Tempera and gold ground on poplar wood. H. 313; W. 163 cm (H. 10 ft 3¼ in.; W. 5 ft 4¼ in.). ⊻ 1813. DP

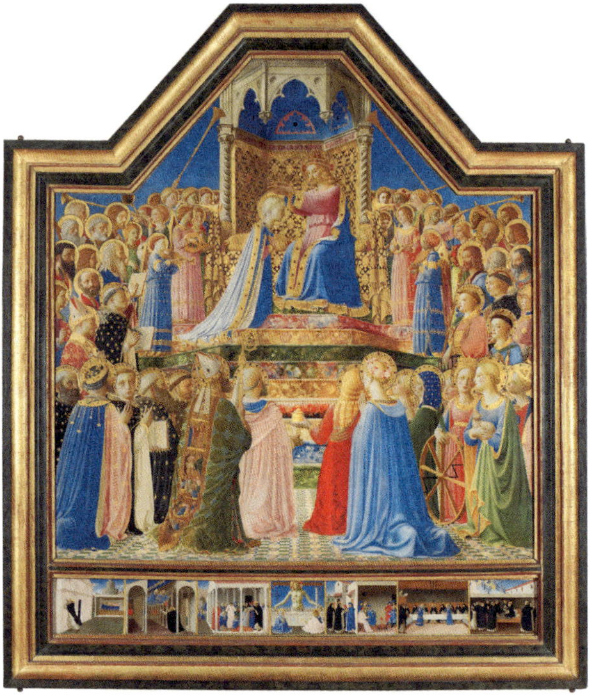

[177]
Guido di Pietro, known as
Fra Giovanni da Fiesole,
known as Fra Angelico
c. 1395/1400–1455
Coronation of the Virgin
c. 1425–1450
Tempera and gold
on poplar wood
H. 209; W. 206 cm
(H. 6 ft 10¼ in.; W. 6 ft 9 in.)
⊻ 1812
DP

Jan van Eyck, painter at the court of Philip the Good, Duke of Burgundy, in Bruges, was another innovator, both in technique – such as the use of oil, which enabled him to make alterations as he worked – and aesthetically. The *Madonna of Chancellor Rolin* **[175]** shows the commissioner of the painting, the duke's Autun-born chancellor, kneeling before the seated Virgin who holds the Infant Jesus. The chancellor, who is depicted level with the Virgin, is richly dressed in fur-lined brocade. Rather than being idealised, his facial features are reproduced with a certain degree of realism. The loggia where the scene unfolds looks onto a vast landscape. The viewer's eye is drawn into the distance, beyond the sumptuous buildings of a city on the banks of a river. Van Eyck portrays the scene with the infinite detail of a medieval miniature, while at the same time paying close attention to the successive planes and the light sources. This artist would have a major influence on Flemish painting of the fifteenth and sixteenth centuries, and on late fifteenth-century Italian painting.

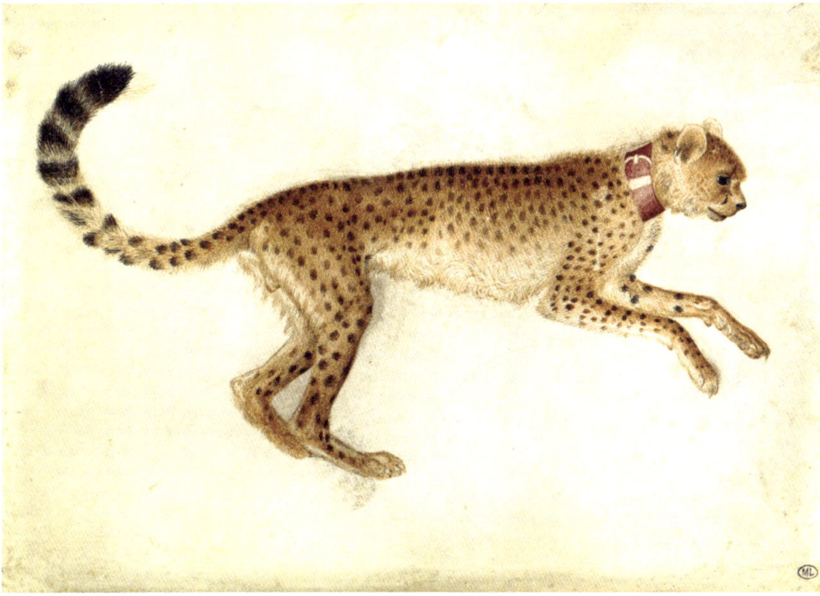

[178] Antonio di Puccio di Giovanni de Cereto, known as Pisanello. Before 1395–1455. ***Leaping Cheetah***
Watercolour on parchment. H. 16; W. 23 cm (H. 6¼; W. 9 in.). ⊻ 1856. DPD

Painter, theologian and friar, Fra Angelico continues to fascinate artists and art historians alike. His work is characterised by his command of light, spareness of style, simplicity of form and a sense of overall composition. *Coronation of the Virgin* **[177]**, the main panel from an altarpiece, probably from the Dominican church in Fiesole, is astonishing for the number of figures, their positioning within the space, and the beauty of their features and silhouettes. Fra Angelico's art coincided with a humanist awakening that gave particular importance to aesthetic creation. This was reflected politically, with each of the great families at the head of the different Italian cities looking to assert their authority through patronage of the arts, such as the Medici in Florence and the Este in Padua. The painter, draughtsman and sculptor Pisanello worked for several of these courts. His art combines real – animal **[178]** or human – and imaginary figures. In his *Portrait of a Princess of the House of Este* **[179]** the artist has skilfully combined various inspirations to make the young princess's profile emerge from the background of leaves and flowers. Born in Florence, the sculptor Donatello trained under fellow Florentine Lorenzo

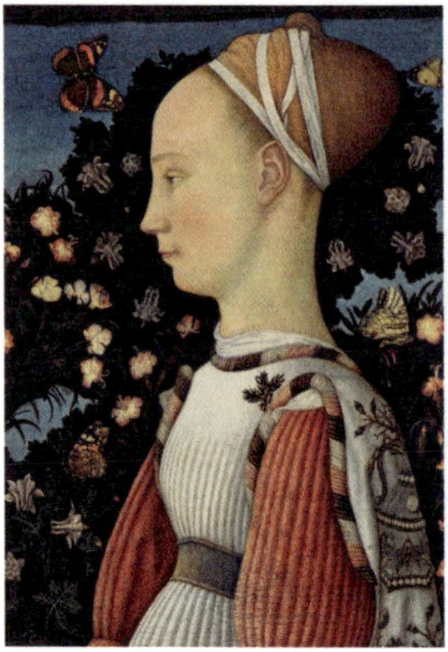

[179]
Antonio di Puccio di Giovanni
de Cereto, known as Pisanello
Before 1395–1455
Portrait of a Princess of the House of Este
c. 1425–1450
Oil on poplar wood
H. 43; W. 30 cm
(H. 17; W. 11¾ in.)
⩡ 1893
DP

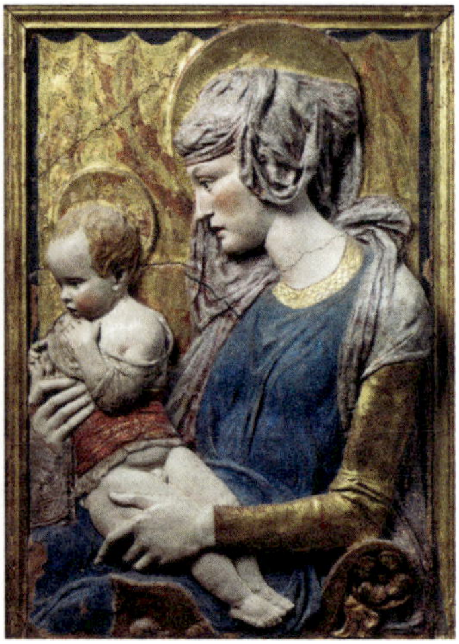

[180]
Donato di Niccolò di Betto Bardi, known
as Donatello
c. 1386–1466
Madonna and Child
Chapel of San Lorenzo, Vigliano, Italy
c. 1445–1455
Polychrome terracotta
H. 102; W. 64; D. 12 cm
(H. 3 ft 4¼ in.; W. 2 ft 1¼ in.; D. 4¾ in.)
⩡ 1881
DS

Ghiberti; he was also close to the architect Filippo Brunelleschi, designer of the dome of Florence Cathedral. Donatello's work is steeped in a new concept of perspective, and brilliantly conveys his attention to the beauty of facial features and the human body, as well as his understanding of emotions. *Madonna and Child* **[180]**, a high relief in painted terracotta, demonstrates his ability to portray attitudes and expressions with veracity.

[181]
Arras, France
Offering of a Heart
c. 1400–1410
Wool
H. 242/245.5 (left/right); W. 211.5/208.5 cm (top/bottom)
(H. 7 ft 11¼ in./8 ft ¾ in. [left/right]; W. 6 ft 11¼ in./6 ft 10 in. [top/bottom])
⩡ 1883 (bequest of Jean-Charles Davillier)
DDA

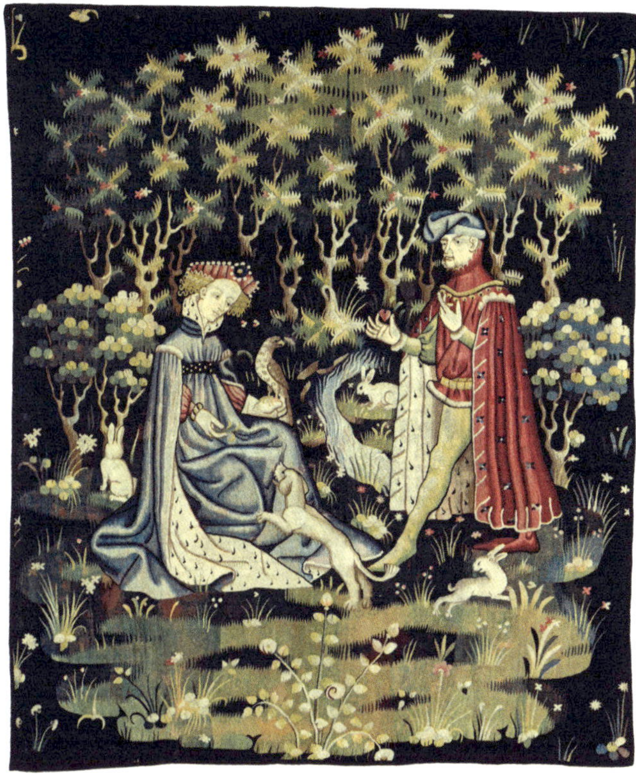

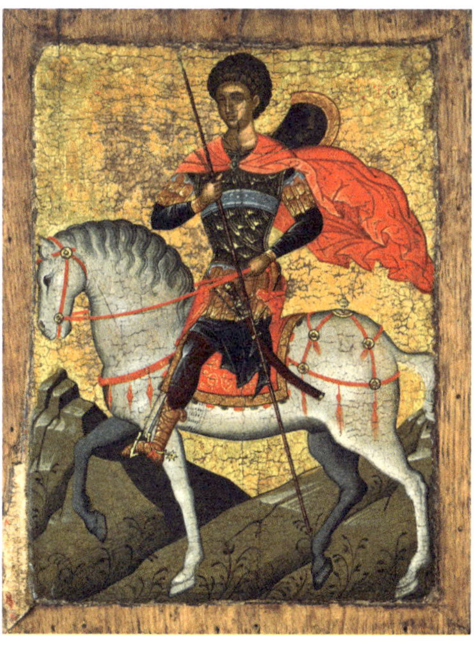

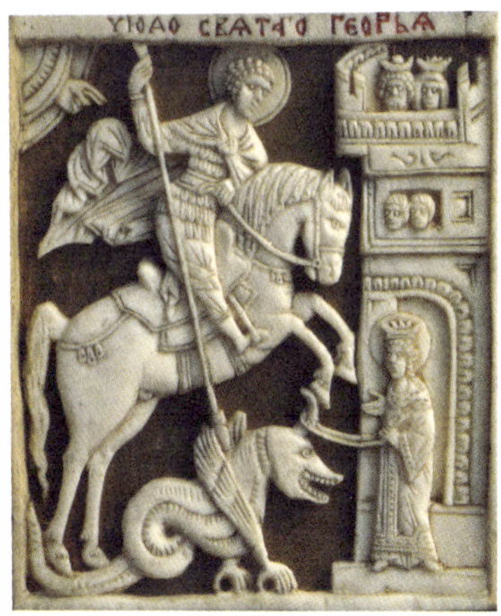

[182]
Cretan School, Greece
Saint George on Horseback
c. 1400–1450
Gold ground on wood
H. 28; W. 21 cm
(H. 11; W. 8¼ in.)
⩡ 1862 (former collection of Giampetro Campana)
DBECA

[183]
Russia
Bas-relief: Saint George and the Dragon
c. 1400–1600
Elephant ivory and wood
H. 5.5; W. 4.6 cm
(H. 2⅛; W. 1¾ in.)
⩡ 1856 (gift of Alexandre-Charles Sauvageot)
DBECA

From the very first writing systems, ways to record thoughts and ideas have been central to much human endeavour. The diffusion of knowledge is closely tied to the development of the civilisations found in the Louvre, where narratives, both historical and imaginary, have an important place. In the mid-fifteenth century Johannes Gutenberg invented the first mechanical printing press, in present-day Germany. It was a type of screw press combined with movable type. A different process had already been developed in China, but had not reached Europe.

Thanks to an exceptional gift by Edmond de Rothschild, the Louvre holds a collection of prints and printed works of remarkable quality. The book shown here **[184]** is illustrated with woodcuts. It recounts the story of the Apocalypse, as told in the Book of Revelation, the last book of the Bible. Even though printing allowed texts to be circulated at a much greater rate than the hand copying of manuscripts by monks, it was still a time-consuming process. Works printed before 1500 – highly prized by collectors – are referred to as incunables, from the title of a 1688 catalogue, *Incunabula typographiæ*, literally the "cradle of typography" (*incunabula* means "swaddling clothes" or "cradle"), hence the metaphorical meaning, "the infancy of typography".

During this same period the art of the miniature in Persia – present-day Iran – reached its highest degree of perfection. This copy of *Shahnameh* – the *Book of Kings*, an eleventh-century epic poem – is illuminated with finely executed ink drawings that have been coloured and heightened with gold. Shown here, Rustam finds Kay Qubad and takes him to be crowned **[187]**.

For almost one hundred years, the kingdoms of France and England had waged an exhausting and seemingly endless war fuelled by dynastic disputes on both sides, and which evolved alongside the succession of alliances formed with other European powers. Despite his almost excessive prudence, the conflict was brought to an end early in the reign of Charles VII. The portrait of the French king by Jean Fouquet **[188]** – an illuminator of immense talent **[197]** who had travelled in Italy – is one of the most remarkable of its day, for its composition and life-size dimensions, as well as for the subject's attitude and three-quarter pose. The inscription "le très victorieux

[184]
Master from the Old Netherlands
15th century
The Apocalypse: Adoration of the Beast. The Beast Wages War on the Saints
c. 1466–1470
Woodcut heightened with colour
H. 26.5; W. 20.5 cm
(H. 10½; W. 8 in.)
⩡ 1935 (gift of Edmond de Rothschild)
PDG

[185]
Manises, Spain
Albarello: Deer and Tree
c. 1440–1450
Lustreware
H. 28.2; Diam. 13.3 cm
(H. 11; Diam. 5¼ in.)
⩡ Bequest of Marie-Françoise Côte, in memory of her husband
DDA

[186]
Agostino di Duccio
1418–1481
Madonna of Auvillers
c. 1464–1469
Marble
H. 81.8; W. 76.6; D. 14.7 cm
(H. 32¼; W. 30¼; D. 5¾ in.)
⩡ 1903
DS

[187]
Fars (?), Shiraz (?), Iran
***Rustam Finds Kay Qubad* (page from the *Book of Kings*)**
c. 1440
Ink, colours and gold on paper
H. 32; W. 23.2 cm
(H. 12½; W. 9¼ in.)
⩡ 1934 (gift of the Société des Amis du Louvre)
DIA

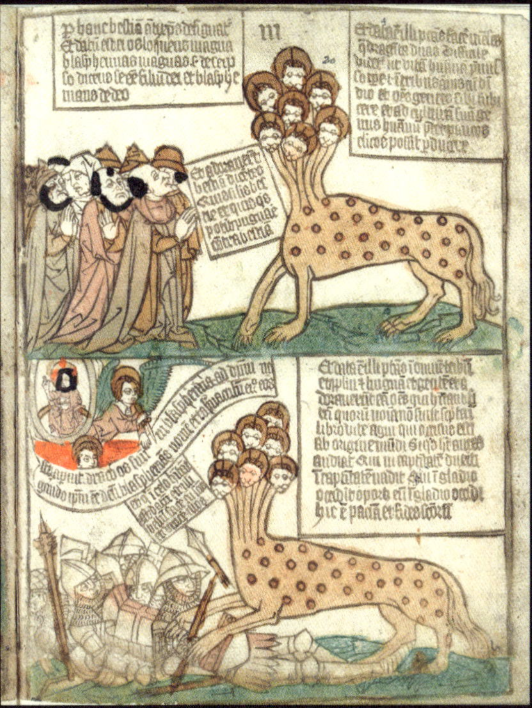

184

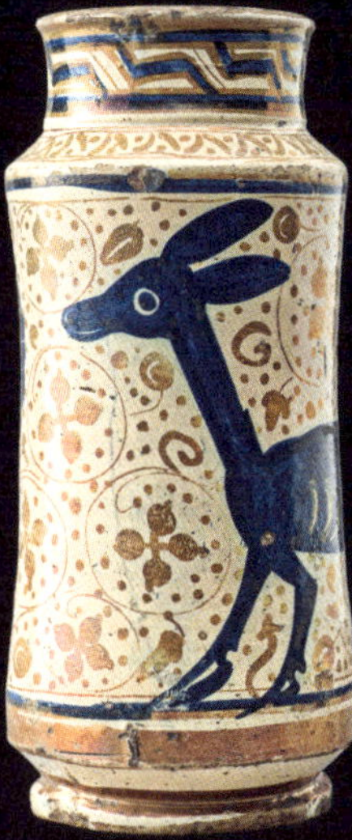

185

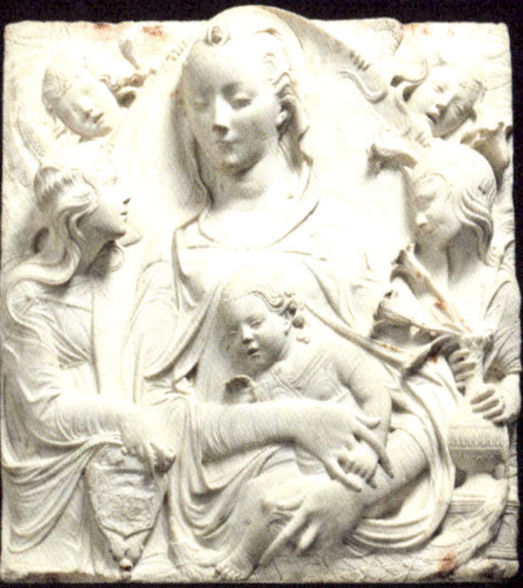

186

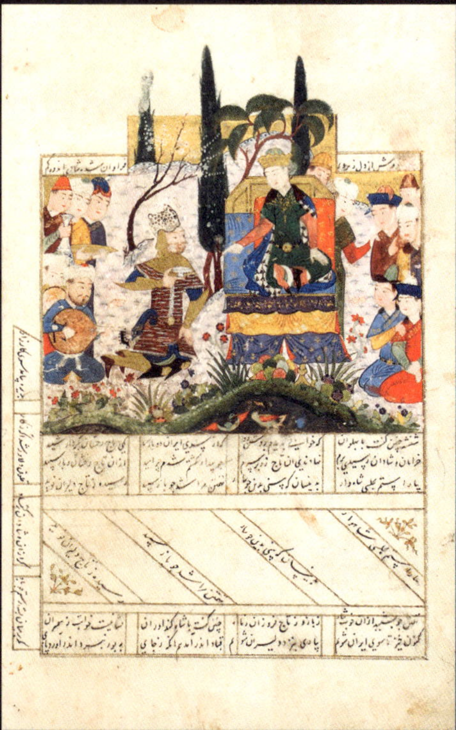

187

roi de France" (the most victorious king of France) alludes to the Hundred Years' War and may have been added at a later date. The painting, which is important to French history and the history of art, was acquired by the Louvre in 1838. When Fouquet depicted himself on an enamelled copper medallion, he created the oldest known self-portrait in French painting **[190]**.

Similarly, the *Madonna of Auvillers* **[186]**, a relief by Agostino di Duccio, marked a new stage for the arts in Italy, with its hieratic yet peaceful portrayal of the Virgin and the naturalistic modelling of the faces. The sculpture almost certainly belonged to the Medici, the great Florentine family whose coat of arms may have been carved into the marble and subsequently erased.

The Americas, at that time a continent still unknown to Europeans, were also home to brilliant civilisations such as the Aztecs in Central America, whose culture would be wiped out by the Spanish conquistadors. The Aztecs worshipped Quetzalcoatl, one of the founding deities of the Central American pantheon and generally depicted as a feathered serpent, symbolising earth – the serpent – and sky – the feathers. This sculpture of Quetzalcoatl **[191]** became part of the Louvre's collections in the mid-nineteenth century. Prior to that, it belonged to Latour Allard, a Frenchman living in Louisiana who collected Mexican artefacts. The museum acquired Allard's collection in 1849 and exhibited pieces from it in its galleries for around a decade. Some are now in the Musée du Quai Branly – Jacques Chirac.

From the same period, the carved male figure holding a bowl **[189]** is another example of accomplished artistic expression from a different corner of the globe, in this instance what is now the Philippines. Made from patinated wood, bulul such as this guarded rice plantations and the harvested crop, and are associated with prosperity. Rice-growing is one aspect of their culture that the peoples settled on these Southeast Asian islands appear to have inherited from a population who migrated there from Taiwan more than four thousand years earlier.

[188]
Jean Fouquet
c. 1420–between 1477 and 1481
Charles VII
c. 1440–1460
Paint on oak wood
H. 85.7; W. 70.6 cm
(H. 33¾; W. 27¾ in.)
⩡ 1838
DP

[189]
Statue
Ifugao culture
Philippines
15th century
Narra wood and sacrificial patina
H. 48; W. 35; D. 42 cm
(H. 19; W. 13¾; D. 16½ in.)
⩡ Gift of Anne and Jacques Kerchache
MQB–JC

[190]
Jean Fouquet
c. 1420–between 1477 and 1481
Medallion, Self-Portrait of Jean Fouquet
c. 1452–1455
Enamelled and gilded copper
Diam. 7.5 cm
(Diam. 3 in.)
⩡ 1860 (gift of Jean Isidore Hippolyte Janzé)
DDA

[191]
Zoomorphic Sculpture, Quetzalcoatl ("Feathered Serpent")
Mexico
c. 1350–1521
Volcanic rock
H. 30; W. 41; D. 49 cm
(H. 11¾; W. 16¼; D. 19¼ in.)
⩡ Former collection of the Musée de l'Homme
MQB–JC

[192]
Cretan School, Greece
Madonna and Child between Saint Cyriac and Saint George
c. 1440–1460
Tempera on spruce wood
H. 94; W. 113 cm
(H. 3 ft 1 in.; W. 3 ft 8½ in.)
⩡ 1963
DBECA

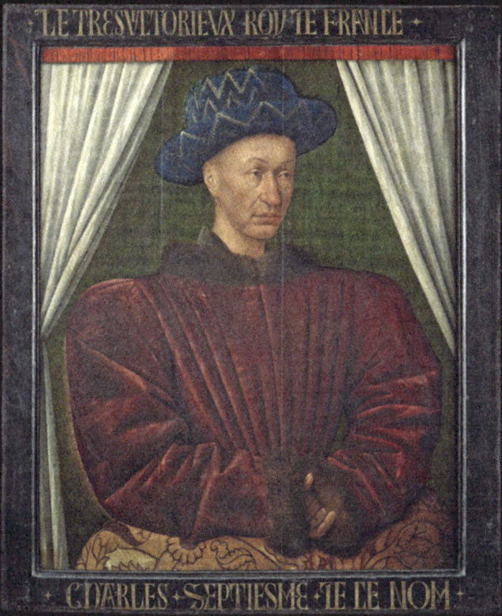

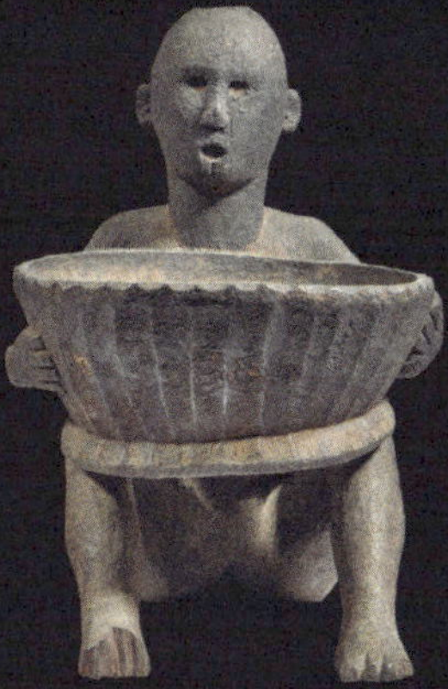

189

188

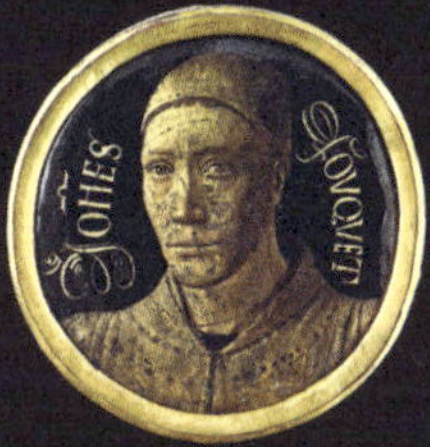

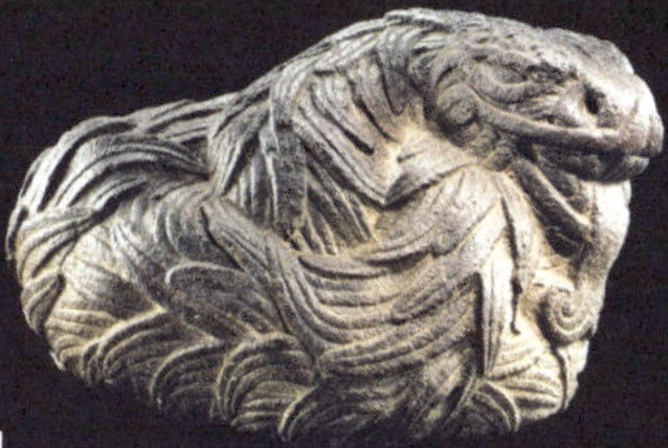

190

191

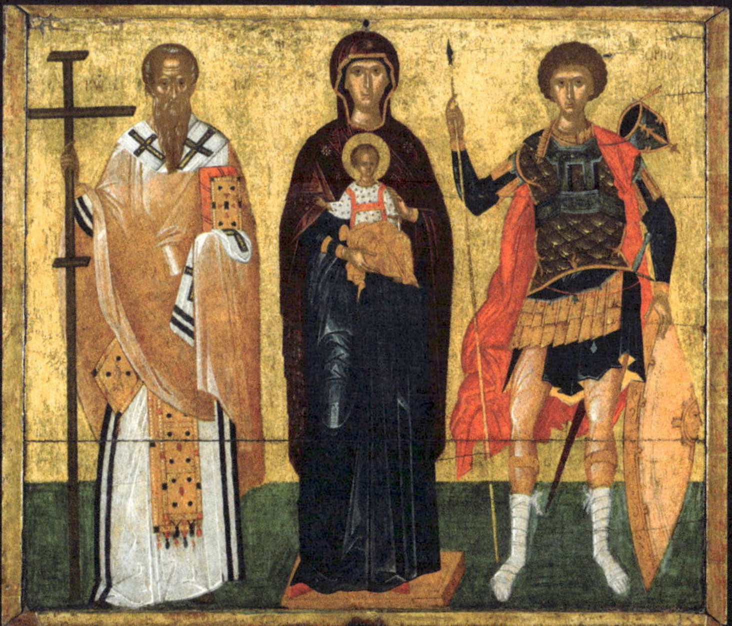

192

Renaissances

Across Europe, the fifteenth and sixteenth centuries were years of artistic renewal grounded in a changing philosophical conception of the individual, considered for themself and no longer solely for their relationship to the divine. This humanist principle distinguishes the artists of this period, and their accomplishments, in the singularity of their vision, a view substantiated by Vasari's *Lives*, published in the mid-sixteenth century. Indeed, we can consider Vasari the first art historian. His text was an important source of information on Italian artists of the fifteenth and sixteenth centuries: the quattrocento and cinquecento, respectively. The name "renaissance" reflects a view of history as an evolving trajectory. It also alludes to an awakened interest in antique art and philosophy, held up as models and reinforced by the discovery of Roman ruins, including many in Rome itself. This "rebirth" – evidence of which was perceptible on the Italian Peninsula from the early years of the fifteenth century – took different stylistic forms.

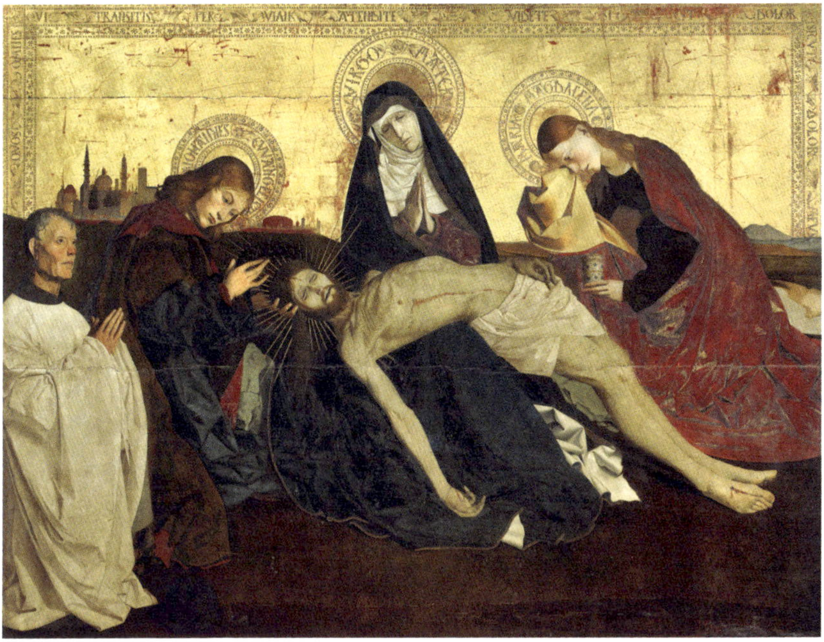

[193] Enguerrand Quarton. 1410–1466. ***Pietà of Villeneuve-lès-Avignon***. c. 1450–1475. Gold ground on walnut wood H. 163; W. 218.5 cm (H. 5 ft 4¼ in.; W. 7 ft 2 in.). ⩡ 1905 (gift of the Société des Amis du Louvre). DP

These renaissances benefitted from environments that encouraged the diffusion of new knowledge. Expeditions financed by the Spanish and Portuguese sovereigns opened up a world that stretched across the oceans. The euphoria of conquest was made more intense by the new sensation that humanity had dominion over nature (unaware of the consequences to come). Artists, and their work, travelled between countries, bringing with them different models, innovations and techniques. For example, oil, which allows greater freedom of execution and the possibility to rework details, was an innovation of the Flemish that was taken up by the Italians.

Protection of the arts became the sign of an enlightened sovereign. Monarchs commissioned works from the artists of their day, invited them to spend time at royal residences, observed and coveted the choices made by other rulers and sought to acquire works of art with which to form exceptional collections. Many were acquired in the seventeenth century for the collection of Louis XIV. This constitution of royal collections, in France in particular, was instrumental

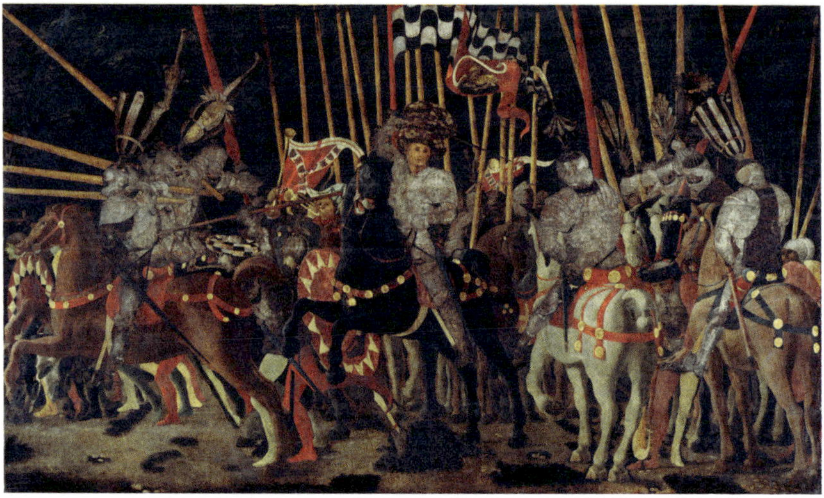

[194]
Paolo di Dono, known as Uccello
c. 1397–1475
The Counterattack of Michelotto da Cotignola at the Battle of San Romano
c. 1450–1475
Tempera (?) on wood
H. 182; W. 317 cm (H. 5 ft 11¾ in.; W. 10 ft 4¾ in.)
⩡ 1862 (former collection of Giampietro Campana)
DP

in establishing Renaissance art as a model that continues to this day.

NEW CONVENTIONS The Renaissance did not put an end to an era of darkness, unwelcoming of artistic expression. Rather, it enabled original points of view and new conventions to emerge, thanks to the economic, social, geographic and philosophical changes taking place. The majestic *Pietà of Villeneuve-lès-Avignon* **[193]** by Enguerrand Quarton, shows the Virgin cradling the body of her son after he has been taken down from the cross. Quarton, native to northern France, was active during the mid-fifteenth century in Provence. A century earlier Avignon had become a busy centre for the arts, thanks to the pope's decision to reside there. *The Battle of San Romano* **[194]** is one of three panels commemorating Florence's victory over Sienna in 1432. Its painter, Uccello, was profoundly interested in the novel technique of linear perspective, which he employs in his depiction of a battle scene in which we can almost hear the lances clashing.

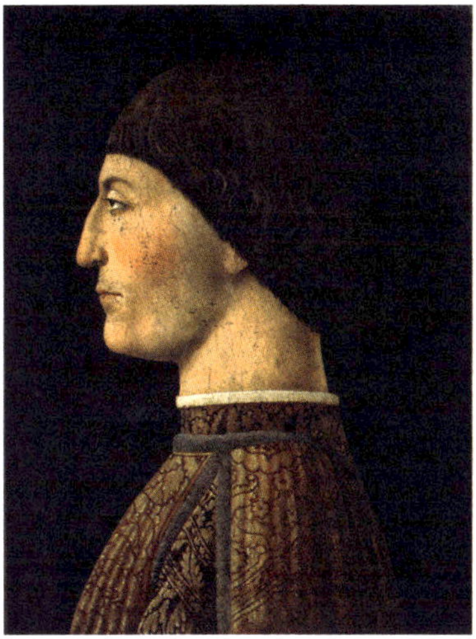

[195]
Piero della Francesca
c. 1415–1492
Portrait of Sigismondo Pandolfo Malatesta
c. 1450–1475
Oil on poplar wood
H. 44.9; W. 34 cm
(H. 17¾; W. 13½ in.)
⊻ 1978
DP

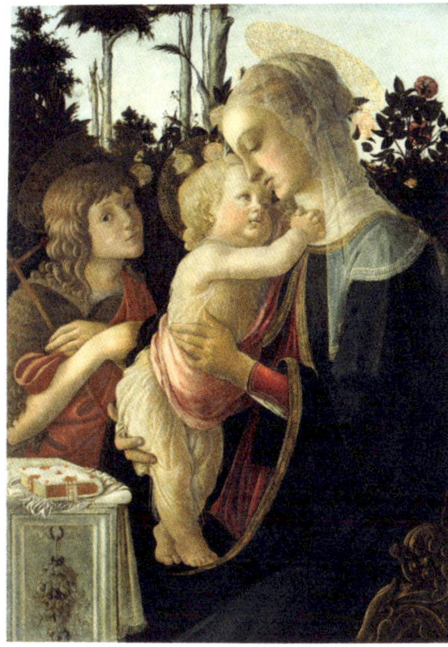

[196] Alessandro di Mariano di Sandro Filipepi, known as Sandro Botticelli. c. 1445–1510. ***Madonna and Child with the Young Saint John the Baptist***. c. 1450–1475. Tempera (?) on poplar wood. H. 90.7; W. 67 cm (H. 35¾; W. 26½ in.). ⊻ 1824 (former royal collection, collection of Louis XVIII). DP

Piero della Francesca was also recognised by his peers as one of the great theorists of pictorial perspective. His love of simple, sculptural forms, enhanced by a masterful use of light, is evident in his *Portrait of Sigismondo Pandolfo Malatesta* **[195]**. Its acquisition by the Louvre in 1978 filled a gap in the museum's collection. Another key Renaissance artist, Sandro Botticelli was among the great Florentine artists of the latter half of the fifteenth century. He produced several works for the Medici, one of the city's most powerful ruling families. Celebrated for *The Birth of Venus* (Uffizi, Florence), he also brought his talent to bear on religious paintings such as *Madonna and Child with the Young Saint John the Baptist* **[196]**. The Virgin is portrayed as a young woman of solemn beauty. Botticelli accentuates the child's attachment to his mother, while the cross carried by the infant John portends Christ's suffering and points to how fragile this happiness is: an indication of the Holy Family's human nature that is reinforced by the painting's soft lines and muted palette. Esteemed by his contemporaries, Botticelli's talent would be eclipsed by that of his successors.

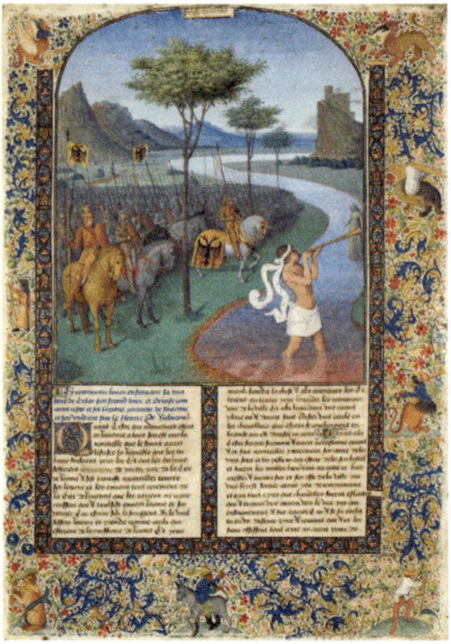

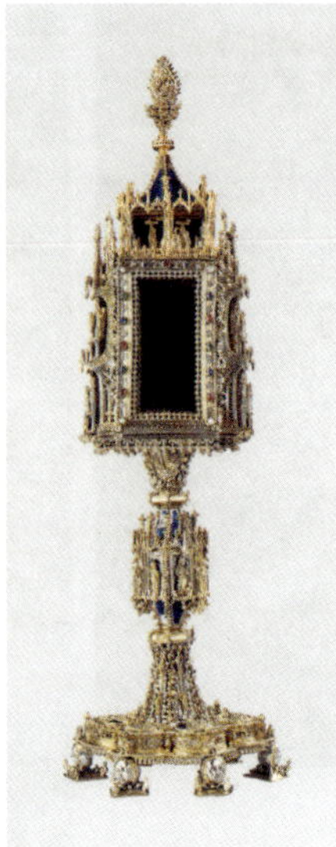

[197]
Jean Fouquet
c. 1420–between 1477 and 1481
Caesar Crossing the Rubicon
c. 1470–1475
Illuminated manuscript on parchment, gold leaf and brown ink
H. 45.1; W. 33 cm
(H. 17¾; W. 13 in.)
⩡ 1941 (bequest of Mrs Thompson)
DPD

[198]
Giovanni Lion da Colonia
Reliquary for the Hand of Saint Martha
Monastery of Saint Martha, Venice, Italy
c. 1472–1474
Enamelled and gilded silver
H. 70.9; W. 23.3; D. 19.3 cm
(H. 28; W. 9¼; D. 7½ in.)
⩡ 1901 (bequest of Adolphe de Rothschild)
DDA

Nineteenth-century artists and connoisseurs rekindled interest in his work; this panel was acquired in 1824 for the collection of Louis XVIII.

Born in Venice, Jacopo Bellini spent time in Florence, a city alive with artistic and intellectual activity. His humanist sensibility can be seen in his drawings, which are freely elaborated and, a rare practice during this period, not made in preparation for a later work. The story of the album containing the vellum for *The Funeral of the Virgin* **[199]**, situated in an imaginary urban landscape, illustrates the ties that existed between East and West, as Gentile Bellini, one of Jacopo's sons and himself a painter, gifted the drawing to Mehmed II, sultan of the Ottoman Empire. Venice, a city-state at the centre of intense maritime trade, fostered some of the strongest links of any western Mediterranean region with the shores of the eastern Mediterranean. Andrea Mantegna, who married Jacopo Bellini's daughter, played a part in the revival of Venetia's artistic life. The large *Saint Sebastian* **[200]**, which Mantegna painted while in the service of the Gonzaga family in Mantua, is a twofold

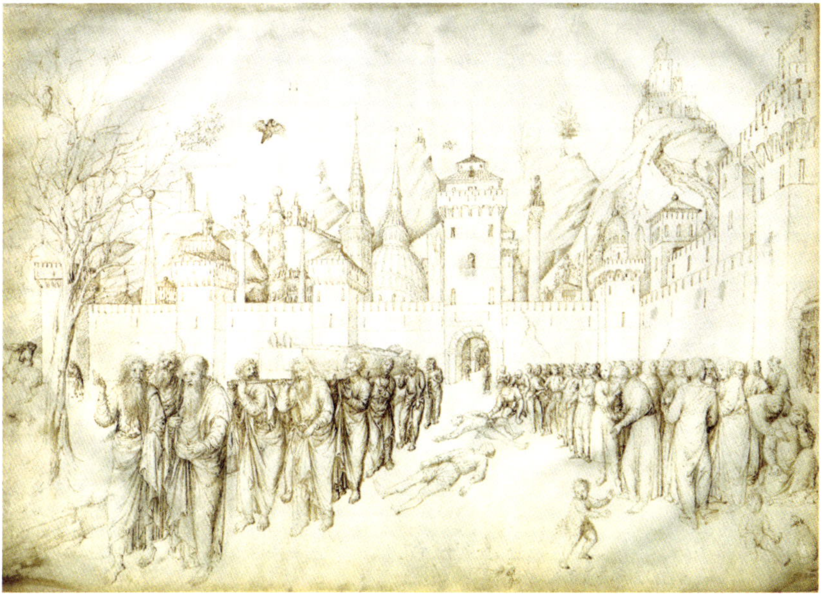

[199] Jacopo di Niccolo Bellini. c. 1390/1400–c. 1470/1471. ***The Funeral of the Virgin***
Pen and ink on parchment. H. 38; W. 26 cm (H. 15; W. 10¼ in.). ⩡ 1884. DPD

homage to ancient art. The Christian martyr, riddled with arrows, is tied to a pillar among ancient ruins, while the saint's almost naked body, bleeding yet having lost none of its youthful vigour, returns to the naturalist forms of antique sculpture.

FIGURES OF GENIUS Apprenticed to the workshop of the Florentine painter and sculptor Andrea del Verrocchio **[203]**, Leonardo da Vinci's talent came quickly to the fore. Vasari considered him a genius. *Drapery for a Seated Figure* **[204]**, a study made probably for the figure of the Virgin in *Annunciation*, painted in Florence, reveals the care the young artist took in depicting volume, light and shadow. An accomplished draughtsman, Leonardo was fascinated by facial expressions and how they transform with age **[206]**. He was also a keen observer of nature, who explored his understanding of the natural world and physical phenomena in swift lines, all the while imagining extraordinary inventions, such as his unrealised flying machines. Fewer than twenty paintings have been attributed

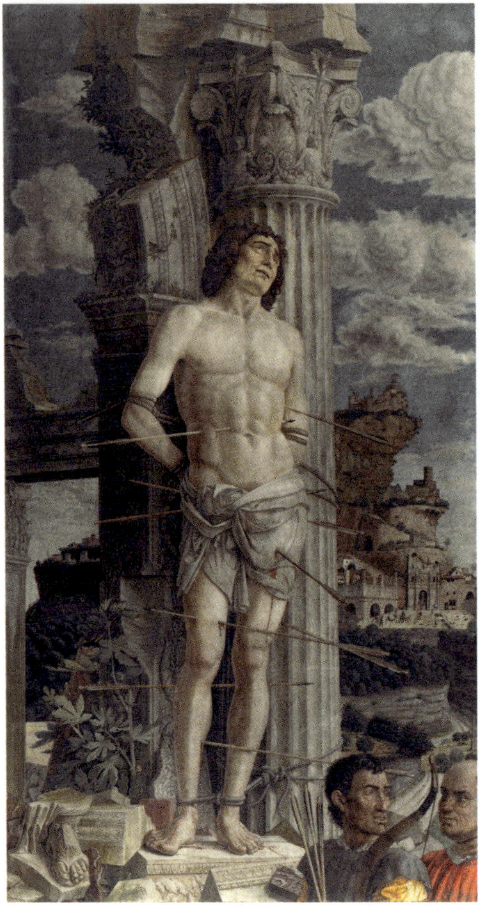

[201]
The della Robbia Workshop, Italy
Saint Sebastian
c. 1500–1515
Glazed terracotta
H. 156; W. 93.5; D. 7.5 cm
(H. 5 ft 1½ in.; W. 3 ft¾ in.; D. 3 in.)
⊻ 1852
DS

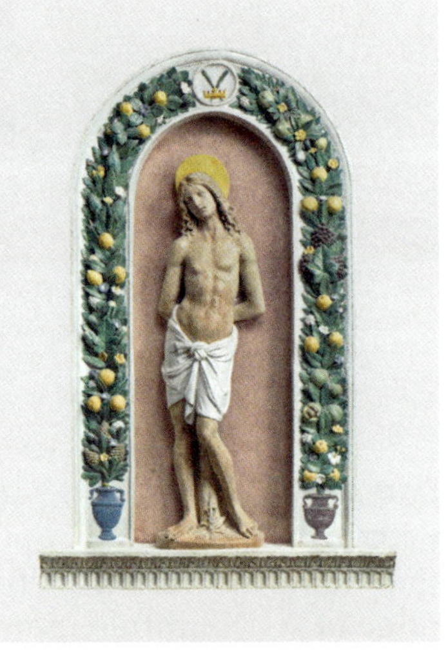

[200]
Andrea Mantegna
1431–1506
Saint Sebastian
c. 1475–1500
Tempera on canvas
H. 255; W. 140 cm
(H. 8 ft 4½ in.;
W. 4 ft 7 in.)
⊻ 1910
DP

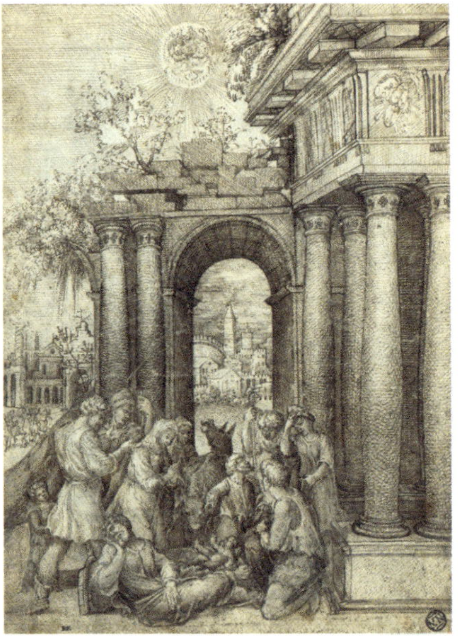

[202]
Girolamo Marchesi
c. 1480–c. 1549/1550
Adoration of the Shepherds
c. 1520
Pen and black ink, grey wash
H. 31; W. 22.6 cm
(H. 12¼; W. 9 in.)
⊻ 1793 (former royal collection)
DPD

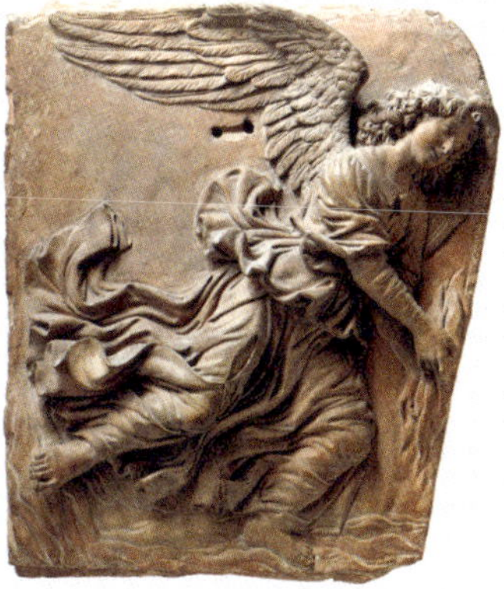

[203]
Andrea di Michele Cioni, known as
Andrea del Verrocchio
1435–1488
A Flying Angel
c. 1475
Terracotta
H. 37; W. 34; D. 4.5 cm
(H. 14½; W. 13½; D. 1¾ in.)
⩡ 1881 (bequest of Élise Dosne-Thiers)
DS

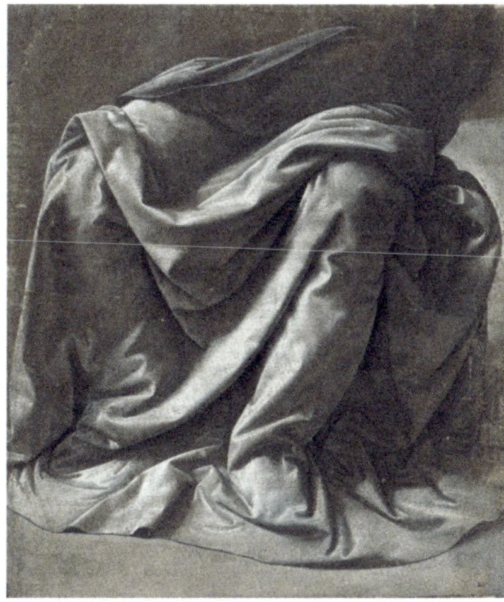

[204]
Leonardo da Vinci
1452–1519
***Drapery for a Seated Figure*, known as**
Saint-Morys Drapery
c. 1475–1482
Brush and grey tempera, heightened with white
on prepared linen canvas
H. 19.6; W. 15.3 cm (H. 7¾; W. 6 in.)
⩡ 1793
DPD

to him. In the early sixteenth century, at the invitation of Francis I, Leonardo came to the French court, bringing a number of his paintings with him. It is thanks to their acquisition that the French royal collections, and later the Louvre, became the world's largest repository of his works. *Mona Lisa* **[207]** – the life-size portrait of Lisa Gherardini, wife of the Florentine merchant Francesco del Giocondo – is famous the world over. Leonardo felt a particularly strong attachment to this work, in which he employed numerous innovations. Rather than show his sitter in profile, a tradition inherited from medals and fashionable in Italy at that time, he preferred the three-quarter pose used by Flemish artists. Furthermore, the still recent technique of oil enabled him to make multiple adjustments; in all likelihood, the *Mona Lisa* is unfinished. Also, the mysterious landscape in the background, drawn partly from his observations and partly from his imagination, carries the viewer's eye towards a distant perspective. Whether Leonardo painted *The Virgin and Child with Saint Anne* **[205]** as a commission is unknown. Of his paintings, it is the one with the most

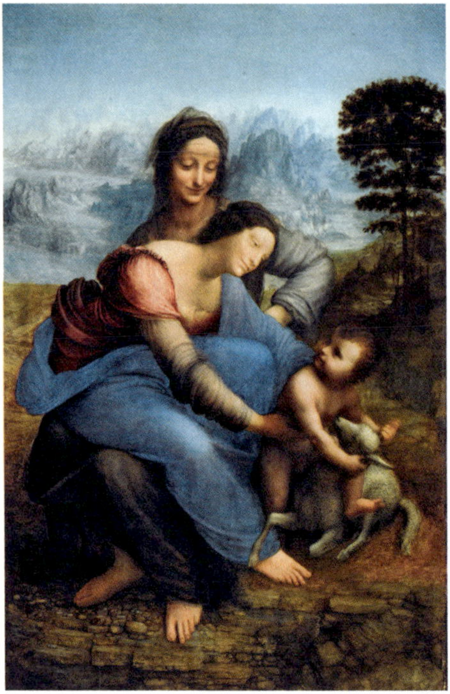

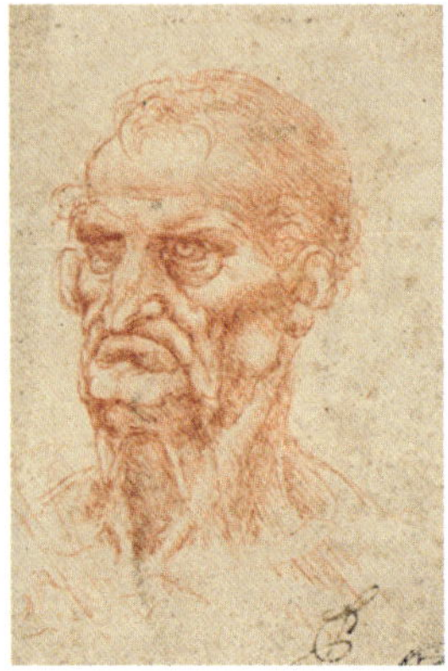

[205]
Leonardo da Vinci
1452–1519
The Virgin and Child with Saint Anne
c. 1503–1519
Oil on poplar wood
H. 168; W. 113 cm
(H. 5 ft 6¼ in.;
W. 3 ft 8½ in.)
⩡ 1793 (former royal collection, collection of Francis I)
DP

[206]
Leonardo da Vinci
1452–1519
Head of an Old Man
c. 1482–1499 or 1500–1508
Red chalk, brown ink and gold
H. 9.4; W. 6.1 cm
(H. 3¾; W. 2⅜ in.)
⩡ 1793 (former royal collection)
DPD

surviving preparatory drawings. The overall composition has been carefully planned: at its apex is the head of Saint Anne, the Virgin's mother, attentive and protective. The Virgin's twisting motion as she reaches for her son imparts movement and also emphasises the older woman's restraint. The blues and browns of their clothes echo the colours in the landscape behind them.

Born near Florence, Michelangelo Buonarroti, known as Michelangelo, is another of the great Renaissance artists. He expressed his genius through sculpture, painting, drawing **[208, 209]** and poetry; he dared to take liberties with his patrons' commissions and endowed his painting – in particular that for the ceiling of the Vatican's Sistine Chapel – and sculpture with extraordinary presence. For all these reasons, he was a model for other artists. The *Rebellious Slave* **[210]** and the *Dying Slave* **[211]** are male nudes that he created for the tomb of Pope Julius II. More than life-size, both sculptures are informed by, though not subservient to, ancient art. Michelangelo brings his own manner to the movement of their bodies – the contorted position

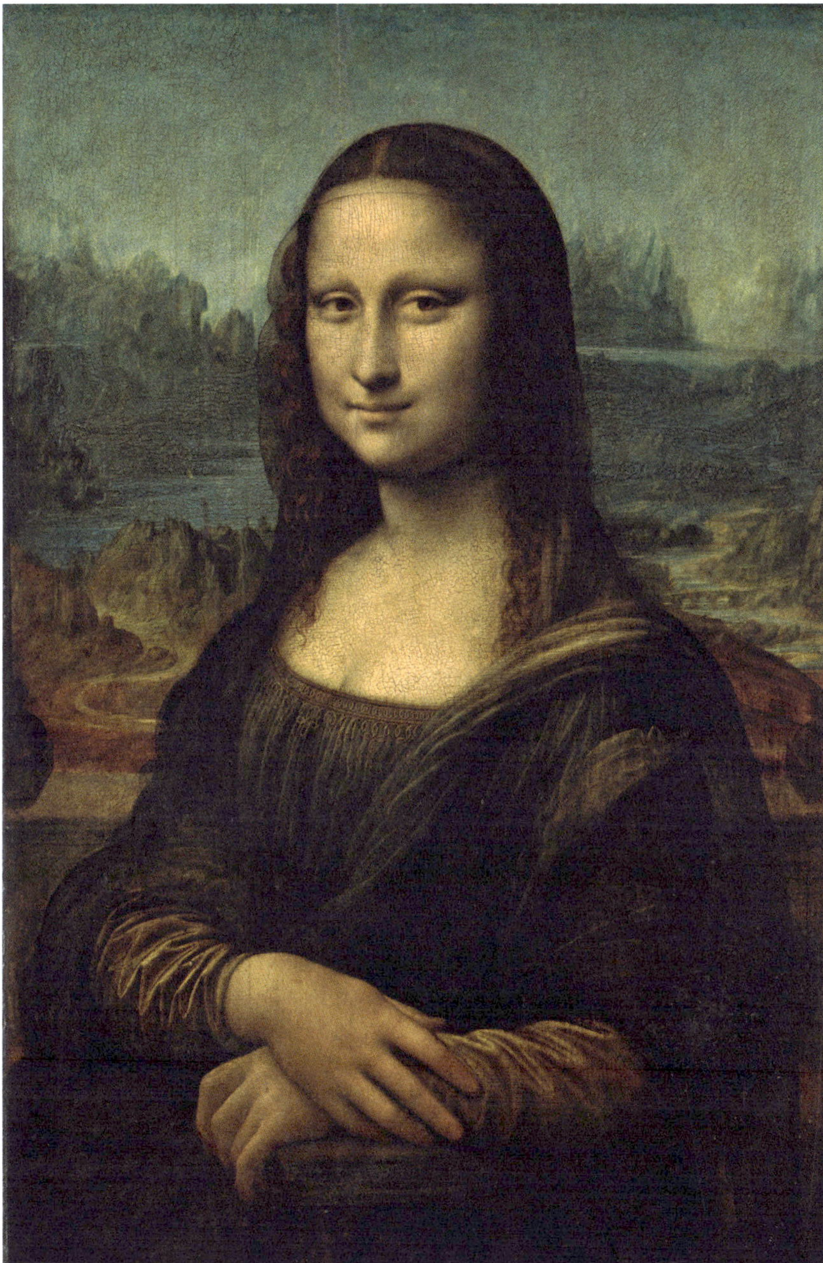

[207]
Leonardo da Vinci
1452–1519
Mona Lisa
c. 1503–1519
Oil on poplar wood
H. 79.4; W. 53.4 cm
(H. 31¼; W. 21 in.)
⊻ 1793 (former royal collection,
collection of Francis I)
DP

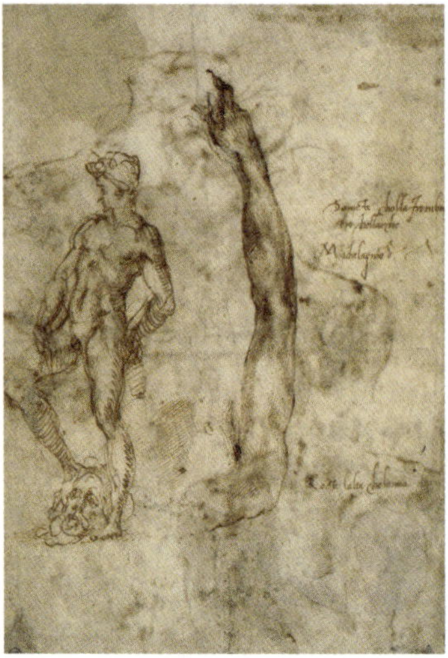

[208]
Michelangelo Buonarroti,
known as Michelangelo
1475–1564
Studies for the Figure of David
c. 1502–1503
Pen and brown ink
H. 26.4; W. 18.5 cm
(H. 10½; W. 7¼ in.)
⩡ 1850
DPD

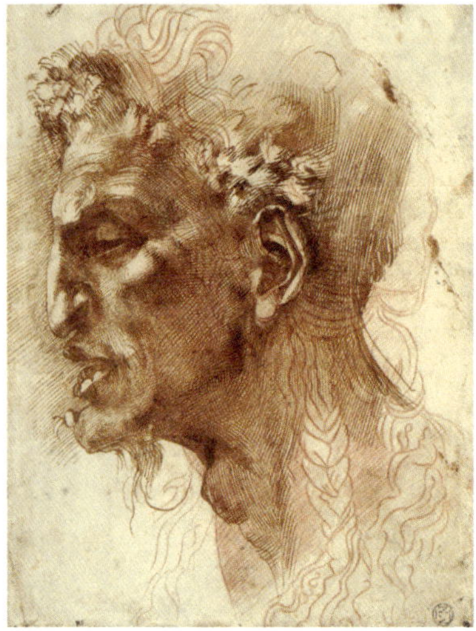

[209]
Michelangelo Buonarroti,
known as Michelangelo
1475–1564
Head of a Satyr in Profile
Pen and brown ink, red chalk
H. 28; W. 21 cm
(H. 11; W. 8¼ in.)
⩡ 1793 (former royal collection)
DPD

of the *Rebellious Slave*, the sensual abandon of the *Dying Slave* – as well as to their stance and facial expression. Each carved from a single block of marble, they extol the virtuosity of an artist who breathed life into stone. The statues remained unfinished and were gifted to the king of France. They were then given, by Henry II, to Anne de Montmorency, the Constable of France, who added them to the facade of his palace in Écouen. Confiscated during the French Revolution, they were placed in the keeping of Alexandre Lenoir before entering the Louvre. They are, as we all are, slaves to their human emotions.

Raffaello Santi, known as Raphael, also stands among the Italian Renaissance geniuses. Born in Urbino, he was instructed first by his father then by Perugino. On moving to Florence, he met Leonardo da Vinci. In a series of paintings commissioned by Pope Julius II to decorate four rooms in his apartments at the Vatican, Raphael excels in his creation of the overall architectural composition and his placement of the various protagonists. His *Annunciation* **[213]**, a drawing illustrating the moment when the archangel

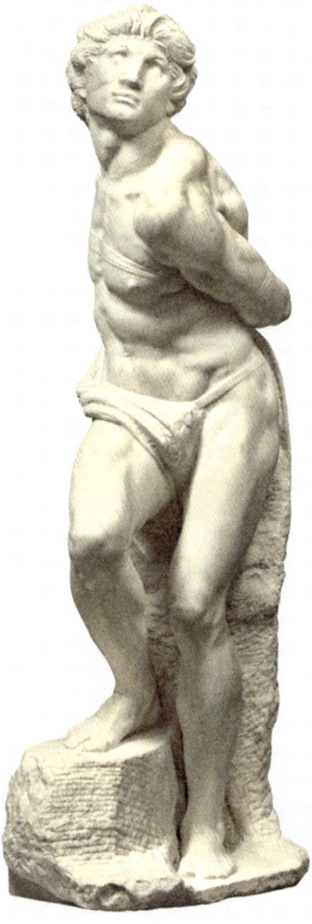

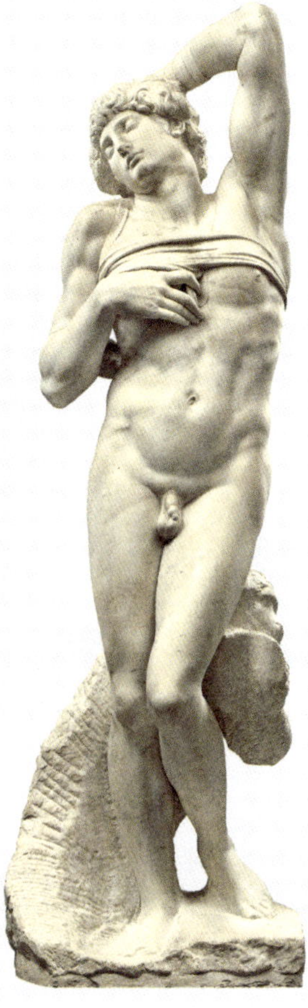

[210]
Michelangelo Buonarroti,
known as Michelangelo
1475–1564
Rebellious Slave
c. 1513–1516
Marble
H. 215; W. 49; D. 75.5 cm
(H. 7 ft ¾ in.; W. 1 ft 7¼ in.;
D. 2 ft 5¾ in.)
⊻ 1794
DS

[211]
Michelangelo Buonarroti,
known as Michelangelo
1475–1564
Dying Slave
c. 1513–1516
Marble
H. 227.7; W. 72.4; D. 53.5 cm
(H. 7 ft 5¾ in.; W. 2 ft 4½ in.;
D. 1 ft 9 in.)
⊻ 1794
DS

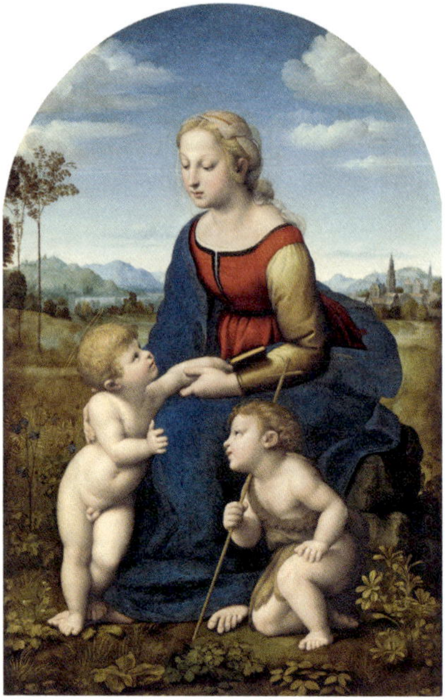

[212]
Raffaello Sanzio, known as Raphael
1483–1520
Madonna and Child with Saint John the Baptist*, known as *La Belle Jardinière
c. 1507–1508
Oil on poplar wood
H. 122; W. 80 cm
(H. 4 ft; W. 2 ft 7½ in.)
⩡ 1793 (former royal collection, collection of Francis I)
DP

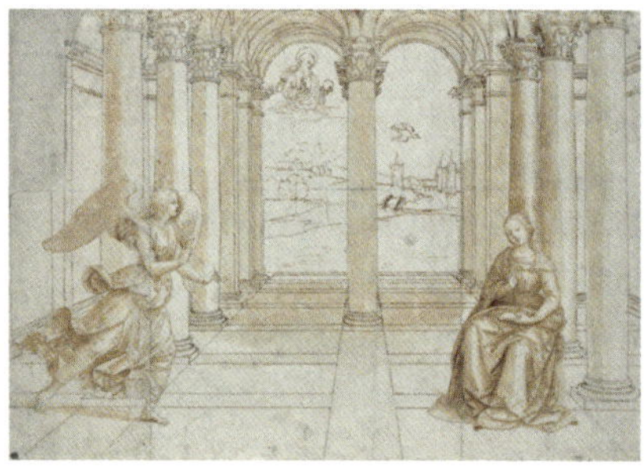

[213]
Raffaello Sanzio, known as Raphael
1483–1520
The Annunciation
c. 1502
Pen and brown ink, brown wash and black chalk
H. 28.5; W. 42.3 cm
(H. 11¼; W. 16¾ in.)
⩡ 1850
DPD

Gabriel announces to Mary that she will bear a son through a virgin birth, shows this same talent for rendering space and proportion. Raphael's clear, calm mastery earned him the admiration of his contemporaries and, lastingly, that of artists and art enthusiasts. *Madonna and Child with Saint John the Baptist*, also known as *La Belle Jardinière* **[212]**, was acquired by Francis I. Its alternative name, "the beautiful gardener", makes reference to the simple garments, those of a young peasant woman, worn by the Virgin, who watches attentively over the two children in a country landscape. The layering of the background points to Leonardo's influence. *Portrait of Baldassare Castiglione* **[214]** shows its subject in a serene, regal attitude, underlined by the choice of pose, the seating of the model, in tight focus against the plain backdrop, and the subtle harmony between the various browns of his doublet and cap. The portrait was owned by Cardinal Mazarin before passing into the collection of Louis XIV.

CROSSED INFLUENCES Born in Nuremberg, in the Holy Roman Empire, Albrecht Dürer was among the artists who brought

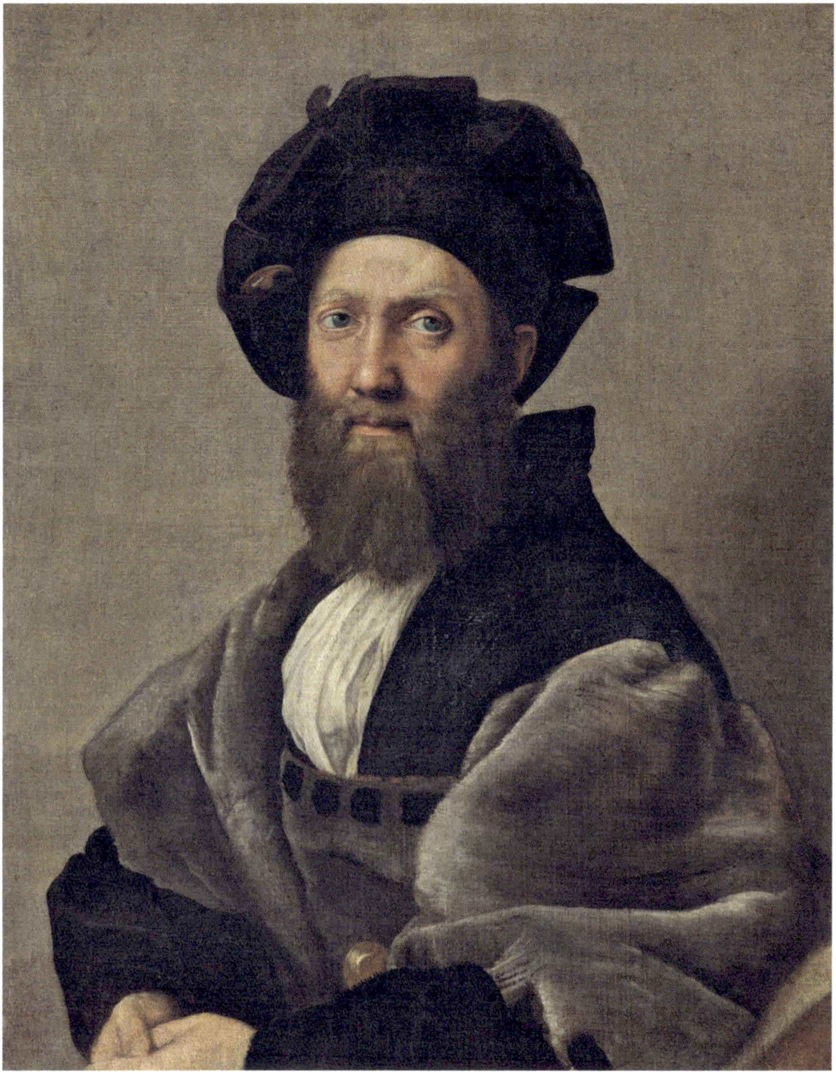

[214]
Raffaello Sanzio, known as Raphael
1483–1520
Portrait of Baldassare Castiglione
c. 1514–1515
Oil on canvas
H. 82; W. 67 cm
(H. 32¼; W. 26½ in.)
⊻ 1793 (former royal collection)
DP

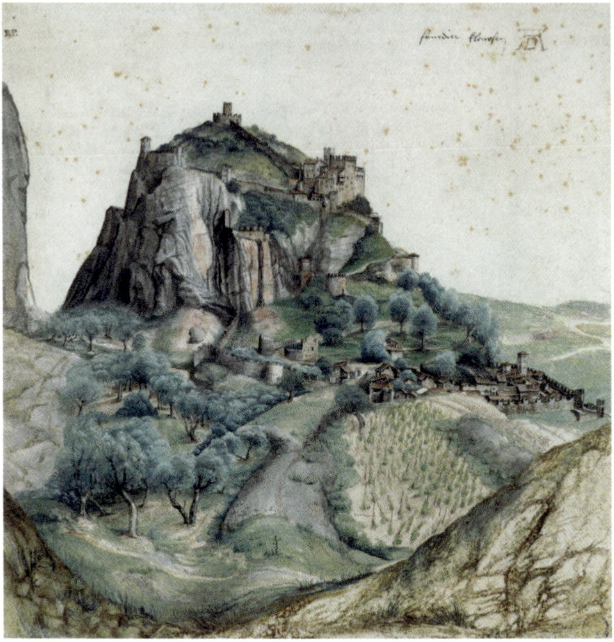

[215]
Albrecht Dürer
1471–1528
View of the Arco Valley in the Tyrol
c. 1495
Pen and brown and black ink, watercolour, heightened with brown
H. 22.3; W. 22.3 cm
(H. 8¾; W. 8¾ in.)
⩡ 1793 (former royal collection)
DPD

printmaking to life. Steeped in the culture of his time, Dürer made several trips to Italy – to Venice and Mantua in particular, where he studied works by Giovanni Bellini and Mantegna, among others. *Portrait of the Artist Holding a Thistle* **[216]** is his first painted self-portrait. He is seated in a three-quarter pose, his hair loose on either side of his face, his quizzical expression firmly drawn. The thistle he holds could be a symbol of fidelity, suggesting the painting is connected to his betrothal. *View of the Arco Valley in the Tyrol* **[215]** is one of a series of sketches that Dürer made during his first travels to Italy. Executed in pen and ink, the mountain landscape is in green and blue watercolour with brown highlights. It was purchased by German-born banker Everhard Jabach, a major seventeenth-century collector, and later acquired for the Cabinet du Roi during the reign of Louis XIV. The constitution of a royal drawings collection is indicative of growing interest in the genre; the Italian *disegno* meaning both "design" and "drawing", that is the intellectual capacity to form a work in the mind and the technical mastery to create it. Alongside Dürer,

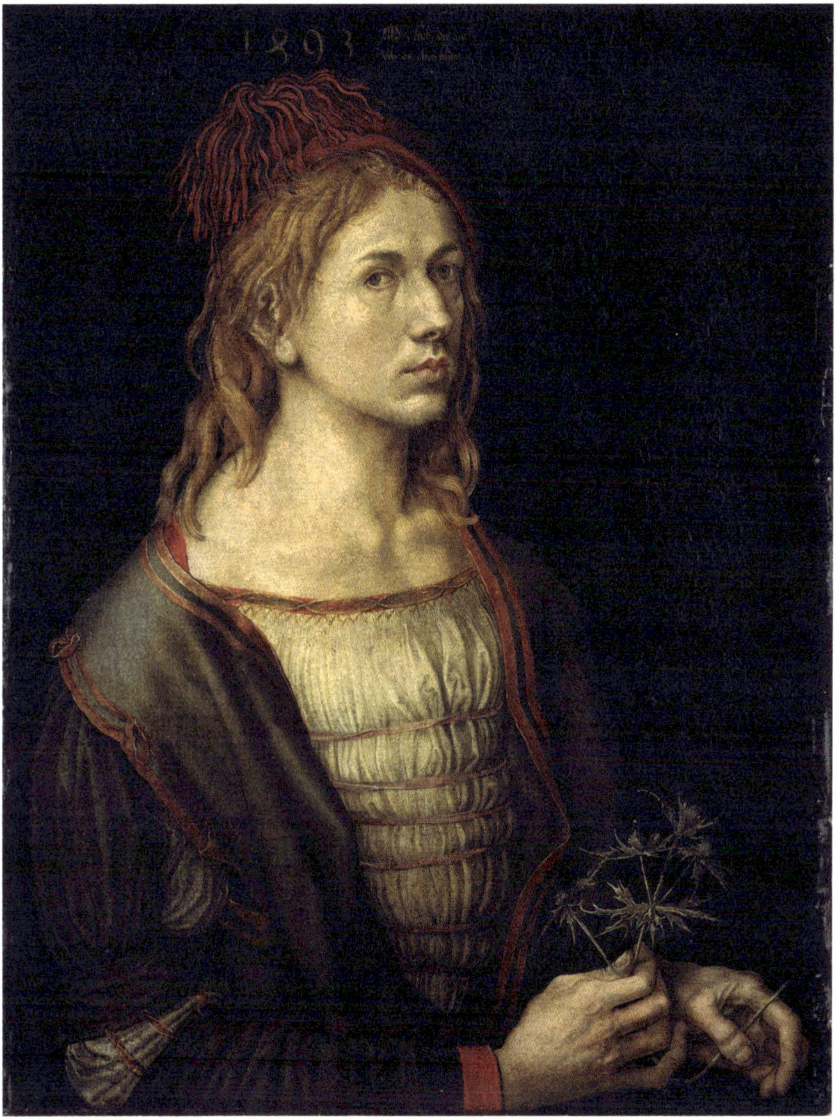

[216]
Albrecht Dürer
1471–1528
Portrait of the Artist Holding a Thistle
1493
Oil on parchment pasted on canvas
H. 56.5; W. 44.5 cm
(H. 22¼; W. 17½ in.)
⩡ 1922
DP

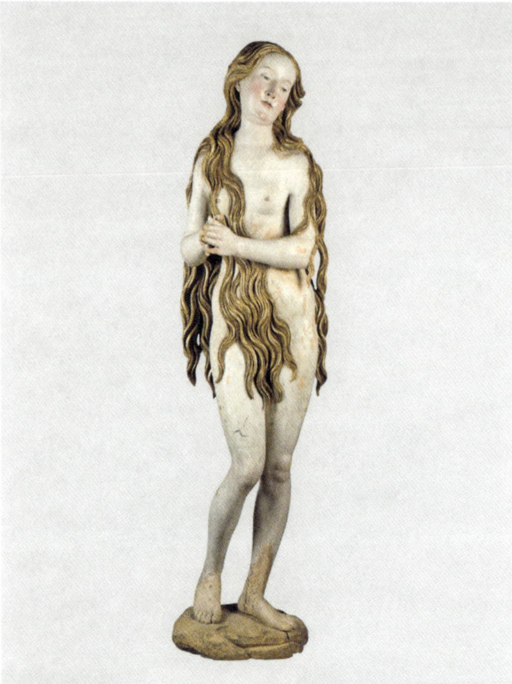

[217]
Gregor Erhart
c. 1470–1540
Saint Mary Magdalene
Mary Magdalene
Church of Saint Mary Magdalene, Augsburg, Germany
c. 1515–1520
Polychrome lime wood
H. 177; W. 44; D. 43 cm
(H. 5 ft 9¾ in.; W. 1 ft 5¼ in.; D. 1 ft 5 in.)
⊻ 1902
DS

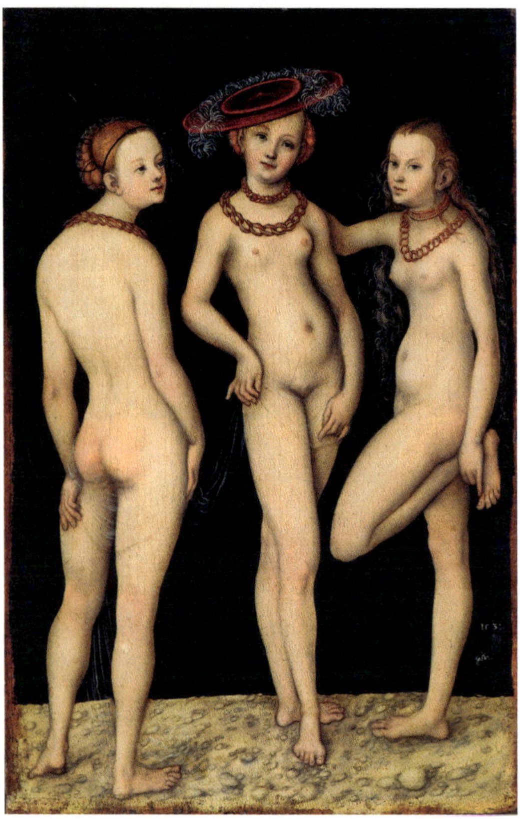

[218]
Lucas Cranach the Elder
1472–1553
The Three Graces
c. 1500–1600
Oil on beech wood
H. 36.6; W. 24.4 cm
(H. 14½; W. 9½ in.)
⊻ 2011 (gift through crowdfunding)
DP

[219]
Hans Holbein the Younger
1497–1543
Portrait of Erasmus of Rotterdam Writing
1528
Oil on lime wood
H. 43; W. 33 cm
(H. 17; W. 13 in.)
⊻ 1793 (former royal collection, collection of Louis XIV)
DP

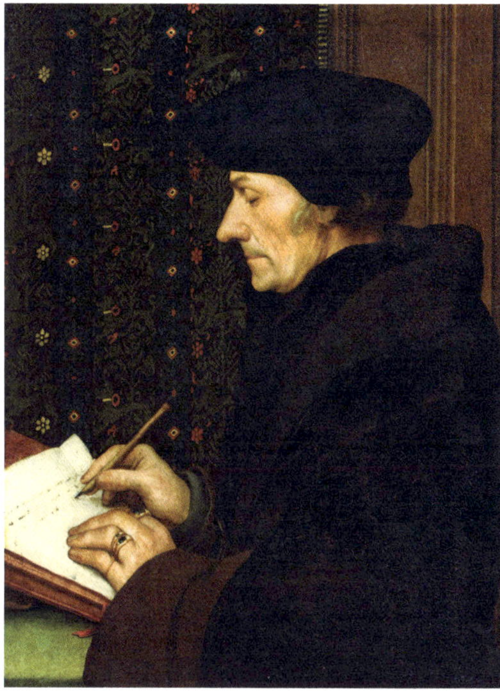

many other artists in the Louvre illustrate the artistic vitality of the Holy Roman Empire during the Renaissance. Sculptor Gregor Erhart is one. Born in Augsburg, we owe him *Saint Mary Magdalene* **[217]**, a superb religious statue in painted wood, also known as the *Beautiful German Woman*. This representation of the saint, celebrated for her beauty, echoes the story that she lived out her life in a cave in Saint-Maximin-la-Sainte-Baume in southern France, with her hair as her only clothing. *The Three Graces* **[218]** by Lucas Cranach the Elder, a Bavarian-born painter, returns to a mythological theme but with the intent of moral and Christian elevation. The Greco-Roman goddesses Aglaia, Euphrosyne and Thalia show Cranach's conception of the female body as long, slender and supple with rounded breasts. Like Erhart, Hans Holbein the Younger hailed from Augsburg. His travels took him to Basel, a centre of humanist thinking, to France and twice to London, where in 1536 he was appointed court painter to Henry VIII. In Holbein's *Portrait of Erasmus of Rotterdam Writing* **[219]**, the philosopher, who also spent time in several European countries, is shown

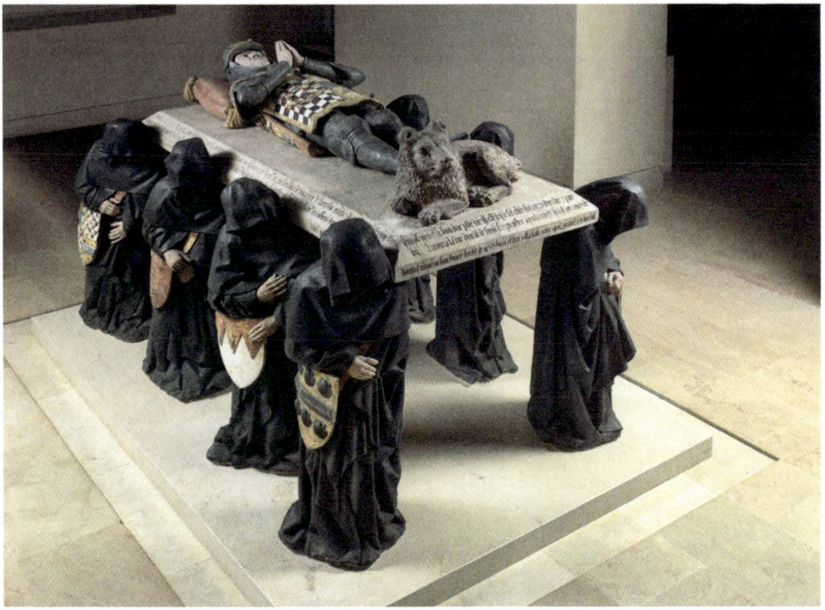

[220] Bourgogne region, France. ***Tomb of Philippe Pot, Grand Seneschal of Burgundy***. Cîteaux Abbey, France. c. 1475–1500. Polychrome limestone and gilding. H. 181; W. 260; D. 167 cm (H. 5 ft 11¼ in.; W. 8 ft 6¼ in.; D. 5 ft 5¾ in.). ⩡ 1889. DS

elegantly attired, pen poised. While the ideas expounded by the author of *In Praise of Folly* were close to those of the Protestant Reformer Martin Luther, Erasmus did not convert to the new religion. The portrait was acquired by Charles I of England then, following the king's execution, by Jabach who sold it to Louis XIV.

The magnificence of the *Tomb of Philippe Pot* **[220]** reflects the refinement of the court of the Dukes of Burgundy whose territory in the fifteenth century extended as far as Flanders. The monument, in painted stone, was made for the final resting place of Philippe Pot, grand seneschal of Burgundy, at Cîteaux Abbey. *Saint George Slaying the Dragon* **[221]**, an allegory for the triumph of good over evil, is by Michel Colombe, a French sculptor, born in Bourges, whose work marked a first renaissance. Originally an altarpiece for the Château de Gaillon, the Cardinal of Rouen's residence, it was displayed at the Musée des Monuments Français before its transfer to the Louvre.

Born in 's-Hertogenbosch in the Duchy of Brabant – at that time ruled by the Dukes of Burgundy, then

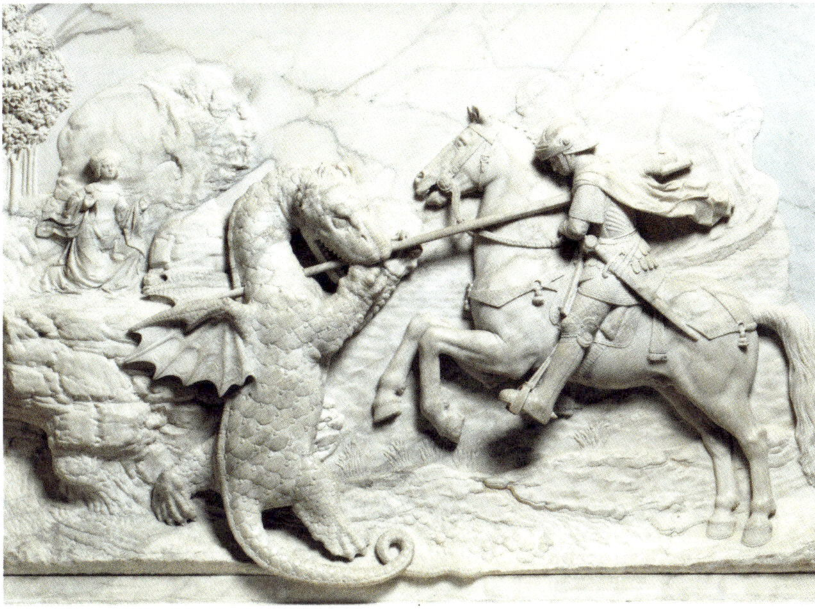

[221] Michel Colombe. c. 1430–1513. ***Saint George Slaying the Dragon*** (detail). High chapel, Château de Gaillon, France. 1508. Marble. H. 128.5; W. 182.5; D. 17 cm (H. 4 ft 2½ in.; W. 5 ft 11¾ in.; D. 6¾ in.). ⩡ 1818 (former collection of the Musée des Monuments Français). DS

by the House of Habsburg and now part of the Netherlands – Jheronimus van Aken, known as Hieronymus Bosch, imagined a world in which strange and fantastical creatures gnaw at the inner tranquillity of religious hermits. His painting is rooted in an acute awareness of the torments that sin inflicts on the human mind, while its inventiveness and minutely detailed narratives inspire today's popular culture, graphic novels and video games in particular. *Ship of Fools* **[224]**, an upper fragment from a long-dispersed triptych, portrays a group of gluttonous, drunken fools cast adrift. Also originating from the Duchy of Brabant, Antwerp to be precise, Quentin Metsys painted *The Money Changer and his Wife* **[223]**, a complex work whose subject most likely came from his observations of the daily dealings of this wealthy town. Its evocation of the vanity of wealth in light of the brevity of life instils a more spiritual dimension. Metsys skilfully incorporates interior and exterior space in the convex mirror whose surface reflects a cross window that opens onto the town, a customer silhouetted against it. Greatly admired at the time of its creation,

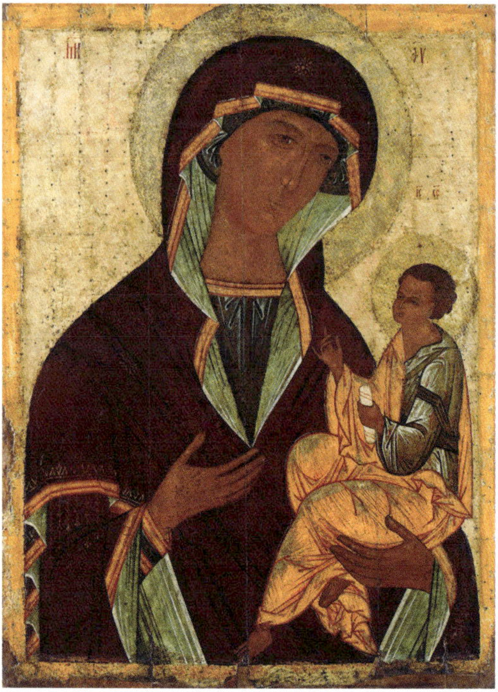

[222]
Novgorod School, Russia
Madonna and Child
c. 1500–1550
Tempera on gold ground and lime wood
H. 109; W. 83 cm
(H. 3 ft 7 in.; W. 2 ft 8¾ in.)
⩡ 1971
DBECA

and by its successive owners, the painting was acquired by the Louvre in 1806, under the First Empire. In *The Beggars* or *The Cripples* **[225]**, executed in Brussels – at one time the capital of the Duchy of Brabant – Pieter Bruegel the Elder paints a world of carnival and derision. *Hunts of Maximilian*, made to cartoons by the Brussels-born painter Bernard van Orley, is a suite of twelve tapestries, one for each month of the year and for each sign of the zodiac. They were woven in Brussels, whose workshops were renowned for their quality. The different scenes allude to the refinement of courtly life at the time of Charles V, shown here **[226]** in the foreground, in red.

VENETIAN LIGHTS *Allegory of Vice* **[227]** and its counterpart, *Allegory of Virtue*, are two gouaches on canvas painted for the studiolo of Isabella d'Este in Mantua by Correggio, the byname of Antonio Allegri. Part of Cardinal Mazarin's collection, they then passed to Louis XIV. Correggio invested his painting with a confluence of sensual grace and spiritual elevation. His work won the admiration of Tiziano Vecellio,

[223]
Quentin Metsys
c. 1465–1466/1530
The Money Changer and His Wife
1514
Oil on wood
H. 70.5; W. 67 cm
(H. 27¾; W. 26½ in.)
⩡ 1806
DP

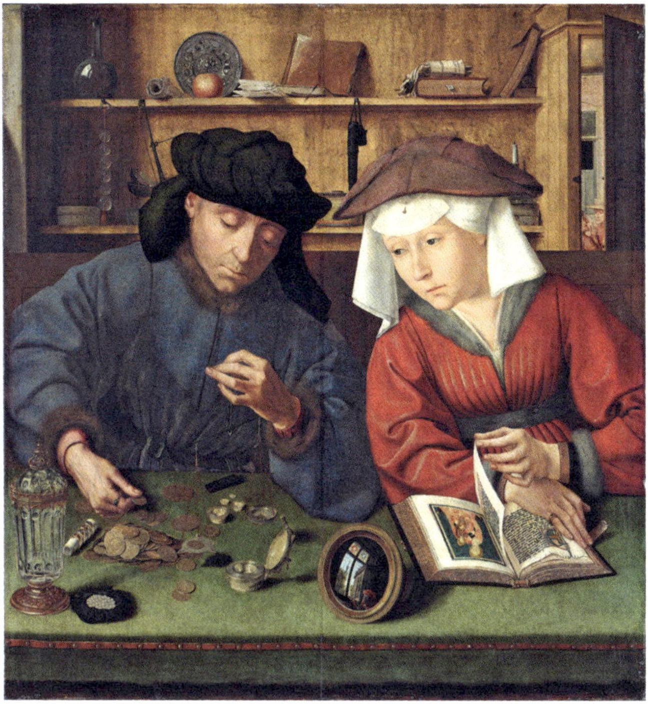

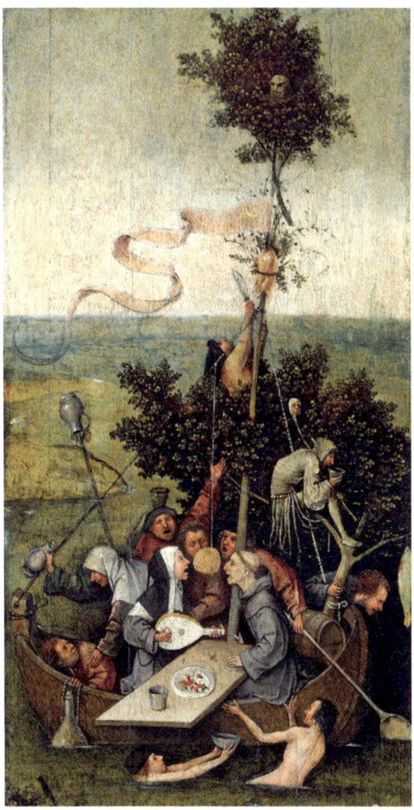

[224]
Jheronimus van Aken, known as Hieronymus Bosch
c. 1450–1516
Ship of Fools
c. 1475–1500
Oil on oak wood
H. 58; W. 33 cm
(H. 22¾; W. 13 in.)
⩡ 1918 (gift of Camille Benoît)
DP

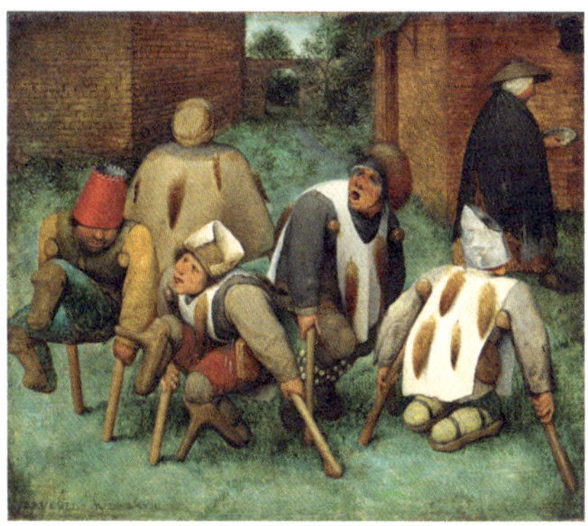

[225]
Pieter Bruegel the Elder
1525–1569
The Beggars or ***The Cripples***
1568
Oil on wood
H. 18.5; W. 21.5 cm
(H. 7¼; W. 8½ in.)
⩡ 1892 (gift of Paul Mantz)
DP

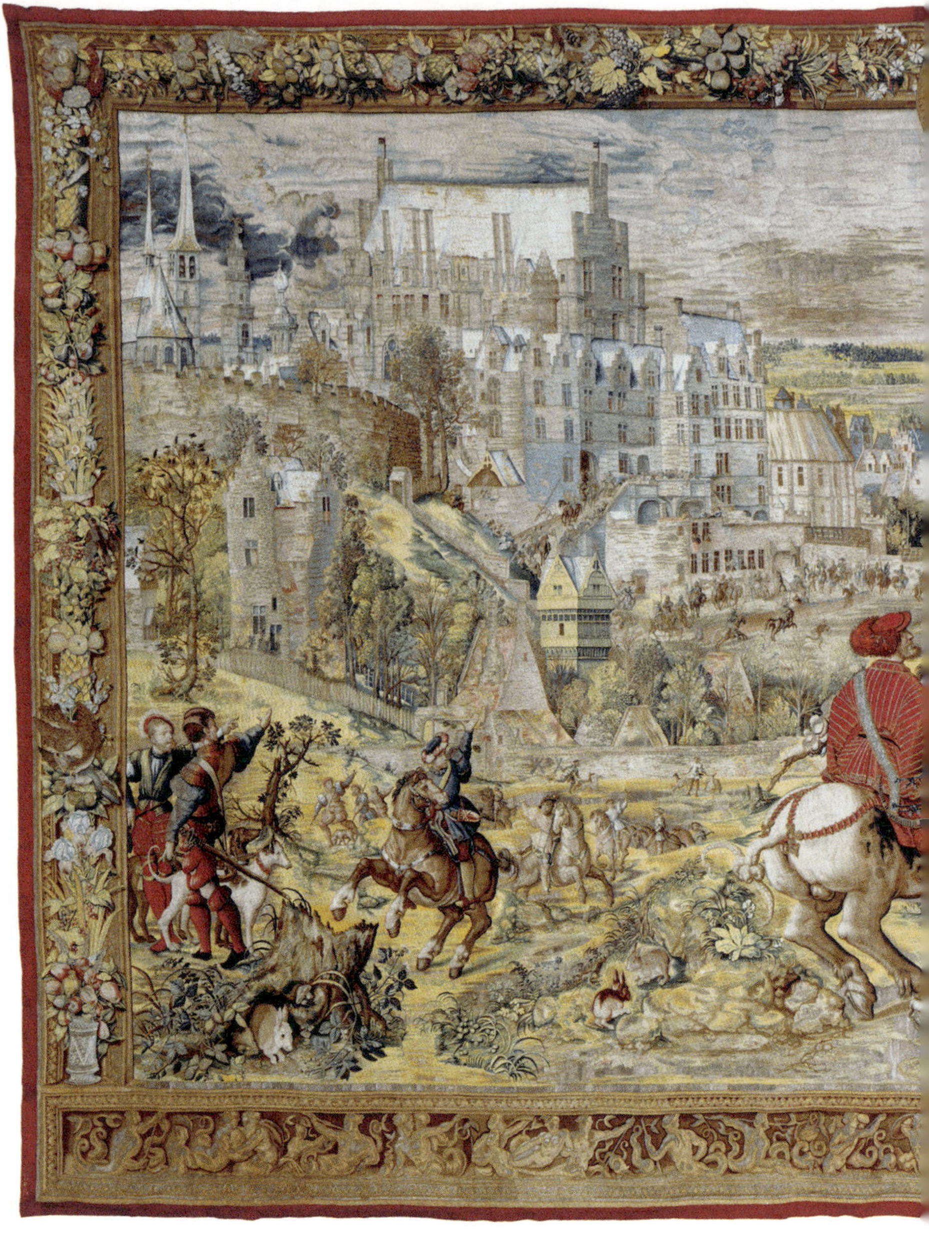

[226]
After Bernard van Orley, c. 1488–1541;
weaving workshop, Brussels, Belgium
March* or *Aries* or *The Falcon Hunt* from the tapestries known as the *Hunts of Maximilian
c. 1531–1533
Wool, silk, silver and gold
H. 445/429 (left/right); W. 756/752 cm (top/bottom)
(H. 14 ft 7¼ in./14 ft 1 in. [left/right]; W. 24 ft 9¾ in./24 ft 8 in. [top/bottom])
⊻ 1793 (former royal collection)
DDA

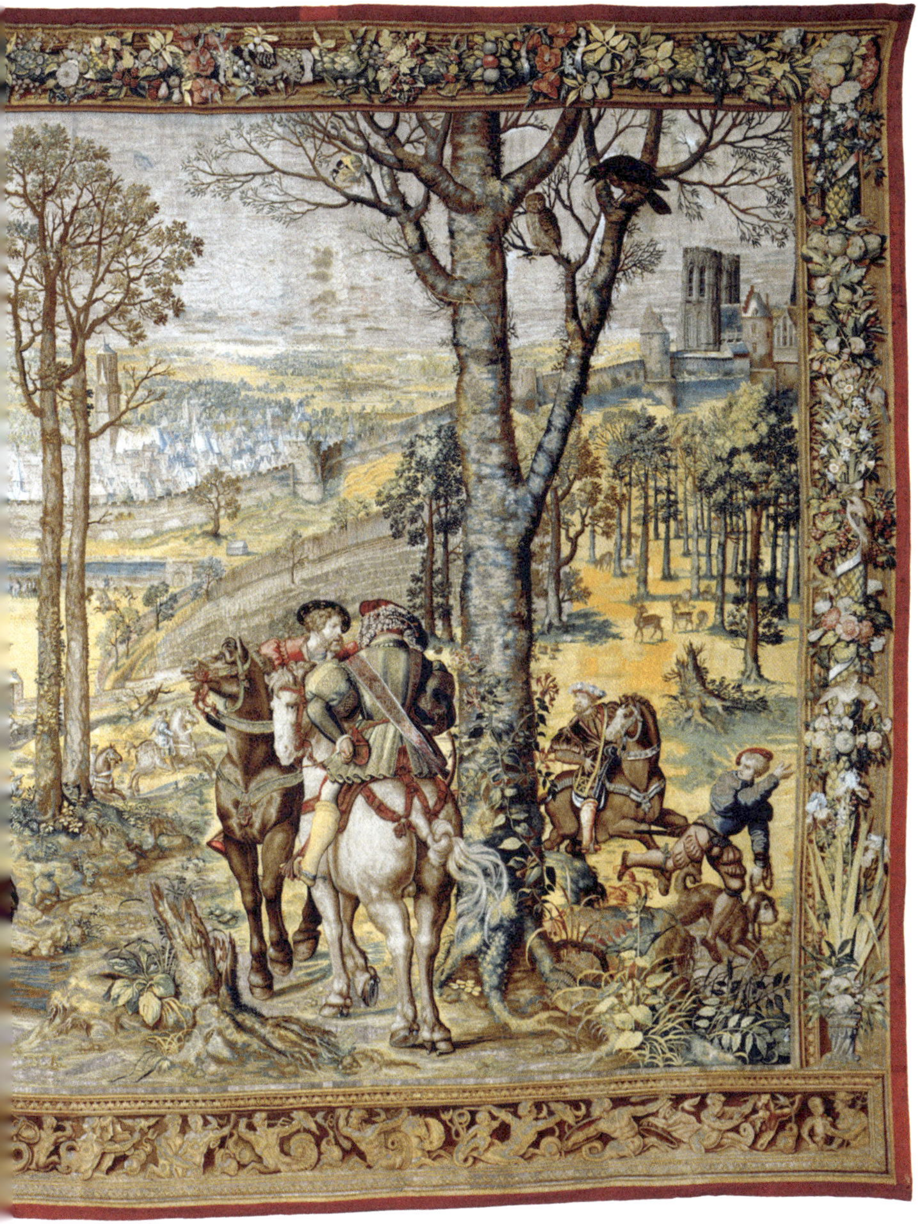

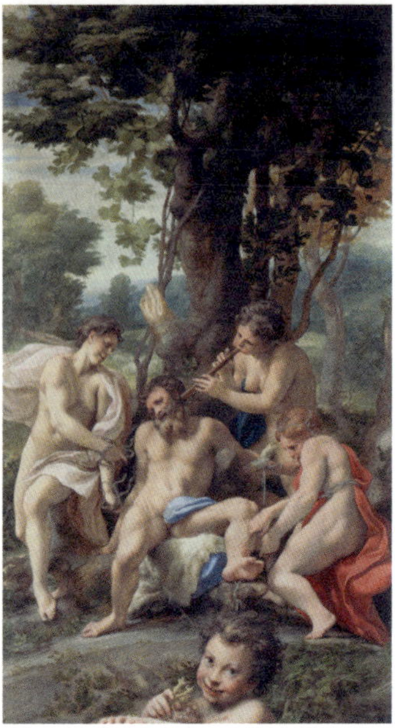

[227]
Antonio Allegri, known as Correggio
1489–1534
Allegory of Vice
c. 1530
Gouache on canvas
H. 142; W. 85.5 cm
(H. 4 ft 8 in.; W. 2 ft 9¾ in.)
⊻ 1793 (former royal collection, collection of Louis XIV)
DPD

better known as Titian. Born in Venice and one of the most celebrated painters of his day, Titian's sense of colour and light introduces a new level of intensity to the scenes he portrayed. *The Entombment of Christ* **[228]**, which captures the painful moments preceding Christ's burial, takes its compositional organisation from ancient friezes. The artist's painterly skill is evident in the deliberate contrasts of red and blue, the light that grazes the tormented body and the sky that opens in the background. Commissioned by Federico II Gonzaga, Duke of Mantua, the painting was owned by Charles I of England then by Jabach, who sold it to Louis XIV. The subject of *Jupiter and Antiope,* also known as the *Pardo Venus* **[230]** – El Pardo is a palace in Madrid – is somewhat enigmatic. Titian shipped the painting to Philip II of Spain, son of Charles V. It shows a sleeping Antiope assailed by Jupiter in the form of a satyr. However, the other figures are not part of the ancient fable, suggesting that Titian has taken the mythological story as a basis from which to develop a reflection on love: peaceful, mutual love opposed

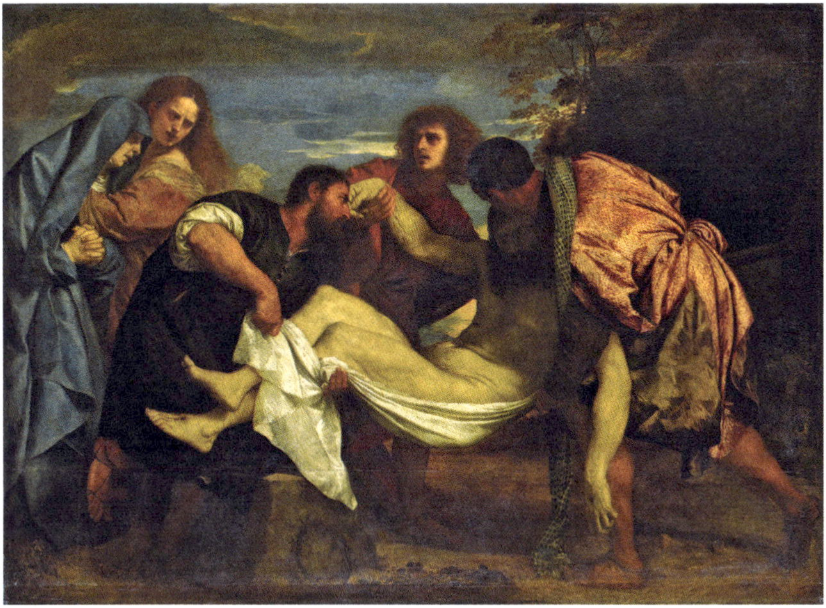

[228] Tiziano Vecellio, known as Titian. c. 1488–1490/1576. ***The Entombment of Christ***. c. 1500–1525. Oil on canvas H. 148; W. 212 cm (H. 4 ft 10¼ in.; W. 6 ft 11½ in.). ⍌ 1793 (former royal collection, collection of Louis XIV). DP

to the violence inflicted on the sleeping woman, unaware and unable to escape the satyr's lecherous gaze. Titian's *Venus* travelled through Europe, leaving Spain for England and the collection of Charles I, before its acquisition by Louis XIV. The positioning of the figures in the landscape and the dynamic of the painting were praised by artists from Antoine Coypel to Gustave Courbet. Another illustration of Venetian painting of the cinquecento, *The Wedding Feast at Cana* **[229]** by Paolo Caliari, known as Paolo Veronese, is the largest painting to hang in the Louvre. Executed for the San Giorgio Monastery in Venice, it represents, in the earthly setting of a banquet, the moment when Christ miraculously turns water into wine. Viewers of this immense painting are struck by the teaming crowd, the vivid colours of their clothing, the sense of agitation and movement, and Veronese's masterful use of light. Its magnificence is a hymn to the glory of La Serenissima. The artist is said to have included himself in the foreground of the painting, as the viola player dressed in white. Also by Veronese, *Jupiter Hurling Thunderbolts at the Vices* **[231]**, for the ceiling of the Council Chamber

[229]
Paolo Caliari,
known as Veronese
1528–1588
The Wedding Feast at Cana
Refectory of the San
Giorgio Benedictine
Monastery, Venice, Italy
1562–1563
Oil on canvas
H. 677; W. 994 cm
(H. 22 ft 2½ in.;
W. 32 ft 7¼ in.)
⩡ 1798
DP

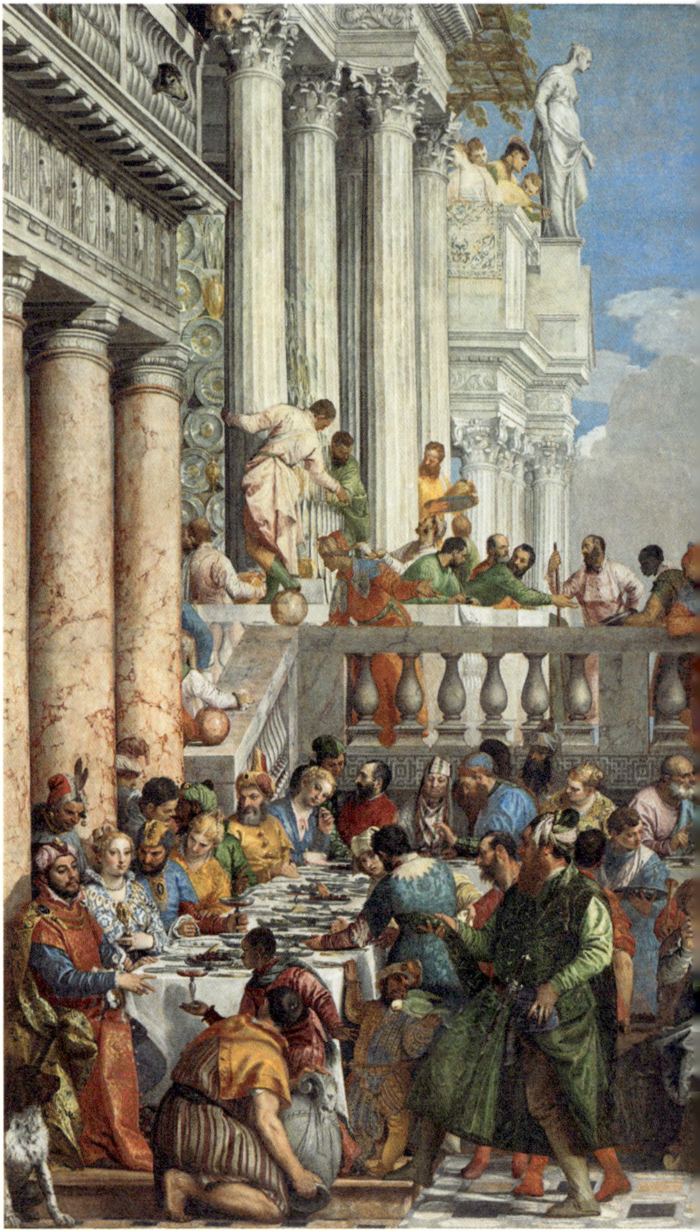

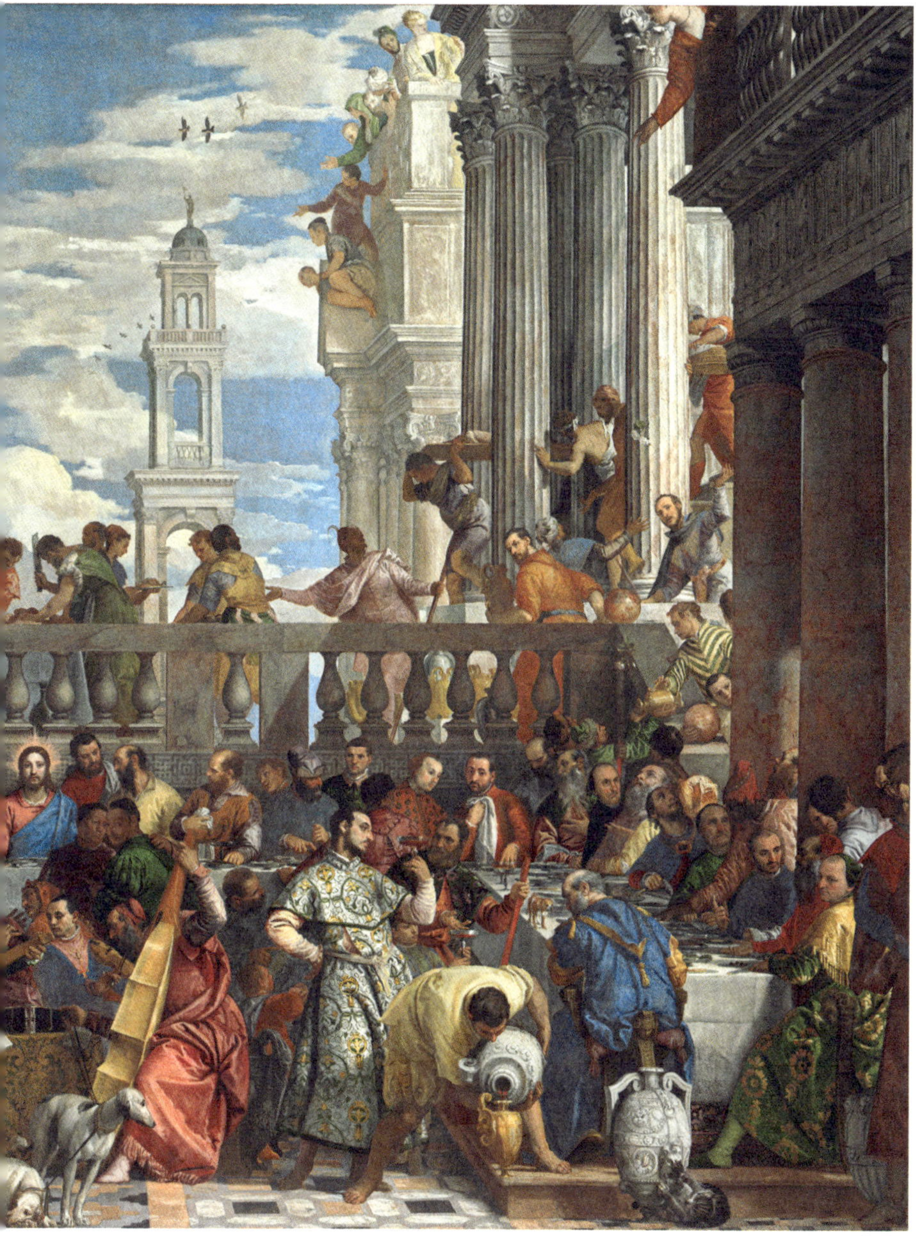

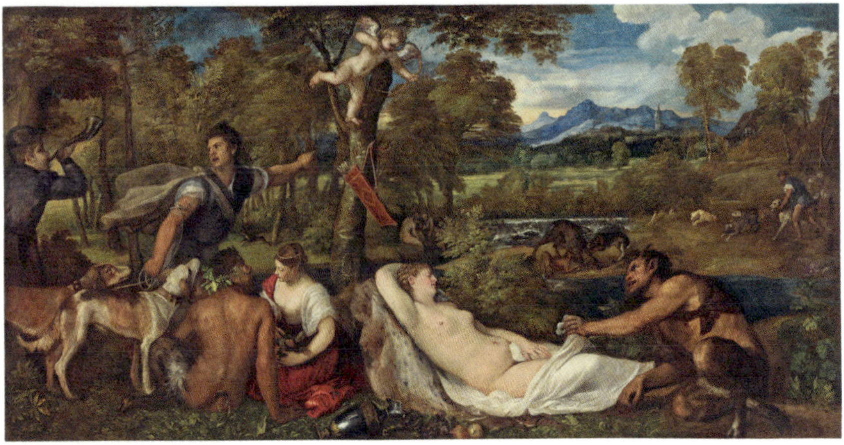

[230] Tiziano Vecellio, known as Titian. c. 1488–1490/1576. ***Jupiter and Antiope*, also known as *Pardo Venus***
c. 1525–1550. Oil on canvas (transposed). H. 196; W. 385 cm (H. 6 ft 5¼ in.; W. 12 ft 7½ in.). ⊻ 1793 (former royal collection, collection of Louis XIV). DP

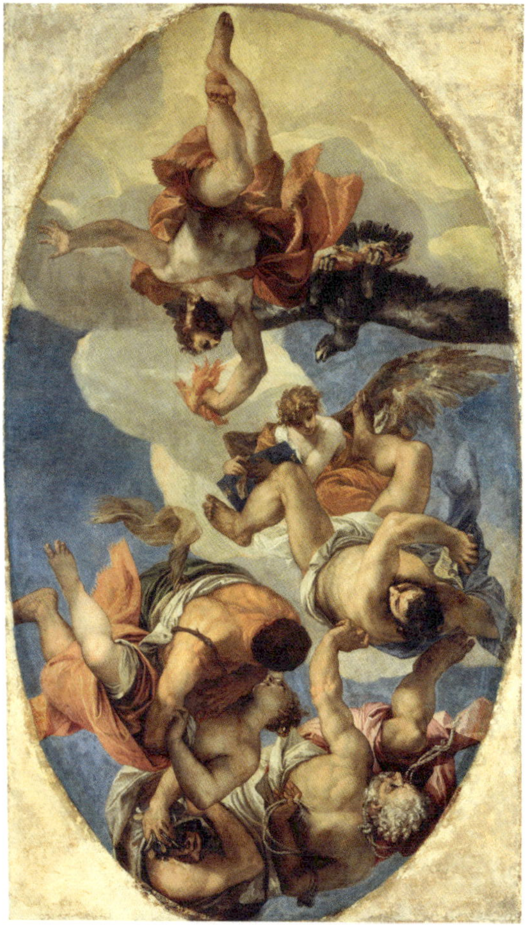

[231]
Paolo Caliari,
known as Veronese
1528–1588
Jupiter Hurling Thunderbolts at the Vices
Central compartment,
ceiling of the Council
Chamber, Doge's Palace,
Venice, Italy
c. 1500–1600
Oil on canvas (transposed)
H. 560; W. 330 cm
(H. 18 ft 4½ in.; W. 10 ft 10 in.)
⊻ 1798
DP

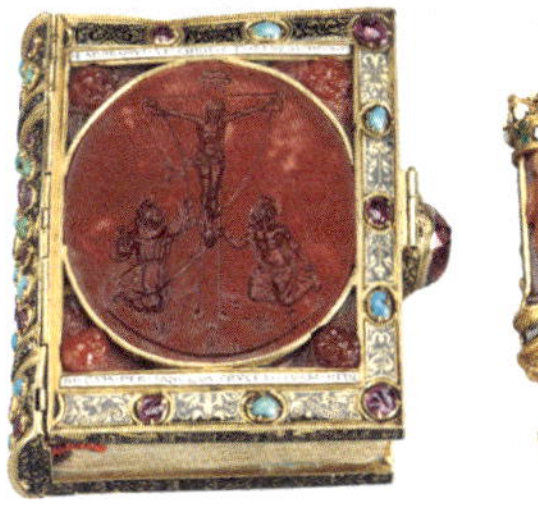

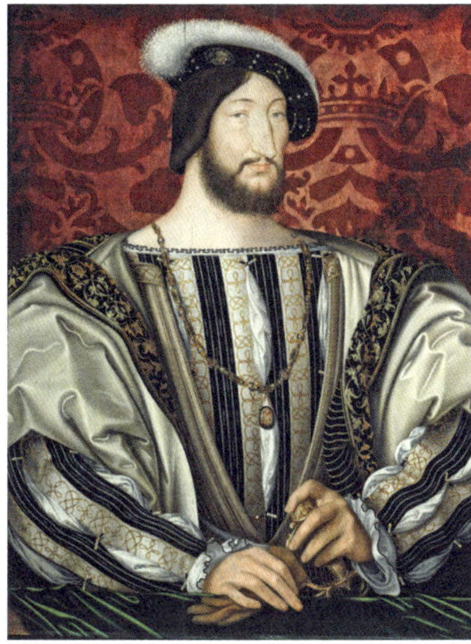

[232]
France
Francis I's Book of Hours
c. 1532–1537
Enamelled gold, cornelian, ruby, turquoise and tourmaline
H. 8.5; W. 8; D. 2.6 cm
(H. 3⅜; W. 3⅛; D. 1 in.)
⩡ 2017
DDA

[233]
Jean Clouet
1486–1540
Francis I, King of France
c. 1525–1550
Oil on oak wood
H. 96; W. 74 cm
(H. 3 ft 1¾ in.; W. 2 ft 5¼ in.)
⩡ 1793 (former royal collection, collection of Francis I)
DP

in the Doge's Palace, the seat of political power in the city-state in the sixteenth century, illustrates his particular genius for adapting the painting's composition to its use – a talent that was not lost on Eugène Delacroix, three centuries later.

MANIERA The patronage of Francis I **[232, 233]** and of his son, Henry II, brought Italian artists to France. Among them, Rosso Fiorentino took charge of the decoration for the Château de Fontainebleau. His *Pietà* **[234]** is a blaze of colour which, breaking with the frieze composition, emphasises the swirling motion of the figures. Benvenuto Cellini's monumental *Nymph of Fontainebleau* **[235]** was commissioned for the same royal residence. Following the sculptor's fall from grace, the architect Philibert Delorme placed the unfinished work at the Château d'Anet, residence of Diane de Poitiers, favourite of Henry II. This is also where the sculpted group *Diana of Anet* was installed, as a decoration for a fountain in the château's grounds. It was commissioned from Jean Goujon, who had previously sculpted the reliefs for the Fontaine des Innocents **[236]**,

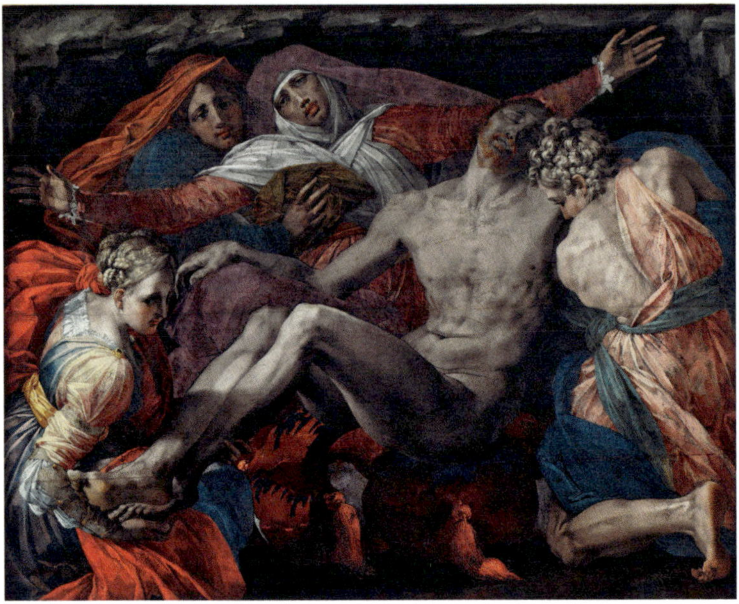

[234] Giovanni Battista di Jacopo, known as Rosso Fiorentino. 1496–1540. ***Pietà***. c. 1530–1540
Oil on canvas (transposed). H. 127; W. 163 cm (H. 4 ft 2 in.; W. 5 ft 4¼ in.). ⩡ 1793. DP

a monumental fountain built to commemorate Henry II's entry into Paris. Goujon's sculptures, inspired by antique forms, reveal his characteristically graceful, fluid style. The Fontaine des Innocents is the work of architect Pierre Lescot who commissioned Goujon for certain sculptural decorations on the facade he designed for the Louvre, inspired by Italian palazzi. Lescot also entrusted him with the monumental caryatids, influenced by ancient sculptures, for the vast ballroom created by Henry II, which is now the Louvre's Salle des Cariatides **[p. 12]**.

Catherine de' Medici, widow of Henry II, commissioned *The Three Graces* **[238]** from sculptor Germain Pilon as part of the funerary monument that would contain her royal husband's heart. Encouraged by the choice of this ancient motif, the sculpture extends gracefully upwards – a refinement borrowed from Italian Mannerism. Pilon also created the funerary monument for Valentine Balbiani, wife of René de Birague **[237]**. It shows the young woman resting on one elbow, accompanied by a small dog, a symbol of faithfulness, and two cherubs. In the lower

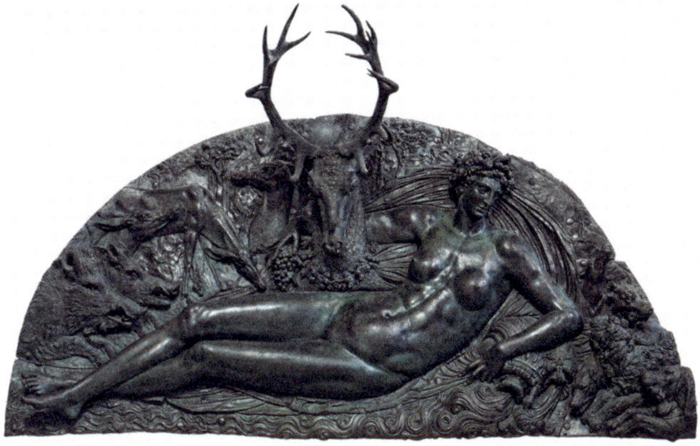

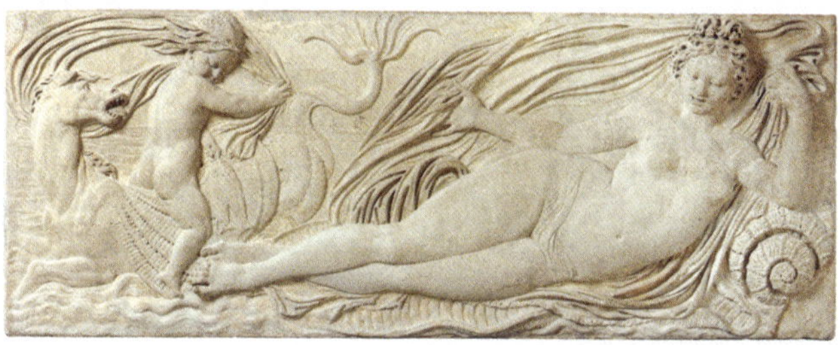

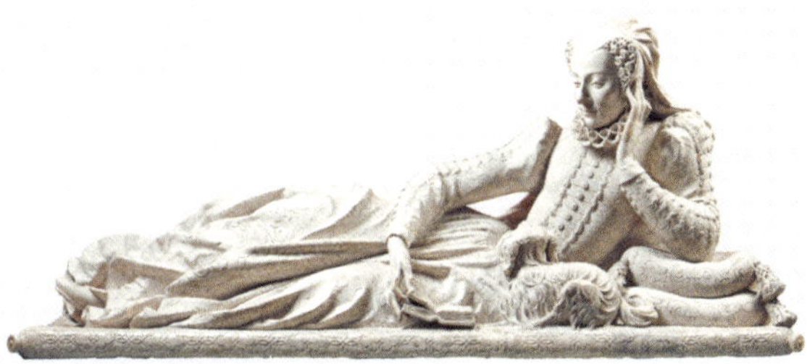

[235]
Benvenuto Cellini, 1500–1571;
Pierre Bontemps, 1507–1568
Nymph of Fontainebleau
c. 1542–1543
Bronze
H. 205; W. 409 cm
(H. 6 ft 8¾ in.; W. 13 ft 5 in.)
⩡ 1794
DS

[236]
Jean Goujon
c. 1510–1572
Nymph and Spirit on a Marine Horse
Fontaine des Innocents,
Paris, France
1547
Stone
H. 74; W. 195; D. 12.5 cm
(H. 2 ft 5¼ in.; W. 6 ft 4¾ in.; D. 5 in.)
⩡ 1818
DS

[237]
Germain Pilon
c. 1528–1590
Valentine Balbiani,
Wife of René de Birague
(partial view)
Church of Saint Catherine-du-Val,
Paris, France
1573
Marble
H. 83; W. 191.5; D. 49 cm
(H. 2 ft 8¾ in.; W. 6 ft 3½ in.;
D. 1 ft 7¼ in.)
⩡ 1834 (former collection of the
Musée des Monuments Français)
DS

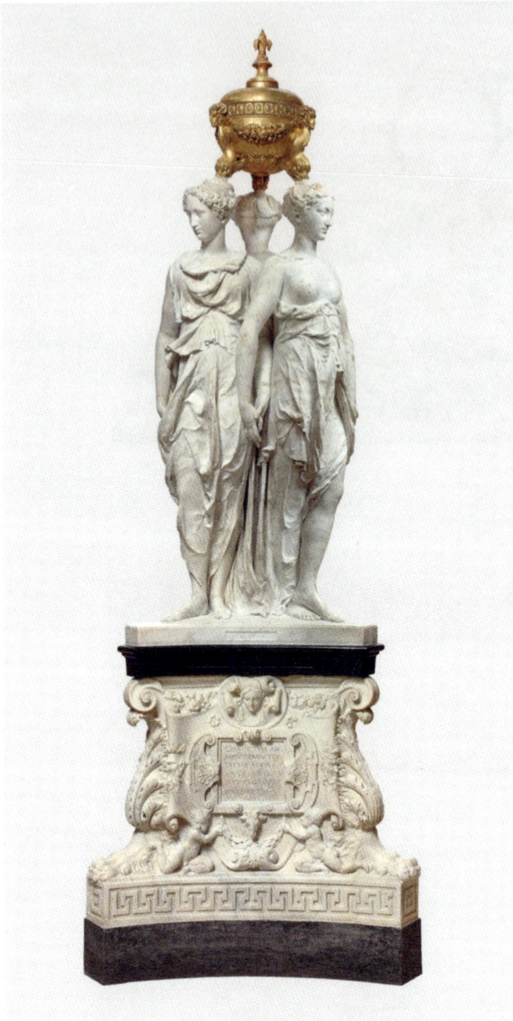

[238]
Germain Pilon
c. 1528–1590
The Three Graces.
Part of the Funerary Monument for the Heart of King Henry II
Orléans Chapel at the church of the Celestine Convent, Paris, France
c. 1500–1600
Marble
H. 150; W. 75.5; D. 75.5 cm
(H. 4 ft 11 in.; W. 2 ft 5¾ in.; D. 2 ft 5¾ in.)
⩡ 1817 (former collection of the Musée des Monuments Français)
DS

[239]
Iznik, Turkey
Peacock Dish
c. 1540–1555
Painted ceramic
H. 8.1; Diam. 37.4 cm
(H. 3⅛; Diam. 14¾ in.)
⩡ 1932 (bequest of Raymond Koechlin)
DIA

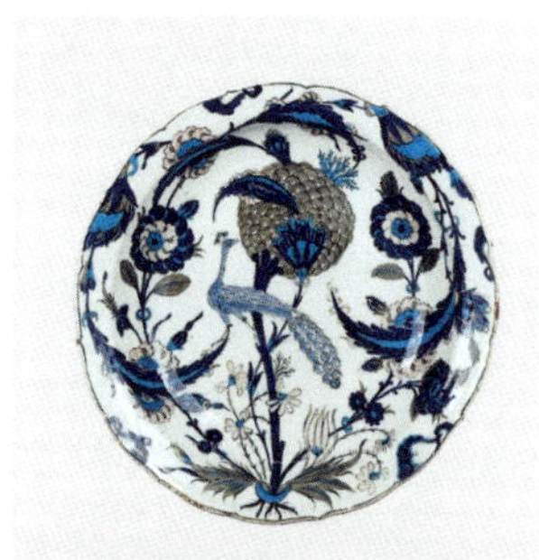

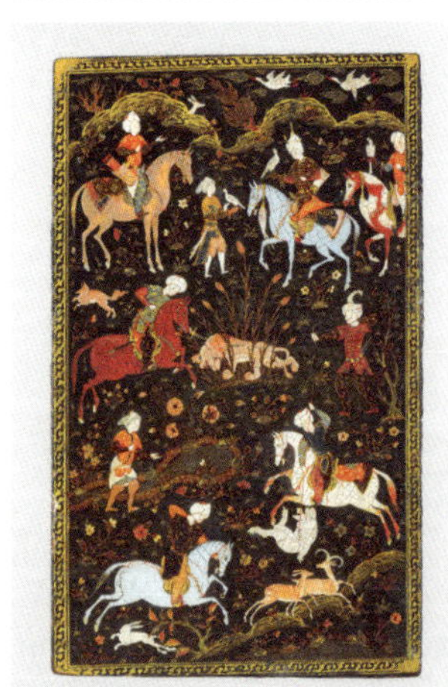

[240]
Attributed to Sultan Muhammed, Iran
Active in the 16th century
Binding:
Hunting Scene
c. 1560–1588
Leather, papier mâché and painted decoration
H. 32; W. 19.9; D. 0.4 cm
(H. 12½; W. 7¾; D. ⅛ in.)
⩡ 2012 (deposit from the Union Centrale des Arts Décoratifs, Paris, bequest of Gaston Migeon)
DIA

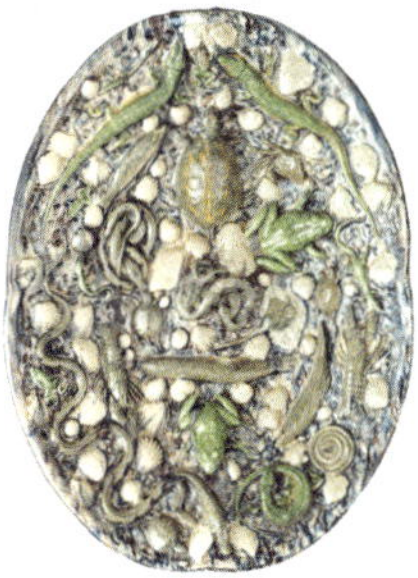

[241]
Attributed to
Bernard Palissy
c. 1510–1589/1590
Oval Dish: "rustiques figulines"
c. 1550–1560
Painted terracotta
H. 9.5; L. 48; W. 37 cm
(H. 3¾; L. 19; W. 14½ in.)
⩡ 1825 (former collection of Edme Antoine Durand)
DDA

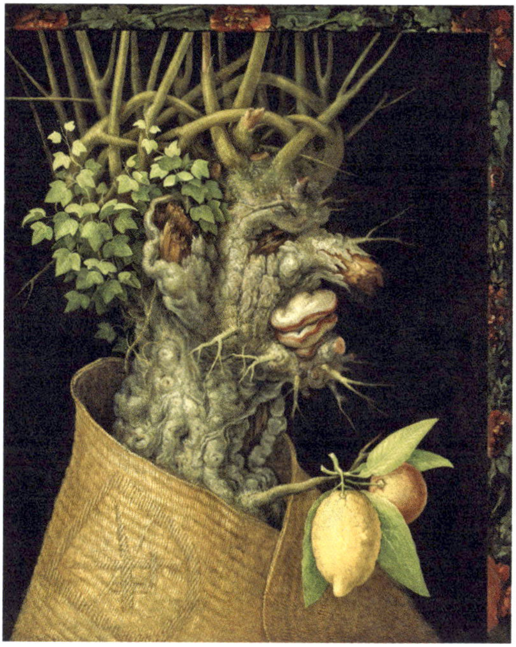

[242]
Giuseppe
Arcimboldo
1527–1593
Winter
1573
Oil on canvas
H. 76; W. 63.6 cm
(H. 30; W. 25 in.)
⩡ 1964
DP

register, a transi – a sculpted figure of a decomposed cadaver – is a reminder of the ravages of death and its inevitability. During this same period, Bernard Palissy looked to the vocabulary of nature for his *rustiques figulines* (rustic ceramics) **[241]**, which he decorated with casts of fish, reptiles, plants and leaves in coloured glazed ceramic. The artist imagined other fauna and flora for his artificial grottos, one of which Charles IX commissioned from this devoted Protestant for the Jardin des Tuileries. The same king ordered the massacre of the Huguenots in Paris on Saint Bartholomew's Day in 1572, one of the most dramatic episodes in the Wars of Religion that opposed Catholics and Protestants in the latter half of the sixteenth century.

MANNERISM Originally from Milan, Giuseppe Arcimboldo settled in Vienna, at the service of Emperor Ferdinand I of Habsburg, then his son Maximilian II. In his *Four Seasons* series, he observes the conventional profile format while replacing facial features with a virtuoso arrangement of flowers and fruit **[242]**. Gifted to Augustus, Elector

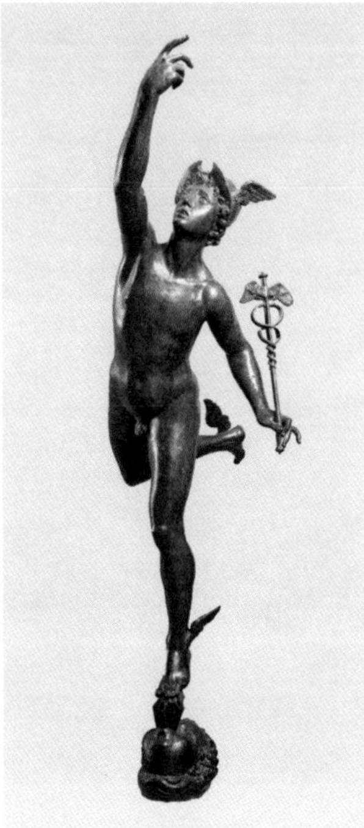

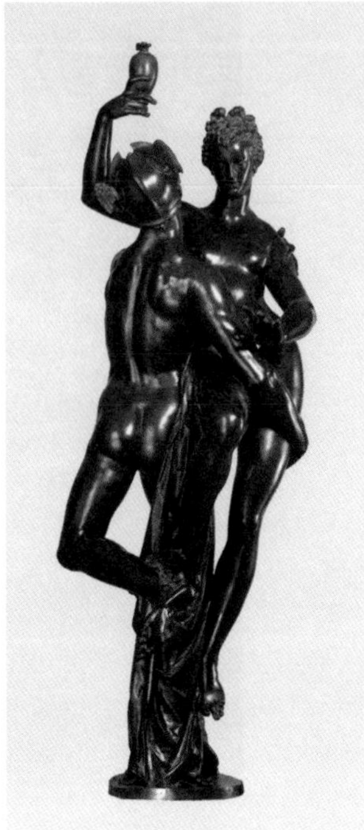

[243]
Attributed to Giovanni da Bologna, known as Giambologna
1529–1608
Mercury
1574–1700
Bronze
H. 169; W. 54; D. 110 cm
(H. 5 ft 6½ in.; W. 1 ft 9¼ in.; D. 3 ft 7¼ in.)
⊻ 1872
DS

[244]
Adriaen de Vries
c. 1556–1560–before 1626
Mercury and Psyche
1593
Bronze
H. 215; W. 92; D. 72 cm
(H. 7 ft ¾ in.; W. 3 ft ¼ in.; D. 2 ft 4¼ in.)
⊻ 1794 (former royal collection, collection of Louis XIV)
DS

of Saxony, this suite also delivers a political message, suggesting that like the endless cycle of the seasons, the power of the Holy Roman Empire will extend infinitely. The same skilful pursuit of subtly balanced forms can be seen in the work of Giambologna, a sculptor born in Flanders, in Douai – now in France – who worked for the Medici in Florence and was also active in Bologna. Inspired by Cellini, his *Mercury* **[243]** appears to defy gravity, the fleetness of this winged messenger of the gods brilliantly rendered by the artist's virtuosity. Giambologna's sculptures were greatly admired and frequently reproduced as small decorative bronzes. Another sculptor, Adriaen de Vries was born in The Hague and became a student of Giambologna in Florence. His *Mercury and Psyche* **[244]**, which plays on the way the two figures expand into the space around them, was originally installed in the gardens of the palace of Emperor Rudolf II in Prague. The statue was then owned by Christina, Queen of Sweden, then Jean-Baptiste Colbert, minister under Louis XIV, before entering the royal collections, at one time adorning the Louvre's Jardin de l'Infante.

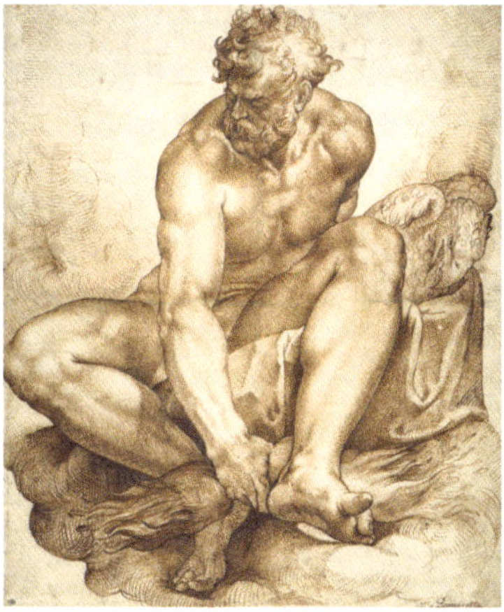

[245]
Bartolomeo Passarotti
1529–1592
Jupiter Sitting on Clouds
c. 1574
Pen and brown ink,
black chalk
H. 44.2; W. 38.1 cm
(H. 17½; W. 15 in.)
⩡ 1793
DPD

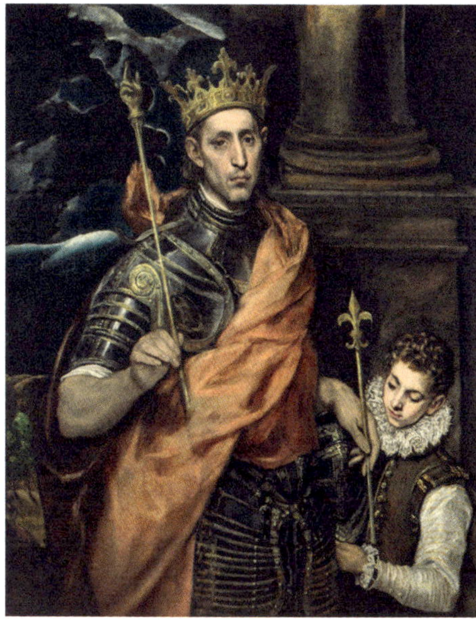

[246] Dominikos Theotokopoulos, known as El Greco. 1541–1614. ***Saint Louis, King of France, and a Page***. c. 1585–1590. Oil on canvas. H. 120; W. 96.5 cm (H. 3 ft 11¼ in.; W. 3 ft 2 in.). ⩡ 1903. DP

Domenikos Theotokopoulos, better known as El Greco, was born in Crete – at that time ruled by the Republic of Venice – where he initially trained as an icon painter. From there, he travelled to Venice, where he admired the work of Titian and Tintoretto, before accepting the invitation of Philip II to visit the Spanish court. His singular style, marked by elongated bodies and a personal interpretation of the human form, sought inspiration as much in Byzantine works as those of the Italian Renaissance. During his lifetime, he had a strong influence on Spanish art and remains one of the painters most admired by today's artists. His *Saint Louis* **[246]** depicts Louis IX, the French king who led one of the crusades. There was very little Spanish art in the French royal collections until the 1830s when, at the behest of Louis-Philippe I, numerous works by Spanish artists were purchased and a Spanish gallery opened inside the Louvre. The collection was dispersed after Louis-Philippe's reign came to an end in 1848. One of the works, El Greco's *Christ on the Cross Adored by Two Donors*, was bought back by the Louvre in 1908.

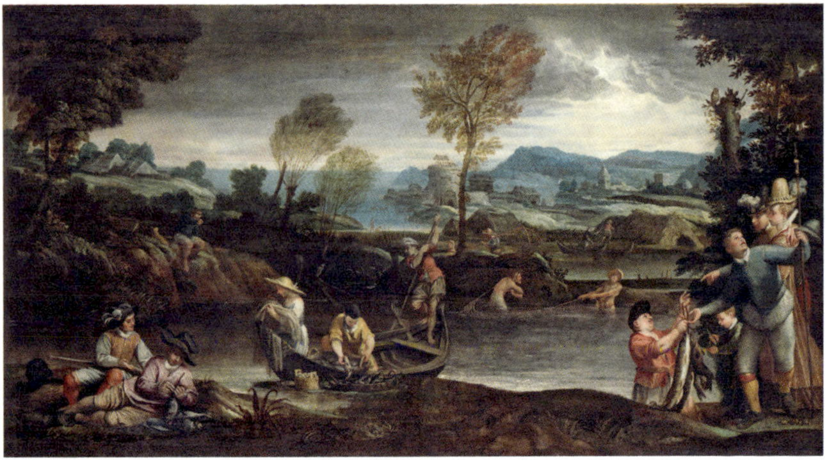

[247]
Annibale Carracci
1560–1609
Fishing
c. 1575–1600
Oil on canvas
H. 136; W. 255 cm
(H. 4 ft 5½ in.; W. 8 ft 4½ in.)
⊻ 1793 (former royal collection, collection of Louis XIV)
DP

CLASSICAL REFORM Annibale Carracci, along with his brother and cousin, was one of the instigators of a new strand of Italian art in the late sixteenth and early seventeenth centuries. His work is marked by a renewed classical and naturalist conception of painting. The Carracci family's school in Bologna played an important role in the instruction of artists and established rules that would be taken up by other institutions. *Fishing* **[247]**, along with its companion *Hunting*, shows country life in a perfectly structured composition. The painting was a gift to Louis XIV from Prince Camillo Pamphili. The Carracci would have a clear and lasting influence on French pictorial conception, in particular landscapes.

“Posterity makes a great difference between power and glory.”

Voltaire,
An Essay on Universal History, the Manners, and Spirit of Nations,
1756

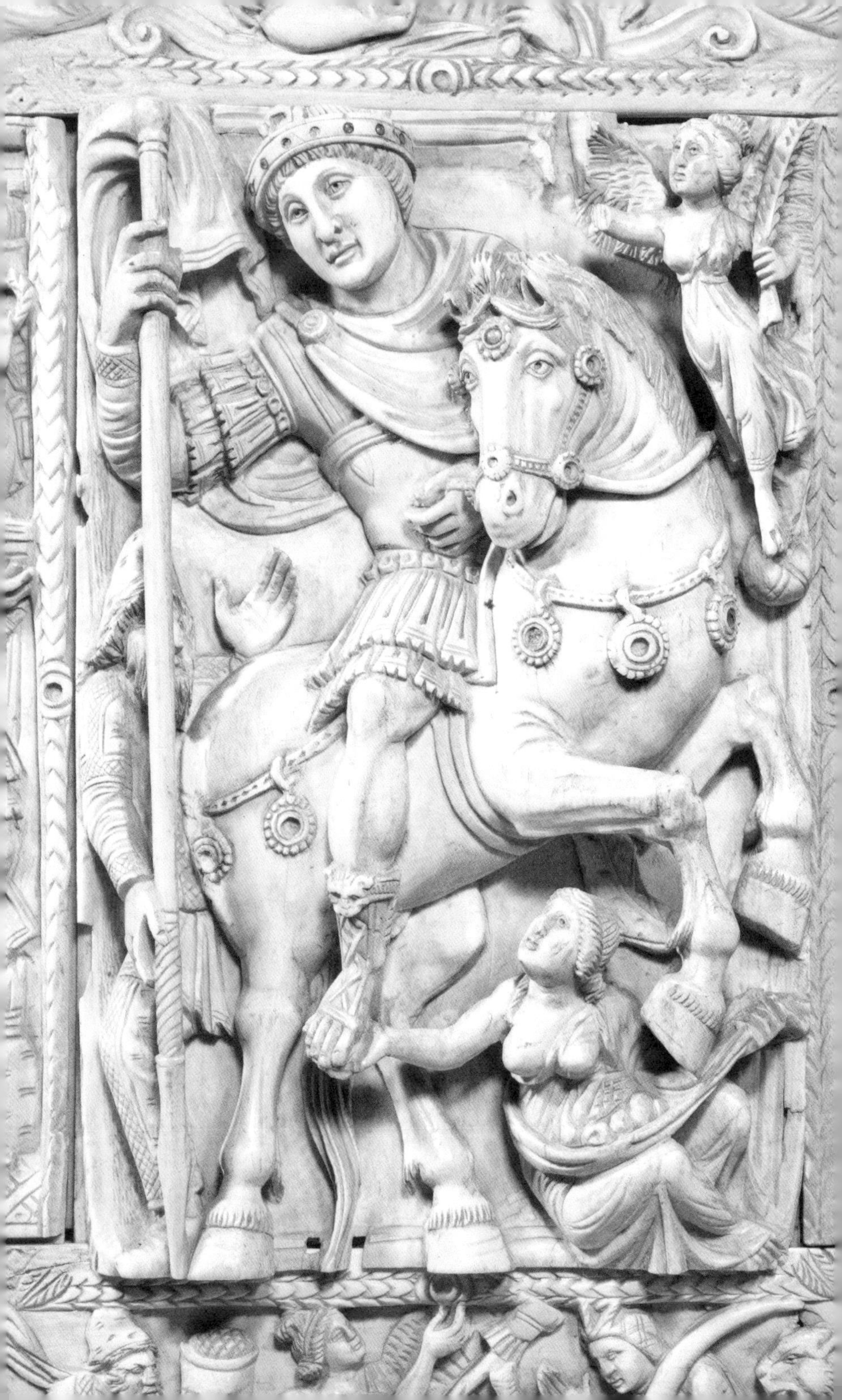

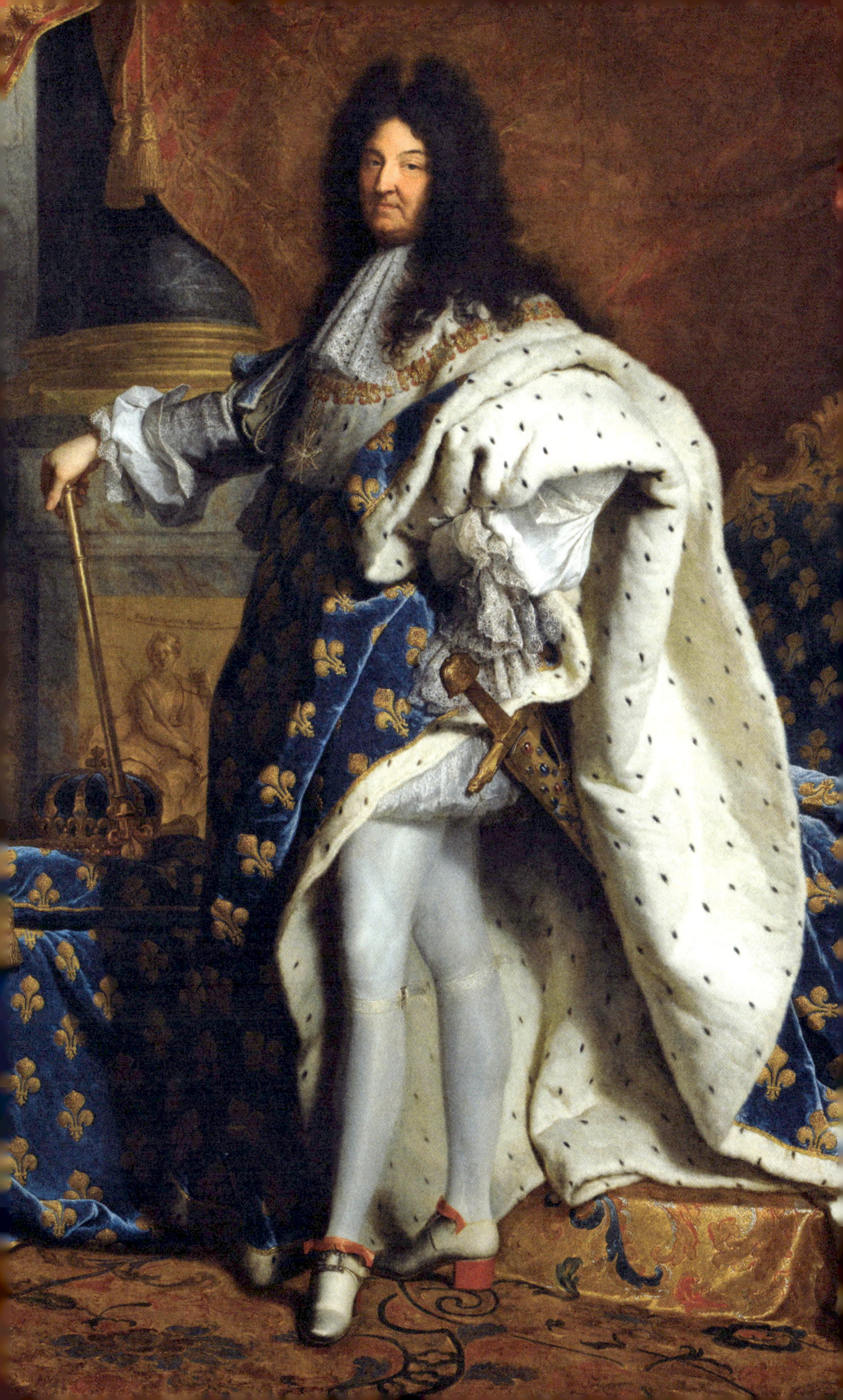

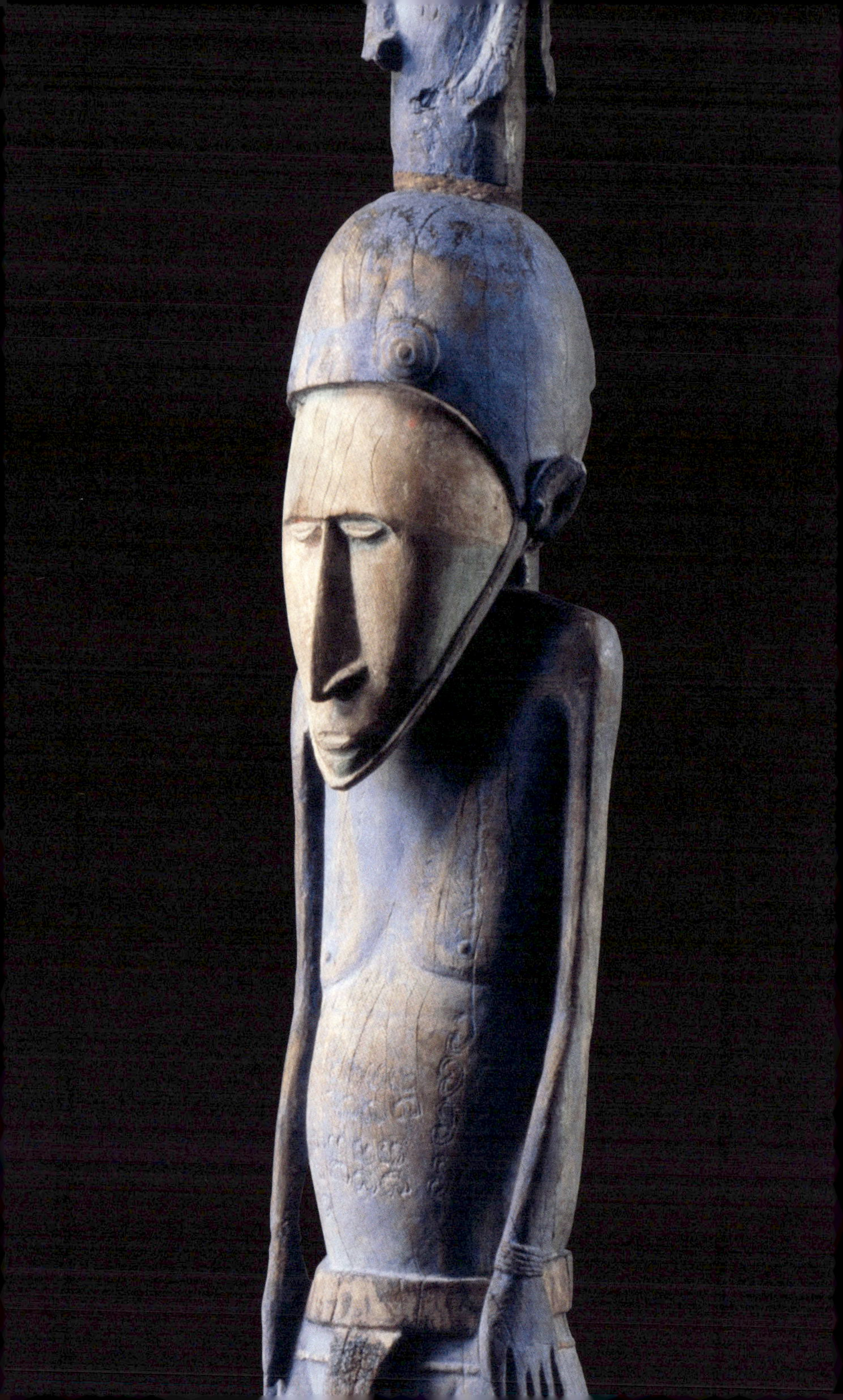

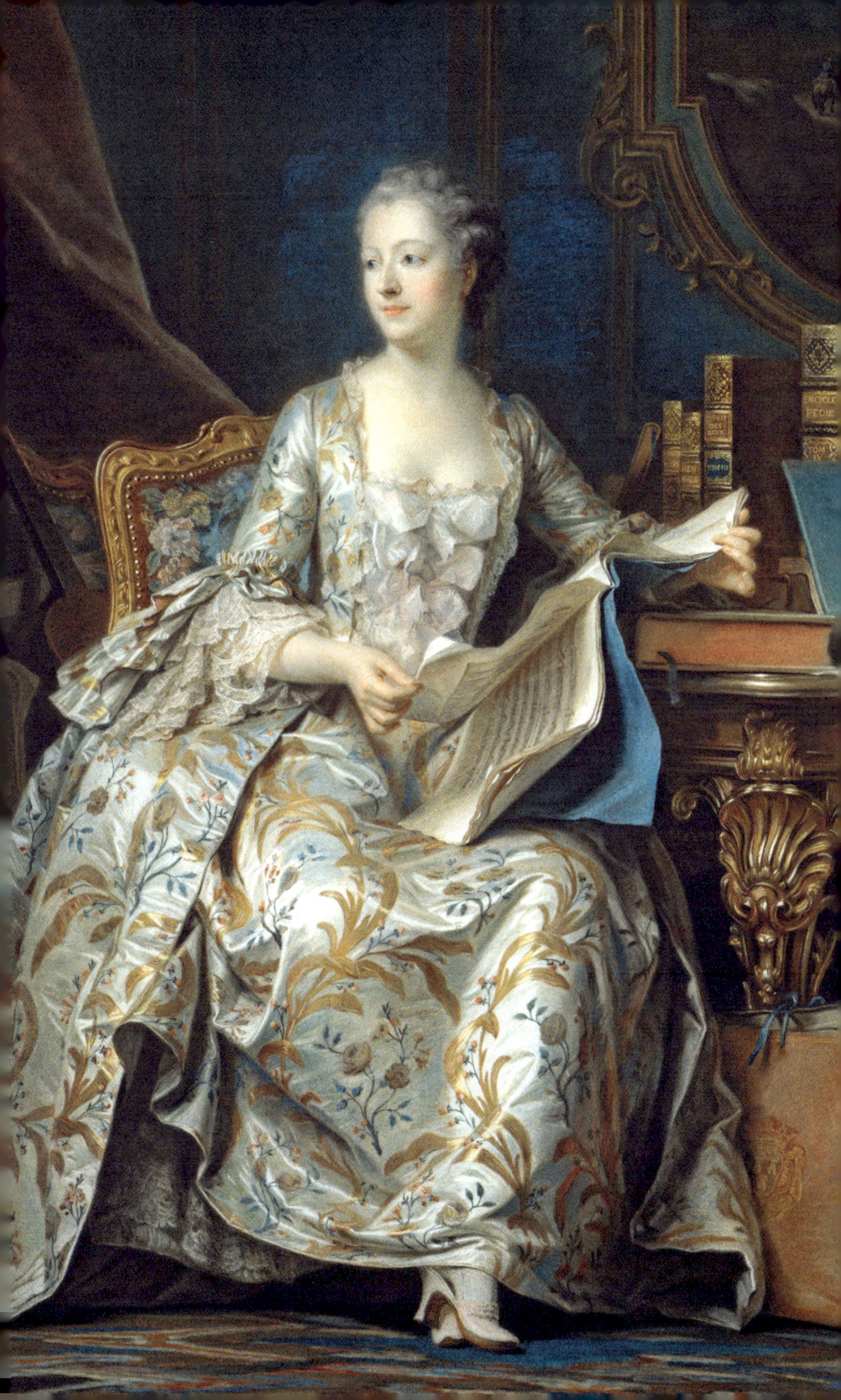

In 1598 Henry IV of France enacted the Edict of Nantes, a proclamation intended to end the decades-long Wars of Religion between Protestants – who followed a reformed Christianity that had originated in Germany early that century – and Catholics who opposed this new doctrine. This royal edict was an act of tolerance, designed to restore peace. Henry IV was himself a Protestant who had converted to Catholicism in order to ascend the French throne.

The large painted panel *Gabrielle d'Estrées and One of Her Sisters* **[248]** alludes to the relationship between Henry IV and Gabrielle d'Estrées. The painting's naturalist style highlights the beauty of its subjects while, symbolically, the sister's delicate pinching of Gabrielle's breast is almost certainly a reference to the birth of a child borne by the king's favourite, as would suggest the presence in the background of a lady-in-waiting who is embroidering for the royal infant.

Aesthetic conceptions were profoundly shaped by artists at the turn of the seventeenth century. Michelangelo Merisi da Caravaggio, known simply as Caravaggio, was one of the greatest painters of his day, whose work – distinguished by naturalism, dramatic use of colour, shadow and a powerful, not to say violent, depiction of religious scenes – would have a lasting influence. He led a tumultuous life, including frequent run-ins with authority, and this disregard for convention helped forge his singular reputation. *Death of the Virgin* **[251]** was commissioned by the clergy of the church of Santa Maria della Scala in Trastevere, Rome. It was rejected by the clerics, who were shocked to see the lifeless body of the mother of Christ portrayed as though it were that of an ordinary woman. However, the painting's beauty did not escape the seasoned eye of collectors. It was acquired first by Vincenzo I Gonzaga, Duke of Mantua, then owned by Charles I of England and later by Louis XIV of France, who bought it from the banker Everhard Jabach for the royal collection. Caravaggio would have an unmistakable influence on Italian and French painters of the seventeenth century. His sense of chiaroscuro, along with the scenes he chose to portray, characteristic of his unique point of view, captured the interest of countless artists.

[248]
School of Fontainebleau, France
Gabrielle d'Estrées and One of Her Sisters
c. 1575–1600
Oil on oak wood
H. 96; W. 125 cm
(H. 3 ft 1¾ in.; W. 4 ft 1¼ in.)
⊻ 1937
DP

[249]
India
Pen Box in the Name of Shah Abbas
Present-day Iran
c. 1575–1625
Bone, metal, turquoise and silk
H. 2.1; L. 12.2; W. 2.5 cm
(H. ⅞; L. 4¾; W. 1 in.)
⊻ 2018
DIA

[250]
Russia
Fragment of an Engolpion: The Hospitality of Abraham / Christ on the Cross
c. 1500–1700
Elephant ivory
Diam. 4.6; D. 0.7 cm
(Diam. 1¾; D. ¼ in.)
⊻ 1856 (gift of Alexandre-Charles Sauvageot)
DBECA

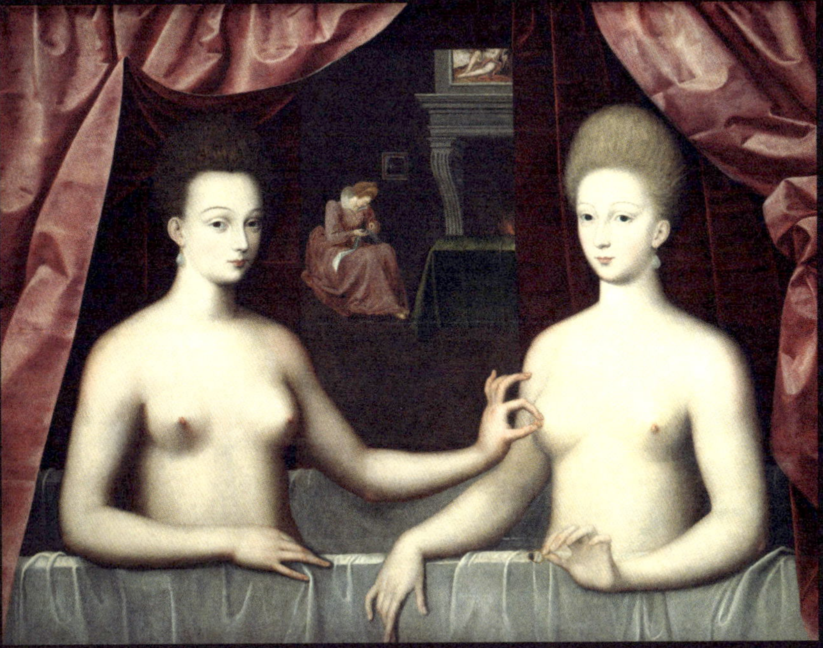

248

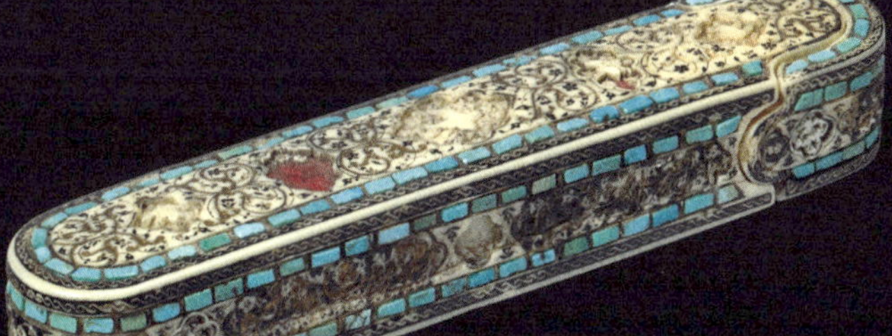

249

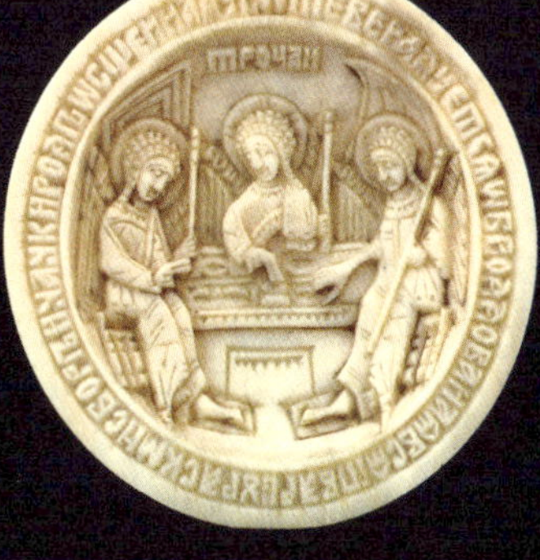

250

Peter Paul Rubens, a painter whose career was then just beginning, would become a favourite of every major European court. Born in Antwerp, from 1600 until 1608 he travelled through Italy, spending time at the court of the Gonzagas in Mantua. His admiration for the powerful human figures that Michelangelo painted for the Sistine Chapel in the Vatican Palace was such that he made his own copies, anxious to have faithful reproductions. Executed by Rubens after Michelangelo, *The Prophet Ezekiel* **[253]** – a drawing owned by Jabach and later sold to Louis XIV – shows how one great artist influenced the other.

During this same period, Persia was governed by Shah Abbas. A protector of the arts and literature, his reign marked the height of the Safavid Dynasty who established Isfahan, in the centre of the country, as their capital. The shah was renowned for his wisdom and moral elevation, illustrated by the elegantly shaped *Pen Box in the Name of Shah Abbas* **[249]**. Its intricate decoration includes an inscription that highlights the link between writing and thought, virtue and the proper use of power. It belonged to the jeweller Louis Cartier: an illustration of how artists and artisans in the nineteenth and early twentieth centuries took inspiration from Persian and Eastern arts.

From this same period, the carved ivory fragment of an engolpion **[250]** formed, with its missing part, a ritual object worn by Orthodox bishops. It shows Abraham, father of the faithful and a central figure in Judaism, Christianity and Islam, welcoming three strangers, in fact three angels sent by God. For the faithful, this episode is a reminder to show hospitality, tolerance and gratitude. The object was gifted to the Louvre by Alexandre-Charles Sauvageot, a characteristic nineteenth-century collector who assembled unusual and little-known artefacts that might otherwise have disappeared from memory.

[251]
Michelangelo Merisi da Caravaggio, know as Caravaggio
1571–1610
Death of the Virgin
c. 1601–1606
Oil on canvas
H. 369; W. 245 cm
(H. 12 ft 1¼ in.; W. 8 ft ½ in.)
⩡ 1793 (former royal collection, collection of Louis XIV)
DP

[252]
Workshop of Giovanni da Bologna, known as Giambologna
1529–1608
Sculpted Group, Rape of Deianara
17th century
Bronze
H. 43.6; W. 30.2; D. 23 cm
(H. 17¼; W. 12; D. 9 in.)
⩡ 1950
DDA

[253]
Peter Paul Rubens
1577–1640
The Prophet Ezekiel
1600–1608
Black and red chalk
H. 46; W. 38 cm
(H. 18; W. 15 in.)
⩡ 1793 (former royal collection, collection of Louis XIV)
DPD

251

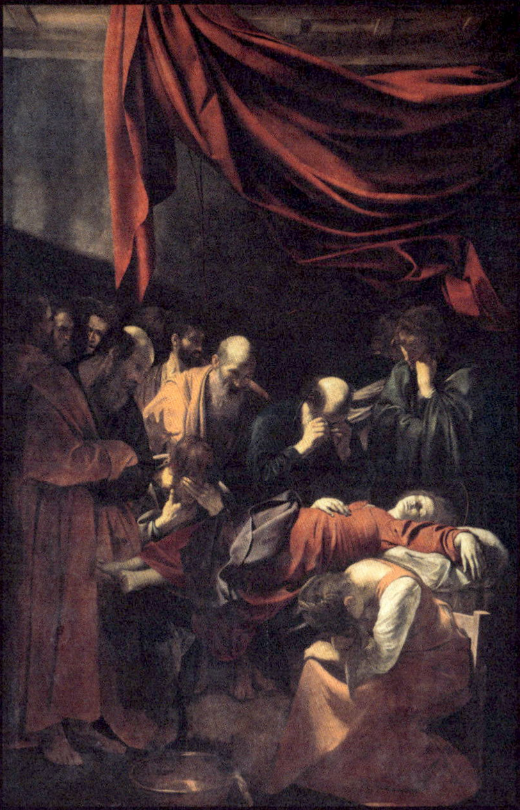

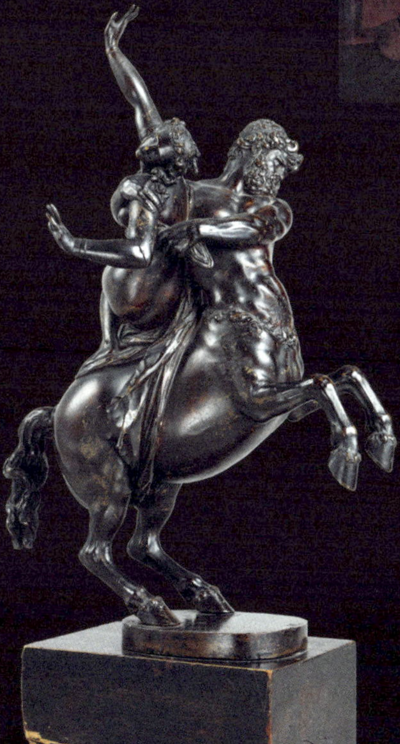

252

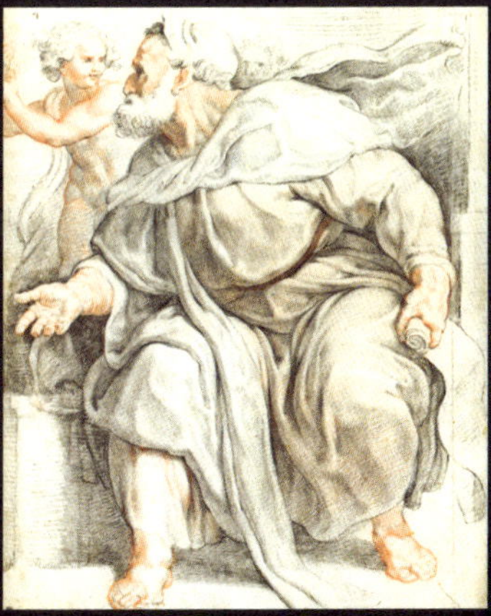

253

Accomplished masters

The role given to artists in Europe and their prominence at royal courts established them as masters of their craft: admired by their contemporaries and models for generations to come. Reputations were forged that have often continued to this day, fuelling debate over creation, between drawing and colour, intention and emotion. The founding of the Académie Royale de Peinture et de Sculpture in Paris in 1648 contributed to lively aesthetic discussion, while its dual mission, to instruct young artists and dispense knowledge, was crucial. Its legacy has been taken up by the Louvre, whose collections largely originate with those assembled by the French monarchy, in particular Louis XIV. In the years since its founding in 1793, the museum has also opened its galleries to artists who had been overlooked, reviving interest in Johannes Vermeer, the Le Nain brothers and Georges de La Tour.

[254]
Guido Reni
1575–1642
The Rape of Deianeira by the Centaur Nessus
c. 1617–1621
Oil on canvas
H. 262; W. 192 cm
(H. 8 ft 7¼ in.; W. 6 ft 3½ in.)
⩡ 1793 (former royal collection, collection of Louis XIV)
DP

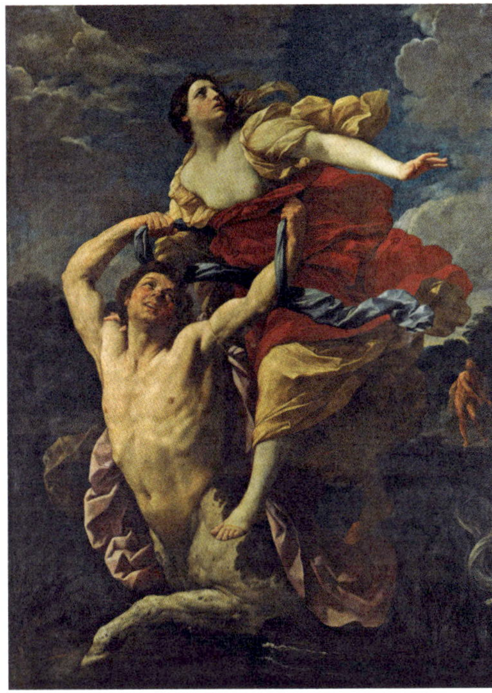

Private collectors have also played an essential role. For example, in the mid-nineteenth century Louis La Caze bequeathed hundreds of paintings to the museum, including Rembrandt's *Bathsheba at Her Bath* **[263]** and Antoine Watteau's *Pierrot* **[287]**. Proof of its vitality, the museum continues to enrich its collections, strengthening specific areas, such as the representation of works by women artists, and developing the British and American collections.

Guido Reni was born in Bologna and studied at the school founded by the Carracci family. His interest in the work of two artists in particular, Michelangelo and Caravaggio, is reflected in his painting. Reni's command of every aspect of his art brilliantly serves his depictions of religious and mythological scenes, such as the Hercules series, which he painted for Ferdinando Gonzaga, Duke of Mantua. Along with the rest of the series, *The Rape of Deianeira by the Centaur Nessus* **[254]** was acquired by Charles I of England, then by Louis XIV. Deianeira, the wife of Hercules, was abducted by the half-human, half-horse centaur who was seduced by her beauty.

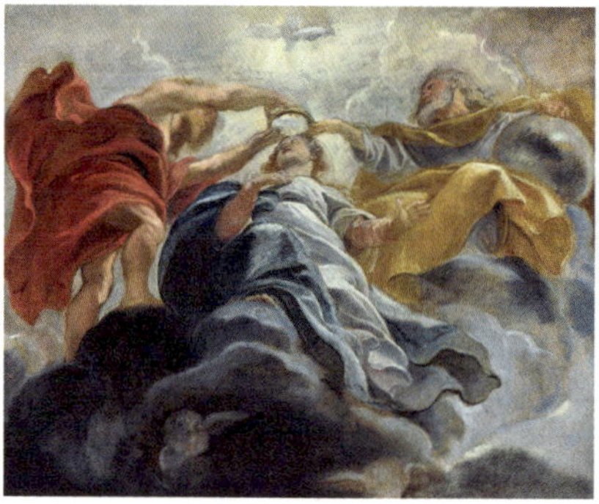

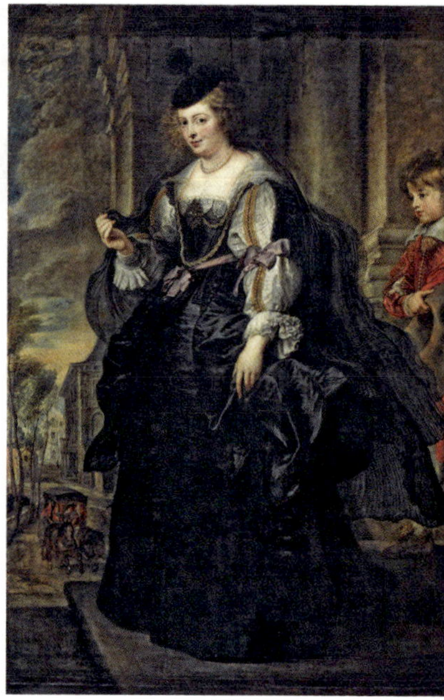

[255]
Peter Paul Rubens
1577–1640
The Coronation of the Virgin
c. 1600–1625
Oil on wood
H. 38; W. 48 cm
(H. 15; W. 19 in.)
⩡ 1869 (bequest of Louis La Caze)
DP

[256]
Peter Paul Rubens
1577–1640
Portrait of Hélène Fourment with a Carriage, followed by Her Son Frans as a Page
c. 1639
Oil on wood
H. 195; W. 132 cm
(H. 6 ft 4¾ in.; W. 4 ft 4 in.)
⩡ 1977 (dation)
DP

Hercules then shot and killed the centaur using an arrow poisoned with the blood of the Hydra of Lerna.

One of the most esteemed artists of his day, Peter Paul Rubens intended that his religious paintings should stir the viewer's emotions. Rubens worked against the backdrop of the Counter-Reformation, promulgated by the Council of Trent in the mid-sixteenth century in response to the new religious aspirations that came with the Protestant Reformation. *The Coronation of the Virgin* **[255]**, painted for the ceiling of the Jesuit church in Antwerp, brilliantly illustrates Rubens's talent as a colourist. The sense of movement invoked in the swirling robes, each distinguished by red, blue or yellow jewel tones, instils a feeling of elevation and exaltation in keeping with the scene. Following Henry IV's death in 1610, Marie de' Medici acted as regent to her son Louis XIII. She would prove an authoritarian ruler and, after Louis came of age, the young king's difficult relationship with his mother became apparent. The queen commissioned Rubens to paint a cycle of twenty-four scenes that would illustrate the great events of her life, to be installed in her residence, the Palais

[257]
Peter Paul Rubens
1577–1640
The Arrival of Marie de' Medici at Marseilles
Galerie Médicis,
Palais du Luxembourg,
Paris, France
c. 1600–1625
Oil on canvas
H. 394; W. 295 cm
(H. 12 ft 11 in.; W. 9 ft 8¼ in.)
⊻ 1790/1793
(former royal collection)
DP

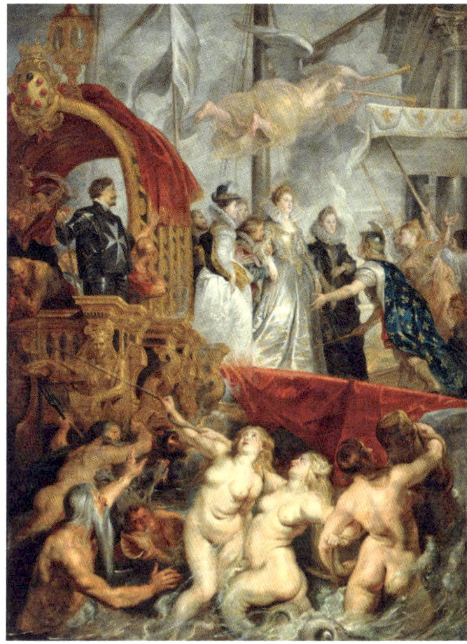

de Luxembourg in Paris. The painter knew he must glorify his patron while eclipsing certain less favourable episodes, and so imagined an allegory that allowed Rubens to cite historical fact as well as mythology, where the queen is portrayed as Juno and Henry IV as Jupiter. This artistic device, which benefited from his skill in selecting scenes, and from his mastery of light and colour, is remarkable, as illustrated by *The Arrival of Marie de' Medici at Marseilles* **[257]**, which immortalises her disembarking in France. The naiads in the foreground inspired Eugène Delacroix for the damned in the waters of the Styx in his *Dante and Virgil in Hell*, his first exhibited work, shown at the 1822 Salon.

Born in Antwerp, Anthony van Dyck became assistant to Rubens in 1618. His portraits are characterised by a deft blend of resemblance and idealisation, an effortless elegance in the pose and dress of his subjects, and a sensitive use of light and colour. Appointed Principal Painter in Ordinary to Charles I of England, his *Charles I at the Hunt* **[259]** was almost certainly produced at the king's

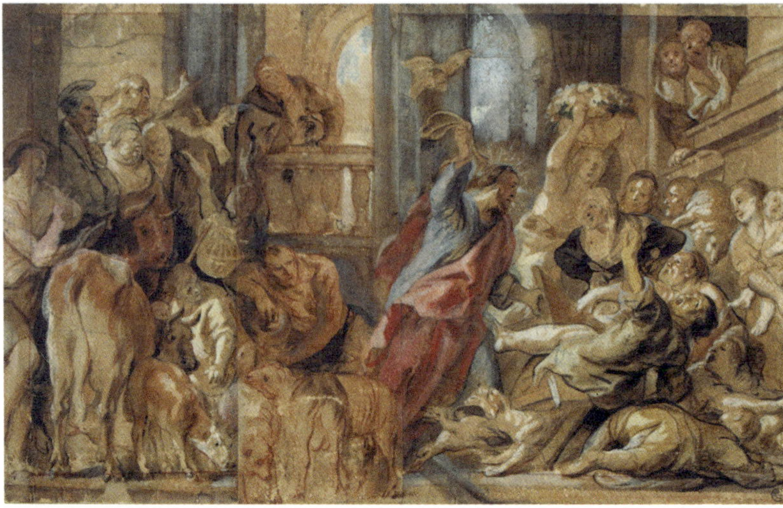

[258]
Jacob Jordaens
1593–1678
Christ Driving the Merchants from the Temple
c. 1645–1650
Watercolour and gouache on a pencil and red chalk sketch
H. 24.1; W. 39.9 cm (H. 9½; W. 15¾ in.)
⩡ 1905
DPD

request. The sovereign's aristocratic grace, the sweeping landscape, and the subtle interplay between shape and colour are captivating. Charles I was executed on 30 January 1649, during the English Civil War. By the early eighteenth century, his portrait by van Dyck had made its way to France, the property first of Jeanne du Barry, mistress of Louis XV, before its acquisition by Louis XVI. Also from Antwerp, Jacob Jordaens was influenced by Rubens and Caravaggio. He excelled in scenes whose multiple figures are depicted without idealisation, investing them with immense energy and force. This is evidenced by his gouache and watercolour preparatory study **[258]** for *Christ Driving the Merchants from the Temple*. Acquired by Louis XV, it accentuates Christ's forceful gestures and the merchants' fearful expressions.

"GOLDEN AGES" The period from 1492, the date of Christopher Columbus's first voyages across the Atlantic, to the mid-seventeenth century has been dubbed the Spanish Golden Age: literally, for the riches brought by the conquistadors from the Americas, whose populations suffered at the hands

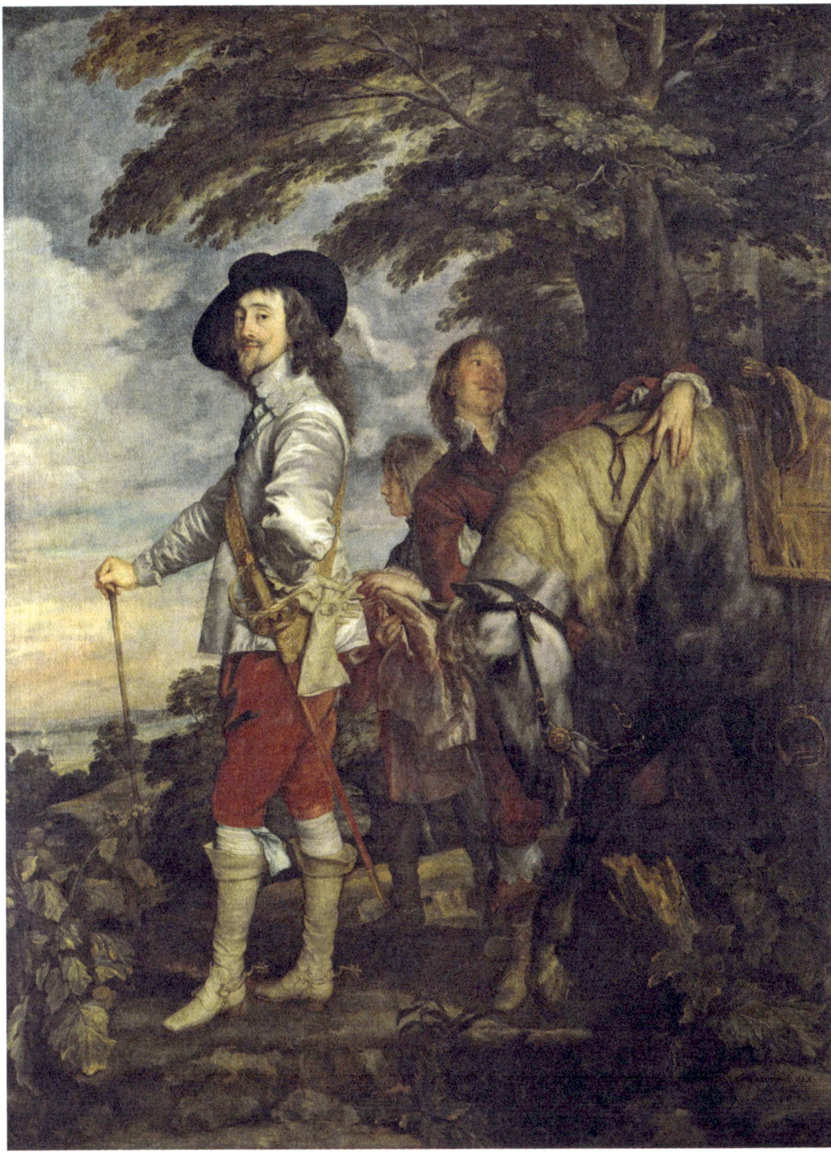

[259]
Anthony van Dyck
1599–1641
Charles I at the Hunt
c. 1625–1650
Oil on canvas
H. 266; W. 207 cm
(H. 8 ft 8¾ in.; W. 6 ft 9½ in.)
⩡ 1793 (former royal
collection, collection
of Louis XVI)
DP

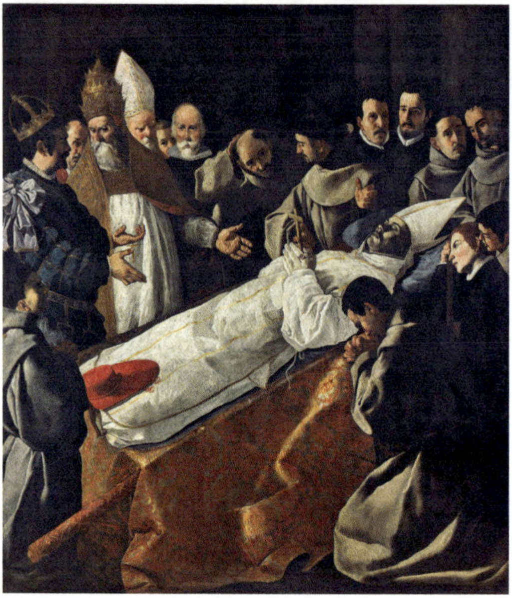

[260] Francisco de Zurbarán. 1598–1664. ***Saint Bonaventure's Body Lying in State***. c. 1629. Oil on canvas. H. 245; W. 220 cm (H. 8 ft ½ in.; W. 7 ft 2½ in.). ⩡ 1858. DP

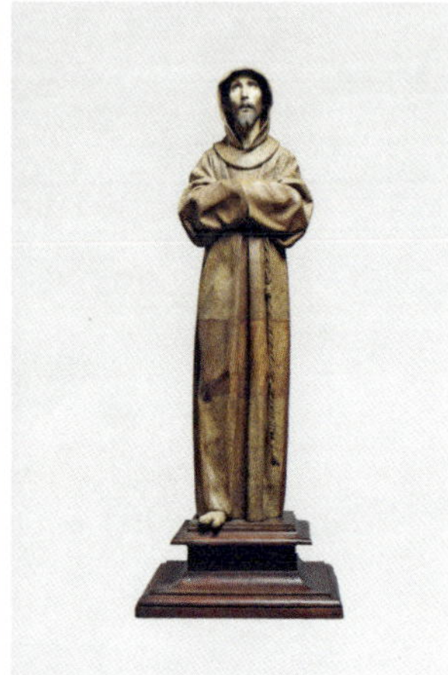

[261]
Spain
Saint Francis Dead
c. 1640–1660
Polychrome walnut, plant fibre, bone and glass
H. 87; W. 26; D. 24 cm
(H. 34¼; W. 10¼; D. 9½ in.)
⩡ 1988
DS

of Spain's armies, and figuratively, thanks to the country's flourishing literary – not least *Don Quixote* by Miguel de Cervantes – and artistic production. Although the Louvre was unable to conserve the works in Louis-Philippe's Spanish gallery when it was dispersed in 1848, the museum does hold several masterful examples of Spanish painting, including Bartolomé Esteban Murillo's *The Young Beggar* **[262]**. The work, acquired by Louis XVI at the end of the eighteenth century, reflects the painter's interest in ordinary subjects. Murillo uses chiaroscuro – light and shade – to spiritually elevate his young model. It is one of the Louvre's most copied works. His contemporary, Francisco de Zurbarán, is renowned for the intense spirituality of his religious paintings, which invite contemplative viewing. His work is devoid of anecdotal devices, focusing instead on the effect the painting has thanks to his carefully chosen palette and command of light. *Saint Bonaventure's Body Lyin g in State* **[260]** was acquired during the Second Empire, in 1858.

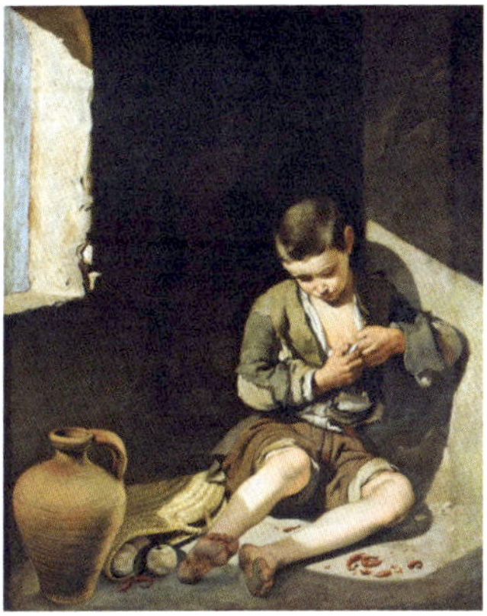

[262]
Bartolomé Esteban Murillo
1618–1682
The Young Beggar
c. 1647–1648
Oil on canvas
H. 134; W. 110 cm
(H. 4 ft 4¾ in.; W. 3 ft 7¼ in.)
⩡ 1793 (former royal collection, collection of Louis XVI)
DP

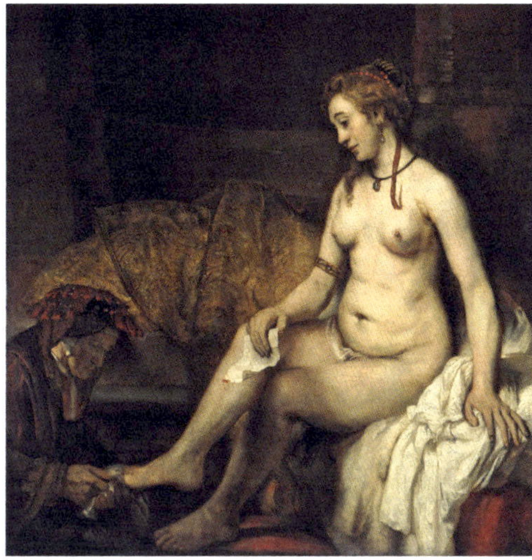

[263]
Rembrandt Harmenszoon van Rijn, known as Rembrandt
1606–1669
Bathsheba at Her Bath
1654
Oil on canvas
H. 142; W. 142 cm (H. 4 ft 8 in.; W. 4 ft 8 in.)
⩡ 1869 (bequest of Louis La Caze)
DP

In the Netherlands too, the seventeenth century was a time of economic prosperity – the Dutch dominated maritime trade – and artistic excellence, exemplified by Rembrandt Harmenszoon van Rijn. Rembrandt sought the greatest possible verisimilitude in paintings that also express an inner truth. *Bathsheba at Her Bath* **[263]** evokes an episode from the Bible: entranced by the young woman's beauty, King David wrote a letter summoning her to his side, even though she was married to one of his generals. Rembrandt makes Bathsheba the focus of attention, her beauty and radiance seemingly illuminating the entire scene. Her emotions are palpably portrayed; chosen by the king, her expression betrays her inner turmoil. *Slaughtered Ox* **[264]** shows the butchered carcass of an ox, strung up in a dark room. The choice of subject, depicted with no wish to soften the scene's brutality, and the palette of reds, browns and blacks, elevate the work beyond a simple genre painting or still life. Renewed interest in Rembrandt's work in France in the late eighteenth century reached a pinnacle in the nineteenth century;

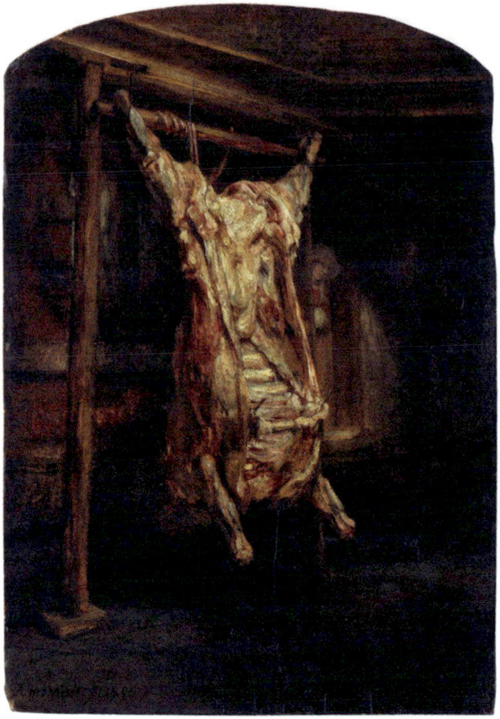

[265]
Rembrandt Harmenszoon van Rijn,
known as Rembrandt
1606–1669
The Three Crosses
1653
Etching and drypoint on vellum
H. 37.3; W. 44.8 cm
(H. 14¾; W. 17¾ in.)
⊻ 1935 (gift of Baron
Edmond de Rothschild)
DPD

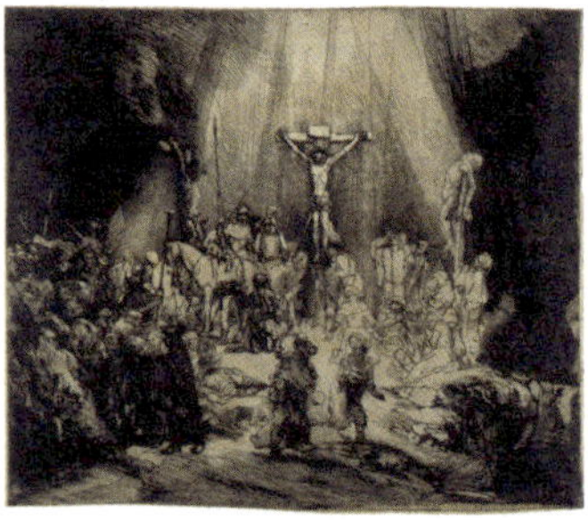

[264]
Rembrandt Harmenszoon
van Rijn, known as
Rembrandt
1606–1669
Slaughtered Ox
1655
Oil on beechwood
H. 94; W. 69 cm
(H. 3 ft 1 in.; W. 2 ft 3¼ in.)
⊻ 1857
DP

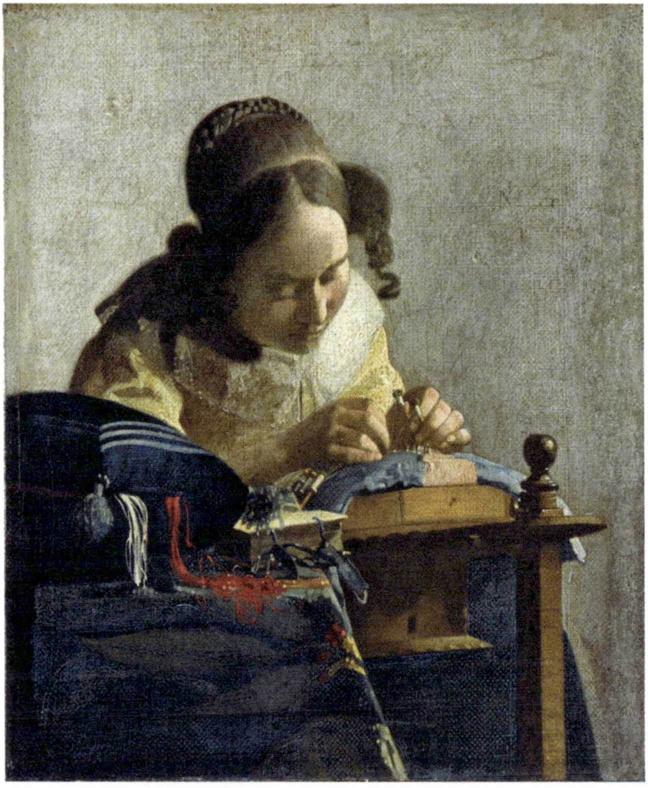

[266]
Johannes Vermeer
1632–1675
The Lacemaker
c. 1669–1670
Oil on canvas
mounted on wood
H. 24; W. 21 cm
(H. 9½; W. 8¼ in.)
⊻ 1870
DP

[267]
Jacob Isaacksz
van Ruisdael
c. 1628/1629–1682
The Ray of Light
c. 1660–1670
Oil on canvas
H. 83; W. 99 cm
(H. 2 ft 8¾ in.;
W. 3 ft 3 in.)
⪯ 1793 (former royal collection, collection of Louis XVI)
DP

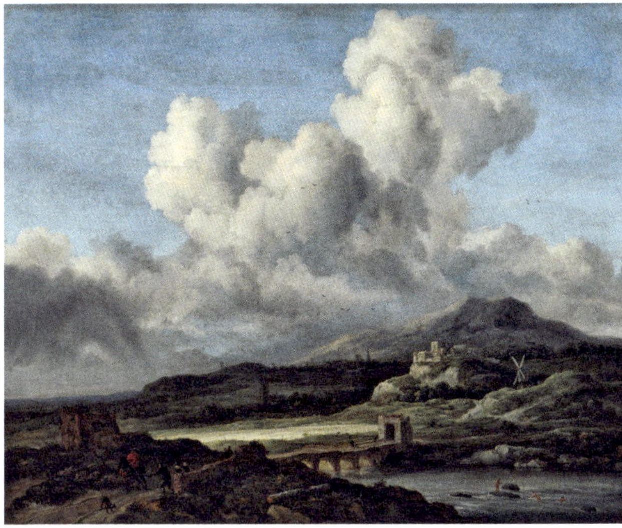

Gustave Courbet was among the painter's most ardent admirers. Rembrandt was also a talented engraver, whose etchings are distinguished by their strong lines and sense of staging **[265]**.

Dutch artists were master landscape painters, particularly observant of how atmospheres were influenced by changing weather conditions. In Jacob van Ruisdael's *The Ray of Light* **[267]**, the panoramic format and sudden burst of sunlight form the subject suggested by the title, which was given to the painting in the nineteenth century.

Today, Vermeer is one of the most popular seventeenth-century Dutch artists **[p. 294]**. His (very few) paintings fascinate in their simplicity of means, and because they resist a too literal interpretation: his genre scenes have no narrative intent. *The Lacemaker* **[266]** is absorbed by her work. Like colours on an artist's palette, the criss-crossing threads appear to form a metaphor for painting. It was only in the mid-nineteenth century that Vermeer's art was recognised in France, an enthusiasm expressed many times over since then, in painting and literature.

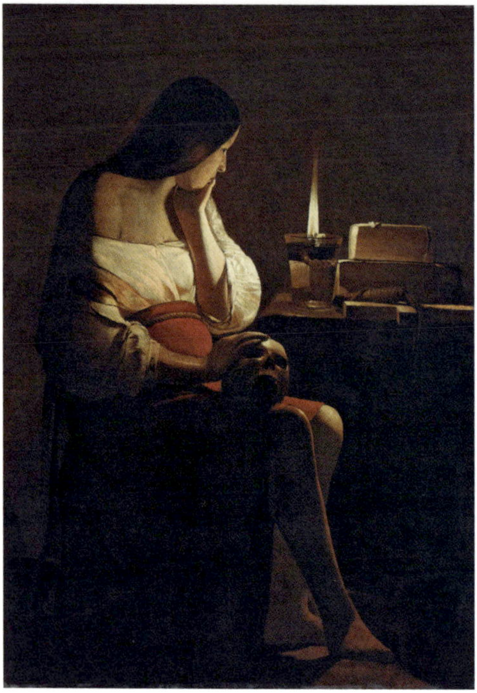

[268]
Georges de La Tour
1593–1652
Magdalene with the Smoking Flame
c. 1642–1644
Oil on canvas
H. 128; W. 94 cm
(H. 4 ft 2½ in.; W. 3 ft 1 in.)
⊻ 1949
DP

SHADOW AND LIGHT Born in the Duchy of Lorraine in the first half of the seventeenth century, Georges de La Tour was another artist to fall into obscurity. It wasn't until the beginning of the twentieth century that his talent was acknowledged and his works attributed to him. *Card Sharp with the Ace of Diamonds* **[269]** is steeped in the painting of Caravaggio, whom La Tour admired. It shows a card game in which the young man on the right is being duped by the other players. The artist is meticulous in his depiction of the various characters' gestures and sideways glances; the viewer is complicit, seeing the cards which the player on the left has tucked into the back of his belt. *Magdalene with the Smoking Flame* **[268]** offers a contemplative view of the saint, alone with a single candle that casts a shadow along her body and over the rudimentary interior. The skull she holds on her lap is a memento mori, a reminder of the brevity of life and the vanity of existence. The Le Nain brothers were also forgotten by history until the nineteenth century when their genre scenes, portrayals of rural life instilled with a form of quiet fervour, were praised by critics and, subsequently, admired by artists. The brothers' *Peasant*

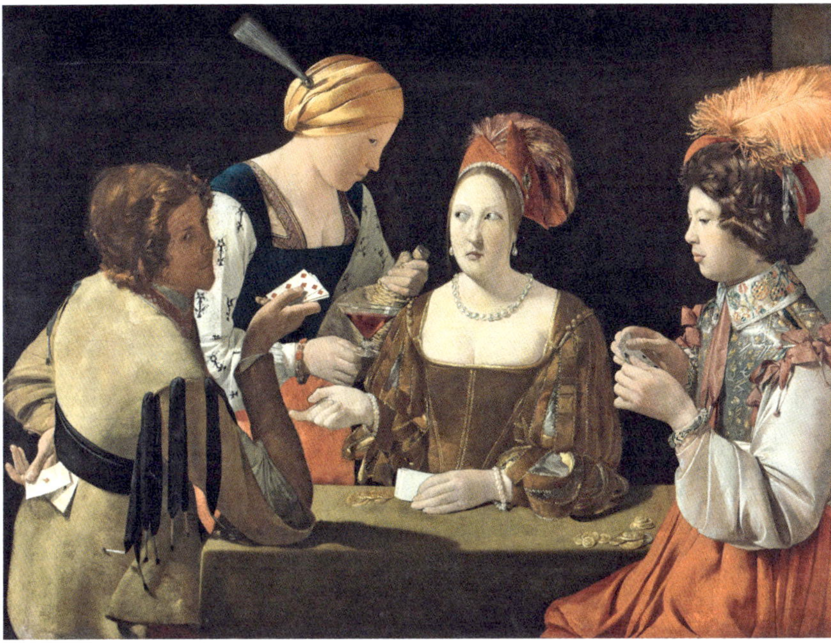

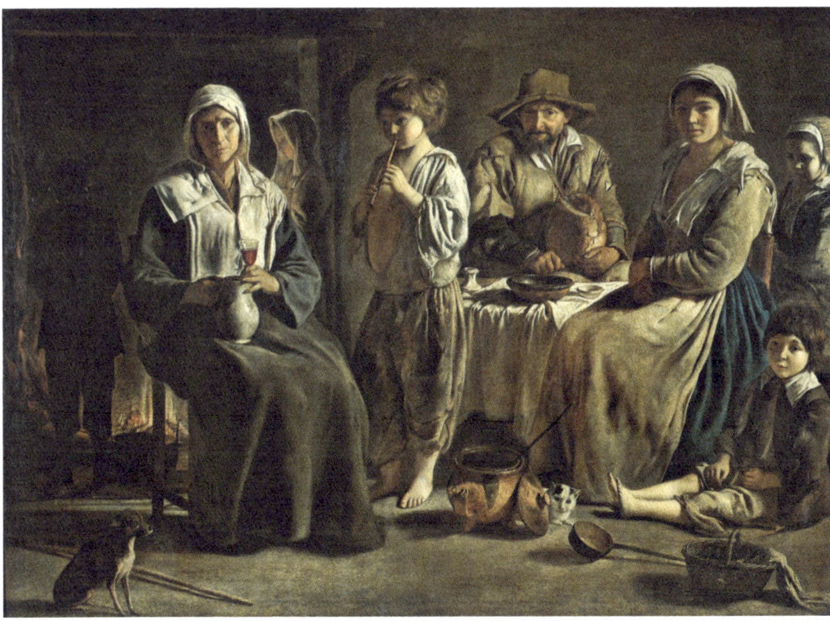

[269]
Georges de La Tour
1593–1652
Card Sharp with the Ace of Diamonds
c. 1636–1640
Oil on canvas
H. 106; W. 146 cm
(H. 3 ft 5¾ in.; W. 4 ft 9½ in.)
⊻ 1972
DP

[270]
Louis Le Nain, c. 1593–1648;
Antoine Le Nain?, c. 1600/1610–1648
Peasant Family
c. 1642
Oil on canvas
H. 113; W. 159 cm
(H. 3 ft 8½ in.; W. 5 ft 2½ in.)
⊻ 1915
DP

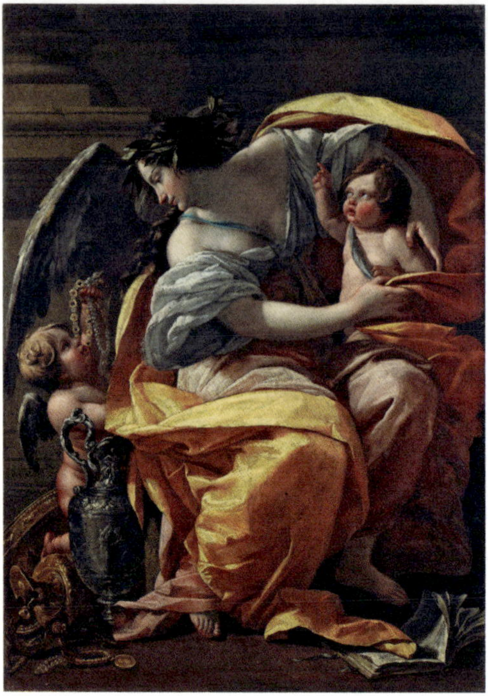

[271]
Simon Vouet
1590–1649
Allegory of Wealth
Château Neuf, Saint-Germain-en-Laye, France
c. 1638–1640
Oil on canvas
H. 170; W. 124 cm
(H. 5 ft 7 in.; W. 4 ft ¾ in.)
⩡ 1793 (former royal collection, collection of Louis XIII)
DP

Family **[270]** is noteworthy for its sense of composition and for the dignity and solemnity with which its subject, a simple gathering of family members, is portrayed. It was acquired by the Louvre in 1915.

Not all artists had to wait for recognition. Simon Vouet painted *Allegory of Wealth* **[271]** for the Château de Saint-Germain-en-Laye. Vouet, who had admired the Baroque painting of his contemporaries in Rome, demonstrates his painterly skill in the swathes of fabric and the wings that envelop the group formed by the woman and the putto pointing to the heavens, the only place where true wealth is found. Nicolas Poussin remains one of the greatest painters of the seventeenth century. A prolific artist, his many works illustrate the extent of his talent and convey a form of classical restraint in their carefully ordered compositions, with precise lines and a strong sense of balance. In *The Arcadian Shepherds* **[272]**, figures dressed in ancient robes, in a landscape that suggests Italy, try to decipher the words "Et in Arcadia ego" ("I too am in Arcadia"), carved into the tomb. This inscription shows Poussin's

[272]
Nicolas Poussin
1594–1665
The Arcadian Shepherds
c. 1638
Oil on canvas
H. 85; W. 121 cm
(H. 2 ft 9½ in.; W. 3 ft 11¾ in.)
⊻ 1793 (former royal collection, collection of Louis XIV)
DP

[273]
Nicolas Poussin
1594–1665
Apollo Sauroctonos
c. 1660
Pen and brown ink, grey and brown wash, black chalk
H. 19; W. 25.7 cm
(H. 7½; W. 10 in.)
⊻ 1878 (gift of Horace His de La Salle)
DPD

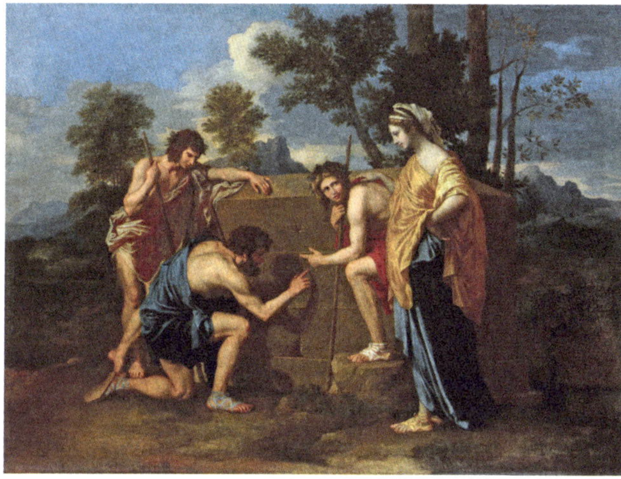

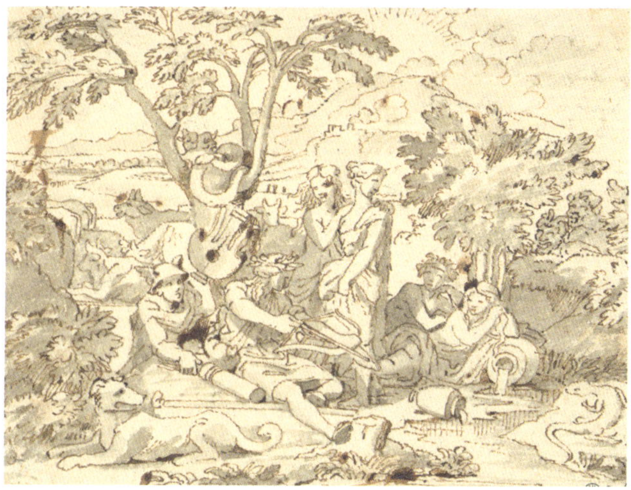

[274]
Philippe de Champaigne
1602–1674
The Dead Christ
c. 1650–1654
Oil on wood
H. 68; W. 197 cm
(H. 2 ft 2¾ in.; W. 6 ft 5½ in.)
⊻ 1793
DP

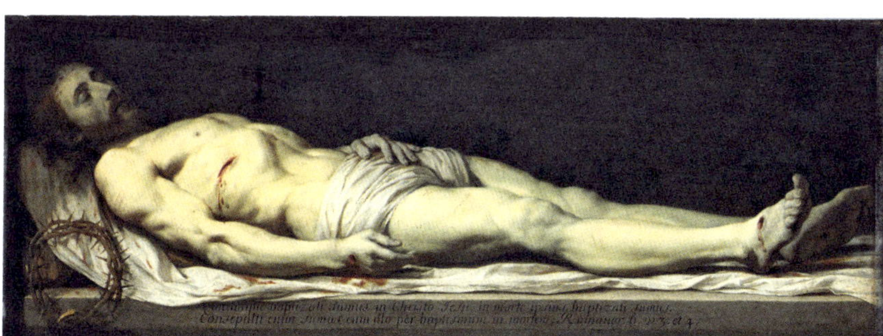

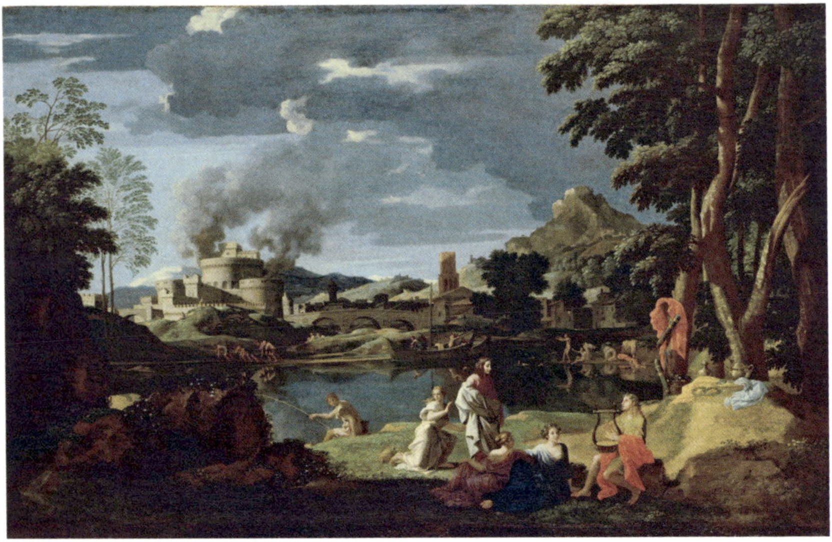

[275] Nicolas Poussin. 1594–1665. ***Landscape with Orpheus and Eurydice***. c. 1648. Oil on canvas H. 124; W. 200 cm (H. 4 ft ¾ in.; W. 6 ft 6¾ in.). ⊻ 1793 (former royal collection, collection of Louis XIV). DP

familiarity with classical mythology and literature: Arcadia is a mythical province, extolled by ancient poets, where peace and happiness reign. The sentence can be read as an evocation of death, present even in Arcadia, or a reference to the joys experienced by the deceased, who had the good fortune to live out his existence in this idyllic place. *Landscape with Orpheus and Eurydice* **[275]** is both a reflection on death and a musing on love. Poussin evokes the story of Orpheus, the very first poet, whose lyre-playing charmed gods, humans and animals alike, and of his wife Eurydice. The vast landscape takes in both the moment of their marriage and the dramatic instance of the young bride's death; Orpheus would later fail in his attempt to bring her back from the Underworld. Another artist, Philippe de Champaigne, was close to the Jansenist theological current whose rigorous principles, in both life and worship, were in contrast with the ostentation of certain religious figures. *The Dead Christ* **[274]** is visually striking in its portrayal of Christ as an isolated figure whose presence is made all the more intense by a powerful relief effect, his body exposed to the viewer's gaze. This visual treatment

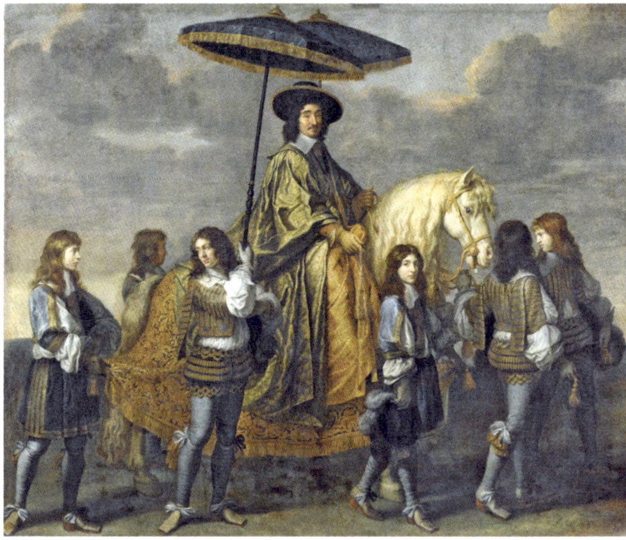

[276]
Charles Le Brun
1619–1690
Chancellor Séguier
c. 1660–1661
Oil on canvas
H. 295; W. 357 cm
(H. 9 ft 8¼ in.;
W. 11 ft 8½ in.)
⊻ 1942 (with the participation of the Société des Amis du Louvre)
DP

elevates his sacrifice by insisting on his very real death, before his Resurrection.

THE SUN KING The arts in France flourished under Louis XIV. The king had architectural ambitions and ordered new constructions to be added to the Louvre, before moving the royal household to Versailles. Charles Le Brun played an active role alongside the king, as his First Painter and as the administrator for royal commissions. In this capacity, he devised the Louvre's Galerie d'Apollon, named for Apollo, god of the arts. Le Brun's painting of *Chancellor Séguier* **[276]** possibly relates to the entry into Paris of Louis XIV and his wife, Maria Theresa of Spain. The composition is devoid of anecdotal details, focused entirely on the chancellor, sumptuously attired, and his entourage. Louis XIV also held military ambitions and waged battle on a number of fronts. In his *Entry of Alexander into Babylon* **[277]**, Le Brun celebrates the Greek conqueror but also the French sovereign. History painting thus alluded to victories past and present, covering Louis XIV in lasting,

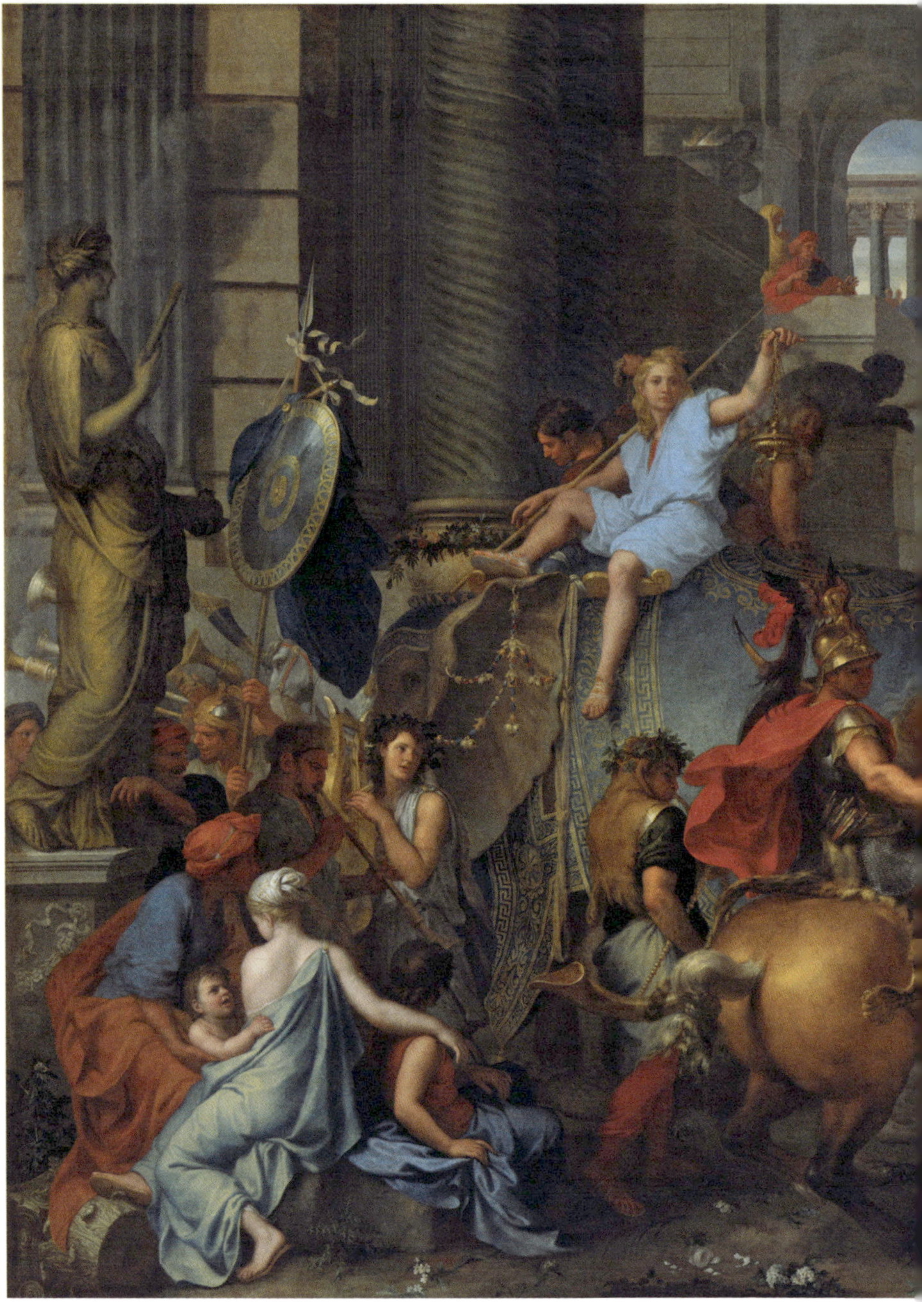

[277]
Charles Le Brun
1619–1690
Entry of Alexander into Babylon
1664–1665
Oil on canvas
H. 450; W. 707 cm (H. 14 ft 9¼; W. 23 ft 1½ in.)
⩡ 1793 (former royal collection, collection of Louis XIV)
DP

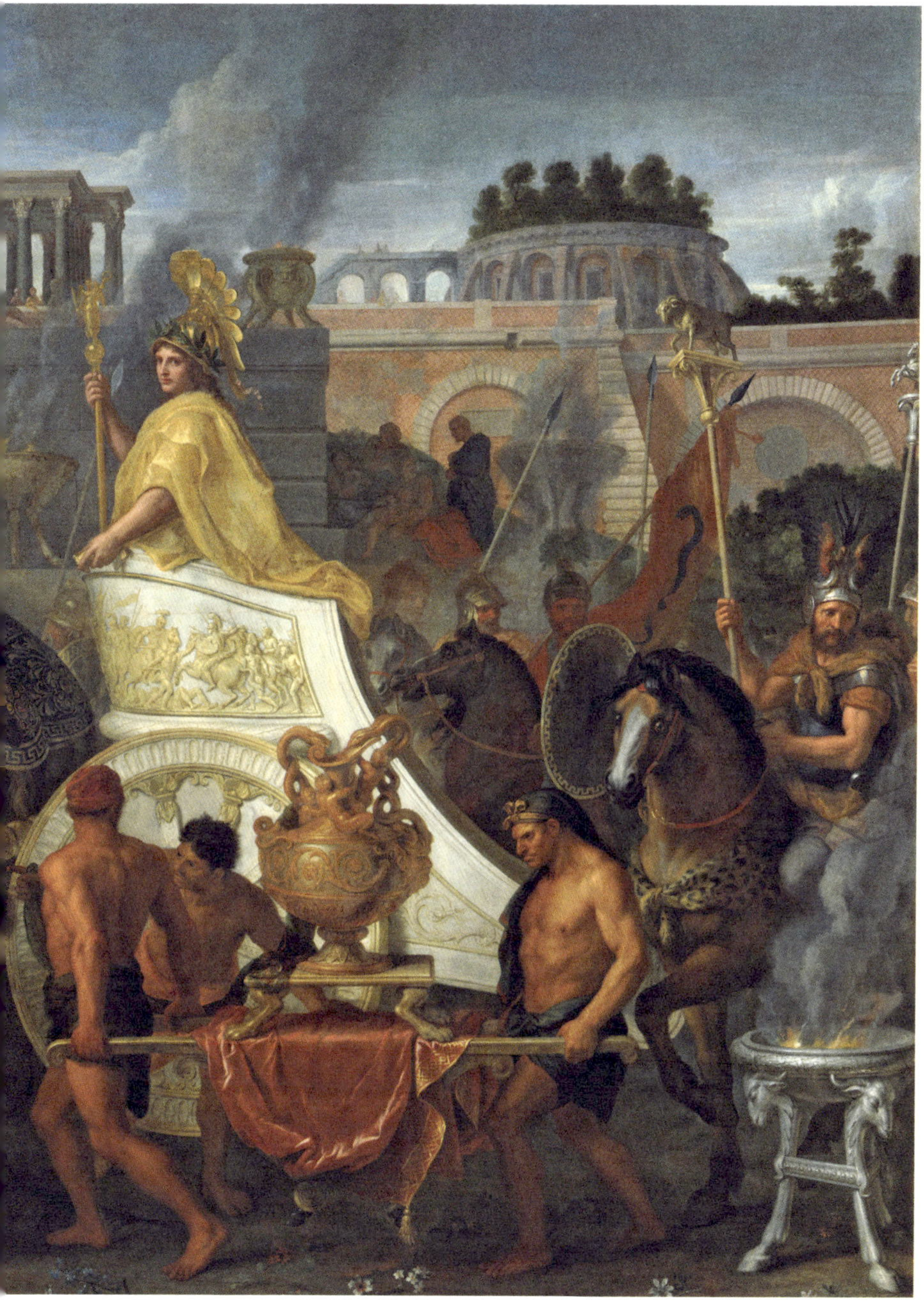

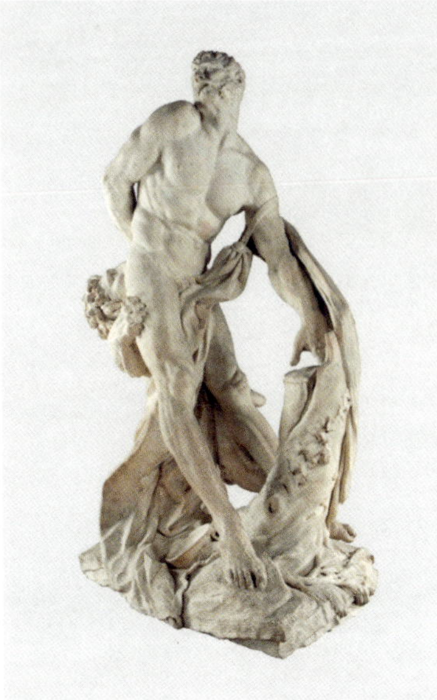

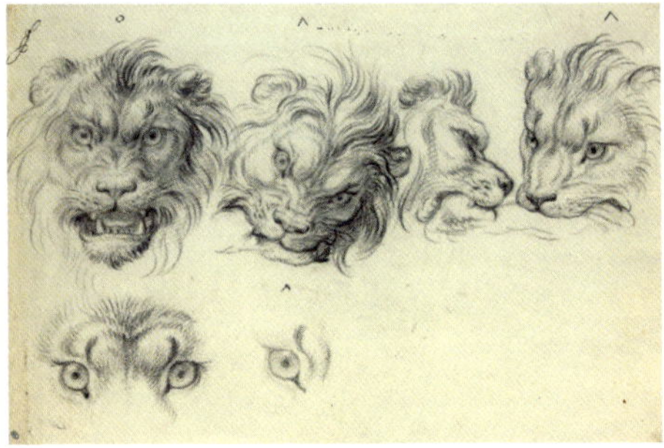

[278]
Pierre Puget
1620–1694
Milo of Croton
Château de Versailles gardens
c. 1672–1682
Carrara marble
H. 270; W. 140; D. 80 cm
(H. 8 ft 10¼ in.; W. 4 ft 7¼ in.;
D. 2 ft 7½ in.)
⊻ 1819 (former royal collection,
collection of Louis XIV)
DS

[279]
Charles Le Brun
1619–1690
Four Lion Heads and Studies of Lion Eyes
c. 1670
Black chalk on white paper
H. 27.4; W. 42.6 cm
(H. 10¾; W. 16¾ in.)
⊻ 1793 (former royal
collection, collection
of Louis XIV)
DPD

mythical glory. Le Brun was also active in the instruction of artists, particularly through his lectures, and instrumental in the creation of the Académie Royale de Peinture et de Sculpture, while his physiognomic studies, which were reproduced as engravings, sought to illustrate the relation between animal features and human expressions **[279]**. Gian Lorenzo Bernini, who worked in Rome, was one of the great Italian sculptors of the first half of the seventeenth century. His bust of Pope Urban VIII **[282]** was bequeathed to Louis XIV by the pontiff's nephew. The young king asked Bernini to propose a design for the Louvre's eastern facade, though he ultimately chose Claude Perrault, who created the monumental colonnade that opens onto the Cour Carrée. Later, in collaboration with François Girardon, Bernini sculpted the sovereign's equestrian statue. A copy in lead was installed in the Louvre's Cour Napoléon in the late 1980s.

Numerous sculptures were commissioned to adorn royal residences and their grounds. Contemporary statues were placed alongside copies of ancient works. Pierre Puget's *Milo of Croton* **[278]** describes the cruel fate that

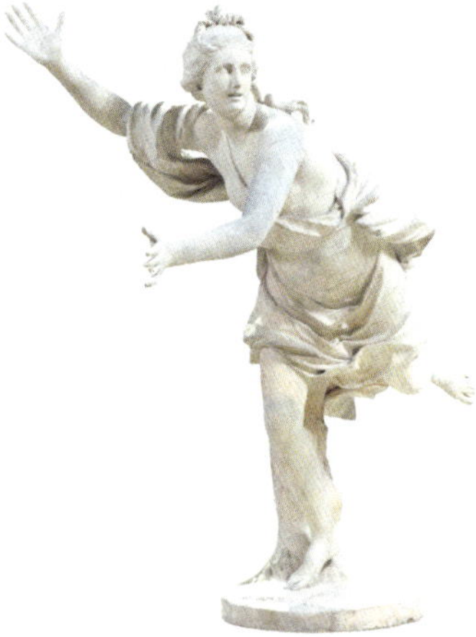

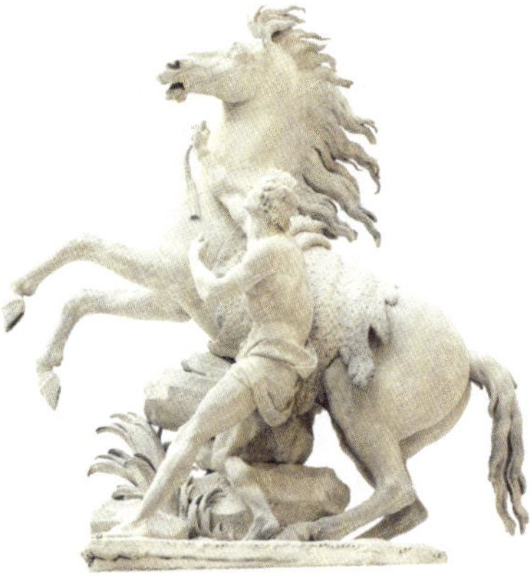

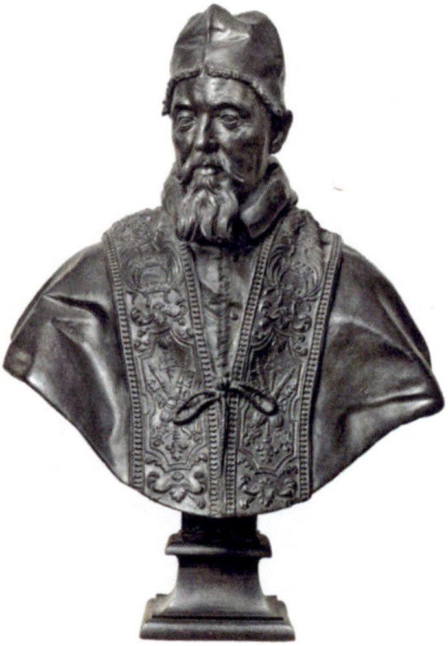

[280]
Guillaume Coustou
1677–1746
Daphne (Chased by Apollo)
Château de Marly gardens
c. 1713–1715
Carrara marble
H. 132; W. 135.5; D. 65 cm
(H. 4 ft 4 in.; W. 4 ft 5¼ in.; D. 2 ft 1½ in.)
⩡ 1940 (former royal collection)
DS

[281]
Guillaume Coustou
1677–1746
Horse Restrained by a Groom
Château de Marly gardens
1745
Carrara marble
H. 340; W. 284; D. 127 cm
(H. 11 ft 1¾ in.; W. 9 ft 3¾ in.; D. 4 ft 2 in.)
⩡ 1984 (former royal collection)
DS

[282]
Gian Lorenzo Bernini
1598–1680
Pope Urban VIII, Maffeo Barberini
c. 1640
Bronze
H. 105; W. 75; D. 42 cm
(H. 3 ft 5¼ in.; W. 2 ft 5½ in.; D. 1 ft 4½ in.)
⩡ 1793 (former royal collection, collection of Louis XIV)
DS

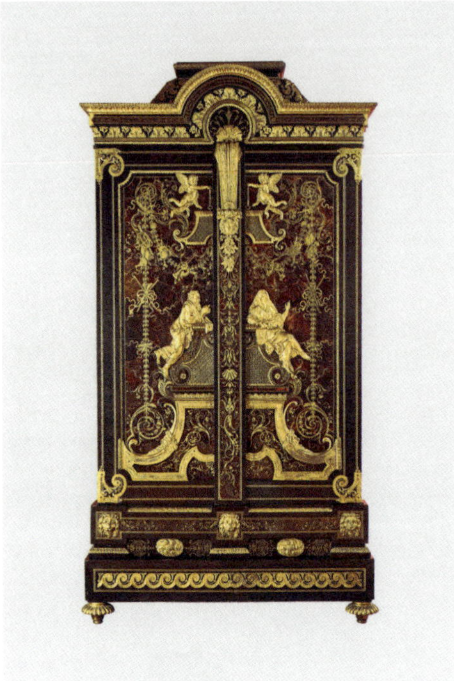

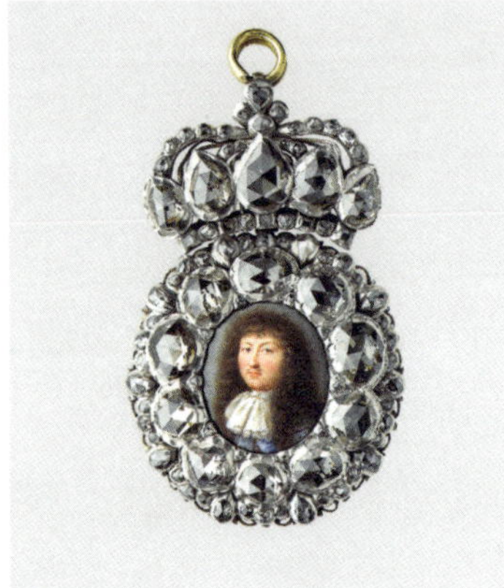

[283]
André Charles Boulle
1642–1732
Armoire, one of a pair
c. 1700–1715
Bamboo, wood, horn, ivory, shell, copper, tin, oak and gilded bronze
H. 286.7; W. 152; D. 59 cm
(H. 9 ft 4¾ in.; W. 4 ft 11¾ in.; D. 1 ft 11¼ in.)
⊻ 1950
DDA

[284]
Laurent Le Tessier de Montarsy, ?–1684; Jean Petitot I ?, 1607–1691
Portrait Box of Louis XIV
c. 1680
Gold, silver, enamel and diamond
H. 7.2; W. 4.6 cm
(H. 2⅞; W. 1⅞ in.)
⊻ 2009
DDA

befell the ancient Greek athlete, prisoner of an oak tree he had tried to split open with his bare hands, making him a helpless prey for a ferocious lion. Sculptor Antoine Coysevox was commissioned for two equestrian groups, *Fame Riding Pegasus* and *Mercury Riding Pegasus*. They reference the imperial art of ancient Rome and the legendary winged stallion, created from the blood of Medusa after she was decapitated by Perseus. Originally intended to stand on either side of the balustrade overlooking the Bassin de l'Abreuvoir at the Château de Marly, one of the first royal palaces built for Louis XIV, both works were removed and taken to the Tuileries in 1719, and two new groups were subsequently commissioned from Guillaume Coustou. In *Horse Restrained by a Groom* **[281]** the sculptor captures the spirit and vitality of the steed the groom struggles to contain. The same ability to capture movement appears in *Daphne (Chased by Apollo)* **[280]**. Here, Coustou cites the Roman poet Ovid, who in his *Metamorphoses*, tells how the nymph fled the god's advances and how she was transformed into a laurel tree, delivering her from her pursuer once and for all.

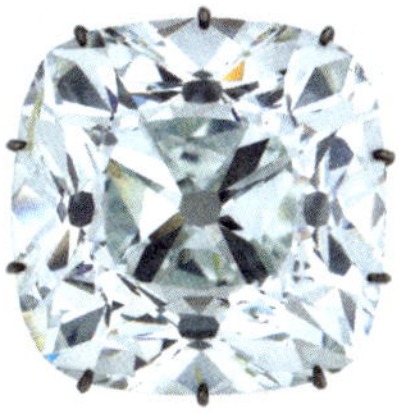

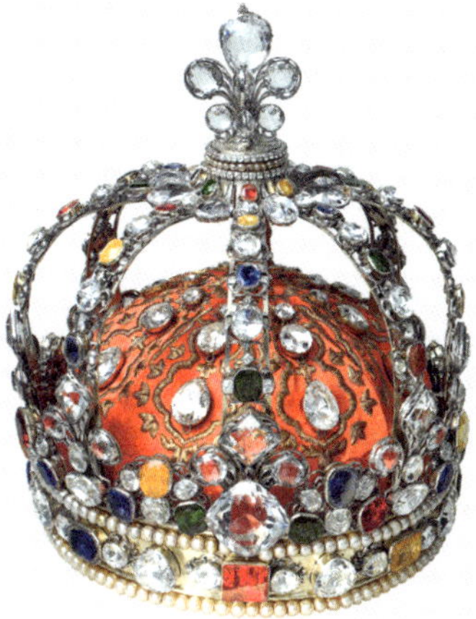

[285]
Joseph Cope (lapidary)
1645–1710
***Diamond*, known as**
The Regent
c. 1704–1706
Diamond
H. 3.2; W. 3.1 cm
(H. 1¼; W. 1¼ in.)
⊻ Former royal collection, collection of Philippe d'Orléans
DDA

[286]
Augustin Duflos, c. 1700–before 1781; Laurent Rondé; Claude Rondé
Louis XV's Crown
Treasury of Saint-Denis, France
1722
Silver, embroidered satin, imitation pearls and gemstones
H. 24; W. 22; Diam. 20 cm
(H. 9½; W. 8¾; Diam. 7¾ in.)
⊻ 1852
DDA

The decorative arts contributed their share to the royal court's splendour, for example the *Portrait Box of Louis XIV* **[284]**, a magnificent example of the jeweller's art. An oval miniature of the king in armour sits at the centre of a mount formed by ten large rose-cut diamonds and forty small diamonds, topped by a crown composed of five diamonds with nine facets and twenty-three small diamonds. The back is enamelled with the royal cypher (two intertwined "L"s). Another craft, cabinetmaking, reached a rare degree of refinement in the hands of André Charles Boulle, whose furniture was richly decorated with inlays in various woods, pewter, brass, horn or ivory using the marquetry technique he perfected. A piece of Boulle furniture was a highly prized possession **[283]**. Certain materials, brought from Africa and South America, such as ebony and ivory, were the result of a lucrative commerce that was linked to the slave trade. Boulle's style was imitated during the nineteenth century but never equalled. The Galerie d'Apollon is home to the French Crown Jewels, which were dispersed at the time of the French Revolution **[286]**.

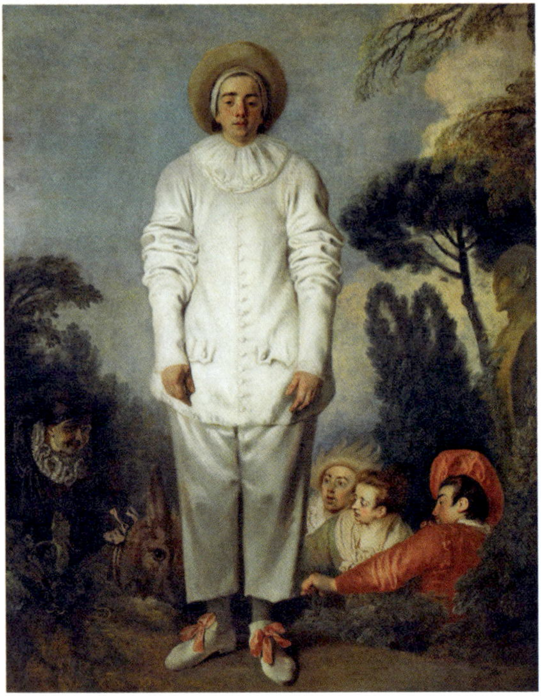

[287]
Jean-Antoine Watteau
1684–1721
Pierrot*, formerly also known as *Gilles
c. 1718–1719
Oil on canvas
H. 185; W. 150 cm
(H. 6 ft ¾ in.; W. 4 ft 11 in.)
⊻ 1869 (bequest of Louis La Caze)
DP

The so-called *Regent Diamond* **[285]**, named in honour of Philippe II, Duke of Orleans, who became regent at the death of Louis XIV, was discovered in 1698 in Golconda, India, and immediately caught the interest of Thomas Pitt, the British governor of Madras, who took the stone to England to be cut. It was acquired for the French Crown at the request of Philippe II in 1717. The *Regent* surpassed every other diamond then known in the West in both beauty and size. Its purity and the quality of its cut are such that it is still considered the most beautiful diamond in the world.

ACCOMPLISHMENTS Antoine Watteau was active in the early eighteenth century, painting works that juxtapose landscape, seduction and contemplation. His *Pierrot*, previously known as *Gilles* **[287]**, illustrates characters from the commedia dell'arte, a form of open-air theatre that originated in Italy. Dressed in white, Watteau's Pierrot stands on a wall that doubles as a stage, indifferent to the people behind him. An aura of mystery surrounds the painting. Pierrot's pose is stiff, his arms hang loosely by his sides. Possibly he feels

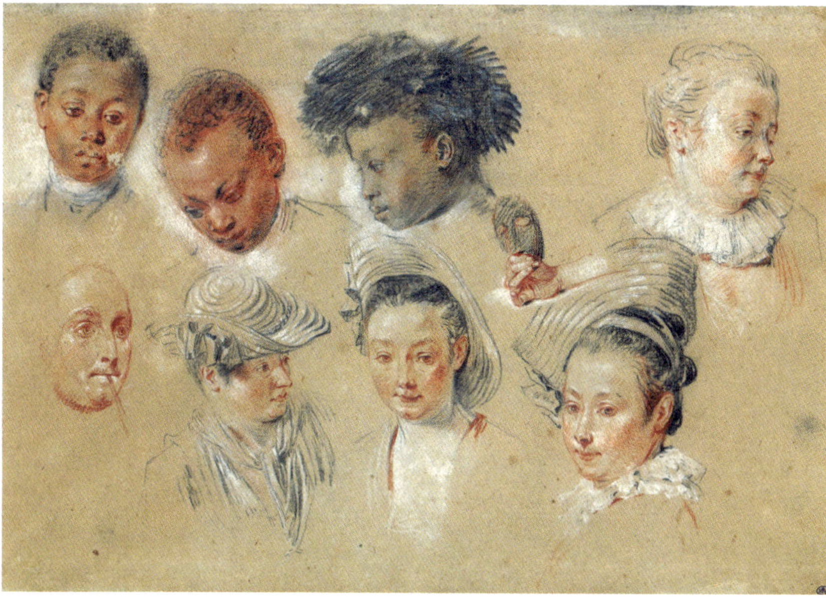

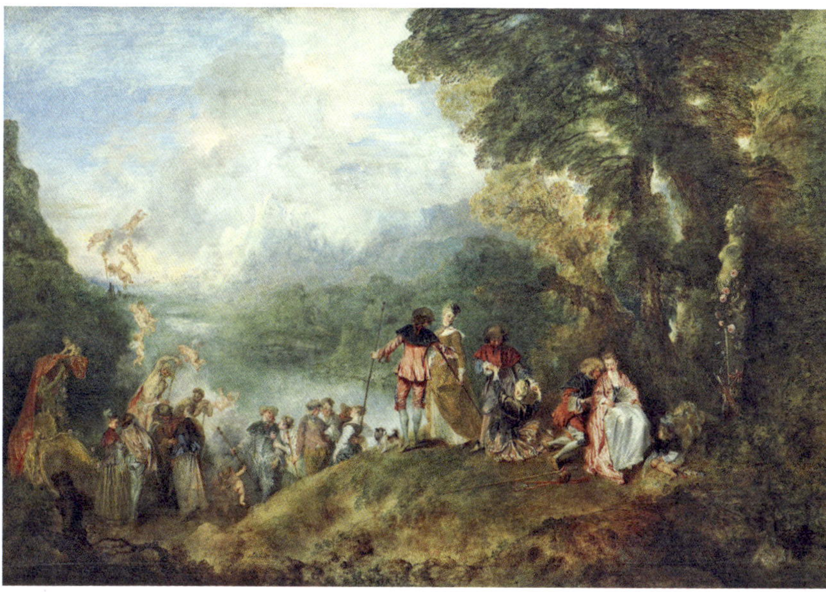

[288]
Jean-Antoine Watteau
1684–1721
Eight Head Studies
Red, black and white chalk, heightened with brown pastel and wash on paper
H. 26.7; W. 39.7 cm
(H. 10½; W. 15¾ in.)
⊻ 1858
DPD

[289]
Jean-Antoine Watteau
1684–1721
Pilgrimage to the Isle of Cythera
1717
Oil on canvas
H. 129; W. 194 cm
(H. 4 ft 2¾ in.; W. 6 ft 4½ in.)
⊻ 1795 (former collection of the Académie Royale de Peinture et de Sculpture)
DP

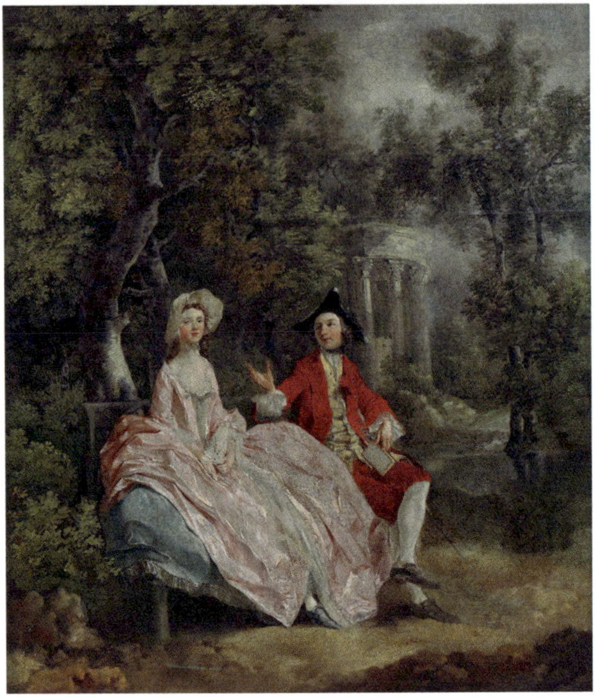

[290]
Thomas Gainsborough
1727–1788
Conversation in a Park
c. 1746–1748
Oil on canvas
H. 73; W. 68 cm
(H. 28¾; W. 26¾ in.)
⩡ 1952 (gift of
Jean Groult)
DP

ill at ease in a costume that is too large, too elaborate for him. Pierrot would go on to embody the image of the artist as clumsy, naïve, a misfit. Watteau was also an accomplished draughtsman. *Eight Head Studies* **[288]** – a sheet in red, black and white chalk – are sketches for various later compositions. His talent was officially recognised by his peers in 1717 when he was elected to the Académie Royale de Peinture et de Sculpture, having presented *Pilgrimage to the Isle of Cythera* **[289]**, prompting the academy to create a new genre, the "fête galante". Cythera was associated with Venus, the goddess of love. The couples in Watteau's painting are leaving for, or perhaps returning from, this enchanted island. Despite its frivolity, the scene is bathed in a poetic melancholy that gives this delightful painting unexpected depth.

Artists wishing to join the academy were required to submit work for approval. These were known as reception pieces. In 1728 Jean Siméon Chardin, a painter of still lifes, proposed *The Ray* **[291]**. Hung from a hook, the dead fish resembles a sea monster and appears twice the size of a frightened kitten

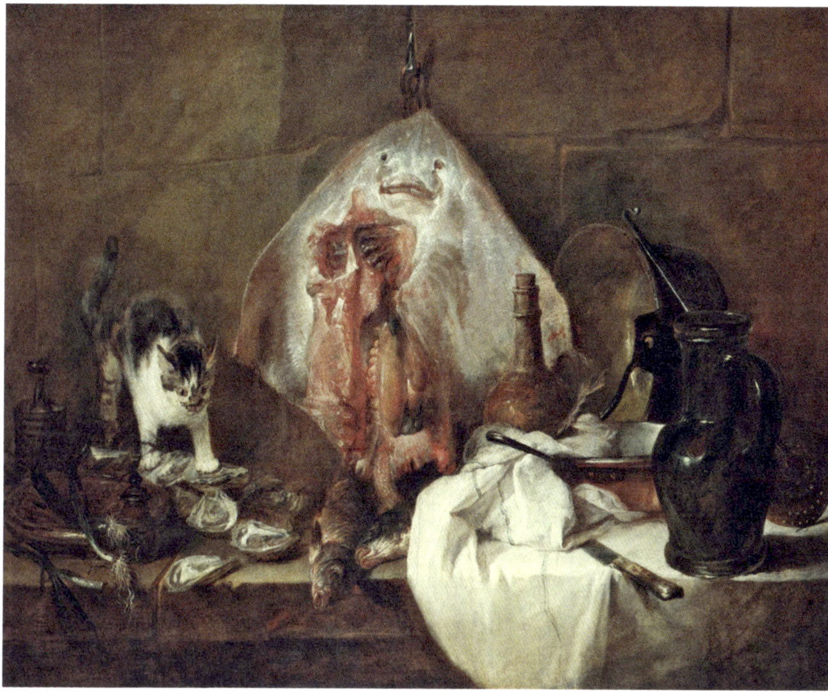

[291]
Jean Siméon Chardin
1699–1779
The Ray
1728
Oil on canvas
H. 114.5; W. 146 cm
(H. 3 ft 9 in.; W. 4 ft 9½ in.)
⊻ 1796 (former collection of the Académie Royale de Peinture et de Sculpture)
DP

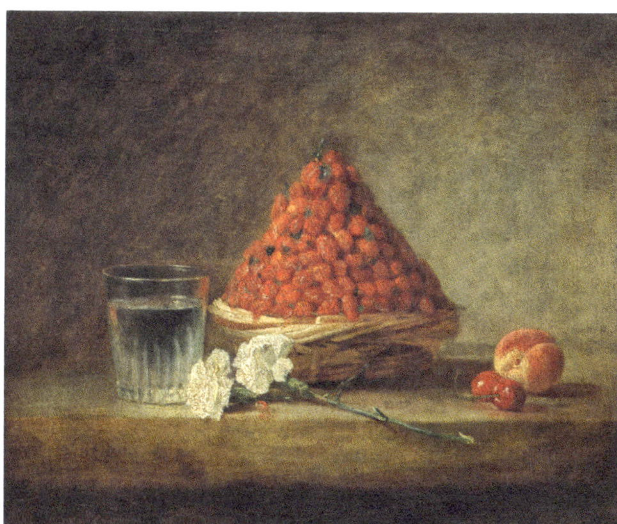

[292]
Jean Siméon Chardin
1699–1779
Basket of Strawberries
1761
Oil on canvas
H. 38; W. 46 cm
(H. 15; W. 18 in.)
⊻ 2024 (acquired with the exceptional support of LVMH, and that of 10,000 donors to the "Become a Patron!" crowdfunding campaign, the Société des Amis du Louvre, Laplace architecture agency and Laboratoires Septodont)
DP

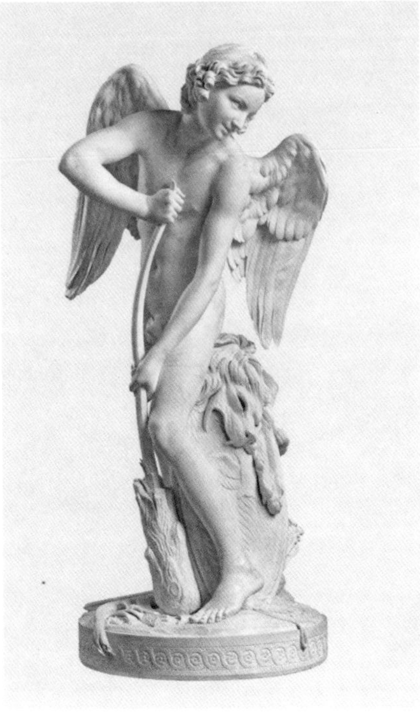

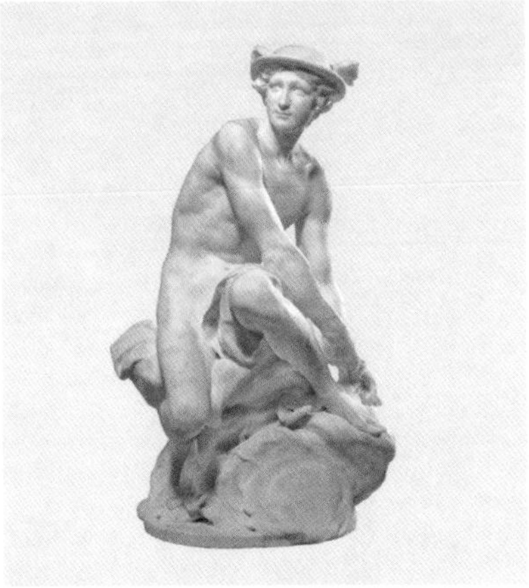

[293]
Edme Bouchardon
1698–1762
Cupid Cutting His Bow from the Club of Hercules
1750
Marble
H. 173; W. 75; D. 75 cm
(H. 5 ft 8 in.; W. 2 ft 5½ in.; D. 2 ft 5½ in.)
⩡ 1824
DS

[294]
Jean-Baptiste Pigalle
1714–1785
Mercury Attaching His Winged Sandals
1744
Marble
H. 58; W. 35.5; D. 33 cm
(H. 22¾; W. 14; D. 13 in.)
⩡ 1848–1850 (former collection of the Académie Royale de Peinture et de Sculpture)
DS

teetering on some oysters. Chardin elevates this ordinary scene into a moment worthy of our attention. The red of the skate's viscera stands out against the white of its skin and, underneath, the pink tones of its flesh. In 1761 Chardin exhibited a carefully composed still life depicting a basket of wild strawberries **[292]**. It would be one of the last works by an artist at the height of his fame as an accomplished master of the genre. Denis Diderot was one of the many to admire the remarkable skill with which Chardin was able to render light and the very substance of the objects he portrays. In 1744 sculptor Jean-Baptiste Pigalle presented *Mercury Attaching His Winged Sandals* **[294]**. The nude figure and explicit references to the god's attributes – the petasos (wide-brimmed hat) and the winged footwear that allows him to fly – anchor the subject in Roman mythology; that we see him sitting, fastening his sandals, a rather ordinary scene, introduces a realistic tone. Edmé Bouchardon sculpted *Cupid Cutting His Bow from the Club of Hercules* **[293]** not in the hope of being accepted into the academy, but as a commission for the Salon de la Guerre at the Château de Versailles. That the artist should have chosen

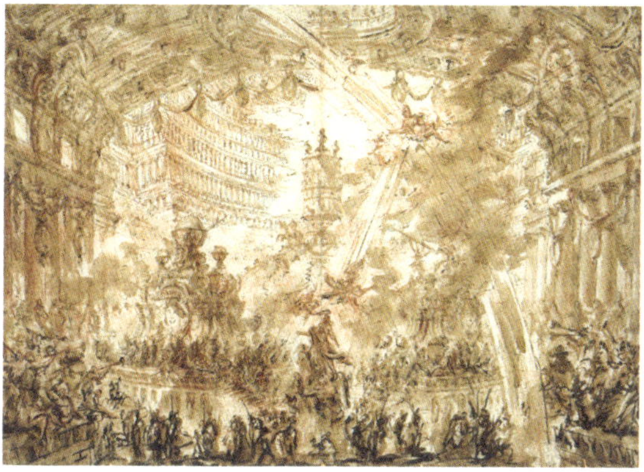

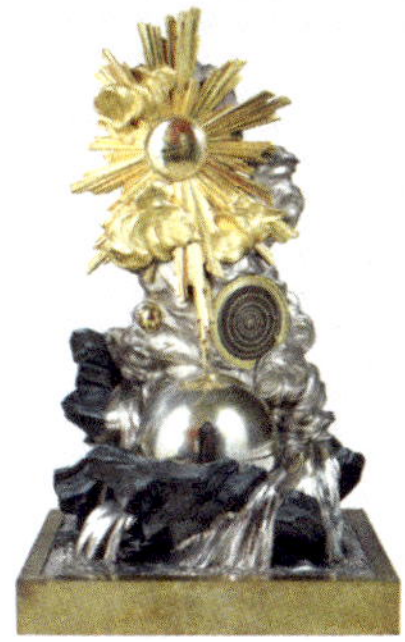

[295]
Giovanni Battista Piranesi
1720–1778
Palace Interior: Two Winged Phemes Crowning a Figure
c. 1748
Pen and ink
H. 51.2; W. 76.5 cm
(H. 20¼; W. 30 in.)
⩡ 1983
DPD

[296]
Claude-Siméon Passemant, 1702–1769;
François Thomas Germain, 1726–1791
Clock of the Creation of the World
1754
Silver and bronze
H. 143; W. 92; D. 77 cm
(H. 4 ft 8¼ in.; W. 3 ft ¼ in.; D. 2 ft 6¼ in.)
⩡ 2014 (deposit from the Établissement Public du Château, du Musée et du Domaine National de Versailles)
DDA

the most whimsical episode in the myth of Hercules suggests his intention was to implicitly extol love's dizzying pleasures more than military courage.

ARTS AND SCIENCES Important advances in science were made during the seventeenth and eighteenth centuries and this progress piqued the curiosity of artists. For example, the architect and draughtsman Giovanni Battista Piranesi, famed for his drawings of imagined buildings, created a vast palace as the scene for two winged figures, symbolising Pheme (also known as Fame), crowning a person who has been identified as the mathematician Isaac Newton **[295]**. The protagonist stands in a broken shaft of light, believed to be an allusion to Newton's theory on the refraction and colours of light. The peculiar cylinder is thought to represent the polymath's law of universal gravitation. Piranesi's drawings helped shape his contemporaries' tastes, especially as many were circulated as prints. The *Clock of the Creation of the World* **[296]** further illustrates how the arts drew on scientific discoveries. It was designed by Claude-Siméon

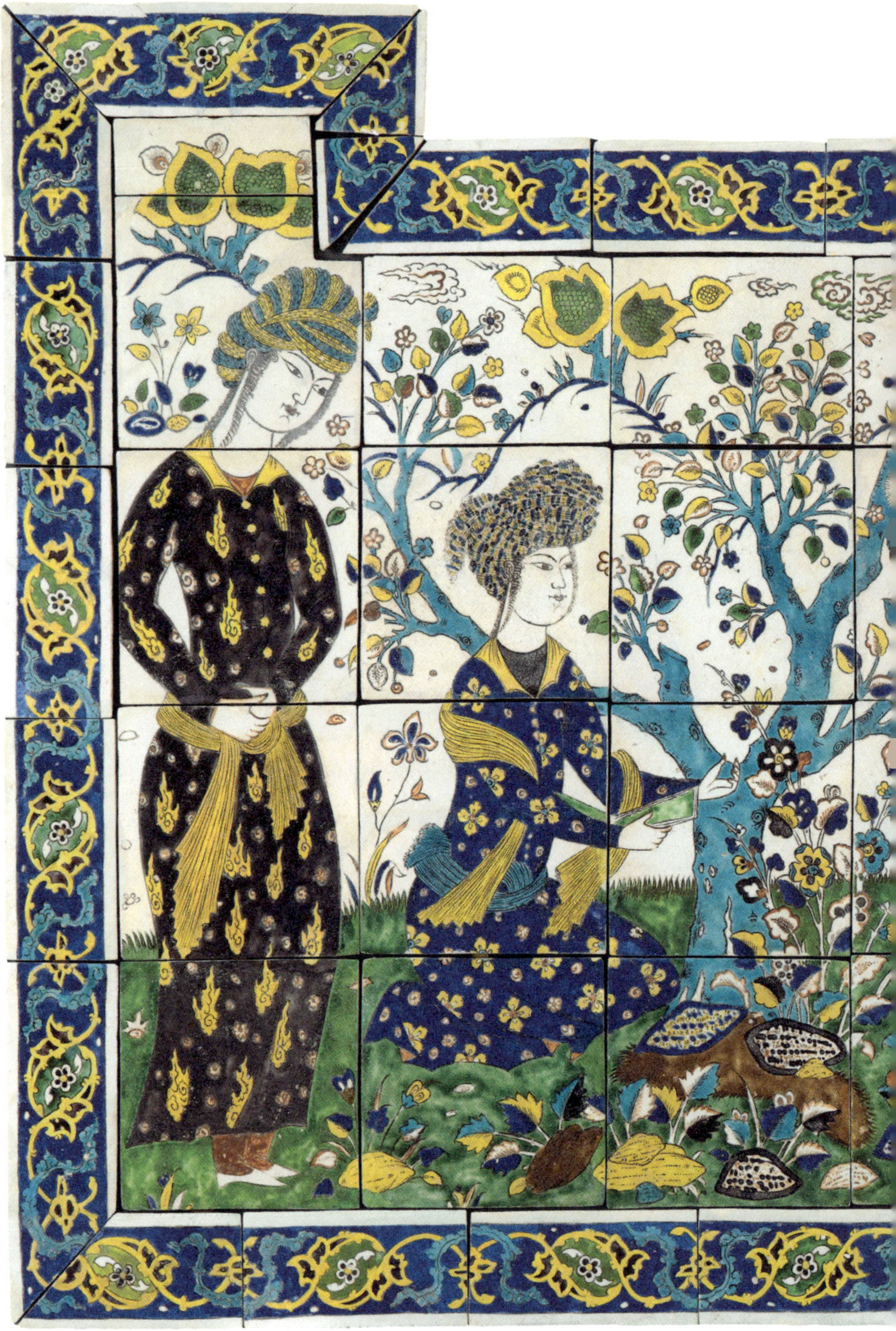

[297] Isfahan, Iran. ***Reciting Poetry in a Garden.*** Palace of Chehel Sotoun (?), Isfahan, Iran. c. 1600–1700
Painted ceramic. H. 118; W. 175.7; D. 6 cm (H. 3 ft 10½ in.; W. 5 ft 9¼ in.; D. 2⅜ in.). ⊻ 1893. DIA

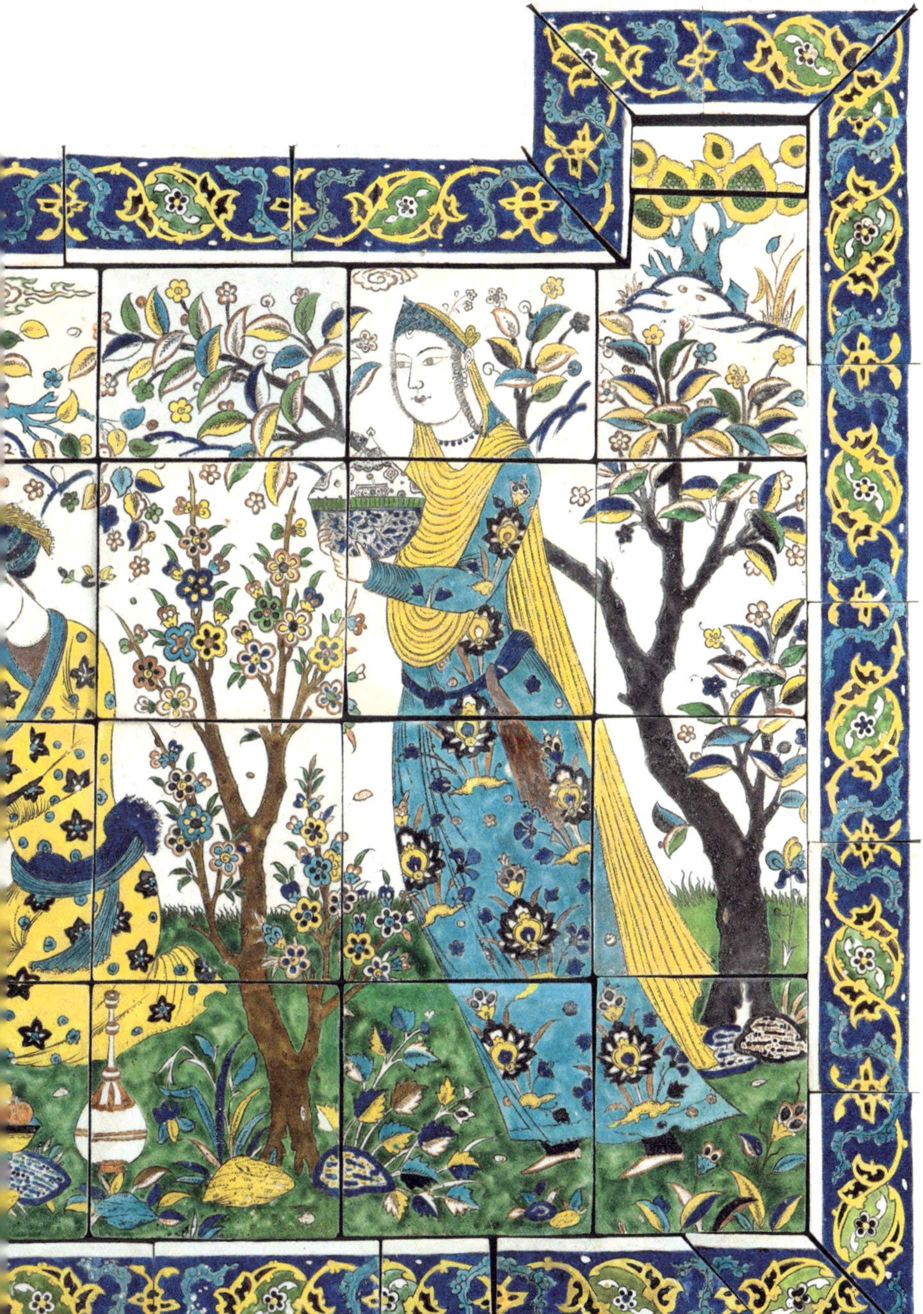

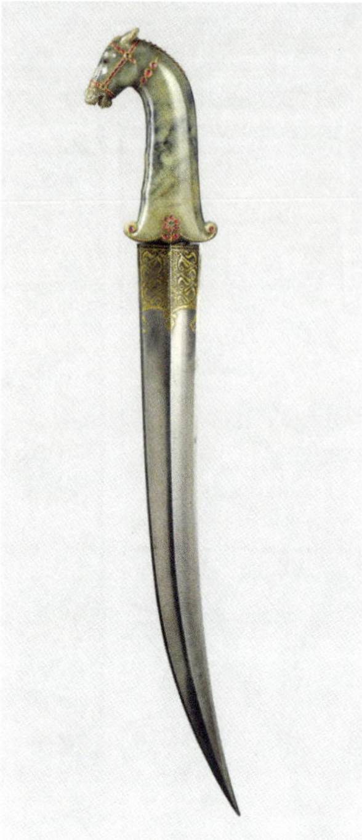

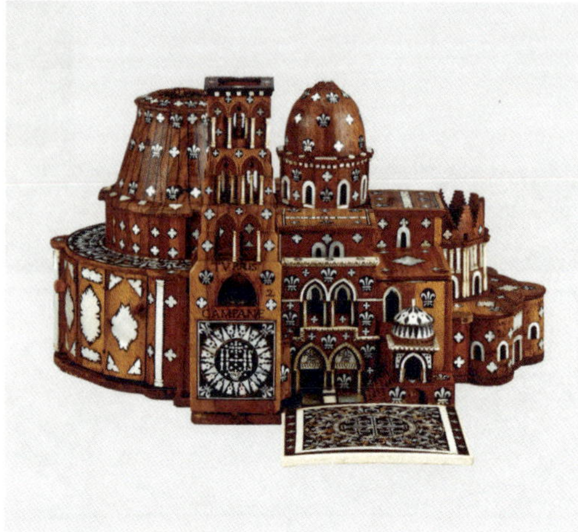

[298]
India
Horse-Head Dagger (Khanjar)
c. 1600–1800
Steel, gold, jade and precious stones
L. 50.5; W. 9.1; D. 2.4 cm
(L. 20; W. 3⅝; D. 1 in.)
⩡ 1927 (bequest of Baroness Salomon de Rothschild)
DIA

[299]
Bethlehem, West Bank
Model of the Holy Sepulchre
c. 1650–1700
Olive wood, mother-of-pearl, bone and boxwood
H. 22; W. 41; D. 35 cm
(H. 8¾; W. 16¼; D. 13¾ in.)
⩡ 2022
DBECA

Passemant, the king's official instrument maker. The clock's case, in patinated, silvered and gilded bronze, depicts the four classical elements of earth, water, air and fire to symbolise the first moments in the Book of Genesis, following the creation of light. Mechanisms in the base drive displays that illustrate the Earth's rotation and the tilt of its axis, the phases of the moon and the motion of the planets. The clock was presented to Louis XV at Versailles in February 1754.

THE LOUVRE, OPEN TO THE WORLD In 2022 the new Department of Byzantine and Eastern Christian Art acquired a model of the Church of the Holy Sepulchre in Jerusalem in olive wood with bone and mother-of-pearl inlays **[299]**. The double doors of the Crusader-era church open onto the parvis, which is bordered to the east by the two-storey Calvary Chapel and, on its west side, by the bell tower. This model is part of a small body of some thirty similar objects, all dated to the seventeenth and eighteenth centuries. They would have been part of the renewed production of devotional objects for pilgrims by workshops in Bethlehem.

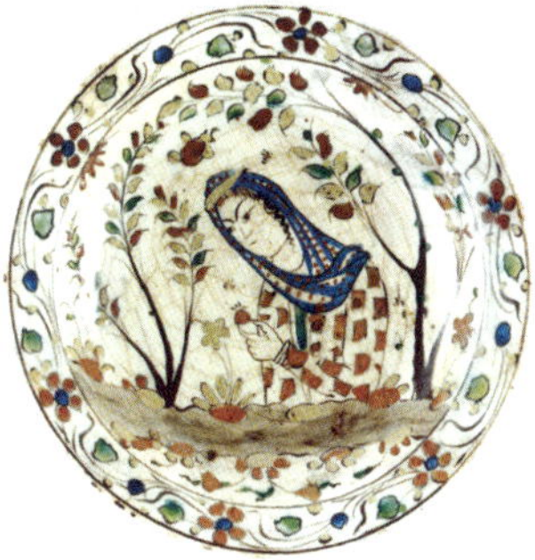

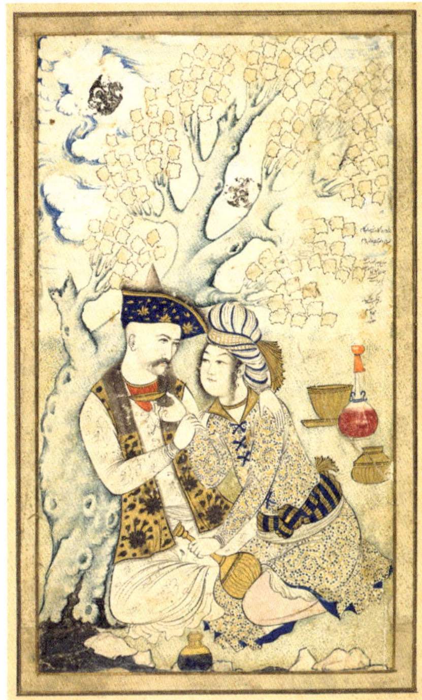

[300]
Iran
Dish with a Young Woman and Fruit
c. 1585–1615
Painted ceramic
H. 6; Diam. 33 cm
(H. 2⅜; Diam. 13 in.)
⊻ 2012 (deposit from the Union Centrale des Arts Décoratifs, Paris)
DIA

[301]
Muhammad Qasim
c. 1575–1659
Shah Abbas I and His Page
1627
Ink, colours, gold and silver on paper
H. 25.5; W. 15 cm
(H. 10; W. 5⅞ in.)
⊻ 1975
DIA

The creation of the Louvre's Department of Islamic Art opened a wider window onto the world. Iranian pottery is recognisable for its craftsmanship and harmonious decoration. Objects such as the beautiful *Dish with a Young Woman and Fruit* **[300]** and wall panels such as *Reciting Poetry in a Garden* **[297]** demonstrate a bold artistic vision. The poets are practising their art in a luxuriant garden, a reminder of the refinement that prevailed in the Persian court in Isfahan. As early as the thirteenth and fourteenth centuries, relations between Iran and China introduced different forms, materials and methods for potters on both sides. Mughal India continues to fascinate for its sumptuous court life and splendid palaces. This prestige is displayed in the *Horse-Head Dagger (Khanjar)* **[298]**, with its gold damascene blade and gold-encrusted, marbled jade hilt.

A major conflict between European powers, opposing France and Austria on one side, Great Britain and Prussia on the other, the Seven Years' War can be viewed as the first global confrontation. The theatre of battle extended to North America, where French troops suffered terrible defeats. The war ended in victory for the British and Prussian alliance, resulting in France's loss of its colonies in America and India, and greater Prussian dominance within the Holy Roman Empire. The balance of power in Western Europe changed, with lasting consequences, from France's support of the future United States of America against Britain in 1776 to the shifting alliances of the late eighteenth century. The war cost France heavily – financially, militarily and commercially – yet appears to have made little impact on the country's artists. In *Vulcan Presenting Venus with Arms for Aeneas* **[302]**, François Boucher treats war and weaponry with an almost frivolous touch, taking inspiration from ancient mythology: Venus, the goddess of love, asked her husband Vulcan to forge the weapons of Mars, the god of war, for her son Aeneas. Boucher's painting was part of a commission by Louis XV for a tapestry cycle illustrating the loves of the gods.

The same virtuosity can be admired in the exceptional *Pot-Pourri Vase in the Form of a Ship* **[306]**, which belonged to the king's favourite, Madame de Pompadour. Its decorative motifs recall the Chinese origin of porcelain, which was prized for its delicacy, translucency, textures and colours. For a very long time the secrets of its production eluded European artists and makers. Ultimately, the Manufacture Royale de Sèvres, founded in 1740, succeeded in mastering the manufacturing process with magnificent results. This pink and green ship – unusual colours for a maritime theme but eminently subtle – was part of major collections: that of the Rothschilds and later the collection of the Grog-Carvens, generous donors to the Louvre.

Classical inspiration and delicacy of execution are also at work in *Pygmalion and Galatea* **[305]**, a marble group sculpted by Étienne Maurice Falconet in 1761. In his *Metamorphoses*, the Roman author Ovid, who lived during the reign of Augustus, tells the story – an allegory of art – of the sculptor and his statue. Enraptured by its

[302]
François Boucher
1703–1770
Vulcan Presenting Venus with Arms for Aeneas
1757
Oil on canvas
H. 320; W. 320 cm
(H. 10 ft 6 in.; W. 10 ft 6 in.)
⊻ 1793 (former royal collection, collection of Louis XV)
DP

[303]
Figure of a god, Ki'i hulu manu
Hawaii, United States
18th century
Plant fibres, dog teeth, mother-of-pearl, vines and wood
H. 67; W. 32; D. 32 cm
(H. 26½; W. 12½; D. 12½ in.)
⊻ Former collection of the Bibliothèque Nationale, Paris
MQB-JC

[304]
Iran
Panel with Four Mystics
c. 1750
Ceramic
H. 120; W. 96; D. 5 cm
(H. 3 ft 11¼ in.; W. 3 ft 1¾ in.; D. 2 in.)
⊻ 1982
DIA

302

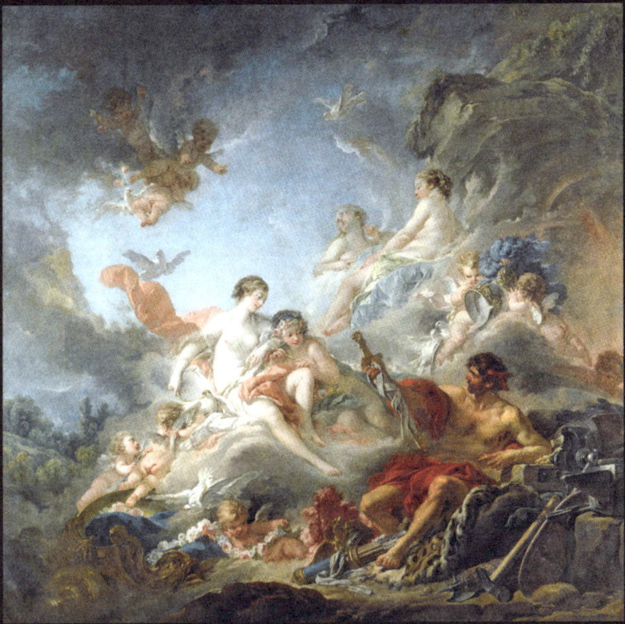

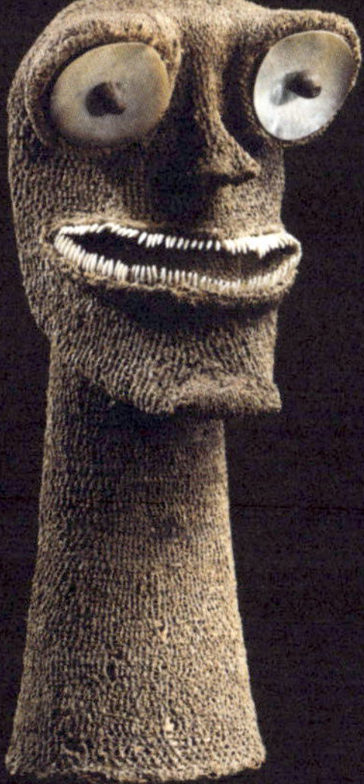

303

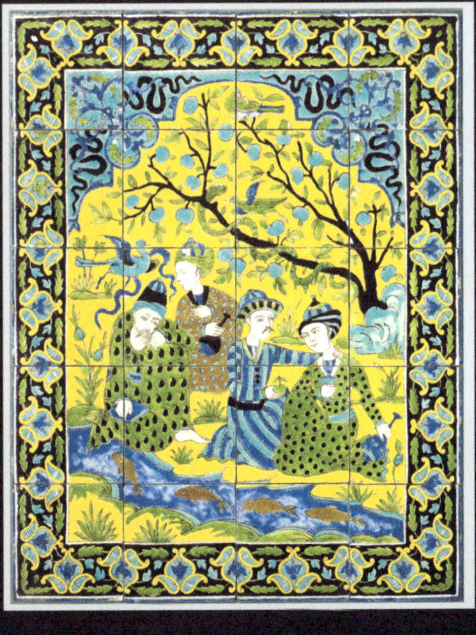

304

beauty, Pygmalion fell in love with his creation, whose marble turned into soft, warm flesh as the sculpture came to life. Widely celebrated, Falconet's work was reproduced in biscuit porcelain, the perfect medium to render Galatea's soft curves and white complexion. One of these reproductions is conserved at the Louvre.

During this time, under the Safavid Dynasty, Persian artists continued to create magnificent panels in coloured ceramic. Their talent is evident in *Panel with Four Mystics* **[304]**. The four figures are shown seated, surrounded by nature's bounty in a landscape that suggests a heavenly garden or "paradise", a word derived from the ancient Iranian language Avestan.

In the eighteenth century, exploratory voyages set sail from Europe to the southern seas, made possible by advances in navigational techniques. England's Captain James Cook led several expeditions to the Pacific Ocean, which took him to lands previously unknown to Europeans. It was no doubt during one of these voyages that the representation of the god Ki'i hulu manu **[303]** was taken from Hawaii to Europe. The figure was originally covered in red feathers, making it even more formidable. It is known to have featured in the public collections of the Muséum d'Histoire Naturelle as of 1796, shortly after the museum's opening in 1793.

The *Nkisi Nkondi* statuette **[307]**, made some time between the late eighteenth and early nineteenth centuries, was brought back from the Congo at the end of the nineteenth century by Joseph Cholet, who sailed with the explorer Pierre Savorgnan de Brazza. The latter made several voyages in Central Africa and founded a first French colony on the Congo River, later named Brazzaville. The nkisi nkondi dog is reputed to defend against witches and witchcraft. Its force is activated by hammering a nail into the statue.

[305]
Étienne Maurice Falconet
1716–1791
Pygmalion and Galatea
1761
Marble
H. 83.5; W. 48.2; D. 38 cm
(H. 32¾; W. 19; D. 15 in.)
⊻ 1930 (bequest of Casimir-Jean-Félix Guyon)
DS

[306]
Manufacture de Sèvres, France
Charles Nicolas Dodin, 1734–1803; Jean Claude Thomas Duplessis, 1730–1783
Pot-Pourri Vase in the Form of a Ship
c. 1760
Soft-paste porcelain
H. 37; W. 33.5; D. 17 cm
(H. 14½; W. 13¼; D. 6¾ in.)
⊻ 1984 (gift of Marie-Louise Jeanne Carmen Carven and René Grog)
DDA

[307]
Zoomorphic Statuette, Nkisi Nkondi
Congo
18th–early 19th century
Wood, metal, earthenware, iron nails and blades, fabric, rope and plant fibres
H. 35; W. 90; D. 41 cm
(H. 13¾; W. 35½; D. 16¼ in.)
⊻ Gift of Joseph Cholet, former collection of the Muséum d'Histoire Naturelle, Paris
MQB-JC

[308]
Hubert Robert
1733–1808
Women Washing Laundry Inside an Ornate Ancient Building
1760
Red chalk
H. 52.2; W. 63.8 cm
(H. 20½; W. 25 in.)
⊻ 1930 (gift of Princess Louis de Croÿ-Dulmen)
DPD

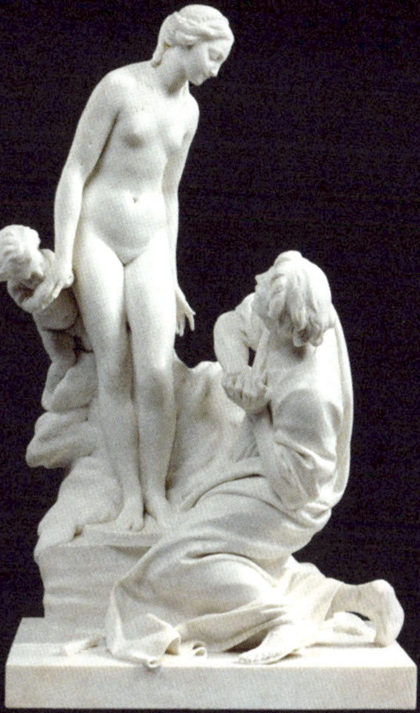

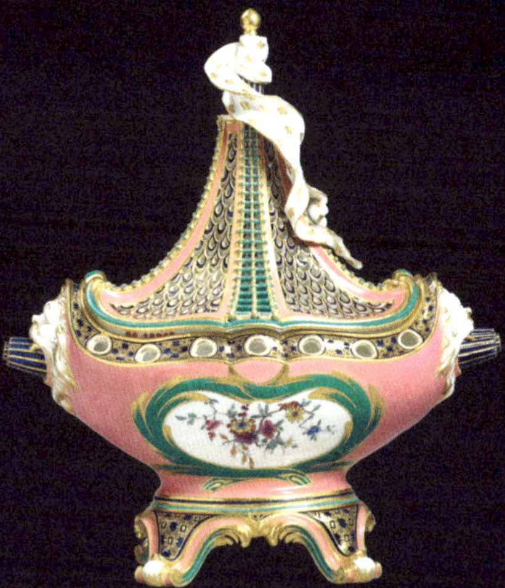

306

305

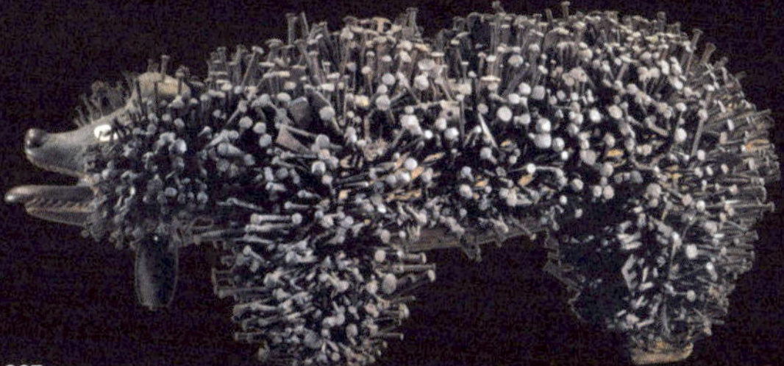

307

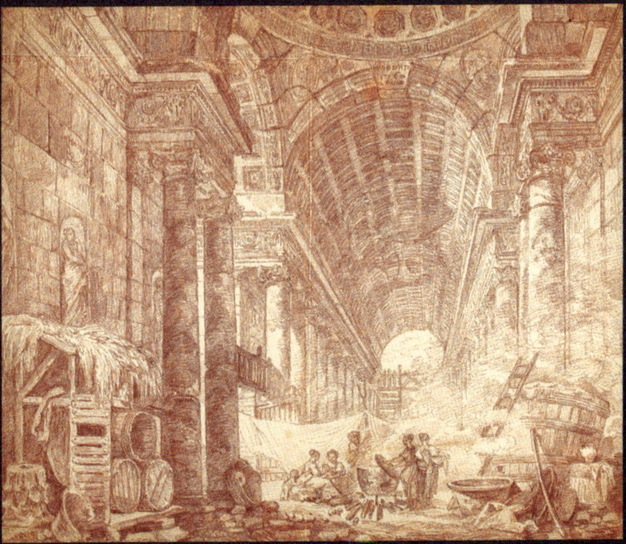

308

Virtuosities

In Europe and North America, the end of the eighteenth century was an intense period in terms of intellectual history, while the United States of America's independence in 1776 and the French Revolution of 1789 marked a time of political upheaval. In France the advancement of knowledge and the desire to explain natural and technical phenomena prompted a vast undertaking: that of the *Encyclopédie*, an enlightened attempt to give order to the world led by Denis Diderot and Jean Le Rond d'Alembert. Published in ten volumes between 1751 and 1772, its long entry on the notion of the "museum" contains the seeds for the future founding of the Louvre. Near Naples, the discovery of Pompeii and Herculaneum, buried under ash following the eruption of Vesuvius in 79, revived interest in antique art. What Johan Joachim Winckelmann, one of art history's pioneers, described as the "quiet grandeur" of ancient works, together with their natural and humanist conception, singled them out once more as models for artists.

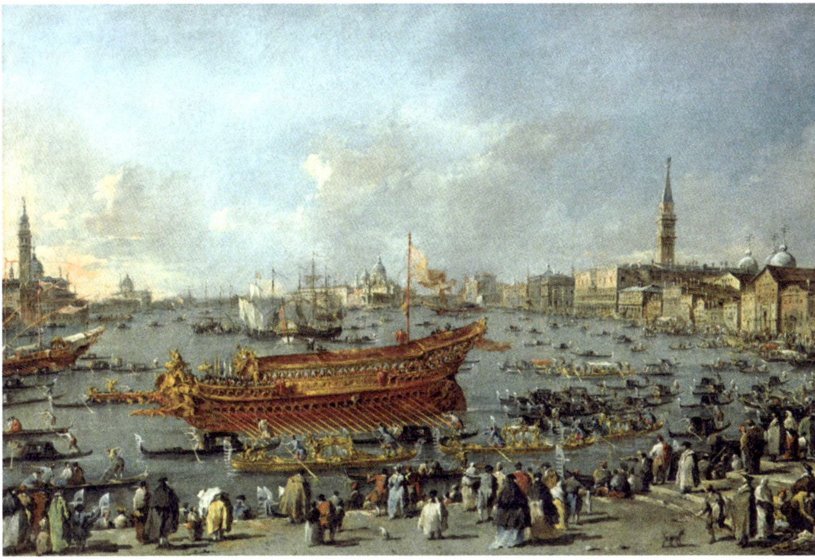

[309] Francesco Guardi. 1712–1793. ***The Departure of the Bucentaur to the Venice Lido on Ascension Day***
c. 1770–1780. Oil on canvas. H. 66; W. 101 cm (H. 2 ft 2 in.; W. 3 ft 3¾ in.). ⊻ 1797. DP

Philosophical thought was centred on the human being, now viewed as a free-thinking individual – though not everyone was at liberty to exercise the privilege of this free will. Jean-Jacques Rousseau's autobiographical *Confessions* stands as one of the major stages in the nascent recognition given to artists; each was encouraged to take control of their own creation, with themselves at its centre.

SOPHISTICATION Much of the period's art was conceived as a demonstration of virtuosity, for example Francesco Guardi's series of ten paintings to commemorate the festivities held for the election of the new doge of Venice in 1763. *The Departure of the Bucentaur* **[309]** captures the crowd gathered along the quay, the dozens of boats on the Grand Canal and the palaces lining the waterside. The *Choiseul Snuffbox* **[311]** is another work of great craftsmanship. Made to hold tobacco leaves, snuffboxes were very personal and precious objects. This one, which was acquired by the Louvre in 2022, is decorated with finely painted gouaches depicting the apartment and office of the Duke de Choiseul, minister

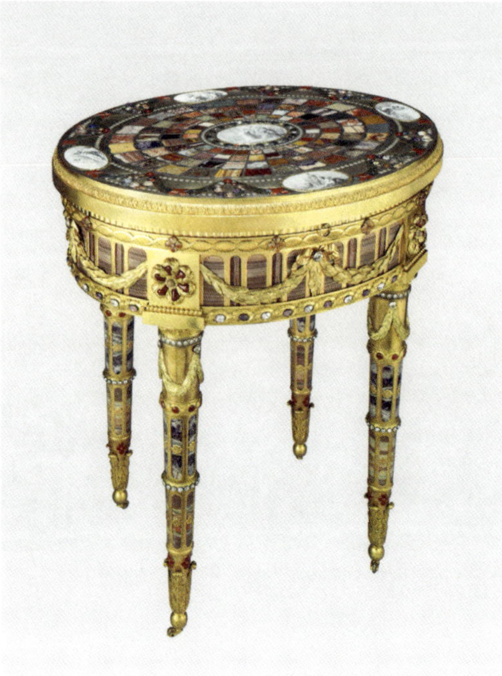

[310]
Johann Christian Neuber
1732–1808
Breteuil Table
c. 1775–1800
Gilded bronze, hard stone and
Saxony porcelain on wood frame
H. 81.5; W. 70.5 cm
(H. 32; W. 27¾ in.)
⩡ 2016
DDA

to Louis XV. The *Breteuil Table* **[310]**, presented to the Baron de Breteuil on the signing of a peace treaty between Austria and Prussia in 1779, is a masterpiece; its decorative inlay of 128 stones echoes Saxony's abundant mineral deposits. The taste for ancient civilisations was stimulated as more objects and monuments were uncovered. From their workshops in Rome, silversmiths Giuseppe and Luigi Valadier were called upon to mount ancient artefacts and to imagine new pieces alluding to Roman civilisation **[312]**. The late 1770s saw a surge in interest in ancient Egypt. Clodion's *Egyptian Woman with Naos* **[313]** is freely inspired by statues discovered during archaeological excavations.

A NEW SENSIBILITY The study of individual emotions, combined with a more detailed understanding of the human anatomy, gave fresh impetus to artistic creativity. Following his death, sixty-nine *Character Heads* **[315]** were found in the studio of Franz Xaver Messerschmidt. Taking himself as his model, the sculptor set out to capture the range of human feeling, from pain to melancholy, conveying these sensations in exaggerated expressions, at times

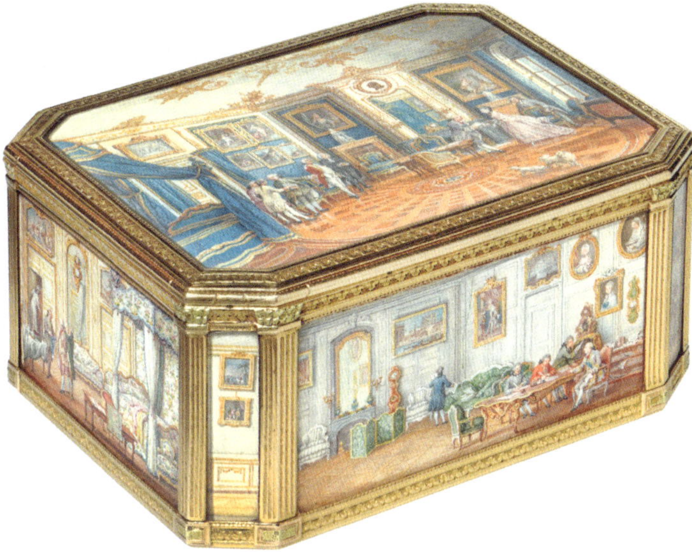

[311]
Louis Roucel; Louis Nicolas Van Blarenberghe, c. 1716/1717–1794
Choiseul Snuffbox
c. 1770–1771
Gold, gouache on vellum and crystal plaques
H. 2.4; W. 8; D. 6 cm
(H. 1; W. 3⅛; D. 2⅜ in.)
⊻ 2022 (with the participation of the Société des Amis du Louvre and crowdfunding)
DDA

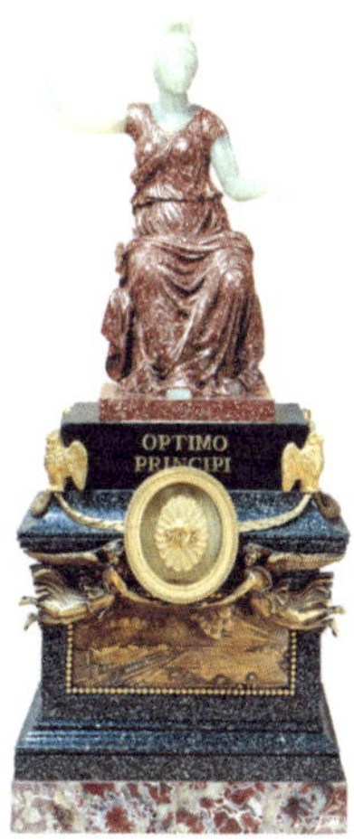

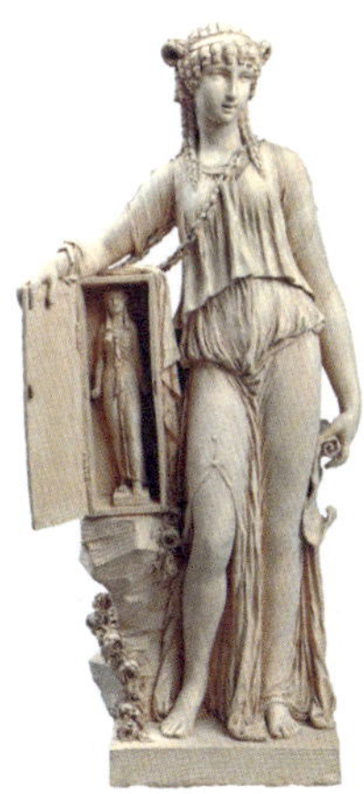

[312]
Luigi Valadier, 1726–1785;
Giuseppe Valadier, 1762–1839;
Giacinto Frey, 1761–1824
Rome Seated
1788
Gilded silver, gilded bronze, jade, jasper, lapis lazuli, marble and porphyry
H. 46; W. 19; D. 19 cm
(H. 18; W. 7½; D. 7½ in.)
⊻ 1798
DDA

[313]
Claude Michel, known as Clodion
1738–1814
Egyptian Woman with Naos
c. 1789
Terracotta
H. 48; W. 19.5; D. 13 cm
(H. 19; W. 7¾; D. 5⅛ in.)
⊻ 1944 (bequest of Marie Dol-Lair)
DS

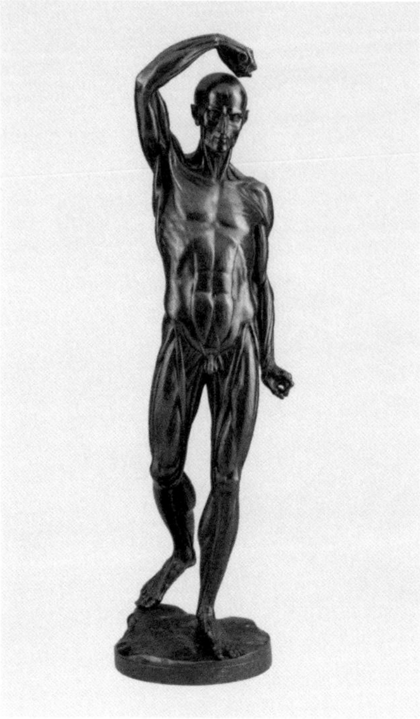

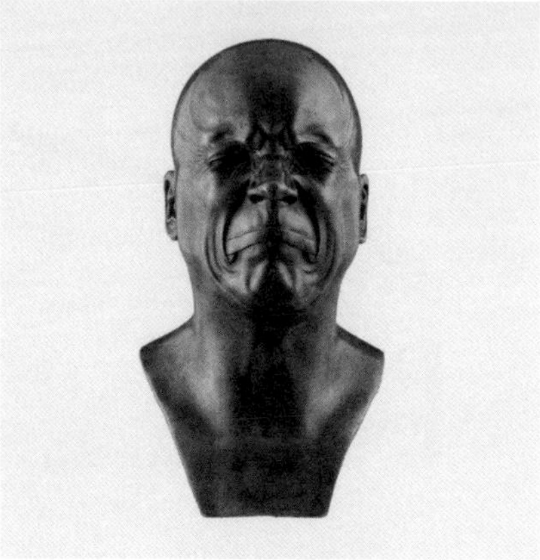

[314]
Jean-Antoine Houdon, 1741–1828; Pierre Philippe Thomire, 1751–1843
Standing Écorché with Raised Arm
1776
Bronze
H. 48.3; W. 16; D. 15 cm
(H. 19; W. 6¼; D. 6 in.)
⊻ 2022
DS

[315]
Franz Xaver Messerschmidt
1736–1783
Character Head
c. 1771–1783
Lead and tin
H. 38.7; W. 23; D. 23 cm
(H. 15¼; W. 9; D. 9 in.)
⊻ 2005
DS

with tendons pulled impossibly tight. His motivations for creating the heads are unknown: anxiety, madness, an exploration of human emotions? *Standing Écorché with Raised Arm* **[314]** is a bronze replica of Jean-Antoine Houdon's sculpture of the same name. Houdon was one of the most celebrated sculptors of his day and casts of his écorchés (flayed figures) circulated widely. Copies similar to the one in the Louvre could be found in the studios of many artists, to study the arrangement and shape of the muscles beneath the skin and, subsequently, reproduce the outstretched movement of an arm or leg as accurately as possible. Houdon produced his first écorché in plaster while in Rome, where he would have had the opportunity to view many ancient and Renaissance works.

A new sensibility emerged in art and literature that gave unprecedented emphasis to representations of the sentiments, whether between family members, friends or lovers. Painting, like theatre, sought to stir the emotions and elevate the mind. In *The Bolt* **[316]**, Jean-Honoré Fragonard shows what the locked door was intended to conceal: the young couple's passionate embrace. The red canopy above the bed highlights the theatricality

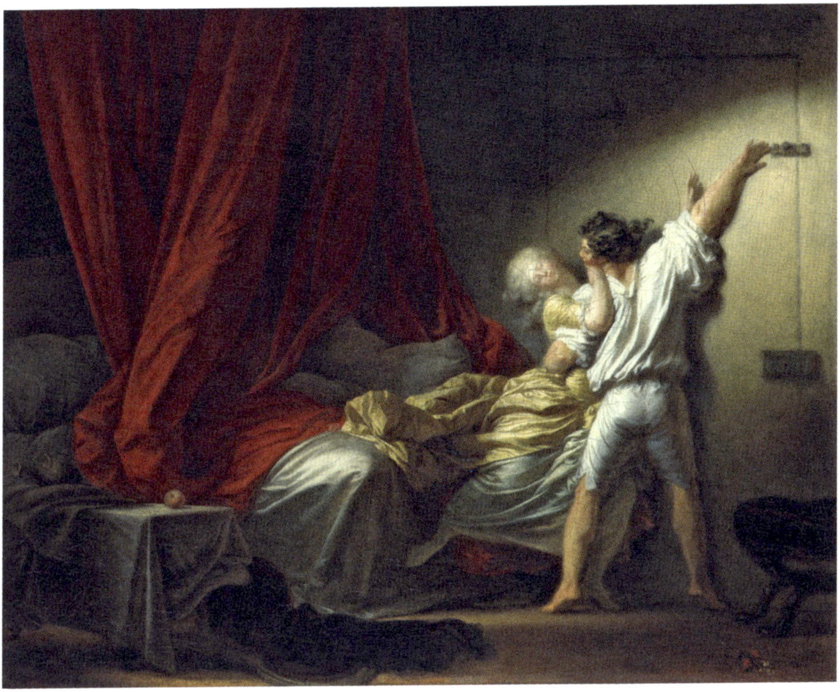

[316]
Jean-Honoré Fragonard
1732–1806
The Bolt
c. 1777–1778
Oil on canvas
H. 74; W. 94 cm
(H. 2 ft 5¼ in.; W. 3 ft 1 in.)
⊻ 1974
DP

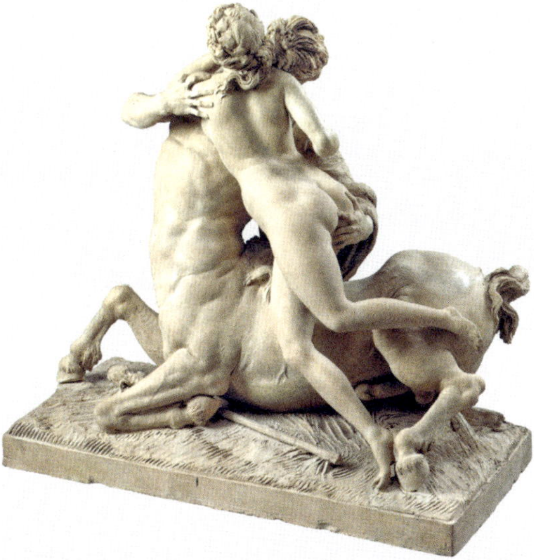

[317]
Johan Tobias Sergel
1740–1814
Centaur Embracing a Bacchante
c. 1767–1778
Terracotta
H. 36.5; W. 39.5; D. 17.5 cm
(H. 14¼; W. 15½; D. 7 in.)
⊻ 1998
DS

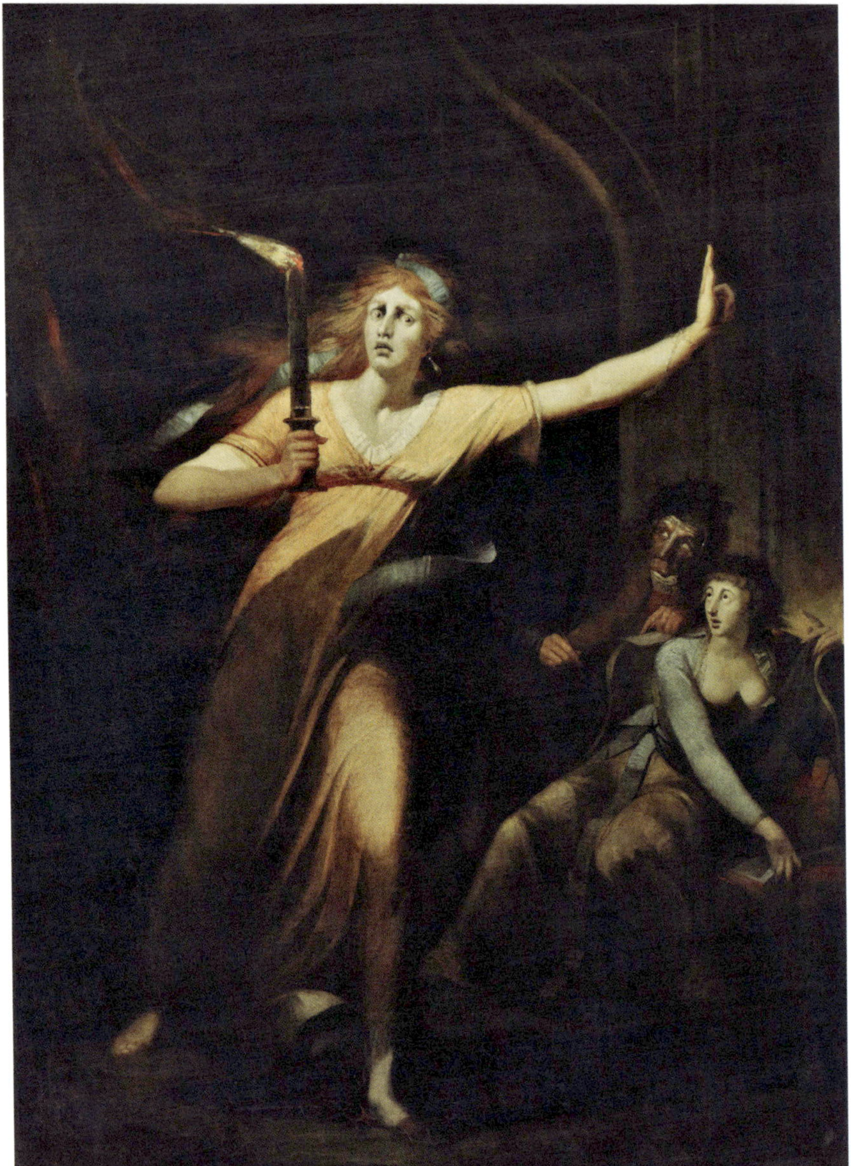

[318]
Henry Fuseli
1741–1825
Sleepwalking
Lady Macbeth
c. 1784
Oil on canvas
H. 221; W. 160 cm
(H. 7 ft 3 in.; W. 5 ft 3 in.)
⩡ 1970
DP

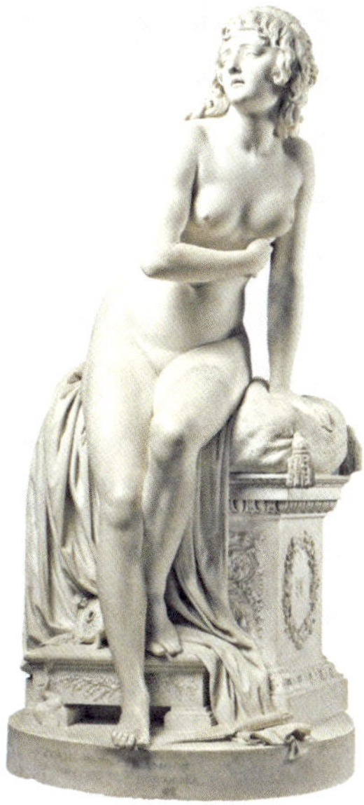

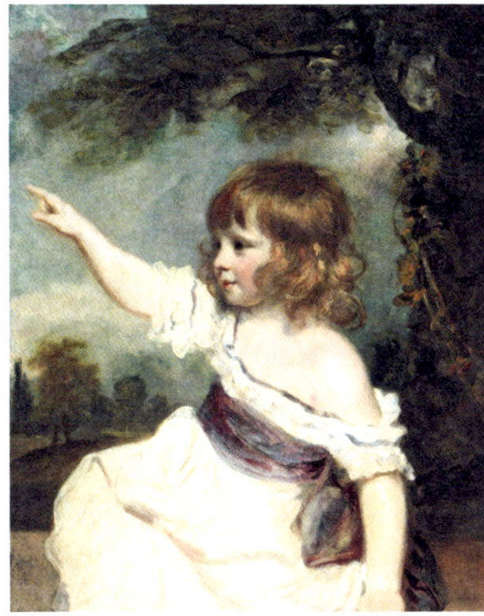

[319]
Augustin Pajou
1730–1809
Psyche Abandoned
1790
Marble
H. 177; W. 86; D. 86 cm
(H. 5 ft 9¾ in.;
W. 2 ft 9¾ in.;
D. 2 ft 9¾ in.)
⩡ 1829
DS

[320]
Sir Joshua Reynolds
1723–1792
Portrait of Francis George Hare
c. 1788–1789
Oil on canvas
H. 77; W. 64 cm
(H. 30¼; W. 25¼ in.)
⩡ 1905 (bequest of Baron Mayer Alphonse de Rothschild)
DP

of the scene. Similarly, the Swedish sculptor Johan Tobias Sergel reinterprets the mythological theme of nymph and satyr to compose the consensual and sensual entwining of *Centaur Embracing a Bacchante* **[317]**. Henry Fuseli's *Sleepwalking Lady Macbeth* **[318]** shows the title figure overcome by madness, plagued by visions and guilt over the murder of Scotland's King Duncan. In the late eighteenth century Shakespeare's work experienced a resurgence in popularity that would continue, thanks to the universal emotions his characters express in plays that range from tragic to comic, from the horrible to the sublime. Jacques-Louis David painted his *Oath of the Horatii* **[321]** in Rome, and by showing the finished piece in his studio, launched a new mode of exhibition whereby artists displayed their work themselves. The painting was inspired by the legend of the Horatii, three Roman brothers, and the Curiatii, three brothers from the rival city of Alba Longa. David shows the Horatii making an oath to their father that they will battle to the death for Rome, a scene that exists neither in ancient narratives nor in Pierre Corneille's seventeenth-century tragedy *Horace*. By choosing to represent a pledge, David highlights

[321]
Jacques-Louis David
1748–1825
Oath of the Horatii
1784
Oil on canvas
H. 330; W. 425 cm
(H. 10 ft 10 in.; W. 13 ft 11¼ in.)
⩡ 1793 (former royal collection, collection of Louis XVI)
DP

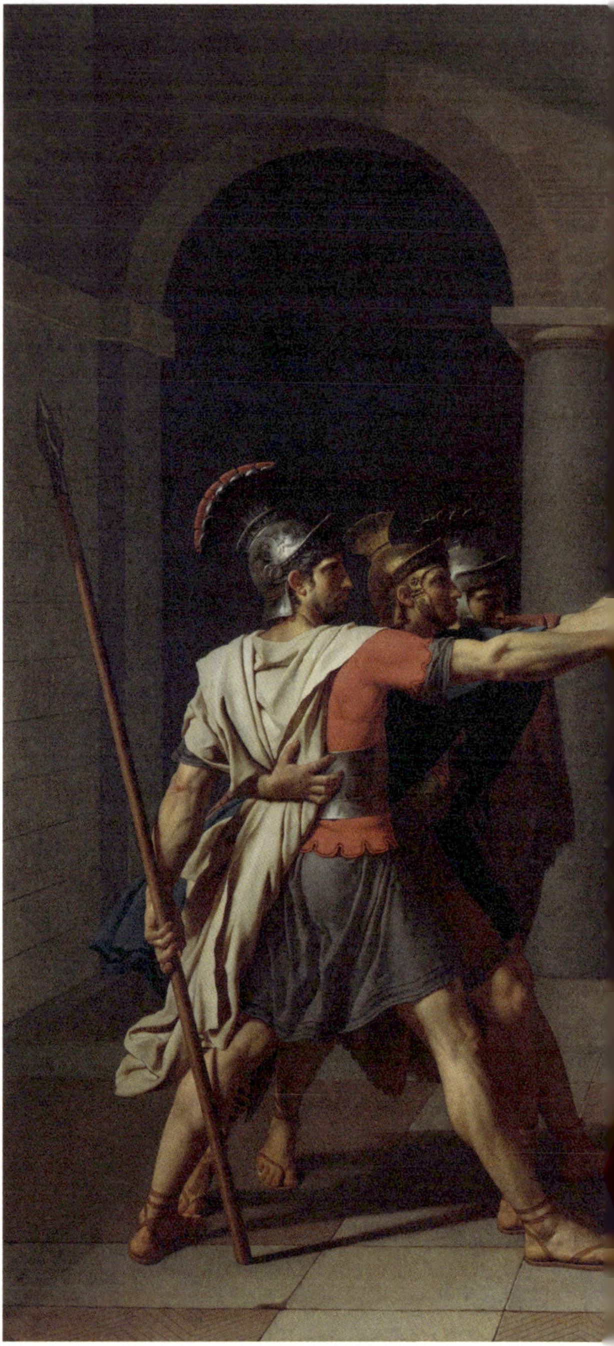

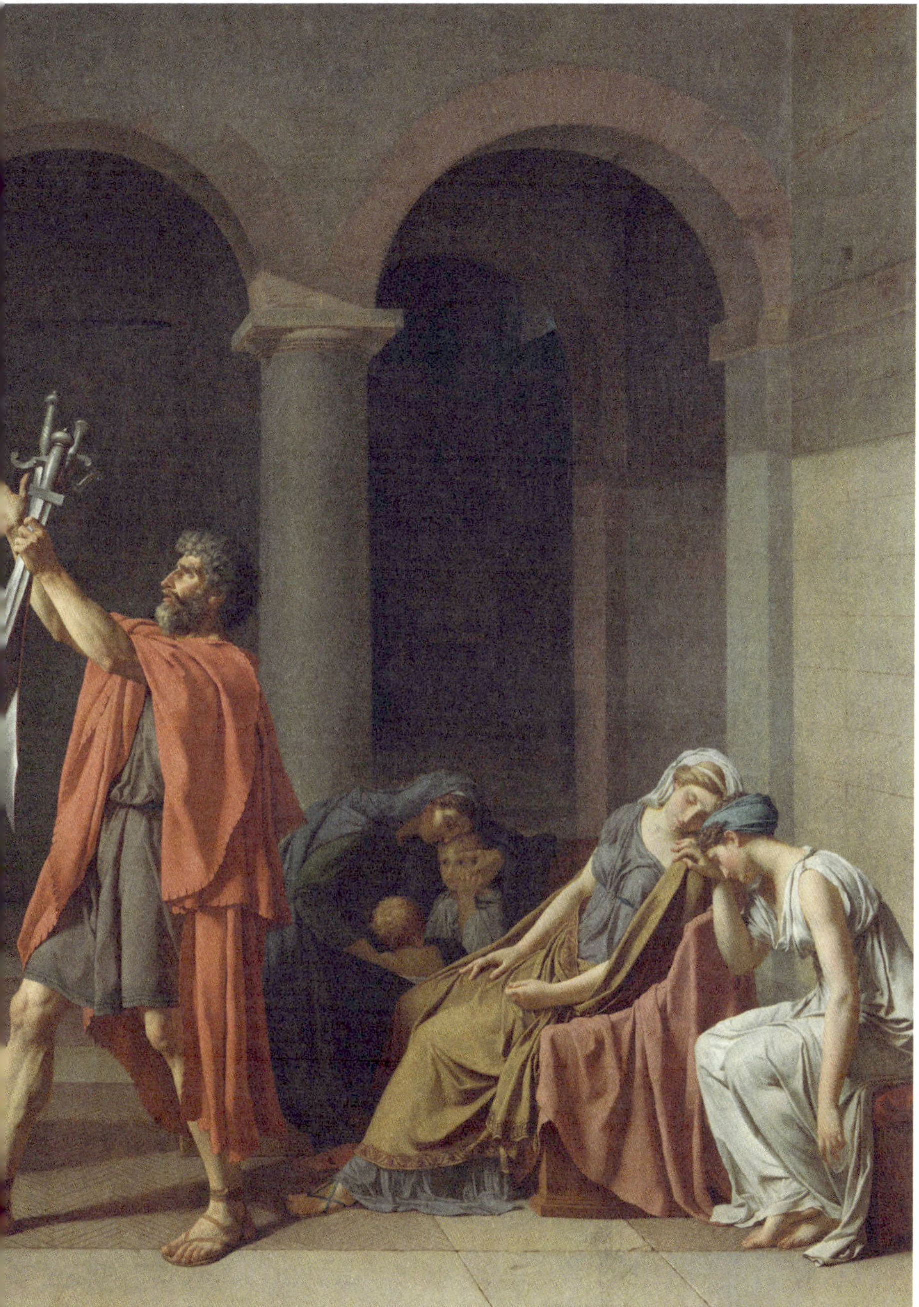

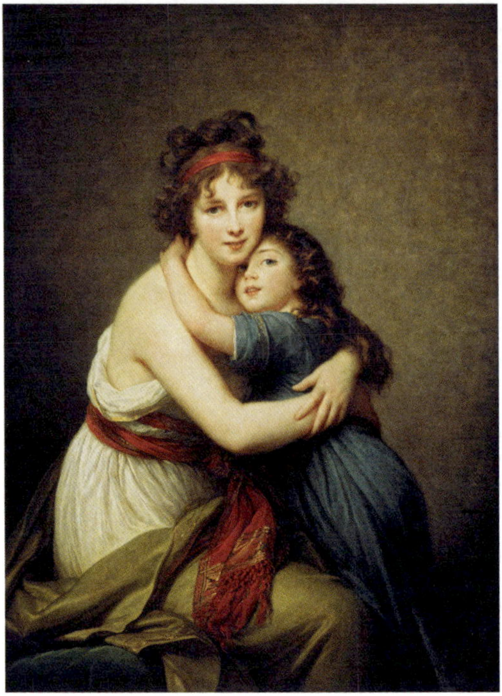

[322]
Élisabeth Vigée Le Brun
1755–1842
Self-Portrait with Her Daughter, Julie
1789
Oil on wood
H. 130; W. 94 cm
(H. 4 ft 3¼ in.; W. 1 ft 1 in.)
⊻ 1793
DP

the men's bravery. As further reinforcement of the brothers' sacrifice, the painter employs a three-part composition to give equal emphasis to the sobbing women's despair and the swearing of the oath.

Around the same time, attitudes towards children's education were changing. The relationship between adult and child was no longer conditioned solely by authority and obedience. In his *Portrait of Francis George Hare* **[320]**, Joshua Reynolds treats his subject with sympathy and sensitivity, not least through his rendering of the boy's sweetness and charming gesture. One of the very few women of her day to be accepted into the Académie Royale de Peinture et de Sculpture, Élisabeth Vigée Le Brun's remarkable talent as a portraitist earned her numerous commissions. Her self-portrait with her daughter **[322]** makes clear her ability to capture the deepest affection with sincerity.

“I am lovely,
O mortals!
Like a dream
of stone.”

Baudelaire,
“Beauty”,
1857

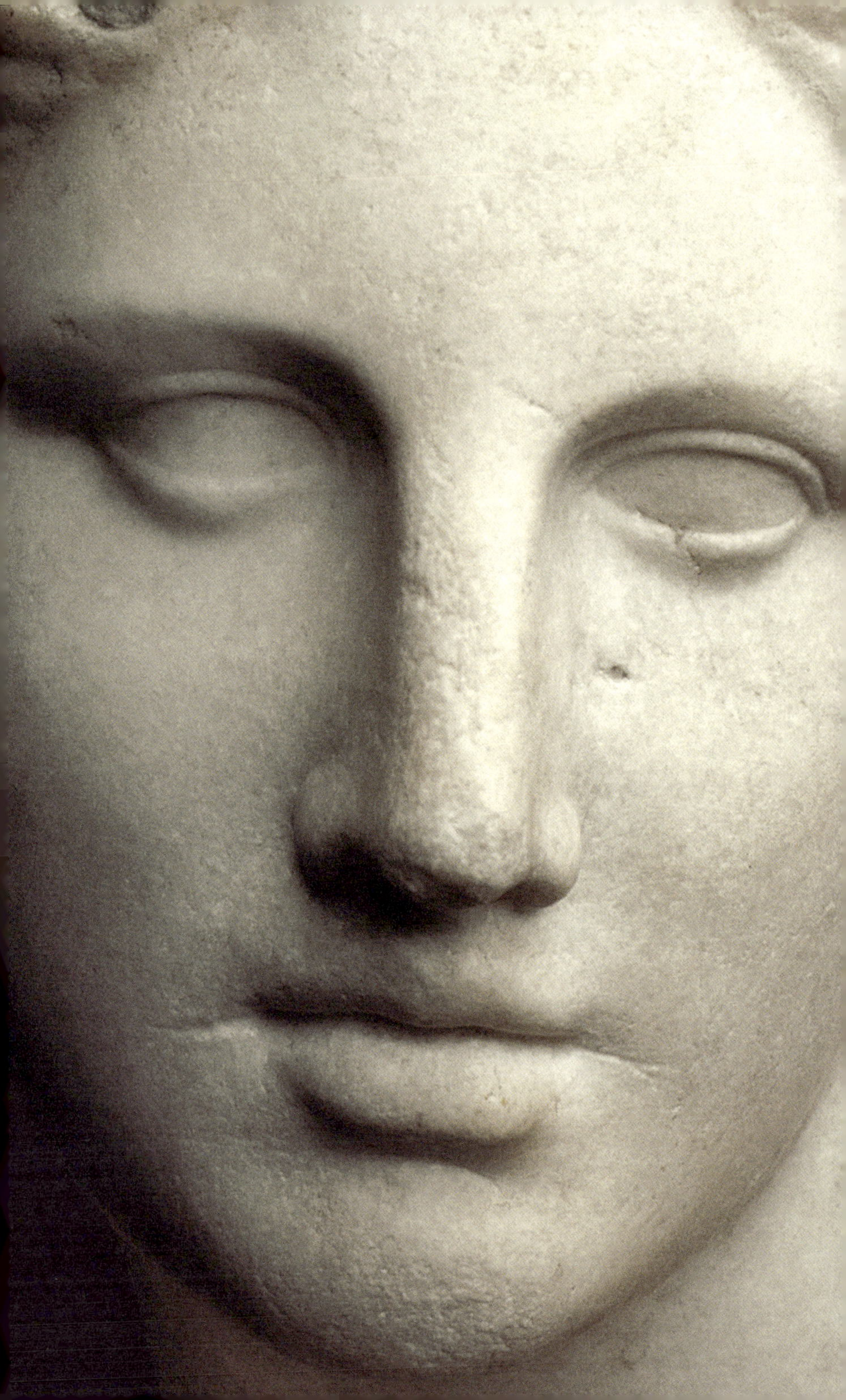

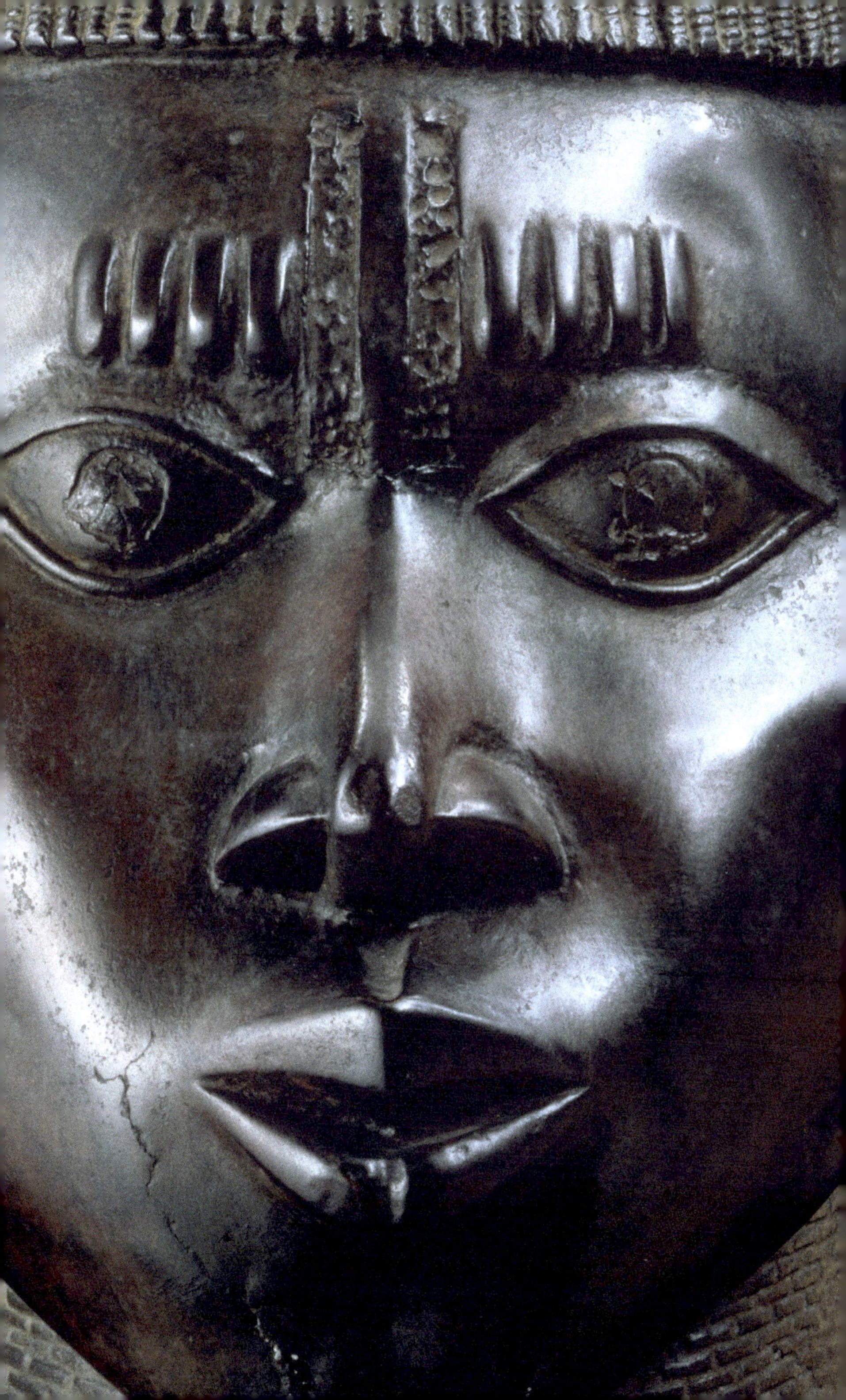

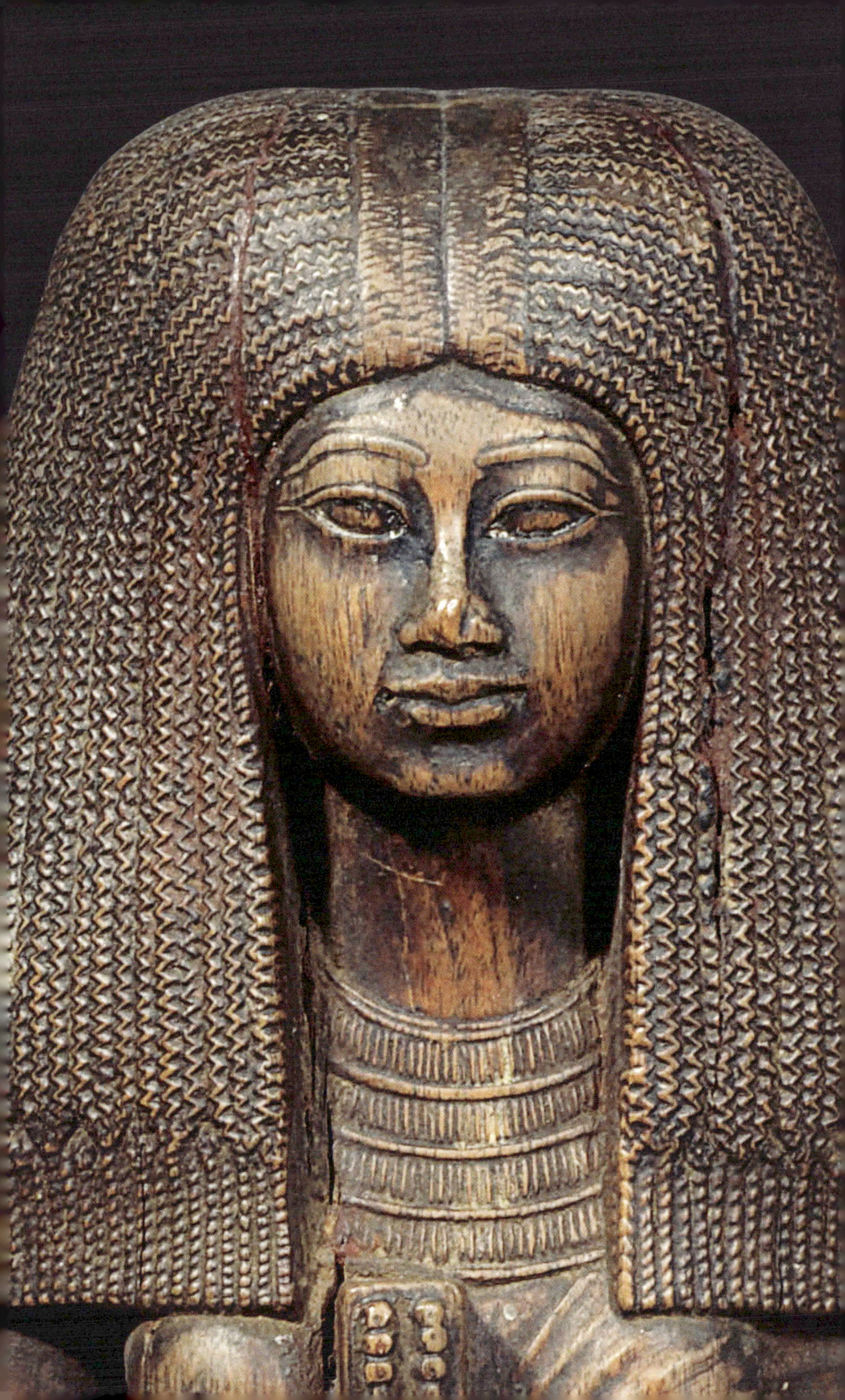

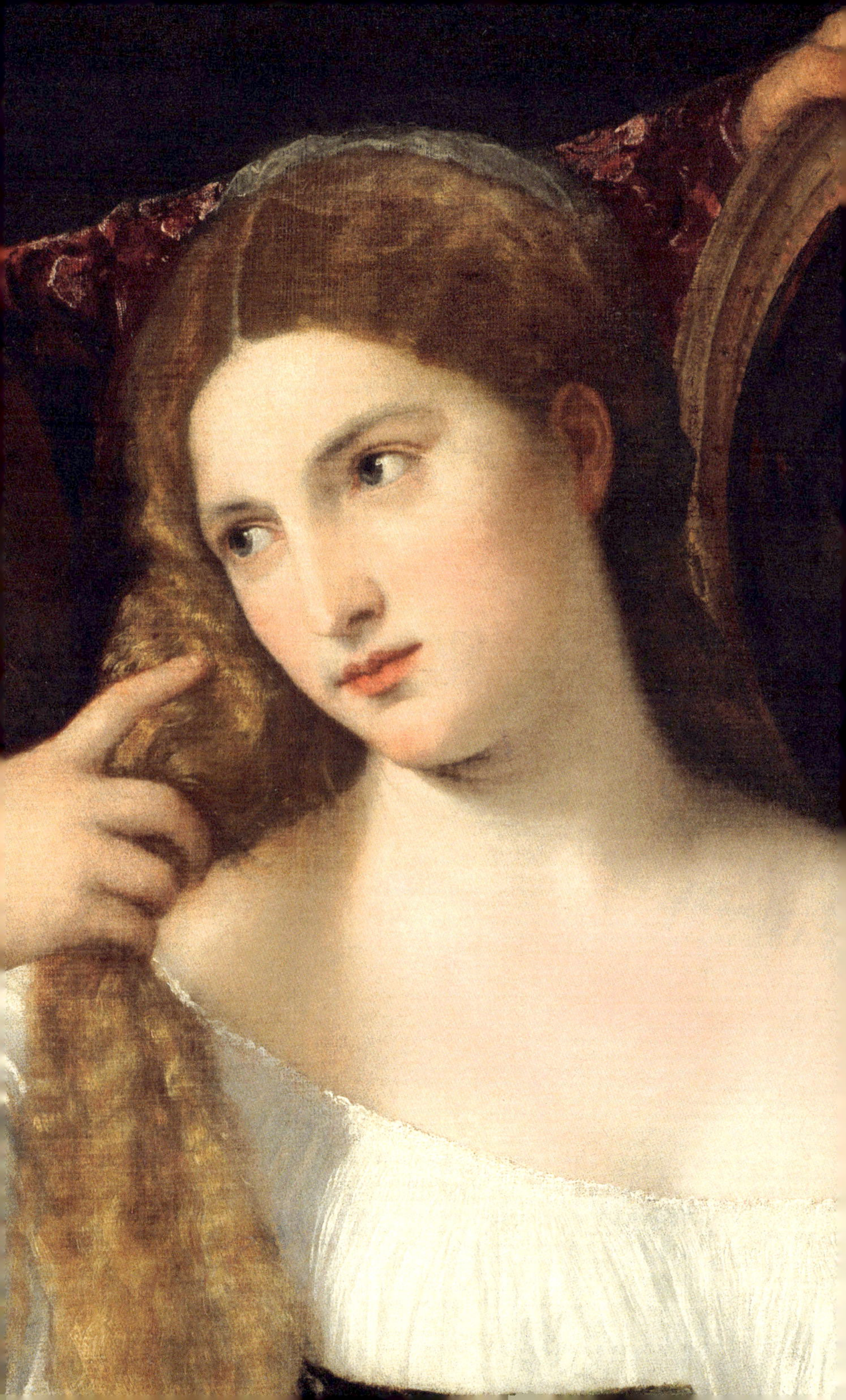

Creation of the Muséum Central at the Louvre

The Muséum Central des Arts opened its doors in 1793. Located inside the Louvre, the former royal residence, it gave first artists, then the public at large, the opportunity to view the collections of paintings, sculptures and ancient works amassed by France's monarchs since Charles V in the fourteenth century. This was not a new idea. Already in the mid-eighteenth century, an entry in the *Encyclopédie* outlined a first project for a national museum, although it would be the French Revolution that ultimately gave form to the modern museum as it appeared at the Louvre. This new institution was designed to be universal both in its collections – an assembly of the most remarkable artworks and objects across eras and civilisations – and its audience – bringing knowledge and the joy of discovery to all.

A new vision emerged in the 1780s that was both formal, reaffirming classical works as a model **[323]**, and political, using art to set examples of personal virtue and civic duty. Both these dimensions are contained in Jacques-Louis David's *The Lictors Bringing to Brutus the Bodies of His Sons* **[324]**, completed in 1789. This huge canvas shows Brutus, considered the founder of the Roman Republic, in the sixth century BCE. True to his convictions, the consul ordered the execution of his own sons, who were plotting to overthrow the new regime. David depicts the dramatic moment when their lifeless bodies are returned to the family home. Brutus, torn between patriotic duty and a father's love, sits tense and isolated in shadow, while the group formed by his distraught wife and daughters is brightly lit. The work was acquired by Louis XVI in 1789, the year the Bastille was stormed in Paris. A few years later, while imprisoned for his support of Revolutionary politics, David drew *Homer Reciting His Poems* **[325]** in honour of the author of the *Odyssey* and the *Iliad*, though a planned painting of the Greek poet was never made.

The portrait of *Mirabeau (Honoré Gabriel Riqueti, Count of), Politician* **[327]** by the sculptor Jean-Antoine Houdon references ancient art in its form – a bust – and, in its subject, acts as an example to follow. Mirabeau was an important voice in the early days of the French Revolution. A writer and a statesman, he was a member

[323]
Charles Percier
1764–1838
Various Antique and Modern Fragments, Drawn from Life
1791
Pen and brown ink, grey and ochre wash
H. 66.3; W. 101.9 cm
(H. 2 ft 2 in.; W. 3 ft 4 in.)
⩡ 2002 (gift of the Société des Amis du Louvre)
DPD

[324]
Jacques-Louis David
1748–1825
The Lictors Bringing to Brutus the Bodies of His Sons
1789
Oil on canvas
H. 323; W. 422 cm
(H. 10 ft 7¼ in.;
W. 13 ft 10¼ in.)
⩡ 1793 (former collection of Louis XVI)
DP

[325]
Jacques-Louis David
1748–1825
Homer Reciting His Poems
1794
Graphite, black ink, grey wash and red chalk on paper
H. 27.2; W. 34.5 cm
(H. 10¾; W. 13½ in.)
⩡ 1878 (gift of Horace His de La Salle)
DPD

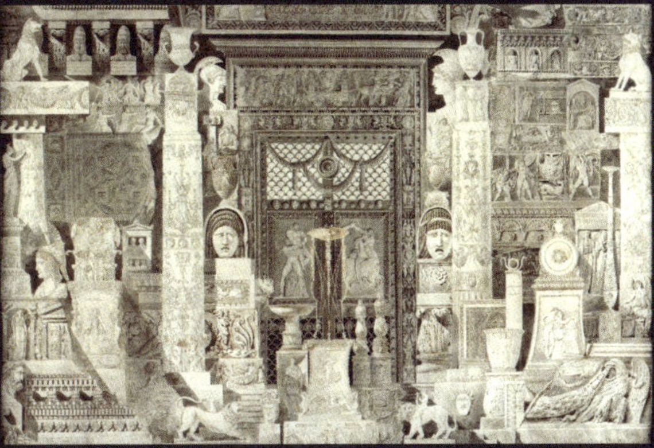

323

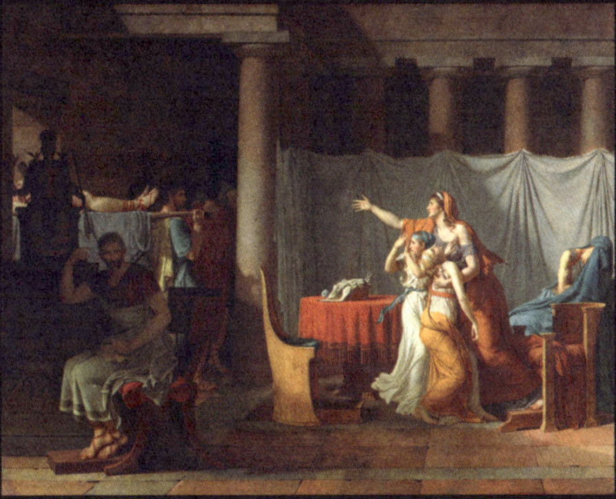

324

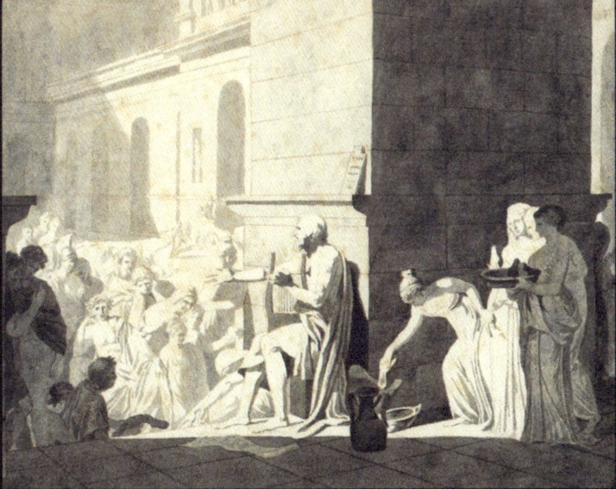

325

of the Third Estate, one of the three orders – the others being the nobility and the clergy – that were present at the Château de Versailles in June 1789 for the meeting of the Estates-General that, under duress, Louis XVI had summoned. A compelling orator, Mirabeau stood up to all those who opposed the proposed reforms, which earned him immense popularity; thousands gathered for his funeral in Paris in 1791. Jean-Antoine Houdon paid tribute to the political figure with a terracotta bust, made from a cast of his face taken after death. Mirabeau was known for his spirit and self-assurance, and these are the traits Houdon captures, never seeking to idealise his subject, who was not a handsome man.

During this same period, Muslim artists in India, influenced by the work of their Arab and Persian counterparts, excelled in the art of the miniature. In 1792, as indicated by an inscription in Arabic and Persian on the work, the Indian draughtsman Hajji Madani sketched this powerful and instantly familiar buffalo **[328]**. Part of the collection at the Union Centrale des Arts Décoratifs, it illustrates the interest artists and creators of the nineteenth century showed for Islamic arts.

In the late eighteenth century, people in the Marquesas Islands used volcanic rock to sculpt statuettes such as this representation of Tiki **[326]**, a civilising hero and the inventor of sculpture and the visual arts. Brought back from an expedition to Oceania, it was displayed in the maritime and ethnographic museum that opened inside the Louvre in 1827, the first of its kind in France. In Papua in the late eighteenth century, wood was carved into works such as the *Korwar Reliquary* **[330]**. One of several objects brought back by Louis-Isidore Duperrey, commander of the *Coquille*, it was previously part of the Muséum d'Histoire Naturelle's collections. Paradoxically, the West became familiar with artistic expressions practised in Oceania through the objects collected by the maritime expeditions that set out to discover and conquer new lands, while the artistic production of Africa, both contemporary and from earlier periods, remained largely unknown despite the continent's greater geographic proximity.

[326]
Anthropomorphic Sculpture, Tiki
Marquesas Islands, French Polynesia
Late 18th–early 19th century
Carved volcanic rock
H. 15.1; W. 9.45; D. 6.3 cm
(H. 6; W. 3¾; D. 2½ in.)
⊻ Former collection of the Louvre, 1851, former collection of the Musée d'Ethnographie du Trocadéro, Paris
MQB–JC

[327]
Jean-Antoine Houdon
1741–1828
Mirabeau (Honoré Gabriel Riqueti, Count of), Politician
1791
Terracotta
H. 53.7; W. 38.5; D. 34.7 cm
(H. 21¼; W. 15¼; D. 13¾ in.)
⊻ 1880
DS

[328]
Attributed to Hajji Madani Musawwir?
Active late 18th century
Buffalo (page from an album)
1792
Ink and colours on paper
H. 11.5; W. 20 cm
(H. 4½; W. 7¾ in.)
⊻ 2012 (deposit from the Union Centrale des Arts Décoratifs, Paris)
DIA

[329]
Workshop of Jean-Baptiste-Claude Sené
1747–1803
Cabriolet Chair
1790
Gilded walnut
H. 91; W. 54; D. 50 cm
(H. 35¾; W. 21¼; D. 19¾ in.)
⊻ 1946
DDA

[330]
Korwar Reliquary
Papua, Indonesia
Late 18th century
Sculpted wood, bone and blue glass
H. 60; W. 20.5; D. 23 cm
(H. 23½; W. 8; D. 9 in.)
⊻ Former collection of the Muséum d'Histoire Naturelle, Paris, collected by Louis-Isidore Duperrey
MQB–JC

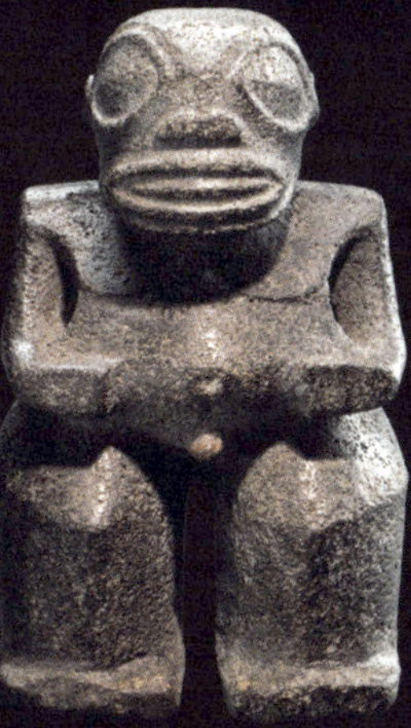

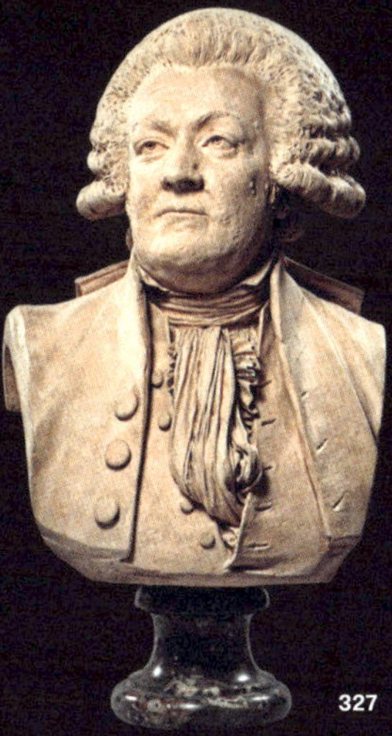

327

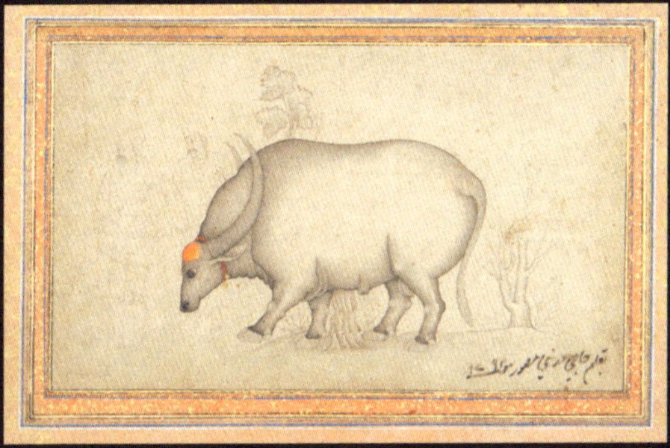

328

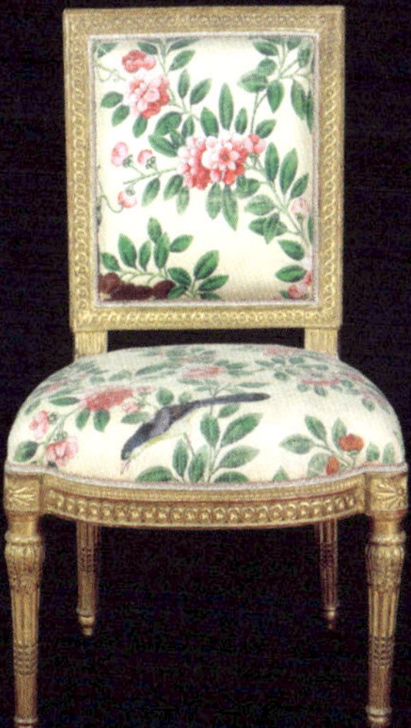

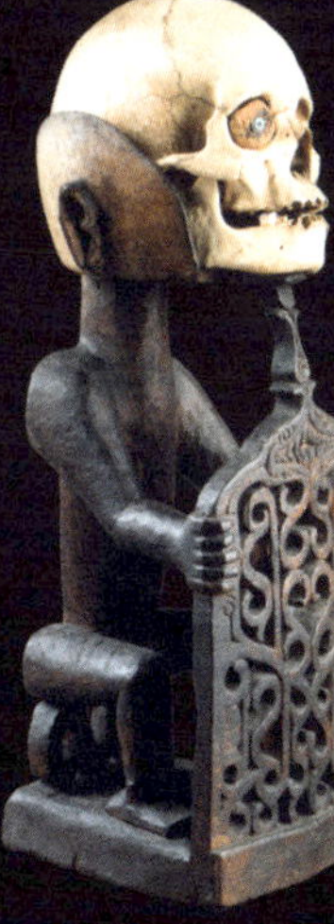

Inventing the museum

The opening of the Muséum Central des Arts in the summer of 1793 was a defining moment. The royal collections went on display in what had been the home of France's kings: the symbol could not have been more powerful. The new museum gave artists, and soon the public at large, the possibility to observe, study and admire at leisure masterpieces of centuries past. Already the collections were a sight to behold and this was just the beginning, as the desire to add to this remarkable ensemble soon became apparent. The uncovering of new objects, the recent familiarisation with distant lands – Egypt had fired the public's imagination since Napoleon Bonaparte's military expedition of 1798 **[331]** – not forgetting the confiscation of works during the French Revolution, all played a part in expanding the museum's holdings. For the armies of Napoleon Bonaparte, victory extended to the possession of the most prized artworks from conquered territories, which were placed at the Louvre for all to see. The museum now held works from every European country. Many would be repatriated following the collapse of the Empire.

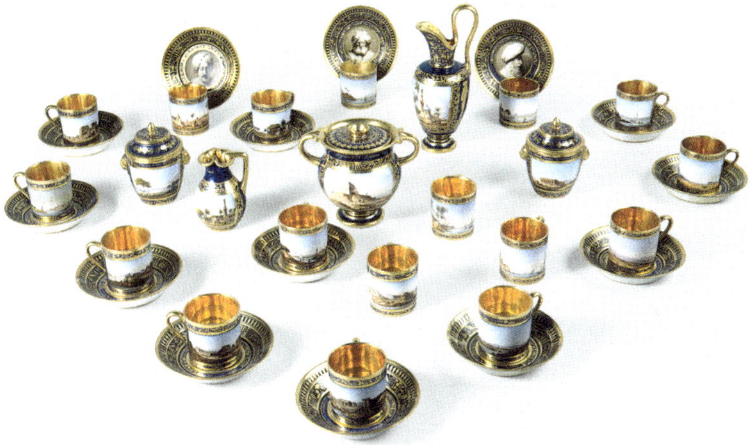

[331] Manufacture de Sèvres. Antoine Béranger, 1785–1867; Antoine Lebel, 1705–1793. ***Napoleon I's Egyptian Cabaret Service***. 1810. Painted and gilded porcelain. 36 pieces. ⊻ 1949. DDA

Rather than returning to their initial locations, most were put on display in the museums that were opening across Europe. The idea of an institution where art could be enjoyed by all was taking shape.

A dynamic had begun that continued after the end of the First French Empire in 1815. The Louvre's collections continued to grow during the Bourbon Restoration, with the arrival of artefacts uncovered by the archaeological excavations conducted throughout the nineteenth century. The museum created a new perspective for living artists, who aspired that their work one day be exhibited there, alongside the ancient masters they admired. For them the Louvre was a vast studio where they could sharpen their gaze, a place where new sources of inspiration blossomed and grew. The Musée du Luxembourg, which opened in Paris in 1818, acted as an anteroom. It showed state acquisitions of works by living artists, which were transferred to the Louvre only after the death of their creators. A former student of David, from the late 1810s Louis Nicolas Philippe Auguste, Comte de Forbin, led an ambitious policy that was instrumental in the Louvre's acquisition of works by young artists.

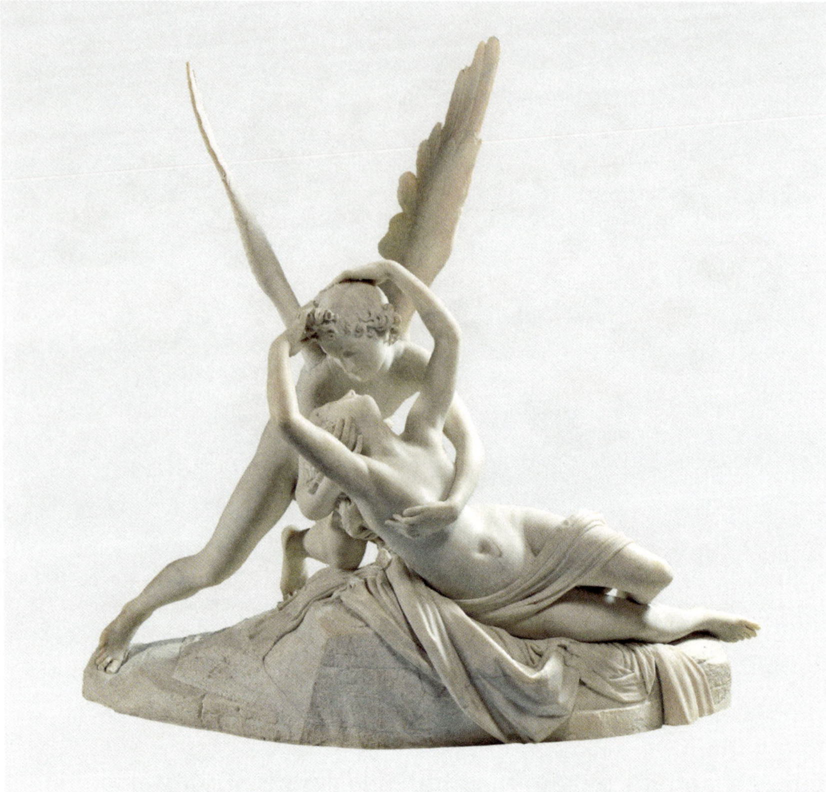

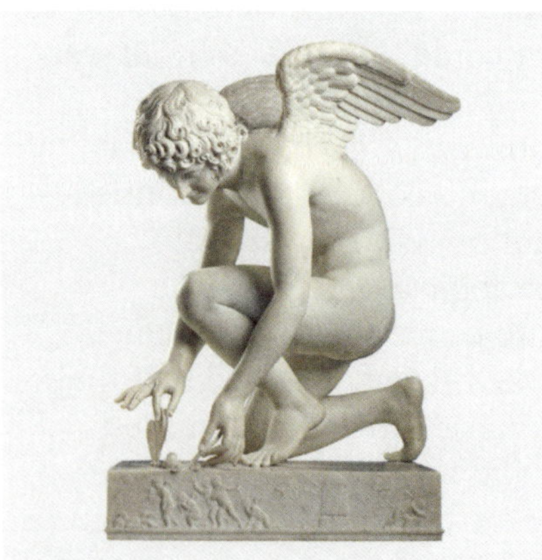

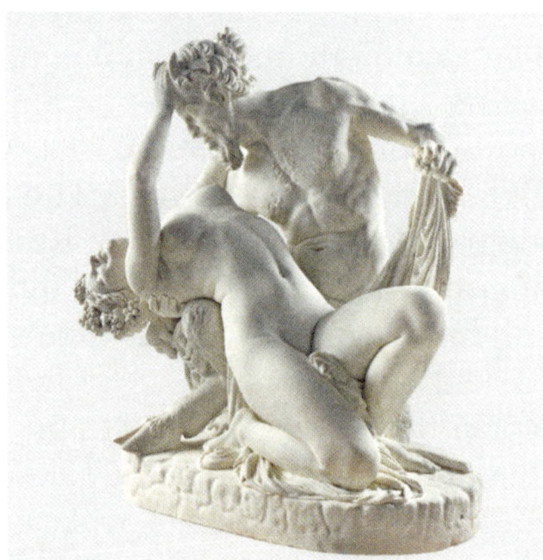

[332]
Antonio Canova
1757–1822
Psyche Revived by Cupid's Kiss
c. 1787–1793
Marble and metal
H. 155; W. 168; D. 101 cm
(H. 5 ft 1 in.; W. 5 ft 6¼ in.; D. 3 ft 3¾ in.)
⏚ 1822 (former collection of Napoleon I)
DS

[333]
Antoine Denis Chaudet, 1763–1810; Pierre Cartellier, 1757–1831
Cupid
1817
Marble
H. 77.5; W. 64; D. 44 cm
(H. 30½; W. 25¼; D. 17¼ in.)
⏚ 1847 (former royal collection)
DS

[334]
James Pradier
1790–1852
Satyr and Bacchante
1834
Marble
H. 125; W. 112; D. 78 cm
(H. 4 ft 1¼ in.; W. 3 ft 8 in.; D. 2 ft 6¾ in.)
⏚ 1980 (with the participation of the Société des Amis du Louvre)
DS

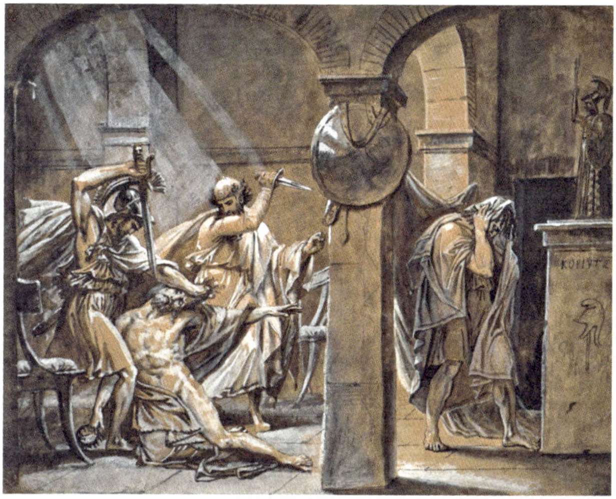

[335]
Antoine-Jean Gros
1771–1835
Death of Timophanes
c. 1793–1800
Pen and brown ink, brown, grey and black wash, black chalk, heightened with white on laid paper
H. 44.4; W. 57.7 cm
(H. 17½; W. 22¾ in.)
⊻ 1842 (bequest of Augustine Dufresne)
DPD

THE MUSEUM AS A STUDIO The taste for classical art took on sensual, graceful new forms. Both the subject and the medium – marble – of *Psyche Revived by Cupid's Kiss* **[332]**, by the Italian sculptor Antonio Canova, hark back to antique statuary. The sculpture leads the eye upwards, swirling through the surrounding space with extraordinary lightness. In the late eighteenth century, the god of love was a popular subject, in the guise of a young man or a charming infant **[333]**. In 1834 James Pradier gave his personal interpretation of passionate love between two mythological beings in *Satyr and Bacchante* **[334]**, portraying himself as the satyr and his companion, Juliette Drouet, as the bacchante; Juliette would later become Victor Hugo's devoted mistress.

References to antiquity also served as examples of moral virtue. While in Rome, Antoine-Jean Gros began preparations for a painting (which never materialised) that would depict the death of Timophanes, whose brother Timoleon, a Corinthian general, had him murdered to save the city from his plot to seize power and rule as a tyrant. In the preparatory study *Death of Timophanes* **[335]** the two assassins stand in shafts of light

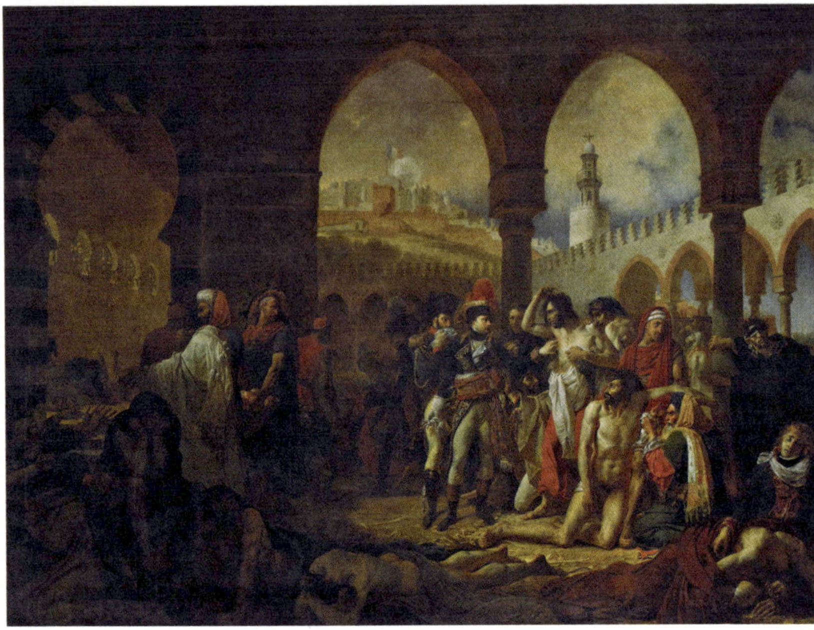

[336] Antoine-Jean Gros. 1771–1835. ***Napoleon Bonaparte Visiting the Plague-Stricken in Jaffa***
1804. Oil on canvas. H. 523; W. 715 cm (H. 17 ft 2 in.; W. 23 ft 5½ in.). ⩝ 1804. DP

while Timoleon, his hands over his ears to muffle his brother Timophanes's screams, disappears into the shadows. Parallels were also drawn between ancient virtue and that of the rulers of the time. Also by Gros, *Napoleon Bonaparte Visiting the Plague-Stricken in Jaffa* **[336]** shows the general, portrayed as benevolent and courageous, visiting victims of bubonic plague at a makeshift pesthouse and allowing them to touch him, despite the risk of contagion. Gros depicts Napoleon as heir to the sovereigns who were said to cure the sick with their touch. Following Napoleon's coronation in 1804, the emperor and his deeds were at the heart of artistic creation, orchestrated by Dominique Vivant Denon, the Louvre's first director. Jacques-Louis David painted the imposing *Coronation of Napoleon* **[339]** between 1805 and 1808. For this pictorial homage, the artist drew inspiration from *The Coronation of Marie de' Medici*, executed by Rubens for the titular queen. Testimony to David's painterly skill, the scene and its multiple protagonists are rendered true to life, while the moment the artist has chosen to immortalise points not only to his compositional genius but also his grasp of the work's political implications. Napoleon crowned himself,

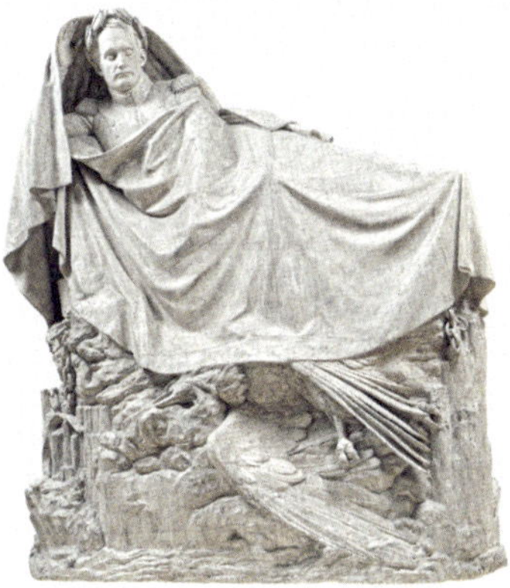

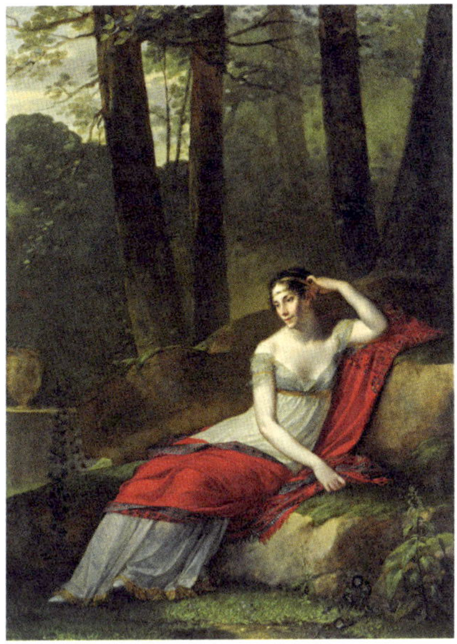

[337]
François Rude
1784–1855
Napoleon Awakening to Immortality
1846
Plaster
H. 220; W. 205; D. 116 cm
(H. 7 ft 2½ in.;
W. 6 ft 8¾ in.; D. 3 ft 9¾ in.)
⊻ 1892
DS

[338]
Pierre-Paul Prud'hon
1758–1823
Empress Josephine
1805
Oil on canvas
H. 244; W. 179 cm
(H. 8 ft; W. 5 ft 10½ in.)
⊻ 1879 (former collection of Napoleon III)
DP

an instant David captured in several preliminary drawings, but the scene lacked grandeur and so the artist recreates the moment when the newly consecrated emperor places the crown on the head of his wife, Josephine. The imperial couple become the focal point of the painting. Though Napoleon's mother Letizia Bonaparte was absent from the ceremony, David gives her a place of honour in the stands. Her imagined presence is a powerful dynastic symbol for the new imperial regime. Following his death in exile on the island of Saint Helena, Napoleon became a romantic hero once again and the return of his remains to Paris in 1841 saw an outpouring of emotion. In *Napoleon Awakening to Immortality* **[337]**, sculpted by François Rude as a monument to his glory, the former emperor is seen rising from his funeral pall.

THE ARTIST AS NARRATOR From his very first submissions to the Salon – an exhibition of works by contemporary artists held in the Louvre's Salon Carré – Théodore Géricault made his ambition clear. The young artist set out to renew history painting through his choice of subjects and through a more

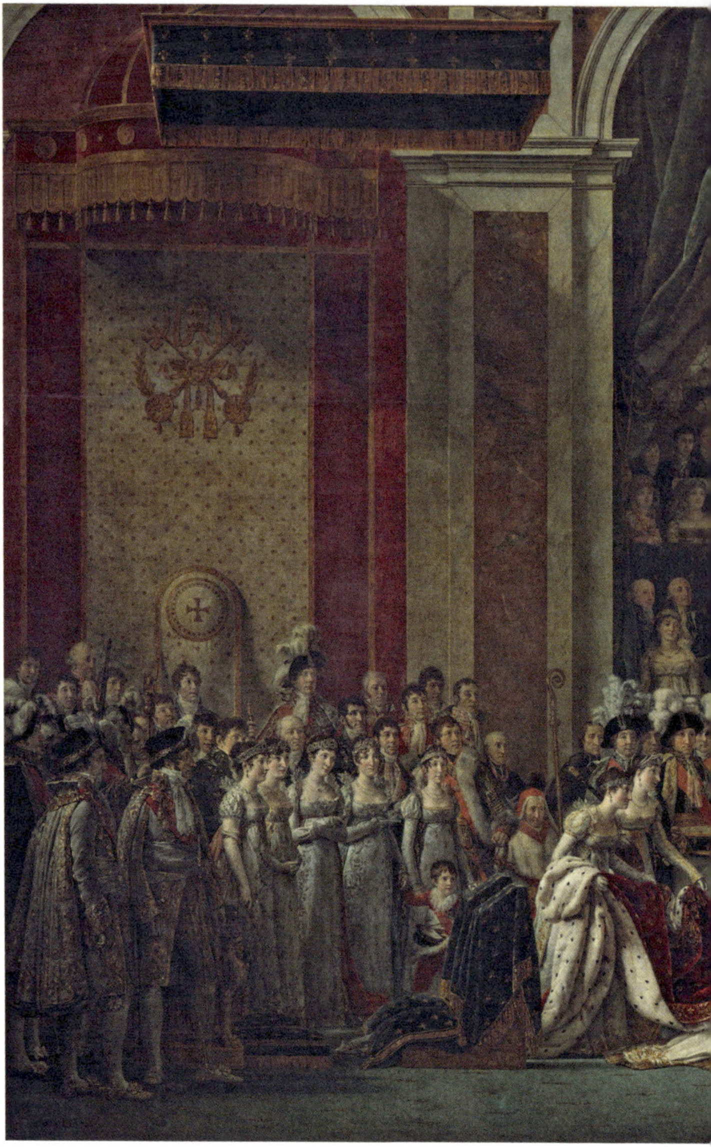

[339]
Jacques-Louis David
1748–1825
The Coronation of Napoleon and the Coronation of Josephine at Notre Dame de Paris
1806–1807
Oil on canvas
H. 621; W. 979 cm
(H. 20 ft 4½ in.; W. 32 ft 1½ in.)
⊻ 1808
DP

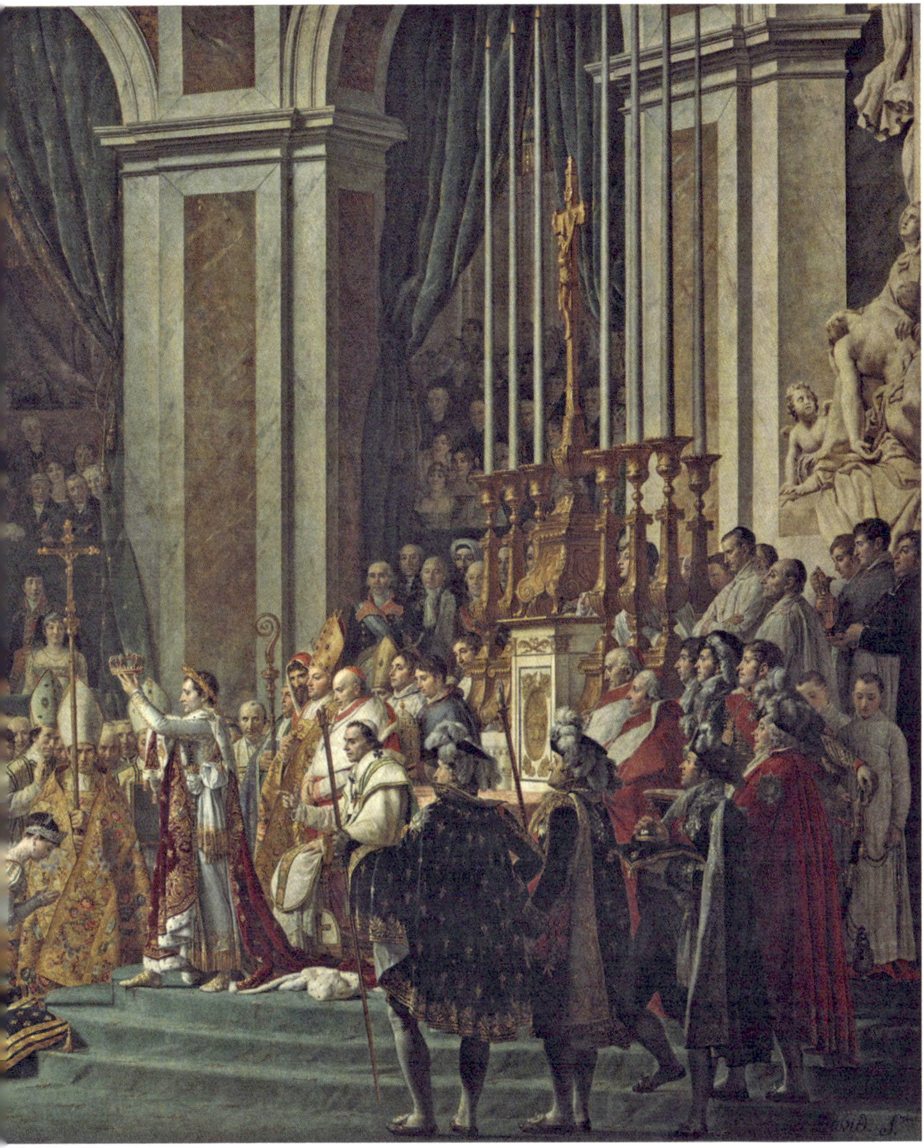

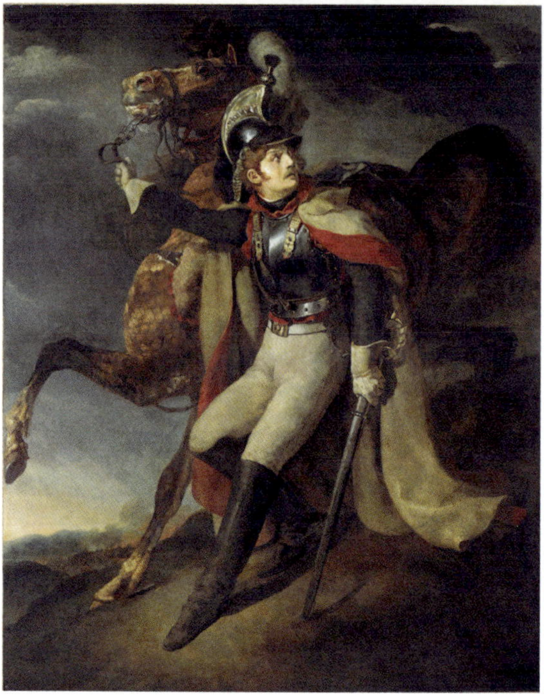

[340]
Théodore Géricault
1791–1824
Wounded Cuirassier Leaving the Field of Battle
1814
Oil on canvas
H. 358; W. 294 cm
(H. 11 ft 9 in.; W. 9 ft 7¾ in.)
⩡ 1851
DP

realistic treatment of the individuals he portrayed. His *Wounded Cuirassier Leaving the Field of Battle* **[340]** of 1814 shows Napoleon's military campaigns in a different light. Instead of portraying the emperor or one of his generals, he paints an anonymous soldier struggling to restrain his mount. The nature of his injury is unknown but his heavy gait and worried expression as he looks back over his shoulder suggest his inner torment, underscored by the dark clouds swirling in the background. In 1819 Géricault exhibited *The Raft of the Medusa* **[341]**, a huge painting inspired by an event three years earlier, when the French frigate *Méduse* was grounded off the coast of Mauritania. The ship's captain abandoned some of his crew and passengers on a raft, which drifted for weeks on the open sea. Many died and survivors were forced to eat their bodies or starve. Géricault chose not to depict glory but the darkest days of the newly restored monarchy. His painting shocked in its message but impressed in its energised composition, which culminates in the figure of the sailor desperately waving a cloth at a passing ship, just visible on the horizon. Eugène Delacroix deeply admired Géricault's art. Following the latter's

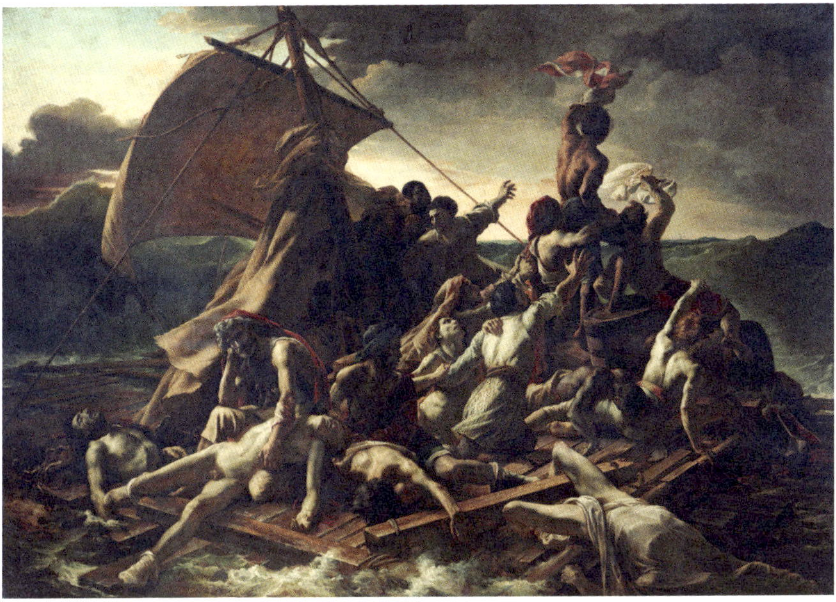

[341]
Théodore Géricault
1791–1824
The Raft of the Medusa
1818–1819
Oil on canvas
H. 491; W. 716 cm
(H. 16 ft 1¼ in.; W. 23 ft 6 in.)
⊻ 1824
DP

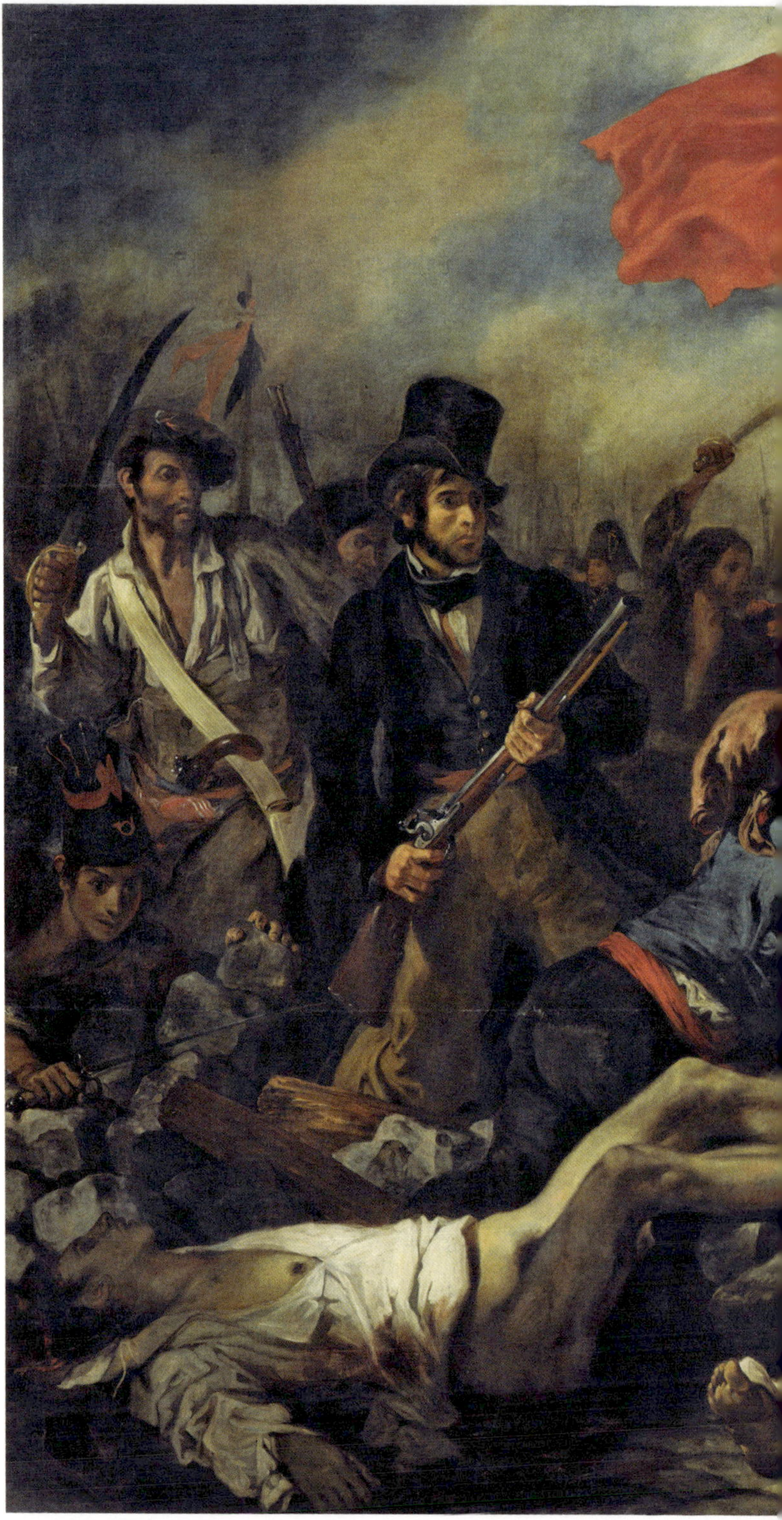

[342]
Eugène Delacroix
1798–1863
Liberty Leading the People
1830
Oil on canvas
H. 260; W. 325 cm
(H. 8 ft 6¼ in.;
W. 10 ft 8 in.)
⊻ 1831
DP

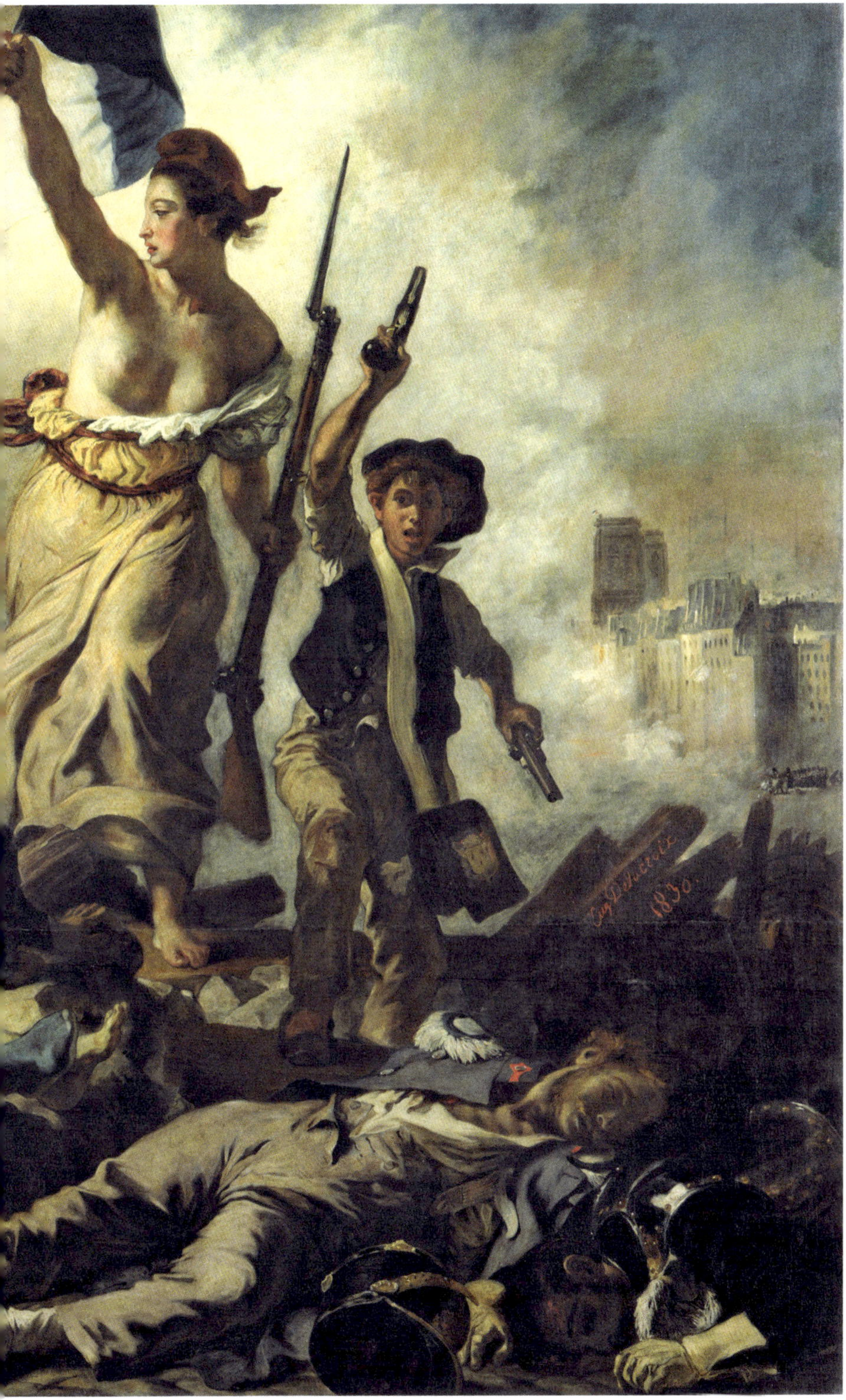
1830

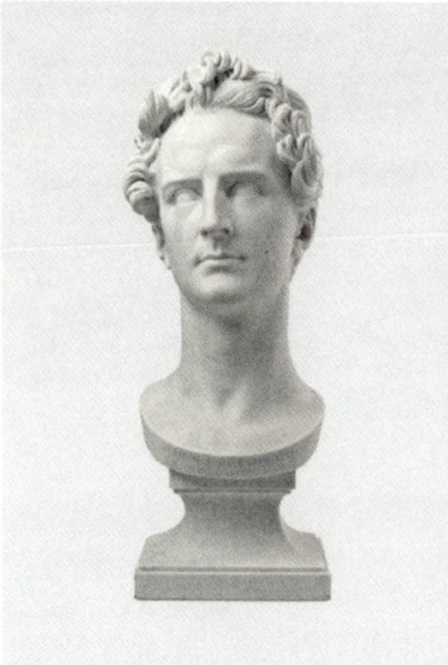

[343]
Pierre-Jean David,
known as David d'Angers
1788–1856
Alphonse de Lamartine
1830
Marble
H. 58; W. 27.5; D. 32 cm
(H. 22¾; W. 10¾; D. 12½ in.)
⩡ 1986
DS

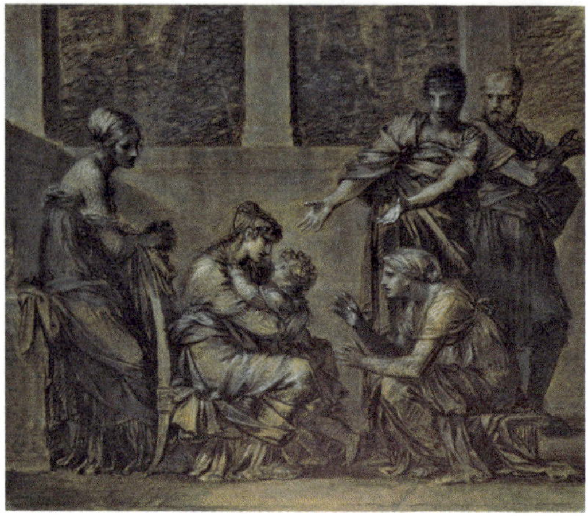

[344]
Pierre-Paul Prud'hon
1758–1823
Andromache
c. 1780–1800
Black and white chalk on faded blue paper
H. 38; W. 46.3 cm
(H. 15; W. 18¼ in.)
⩡ 1883 (gift of Coutan-Hauguet-Schubert-Milliet)
DPD

untimely death in 1824, Delacroix emerged as the most promising artist of his generation. His *Liberty Leading the People* **[342]** borrows from Rubens in its association of a female allegory inspired by Greek sculpture with an historical event, here the Paris uprisings of July 1830. The painting became a manifesto in the twentieth century and remains a symbol of revolution, widely admired and frequently hijacked by popular culture.

Exposure to new knowledge and a broadening of horizons, the close ties between painting and theatre, together with the increased freedom with which they could choose their subjects, gave artists opportunities to draw inspiration from original sources. The ancient models that the playwright Jean Racine chose for his tragedies, whose personal dimension forms part of the dramatic apparatus, were reprised by Pierre-Narcisse Guérin, Girodet and Pierre-Paul Prud'hon. Their drawings **[344, 345]**, featuring a carefully scripted dramaturgy, espouse an idealised representation of the human body. François-René de Chateaubriand's recently published novella gave Girodet the idea for *The Burial of Atala* **[346]**. Borrowing its frieze composition and Chactas's muscular physique from antique

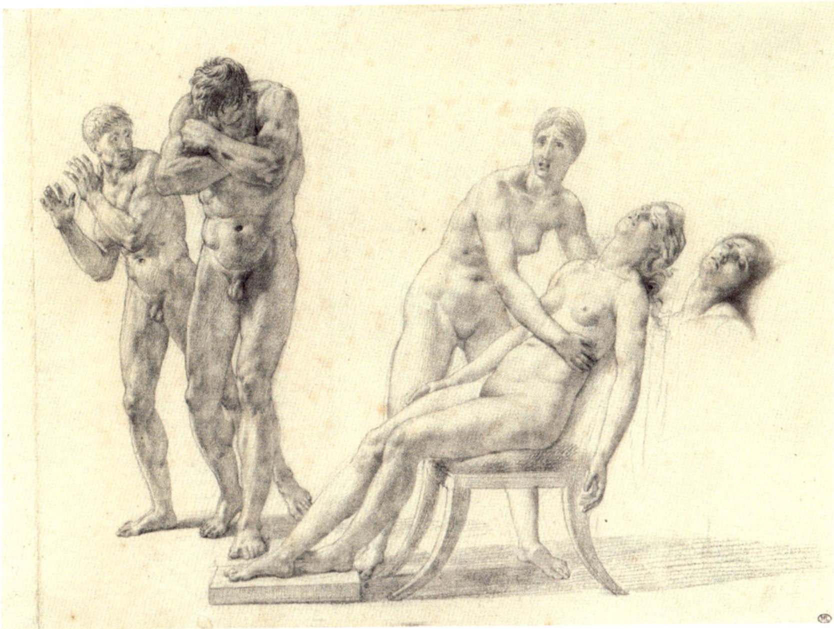

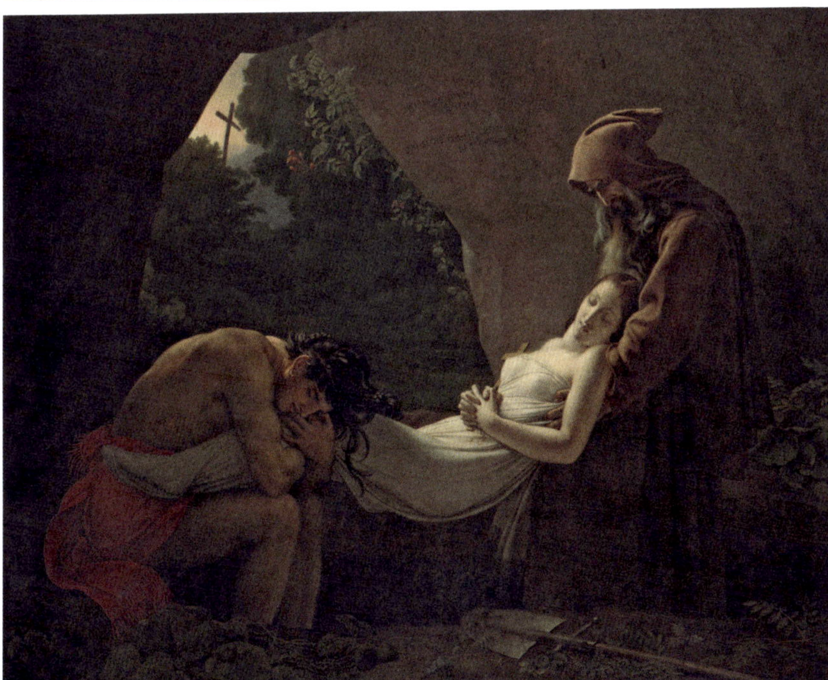

[345]
Anne-Louis Girodet de Roucy-Trioson
1767–1824
Death of Phaedra
1801
Black chalk
H. 26.5; W. 36.7 cm (H. 10½; W. 14½ in.)
⩡ 1851
DPD

[346]
Anne-Louis Girodet de Roucy-Trioson
1767–1824
The Burial of Atala
1808
Oil on canvas
H. 207; W. 267 cm (H. 6 ft 9½ in.; W. 8 ft 9¼ in.)
⩡ 1818 (former royal collection, collection of Louis XVIII)
DP

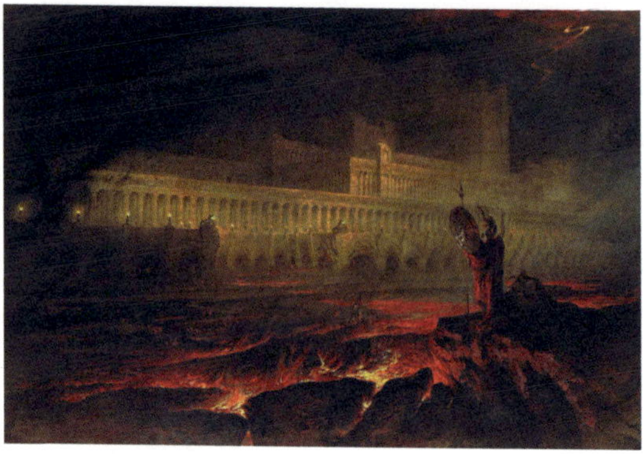

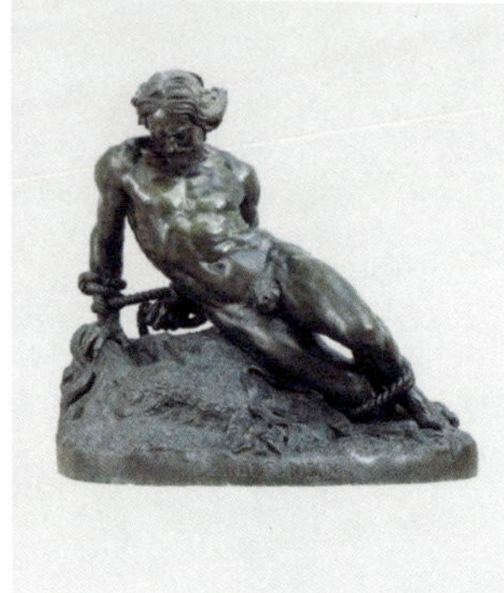

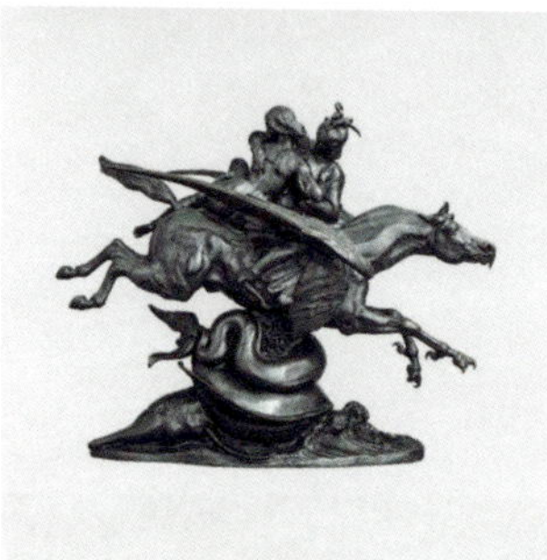

[347]
John Martin
1789–1854
Pandemonium
1841
Oil on canvas
H. 123; W. 185 cm
(H. 4 ft ½ in.;
W. 6 ft ¾ in.)
⊻ 2006
DP

[348]
Jean-Bernard
Duseigneur, known as
Jehan Duseigneur
1808–1866
The Frenzy of Orlando
1867 (plaster:
Salon 1831)
Bronze
H. 130; W. 140; D. 90 cm
(H. 4 ft 3¼ in.;
W 4 ft 7¼ in.;
D. 2 ft 11½ in.)
⊻ 1868
DS

[349]
Antoine-Louis Barye
1795–1875
Angelica and Roger on the Hippogriff
c. 1840
Bronze with green
patina
H. 51.5; W. 69; D. 29 cm
(H. 20¼; W. 27¼;
D. 11½ in.)
⊻ 1902 (bequest of
George Thomy Thiéry)
DS

[350] Paul Delaroche. 1797–1856. ***Edward V and His Younger Brother Richard, Duke Of York in the Tower (1483)*, known as *The Children of Edward***. 1830. Oil on canvas. H. 181; W. 215 cm (H. 5 ft 11¼ in.; W. 7 ft ¾ in.). ⊻ 1831. DP

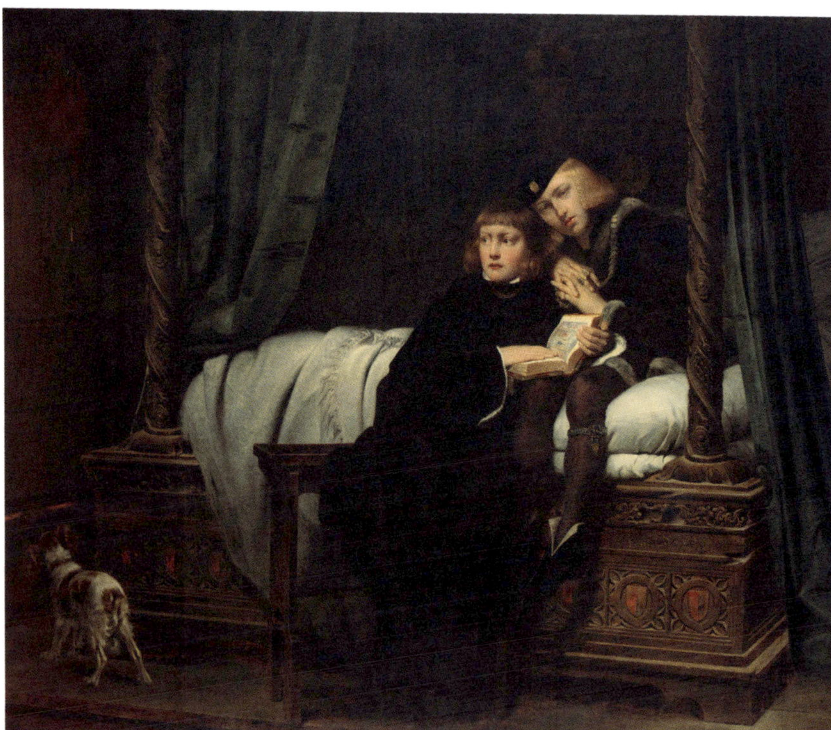

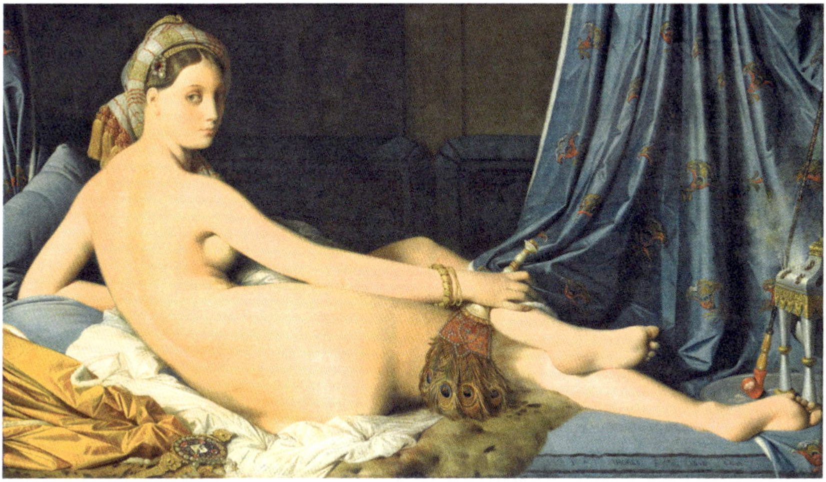

[351]
Jean-Auguste-Dominique Ingres
1780–1867
An Odalisque*, known as *Grande Odalisque
1814
Oil on canvas
H. 91; W. 162 cm
(H. 2 ft 11¾ in.; W. 5 ft 3¾ in.)
⊻ 1899
DP

art, the painting tells of the Native American heroine's sad fate. Renaissance epic poems, including *Orlando Furioso* by Ludovico Ariosto **[348, 349]** and *Jerusalem Delivered* by Torquato Tasso, were also frequent sources of inspiration for artists in the nineteenth century. Paul Delaroche, meanwhile, looked to Shakespeare for the subject of *The Children of Edward* **[350]**, a scene taken from *Richard III*. The terror of the young princes, the sons of the titular Richard's brother and the heirs to the throne, is palpable as they hear the approaching assassins. A shadow cast in the light under the door signals the latters' presence with dramatic suspense.

Ever since the publication of *The Arabian Nights* in the early eighteenth century, the East has continued to be a source of fascination in the West. An imaginary, fantasised Orient gave rise to new representations of the female body. This was a Western construction of the East, unrelated to reality. In her languid pose, the odalisque encapsulated imagined images of Eastern seduction while conforming to the Italian Renaissance canon of the reclining nude. Ingres exhibited his *Grande Odalisque* **[351]** at the 1819 Salon. The painting, in which the artist takes liberties with anatomical constraints, adding vertebrae in order to emphasise the elegance

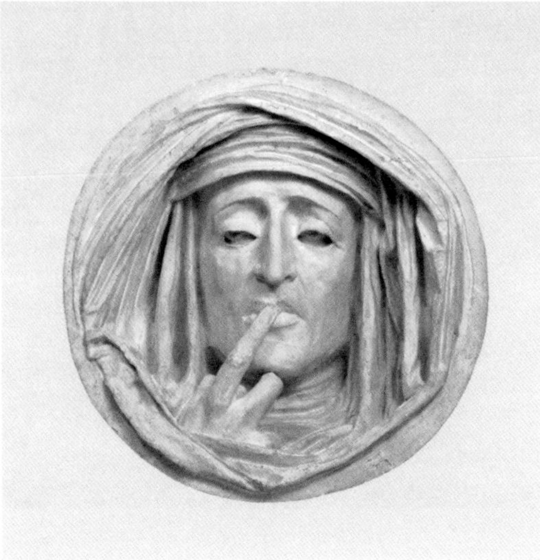

[352]
Auguste Préault
1809–1879
Silence
c. 1842
Plaster
Diam. 41; D. 19.5 cm
(Diam. 16¼; D. 7¾ in.)
⊻ 1985
DS

of the female form, marked the beginning of the female nude as a genre, separate from the figures represented in mythological or religious painting. Delacroix demonstrated his boldness and creative freedom with another Eastern subject: *The Death of Sardanapalus* **[353]** caused an outcry when it was shown at the 1827 Salon. Inspired by the story of one of the last kings of Assyria, the subject of a play by Lord Byron, the painting shows Sardanapalus on a vast divan, surrounded by his possessions, concubines and horses, waiting to be devoured by the fire he himself has lit. Delacroix's depiction of the cynical courage of a man known for a life of debauchery flew in the face of pictorial convention. The feverish composition and riotous colour – revived by restoration in 2023 – of a painting that did nothing to promote virtuous conduct scandalised the Salon's public. But Delacroix was now the name on everyone's lips. The painter would later experience the Orient first-hand, when he accompanied a French diplomatic mission to Morocco in 1832. This eye-opening encounter with the Cherifian kingdom's inhabitants and landscapes would enrich his art. Delacroix filled notebooks with writings along with watercolour sketches **[354]**

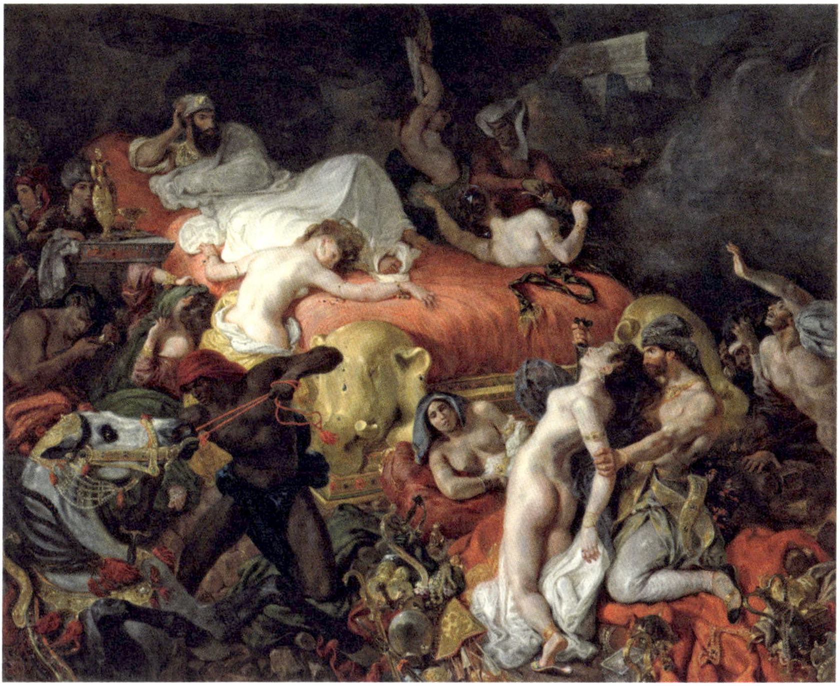

[353]
Eugène Delacroix
1798–1863
The Death of Sardanapalus
1827
Oil on canvas
H. 392; W. 496 cm
(H. 12 ft 10¼ in.; W. 16 ft 3¼ in.)
⊻ 1921
DP

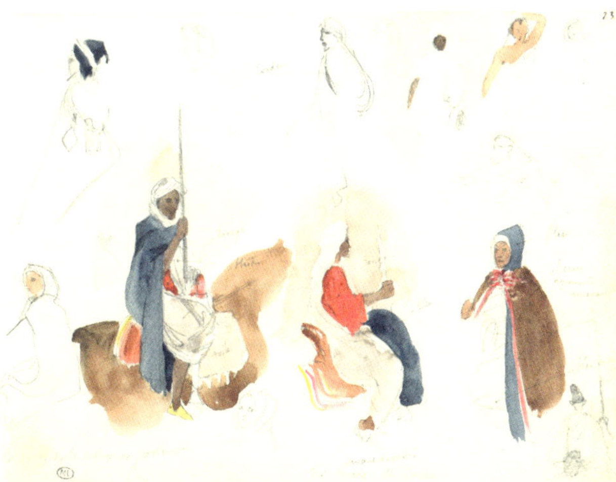

[354]
Eugène Delacroix
1798–1863
Studies of Arab Horsemen and Figures
1832
Pencil and watercolour on paper (album)
H. 15.8; W. 21.2 cm
(H. 6¼; W. 8¼ in.)
⊻ 1927 (bequest of Étienne Moreau-Nélaton)
DPD

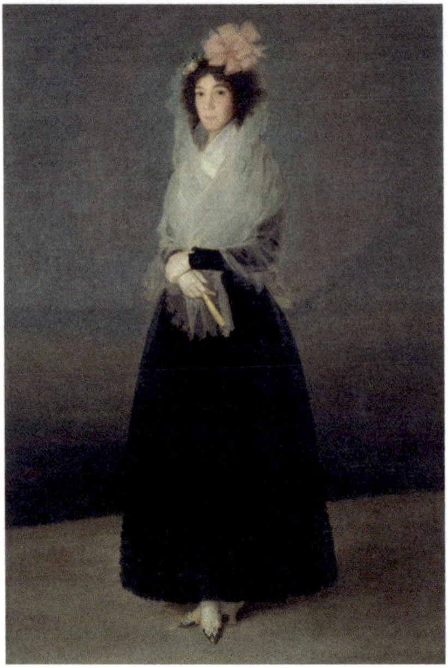

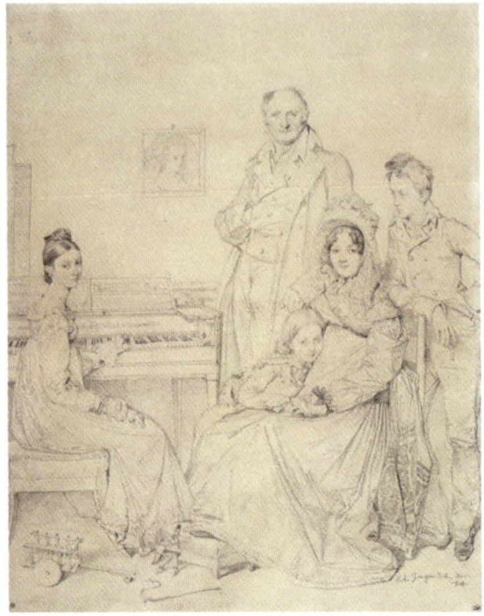

[355]
Francisco de Goya y Lucientes
1746–1828
Portrait of the Marquise de la Solana
c. 1794–1795
Oil on canvas
H. 181; W. 122 cm
(H. 5 ft 11¼ in.; W. 4 ft)
⊻ 1953 (gift of Carlos Beistgui)
DP

[356]
Jean-Auguste-Dominique Ingres
1780–1867
The Stamaty Family
1818
Pencil on paper
H. 46.3; W. 37.1 cm
(H. 18¼; W. 14½ in.)
⊻ 1912 (gift of Léon Bonnat)
DPD

whose luminous colours and vitality convey the emotion sparked by these discoveries.

AESTHETIC LIBERTIES History painter Francisco Goya left a deep imprint on Spanish art. He was also a gifted portraitist. His full-length *Portrait of the Marquise de la Solana* **[355]** demonstrates the skill with which he was able to render the contrast between black and white, the beauty of materials and luminosity. Trained under Vigée Le Brun and David, Marie-Guillemine Benoist was one of the few women artists of the time to show their work at the Salon. Her *Portrait of Madeleine* **[358]**, a young Parisian of the early nineteenth century, highlights the model's regal beauty while the draped garments accentuate her classical pose. This was one of the first depictions of a woman of colour as an individual rather than in a subservient role of servant, nursemaid or cook. Like this work, Jean-Baptiste Camille Corot's *Woman with a Pearl* **[359]** looks to the *Mona Lisa* for the sitter's expression and pose. Ingres painted three members of the Rivière family. His portrait of *Mademoiselle Caroline Rivière* **[357]**, the daughter of the family, was completed the year of the sitter's

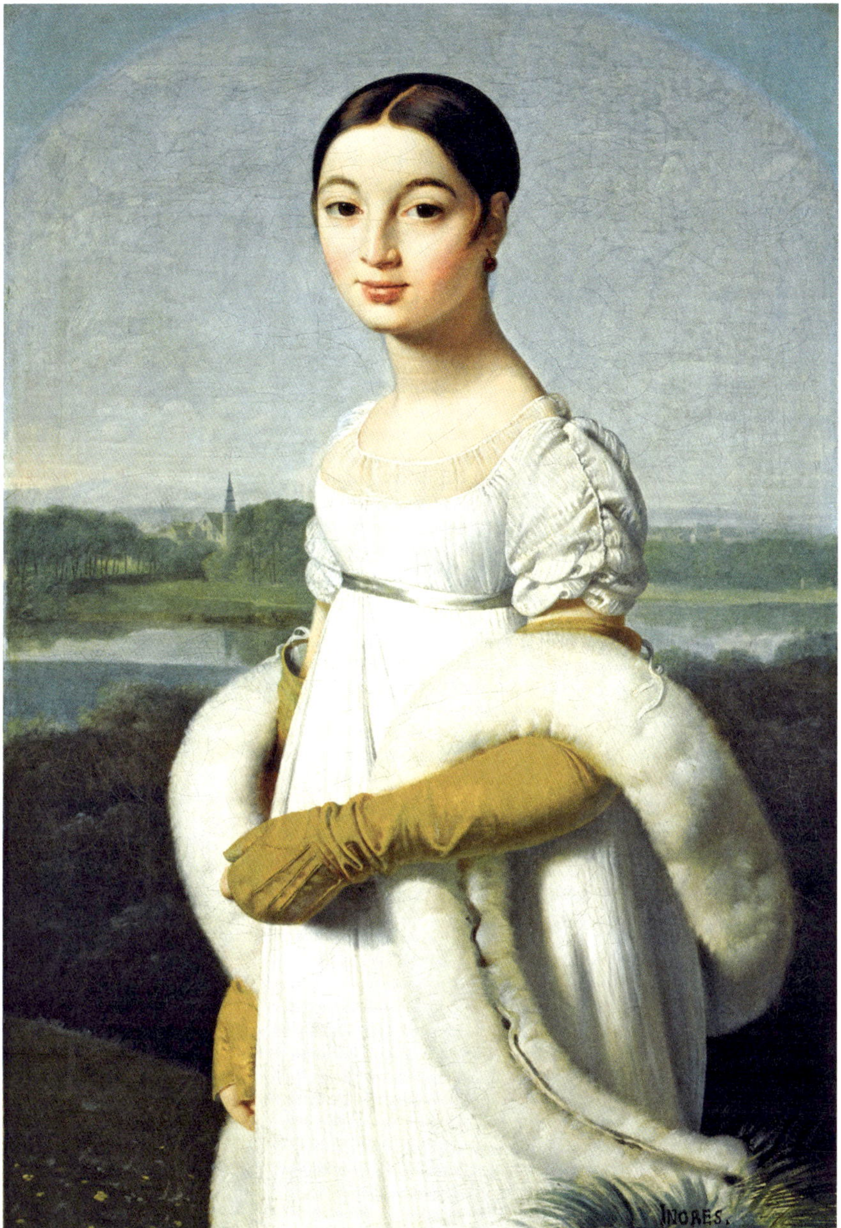

[357]
Jean-Auguste-Dominique Ingres
1780–1867
Mademoiselle Caroline Rivière
1805
Oil on canvas (transposed)
H. 100; W. 70 cm
(H. 3 ft 3¼ in.; W. 2 ft 3½ in.)
⊻ 1870 (bequest of Sophie Robillard)
DP

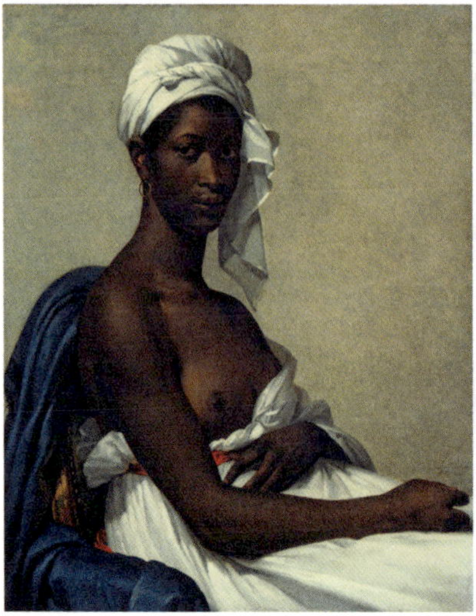

[358]
Marie-Guillemine Benoist
1768–1826
Portrait of Madeleine
1800
Oil on canvas
H. 81; W. 65 cm (H. 32; W. 25½ in.)
⩡ 1818 (former royal collection, collection of Louis XVIII)
DP

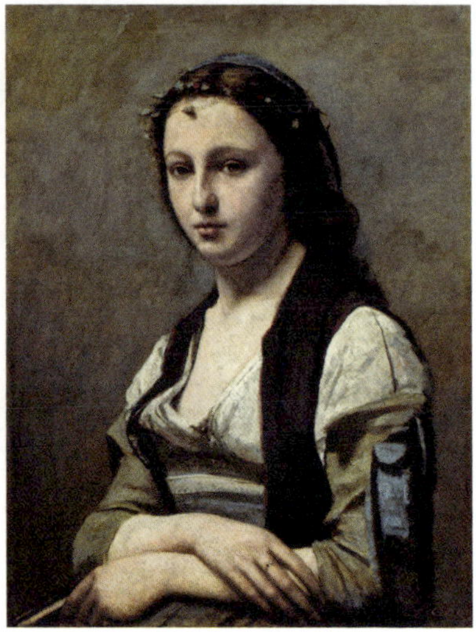

[359]
Jean-Baptiste Camille Corot
1796–1875
Woman with a Pearl
c. 1850–1875
Oil on canvas
H. 70; W. 55 cm
(H. 27½; W. 21¾ in.)
⩡ 1912
DP

death. Ingres celebrates the young woman's fragile beauty in a subtle palette of whites and beiges, combining physical resemblance with a rare freedom of interpretation: Caroline's shoulders have been narrowed whereas her arms appear longer and, enveloped in mustard-yellow leather gloves, lend the young model an unexpected force. As a landscape artist, Corot's paintings **[360]** are suffused with the melancholy of contemplation; as a portraitist, he was an attentive observer of the human figure.

A DESIRE FOR NATURE For a long time deemed a lesser genre, landscape painting came into its own in the nineteenth century as uniquely qualified to express the artist's personal sensibility. Demand for landscapes increased among buyers whose craving for nature was partly in reaction to urban industrialisation. Caspar David Friedrich embodies a German vision of the landscape, in which the transcription of nature extends into a philosophical meditation **[361]**. It was some time before his work became known in France, and few examples are held in the country's museums. The English

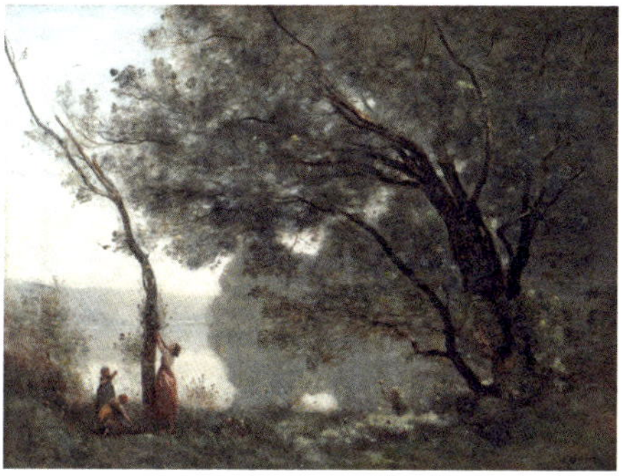

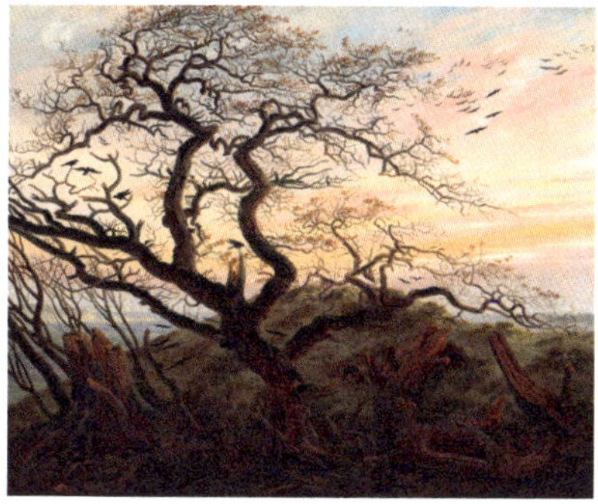

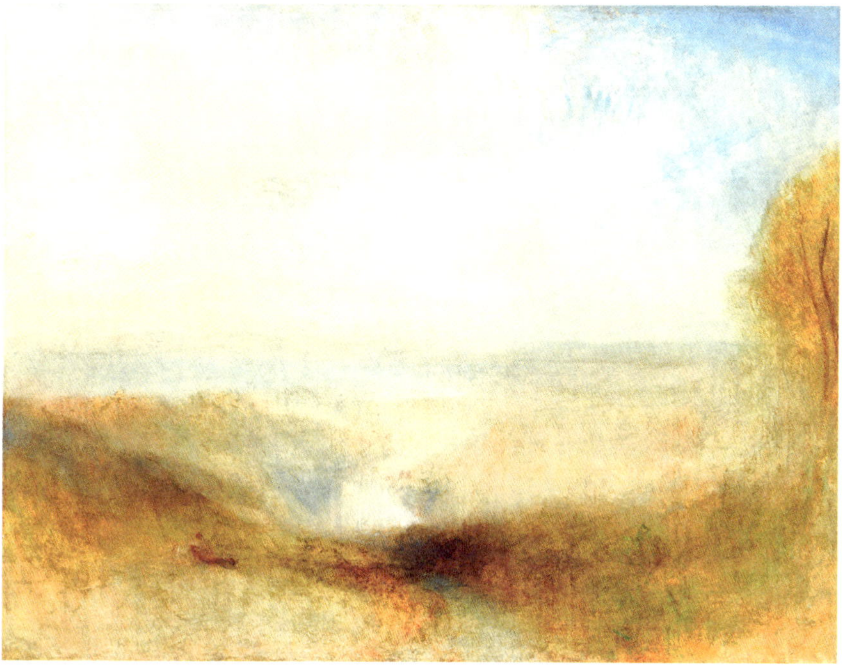

[360]
Jean-Baptiste Camille Corot
1796–1875
Souvenir of Mortefontaine (Oise)
1850–1875
Oil on canvas
H. 65; W. 89 cm
(H. 25½; W. 35 in.)
⊻ 1889 (former collection of Napoleon III)
DP

[361]
Caspar David Friedrich
1774–1840
Tree of Crows
c. 1822
Oil on canvas
H. 59; W. 73 cm
(H. 23¼; W. 28¾ in.)
⊻ 1975
DP

[362]
J. M. W. Turner
1775–1851
Landscape with a River and a Bay in the Distance
c. 1845
Oil on canvas
H. 94; W. 124 cm
(H. 3 ft 1 in.; W. 4 ft ¾ in.)
⊻ 1967
DP

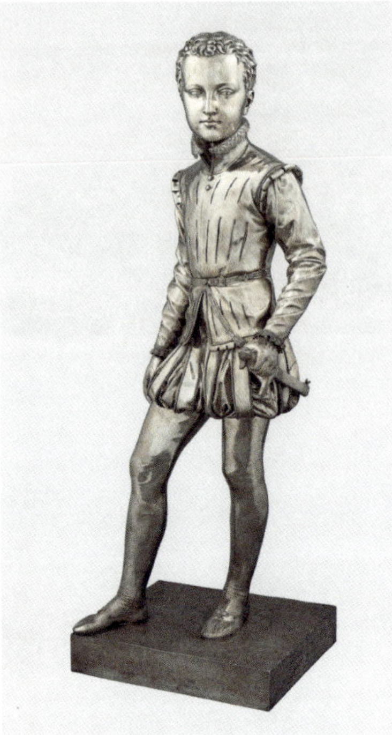

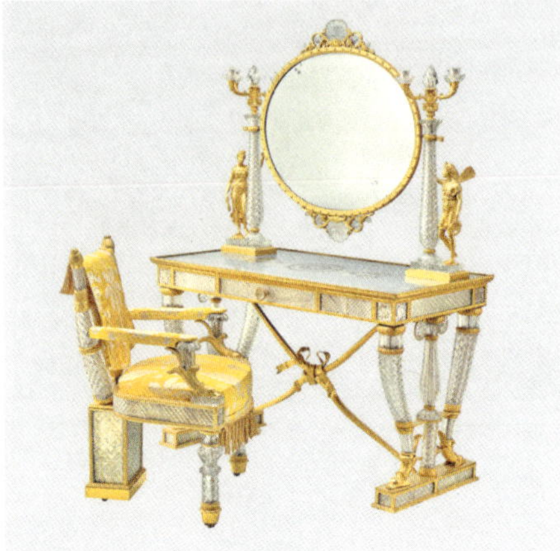

[363]
After François
Joseph Bosio
1768–1845
Young Henry IV
1824
Silver
H. 125; W. 42;
D. 45 cm (H. 4 ft 1¼ in.;
W. 1 ft 4½ in.;
D. 1 ft 5¾ in.)
⊻ 1829
DS

[364]
Marie-Jeanne-Rosalie
Désarnaud-Charpentier
1775–1842
Duchess of Berry's Dressing Table
c. 1819
Gilded bronze, beech, crystal and glass
H. 78.5; W. 122.5; D. 64.3 cm
(H. 2 ft 7 in.; W. 4 ft ¼ n.; D. 2 ft 1¼ in.)
⊻ 1822
DDA

artist J. M. W. Turner was fascinated by the changing elements and their effects on nature **[362]**. He excelled in translating these fleeting instances into atmospheric paintings that break with the tradition of the classic, timeless landscape. His work would have an undeniable influence on later French painting, in particular Impressionism.

HISTORICISM While the French Revolution temporarily halted the trade in objets d'art, the Exposition des Produits de l'Industrie Française, which was held periodically from 1798 until 1849, showcased the country's industry and artisans. At the same time, the large manufactories were experiencing a revival, busy furnishing the grand residences of the Empire. Interest in earlier centuries manifested itself in reinvented forms and decoration, furthered by technical progress such as the introduction of new materials. The refined taste of renowned socialite Juliette Récamier is evident in the classically inspired furniture that was made for her by the cabinetmakers Jacob Frères **[365]**. The *Large Jewellery Cabinet* **[366]** crafted for Empress Josephine is similar in appearance to the one made for Marie-Antoinette.

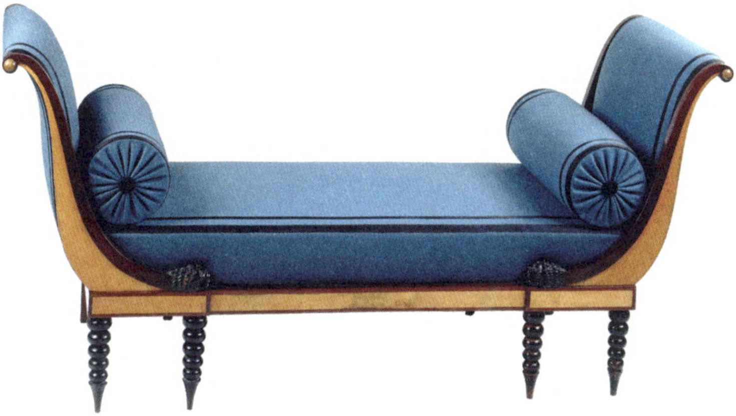

[365]
Attributed to Jacob Frères
Daybed from the Salon of Madame Récamier
c. 1800
Walnut frame, San Domingan satinwood and amaranth veneer, solid satinwood, painted solid walnut
H. 78; L. 171; D. 60 cm
(H. 2 ft 6¾ in.;
L. 5 ft 7¼ in.; D. 1 ft 11½ in.)
⊻ 1994 (gift)
DDA

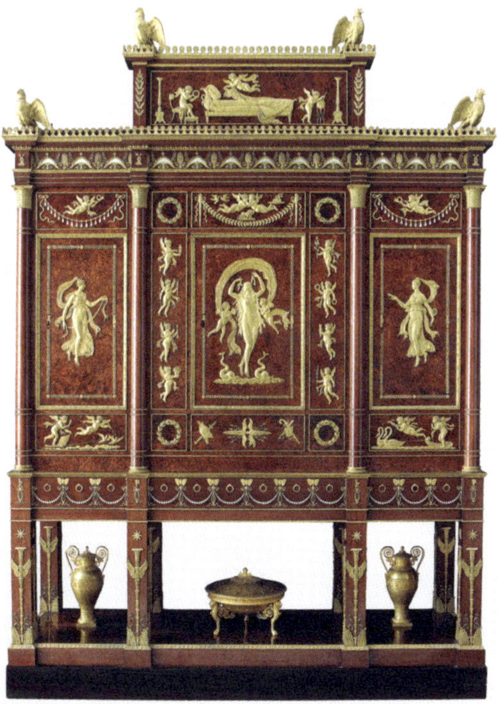

[366]
François-Honoré-Georges Jacob, known as Jacob-Desmalter
1770–1841
Empress Josephine's Jewellery Cabinet
1809
Gilded bronze, mahogany, amaranth, ebony, yew and mother-of-pearl
H. 276; W. 200; D. 60 cm
(H. 9 ft ¾ in.; W. 6 ft 6¾ in.;
D. 1 ft 11½ in.)
⊻ 1965 (former imperial collection)
DDA

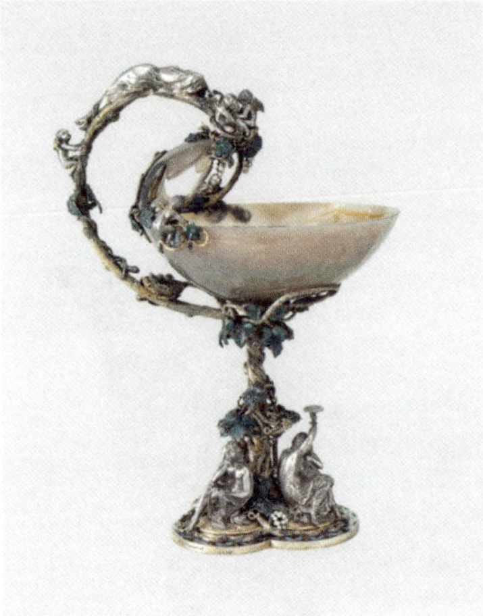

[367]
François Désiré Froment-Meurice,
1801–1855, and others
Wine Harvest Cup
c. 1844
Enamelled and gilded silver, agate and shell
H. 35; W. 27; D. 15 cm
(H. 13¾; W. 10¾; D. 5⅞ in.)
⊻ 1984
DDA

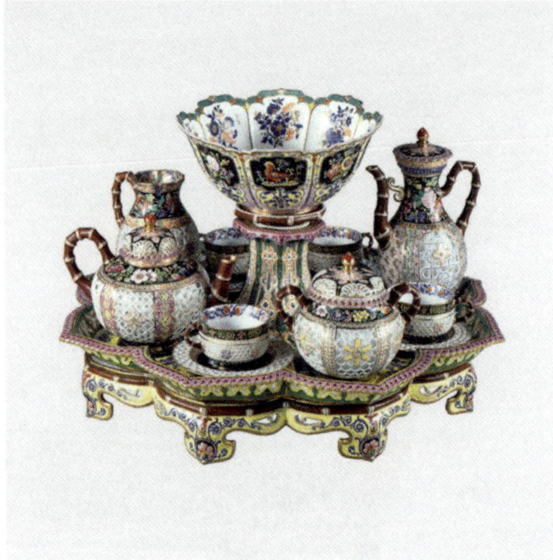

[368]
Manufacture de Sèvres
Queen Maria Amalia's Reticulated Chinese Coffee and Tea Service
1840
Hard-paste porcelain
Ten pieces
⊻ 1986
DDA

Its bronze embellishments are an imaginative combination of antique references with allusions to femininity; the central motif, for example, depicts "Cupid and the goddesses hurrying to present their offerings to the queen of the Earth". The *Duchess of Berry's Dressing Table* **[364]** is remarkable in its fabrication. Supported by an iron frame, it is composed of cut crystal plaques and casings with gilt bronze mounts. The transparency of the crystal contrasts with the monumental nature of the whole, which is still reminiscent of the Empire style. The *Wine Harvest Cup* **[367]** freely interprets classical and Renaissance bowls and vases, themselves often assemblies of objects from different eras. The bowl is in agate while the mount is partially gilded and enamelled silver. The *Reticulated Chinese Coffee and Tea Service* **[368]** is one of the most daring creations to come out of the Manufacture de Sèvres – under the directorship of Alexandre Brogniart since 1800 – and symbolic of the multiple inspirations that the manufactory's ceramists explored. The Chinese influence is clearly evident, not least in the faux bamboo spouts and handles. Elaborate openwork, or reticulation, together with the exuberant colour scheme distinguish this exceptional service.

“The vast space
in which the stars
accomplish their revolution;
from this point of view,
Earth, being a planet,
is in the sky.”

Émile Littré,
Dictionnaire de la langue française,
1873–1877

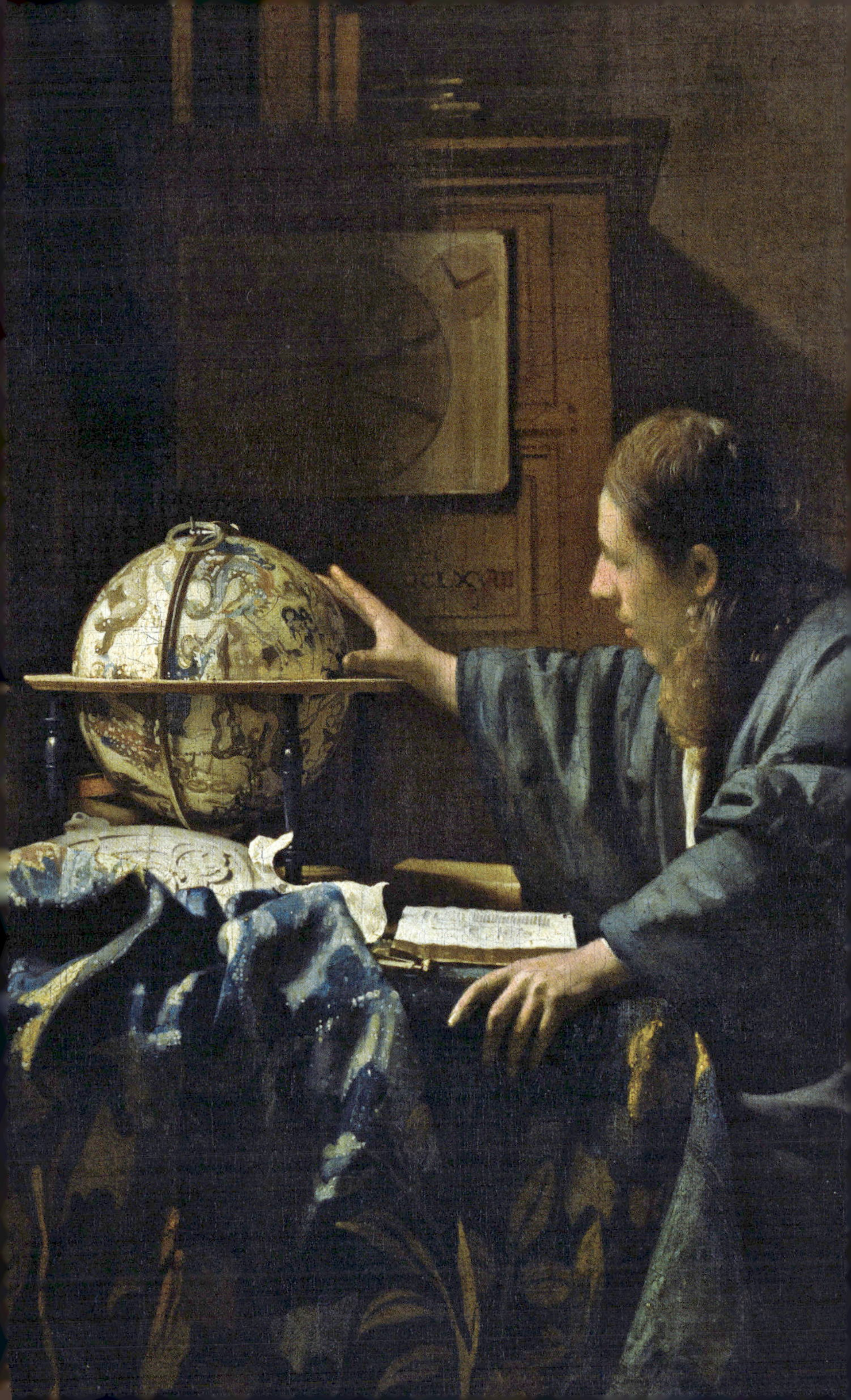

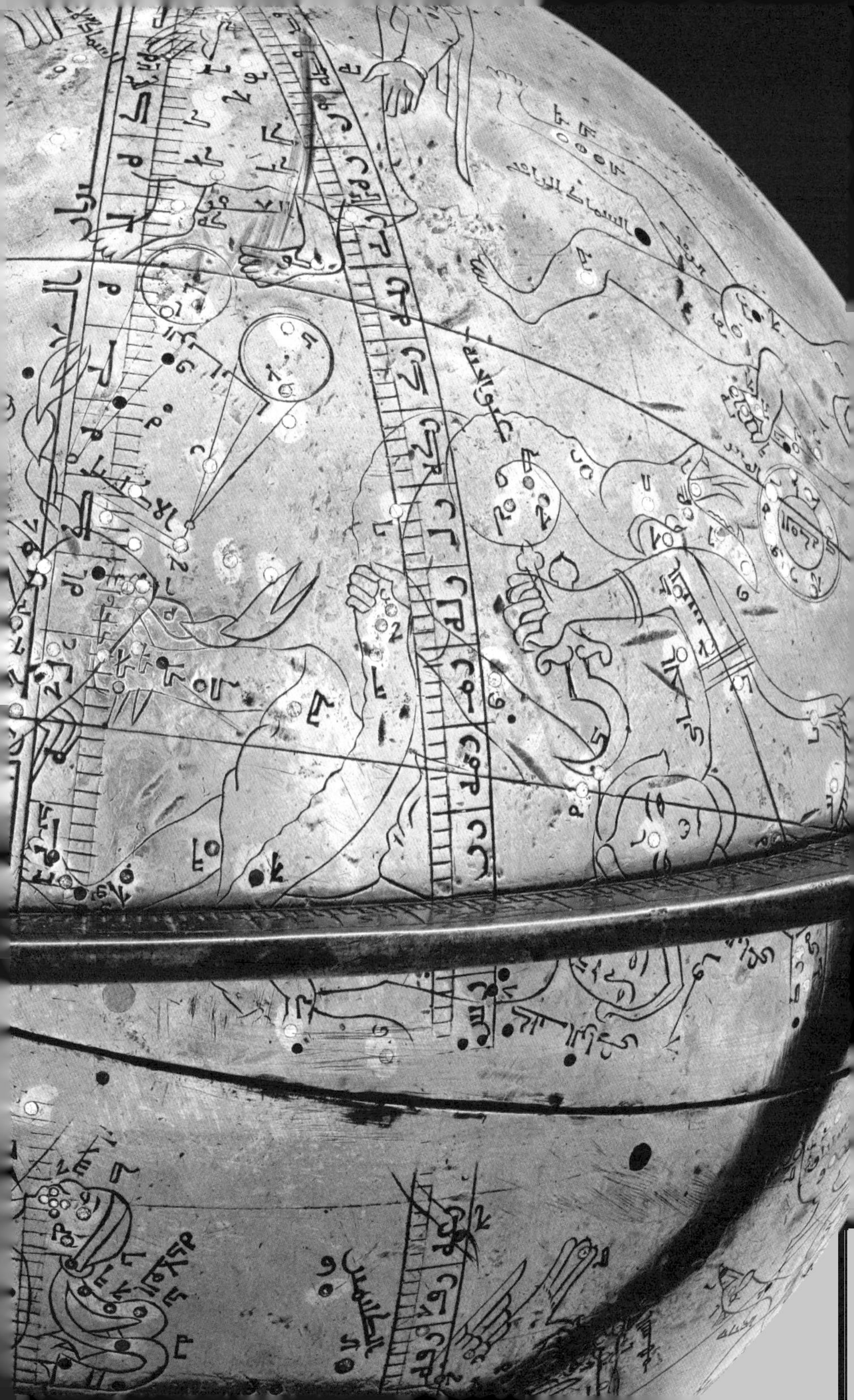

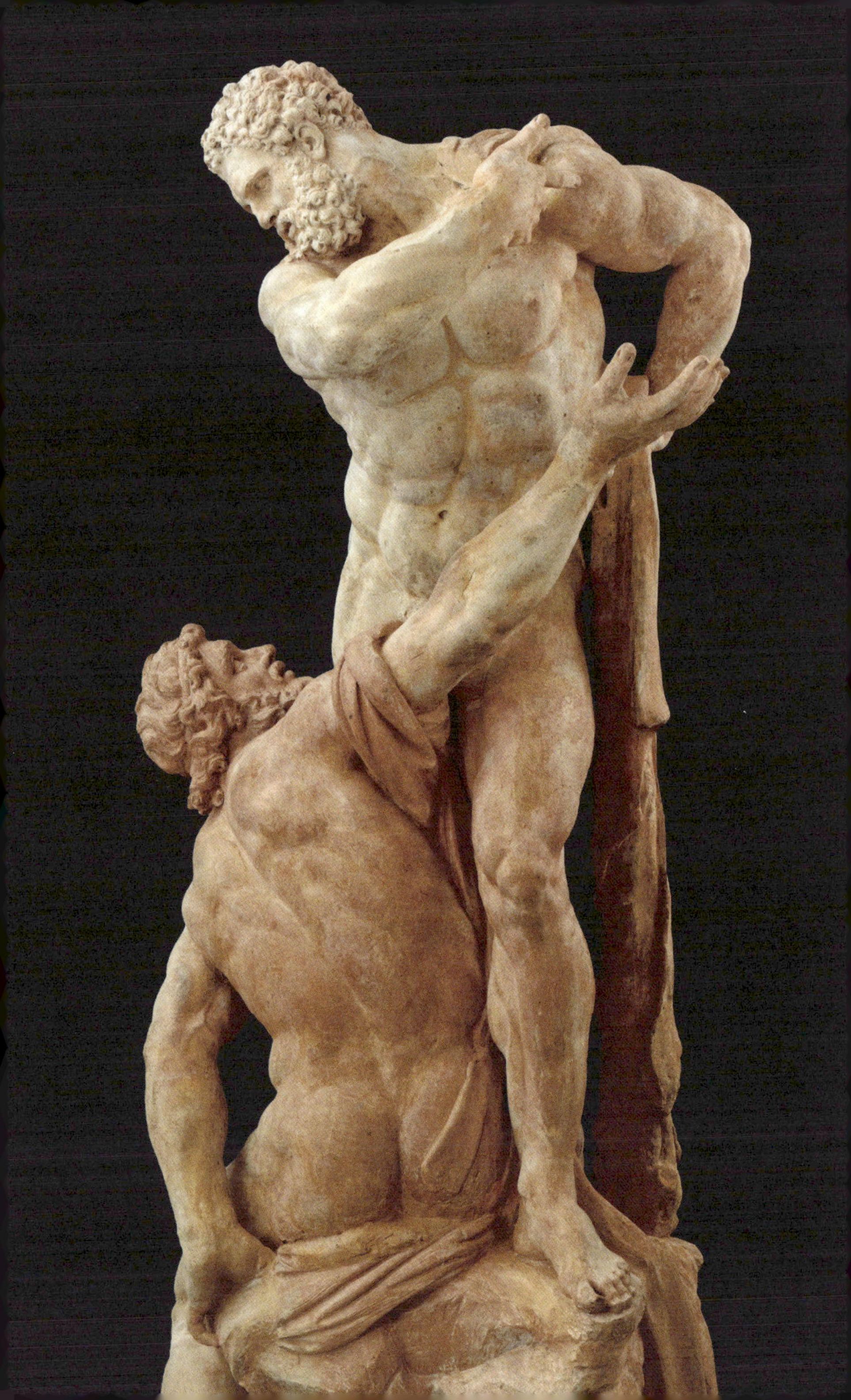

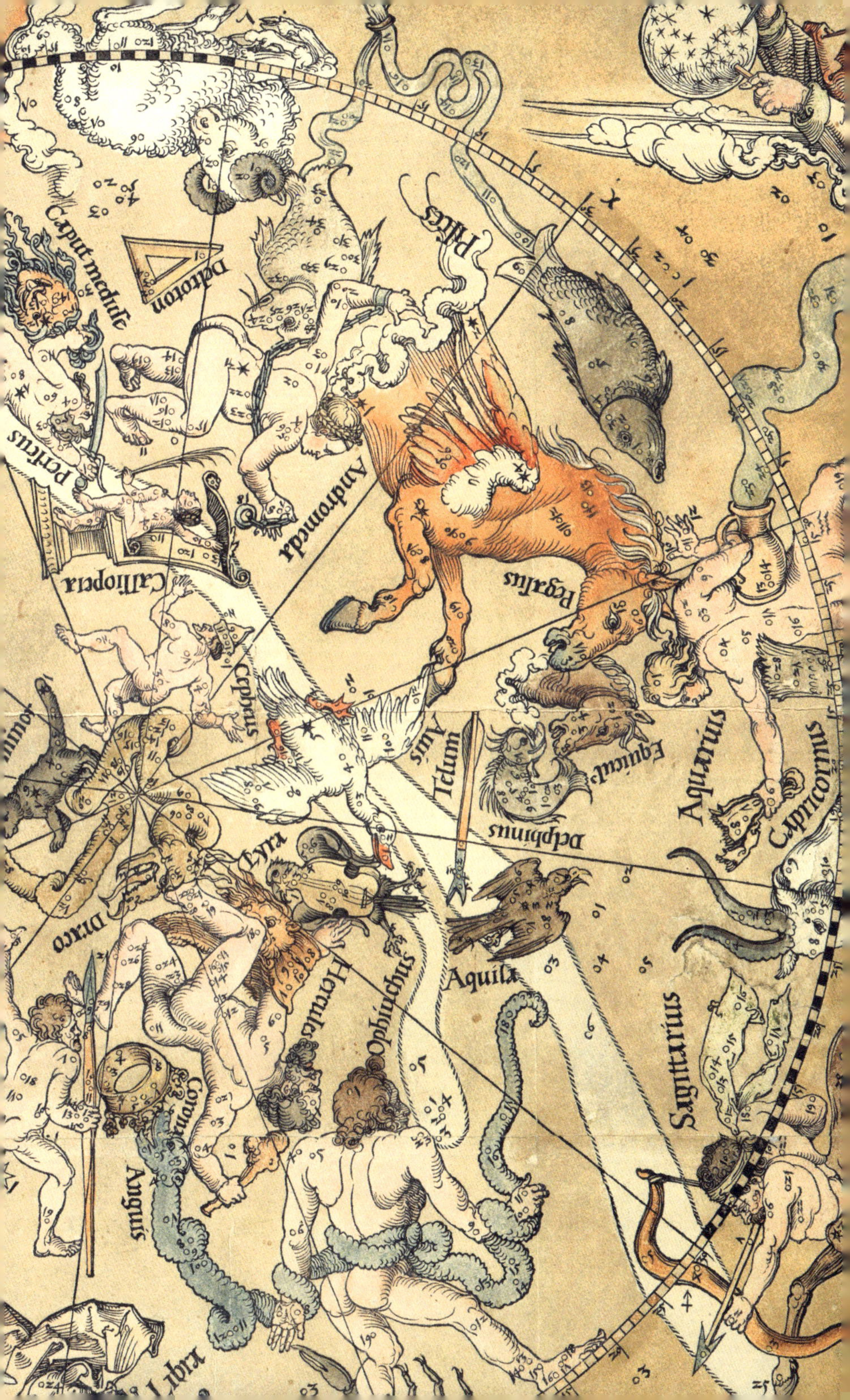
Caput medusę
Deltoton
Pisces
Perseus
Andromeda
Cassiopea
Pegasus
Cephus
Telum
Equiculus
Delphinus
Aquarius
Capricornus
Lyra
Draco
Aquila
Hercules
Ophiuchus
Sagittarius
Corona
Angus
Libra

On 4 February 1794, slavery was abolished in French colonies, five years after the 1789 Declaration of the Rights of Man and of the Citizen. It was reinstated by Napoleon Bonaparte in 1802. Slavery and human trafficking were legally abolished in France in 1848, thanks to campaigning by the journalist and politician Victor Schœlcher. France thus aligned itself with the many countries, including Denmark and Chile, which had already abolished slavery. The decree was signed at Place de la Concorde, not far from the Louvre and the Tuileries gardens. Despite this, France continued its colonial conquests in Algeria and, over the following decades, in other African countries and Asia. Théodore Chassériau's *Qaid Visiting a Douar* **[369]** is more pictorial than political. A student of Jean-Auguste-Dominique Ingres, Chassériau merges the light and colours of Santo Domingo (now the Dominican Republic) where he was born, with those of Morocco, a country celebrated by Eugène Delacroix, whose work he admired.

Having reigned over France, conquered part of Europe, founded an empire and enacted a set of laws that remains the basis for the French civil code today, in 1815 Napoleon Bonaparte was defeated at the Battle of Waterloo and exiled to the remote island of Saint Helena in the Atlantic Ocean, where he died in 1821. Despite the opposition he attracted at home and in Europe, his extraordinary life, a succession of rapid victories then a fall from grace, made him a romantic figure. The return of his remains in December 1840, aboard the *Belle Poule*, and their laying to rest inside the Hôtel des Invalides, a military monument built in the seventeenth century under Louis XIV, left an indelible mark on history. Painted in 1848, Paul Delaroche's *Bonaparte Crossing the Alps* **[374]**, depicting the future emperor during the Italian campaign, radically differs from Jacques-Louis David's painting of the same scene. In sharp contrast to the latter's idealised image of the general mounted on a majestic stallion, a glorious successor to the Carthaginian general Hannibal and Emperor Charlemagne, Delaroche paints Bonaparte astride a mule that struggles forward through the icy cold, led by a peasant.

The Second French Republic would be short-lived: established in 1848, it was ended by the coup d'état of 2 December 1851. In late 1852, under the new constitution

[369]
Théodore Chassériau
1819–1856
Qaid Visiting a Douar
1849
Oil on canvas
H. 142; W. 200 cm
(H. 4 ft 8 in.; W. 6 ft 6¾ in.)
⩡ 1918 (gift of Baron and Baroness Arthur Chassériau)
DP

[370]
Statue of a Guardian Figure, Mbulu-ngulu
Mahongwe culture
Gabon
c. 1800–1850
Wood, brass, copper and plant fibres
H. 52; W. 17; D. 9,5 cm
(H. 20½; W. 6¾; D. 3¾ in.)
⩡ Former collection of the Musée de l'Homme, Paris, gift of Joseph Michaud
MQB–JC

[371]
Manufacture de Sèvres
Jean-Baptiste-Jules Klagmann, 1810–1867;
Alexandre Evariste Fragonard, 1780–1850
Cabinet
1848
Ebony, porcelain, painted enamel and gilded bronze
H. 87; W. 83; D. 45 cm
(H. 34¼; W. 32¾; D. 17¾ in.)
⩡ 2004 (gift of the Société des Amis du Louvre)
DDA

369

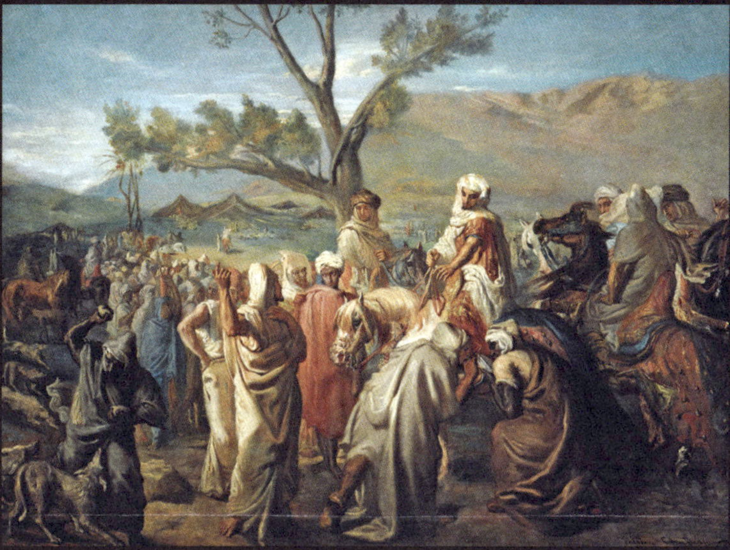

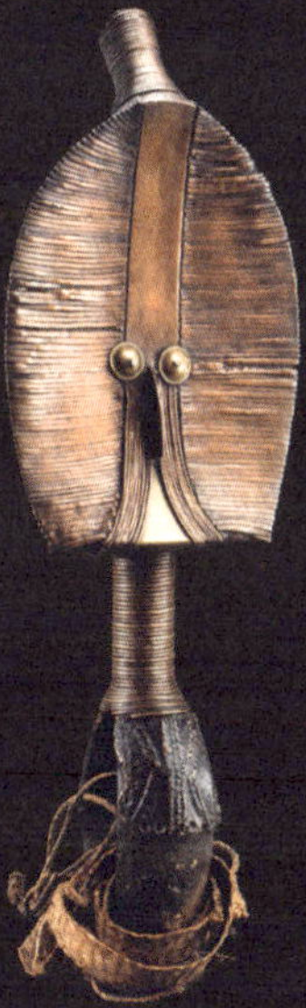

370

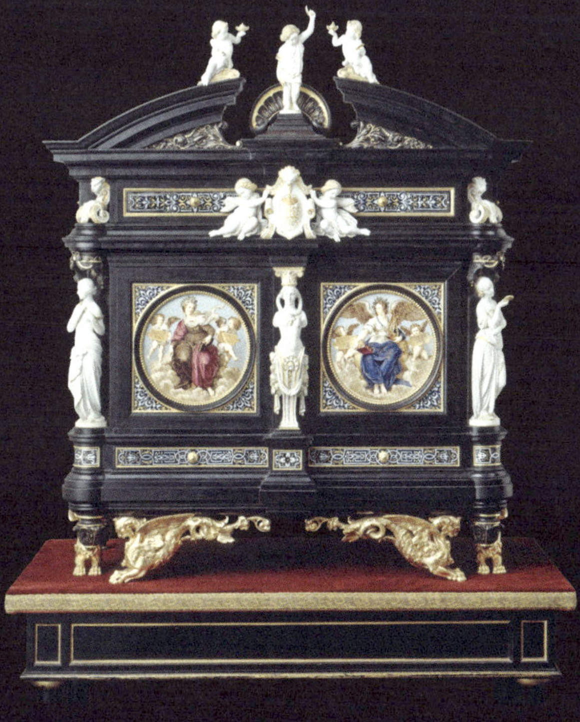

371

enacted in January that year, Louis Napoleon Bonaparte became Emperor Napoleon III. Victor Hugo had vigorously opposed the man he considered a tyrant and referred to as “Napoleon the small”. On 11 December 1851 the writer left Paris first for Brussels then Jersey and Guernsey, two of the Channel Islands, where he lived out his exile. This great author was also a talented draughtsman; executed in May 1855, this wash **[372]** entwines Hugo's initials with those of Juliette Drouet, his loyal mistress. Together they fly above Marine Terrace, home to the writer and his family in Jersey.

The nineteenth century also saw the development of major historic disciplines. Art and creativity were informed by a desire to understand the past, itself fuelled by the creation of museums and the conservation of ancient monuments. Jean-Baptiste-Jules Klagmann's sculpted cabinet **[371]** is a wonderful mélange of inspirations. Its shape is borrowed from the sixteenth century, while the decorative plaques in porcelain and the biscuit-porcelain sculptures treat Renaissance motifs in a modern manner. Part of the cabinet, which was shown at the 1850 Exposition des Manufactures, was made at the Sèvres porcelain manufactory, where technical innovation and creativity were flourishing.

The area that is now Alaska – first sighted by Europeans in the eighteenth century, by Vitus Bering, a Danish explorer in Russian service – was purchased by the United States in 1867 and became an American territory in 1912. The French ethnologist and linguist Alphonse Pinart travelled there several times to study the languages and mythological cultures relating to nature along with the conditions of the people who lived in these often hostile climates. The objects he brought back to France include this wooden Inuit ritual mask **[373]**. The smooth outlines suggest a human face, its sentiments entirely interiorised.

Sculpted in Gabon in the nineteenth century, the *Statue of a Guardian Figure, Mbulu-ngulu* **[370]** would have watched over an ancestor's remains. Its long, sinuous neck and raised head are taken from the Naja, a genus of snake commonly known as cobras.

[372]
Victor Hugo
1802–1885
Marine Terrace
1855
Pen, brush and brown ink, red gouache, rubbed with red chalk, on paper
H. 42; W. 33 cm
(H. 16½; W. 13 in.)
⊻ 2023 (gift of the Société des Amis du Louvre)
DPD

[373]
Ritual Mask
Inuit culture
Alaska, present-day United States
c. 1800–1850
Wood
H. 49; W. 18; D. 15 cm
(H. 19¼; W. 7; D. 5⅞ in.)
⊻ Gift of Alphonse Pinart
MQB-JC

[374]
Paul Delaroche
1797–1856
Bonaparte Crossing the Alps
1848
Oil on canvas
H. 289; W. 222 cm
(H. 9 ft 5¾ in.;
W. 7 ft 3½ in.)
⊻ 1982 (gift of Mr and Mrs Robert Raymond Birkhauser)
DP

[375]
Denis Foyatier
1793–1863
Siesta
1848
Marble
H. 76; W. 154.5; D. 59 cm
(H. 2 ft 6 in.; W. 5 ft ¾ in.;
D. 1 ft 11¼ in.)
⊻ 1897 (gift of Denis François-Félix Deloye)
DS

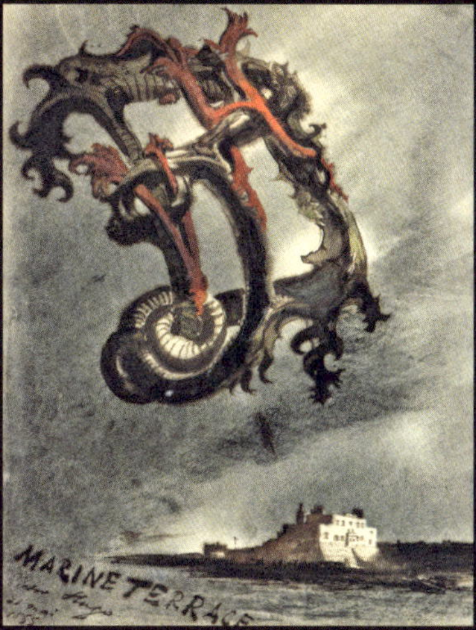

372

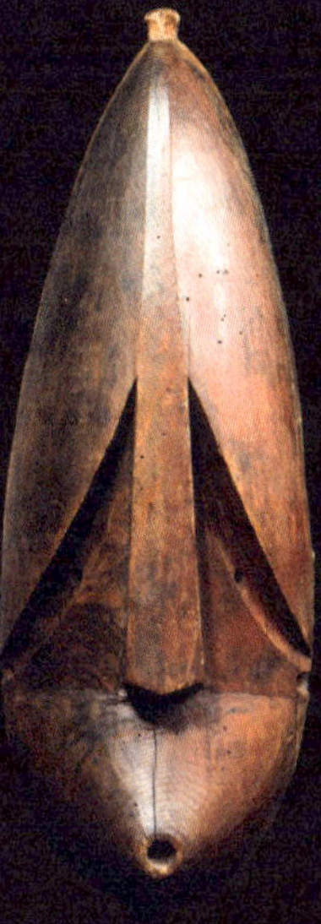

373

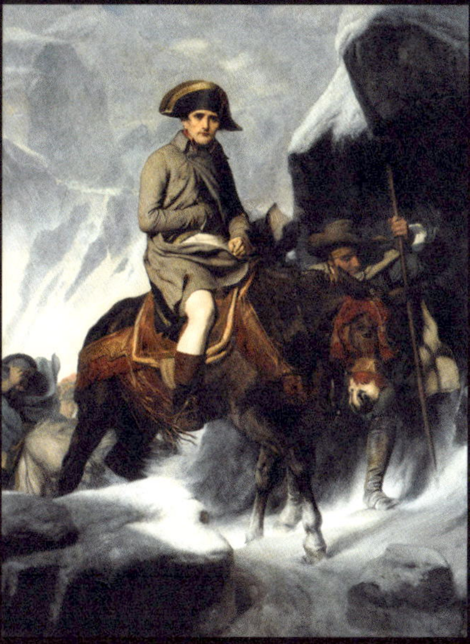

374

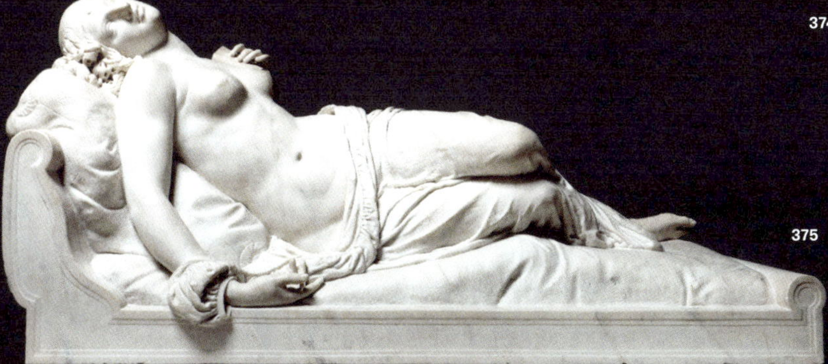

375

From one museum to another

Since the opening of the Musée d'Orsay in 1986, the Louvre's collections have stopped at 1848, although there are exceptions. Among these, the *Crown of Empress Eugenie* **[376]** is part of the French Crown Jewels that are conserved at the Louvre. Characteristic of the spectacular creativity of Second Empire jewellers, it was commissioned in 1855 by Napoleon III and shown with other royal treasures at that year's Universal Exposition in Paris as a symbol of France's prestige. Its eight arches are formed by the outstretched wings of eight imperial eagles. From the same period, *Empress Eugenie's Stomacher* **[377]** dazzles as much for the virtuosity of its tassels and bow shape as for the beauty of the diamonds from which it is made.

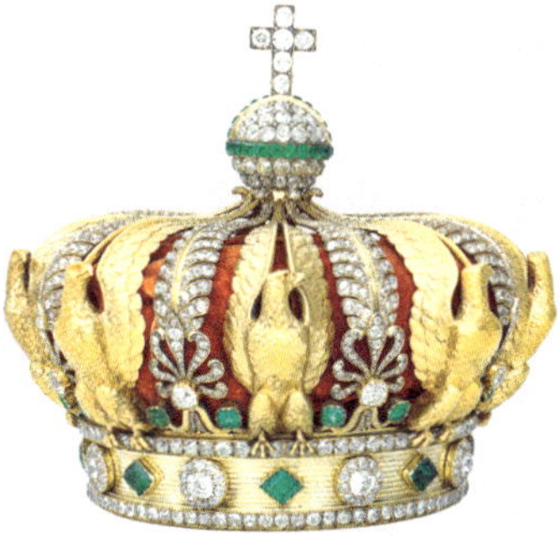

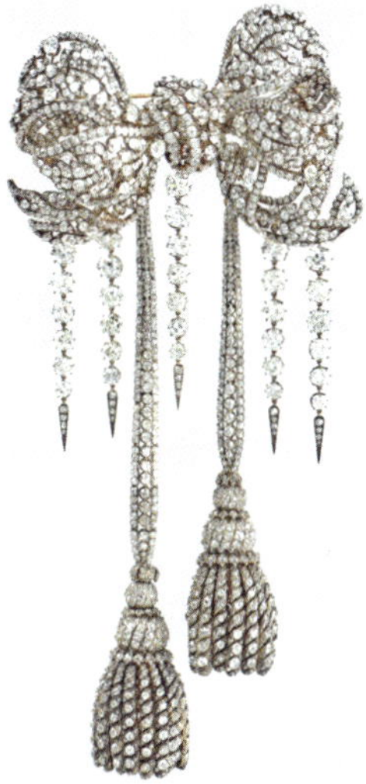

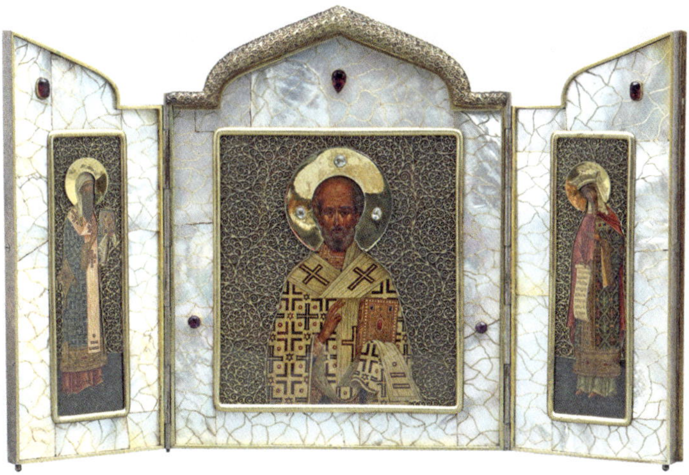

[376]
Alexandre-Gabriel
Lemonnier
c. 1808–1884
Crown of Empress Eugenie, with case
1855
Gold, leather, diamonds and emeralds
H. 13; W. 15; Diam. 16.5 cm
(H. 5⅛; W. 5⅞; Diam. 6½ in.)
⩡ 1855
DDA

[377]
François Kramer
Empress Eugenie's Stomacher
1855
Silver, gold and diamonds
H. 22.2; W. 10.5; D. 3.5 cm
(H. 8¾; W. 4⅛; D. 1⅜ in.)
⩡ 2008
DDA

[378]
Kuzma Ivanovich Konov
Active early 20th century
Triptych Icon Representing Saint Nicolas, Saint Alexandra and Saint Alexis
c. 1908–1910
Silver, silver gilt, mother-of-pearl, amethysts, garnets, aquamarines and mica
H. 21; W. 18/36 cm (open/closed)
(H. 8¼; W. 7/14¼ in. [open/closed])
⩡ 2022 (former collection of Hélène and Jurgis Baltrušatis)
DBECA

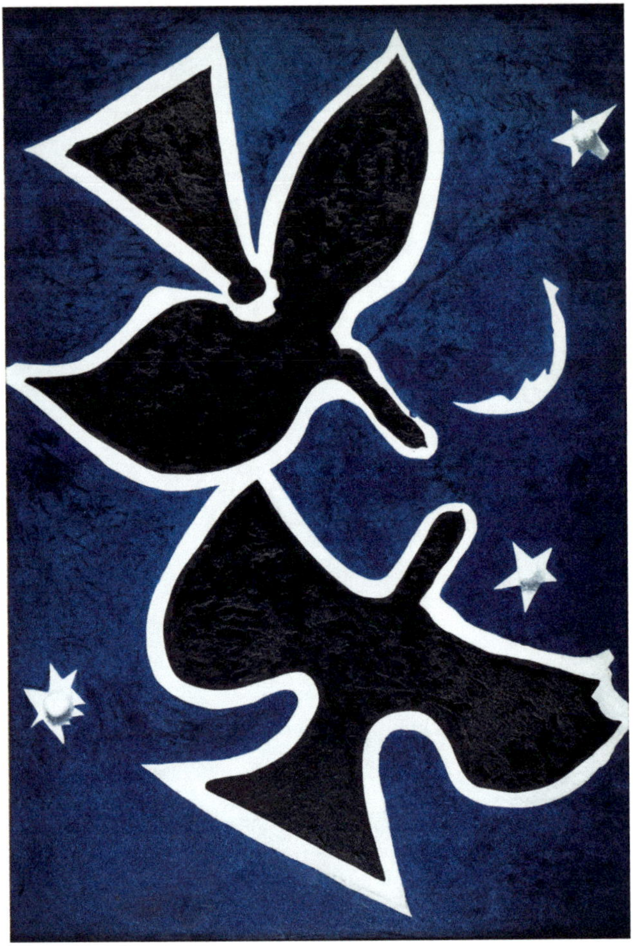

[379]
Georges Braque
1882–1963
Ceiling: The Birds
1953
Oil on canvas
H. 505; W. 346 cm
(H. 16 ft 6¾ in.; W. 11 ft 4¼ in.)
⊻ 1953
DP

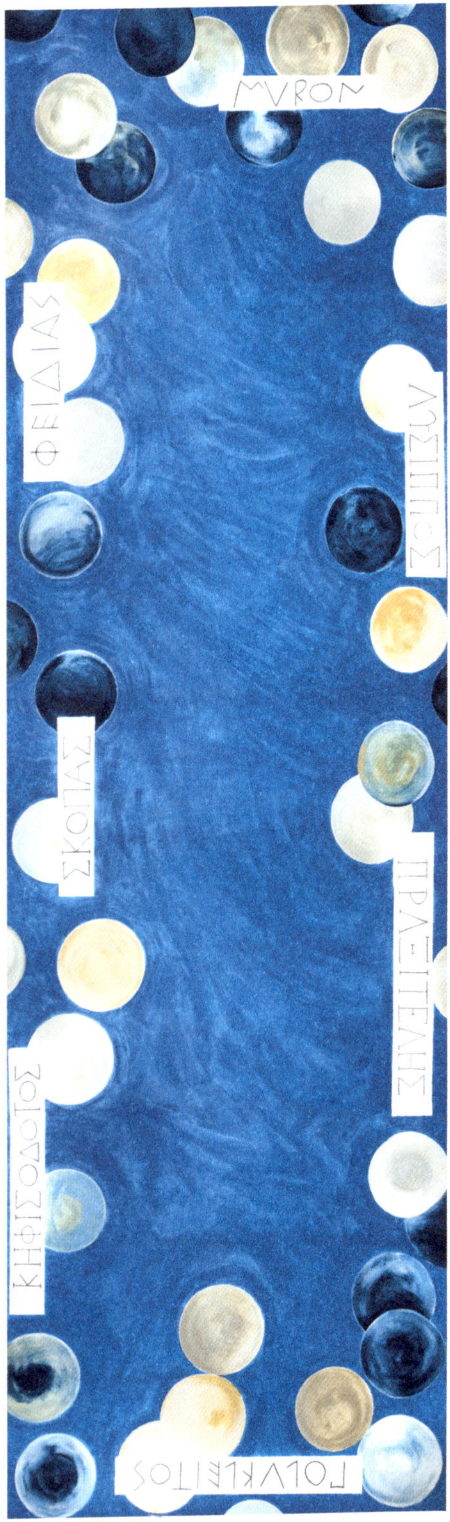

[380]
Edwin Parker Twombly Jr,
known as Cy Twombly, and studio
1928–2011
The Ceiling
Mounted canvas
L. 34; W. 11 m
(L. 111 ft 6 in.; W. 36 ft)
⊻ 2010 (gift)
DP

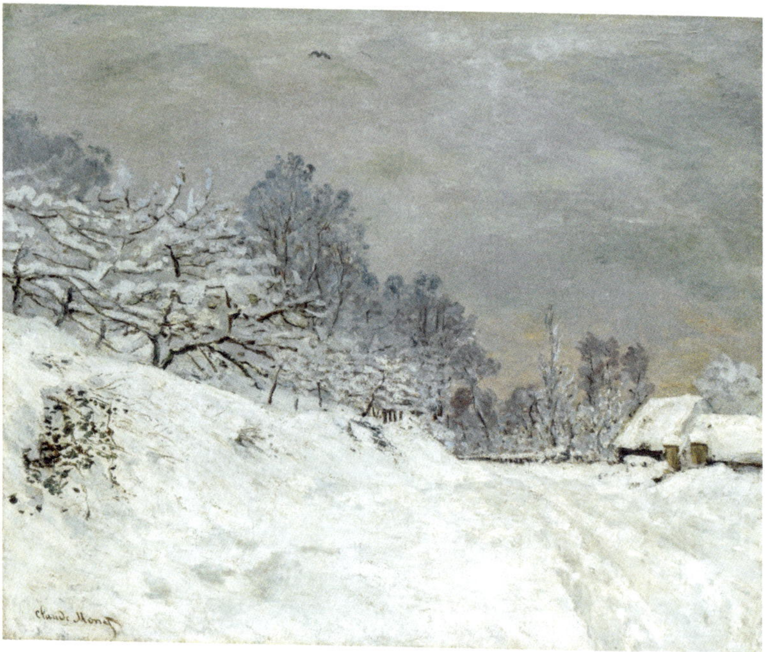

[381] Claude Monet. 1840–1926. ***Snow Near Honfleur***. 1867. Oil on canvas
H. 81.5; W. 102 cm (H. 2 ft 8 in.; W. 3 ft 4¼ in.). ⩡ 1977 (gift of Hélène and Victor Lyon). DP

A number of Impressionist paintings were gifted to the Louvre in 1977 by Victor and Hélène Lyon, including Claude Monet's *Snow Near Honfleur* **[381]**. In accordance with these generous collectors' wishes, they are shown together at the Louvre.

The creation of the Department of Byzantine and Eastern Christian Art in 2022 extended the Louvre's temporality, as demonstrated by the department's first acquisition. A superb example of early twentieth-century Russian silverwork, this imperial icon in silver and silver gilt set with gemstones is mounted as a triptych. It depicts Saint Nicholas, Saint Alexandra and Saint Alexis **[378]**, and originates from the prestigious collection of the poet Jurgis Baltrušaitis, Lithuania's ambassador to Moscow from 1920 until 1939.

Similarly, permanent works by contemporary artists, in particular the ceiling paintings commissioned from Georges Braque **[379]** in 1952 and Cy Twombly **[380]** in 2010, remind us that the Louvre is a home for artists and a museum in unison with the present.

"How beautiful
the woods were!
How soft the light! ...
I was penetrated with
sunlight, rustling
with breezes, echoing
with crickets and birdsong,
like a room open
on a garden."

Colette,
Claudine Married,
1902

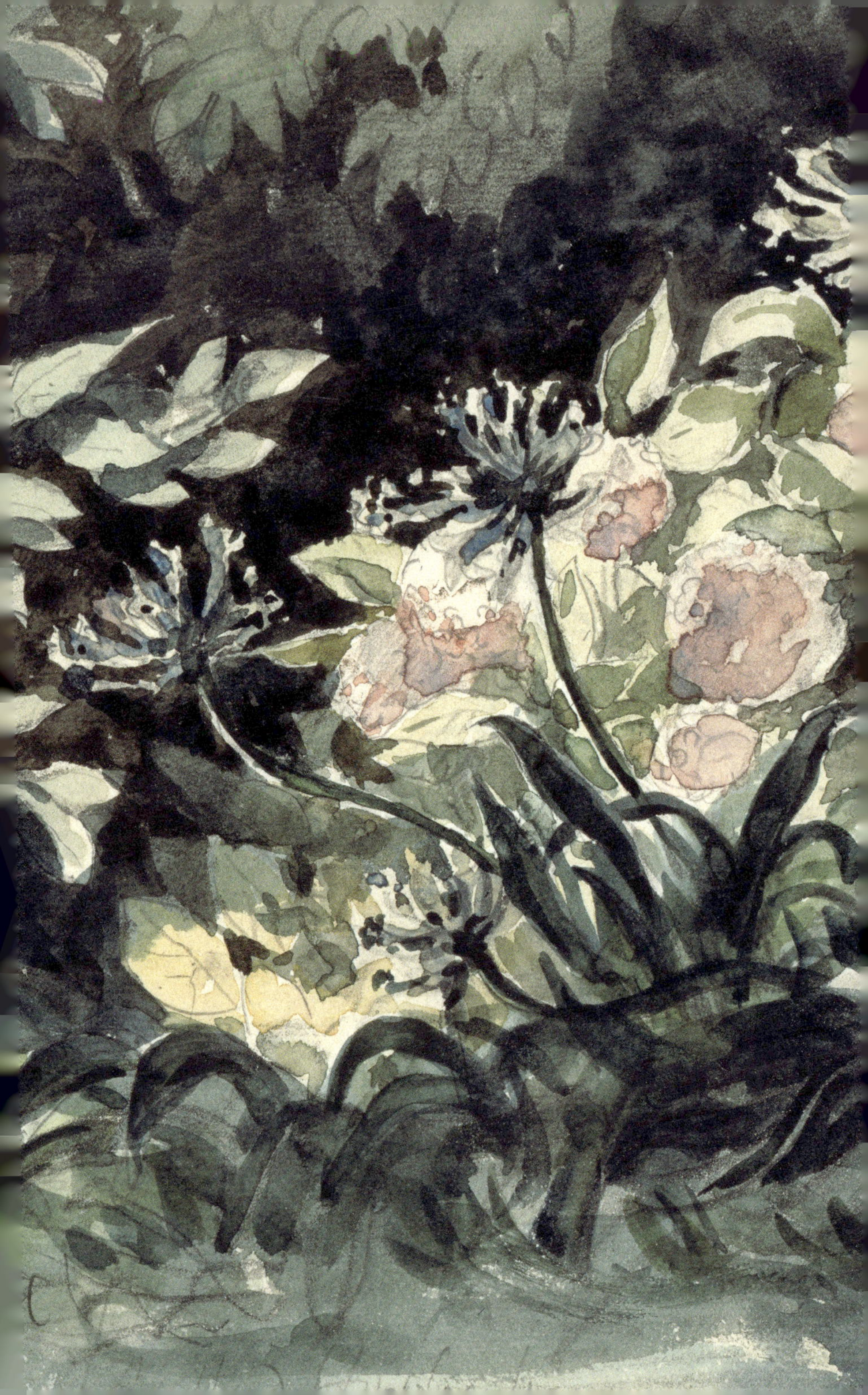

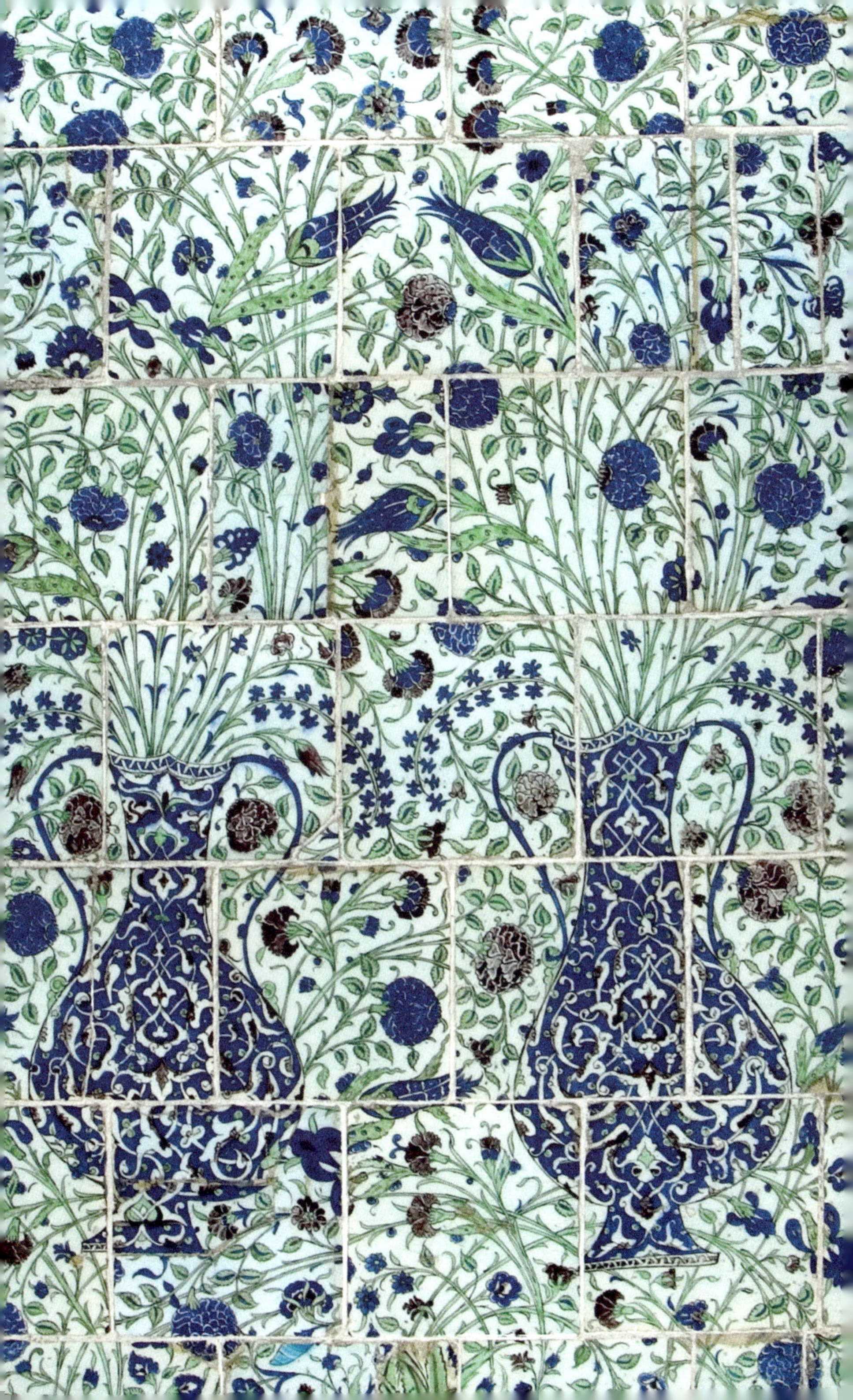

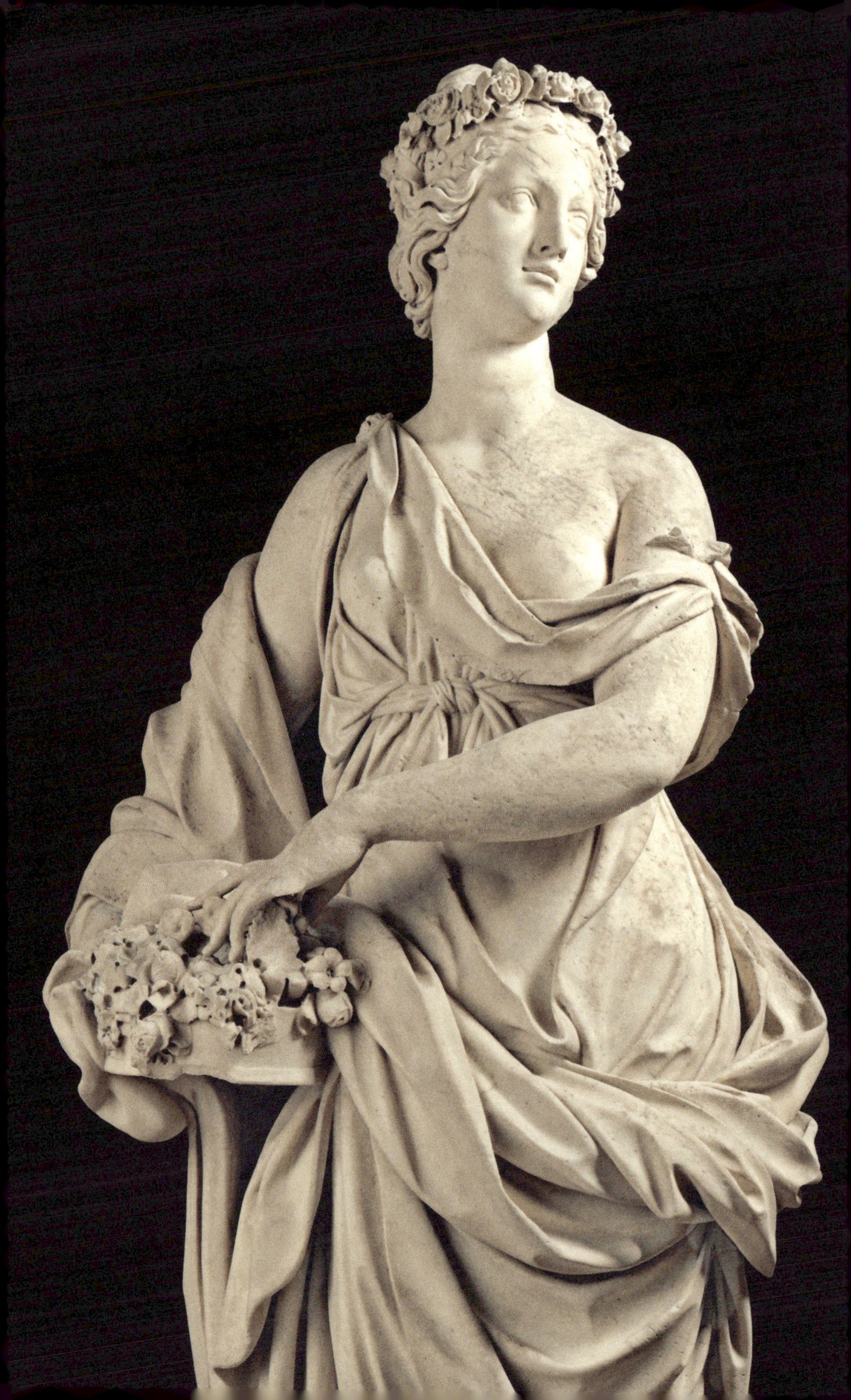

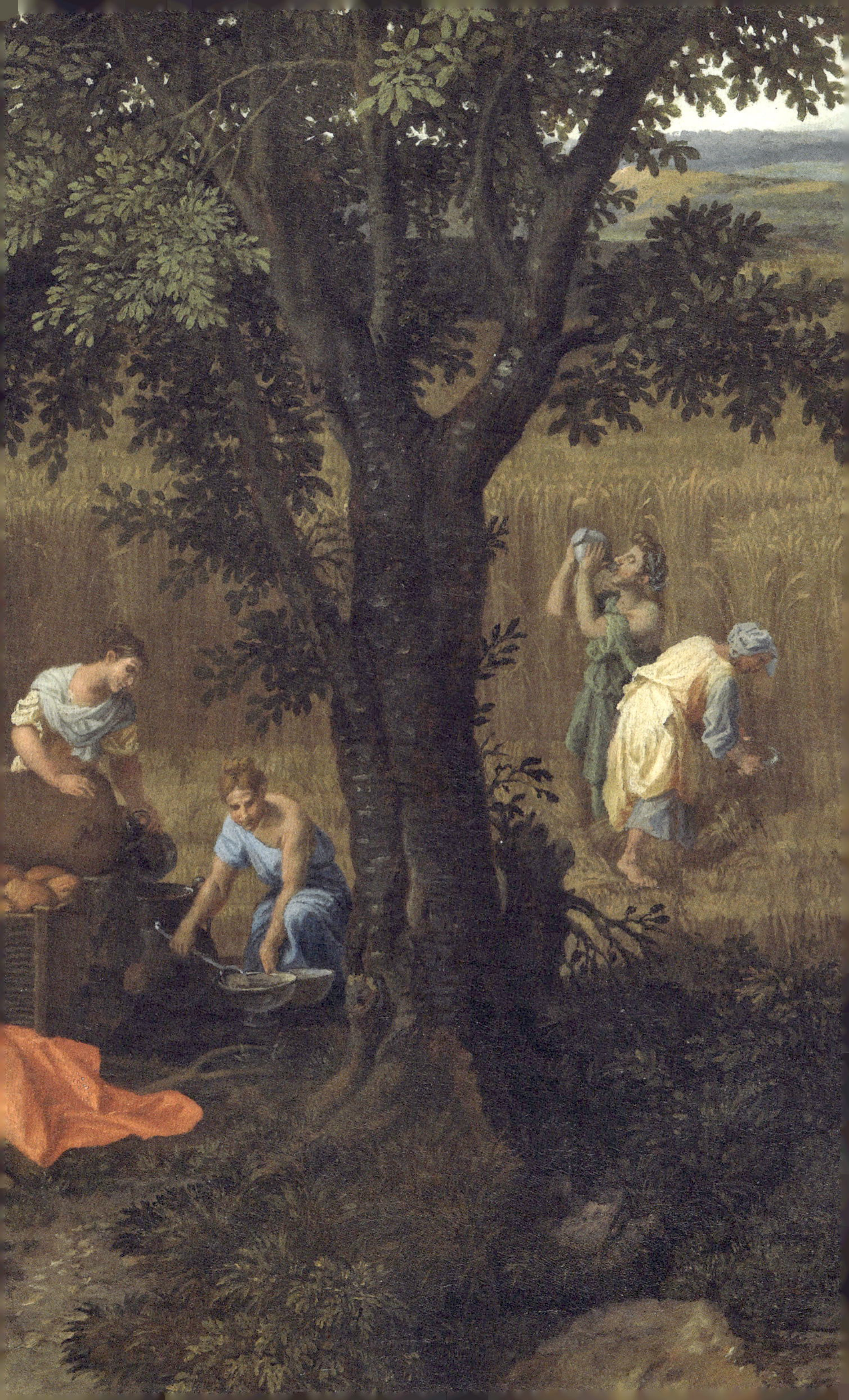

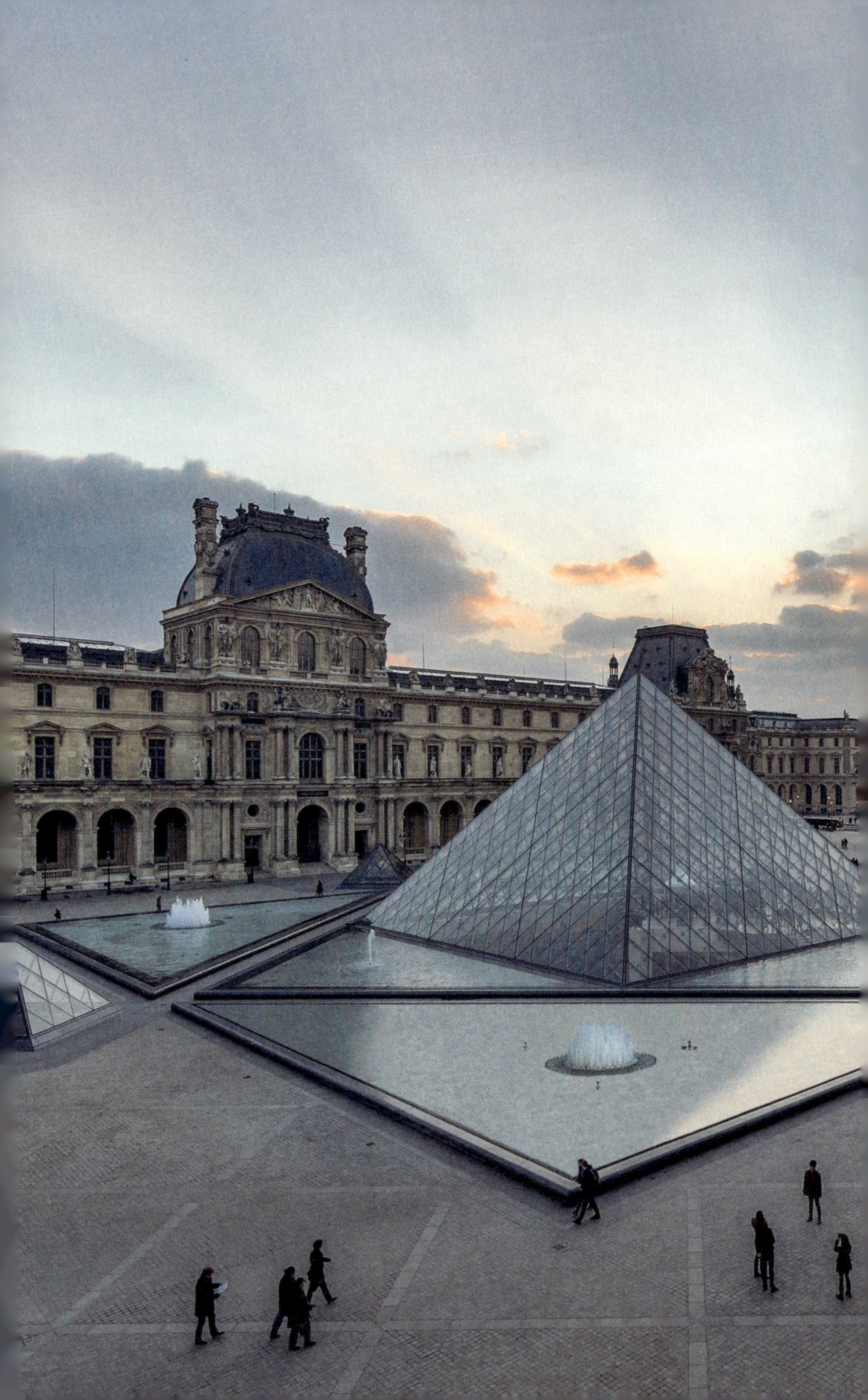

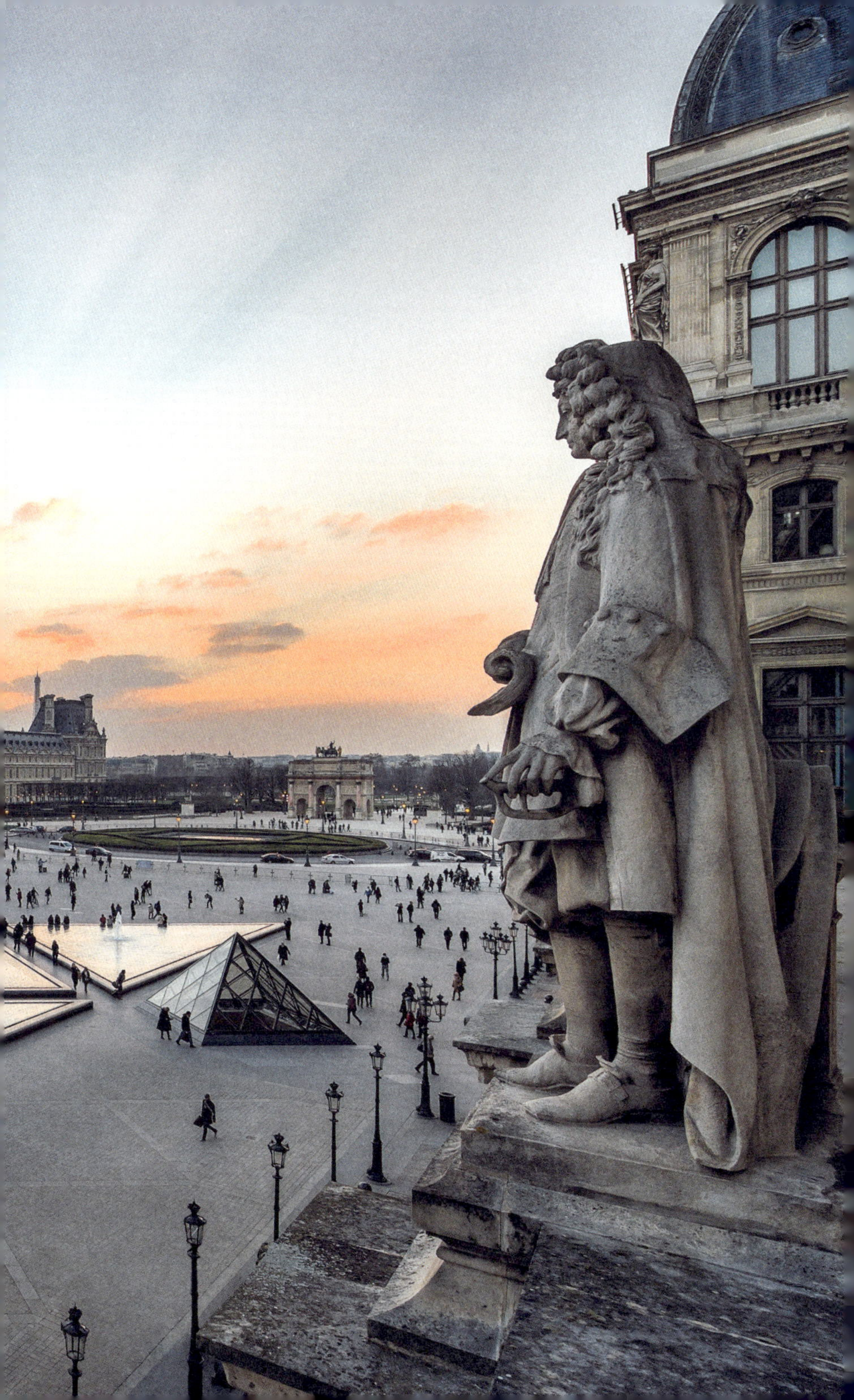

INDEX

A

Agasias, no. 58
Anguier, Michel, p. 296
Arcimboldo, Giuseppe, no. 242

B

Barye, Antoine-Louis, no. 349
Bellini, Jacopo di Niccolo, no. 199
Benoist, Marie-Guillemine, no. 358
Bernini, Gian Lorenzo, no. 282
Béranger, Antoine, no. 331
Béroud, Louis, p. 18
Biennais, Martin Guillaume, no. 168
Blancard, Hippolyte, p. 6
Blarenberghe, Louis Nicolas Van, no. 311
Bonaguida, Pacino di, no. 163
Bontemps, Pierre, no. 235
Bosch, Hieronymus. Jheronimus van Aken, known as, no. 224
Bosio, François Joseph, no. 363
Botticelli, Sandro. Alessandro di Mariano Filipepi, known as, no. 196
Bouchardon, Edme, no. 293
Boucher, François, no. 302
Boulle, André Charles, no. 283
Braque, Georges, no. 379
Bruegel, Pieter, known as the Elder no. 225

C

Canova, Antonio, no. 332
Caravaggio. Michelangelo Merisi da Caravaggio, known as, no. 251
Carracci, Annibale, no. 247
Cartellier, Pierre, no. 333
Castiglione, Giuseppe, pp. 4–5
Cellini, Benvenuto, no. 235
Champaigne, Philippe de, no. 274
Chardin, Jean Siméon, nos 291, 292
Chassériau, Théodore, no. 369
Chaudet, Antoine Denis, no 333
Cimabue. Cenni di Pepe, known as, no. 157
Clodion. Claude Michel, known as, no. 313
Clouet, Jean, no. 233
Colombe, Michel, no. 221
Cope, Joseph, no. 285
Corot, Jean-Baptiste Camille, nos 359, 360
Correggio. Antonio Allegri, known as, no. 227
Coustou, Guillaume, nos 280, 281
Cranach, Lucas, known as the Elder, no. 218

D

David, Jacques-Louis, nos 321, 324, 325, 339
David d'Angers. Pierre-Jean David, known as, no. 343
Delacroix, Eugène, nos 342, 353, 354, and p. 308
Delaroche, Paul, nos 350, 374
Della Robbia, family, no. 201
Désarnaud-Charpentier, Marie-Jeanne-Rosalie, no. 364
Dodin, Charles Nicolas, no. 306
Donatello. Donato di Niccolò di Betto Bardi, known as, no. 180
Duccio, Agostino di, no. 186
Duflos, Augustin, no. 286
Duplessis, Jean Claude Thomas, no. 306
Dürer, Albrecht, nos 215, 216
Duseigneur, Jehan. Jean-Bernard Duseigneur, known as, no. 348
Duval, Victor, p. 9
Dyck, Anton van, no. 259

E

El Greco. Dominikos Theotokopoulos, known as, no. 246
Erhart, Gregor, no. 217
Euphronios, no. 70
Eyck, Jan van, no. 175

F

Falconet, Étienne Maurice, no. 305
Fouquet, Jean, nos 188, 190, 197
Foyatier, Denis, no 375
Fra Angelico. Guido di Pietro, known as Fra Giovanni da Fiesole, known as, no. 177
Fragonard, Alexandre Evariste, no. 371
Fragonard, Jean-Honoré, no. 316
Francesca, Piero della, no. 195
Frey, Giacinto, no. 312
Friedrich, Caspar David, no. 361
Froment-Meurice, François Désiré, no. 367
Fuseli, Henry, no. 318

G

Gainsborough, Thomas, no. 290
Gérardin, Auguste, p. 2
Géricault, Théodore, nos 340, 341
Germain, François Thomas, no. 296
Giambologna. Jean Bologne, known as, nos 243, 252
Giotto di Bondone, no. 176
Girodet de Roucy-Trioson, Anne Louis, nos 345, 346
Goujon, Jean, no. 236
Goya y Lucientes, Francisco de, no. 355
Gros, Antoine-Jean, nos 335, 336
Guardi, Francesco, no. 309

H

Hajji Madani Musawwir, no. 328
Holbein, Hans, known as the Younger, no. 219
Houdon, Jean-Antoine, nos 314, 327
Hugo, Victor, no. 372

I

Ibn al-Husayn al-Asturlabi, Yunus, p. 295
Ibn al-Zayn, Muhammad, no. 172
Ibn Husayn ibn Muhammad al-Mawsili, Ali, no. 154
Ingres, Jean-Auguste-Dominique, nos 351, 356, 257

J

Jacob Frères, no. 365
Jacob-Desmalter. François-Honoré-Georges-Jacob, known as, no. 366
Jordaens, Jacob, no. 258

K

Klagmann, Jean-Baptiste-Jules, no. 371
Konov, Kuzma Ivanovich, no. 378
Kramer, François, no. 377

L

La Tour, Georges de, nos 268, 269
La Tour, Maurice Quentin de, p. 207
Lebel, Antoine, no. 331
Le Brun, Charles, nos 276, 277, 279
Le Nain, Antoine, no. 270
Le Nain, Louis, no. 270
Le Tessier de Montarsy, Laurent, no. 284
Legros, Pierre, p. 310
Lemonnier, Alexandre-Gabriel, no. 376
Léon, Auguste, p. 20
Leroux, Georges, p. 16
Lion da Colonia, Giovanni, no. 198
Littemont, Jacob de, no. 170

M

Master Alpais, no. 149
Master from the Old Netherlands, no. 184
Mangot, Pierre, p. 145
Mantegna, Andrea, no. 200
Marchesi, Girolamo, no. 202
Martin, John, no. 347
Martini, Simone, no. 159
Messerschmidt, Franz Xaver, no. 315
Metsys, Quentin, no. 223
Michelangelo Buonarroti, known as Michelangelo, nos 208, 209, 210, 211
Monet, Claude, no. 381
Mounicq, Jean, p. 3
Murillo, Bartolomé Esteban, no. 262

N

Neuber, Johann Christian, no. 310
Normand, Alfred-Nicolas, p. 12

O

Orley, Bernard van, no. 226

P

Pajou, Augustin, no. 319
Palissy, Bernard, no. 241
Passarotti, Bartolomeo, no. 245
Passemant, Claude-Siméon, no. 296
Percier, Charles, no. 323
Petitot I, Jean, no. 284
Phidias, no. 65
Pigalle, Jean-Baptiste, no. 294
Pilon, Germain, nos 237, 238
Piranesi, Giovanni Battista, no. 295
Pisanello. Antonio di Puccio di Giovanni de Cereto, known as, nos 178, 179
Poussin, Nicolas, nos 272, 273, 275, and p. 311
Pradier, James, no. 334
Préault, Auguste, no. 352

Prud'hon, Pierre-Paul, nos 338, 344
Puget, Pierre, no. 278

Q

Qasim, Muhammad, no. 301
Quarton, Enguerrand, no. 193

R

Raphael, Raffaello Sanzio, known as, nos 212, 213, 214
Rembrandt. Rembrandt Harmenszoon van Rijn, known as, nos 263, 264, 265
Reni, Guido, no. 254
Reynolds, Sir Joshua, no. 320
Rigaud, Hyacinthe, p. 205
Robert, Hubert, no. 308, and p. 13
Rondé, Claude, no. 286
Rondé, Laurent, no. 286
Rosso Fiorentino, Giovanni Battista di Jacopo, known as, no. 234
Roucel, Louis, no. 311
Rubens, Peter Paul, nos 253, 255, 256, 257
Rude, François, no. 337
Ruisdael, Jacob Isaacksz Van, no. 267

S

Sené, Jean-Baptiste-Claude, no. 329
Sergel, Johan Tobias, no. 317
Soltan, Mohammed, no. 240

T

Thomire, Pierre Philippe, no. 314
Titian. Tiziano Vecellio, known as, nos 228, 230, and p. 263
Turner, Joseph Mallord William, no. 362
Twombly, Cy, Edwin Parker Twombly Jr, known as, no. 380

U

Uccello, Paolo di Dono, known as, no. 194

V

Valadier, Guiseppe, no. 312
Valadier, Luigi, no. 312
Vermeer, Johannes, no. 266, and p. 294
Veronese, Paolo Caliari, known as Veronese, nos 229, 231
Verrocchio, Andrea del. Andrea di Michele Cioni, known as, no.203
Vigée Le Brun, Élisabeth, no. 322
Vinci, Leonardo da, nos 204, 205, 206, 207
Vivier, Hennequin du, no. 168
Vouet, Simon, no. 271
Vries, Adriaen de, no. 244

W

Watteau, Antoine, nos 287, 288, 289

Z

Zurbarán, Francisco de, no. 260

ADDITIONAL CAPTIONS AND QUOTATION SOURCES

Front cover
Leonardo da Vinci
1452–1519
Mona Lisa
(detail)
c. 1503–1519
Oil on poplar wood
H. 79.4; W. 53.4 cm
(H. 31¼; W. 21 in.)
⪯ 1793 (former royal collection, collection of Francis I)
DP

Back cover
Jean Clouet
1486–1540
Francis I, King of France
(detail)
c. 1525–1550
Oil on oak wood
H. 96; W. 74 cm
(H. 3 ft 1¾ in.; W. 2 ft 5¼ in.)
⪯ 1793 (former royal collection, collection of Francis Iᵉʳ)
DP

p. 1
Pavillon de Flore, seen from the Tuileries Gardens

p. 2
Auguste Gérardin
1849–after 1901
Galerie d'Apollon at Night
(detail)
Charcoal, wash and ink
H. 31.8; W. 42.5 cm
(H. 12½; W. 16¾ in.)
⪯ 2004 (gift of Marc Fumaroli)
DAG

p. 3
Jean Mounicq
born 1931
The Louvre, the* Winged Victory of Samothrace*, Paris, 1989
(detail)
1989
Gelatin silver print
H. 24; W. 18 cm
(H. 9½; W. 7 in.)
Médiathèque du Patrimoine et de la Photographie, Charenton-le-Pont, inv. 1930T001737

pp. 4–5
Giuseppe Castiglione
1829–1908
The Salon Carré in 1861
(detail)
1861
Oil on canvas
H. 69; W. 103 cm
(H. 2 ft 3¼; W. 3 ft 4½ in.)
⪯ 1861
DP

p. 6
Hippolyte Blancard
1843–1924
Grande Galerie
(detail)
c. 1890
H. 15; W. 19 cm
(H. 5⅞; W. 7½ in.)
⪯ Gift of Maurice Rousseau
Musée Carnavalet, Histoire de Paris, Paris, inv. PH77972

p. 7
The Grande Galerie

p. 8
The Galerie d'Apollon

p. 9
Victor Duval
1795–1889
View of the Galerie d'Apollon at the Louvre
(detail)
1874
Oil on canvas
H. 65; W. 81 cm
(H. 25½; W. 32 in.)
⪯ 1993 (gift of Claude Sère)
DP

pp. 10–11
Cour Marly

p. 12
Alfred-Nicolas Normand
1822–1909
Musée du Louvre: Tribune des Cariatides
(detail)
1889
Albumen print
H. 17; W. 22.5 cm
(H. 6¾; W. 8¾ in.)
Médiathèque du Patrimoine et de la Photographie, Charenton-le-Pont, inv. NRM00940

p. 13
Hubert Robert
1733–1808
The Salle des Saisons at the Louvre, in 1802–1803
(detail)
1802–1803
Oil on canvas
H. 37; W. 46 cm
(H. 14½; W. 18 in.)
⪯ 1964
DP

p. 14
The colonnade at the Louvre

p. 16
Georges Leroux
1877–1957
Inside the Grande Galerie at the Musée du Louvre
(detail)
c. 1947
Oil on canvas
H. 89; W. 151 cm
(H. 2 ft 11 in.; W. 4 ft 11½ in.)
⪯ 1974 (gift of Pierre Massenet)
DP

p. 18
Louis Béroud
1852–1930
The Salle Rubens at the Musée du Louvre, Laid Out by Gaston Redon
(detail)
1904
Oil on canvas
H. 200; W. 300 cm
(H. 6 ft 7¾ in.; W. 9 ft 10 in.)
⪯ 1978 (long-term loan from the Fine Arts Museums of San Francisco)
DP

p. 20
Auguste Léon
1857–1942
The Salle des États, currently host to the *Mona Lisa*, 5 September 1921
(detail)
Autochrome
H. 9; W. 12 cm
(H. 3½; W. 4¾ in.)
Archives de la Planète collection, Musée Albert-Kahn, Boulogne-Billancourt

Writing

p. 63
Voltaire, *Dictionnaire philosophique*, edited by Raymond Naves and Olivier Ferret (Paris: Classiques Garnier, 2008), p. 96.

p. 64
Tablet
(detail)
Susa, present-day Iran
c. 2250 BCE
Clay
H. 16; W. 15; D. 2.5 cm
(H. 6¼; W. 5⅞; D. 1 in.)
⩡ 1906–1908
DNEA

p. 65
Lamp in the name of Ma'tuq ibn Mahfuz ibn Ma'tuq ibn al-Buzuri al-Baghdadi
(detail)
Damascus, Syria
c. 1294
Blown glass, enamelled and gilded decoration
H. 26.7; Diam. 24.6 cm
(H. 10½; Diam. 9¾ in.)
⩡ 1973 (bequest of André Maggiar)
DIA

p. 66
The Evangelist Saint Matthew Writing under the Guidance of an Angel
(detail)
Chartres Cathedral, France
c. 1230
Limestone
H. 64.5; W. 50; D. 15 cm
(H. 25½; W. 19¾; D. 5⅞ in.)
⩡ 1905
DS

p. 67
The Seated Scribe
(detail)
Saqqara, Memphis, Egypt
c. 2620–2500 BCE
Painted limestone, Egyptian alabaster, rock crystal and copper
H. 53.7; W. 44; D. 35 cm
(H. 21¼; W. 17¼; D. 13¾ in.)
⩡ 1854
DEA

Humanity

p. 111
Aimé Césaire, speech made in Dakar on 6 April 1966, for the opening of the First World Festival of Negro Arts.

p. 112
Statue of Sepa
(detail)
Egypt
c. 2700–2620 BCE
Painted limestone
H. 165.5; W. 40; D. 55 cm
(H. 5⅝; L. 8¼; D. 6¼ in.)
⩡ 1837
DEA

p. 113
Hera of Samos
(detail)
Sanctuary of the goddess Hera, Samos, Greece
c. 570–560 BCE
Marble
H. 192; W. 58; D. 38 cm
(H. 6 ft 3½ in.;
W. 1 ft 10¾ in.; D. 1 ft 3 in.)
⩡ 1881
DGERA

p. 114
Monumental Head, Moai
(detail)
Easter Island, Chile
11th–15th century
Lithic and andesite from the Rano Raraku volcano
H. 170; W. 100; D. 90 cm
(H. 5 ft 7 in.; W. 3 ft 3¼ in.;
D. 2 ft 11½ in.)
MQB–JC

p. 115
Sculpture, Tino Aitu
(detail)
Nukuoro Atoll, Micronesia, Oceania
Late 18th century
Wood
H. 35; W. 10.2; D. 7 cm
(H. 13¾; W. 4; D. 2¾ in.)
⩡ Gift of Georges Henri Rivière
MQB–JC

Interweaving

p. 141
Jean-Marie Gustave Le Clézio, in *Les musées sont des mondes*, edited by Marie-Laure Bernadac (exh. cat. Paris: Gallimard / Éditions du Louvre, 2011).

p. 142
Nef in lapis lazuli
(detail)
Stone from Italy (?), mounted in Paris, France, 1670
Lapis lazuli, enamelled gold and silver gilt
H. 41.5; W. 37.5; D. 18.5 cm
(H. 16¼; W. 14¾; D. 7¼ in.)
⩡ 1796 (former royal collection)
DDA

p. 143
Calabash from the Indies
(detail)
Calabash from India, mounted in Germany in 1585–1615
Calabash, silver gilt, amethyst, blood jasper, topaz and garnet (mount)
H. 13.5; W. 21; D. 16 cm
(H. 5⅜; W. 8¼; D. 6¼ in.)
⩡ 1796 (former royal collection)
DDA

p. 144
France, c. 1840
Chest decorated with 49 intaglios
(detail)
Engraved and gilded metal, carnelian, jasper, agate, amethyst and chrysoprase
H. 15.7; W. 19.5; D. 13.2 cm
(H. 6¼; W. 7¾; D. 5¼ in.)
⩡ 1881 (bequest of Élise Dosne-Thiers)
DDA

p. 145
Pierre Mangot
16th century
Chest
(detail)
1532–1533
Wood, mother-of-pearl, silver gilt and precious stones
H. 28.3; W. 40.8; D. 27.3 cm
(H. 11¼; W. 16; D. 10¾ in.)
⩡ 2000
DDA

Power

p. 203
Voltaire, *An Essay on Universal History and the Manners and Spirit of Nations*, translated by Mr Nugent (Edinburgh: J. Balfour and Co., 1777), p. 2.

p. 204
Constantinople, now Istanbul, Turkey
Panel, in five parts, from a diptych: The Triumphant Emperor (Justinian?)
(detail)
Byzantium
c. 525–550
Elephant ivory
H .34.2; W. 26.8; Th. 2.8 cm
(H. 13½; W. 10½; Th. 1⅛ in.)
⩡ 1899 (former Barberini collection)
DDA

p. 205
Hyacinthe Rigaud
1659–1743
Louis XIV
(detail)
1701
Oil on canvas
H. 277; W. 194 cm
(H. 9 ft 1 in.; W. 6 ft 4½ in.)
⩡ 1793 (former royal collection, collection of Louis XIV)
DP

p. 206
Sculpture, Trrou Korrou*, known as *The Blue Man
(detail)
Sanakas, Malo island, Vanuatu
Early 19th century
Sculpted and carved intsia bijuga wood, blue (washing blue), white, green and red pigments
H. 300; W. 35; D. 34 cm
(H. 9 ft 10 in.; W. 1 ft 1¾ in.; D. 1 ft 1½ in.)
⪯ Gift of Gabriel Gomichon des Granges, 1935, La Korrigane expedition
MQB–JC

p. 207
Maurice Quentin de La Tour
1704–1788
Portrait of the Marquise de Pompadour
(detail)
c. 1752–1755
Pastel heightened with gouache on blue paper
H. 177.5; W. 131 cm
(H. 5 ft 10 in.; W. 4 ft 3½ in.)
⪯ 1803
DAG

Beauties

p. 259
Charles Baudelaire, "Beauty", *The Flowers of Evil*, translated by Cyril Scott (London: Elkin Mathews, 1909).

p. 260
The Kaufmann Head, Head of Aphrodite
(detail)
Tralles, present-day Turkey
c. 150–130 BCE
Marble
H. 34; W. 22; D. 33 cm
(H. 13½; W. 8¾; D. 13 in.)
⪯ 1951
DGERA

p. 261
Anthropomorphic Head
(detail)
Nigeria
c. late 15th century–early 16th century
Copper alloy
H. 21; W. 15.5; D. 13.5 cm
(H. 8¼; W. 6; D. 5⅜ in.)
⪯ Former collection of the Musée des Arts d'Afrique et d'Océanie, gift of the Barbier-Mueller collection
MQB–JC

p. 262
Statue de Touy
(detail)
Egypt
c. 1390–1352 BCE
Wood
H. 33.4; W. 8.3; D. 17 cm
(H. 13¼; W. 3¼; D. 6¾ in.)
⪯ 1895
DEA

p. 263
Tiziano Vecellio, known as Titian
c. 1488/1490–1576
Woman with a Mirror
(detail)
1525–1550
Oil on canvas
H. 49; W. 49 cm (H. 19¼; W. 19¼ in.)
⪯ 1793 (former royal collection, collection of Louis XIV)
DP

Sky

p. 293
Émile Littré, "Ciel", *Dictionnaire de la langue française* (Paris: Librairie Hachette et Cie, 1873–1877).

p. 294
Johannes Vermeer
1632–1675
The Astronomer
(detail)
1668
Oil on canvas
H. 51; W. 45 cm
(H. 20; W. 17¾ in.)
⪯ 1982 (dation)
DP

p. 295
Yunus ibn al-Husayn al-Asturlabi
12th century
Celestial Globe
(detail)
Isfahan (?), Iran
1144
Cast brass, engraved decoration with inlaid silver
H. 27; Diam. 21.6 cm
(H. 10¾; Diam. 8½ in.)
⪯ 1985 (dation)
DIA

p. 296
Michel Anguier
1612–1686
Hercules Helping Atlas to Hold Up the Heavens
(detail)
1668
Terracotta
H. 130; W. 58; D. 60 cm
(H. 4 ft 3¼ in.; W. 1 ft 10¾ in.; D. 1 ft 11½ in.)
⪯ 1873/1889 (former collection of the Académie Royale de Peinture et de Sculpture)
DS

p. 297
Albrecht Dürer
1471–1528
The Celestial Map – Northern Hemisphere
(detail)
1515
Woodcut heightened with watercolour and gold
H. 45.6; W. 43 cm
(H. 18; W. 17 in.)
⪯ 1935 (gift of Edmond de Rothschild)
DPD

Nature

p. 307
Colette, *Claudine en ménage* (Paris: Mercure de France, 1902).

p. 308
Eugène Delacroix
1798–1863
Flower Bed with Pink Hydrangeas, Blue Squills and Red Anemones
(detail)
1849
Watercolour over graphite on paper
H. 18.7; W. 29.6 cm
(H. 7¼; W. 11¾ in.)
⪯ 1918 (former Edgar Degas collection)
DPD

p. 309
Panel with Two Large Vases of Flowers. Bordered with Scrolls of Flowers and Dentate Leaves
(detail)
Damascus, Syria (?)
c. 1560–1600
Ceramic, painted decoration on slip under transparent glaze
H. 187; W. 120; D. 4 cm
(H. 6 ft 1½ in.; W. 3 ft 11¼ in.; D. 1⅝ in.)
⪯ 1890
DIA

p. 310
Attributed to Pierre Legros
1629–1714
Spring
(detail)
Château de Saint-Cloud gardens
1685–1700
Marble
H. 265; W. 100; D. 70 cm
(H. 8 ft 8¼ in.; W. 3 ft 3¼ in.; D. 2 ft 3½ in.)
⪯ 1872
DS

p. 311
Nicolas Poussin
1594–1665
Summer* or *Ruth and Boaz
(detail)
c. 1660–1664
oil on canvas
H. 118; W. 160 cm
(H. 3 ft 10½ in.; W. 5 ft 3 in.)
⪯ 1793 (former collection of Louis XIV)
DP

pp. 312–313
The Louvre Pyramid, designed by architect I. M. Pei, in the centre of the Cour Napoléon with the Denon Wing in the background

Unless otherwise stated, the quotes were translated from the French by the publisher.

UNDERSTANDING THE CAPTIONS

Above the title of each work is the name and dates of its artist or maker, or the place and date of its creation. Geographical areas mentioned under the title of certain works correspond to where the work was discovered. The date and/or means of acquisition by the Musée du Louvre or the Musée du Quai Branly – Jacques Chirac are indicated after the ⊻ symbol.

The last line corresponds to the department that conserves the work, abbreviated as follows:

- DBECA: Department of Byzantine and Eastern Christian Art. At the time of writing, this department was still being established, and certain works will be assigned to it from other departments.
- DEA: Department of Egyptian Antiquities
- DPD: Department of Prints and Drawings
- DGERA: Department of Greek, Etruscan and Roman Antiquities
- DIA: Department of Islamic Art
- DNEA: Department of Near Eastern Antiquities
- DDA: Department of Decorative Arts
- DP: Department of Paintings
- DS: Department of Sculptures
- MQB-JC: Musée du Quai Branly – Jacques Chirac. Works from this museum are presented in the Pavillon des Sessions at the Louvre.

FOR MORE INFORMATION

If you would like to learn more about the works featured in this guide, the Louvre Collections database contains details of more than 500,000 works, on display and not, from the Musée du Louvre and the Musée National Eugène-Delacroix. New information is added each day, thanks to ongoing research and cataloguing by the staff of the two museums.

https://collections.louvre.fr/en/

This guide would not have been possible without the work of colleagues past and present. Their publications, research and hypotheses were the impetus behind its writing. It is, therefore, also a tribute to the people who, over the last 230 years, have made the Louvre what it is today and what it will be tomorrow.

The publishers and Dominique de Font-Réaux extend their sincere thanks to Marine Guyé, Anthony Petiteau, Anne-Solène Rolland and David Seguin for their invaluable assistance in producing this guide.

PHOTO CREDITS

Collection des Archives de la Planète, Musée Départemental Albert-Kahn / Département des Hauts-de-Seine: p. 20 • Musée Carnavalet / CC0 Paris Musées: p. 6 • Photo Emmanuel Watteau: no. 299 • Rama / CC BY-SA 3.0 fr: no. 1 • *GrandPalaisRmn, Paris*: GrandPalaisRmn (Musée du Louvre) / Daniel Arnaudet: nos 119, 140, 142, 160, 226, 329, 365, 368, and pp. 142, 143 / Martine Beck-Coppola: nos 81, 123 / Michèle Bellot: nos 178, 209, 215 / Jean-Gilles Berizzi: nos 133, 136, 137, 146, 149, 168, 169, 194, 241, 284, 302, 366, 371, and pp. 13, 64, 261, 308, 311 / Gérard Blot: nos 38, 199, 265, 347, and p. 207 / Gérard Blot/Christian Jean: no. 152 / Sylvie Chan-Liat: nos 2, 364 / Christophe Chavan: no. 253 / Maurice and Pierre Chuzeville: p. 204 / Adrien Didierjean: nos 122, 139, 148, 164, 185, 186, 242, 269, 349, and pp. 9, 263 / Adrien Didierjean/Mathieu Rabeau: no. 277 / Philippe Fuzeau: p. 297 / Béatrice Hatala: no. 35 / Christian Jean: p. 66 / Thierry Le Mage: nos 163, 197, 208, 258, 308, 323, 325, 356 / Hervé Lewandowski: nos 30, 42, 49, 50, 66, 68, 74, 78, 83, 87, 91, 94, 98, 105, 115, 116, 147, 227, 257, 282, 317, 372, and p. 113 / Stéphane Maréchalle: nos 70, 73, 85, 114, 118, 121, 124, 128, 144, 150, 151, 170, 190, 228, 236, 250, 262, 272, 283, 285, 355, 359, 363, 376, 377, 378, 381, and pp. 4–5, 16, 144, 145, 205, 296 / René-Gabriel Ojeda: nos 60, 200, 203, 205, 251, 281, 315, 360 / Thierry Ollivier: nos 237, 274, 318, 324 / Tony Querrec: nos 97, 104, 110, 145, 184, 188, 196, 212, 216, 225, 246, 248, 259, 264, 271, 275, 322, 343, 350, 375, and p. 310 / Mathieu Rabeau: nos 21, 62, 117, 154, 193, 247, 263, 301, 338, 358, 362 / Franck Raux: nos 7, 8, 22, 23, 28, 32, 33, 48, 51, 64, 159, 172, 179, 192, 222, 224, 254, 256, 268, 276, 287, 336, 340, 351, 357, 361, 369, 374, and pp. 18, 293 / Benoît Touchard: nos 255, 260 / Michel Urtado: nos 165, 175, 182, 202, 204, 206, 207, 213, 214, 219, 229, 230, 233, 245, 273, 305, 309, 316, 320, 321, 335, 339, 341, 342, 345, 346, 353, 354 / Image GrandPalaisRmn: nos 3, 101, 138, 143, 181, 198, 231, 312 • Ministère de la Culture – Médiathèque du Patrimoine et de la Photographie, Dist. GrandPalaisRmn / Jean Mounic / GrandPalaisRmn – Copyright management: p. 3 / Alfred-Nicolas Normand: p. 12 • Musée du Quai Branly – Jacques Chirac, Dist. GrandPalaisRmn / Hughes Dubois : nos 82, 134, 162, 303 / Patrick Gries: no. 141 / Pauline Guyon: no. 189 / Image Musée du Quai Branly – Jacques Chirac: nos 54, 161, 191, 307, 326, 330, 370, 373, and pp. 114, 115, 206 • Musée du Louvre, Dist. GrandPalaisRmn / Alain Basset: no. 111 / Martine Beck-Coppola: nos 183, 195, 218, 286, 295, 331, 344, 367 / Harry Bréjat: p. 2 / Laurent Chastel: no. 279 / Anne Chauvet: nos 10, 92, 102 / Raphaël Chipault: nos 6, 17, 18, 31, 126, 201, 297, 300, 332, and p. 65 / Christian Decamps: front cover, nos 5, 9, 11, 12, 13, 19, 26, 27, 34, 37, 39, 41, 43, 44, 55, 80, and pp. 67, 262 / Michel Denancé: pp. 10–11 / Angèle Dequier: back cover, nos 20, 157, 176, 177, 223, 234, 266, 267, 270, 289, 290, 291, 380 / Hughes Dubois: nos 127, 129, 130, 131, 132, 135, 155, 156, 158, 174, 239, 298 / Philippe Fuzeau: nos 15, 16, 63, 71, 153, 232, 278, 310 / Peter Harholdt: no. 89 / Marc Jeanneteau: no. 288 / Christian Larrieu: no. 106, and p. 112 / Daniel Lebée/Carine Déambrosis: nos 14, 47, 53, 56, 58, 65, 67, 75, 77, 86, 217, and p. 260 / Hervé Lewandowski: nos 103, 109, 167, 171, 173, 210, 211, 220, 238, 249, 292, 293, 311, 313, 334, and p. 295 / Paul Maurer: p. 14 / Thierry Ollivier: nos 25, 46, 57, 59, 61, 69, 72, 76, 79, 84, 88, 90, 93, 95, 96, 113, 125, 166, 180, 221, 243, 244, 252, 261, 280, 296, 304, 306, 314, 319, 333, 337, 348 / Olivier Ouadah: no. 379, and pp. 1, 7, 8, 312–313 / Pierre Philibert: nos 235, 294, 327, 352 / Georges Poncet: nos 4, 29, 36, 40, 45, 52, 99, 100, 112 / Étienne Revault: no. 240 / Claire Tabbagh: p. 309 / Claire Tabbagh/Collections Numériques: nos 120, 187, 328 / Paul Veysseyre: nos 107, 108

Despite our best efforts, we have been unable to identify the authors or copyright holders for all photographs and/or works in this guide. We apologise to the authors or copyright holders whose names we have omitted and would be grateful if they could kindly contact us.

COPYRIGHT CREDIT LINES

Musée du Louvre

Laurence des Cars
President-Director

Kim Pham
Director General

Francis Steinbock
Deputy Director General

Aline François-Colin
Director of Exhibitions and Publications

Valérie Coudin
Deputy Director of Publications

Violaine Bouvet-Lanselle
Head of Publications

Hélène Vassal
Director of Collection Support

Sybille Clochet
Head of Document Engineering, Images and Translation

Maureen Huault-Gavaudo
Head of Images

GrandPalaisRmnÉditions

Sophie Laporte
Publications and Art Studios Manager

Claire Bonnevie
Head of the Book Department

Enzo Dizarn
Editorial Coordinator

Hugues Charreyron
Production Manager

Marianne Lemarignier
Image Editor

Philippe Couton
Documentalist, GrandPalaisRmn Photo Agency

Sandra Petch
Translation from the French

Bronwyn Mahoney
Copy-Editing

Paper! Tiger! (Aurélien Farina)
with Malou Messien
Graphic Design

Text

Dominique de Font-Réaulx
Senior Curator, Special Adviser to the President-Director, Musée du Louvre

Colour Separation by Fotimprim, Paris, France.

Typeset in Baskervville (ANRT, 2017–2018)
and LL Unica 77 (Lineto, 2019).

Printed in April 2024 by Graphius, Ghent, Belgium.

254–256, rue de Bercy
75012 Paris
ISBN: 978-2-7118-6443-0
GK196443

Musée du Louvre
75058 Paris Cedex 01
ISBN: 978-2-35031-811-0

louvre.fr/en

Legal deposit: May 2024